Women in an Insecure World

Violence against Women

Facts, Figures and Analysis

Edited by Marie Vlachová and Lea Biason

Geneva Centre for the Democratic Control of Armed Forces (DCAF)

ISBN 92-9222-028-4

Special thanks to SRO Kundig for the cover design,
layout and support in the publication of the book.

Printed by SRO Kundig
Chemin de l'Etang 49
Geneva, Switzerland

Table of Contents

TABLES

Foreword

Armed conflict continues to stalk the world, becoming ever more vicious. The fundamental principles of international humanitarian law are commonly disregarded. It is an appalling fact that in today's conflicts civilians are not just the accidental victims of war, they are increasingly the deliberate targets.

Women and children suffer disproportionately during and after wars. They form the majority of refugees and internally displaced persons. They endure rape and sexual abuse, which have been used throughout history as weapons of war. It is my firm conviction that much more attention must be given to the consequences of war for women and children, and in particular to the protection of women and girls from gender-based violence.

The history of armed conflict is not only characterised by the horrors of war, but by women's stories of courage and resistance. During and after a conflict, with the adult male population greatly diminished, women often become the main providers for their devastated families. They keep the wheels of society turning. It is therefore also important to recognise that women have an important part to play in peace processes. United Nations Resolution 1325 on women, peace and security, which has been unanimously approved in 2000, is a groundbreaking document. It guides Switzerland's foreign peace policy in its work to promote the participation of women in peace-related activities.

Including women in peace negotiations, peacekeeping operations, and in reconstruction and reconciliation efforts following a conflict will help ensure that women's priorities and needs are addressed. These include ensuring a safe return to their homes; tracing missing relatives; meeting specific health care needs, such as treatment for sexually transmitted diseases, including HIV/AIDS; restoring normality and providing education for their children; and offering justice and redress for atrocities that have been committed against women during the conflict.

The promotion of peace is a priority of Swiss foreign and security policy. My ministry is focusing its peace promotion policy on human security, placing particular emphasis on the security needs of individuals and communities affected by armed conflicts. We are involved in international efforts to control the proliferation of weapons – in particular by banning anti-personnel mines and combating the illicit trade in small arms and light weapons – and to ensure greater protection for the most vulnerable persons of civil society.

Everyone should be able to live without fear. However, for many people, and in particular for women, a secure world remains just a hope. The information and the analysis of gender-based violence in this book are sobering. The book also contains valuable recommendations which aim to make the world more secure for women.

It is for me a pleasure to give patronage to this book on Women in an Insecure World so ably edited by Dr. Marie Vlachová, Ms. Lea Biason, and their team at the Geneva Centre for the Democratic Control of Armed Forces (DCAF). This book is an important contribution to our endeavours to include gender issues in the discussion about human security.

Micheline Calmy-Rey
Federal Councillor
Federal Department
of Foreign Affairs of Switzerland

Preface

Slaughtering Eve - The Hidden Gendercide

I became aware of the necessity for the Geneva Centre for the Democratic Control of Armed Forces (DCAF) to write this book when I was preparing, in the summer of 2002, DCAF's first Occasional Paper[1] dealing with the problems posed by the security sector[2] in an unruly world.

The paper had as a point of departure that human security is today in many parts of the world actually decreasing rather than increasing. There is tragic evidence for this fact. Thus, if in the First World War one victim in ten was a civilian (while nine were soldiers), this ratio had by the end of the century been reversed when civilian victims outstripped in most conflicts military casualties ten to one.[3] Within a single century, the price of conflict had, thus, increased for the civilian population by a factor of 100. Never before have there been so many refugees as today. Never before have there been so many deadly remnants of war – such as unexploded ordnance and anti-personnel mines – waiting to claim their innocent victims long after the guns have fallen silent. Never before has there been so little hesitation to use terror against civilian targets. The horrible phenomenon of 'ethnic cleansing' has, at the end of the last century, reappeared. Organised international crime has become a threat of strategic proportions. The illicit trade in drugs, blood diamonds, tropical woods, cigarettes and human beings is steadily growing. Even piracy is on the rise.[4]

While researching the necessary statistics for my paper, I was struck – time and again – that, regardless of what type of evil I was investigating, a disproportionate number of the victims were women and children and these victims counted not in thousands, but in millions. Every UN agency, every international institution, every non-governmental organisation, which I consulted on the internet, contributed with its data another tragic piece to the picture:

- The United Nations estimate from 113 million up to 200 million women are demographically 'missing'. They have been the victims of infanticide (boys are preferred to girls) or have not received the same amount of food and medical attention as their brothers, fathers and husbands.[5]

- The number of women forced or sold into prostitution is estimated worldwide at anywhere between 700,000 and 4,000,000 per year. Between 120,000 and 500,000 of these victims are sold to brothels and pimps in Europe, 2,000 to 3,000 to brothels in Switzerland. Profits from sex slavery are estimated at seven to twelve billion US dollars per year.[6]

- Nine out of ten victims of anti-personnel mines are civilians.[7]

- Globally, women aged between fifteen and forty-four are more likely to be maimed or die as a result of male violence than through cancer, malaria, traffic accidents or war combined.[8]

- Domestic violence against women is still rampant. In Switzerland alone, close to 3,000 women in 2002 sought shelter in protective houses for women. It is estimated that only a small fraction of female victims made such a step. The cost of domestic violence to the Swiss economy is conservatively estimated at over 400 million Swiss Francs per year.[9] In Austria, fifty per cent of divorces are filed on the grounds of violence against women, while twenty-two per cent of Finnish women claim to have suffered violence from their partners.[10] Marital rape remains the most widespread crime at the global level.

- Systematic rape is used as a weapon of terror in many of the world's conflicts.

- For every woman killed by mankind there are scores that are physically or psychologically wounded if not maimed (there are 2-3 million cases of female genital mutilation alone each year).

The list is endless. The picture is all too clear: we are confronted with the slaughter of Eve, a systematic gendercide of tragic proportions. The number of women killed by males is one of the significant causes of death on this planet. The number of victims is several times larger than the numbers of dead in all the wars of the twentieth century combined. The victims are claimed in conflicts, but also next door. The causes are multiple, but eventually boil down to the simple fact that for all too many a woman's life and dignity are worth less than a man's. This situation is simply intolerable.

We have tried, in this book, to bring the facts together. While we initially played with the idea to write a book about the aspect of this gendercide that directly relates to our work, we soon came to the conclusion that this would be too narrow an approach. Studies that look at the multiple specific aspects of a problem in great detail are, obviously, eminently important. Yet what is, at this juncture, also needed is a comprehensive view of the issue. The data must be seen in their totality for us to be able to even begin to understand what is going on. We hope that the facts, the figures and the analysis we have brought together in this volume will contribute to shake up the international community, mankind – all of us. There cannot be any room for complacency in face of slaughter, maiming, rape, degradation, and social discrimination.

DCAF intends to continue to work in this key area. It has created an international working group on women and children in an insecure world. This working group will, as a next step, embark on a companion volume to this book, dedicated to children in an insecure world. In parallel we shall initiate work on a second edition of this book, bringing together more data and analysis. We hope that we shall be able to further broaden the number of institutions and experts contributing to this research. I would like to invite all readers of this book to become part of this process. Do not hesitate to contact us and to share with us your criticism, your ideas on what additional dimension should be covered, your data and your experience. We are confronted with one of the great crimes of human history. We cannot live with it. We cannot close our eyes from it. We cannot hope that it will simply go away. We must act. Now.

Theodor H. Winkler
Director
Geneva Centre for the Democratic Control of Armed Forces

Endnotes

[1] T. H. Winkler, 'Managing Change. The Reform and Democratic Control of the Security Sector and International Order', *Occasional Paper*, No.1 (Geneva Centre for the Democratic Control of Armed Forces, October 2002).

[2] The security sector includes all the organisations that have the authority to use, or order the use of, force, or the threat of force, to protect the state and its citizens, i.e. the armed forces, police, border guards, customs, intelligence services, government ministries and parliaments, judicial and penal systems, state security agencies, paramilitary or militia forces, non-governmental security organisations, private security firms, etc.

[3] E. Eppler, *Vom Gewaltmonopol zum Gewaltmarkt* (Frankfurt a.M.: Suhrkamp, 2002), 60; cf. also J. Solana,'A Secure Europe in a Better World', *European Security Strategy* (Brussels, 12 December 2003), at http://ue.eu.int/pressdata/EN/reports/78367.pdf

[4] C. Plate, 'Entzauberung der Seeräuber-Romantik: Vor den Küsten Südostasien und Afrikas ist die von Freibeutern ausgehende Gefahr besonders gross', *Neue Zürcher Zeitung (NZZ)* (25 August 2002), 3.

[5] Data cited by Anna Diamantopoulou, Speech at the Conference *Violence against Women: Zero Tolerance*, (Lisbon, 4 May 2000), at http://europa.eu.int/comm/employment_social/equ_opp/news/lisbon_en.htm

[6] Marianne Truttmann, 'Mit vereinten Kräften gegen die Sklaverei', *Der Bund* (21 September 2002), 5.

[7] Geneva International Centre for Humanitarian Demining.

[8] Anna Diamantopoulou, *Violence against Women: Zero Tolerance*.

[9] Switzerland, 'Grenzüberschreitende Ohnmacht Kampf gegen Gewalt an Frauen', *NZZ* (26 November 2003). More women seek shelter from domestic violence. The number of women seeking shelter from domestic violence has hit record levels in Switzerland.

[10] Anna Diamantopoulou, *Violence against Women: Zero Tolerance*.

Acknowledgements

This book would not have been feasible without the support of the Swiss Federal Councillor and Foreign Minister Mrs. Micheline Calmy-Rey. The patronage of the Geneva Centre of the Democratic Control of Armed Forces (DCAF) project entitled 'Women and Children in an Insecure World', taken over in 2003, is one of Mrs. Calmy-Rey's activities in putting women's rights higher on her political agenda and raising public and governmental awareness of the gravity of violence against women. From the very beginning, the project has been warmly supported by the DCAF leadership, namely Ambassador Theodor H. Winkler, DCAF's Director, who put forward the idea to examine the issues of violence against women in the framework of human security. His stubborn support and continuous inputs during the whole time of the book's preparation have been essential, as well as the practical guidance of DCAF's Head of Think Tank, Dr. Heiner Hänggi. We also thank Ms. Anja Ebnöther, DCAF's Head of Special Programmes for her management and valuable assistance in the successful finalisation of the book.

The publication is the product of a broad collaboration of experts from various fields in intergovernmental and non-governmental organisations, research institutes and academia. We are truly indebted to the large number of our authors who had to cope with the specific needs of the publication, showing great flexibility, patience, and devotion to the topic during the demanding process of all the necessary adaptations, completions, merging and style levelling the editors had to undertake to transform about thirty papers into a coherent and compound final text. We thank Lesley Abdela; Ancil Adrian-Paul; Krishna Ahooja-Patel; Augusta Angelucchi; Pamela Bell; Martin Bohnstedt; Valentina Cherevatenko; Laurence Desvignes; Courtney Draggon; Isha Dyfan; Mona Eltahawy; Vanessa Farr; Agnès Hubert; Cecilia Jimenez; Ramina Johal; Nicola Johnston; Adam Jones; Lynn Khadiagala; Avila Kilmurray; Chaula Kothari; Shukuko Koyama; Ida Kuklina; Sonja Licht; Charlotte Lindsey; Megan McKenna; Marlea Muñez; Ndioro Ndiaye; 'Funmi Olonisakin; Leena Parmar; Athena Peralta; Charlotte Ponticelli; Nadine Puechguirbal; Indai Sajor; Josi Salem-Pickartz; Colette Samoya; Aida Santos-Maranan; Mikiko Sawanishi; Darla Silva; Slavica Stojanovic; Biljana Vankovska; Camila Vega; and Charlotte Watts.

We thank the group of external and internal reviewers who generously and at short notice gave us very useful comments on the first and final drafts of the book. Some of them co-operated with us during the whole process of the book's production offering their helpful hand anytime we needed it. Our thanks go to Alyson Bailes, Director of the Stockholm International Peace Research Institute (SIPRI), Krishna Ahooja-Patel, President of the Women's International League for Peace and Freedom (WILPF), Sonja Licht, President of the Belgrade Fund for Political Excellence, Christine Pintat, former Assistant Secretary General of the Inter-Parliamentary Union (IPU), Marina Caparini, DCAF Senior Fellow and Philipp Fluri, DCAF Deputy Director.

The production of this book would not have been possible without DCAF research assistants. Ivana Schellongová and Melina Skouroliakou have provided inestimable help to the editors in all the stages of the work, starting with research, data and statistics collection, photos compilation, technical revisions, and last but not least the essential administrative tasks. Karin Grimm, Jason Powers and interns Hélène Harroff-Tavel and Kimi Porter have provided valuable assistance in the finalisation of the book. Finally, our thanks belong to all DCAF staff who supported the project from the very beginning and gave us a helpful hand any time we needed it.

The opinions and conclusions expressed in the book are those of its authors and editors and do not necessarily reflect the positions of the authors' employers or the Geneva Centre of the Democratic Control of Armed Forces.

Marie Vlachová and Lea Biason

Introduction

Violence against women is firmly established as part of the international agenda dealing with the protection of those suffering most from the insecurities of the present world. Although there are other groups at risk - children, the elderly generation, ethnic minority groups, to name just some of them - women constitute the most numerous part of the world population exposed to systematic and persistent violence. However, what makes their role in combating violence indispensable is not the omnipresence and magnitude of their victimisation, but the fact that women have often demonstrated the capability of overcoming the trauma of violent acts, to survive and help in the survival of others, and to contribute actively to defending and building peace.

The recognition of women's role in making the world more secure can be considered as a part of the process of conceptualisation of security and security providers. Current threats and risks have prompted attempts to revise the traditional meaning of national security as primarily the protection of states, and to introduce a broader concept, recognising security not in terms of the structure of the security sector, but as an indivisible need and value all people have the right to enjoy. The main task of the security sector is to create conditions that would enable all people to satisfy that need. Such a concept goes beyond state-centred military security and focuses on the ability or inability of state institutions to ensure the protection of all citizens. On one hand, it enables the definition of vulnerable groups bearing the brunt of poverty, armed conflict, malfunctioning of the security sector and inefficient legal protection, on the other hand, it recognises the role of non-state, non-governmental organisations from civil-society.

Developing the concept of democratic principles and standards of national security sectors, the Centre for the Democratic Control of Armed Forces (DCAF) had to face the fact that security and safety is not enjoyed equally by men and women, and that after all, violence against women (and other groups at risk) is impeding the process of the creation of a well-functioning security sector - i.e. the institutions capable of the provision of an adequate level of security for all citizens. Moreover, violence against women occurs in varying contexts – at the domestic and community levels, in situations of armed conflict and under repressive governments. In many cases it is a conscious policy, and often deliberate acts of individuals punishable by law. And protection, punishment of perpetrators and redress of injustice are the 'raison d'être' of security sectors.

In January 2003 a working group on 'Women and Children in an Insecure World' was established within DCAF in order to examine the issues of systematic violence within the context of security sector reform. Primarily, DCAF's activities aim at raising awareness of the vulnerability of women and children within the security community, and subsequently the public at large.

This publication is the first product of the working group activities. Our goal was to show the scope and multifaceted nature of gender-based violence, as well as the gravity of its consequences for families, communities and societies. We wanted to avoid declarative or emotional approaches, although escaping compassion, terror and rage proved to be impossible at times. Instead we wanted to bring meaningful information about the topic, to look under the surface of the phenomenon, analysing the diversity of its historical, social and cultural root causes. In addition, we wanted to show that women and men combating the violence are not helpless since the abuse of women and girls has caught the attention of various organisations across the world, many of them founded and run by women themselves. The book presents women both as survivors and actors, bringing evidence of their resilience against adversity and their efficiency if given the chance.

This is a handbook-type volume, encompassing descriptive, analytical and illustrative elements, intended for all those who, by examining issues of security sectors more and more frequently, face the problems of vulnerable groups. The book has been assigned to academics and practitioners, politicians, donors, experts, activists, journalists, etc., who are seeking a useful insight into the complexity and variety of the issues of violence against women.

There are two features that catch attention: the persistence and ubiquity of gender-based violence. Violent acts against women have been committed through all our history regardless of regions and cultures. To give the reader an insight into the persistent and pervasive nature of gender-based violence we begin the book with a chapter examining its main roots. The three parts that follow survey various forms of violence in the different contexts of family, community and society, in times of peace and war. The third part, devoted to women's roles in post-conflict reconstruction, offers a set of varying activities of women's organisations in peace negotiation, peacebuilding and in the processes of reconciliation and justice. In the concluding part of the book the main agendas devoted to curbing the violence are introduced.

The topic of violence against women is extremely broad, as the violence is universal, taking on various forms and affecting women in all stages of their lives. The issues are covered by at least three extensive agendas: human rights, development, and peace studies. A substantial contribution to the understanding of the roots of gender-based violence has been made in numerous feminist studies. A variety of actors have been engaged in the long-lasting struggle for its eradication, and to describe their activities and achievements exceeds the limit of one publication, thus the selection between the topics covered thoroughly and those given more cursory attention had to be done, though we wished to encompass as many issues as possible. Intentionally we avoided topics overloaded with the plethora of complex causes and consequences - such as globalisation and ecology - or too sensitive to be addressed properly in the limited space - such as birth and sexuality control issues. We tried to concentrate on the topics connected with the malfunctioning of the security sector, failing to protect women and their families against war cruelties and post-war insecurities, and on the analysis of domestic and traditional forms of violence whether based on religious practices, customary laws or widespread social norms. Being aware of all the limitations, we hope that those in need of information on security and having the courage to confront the issues of gender-based violence as one of the major sources of insecurities of the present world will benefit from this publication.

ROOTS AND SCOPE

OF

GENDER-BASED

VIOLENCE

Roots and Scope of Gender-Based Violence

'Gender-based violence is a form of discrimination that seriously inhibits women's ability to enjoy rights and freedoms on a basis of equality with men. [...] Gender-based violence is directed against a woman because she is a woman or affects women disproportionately. It includes acts that inflict physical, mental or sexual harm or suffering, threats of such acts, coercion and other deprivations of liberty.'

Committee on the Elimination of Discrimination against Women,
General Recommendation No. 19

Generally, both within academia and among practitioners, it has been accepted that the roots of gender-based violence lie in gender relations, which worldwide are marked by the domination of men and the subordination of women. This explanation appears in official documents on violence against women such as General Recommendation No. 19 of the Committee on the Elimination of All Forms of Discrimination against Women, providing an official interpretation of violence against women as a form of discrimination in 1992. Recent statements made by prominent personalities and organisations use the same explanatory framework when mentioning the roots of gender-based violence. For instance, in her report to the 60th UN Commission of Human Rights Yakin Ertürk, Special Rapporteur of the United Nations Commission on Human Rights on violence against women, its causes and consequences, accentuated that diverse kinds of discrimination against women are based on systems of subordination and inequality. This means that crimes against women are not considered as severe as those against men and the worldwide violent behaviour against women and girls remains unchanged. The pervasive character of the dominance/subordination pattern of gender relations causes that in spite of a variety of forms, violence against women is universal regarding its geographical scope and omnipresence with concerns to its manifestation from the level of the house to the transnational arena.[1]

Since the last decade, through several documents, the international community has made pronouncements on what constitutes violence against women and the scope of this violence. The United Nations, for example, acknowledges that women are vulnerable to violence that may be of a physical, sexual or psychological nature, which is perpetrated in the private sphere, such as in the home, and in public settings (including places of work and educational institutions) and that the state can sometimes legitimise such violence through inaction or action in the form of bad policy and ideology.[2] Violence is largely committed by men - whose victims are mostly, but not exclusively, women and girls. This violence has a pattern and it is manifested at several levels from the domestic to the state and to the international community.

Alice, 20 years old, was gang-raped twice by rebels and pro-government militia fighters as she and her family fled the civil war in Monrovia, Liberia.

Available statistics suggest that domestic violence constitutes the largest form of abuse of women worldwide, without regional exception. For example, it is estimated that one in four women is a victim of domestic violence in the US.[3] In India and Pakistan, thousands of women are reportedly victims of dowry deaths. In Peru, more than half of the cases of reported crime are of women beaten by their spouses.[4] In many parts of Africa, abuse of women is simply taken as the acceptable norm and the majority of cases are not reported.

Woman's fight for survival begins at a very early stage in the life cycle, as corroborated by the mortality rate of girls between the ages of one and four years, which is much higher than that of boys of the same age group. In many countries girls are systematically starved, denied medical care and neglected by their family because of their preference for boys. In some countries – for example in China, India, Korea and parts of North Africa – this results in a demographic misbalance between men and women.

Women, and girls in particular, remain vulnerable to sexual violence, to which they are very frequently exposed in the 'safety' of their homes. For example, a study of a Treatment Centre in Zaria, Nigeria, in 1988 indicated that fifteen per cent of female patients requiring treatment for sexually transmitted diseases (STDs) were under the age of five. In the same sample, six per cent were between the ages of six and fifteen years. Similarly, another study of the Maternity Hospital of Lima, Peru, indicated that 90 per cent of young mothers between ages twelve and sixteen became pregnant through rape and a majority of these girls had been victimised by a close male relative. In a study carried out in Costa Rica, 95 per cent of pregnant girls under fifteen were victims of incest.[5] Girls continue to suffer in other ways depending on their

social environment. A girl who has been sexually assaulted faces further victimisation at home and in the community in varying degrees. She has to confront moral judgement by a community, which is bound by cultural and religious practices that place certain expectations on girls and women. In many societies, greater premium is placed on a girl who remains a virgin - as she is a more dependable asset to be cashed in for forced early marriage. Invariably, the choices open to girls in these situations are limited so they become easy targets for further exploitation through prostitution, slavery, child labour, and trafficking. A publication by UNFPA aptly describes the plight of the adolescent girl: *'In the hierarchy of gender-based power relations, adolescent females occupy the lowest rung. Their opportunities for self-development and autonomy are limited, due to societies denying them access to education, healthcare and gainful employment. On top of this, many are confronted with sexual coercion and abuse, often starting at a very young age.'*[6] All through life, other situations continue to make girls and women vulnerable to gender-based violence. In their workplaces women face other forms of abuse and discrimination ranging from sexual harassment, unequal pay to poor maternity benefits, all of which increase their vulnerability.

Armed conflict, particularly within states, has perhaps drawn the greatest attention to the issue of gender-based violence in recent years. Although the victimisation of women in armed conflict has increased in recent times, so has women's participation in wars as part of armed forces or groups. For example, in revolutionary warfare or counter-insurgencies, which have occurred largely in the Southern Hemisphere, women have increasingly served as part of armed forces, although in some cases this has resulted from coercion.[7]

Women have numbered the most among victims of war. Attacking and victimising women and children, particularly girls, is no longer accidental - it is policy. Now, for the first time in history, this group of civilians is the target of choice for armed groups, particularly irregular forces in their efforts to destabilise society and gain political, military or economic advantages. In wartime the protagonists' intent is often to strike at the hearts of their opponents by destroying that which is most precious to them, which define their pride and position as men within the society – their wives and daughters, who sometimes also have economic value and can be bartered at whim. Much of the rape and sexual assault committed against women in times of war are aimed at demoralising the enemy as a calculated policy. Some of the most shocking manifestations of this were seen in the conflicts in the former Yugoslavia. Rape of women, aimed at purposely infecting them with HIV/AIDS, has been a recent phenomenon. Even when deliberate infection has not been the case, it is often a natural consequence of rape. There has been a notable increase in HIV/AIDS infection along the corridors of armed conflict – a net effect of using rape as a weapon of war.

There is increasing awareness of the victimisation, including harassment and sexual assault of refugees and displaced persons as they flee armed conflict and attempt to cope with life in a new environment. Women and girls form a majority of the world's refugees and internally displaced persons (IDPs). The breakdown in social values, which occurs as a result of the migration from their communities, heightens the vulnerability of displaced women and girls. They not only become victims of domestic violence within their family setting, but they sometimes also face harassment at the hands of some of their supposed protectors – peacekeepers and aid workers. The much publicised cases of sexual exploitation of women and girls in the refugee camps in West Africa in 2001 by peacekeepers and aid workers is a case in point. The victimisation of women and girls in situations of armed conflict is not peculiar to any one geographical location. It is widespread across all regions experiencing armed conflict.

One issue, which is in part an offshoot of armed conflict, is the trafficking of human beings across borders. In some regions, the trafficking of boys and girls for use in armed conflict has been a key feature in, for example, the Mano River area of Liberia, Guinea and Sierra Leone, and the Great Lakes Region of Africa. Women, girls and boys are trafficked for use as labourers, for forced prostitution or as slaves.

Explaining the roots

Do the roots of violence against women lie in inherently violent men and inherently peace-loving women? Traditional explanations for gender-based violence often place the responsibility with men, who control the traditional institutions and often militarise society. Distinctions are made between inherently violent men and inherently peace-loving women. Thus, the common perception is that wars are started by men, who are naturally aggressive and operate in male dominated systems; and that it is men who have institutionalised violence. Women are seen as peace-loving who abhor violence and do not seek to conquer Although sometimes violent, women have not sought to institutionalise violence. It is men who militarise society and the combination of militarism and patriarchy has perpetuated violence against women. Those who advocate greater participation of women in peace processes and in governance have this as their underlying assumption; they argue that women would behave better than men in positions of political power, and that there would be less violence and fewer wars.

However, there is an opposing viewpoint, which finds that women are just as responsible as men for promoting militaristic agendas, which generate much of the violence perpetuated against women. Women are arguably the gatekeepers and channels for promoting cultures and values that lead to war. Gnanadason asks, *'if women are so loving, peaceful and nurturing, why do so many of their sons become violent?'*[8] Women have played crucial parts in war efforts and war machines. Women, like men, are strong defenders of nationalist causes. Nations have gone to war against other nations to defend values that bind them together as a people and women are as passionate as men over the defence of those values. Many times in history they have encouraged their sons and assisted in the mobilisation of entire nations for war.

Some analysts go further to explain that militarism and patriarchy are just as vicious to men as to women, but it is often less recognised that men suffer from these structures as well. According to Cynthia Adcock: 'We have generally portrayed ourselves as the victims of male domination, downplaying the areas in which we ourselves hold power. We have thoroughly described and documented that half of the age-old saga of domination and oppression in which we are the victims. We have not yet fully recognised the effects of maternal power over children as a root cause of resentment, fear and hatred of females. Rarely do we admit that males have sometimes been our victims, as we have been theirs.'[9]

Underpinning the above views, however, is the argument that at the root of this lies patriarchy, a social construct, which ascribes different roles to men and women. From a very early stage, boys and girls are socialised differently in many societies – girls are raised to be obedient and caring, to serve, and fulfil the needs of men, rather than their own. Boys are the dominant, whose role it is to conquer and to be leaders. Although their socialisation over time makes many women natural supporters of peace movements and peaceful resolution of disputes as opposed to violent means of pursuing conflict, these traditional roles have only served to shape their outlook, but not their inherent nature. Thus, women are not inherently less violent and more peaceful than men. They have learned through socialisation processes. Moreover, experiences of childbirth and child rearing also assist the development of their peaceful capabilities.

The state plays a role

Women are not at the helm of affairs in the male dominated patriarchal systems that keep women and girls repressed. While women have played a role in supporting war efforts and transferring values that promote war (and they can at times be as violent as men), the systems and institutions that perpetuate violence against women are largely male dominated. The plight of millions of women and girls all over the world remains bleak and this fate appears sealed under seemingly immutable state structures that legitimise violence against women. If women (and men) are to make better, more peace loving leaders, it will be because structures and governance systems have been altered to allow for equality and equitable distribution of resources.

The state can either be the most important enabler for gender-based violence or greatest driver of change. Through action or inaction, the state plays a role in legitimising abuse of girls and women. In some countries, inheritance laws preclude women from inheriting or owning property. Some states accept so-called crimes of honour, whereby a male relative beats a woman to death for dishonouring the family name. This has sometimes been upheld by courts of law. A woman's right to citizenship is decided by her spouse in some cases thus ensuring that some women remain under the control of abusive spouses. Freedom of movement is impeded in some countries where women must be escorted by a male irrespective of their age. In some countries women are traditionally not allowed to obtain gainful employment. All of these factors further increase the vulnerability of women to violence. Unfair laws, which place restrictions on women's citizenship and economic rights, ensure that

they remain poverty-stricken at the bottom of the social ladder and this invariably encourages the exploitation of women and girls through prostitution, slavery, child labour and trafficking.

It has also been well documented that violations of women's rights are rife under repressive and authoritarian systems of government. It is not unusual to find that in states or regimes where repression and bad governance are the order of the day there are also ready channels for repression of women. The rights of women, as well as of men, are violated, as political opponents and their supporters are harassed, intimidated, tortured and arrested arbitrarily. In some cases, such states collapse or eventually regress into a situation of armed conflict and the abuse of women simply continues in other ways.

Addressing violence against women

The most effective, and perhaps the most visible, driving force behind the recent global efforts to address gender-based violence has been the women's movements around the world. The cause of women has also been championed by unions, various streams of the leftist movement, liberation movements, and churches including freedom theologians, in particular, feminist theologians in the Southern Hemisphere, and female academics and writers.

Women demonstrators carry a banner reading 'Not One More', a reference to the rising number of women killed by their partners in a recent wave of domestic violence in Spain.

The declaration of human rights as universal has been used as an entry point for the women's movements campaign to protect women and eradicate all forms of violence against women. In particular, the view taken within many states that those abuses against women, which occur in the private sphere, such as domestic violence and other harmful cultural practices, should not be part of the concern of the state, has been challenged by women. The women's movements have argued that women's rights are human rights and that states have the obligation to protect women's human rights, thus using human rights as an instrument to combat various forms of abuse including child abuse, domestic violence and other forms of violence against women. The movements have challenged traditions, which upheld abuses against women's sexual and reproductive rights.

Official recognition of gender-based violence and an attempt by the international community to systematically address this problem is only about a decade old. The UN General Assembly's Declaration on the Elimination of Violence against Women of December 1993 marked the first official attempt by the international community to address the problem of gender-based violence. This builds upon the Convention on the Elimination of all forms of Discrimination against Women (CEDAW), which was adopted by the UN General Assembly in 1979. While CEDAW does not deal exclusively with the issue of violence against women, it is the only human rights convention, which acknowledges women's reproductive rights as legitimate and views culture and tradition as critical forces dictating gender and family roles – all of which are critical to understanding and dealing with gender-based violence. These documents form part of the emerging normative framework for understanding and addressing violence against women.

Since then, some tangible progress has been realised. In 1995, the UN Fourth World Conference on Women, held in Beijing further strengthened this normative framework. The document, which resulted from this conference, The Beijing Platform for Action, further elaborated the nature and scope of gender-based violence, acknowledging that there can be no development without equality and as long as violence is tolerated, development becomes more elusive. The Platform for Action identifies twelve critical areas of concern[10] and the document serves as a strategic guide for states in the implementation of their policies around women and equality. Among other things what was new in Beijing, was the identification of the 'girl-child' as a critical area of concern. By highlighting the need of the girl-child, it would be possible to combat the bias against girls in early life, which reduce their opportunities for development. Thus by seeking to address the abuse of women in a holistic manner, it might

be possible to begin to break the chain of violence which occurs throughout a woman's lifecycle. Women's movements and women's organisations were also a driving force in the processes leading to Beijing and afterwards. In New York, five years after Beijing, the Beijing plus 5 conference reviewed progress since the Platform for Action and adopted a political declaration and outcome document, 'Further Actions and Initiatives to Implement the Beijing Declaration and Platform for Action'.[11]

Additionally, some progress has been recorded in the area of international humanitarian law and human rights law, which will contribute to efforts to address the problem of gender-based violence. Rape is now recognised as a crime of war in the Rome Statute establishing the International Criminal Court (ICC). The International Criminal Tribunals for former Yugoslavia and Rwanda also recognise rape as a means of genocide and as crimes against humanity, for which government and military personnel can be held individually responsible.

Why gender-based violence persists

Although work continues at various levels to reverse the trend of violence against women in all its ramifications, women continue to experience violence within the home and community and they remain constant targets in situations of armed conflict, while also in some cases

Table 1:
Gender violence throughout the life cycle

Prenatal phase
Battering during pregnancy (emotional and physical effects on the woman; effects on birth); coerced pregnancy; deprivation of food and liquids; sex-selective abortion

Infancy
Female infanticide; emotional and physical abuse; differential access to food and medical care for girl infants

Childhood
Child marriage; genital mutilation; sexual abuse by family members and strangers; differential access to food and medical care; child prostitution

Adolescence
Rape and marital rape; sexual assault; forced prostitution; trafficking in women; courtship violence; economically coerced sex; sexual abuse in the workplace

Reproductive age
Abuse of women by intimate partners; marital rape; dowry abuse and murders; partner homicide; psychological abuse; sexual abuse in the workplace; sexual harassment; rape; abuse of women with disabilities; legal discrimination

Old-age
Abuse and exploitation of widows

Source:
United Nations Development Programme, Regional Bureau for Latin America and the Caribbean, *A Life Free of Violence: It's our Right: United Nations Inter-Agency Campaign on Women's Human Rights in Latin America and the Caribbean* (1998), at http://www.undp.org/rblac/gender/objectives.htm

repressed by the state. A number of reasons have been advanced for the persistence of gender-based violence despite these on-going efforts, some of which are discussed here.

While conventions and international treaties provide legitimacy for non-governmental entities, including women's organisations and activists to continue their work and campaigns against gender-based violence at national and local levels, their implementation requires time and significant resources. Monitoring states and other actors' compliance with their commitments and obligations, would require a systematic approach and commitment of resources. What is more, there are no enforcement mechanisms even if a party is found to be in violation of these commitments. The international community tends to respond only when situations degenerate and threaten international peace and security as seen in Rwanda and the former Yugoslavia.

Despite the efforts described above and the stated commitments of some states, attitudes of statesmen do not often encourage culture change and implementation of the international conventions. This is perhaps best demonstrated by the continued separation of and different attitudes towards violence which is committed against women in the private and the public spheres. For example, society readily condemns deaths of women (and men), resulting from their public activities while remaining largely silent when women die as a result of domestic violence. In many cultures, violence against women in the home is rarely acknowledged. The treatment of this type of violence as something which should be dealt with in the privacy of the home or family setting and not brought to the public sphere, particularly among politicians and lawmakers (who are often better placed to bring about a change in law and attitudes), has ensured the persistence of this problem.

If the separation of crimes committed in private and in public is still so rampant at the national level, it is doubly difficult to address this when international actors are expected to respond to local occurrences. For example, when women and girls living in refugee camps experience domestic and community violence (which are the most widespread forms of violence confronting female refugees), these acts of violence are considered marginal to global concerns. Yet, very often, programming policies of international organisations and agencies sometimes serve to reinforce these acts of violence.

However, the effective eradication of gender-based violence requires not just institutional change at international and national levels; it also requires a change of mindset and attitudes among individuals and state actors. Dealing with mindsets and age-old cultures and behaviour often entails a long-hurl approach. While progress appears slow, steps are being taken at community and national levels in many countries, which will ultimately contribute to meaningful change.

Endnotes

1 United Nations, *Report of the Special Rapporteur of the Commission on Human Rights on Violence against Women, its Causes and Consequences*, Yakin Ertürk, UN Document E/CN.4/2004/66 and Addenda 1 and 2 (Geneva, 2004).

2 See for example, United Nations, *Declaration on the Elimination of Violence Against Women*, UN Document A/RES/48/104 (1993), at http://www.ohchr.org/english/law/eliminationvaw.htm. See also United Nations, *The Beijing Platform for Action* (Beijing, China, 4-15 September 1995), at http://www.un.org/womenwatch

3 L. Heise, 'International Dimensions of Violence against Women', *Response to the Victimization of Women and Children*, Vol. 12, No. 1 (1989), 3-11.

4 See A. Gnanadason et al. (eds), *Women, Violence and Non-Violent Change* (Geneva: WCC Publications, 1996), 10-11.

5 The Interactive Population Centre, *Forms of Gender-based Violence and their Consequences* (UNFPA, March 1999), at http://www.unfpa.org/intercenter/violence/intro.htm. Statistics quoted from the World Health Organization, at http://www.who.int

6 The Interactive Population Centre, *Forms of Gender-based Violence and their Consequences*.

7 Women have been part of armed groups and armed forces for example in Cambodia, Eritrea, El Salvador, Liberia, Namibia, Nicaragua, South Africa and Uganda, among others.

8 See Gnanadason et al., *Women, Violence and Non-Violent Change*, 4.

9 C. Adcock, 'Fear of "Other": The Common Root of Sexism and Militarism', in P. McAllister (ed) *Reweaving the Web of Life, Feminism and Nonviolence* (Philadelphia: New Society Publishers, 1982), 216. See also Gnanadason et al., *Women, Violence and Non-Violent Change*, 6.

10 These include women and poverty, education and training of women, women and health, violence against women, women and conflict, women and the economy, women in power and decision making, institutional mechanism for the advancement of women, human rights of women, women and the media, women and the environment, and the girl-child.

11 UN Womenwatch, *Follow up to Beijing*, at http://www.un.org/womenwatch/confer/beijing/

PART I

VIOLENCE AGAINST WOMEN IN DAILY LIFE

Introduction

Most of the violence against women is committed in everyday life, often in the private sphere of households where women spend a substantial part of their lives as mothers, wives, daughters, sisters, and caretakers, embedded in the cultural practices of their local communities. Intentional violence and social discrimination against women and girls result in desperation, entrapment in criminal networks and ultimately the termination of their lives. From infancy to adulthood they become vulnerable victims to violence condoned by the family and the community which is rarely recognised as a crime or a violation of their most fundamental humanity.

One of the most extreme forms is gendercide (although 'womencide' or 'feminicide' would be more precise), that is the killing, or violent behaviour leading to the death of girl infants, girl children and women. The chapter on this issue deals with maternal mortality and deliberate abortions of female foetuses (female foeticide) and infanticide, as well as premeditated deficit of health care, nutrition and education to which girls are exposed because of boy preference. Furthermore, it describes the serial killing of women, and another, particularly appalling form of violent behaviour, the rape of girl infants and children.

A wide range of forms of violence, strongly linked to cultural norms, such as honour killing, female genital mutilation, dowry-related killing, acid attacks, stove deaths, and bride burnings, are examined in the chapter on violence and tradition. These mostly unpunished crimes could not have occurred if it had not been for the support of the larger communities and societies. Some of the crimes are committed directly under common law and a religion obliging men to punish disobedience or even kill the women and girls who have transgressed rigid community rules. The fact that these crimes are related to certain cultural beliefs does not exclude them from international human rights law, specifically to the evolution of

the international recognition of women's rights. Although attempts to implement international human rights law into local legislation and justice often meet with strong resistance from national governments and local authorities, some progress has already been achieved, as witnessed by the success in the gradual eradication of one of the cruellest form of violence - female genital mutilation. In communities worldwide and in varying degrees, social discrimination and gender inequalities lead to exploitation of female labour power and violation of women's rights in the socio-economic field. The corresponding chapter on gender-based violence and poverty provides a key analysis on the phenomenon of the 'feminisation of poverty' and provides vital strategies on empowerment. An adequate response is crucial as the problem of women's destitution coupled with culturally ingrained oppression are the basic factors which lock women in cycles of violence such as intimate partner violence, prostitution and human trafficking for bonded labour.

The high number of victims of intimate partner violence, which is probably only the proverbial tip of the iceberg, corroborates the fact that for many women the home, their very domain and assigned place in society, is filled with pain and suffering. Women are battered, raped, abused, mutilated, enslaved and murdered by their intimate partners, fathers, brothers and other relatives, including female ones, as in the case of female genital mutilation or infanticide, usually executed by elderly women of the family or tribal community. The chapter on intimate partner violence elucidates the complexities of the problem where women's emotional and economic dependence on the perpetrator of violence reduces avenues of escape. The roles and involvement of different sectors in society such as the health sector, the legal apparatus and the community in general are thus vital.

When the home becomes an insecure place, many women and girls opt to flee, becoming easy prey to prostitution as a desperate act to escape abuse or lift themselves and their families from poverty. The relevant chapter examines the inherent and wide-ranging forms of violence in the different forms of prostitution and the sex trade and introduces the reader into the present legal debate and societal attitudes towards this age-old phenomenon. A section on trafficking in women and girls for the sex industry and/or domestic slavery follows, highlighting the skill of organised criminal networks in establishing highly profitable and large scale operating systems of women's slavery. It essentially maps out the global magnitude, and national and international trends and legal responses in combating this problem.

Women caught in criminal networks and domestic abuse are rarely treated as victims by the law. On the contrary, they are arrested and detained as violators of immigration laws, regulations prohibiting prostitution and other customary laws. Instead of protecting women the state apparatus – such as the police with its arrest and custodial powers – can be complicit in the oppression of women. The corresponding chapter on custodial violence against women shows how corruption and gender relations lead to violations of women's fundamental rights while in detention or prison.

The scope of violence women are exposed to in their everyday life is shocking, especially when we take into consideration that most of these crimes and human rights violations occur next door, in our neighbourhood, or in our nearby community. But there is hope: due to the permanent sensitisation by the international community, NGOs and media, never before has there been so much public information about the gravity and consequences of violence against women. The subsequent part of the book therefore suggests some solutions and good practices. Nevertheless, redress will be long and difficult considering how deeply violence is entrenched in the fabric of gender relations.

Chapter 1

Gendercidal Institutions against Women and Girls

'State parties shall take all appropriate measures [...] to modify the social and cultural patterns of conduct of men and women, with a view to achieving the elimination of prejudices and customary and all other practices which are based on the idea of the inferiority or the superiority of either of the sexes or on stereotyped roles for men and women.'

Convention on the Elimination of All Forms of Discrimination against Women

In recent years, systematic attention has begun to be paid, from both academic and humanitarian perspectives, to the phenomenon of *gendercide*, or gender-selective mass killing.[1] An important aspect of the study of gendercide is attention to gendercidal institutions. These can be defined as patterned human behaviour, enduring over time that leads to large-scale, disproportionate mortality among a particular gender group. Gender in turn can be understood as 'refer[ring] to the two sexes, male and female, within the context of society.' This is the definition used by the International Criminal Court, which includes gender crimes among forms of persecution against a group or collectivity.[2]

Analysis of gendercidal institutions is particularly important in understanding women's victimisation experiences worldwide and throughout history. In cases of politico-military genocide or other large-scale atrocities, it is generally men, particularly those of a 'battle age', who are most likely to be marked off for selective killing, as in Bangladesh in 1971 or Srebrenica in 1995. Women, although frequently exposed to sexual assaults and other violence (as this volume makes painfully clear), tend to emerge from politico-military genocides more intact, demographically speaking, than their male counterparts. The picture shifts when we turn to consider gendercidal institutions. These are not discrete politico-military 'events', but enduring features of human culture and society extending back millennia. Throughout history and around the world today, the number of women killed by key gendercidal institutions – female infanticide and foeticide, maternal mortality, and gendered deficits of health care, education, and nutrition (hereafter referred to as the 'female deficit') – vastly exceeds the number of women or men killed in politico-military gendercides.[3] Because these phenomena are consigned to the background of analysis and humanitarian action they are rarely explored or integrated into agendas of humanitarian assistance or development. It is striking that there is still no comparative study in English of female infanticide as a global-historical phenomenon. Moreover, there is no such a work on maternal mortality, which claims some 600,000 female lives annually – a holocaust on the order of the Rwanda genocide of 1994, repeated every year. This chapter provides an outline of the scale and character of the three key gendercidal institutions already mentioned and a brief survey of other gendercidal institutions against women that deserve incorporation into humanitarian agendas.

Female infanticide

The phenomenon of female infanticide is as old as many cultures, and has likely accounted for millions of gender-selective deaths throughout history. It remains a critical concern in a number of 'Third World' countries today, but is heavily concentrated in the two most populous countries on earth – China and India.

It hardly needs emphasising that female-specific infanticide reflects the low status accorded to women in most parts of the world. Moreover, we should not overlook the importance of state policy in buttressing discriminatory cultural formations, as R. J. Rummel emphasises in his book *Death by Government*. Rummel calls infanticide a *'type of government killing whose victims may total millions.'* He suspects that *'the death toll from infanticide must exceed that from mass sacrifice and perhaps even outright mass murder.'*[4] How much of this is gender-specific infanticide is uncertain. However, one can reasonably assume that, especially in recent centuries, girl infants are virtually always its targets.

Fortunately, improvements in women's status in many parts of the world have largely suppressed female infanticide – although many other forms of discrimination against women and girls remain. In India, as John-Thor Dahlburg has noted, *'as a whole, according to census statistics, the gender imbalance has moved from 972 females for 1,000 males in 1901, to 929 females per 1,000 males in 1996.'*[5] Ultrasounds followed by gender-selective abortions increasingly account for the demographic deficit in females, but infanticide continues to play a significant role. Female infants are killed by poison, by smothering, or by being fed unhulled rice to puncture their windpipes. In nearly all cases the murderers are women, socially conditioned, propagandised and coerced into doing the 'dirty work' of perpetuating discrimination against their sex.

In China, meanwhile, a longstanding tradition of killing or abandoning infants, especially females, has been addressed, but never fully suppressed by the post-1949 communist regime. The progressive steps towards elimination of this gendercidal institution, which was rampant in the Chinese countryside before the revolution, succeeded in producing a 'decline of excess female mortality after the establishment of the People's Republic.'[6]

A Chinese family poses for pictures in Tiananmen Square. China's top lawmakers want to make it a crime for doctors to detect an unborn baby's sex for non-medical reasons in a bid to combat the abortion of female foetuses.

However, in the 1980s the phenomenon resurged, linked by almost all commentators to the 'one-child' policy introduced by the Chinese government in 1979 to control spiralling population growth. The Chinese government appeared to recognise the linkage by allowing families in rural areas where anti-female bias is stronger, a second child if the first was a girl. Nonetheless, in September 1997, the World Health Organization's Regional Committee for the Western Pacific issued a report claiming that *'more than 50 million women were estimated to be "missing" in China because of the institutionalised killing and neglect of girls due to Beijing's population control program that limits parents to one child.'*[7]

In 1999, Jonathan Manthorpe reported a study by the Chinese Academy of Social Sciences, claiming that the imbalance between the sexes is now so distorted that there are 111 million men in China who will not be able to find a wife. As a result, the kidnapping and slave-trade of women has increased. Since 1990, official Chinese figures state, 64,000 women to 68,000 a year on average – have been rescued by authorities from forced marriages. While the world ratio of women to men is 105 to 100, in China 117 boys were born for every 100 girls in 2003, and more than 30 million women are expected to be missing by 2020 if the unfavourable demographic trend is not reversed. It is expected that when the first generation born under the one-child policy reaches the normal marital age the lack of brides will increase the magnitude of wife-selling, baby-trafficking and prostitution to the extent that these can create serious social tensions especially in rural areas where the demographic imbalance is most apparent. *'The number who have not been saved can only be guessed at. [...] The thirst for women is so acute that the slave-trader gangs are even reaching outside China to find merchandise. There are regular reports of women being abducted in such places as northern Vietnam to feed the demand in China.'*[8] The remedy is seen in the enhancement of state family planning policy, better pension fees, 'caring for girls' campaigns and passing laws banning gynaecologists from telling pregnant women the sex of a foetus once it is confirmed by ultrasound checks, and tighter prohibition over sex-selective abortions.

The 'female deficit'

Mortal discrimination against women 'operates through differential access to health care, education, and leisure above all.'[9] This section focuses on the deficiencies in health care and education, with concluding comments about nutritional deficiency, which is actually less significant in causing excess mortality among women and girls than is generally recognised.

The gendered deficiency in women's health care is perhaps the greatest contributor to excess female mortality around the world. It is important to recognise that the 'female deficit' operates in nearly every area of health care starting with maternal mortality and ending with anaemia from which some 40 per cent of women suffer.[10] According to the World Bank, investing in women's health and nutrition could save millions of women in developing countries from needless suffering and premature death. The wider benefits would also be huge, not only for national development processes, but for the children of the women concerned *'improving the health, nutrition, and maternity care of women would improve the prospects for the seven million infants who die [annually]*

Box 1.1: Some more facts about female infanticide and selective abortion

UNICEF defines female infanticide as the killing of a girl child within the first weeks of her birth. Infanticide has been practised as a brutal method of family planning in societies where boy children are still valued, economically and socially, above girls. Outright infanticide, usually of new-born girls, takes place in some communities in Asia, and medical testing for sex selection, although officially outlawed, has become a booming business in China, India and the Republic of Korea.

There are no reliable statistics on infanticide available. However, substantial disparities in gender population figures in these areas illustrate the extent of the problem. Nobel Prize laureate and economist Amartya Sen coined the term 'missing women' to describe the large number of women in the world who are not alive due to neglect and discrimination, including the practice of selective abortion that targets female foetuses. He estimated that there are 107 million women missing worldwide.

The world average for women to men is about 990 women for every 1,000 men. In Western Europe, there are as many as 1,063 women to every 1,000 men. The 2001 census in India showed 927 girls for every 1,000 boys under age six, a decline from 962 girls twenty years earlier. J. K. Banthia, the Indian census commissioner, estimated that several million foetuses have been aborted in India in the last two decades because they were female. By interpreting census figures of the last century, the commissioner states that as many as 25 million female foetuses and babies have been killed before, during or after birth in India.

Methods of ending a baby girl's life vary. A grain of paddy is forced into the baby's mouth, a table fan switched on at full blast turned towards the infant's face and milk from poisonous weeds fed to the baby are some techniques used. The Tamil Nadu Government launched an initiative in 1992 called the *Cradle scheme*, which allowed a mother to clandestinely leave a baby

she did not want in a cradle outside the Social Welfare Department. Aborting female foetuses is practised in some of India's most prosperous states in spite of the fact that in 1996 India banned the use of ultrasound machines for sex determination. However, the government only began to take broad action after the 2001 census figures appeared. Public health officials are quoted as saying that both economic and cultural forces drive the desire for boys. The greatest disparity in sex ratios existed in the northern Indian agricultural district of Fatehgarh Sahib where there are 754 girls for every 1,000 boys. Taking into account the economic prosperity of the region, it is not poverty that leads to son preference as expressed by selective abortion, but rather cultural forces. In the traditional South Asian family, a son is expected to live with his parents, earn an income, inherit property, care for his forebears in their old age and light their funeral pyre. When a daughter marries, the bride's family pays the bridegroom's family a dowry and she moves in with her husband's family, leaving her parents with nothing or even a debt. The Indian health minister recently proposed that the government begin an advertising campaign warning that there would not be enough women for men to marry if the trend continued. Such a situation exists in some states in northern India as well as in parts of China. Indian officials are also considering paying families a supplement if they have a girl and put up advertising campaigns in states most affected by selective abortion to declare that 'daughters are our pride' and 'female foeticide is illegal'. However, activists and doctors acknowledge that it could take decades to change attitudes towards girls and end the practice of selective abortion.

Sources:
A. Sen, *Development as Freedom* (New York: Alfred A. Knopf, 2000).
D. Rhode, 'India Steps Up Effort to Halt Abortions of Female Foetuses', *The New York Times* (26 October 2003).
D. Leonhardt, 'It's a Girl! (Will the Economy Suffer?)', *The New York Times* (26 October 2003).

during their first week of life and the over twenty million low-birth-weight babies born each year.'[11]

Despite enormous advances in girls' education in recent decades, the deficit of girls in education worldwide currently amounts to about 65 million females, according to an April 2003 report of the Global Campaign for Education (GCE). The deficit not only produces under-educated women, but is also closely associated with a range of other vulnerabilities on the economic and health fronts. According to the GCE, *'getting girls into school is literally a matter of life and death. The children of women who have completed primary education are on average twice as likely to survive beyond the age of five, and half as likely to suffer from malnutrition.'[12]* In sub-Saharan Africa, for example, increasing levels of women's secondary education have led to a steep decline in HIV infection rates. Educated women have fewer children and are less likely to die in pregnancy and childbirth. Educated women also earn substantially higher salaries, greatly boosting the economies of countries that invest in this crucial resource. One such country is Bangladesh, where combined government and NGO efforts to promote access and equity in education have raised girls' secondary enrolment from 13 to 56 per cent in ten years.[13]

The link between nutritional deficiency and excess mortality of girls and women, however, is a matter of controversy. The most recent and detailed surveys suggest, somewhat counter intuitively, that while evidence is plentiful for gender bias in health care, evidence for gender

bias in calorie adequacy is limited. Only in cases of 'frank starvation' does poor nutrition lead directly to increased mortality.[14] Moreover, in many studies of developing societies, boys have been found to exhibit similar or greater levels of underweight, stunting, and muscle-wasting diseases. However, pregnant women who must increase their body weight by eleven to thirteen kilograms by the end of the pregnancy, require an increased intake of calories, protein and calcium. Chronic energy malnutrition increases the likelihood of maternal morbidity, especially in the third trimester.[15] Accordingly, nutritional deficiency should be viewed primarily alongside maternal mortality and the related destructive consequences of pregnancy and childbirth in many parts of the developing world.

Table 1.1:

Number of women to 100 men in the countries where there is 95 or less women per 100 men (2003)

Country	Women per 100 men
United Arab Emirates	54
Kuwait	66
Oman	74
Bahrain	74
Saudi Arabia	86
Jordan	92
Sri Lanka	93
Brunei	93
Western Sahara	93
India	94
Afghanistan	94
Lybian Arab Jamahiriya	94
China	95
Pakistan	95
Bangladesh	95
Côte d'Ivoire	96

Note: The gender disparity in the Gulf states can be ascribed to substantial labour power of foreigners attracted by job opportunities in oil revenues. Most of these non-nationals are men either from other Arabic countries or from Asia (India, Pakistan, Bangladesh, Philippines and Sri Lanka).

Source: UN Statistics Division, *Statistics and indicators on women and men 2003*, at http://unstats.un.org/unsd/demographic/products/indwm/table1a.htm

Table 1.2:

Child mortality rate in selected countries in 1988-2000 (alphabetically)

Country (in alphabetic order)	Child mortality rate Male per 1,000	Child mortality rate Female per 1,000
Bangladesh	28	38
Benin	89	90
Botswana	18	16
Brazil	8	9
Burundi	101	114
Cameroon	69	75
Central African Republic	63	64
China	10	11
Egypt	15	16
El Salvador	17	20
Ethiopia	83	86
Gabon	32	33
Guatemala	15	18
Haiti	52	54
India	25	37
Indonesia	19	20
Kenya	36	38
Kyrgyz Republic	10	11
Malawi	101	102
Mali	136	138
Mexico	15	17
Namibia	30	34
Niger	184	202
Nigeria	66	69
Pakistan	22	37
Paraguay	10	12
Peru	19	20
Sudan	62	63
Togo	75	90
Turkey	12	14
Yemen	33	36

Note: Child mortality rate is the probability of dying between the ages of one and five expressed as a rate per 1,000 boys. Child mortality rates are higher for boys than for girls in countries where parental gender preferences are not significant. Where female child mortality is higher, most probably girls have unequal access to resources due to preferences to boys. The selected countries included in the table are those where the mortality of infant girls are higher than infant boys.

Source: World Bank, *World Development Indicators 2002* (Washington D.C.: World Bank, 2002), 122-25.

Rape of girl infants and children

Abuse, discrimination and violence are rarely conditioned by one variable acting alone. Gendered violence against women and girls is, among other factors, shaped by age, social class and geographical location. Child and infant rape represents a destructive 'gendercidal institution' against women where gendered victimisation is closely linked to age. Rapes of girls (and boys) are widespread in both underdeveloped and developed worlds. They appear to be most common in Africa, where they have attained epidemic proportions alongside another epidemic, that of AIDS. In South Africa alone, an astonishing 31,780 cases of child rape or attempted rape were reported to the police between January 2000 and October 2001. According to Anthony LoBaido, over fifteen per cent of all reported rapes are against children under eleven, and another 26 per cent against children aged between twelve and seventeen. The South African Police Service estimates that 35 rapes are committed in the country for every one that is reported.[16]

Often, men use the privileges associated with their gender – money, power and social status – to lure or coerce girls into sex. A report by Africa Rights, for example, found cases of schoolteachers attempting to obtain sex, in return for good grades or for not failing pupils in the Democratic Republic of the Congo, Ghana, Nigeria, Somalia, South Africa, Sudan, Zambia and Zimbabwe. A South African survey that included questions about the experience of rape before the age of fifteen found that schoolteachers were responsible for 32 per cent of all disclosed child rapes.[17]

A particularly grisly phenomenon is the rape of infant girls, which burst into the media spotlight in South Africa in 2000 and 2001. In one such case in November 2000, reported by LoBaido, *'a nine-month-old baby girl from Kimberley in the Northern Cape who survived a gang rape underwent a full hysterectomy and will require further surgery to repair intestinal damage […] she suffered extensive damage to her colon and anus as well.'* Six men, between 22 and 66 years of age, were charged with rape and indecent assault. Scholars and commentators have adduced various features of these infant rapes. Victims generally range in age from five to eighteen months, while their male assailants' range from adolescents to senior citizens. Attacks tend to be life threatening or outright fatal. They are also one-off and opportunistic rapes - for example, when a mother leaves her infant child in the care of a man. Male family members, for obvious reasons, are especially likely to be perpetrators; alcohol and parental neglect usually fuel the attacks. It is widely recognised that the phenomenon of infant rape differs sharply from paedophilia, which tends to target girls and boys between eight and thirteen years, and usually features an extended period of ingratiating behaviour and coercion before a direct sexual assault is inflicted.

In South Africa and other African countries, such as Zimbabwe and Zambia, men's rape of girls and female infants may be linked to the so-called 'virgin cure' myth: if a man has sex with a virgin, he will be cured of HIV, the virus that causes AIDS. In a recent South African poll, one in four male respondents expressed their belief in the myth, which has deep historical roots extending well beyond the developing world. According to Mike Earl-Taylor, the myth of the virgin cure goes back to sixteenth century Europe, and is also to be found in nineteenth century Victorian England, where, in spite of the emphasis on morality, rectitude and family values, there existed a widespread belief that sexual intercourse with a virgin was a cure for syphilis, gonorrhoea, and other sexually transmitted diseases. A variant of this belief has become especially destructive of girls' lives in Africa and elsewhere - the conviction that virgins and young girls are less likely to carry the AIDS virus and, therefore, can be exploited with less fear by predatory older males.

However, some scholars and medical experts have questioned whether the 'virgin cure' myth is really responsible for the numerous rapes of girl children and infants. Dr. Rachel Jewkes of the Gender and Health Research Group in South Africa acknowledges reported cases of the virgin cure *'as a motivating factor for child rape, but the predominant evidence suggests that this is infrequently the case.'* According to Jewkes, no overall increase is evident in South African infant rapes, despite the 'cluster' of cases that attracted media attention and public outrage at the beginning of the new millennium. Rather than emphasising, as some scholars do, the trauma of apartheid and the dislocations of democratisation in accounting for sexual violence against women and girls, Jewkes assigns greater weight to the entrenched patriarchal features of South African society, including gender inequality, notions of male sexual entitlement, and a climate of impunity for rape. Jewkes argues that *'the root of the problem of infant rape, as with rape of older girls and women, substantially lies at these more mundane doors and should be regarded as part of the spectrum of sexual violence against women and girls.'* She also cites gang initiation rituals, which are notoriously extremely brutal, as underpinning some cases of infant rape.[18]

In analysing rapes of girl children, note should be taken of the developing world's marriage institutions that often legitimise a range of sexual violence against women, particularly through the marrying of young children. According to the WHO, in Ethiopia and areas of West Africa, marriage at the age of seven or eight years is not uncommon, while in Nepal, seven per cent of girls are

Table 1.3:
Reported cases of child rape or attempted rape in South Africa in 1994-2000 (in absolute figures)

Period/Year	Reported cases
1994-1997	7,559
1998	15,732
1999	17,503
2000	31,780

Source: The Baby Rapes of South Africa, at
http://www.dreamwater.org/achildeyes/childrapes/stats.html

Table 1.4:
Data on child abuse (not necessarily sexual) in South Africa in 1994-2002 (in absolute figures)

Year	1994	1995	1996	1997	1998	1999	2000	2001	2002
Cases	2,723	2,905	2,315	2,368	2,083	2,407	2,483	2,532	3,789

Source: South African Police Service data, at
http://www.saps.gov.za/8_crimeinfo/200309/childa.html

Table 1.5:
Percentage of women over 16 years old who reported being sexually assaulted in 1992-1997 (selected cities)

Country	Study Population (city/cities)	Year	Sample size	Percentage of women (over 16 years old) sexually assaulted in the previous 5 years
Africa				
Botswana	Gaborone	1997	644	0.8
Egypt	Cairo	1992	1,000	3.1
South Africa	Johannesburg	1996	1,006	2.3
Tunisia	Grand-Tunis	1993	1,087	1.9
Uganda	Kampala	1996	1,197	4.5
Zimbabwe	Harare	1996	1,006	2.2
Latin America				
Argentina	Buenos Aires	1996	1,000	5.8
Bolivia	La Paz	1996	999	1.4
Brazil	Rio de Janeiro	1996	1,000	8.0
Colombia	Bogotá	1997	1,000	5.0
Costa Rica	San José	1996	1,000	4.3
Paraguay	Asunción	1996	587	2.7
Asia				
China	Beijing	1994	2,000	1.6
India	Budapest	1996	1,200	1.9
Indonesia	Jakarta, Surabaya	1996	1,400	2.7
Philippines	Manila	1996	1,500	0.3
Eastern Europe and Asia				
Albania	Tirana	1996	1,200	6.0
Hungary	Budapest	1996	756	2.0
Lithuania	Diauliai, Kaunas, Klaipeda, Panevezys, Vilnius	1997	1,000	4.8
Mongolia	Ulaanbaatar, Zuunmod	1996	1,201	3.1

Source: Adapted from World Health Organization, World Report on Violence and Health
(Geneva: WHO, 2002), 151.

married before the age of ten. In Rajasthan, India, 56 per cent of women responding to a survey said they had married before the age of fifteen and of these fifteen to seventeen per cent had married before age of twelve. Such customs constitute sexual violence, since the children involved are unable to protect themselves against it.[19]

It must also be recognised that sexual assaults of girls, and even infants, are not restricted to the developing world. Statistics gathered by the US Federal Bureau of Investigations for 1992 – apparently the last year that such statistics were made available – indicated that in the twelve US states surveyed, 51 per cent of female rape victims were under the age of eighteen, nearly double the representation of this age group in the broader population. A calculated sixteen per cent of rape victims, or one in six, were under the age of twelve. The Bureau of Justice statistics estimated that across the United States, some 17,000 girls under twelve were raped in 1992. These assaults bear a strong resemblance to their developing world counterparts, namely heavily structured around abusive and neglectful family relationships and the coercive exercising of social power.

Maternal mortality

The United Nations Children's Fund refers to maternal mortality and morbidity – the death of women in pregnancy or childbirth – as 'in scale and severity the most neglected tragedy of our times.' According to UNICEF, a staggering 585,000 women die annually from complications arising from pregnancy and childbirth. Moreover, *'these are not deaths like other deaths,'* the organisation noted, *'over 200,000 die of haemorrhaging, violently pumping blood onto the floor of a bus or bullock cart or blood-soaked stretcher as their families and friends search in vain for help. About 75,000 more die from attempting to abort their pregnancy themselves. [...]Perhaps 75,000 more die with brain and kidney damage in the convulsions of eclampsia,[20] another 100,000 die of sepsis, the bloodstream poisoned by a rising infection from an unhealed uterus or from retained pieces of placenta, bringing fever and hallucinations and appalling pain.'[21]*

Furthermore, Peter Adamson writes, *'for every woman who dies, approximately 30 more incur injuries, infections and disabilities, which are usually untreated and unspoken of, and which are often humiliating and painful, debilitating and lifelong.'* The ten countries with the highest annual rates of death in childbirth are Sierra Leone, Afghanistan, Bhutan, Guinea, Somalia, Angola, Chad, Mozambique, Nepal, and Yemen.

Some might question whether an institution where mortality is only indirectly caused by an identifiable agent should truly be considered gendercidal. However, the trend in international law and human rights theory in recent decades has been to include indirect infliction of mass death – through famine, disease, privation, or denial of rights and services – as a core pattern of atrocity.[22] 'In criminal law, including international criminal law,' Robert Gellately and Ben Kiernan write in a recent survey of genocide studies, *'the specific motive is irrelevant. Prosecutors need only prove that the criminal act was intentional, not accidental. [...] In this legal definition, genocidal intent also applies to acts of destruction that are not the specific goal, but are predictable outcomes or by-products of a policy, which could have been avoided by a change in that policy.'*[23] Extended to gender-discriminatory 'acts of destruction' – gendercide – a key question will be whether outcomes that dictate levels of maternal mortality are 'predictable', whether alternative policies are available, and whether the destructive policies are repeatedly chosen and thereby perpetuated. If alternatives are rejected and the necessary resources are apportioned elsewhere, with moral recklessness on the part of the government and administrators, then genocidal and gendercidal intent can be imputed.

If the 600,000 fatalities of maternal mortality, along with the millions of related health casualties among women, can be considered gendercidal, then the main culprits are the states that fail to provide the physical protection and health guarantees that women require, notably a safe and hygienic natal environment. Governments and ruling elites, who are able to find money for sophisticated weapons, mysteriously come up short when it comes to funding for hospitals, clinics and midwives; they systematically deny other resources in the fields of education, law, health, and contraception to women. Thereby denying them rights that all human beings must have in order to control their bodies and their destinies. *'Even in the largest and poorest nations,'* as UNICEF points out, *'there are usually health units and district hospitals with the doctors, midwives, nurses, drugs, and equipment that can provide obstetric care when needed. If they cannot, then this usually reflects a lack of priority, or a lack of relatively small amounts of funds for basic training and equipment, rather than the inherent impossibility of the task. [...] Action on this issue has been paralysed for too long by the idea that only the building of hundreds more hospitals and the training of thousands more expensive obstetricians can make the right kind of care available to [those] who need it. But the fact is that properly trained health workers and midwives, working in modern health units with inexpensive equipment and reliable supplies of relatively cheap drugs, can usually cope – and know when to call in obstetricians if a caesarean section is necessary. [...] Reducing maternal deaths and injuries is therefore not a matter of possibilities, but of priorities. The strategies that work have been identified. And the resources will follow if priority lights the way.'*[24]

A poster showing missing women from Vancouver's downtown eastside. The women, all sex trade workers, join the 45 other women reported as missing since 1984.

© Reuters, Andy Clark, 2001

Table 1.6:

Lifetime chance of dying in pregnancy or childbirth by UNICEF regions in 2004

REGION	Lifetime chance of dying in pregnancy or childbirth (affected not only by maternal mortality rates but also by the number of births per women)
Sub-Saharan Africa	1 in 13
Eastern and Southern Africa	1 in 15
Western and Central Africa	1 in 16
Middle East and North Africa	1 in 55
South Asia	1 in 54
East Asia and the Pacific	1 in 283
Latin America and the Caribbean	1 in 157
CEE/CIS and Baltic States	1 in 797
Least developed countries	1 in 16
Developing countries	1 in 61
Industrialised countries	1 in 4,085
World	1 in 75

Source: UNICEF, *The State of the World's Children 2004* (Geneva: UNICEF), 12.

The well-known example of Cuba demonstrates that even poor countries can affect massive transformations in women's health, including maternal mortality. After the 1959 revolution, policies were instituted to extend health infrastructure beyond the cities. The impact was felt in key areas like maternal mortality. Today, nearly all Cuban mothers give birth in hospitals, with trained staff to handle any complications. By 1996 – in the middle of a harsh decade of economic austerity – Cuba's maternal mortality rate stood at 2.4 per 10,000 births, barely higher than North American figures. Globalising grassroots approach would involve training some 850,000 health workers, according to UNICEF and World Health Organization reports, as well as the necessary drugs and equipment. The total cost would be US$200 million – about the price of half a dozen jet fighters.[25]

Domestic and serial killings of women

Domestic and serial killings of women are among the primary forms of fatal violence that women in the developed world confront. For the most part, thanks to social and technological modernisation, some traditional forms of violence that inflict a huge death toll on women in the developing world – such as female infanticide and maternal mortality – have ceased to feature significantly in the lives of western women. However, domestic murders of women and girls, along with the reality and diffuse threat of serial killings, have not disappeared. According to the 2002 World Health Organization's World Report on Violence and Health 40 to 70 per cent of female murder victims were killed by their husbands or boyfriends, frequently in the context of an ongoing abusive relationship.

This contrasts with the situation of male murder victims as evidenced by, for example, the United States where only four percent of men murdered between 1976 and 1996 were killed by their wives, ex-wives or girlfriends. In Australia between 1989 and 1996, the figure was 8.6 per cent.[26]

Serial killings of women, although far less frequent than domestic murders, have nonetheless influenced how women live their lives throughout the developed and developing worlds. In the late nineteenth century, 'Jack the Ripper' stalked the streets of the poor London district of Whitechapel, fuelling a trend – the serial murder of prostitutes – that remains prominent today. In the twentieth century, many serial killers preyed on women in the United States, among them Richard Speck, Albert DeSalvo (the Boston Strangler), Ted Bundy, and Richard Ramirez (the Hillside Strangler). Other developed societies, both capitalist and communist, have known male serial killers of women. They include Germany (where Bruno Ludke killed at least 80 women from 1928 to 1943), Poland (Lucian Staniak, who killed twenty women in the 1960s), and France (Thierry Paulin and Jean-Thierry Mathurin, who targeted elderly Parisian women between 1984 and 1987).

The carnage wreaked by many male serial killers of women and girls almost defies belief. As this text was written, newspapers reported that Gary Ridgway, a blue-collar worker, had pleaded guilty to murdering 48 women, the largest death toll of any serial killer in US history. Ridgway confessed that he was the 'Green River Killer' who, like so many serial killers, chose prostitutes and vagrant women as his victims, because their deaths were less likely to evoke concern and public outrage. Men who serially murder

Police carry the corpse of a woman found outside of Ciudad Juarez, Mexico, where more than 300 women, mostly aged between 15 and 30, have been murdered in the past decade. Most of the victims have been found in outlying areas of the city and usually bear signs of torture and rape.

Gary Ridgway (far right), on trial in 2003 for the Green River Killer case, at that time the largest unsolved serial murder case in American history. He was later convicted.

women are frequently romanticised for their supposed 'charm' and the wiles they display in luring victims to their deaths. With few exceptions, it is these male murderers that history remembers, not their female victims. The sexual dimension that commonly features in male serial killings of women and girls also contributes to the prurient glamorisation of these crimes.

Neither domestic violence nor serial killings exclusively target women and girls, nor are they committed exclusively by men. But specific attention to killings of women in domestic and serial contexts is justified, for two main reasons. First, the relatively lower vulnerability of women to murder in general (in most western societies, women account for one-quarter to one-third of murder victims) means that serial and, especially, domestic killings figure disproportionately in women's murder statistics. Second, when both domestic murderers and serial killers target

victims of the opposite sex, it is overwhelmingly men who target women. These killings, and related crimes such as rape and sexual torture, tend to carry powerful overtones of misogyny or hatred of women in general. In part because these acts reflect a broader hostility, they evoke fear among the general population of women in developed societies, far beyond that justified by statistical measures alone. Every woman who returns home trembling with the thought of the treatment that might await her at her male partner's hands, and every woman who clutches her keys between her fingers as she walks through a parking garage at night, has felt a chill of gendered fear that is more muted or entirely absent in the case of men, even if men can also be victims of domestic homicide and serial killers. This text has not discussed the separate phenomenon of mass killings, defined by the US Federal Bureau of Investigation as 'any murder of four or more victims at

Box 1.2: Marc Dutroux – a serial killer

Marc Dutroux is escorted away after appearing before the Neufchâteau court for kidnapping, sexual abuse and murder of several girls in the mid-1990s in Belgium.

Victim Laetitia Delhez (left) cries in the arms of Sabine Dardenne (right) during a visit of the court to the house where they had been held captive by Marc Dutroux.

On 1 March 2004, the trial of Marc Dutroux started in the town of Arlon in northern Belgium. Dutroux was arrested in 1996, together with three accomplices including his wife, and was accused of the murder, rape, abduction and imprisonment of six girls aged eight to nineteen. Among his victims, two eight-year-old girls were imprisoned in the cellar of his house, sexually abused and later starved to death. Their bodies were found in a garden next to his house. Two other victims, aged seventeen and nineteen, were also tortured and then murdered. Dutroux's arrest was triggered by the disappearance of two more girls in August 1996. These two, aged twelve and fourteen, terrified but alive, were found by the police in a special dungeon constructed in the basement of Dutroux's house. They also found several hundred pornographic videos in different houses Dutroux had bought and used for his 'businesses'.

Sabine Dardenne and Laetitia Delhez, the two surviving victims, testified in the trial. The dreadful crimes shocked the public as much as the inefficiency of the police and justice system, as Dutroux had already been accused twice in the past for kidnapping, rape, and torture, but was first released because of lack of evidence, and the second time after just three years in prison. Dutroux has now been sentenced to life imprisonment.

Sources:
Marc Dutroux, A Pedophile and Child-Killer, *The Crime Library*, at http://crimelibrary.com
A. Fouché, Belgium's trial of shame, *BBC News* (17 June 2004), at http://news.bbc.co.uk
Profile: The Dutroux survivors, *BBC News* (17 June 2004), at http://news.bbc.co.uk
Belgian kidnap victim tells story, *BBC News* (24 February 2003), at http://news.bbc.co.uk. Sabine Dardenne tells her story: One of the victims of the notorious Belgian suspected paedophile Marc Dutroux has for the first time told the horrific story of her kidnapping ordeal.

one time and place.' Mass killings in developed societies have tended to be indiscriminate, or perhaps weighted statistically against males. This reflects the fact that such killings generally occur in public spaces and in contexts where men predominate; think of the terrorist attacks on 11 September 2001 in the US, which killed three times as many men as women. However, recent history does provide us with a particularly grotesque case of mass murder of women in the developed world. This is the so-called 'Montreal Massacre' on 6 December 1989, when a deranged young man with an assault rifle separated female college students from their male counterparts and murdered fourteen young women. The massacre, the worst in Canadian history, shocked a nation accustomed to low homicide rates and limited gun crime. Many saw it as highlighting the broader vulnerability to domestic and public violence that remains a reality for women even in the world's wealthiest and most developed societies.

Endnotes

1 See A. Jones (ed), *Gendercide and Genocide* (Nashville: Vanderbilt University Press, 2004). See also the Gendercide Watch website, at http://www.gendercide.org. It includes 22 detailed case-studies of gendercidal killing, including key gendercidal institutions targeting both females and males. The term 'gendercide' was coined by M. A. Warren in her book, *Gendercide: The Implications of Sex Selection* (Totowa: Rowman and Littlefield, 1985).

2 See Article 7.3 of *the Statute of the International Criminal Court*, at http://www.preventgenocide.org/law/icc/statute/part-a.htm#2

3 However, men also suffer from male-specific institutions that under certain conditions can be gendercidal, notably corvée (forced) labour, military conscription, and incarceration.

4 R. J. Rummel, *Death by Government* (Somerset: Transaction Publishers, 1994), 65-66, emphasis added.

5 J.-T. Dahlburg, 'Where Killing Baby Girls "Is No Big Sin"', *The Los Angeles Times* (28 February 1994).

6 A. J. Coale and J. Banister, 'Five Decades of Missing Females in China', *Demography*, Vol. 31, No. 3 (August 1994), 472.

7 See J. Farah, 'Cover-up of China's Gender-cide', *Western Journalism Center/FreeRepublic* (29 September 1997), at http://www.freerepublic.com/forum/a8896.htm. Farah refers to the gendercide as 'the biggest single holocaust in human history'.

8 J. Manthorpe, 'China Battles Slave Trading in Women: Female Infanticide Fuels a Brisk Trade in Wives', *Vancouver Sun* (11 January 1999).

9 L. F. De Rose et al., 'Does Female Disadvantage Mean Lower Access to Food?', *Population and Development Review*, Vol. 26, No. 3 (New York, September 2000), 539.

10 World Bank, *A New Agenda for Women's Health and Nutrition* (Washington D.C.: World Bank, 1994), at http://www.worldbank.org/html/extdr/hnp/health/newagenda/women.htm

11 World Bank, *A New Agenda for Women's Health and Nutrition*.

12 GCE spokesperson quoted in 'Annan Plea for Girls' Schooling', *BBC Online* (8 April 2003), at http://news.bbc.co.uk/go/pr/fr/-/2/hi/uk_news/education/2929541.stm

13 Global Campaign for Education, *A Fair Chance: Attaining Gender Equality in Basic Education by 2005* (April 2003), 4, at http://www.campaignforeducation.org/_html/actionweek/downloads/AFairChanceFullReport.pdf

14 De Rose et al., *Does Female Disadvantage Mean Lower Access to Food?*, 517-18.

15 World Health Organization, *Women's Health in South-East Asia* (Geneva: WHO, 2000), at http://w3.whosea.org/women2/nutrition.htm

16 M. Earl-Taylor, 'HIV/AIDS, the Stats, the Virgin Cure and Infant Rape', *Science in Africa* (April 2002), at http://www.scienceinafrica.co.za/2002/april/virgin.htm

17 A. C. LoBaido, 'Child-Rape Epidemic in South Africa', *WorldNetDaily* (26 December 2001), at http://www.worldnetdaily.com/news/article.asp?ARTICLE_ID=25806

18 Taylor, 'HIV/AIDS, the Stats, the Virgin Cure and Infant Rape' and 'The "Virgin Myth" and Child Rape in South Africa', *Science in Africa* (April 2002).

19 E. G. Krug et al. (eds), *World Report on Violence and Health* (Geneva: WHO, 2002), 89-121, at http://www.who.int/violence_injury_prevention/violence/world_report/en/FullWRVH.pdf

20 Convulsions, or seizures, occurring during or immediately after pregnancy.

21 P. Adamson, 'Deaf to the Screams', *New Internationalist* (January/February 1997), athttp://www.newint.org/issue287/adamson.html

22 Genocide studies, for example, has increasingly focused on cases such as Stalin's famine imposed on the Ukrainians in the 1930s, the destruction of a large part of East Timor's native population by disease and starvation following the Indonesian invasion of 1975, and the extermination of up to 95 per cent of the indigenous population of the Americas through an intersecting process of large-scale killing, enslavement, exile, and cultural annihilation. 'Indirect' killing through disease and privation is generally recognised as constituting part of the American genocide, as it is in the case of the millions of Jews who died by these proximate causes at the hands of the Nazis.

23 R. Gellately and B. Kiernan, 'Introduction', in R. Gellately and B. Kiernan (eds), *The Spectre of Genocide: Mass Murder in Historical Perspective* (Cambridge: Cambridge University Press, 2003), 15, emphasis added.

24 P. Adamson, 'Commentary: A Failure of Imagination' [on maternal mortality], *The Progress of Nations* (New York: UNICEF, 1996), at http://www.unicef.org/pon96/womfail.htm

25 Other countries, including Indonesia, Iran, Mexico, and Uganda, have taken important steps to confront maternal mortality and related health crises. See United Nations, *Women and Health* (June 2000), at http://www.un.org/womenwatch/daw/followup/session/presskit/fs3.htm

26 WHO, *World Report on Violence and Health*, 87-122.

Chapter 2

Rooted in Tradition : Community-Based Violence against Women

A seven-year old girl dies from an infection she developed after a traditional midwife used a blade to slice off her clitoris and external genitalia.

A young woman who had eloped to marry a man without her father's permission returns to talk to her father in an attempt to change his mind. Her father beheads her, carries her head out onto the streets shouting, 'I have cleansed my family's honour.'

A man throws acid at a woman's face after she rejects his advances.

A woman is doused with gasoline and set on fire by her husband and his family when her family does not pay them more dowry money.

These are examples of traditional forms of violence against women

Tradition is the passing down of elements of a culture from generation to generation. As such, these forms of violence are deeply ingrained in their respective societies and have, to a large extent, gone unquestioned. The victims of such traditional forms of violence are often illiterate and uneducated. Furthermore, women and girls are the weakest members of traditional societies and as such have little recourse to the law or legal help. Many have questioned why women are seemingly so willing to perpetuate violent practices, some of which they suffered from as girls. It is best to remember that as the weakest members of their societies, women have internalised the expectations of their communities and understand that in order to ensure their daughters' survival and acceptance within the community, they must continue to practice traditions that they may not necessarily agree with.

Little will change until women, and their communities, are better educated as to the harmful effect of these traditional practices and are offered alternative rites to replace the harmful traditions that are currently in place. It is also helpful to place these acts of violence within a larger international context of violence against women. Throughout the world, violence is meted out against girls and women. Whether such violence exists in a traditional framework or not, it is still violence and as such should be opposed. Many forms of violence against women are motivated by the desire to control female sexuality – whether it is called an honour killing in a traditional society or a crime of passion in a less traditional community, the end result is the same: a crime has been committed. An issue that often comes up when discussing traditional forms of violence against women is that of cultural relativism. Cultural relativism, issuing from the philosophical belief that all views are equally valid, denies the universality of human rights by arguing that the rights are culturally determined, which logically leads to the idea that in some societies it is acceptable for women to be limited in their freedom and controlled even in their intimate life (control of sexuality). The Women's Rights Division of the Human Rights Watch, strongly commented against such a way of thinking as stated in the following: *'Our duty as activists is to expose and denounce as human rights violations those practices and policies that silence and subordinate women. We reject any law, culture, or religion in which women are systematically discriminated against, excluded from political participation and public life, segregated in their daily lives, raped in armed conflict, beaten in their homes, denied equal divorce or inheritance rights, killed for having sex, forced to marry, assaulted for not conforming to gender norms, and sold into forced labour.'*[1] The United Nations Declaration on the Elimination of Violence against Women, signed by many countries where traditional forms of gender-based violence have been practiced, defines violence against women as any act of gender-based violence that results in physical, sexual or psychological harm or suffering to women, directly pointing out *'female genital mutilation and other traditional practices harmful to women.'*[2]

Female genital mutilation

The World Health Organization estimates that 6,000 girls a day (more than 2 million per year) are genitally mutilated. It has classified female genital mutilation (FGM) into four types:

Type I: Excision of the prepuce, with or without excision of part or all of the clitoris.

Type II: Excision of the clitoris with partial or total excision of the labia minora.

Type III: Excision of part or all of the external genitalia and stitching/narrowing of the vaginal opening (infibulation).

Type IV: Unclassified, which includes pricking, piercing or incising of the clitoris and/or labia; stretching of the clitoris and/or labia; cauterisation by burning of the clitoris and surrounding tissue.

Genital mutilation causes lasting psychological trauma, extreme pain, chronic infections, bleeding, abscesses, tumours, urinary tract infections and infertility. According to the World Health Organization (WHO), the immediate and long-term health consequences of FGM vary according to the type and severity of the procedure performed. Immediate complications include severe pain, shock, haemorrhage, urine retention, ulceration of the genital region and injury to adjacent tissue. Haemorrhage and infection can cause death. Long-term consequences include cysts and abscesses, keloid scar formation, damage to the urethra resulting in urinary incontinence, dyspareunia (painful sexual intercourse) and other sexual dysfunction as well as difficulties with childbirth. The impact of this practice on the psychosexual and psychological health of girls and women is profound.

The practice is not exclusive to one religion or social class. It is older than Christianity and Islam. Egyptian mummies are said to display characteristics of mutilation. As recent as the 1950s, partial or total removal of the clitoris was prescribed in parts of western Europe and the United States in response to hysteria, epilepsy, mental disorders, masturbation, nymphomania, melancholia and lesbianism. Today, girls and women are subjected to genital mutilation in at least twenty-eight countries, mostly in Africa, but as immigrants are taking the practice with them to their destination countries, the practice is spreading to Europe, the United States and Canada. It is carried out for several reasons, including restriction of female sexuality and as a rite of passage not only into womanhood, but also into marriage. Girls who do not undergo the procedure are considered unable to marry. Within the international community there has been a certain reluctance to speak out against FGM, as with many other traditional forms of violence, in deference to cultural relativism. In the 1950s the UN Commission on the Status of Women addressed the issues of FGM and other traditional ceremonies perpetrated against women in the name of customary law asking the member states to vigorously take action against *'…all customs which violate the physical integrity of women, and which thereby violate the dignity and worth of the human person as proclaimed in the Charter and in the Universal Declaration of Human Rights.'*[3] The diffident response of member states indicated that these practices would have long lives - some states considered the effort to abolish them as violations of the UN Charter, whereas others accentuated the necessity of a gradual process of education that could lead to abandoning of the practices. The issues of the adverse effects of the practices on the health and well-being of the victims had not been discussed within the UN until the United Nations' International Women's Year in 1975. The harmful traditional practices became a frequent subject of the women's movement in the 1980s and 1990s spurred on by activities of many grassroots NGOs that sprung up in the countries where these practices prevailed. They asked their international counterparts to be vociferous in opposition, but to leave it to the local groups to come up with the best ways to eradicate the practice. According to their experience, at the grassroots level, the traditional forms of violence against women can be challenged effectively:

- By questioning the reason for their continued existence.
- Through education aimed at raising awareness of the harm such practices have on girls and women.
- By fighting for legislation to outlaw these practices if and where possible.
- By offering alternative rites that do not threaten the well-being or lives of girls and women.
- By understanding the impact of these harmful practices on girls and women.

Activists and organisations who have made headway in eradicating female genital mutilation have found that one of the most effective ways of persuading a community to stop subjecting its girls to it, is by highlighting its harmful physical and emotional consequences (see 'Female genital mutilation' in the list of organisation dealing with women's rights in this volume). One of the most moving examples of the positive effect of using awareness to eradicate FGM that this author has come across involved a young Ethiopian couple who used their wedding as a demonstration against the practice (see box 2.1).

Honour killings

Honour killings are murders that occur in defence of perceived individual, family or community honour. In the case of honour killings of women and adolescent girls, the victim is generally perceived to have behaved in a sexually immoral, undignified or provocative manner. 'Immoral' behaviour may take the form of marital infidelity, refusing to submit to an arranged marriage, demanding a divorce, flirting with or receiving phone calls from men, failing to serve a meal on time, or 'allowing oneself' to be raped. In one notorious case in the Turkish province of Sanliurfa, a young woman's throat was cut because an admirer had arranged for a song to be dedicated to her on the radio.

UNICEF estimates that 130 million girls and women have been genitally mutilated. According to the World Health Organisation more than two million girls are mutilated per year, a rate of once every fifteen seconds.

As such examples indicate, honour killings of women and adolescent girls reflect enduring patriarchal traditions. Paradoxically, women are viewed *'on the one hand as fragile creatures who need protection and on the other as evil Jezebels from whom society needs protection,'* in the words of Canadian journalist Sally Armstrong. In patriarchal tradition, since the male is the sole protector of the female he must have total control of her. If his protection is violated, he loses honour because he failed to protect her.[4]

As commonly defined, most honour killings of women occur in Islamic countries - to the extent that they reflect specifically Islamic features of these societies. However, two qualifications should be noted. First, honour killings are by no means 'Islamic' in the sense that they are sanctioned by Islamic religion or law. There is not a word in the Koran about death in the name of honour. Second, although the forms may differ, honour killings and related crimes against women are a global phenomenon. As Widney Brown of Human Rights Watch notes, the practice goes across cultures and across religions.

Honour killings of women have reached crisis levels in some Islamic societies in the Middle East, North Africa, and West Asia. In Pakistan, a 1999 Human Rights Report cited 888 women murdered in this manner in a single Pakistani province (Punjab). A report by the independent Human Rights Commission of Pakistan stated at least 461 women killed by family members in 2002 in just two of Pakistan's four provinces - Punjab and Sindh. In the first eight months of 2003 at least 637 women and girls were reported murdered in honour killings.[5] Even low estimates suggest that at least three Pakistani women are killed for 'honour' every day. Sometimes the attacks leave the female victim not dead, but disfigured for life, through attacks by fire, gasoline, or acid. The Progressive Women's Association of Pakistan recorded 3,560 hospitalisations of women after such attacks. Authorities generally turn a blind eye to the crimes. *'We deal with these cases every day,'* says Pakistani lawyer and woman activist Nahida Mahbooba Elahi, *'but I have seen very few convictions. The men say the wife did not obey their orders, or was having relations with someone else. The police often say it is a domestic matter and refuse to pursue the case. Some judges even justify it and do not consider it murder.'*[6]

In the Middle East similar patterns prevail. Controversy has especially been pronounced in the case of Jordan, reputed to be one of the more liberal Arab states, where until recently honour killings were actually sanctioned by law. Under Article 340 of the Jordanian penal code, a man could be excused for killing his wife or a female relative, if she was judged to have committed adultery. After international protests the article was grudgingly amended by the Jordanian parliament, dominated by Bedouin traditionalists. However, other legislation grants exemptions to murderers who are 'provoked' into their crimes. The end result is the same - a tacit sanctioning of honour killings of women. Once a murder has been judged an 'honour killing', the usual sentence is from three months to one year. In many, if not most instances, it is an adolescent male who is pressed into committing the crime, since his underage status virtually guarantees that he will be let off lightly. It is not exceptional that such offenders, often under eighteen, are treated by their communities as heroes.

The scale of honour killings in Jordan is difficult to assess, which is a problem that confronts analysts in nearly all instances of violence against women. In the mid-1990s, the liberal Jordan Times, which has played a key role in publicising and condemning honour killings of Jordanian women, estimated that between twenty and sixty women were murdered in this manner every year. However, others argue that the death toll may run into the hundreds, while hundreds of more women are condemned to live in

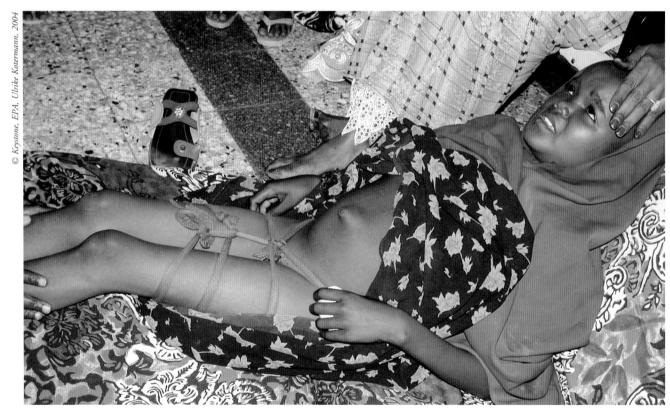

Nine-year old Somalian Fay Mohammed, who was circumcised several days before the picture was taken, lays with her legs bound so that the wound can heal.

© Keystone, EPA, Ulrike Kotermann, 2004

Box 2.1: Two examples of persuading a community to stop female genital mutilation

Genet Girma and her bridegroom Addisie Abosie did the unthinkable in their community when they wore placards clearly stating their positions on FGM. 'I am not circumcised, learn from me,' Genet's placard read. Her groom wore a matching one that said 'I am very happy to be marrying an uncircumcised woman.' Genet was the first known woman in Kembatta, Ethiopia, to marry in public who refused the mutilation of her genitals that is considered a rite of passage for all girls and young women in that part of the country. Between the ages of sixteen and eighteen, young women in that region are subjected to excision - the removal of the clitoris, as well as, of the inner and outer labia. Genet said in an interview, conducted during a visit to New York in January 2003, that before her wedding in 2002 she ran away from home rather than undergoing the ordeal. Both her family and that of Addisie rejected the couple and would not attend their wedding. Because of Genet and Addisie's courage in so openly confronting the practice, some 2,000 other people attended the ceremony, which was televised and covered extensively in Ethiopia's main newspaper. Their families accepted the couple several months after their wedding, when they were expecting their first child. Since their wedding and public stand against FGM, many other couples followed suit. It was obvious from the interview with Genet and Addisie that their stand on FGM was a result of educational and advocacy work of the Kembatta Women's Centre at their school that taught them the harmful effects of the practice. The couple said they were able to use the information the centre gave them to make the link between FGM and their respective mothers' difficulty in giving birth. Several years before he got married, Addisie decided that, unlike all the men in his community who took it for granted that their brides were cut, he would not expect his wife to have undergone the procedure. The turning point for him came when he attended the birth of his mother's sixth child. She gave birth fourteen times, but only eleven of the children survived. At the time, Addisie was a teenager, sitting outside the room waiting for the arrival of his latest sibling. His mother's labour lasted for four days and Addisie left before the actual birth because, he said, he could not bear to stay when he heard the traditional birth attendant ask for a blade. A few years later he went to the same birth attendant, also a bone setter, to treat a soccer injury. He asked her why she had requested the blade all those years ago. The birth attendant told him that as a result of excision, his mother's genitals were scarred so badly they had lost their elasticity and the only way to help the baby out was to cut through the scar tissue.

Making this link between FGM and its physical consequences was also key to a success story in the fight against the practice in Senegal. Ginger Adams Otis recounts how a programme that is on its way to eradicating FGM in Senegal is about to be replicated in other African countries. A non-governmental organisation called Tostan has combined health education and human rights awareness to inform Senegalese about the dangers of genital mutilation. Tostan's founder and director Molly Melching has devised programmes that will be available to other health workers and community leaders. Currently, there are about 4,000 Senegalese villages out of 13,000 that still practice FGM. Ms. Melching estimates FGM could be eradicated from Senegal within two to five years. Tostan's programme began by educating women in basic health and human rights issues. Teaching methods included song, dance and theatre because most women in Senegal have little formal schooling. The human rights dimension of classes changed the way local women viewed their right (and the right of their daughters) to physical integrity. As Ms. Melching affirmed, the programme essentially explained the health factors of FGM, which helped many women understand the linkages between the practice and the experiences of chronic pain and fevers during their childhood after the ceremony. These fevers were caused by infections that wear down otherwise healthy young girls and sometimes end their lives. As women gained more knowledge about the female anatomy, more and more of them came to question the need for female genital mutilation.

Sources:
Kembatta Women's Self-Help Centre, at http://www.kmgselfhelp.org
Tostan, at http://www.tostan.org
Women's eNews, December 2003, at http://www.womensenews.org

---

perpetual fear and isolation, not daring to leave the relative safety of their homes. In spite of the opposition to honour killings by King Abdullah and the widely respected Queen Noor the situation has not improved much. In September 2003 the Parliament of Jordan rejected a proposed law imposing harsher punishment for men who commit honour killings. In neighbouring Syria, legislation (Article 548) exempts a man from punishment if he discovers his wife engaged in adulterous or 'illegitimate' sexual acts.

Overall, the United Nations Population Fund (UNPFA) estimates that 5,000 women are killed annually in honour crimes, the majority of them in the Islamic world. However, crimes with close parallels to the honour killings in Islamic communities are committed worldwide. Honour killings have been reported in Bangladesh, Brazil, Ecuador, Egypt, India, Israel, Italy, Jordan, Morocco, Pakistan, Sweden, Turkey, Uganda and the United Kingdom. In the United Kingdom twelve such killings were recorded in 2002.

It is not always women who are targeted in honour attacks. The blood feuds of the Balkans and Caucasus are closely intertwined with the honour of communities and, in particular, their male members. However, such feuds focus exclusively on vengeance against male enemies, combined with an exaggerated, almost surreal protectiveness towards females. Further complicating the gender picture, honour crimes against women are widely supported by other women in the victim's community. *'Females in the family – mothers, mothers-in-law, sisters, and cousins – frequently support the attacks. It's a community mentality,'* notes Zaynab Nawaz of Amnesty International.[7] This participation illustrates once more that although women may not agree with such harsh

 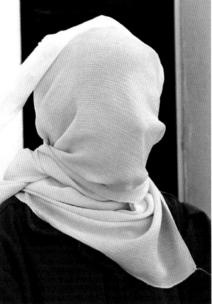 

© Reuters, Ali Jarekji, 1999

Three Jordanian women, who were either raped, assaulted or had relationships outside of marriage, are being kept in jail to protect them from honour killing by their families - mostly the males who are called to perform such acts with the support of the family and the society.

justice, they enable it as a form of protecting their own status when behaving as required of them in these communities. However, there are some examples of local women who raised their voices publicly against traditional forms of violence. The work of Jordanian journalist Rana Husseini is an example of a voice that has long championed the cause for the end of honour killings and for tougher sentencing for the perpetrators of this crime. Rana Husseini began writing about honour killings in 1993 for her newspaper, the English-language daily *Jordan Times*. Despite death threats and harsh criticisms, she has continued to expose the cruelty of honour

Table 2.1 :
Occurrence of female genital mutilation in 1998-2002 among women aged 15-40 years (in percentage)

Country	Percentage
Guinea	99
Egypt	97
Mali	92
Sudan	90
Eritrea	89
Ethiopia	80
Burkina Faso	72
Mauritania	71
Cote d'Ivoire	45
Chad	45
Kenya	38
Central African Republic	36
Nigeria	25
Yemen	23
Tanzania	18
Benin	17
Niger	5

Source : UNICEF, *The Stapte of World's Children 2004* (New York: UNICEF House, 2004), 134-35.

Table 2.2 :
National legislation efforts to eliminate female genital mutilation (year of enactment)

African Nations	
Benin (2003)	Ghana (1994)
Burkina Faso (1996)	Guinea (1965)
Central African Republic (1966)	Kenya (2001)
Chad (2003)	Senegal (1999)
Côte d'Ivoire (1998)	Tanzania (1998)
Djibouti (1994)	Togo (1998)
Egypt (Ministerial Decree, 1996)	Nigeria (multiple states, 1999-2002)
Industrialised Nations	
Australia (6 of 8 states, 1994-97)	Norway (1995)
Belgium (2000)	Sweden (1982, 1998)
Canada (1997)	United Kingdom (1985)
New Zealand (1995)	United States (Federal law, 1996; 16 of 50 states, 1994-2000)
Prosecutions in cases of FGM	
Burkina Faso	Senegal
Egypt	Sierra Leone
Ghana	France

Source : A. Rahman and N. Toubia, *Female Genital Mutilation: A Guide to Laws and Policies Worldwide* (London, New York: Zed Books, 2000), at http://www.crlp.org/pub_fac_fgmicpd.html

killings. She has shown how these acts hold both women and men hostage. In her writing she has often emphasised how Jordanian men are just as much victims of the strict, tribal code of honour as women are.[8]

Dowry-killing, bride burnings and stove deaths

One of the most extreme and destructive of these practices is dowry killings in India, where women are killed because the dowry or bride-wealth that they bring to a marriage is deemed insufficient by the groom's family, and an affront to family honour. According to the United Nations Children's Fund (UNICEF), an astonishing 5,000 women die in dowry killings every year in India. Although these are not normally tabulated as honour killings, they have a similar pattern. Also note that many 'ordinary' forms of domestic violence against women, fatal and otherwise, involve perceived transgressions against a male's sense of personal honour. This often generates pathological possessiveness and homicidal jealousy towards female partners and close relatives.

According to UNICEF, bride burnings are when husbands engineer an accident, frequently the bursting of a kitchen stove, when they feel the obligatory marriage dowry (gifts from in-laws) is not sufficient. A tiny percentage of these murderers are brought to justice.

'Stove deaths' is a term that refers to the punishment of a wife by setting her ablaze. Her death is then often blamed on an accident, such as the explosion of a stove, or on a suicide attempt. Juliette Terzieff writing in *Women's eNews* from Pakistan explains that the reasons for burning women vary, but most cases centre around the failure to give birth to a son, the desire to marry a second wife without having the financial means to support the first and long-running animosity with mothers-in-law. Juliette Terzieff reports that between 1994-2002, some 4,000 women have been doused in kerosene and set alight by family members in the area surrounding the Pakistani capital Islamabad. Less than four percent survive. Human rights campaigners estimate that three women per day die as a result of stove deaths in Pakistan. Activists claim that husbands' families often bribe the police to label cases as suicides. Pakistani activist Shahnaz Bukhari is a leading campaigner against stove deaths in her country. In an interview, she explained that the misery of the victims she encountered spurred her work. As a clinical psychologist, she founded the Progressive Women's Association in 1986 to fight for the rights of abused women and opened a shelter in her ancestral home for female victims of violence and their children. She also campaigns for opening similar centres in Pakistan, as well as, for tougher laws against perpetrators.[9]

Acid attacks

Acid throwing is one particularly vicious and damaging form of violence against women and girls practiced in some Asian countries. Acid violence is a relatively recent phenomenon, with the first documented case occurring in 1967 in Bangladesh. Throwing of sulphuric acid on the face and body of young females has become an increasingly popular way of expressing anger or frustration by refused suitors, jilted lovers, ex-husbands, and the like. Some of these young women are nothing more than at the wrong place at the wrong time.

Such attacks often leave victims disfigured and scarred for life. Nitric and sulphuric acid (the kind found in car batteries) causes skin tissue to melt; in some cases leaving the bones underneath exposed and dissolving the bone. Most seriously, acid striking the eyes permanently damages them, and many survivors lose one or both eyes. Victims

Acid attacks rank among the worst crimes against women living in Pakistan. Shaheena, fifteen years old, was blinded by acid that her brother-in-law threw at her sister Sakeena.

Box 2.2 : The Sharia penalty - stoning to death for adultery : A Nigerian example

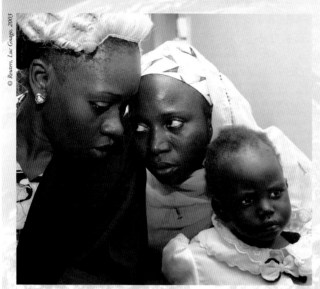

Accused Nigerian mother Amina Lawal (center) holds her baby girl while speaking to her lawyer during the court appeal that overturned her death sentence by stoning for alleged adultery.

The *Sharia* is an Islam-derived law system, a religious set of rules and guidelines governing relations in a Muslim society. It has several sources, the most important ones being the *Qur'an* (the Message from *Allah*), the *Sunna* (the life of the Prophet Muhammad as narrated in the *Hadith*) and the *Ijma*, the consensus of Islamic legal scholars.

In Nigeria, *Sharia* law has been in force for a long time but was limited to personal status and civil law until 2000 when it was extended to apply to criminal law in the twelve (out of thirty-six) Nigerian states with a predominantly Muslim population. One controversial category of crime is the *hadd* (or *hudud* in plural) which hold specific punishments derived from the *Qur'an* and the *Hadith*, such as stoning to death for extra-marital sex and adultery, amputation for theft or armed robbery, and flogging for drinking alcohol. Such severe penalties - seen today as cruel, inhuman, and degrading treatment and punishment - have raised fundamental human rights issues conflicting with international human rights law, in particular with women's rights.

In March 2002, thirty-year-old Nigerian Amina Lawal, a destitute divorced woman, was sentenced to death by stoning - that is to be buried up to her neck and have rocks thrown at her head - for

being pregnant outside of marriage. Amina Lawal's case is but one of many others illustrating evidence of the prejudice of legislation and practice to women. Other examples are Safiya Hussaini, a divorced woman accused of being pregnant with the child of a married lover, who received a death sentence to be stoned; and Bariya Ibrahim Magazu, an eighteen-year-old girl, who, after having been raped by three men and becoming pregnant, was sentenced to 100 lashes. In all three cases the men have been acquitted due to lack of evidence. Bias in the collection of proof of adultery allegations explains this trend as pregnancy is satisfactory evidence for women to be convicted, while for men four eyewitnesses are required, a condition that is highly difficult to satisfy.

Amina Lawal's case has created much anxiety inside Nigeria as well as in the international community, especially as the reinstatement of these forms of punishment was done in spite of Nigeria's ratification of the International Covenant on Civil and Political Rights, the Convention against Torture and Other Cruel, Inhuman or Degrading Treatment and the Convention on the Elimination of All Forms of Discrimination Against Women.

With the help of local women's rights groups Amina hired a lawyer and appealed against her sentence. Although a *Sharia* court of appeal upheld the sentence, in the end, after a massive international campaign and pressure put on the Nigerian government, the sentence was overturned in September 2003.

Amina Lawal has won her case, but in some parts of Nigeria the Islamic penal code allowing degrading treatment still poses a threat to the basic rights of privacy and human dignity. Although the government condemned the cruelest application of the *Sharia* law on the grounds of its unconstitutional character, its power to prevent other similar judgments is limited by the fear of potential religious and ethnic conflicts that threaten northern Nigeria, especially in the states with mixed Christian and Muslim populations.

Sources:
Human Rights Watch, "Political Shari'a'? Human Rights and Islamic Law in Northern Nigeria', *Human Rights Watch Report*, Vol. 16, No. 9 (A) (September 2004), at http://www.hrw.org/reports/2004/nigeria0904/
M. Dan-Ali, Stoking Nigeria's Sharia fires, *BBC News* (22 March 2002), at http://news.bbc.co.uk/1/hi/world/africa/1888584.stm
Reprieve for Nigerian adultery convict, *BBC News* (3 June 2002), at http://news.bbc.co.uk/1/hi/world/africa/2023502.stm
Amnesty International, *Nigeria: Amina Lawal's Victory Welcomed, but Others Threatened* (25 September 2003), at http://www.amnesty.org.uk/action/aminalawal/release.shtml
S. Steiner, 'Sharia Law', *Guardian Unlimited* (20 August 2002), at http://www.guardian.co.uk/theissues/article/0,6512,777972,00.html

often face social isolation, and in case of an unmarried woman attacked with acid it is unlikely that she will ever be able to find a husband.

Acid attacks have been reported mainly in Bangladesh, Burma, Cambodia, India, Kashmir and Pakistan. Accurate statistics on the number of attacks are hard to come by, given the isolated nature of rural communities in these countries, but available evidence from Bangladesh suggests an alarming trend - 47 cases were reported in 1996, 130 in 1997, and 200 in 1998. The number of unreported

cases is thought to be high.[10] According to a 2002 report in the English-language newspaper of the United Arab Emirates *The Gulf News*, authorities in Bangladesh said acid was thrown onto 340 women in 2001, up from 213 in 2000. The court systems in Bangladesh has only recently started to administer stiff punishments to perpetrators, hoping that this will work as a deterrent to others. The Acid Survivors Foundation was established in May 1999 in Bangladesh to tackle the problem. Recently such attacks were also reported from Kashmir, as a part of a terrorist group's campaign to enforce a strict Islamic dress code among women.

International response to traditional practices of violence against women and girls

The 1948 Universal Declaration of Human Rights contains the right of men and women of full age to marry and to found a family, saying they are entitled to equal rights during marriage and at its dissolution. It also states that marriage shall be entered into only with the free and full consent of the intending spouses. According to the Declaration everyone has the right to a standard of living adequate for health and well-being, including food, clothing, housing and medical care and necessary social services. Stating that during motherhood and childhood women and children are entitled to special care and assistance, the Declaration goes on to say that all children, regardless of gender, shall enjoy the same social protection.

In the Convention and Registration on Consent to Marriage, Minimum Age for Marriage, and Registration of Marriages, adopted by the General Assembly in November 1962, important measures concerning marriage were adopted in order to confront the widespread practice of forced child marriage. It stipulates that no marriage should take place without the full and free consent of both parties, however the determination of the minimum age of marriage was left to national governments. Together with provisions in the Declaration on the Elimination of All Forms of Discrimination against Women from 1967, the agreements accepted in the 50s and the 60s represent the core of the international legal tools protecting women's rights in marriage.

The first agreement on the violation of women's rights in customary laws, religious practices and traditional ceremonies were initiated by the Commission on the Status of Women in the 1950s, but the response of member states was at that time mixed. *'Some maintained that only a gradual process of education could lead to the eradication of such practices; some suggested that the effort to abolish traditional practices was in violation of the UN Charter, which proscribes interference in the domestic affairs of member states; and others felt that traditional practices that compromise the health and well-being of women and girls should be abolished.'*[11] Due to the reluctance of national governments, the issues of traditional practices affecting the well-being and health of women and girls were abandoned until the 1970s. A seminar, organised by the WHO in 1979 on traditional forms of violence against women, initiated activities of a growing number of individuals and organisations that led to an overall opinion that neither tradition nor religion can justify female genital circumcision.

Adopted in 1979, the Convention on the Elimination of All Forms of Discrimination against Women (CEDAW) is considered by many as an international bill of rights for women. The states that accept the Convention commit themselves to carry out a series of measures to end discrimination against women in all forms, including:

- To incorporate the principle of equality of men and women in their legal system, abolish all discriminatory laws and adopt appropriate ones prohibiting discrimination against women.
- To ensure the elimination of all acts of discrimination against women by persons, organisations or enterprises.

The Office of the United Nations High Commissioner for Human Rights (OHCHR) described the Convention as the only human rights treaty, which affirms the reproductive rights of women and targets culture and tradition as influential forces shaping gender roles and relations. Countries that have ratified or acceded to the Convention are legally bound to put its provisions into practice. At least every four years, they must submit national reports on measures they have taken to comply with their treaty obligations.

The issues of violence against women based on custom, tradition and religion were addressed during the World Conference on Human Rights held in Vienna in 1993. The Vienna Declaration recognised that although national and regional particularities and historical cultural and religious backgrounds need to be considered, it is the duty and responsibility of states to promote and protect all human rights and fundamental freedoms for all, regardless of their political, economic and cultural systems. Although the Vienna conference was neither the first international platform to discuss women's rights, nor the first to stress the promotion and protection of rights and freedoms for all irrespective of cultural systems, it was the first to so clearly state that women's rights could not be separated from respect for human rights as a whole.

UN human rights bodies have been dealing with the issue of harmful traditional practices during the last decades. In 1983, the issue was taken up by the Sub-Commission on Prevention of Discrimination and Protection of Minorities, which recommended that a working group be established to conduct a profound study of all aspects of the problem. The Working Group on Traditional Practices Affecting the Health of Women and Children, was made up of experts designated by the Sub-Commission, the United Nations Children's Agency, the United Nations Educational, Scientific and Cultural Organization and WHO, as well as members of various non-governmental organisations, and held three sessions in Geneva during 1985 and 1986. The working group's report was submitted to the Commission on Human Rights at its forty-second session in 1986. The Commission requested the Sub-Commission to examine measures to be taken at national and international levels to eliminate traditional harmful practices. The Sub-Commission consequently appointed one of its members, Mrs. Halima Embarek Warzazi as a Special Rapporteur to study developments regarding traditional practices affecting the health of women and children. On the basis of

Waris Dirie, the United Nations Special Ambassador for the UN Population Fund and a Somali-born model, regains her composure while talking about the practice of female genital mutilation, which she underwent at the age of five.

information from governments, specialised agencies and concerned NGOs, as well as field missions to Sudan and Djibouti, and two regional seminars on the subject organised by the Centre for Human Rights in Africa and Asia in Burkina Faso in 1991 and Sri Lanka in 1994, the Special Rapporteur's report shed much needed light on these harmful traditional practices. In its resolution 1994/30 on 26 August 1994, the Sub-Commission adopted the Plan of Action for the Elimination of Harmful Traditional Practices Affecting the Health of Women and Children. On the national level, it calls on governments to legislate against practices harmful to the health of women and children, particularly female genital mutilation. In addition to a focus on FGM, the Plan of Action also covers son preference, early marriage, child delivery practices, as well as violence against women and girl children. Its calls for widespread educational campaigns that include a survey and review of school curricula and textbooks with a view to eliminate prejudices against women. In its recommendations on ways to eliminate FGM, for example, the Plan of Action calls for courses on the ill effects of the practice and other traditional practices to be included in training programmes for medical and paramedical personnel. It says that topics

relating to traditional practices affecting the health of women and children should be introduced into functional illiteracy campaigns. The Plan of Action suggests that audio-visual programmes, sketches and plays should be prepared and articles published in the press on traditional practices that are harmful to the health of young girls and children, particularly female genital mutilation. In its suggestions for international action, the plan states that the question of traditional practices that affect the health of women and girl children should be retained on the agenda of the Commission on Human Rights and the Sub-Commission, so as to keep it under constant review. It calls on the Commission on the Status of Women to give more attention to harmful traditional practices. It also calls on all the organs of the United Nations working for the protection and the promotion of human rights to include on their agenda the issue of harmful traditional practices. In a call to NGOs, national and international, the Plan of Action suggests including in their programmes activities relating to traditional practices affecting the health of women and girl children.

The Commission of Human Rights' Special Rapporteur on Violence against Women, Ms. Radhika Coomaraswamy, provided extensive empirical evidence of the various types of such practices taking place in different parts of the world in her 2002 report to the Commission.[12] She gave particular attention to dominant ideologies and structures that perpetuate cultural practices that are violent towards women, including the regulation of female sexuality and masculinity and violence. The Special Rapporteur recommended that women from various communities should assist to transform harmful practices without destroying the rich cultural legacy of their societies, which makes up their identity. She urged governments not to invoke any custom or tradition to avoid their obligation to eradicate violence against women and suggested effective punishment of perpetrators and redress to victims. Finally, she requested states to provide for education to modify the social and cultural patterns of social conduct fostering violent practices against women.

The Commission also appointed a Special Rapporteur on Freedom of Religion or Belief mandated to examine inconsistencies of governmental actions with the provisions of the Declaration on the Elimination of All Forms of Intolerance and of Discrimination Based on Religion or Belief, and to promote remedial action. The task included a gender perspective in the reporting process, information collection and recommendations. The former Special Rapporteur, Mr. Abdellefatah Amor in his report submitted to the Commission of Human Rights in 1999, strongly condemned discrimination and intolerance of women as supposedly prescribed by religion and tradition. In 2002, the Special Rapporteur presented to the Commission of Human Rights a comprehensive study entitled 'Study on the Freedom of Religion or Belief and the Status of Women from the Viewpoint of Religion and Traditions'. The document elucidates an important collection of juridical instruments and their inadequacies in addressing discrimination of women. Moreover, it details traditional and cultural practices harmful to women, such as cultural stereotypes, prejudice in women's health, discrimination in the family status, disrespect of their right to life, prejudice to dignity and social disqualification, which all demonstrate the inconsistency of such practices with the respect of women's inherent and fundamental human rights. Its conclusions and recommendations advanced national and international measures to be adopted for the prevention and protection of women's rights. Since then, a network of NGOs such as the Women's United Nations Report Network (WUNRN) is campaigning to build on the juridical and factual aspects of the report in order to draw plans of action and practical projects for redress.

Further international research on legislations and decrees in relation to female genital mutilation were examined in July 2003 in Cairo, where more than a hundred experts representing governments, NGOs and international organisations gathered for the Expert Consultation on Legal Tools to Prevent Female Genital Mutilation. At the meeting, experts discussed the importance of law as an element of strategies to stop FGM. They also came up with recommendations for ensuring effective legal responses to the practice. The meeting concluded with the adoption of a final declaration, which affirms that the prevention and the abandonment of FGM can be achieved only through a comprehensive approach promoting behaviour change, and using legislative measures as a pivotal tool.[13]

Specific NGOs have done pioneer work in promoting legislations to prohibit FGM. The following section on legislation worldwide against FGM is based on a June 2003 fact sheet posted by the Centre for Reproductive Rights, a non-profit legal advocacy organisation dedicated to promoting and defending women's reproductive rights worldwide. The centre's fact sheet incorporated information from RAINBO, an African led international non-governmental organisation established in 1994 to work on issues of women's empowerment, gender, reproductive health, sexual autonomy and freedom from violence as central components of the African development agenda. RAINBO specifically strives to enhance global efforts to eliminate the practice of female circumcision / female genital mutilation (FC/FGM) through facilitating women's self-empowerment and accelerating social change.[14] Several governments in Africa and elsewhere have taken steps to eliminate the practice of FGM in their countries. These steps include laws criminalising FC/FGM, education and outreach programmes and the

Box 2.3: Religious and occult sects – abusing women and children

Religious sects and cults can be very destructive to the members and their families; they can change personalities and destroy families. Managed by strong leaders ('gurus'), sects use typically manipulative, antidemocratic methods of isolation, indoctrination, total control, brainwashing and many times physical, sexual and mental abuse. No criticism is tolerated. People who fall under the spell of such cults break with their families, friends, and their communities to make themselves

Lea Saskia Laasner spent almost ten years in the Ramtha sect in Austria, Portugal and Belize before she managed to escape. Laasner describes the humiliating circumstances of living in this sect, how she was sexually mistreated by the guru and how she managed to escape.

slaves to the financial and political objectives of the cult. Women and teenage girls are especially subject to the luring of the gurus, becoming passive objects of sexual abuse, as it happened to Lea Saskia Laasner. Her family had given up everything to become a member of the 'Ramtha' cult. Ramtha, disguised to the outside world as a relief organisation in order to have access to donations, had purchased a ranch in Central America. While thirteen-years-old Lea Saskia Laasner became the guru's favourite and was regularly sexually abused, she lived in complete isolation, without schooling and was, along with other sect members, subject to rituals, indoctrination and humiliation. Having lived ten years with Ramtha, she considered about suicide. At the age of twenty-one she escaped and made her story public.

Sources:
Lea Saskia Laasner with Hugo Stamm, *Allein gegen die Seelenfänger* (Frankfurt: Eichborn Verlag, 2005)
Schweizerische Arbeitsgemeinschaft gegen destruktive Kulte, at www.sekten.ch/sadk/index.html
Evangelische Informationsstelle, at www.relinfo.ch/sekten/kriterien.html

use of civil remedies and administrative regulations to prevent the practice. Twelve countries - Benin, Burkina Faso, Central African Republic, Chad, Côte d'Ivoire, Djibouti, Ghana, Guinea, Kenya, Senegal, Tanzania, and Togo - have enacted laws criminalising FGM. The penalties range from a minimum of six months to a maximum of life imprisonment. Several countries also impose monetary fines. In Egypt, the Ministry of Health issued a decree declaring FGM unlawful and punishable under the Penal Code. As of January 2003, there had been reports of prosecutions or arrests in Burkina Faso, Egypt, Ghana, Senegal, and Sierra Leone.

Eight industrialised countries that receive immigrants from countries where FGM is practised - Australia, Belgium, Canada, New Zealand, Norway, Sweden, United Kingdom, and United States - have passed laws criminalising the practice. In Australia, six out of eight states have passed laws against FGM. In the United States, the federal government and sixteen states have criminalised the practice. Moreover, the United States and Canada consider FGM as a type of harm that could qualify someone for protection under the Convention relating to the Status of Refugees. There have been no known prosecutions in any of these countries. One country, France, has relied on existing criminal legislation to prosecute both practitioners of FGM and parents procuring the service for their daughters.[15]

In many countries in Africa, there now exist strong indigenous movements aimed at stopping the practice of FGM. In Kenya, a ceremony called 'circumcision with words' celebrates a young girls' entry into womanhood by using words and not through genital cutting. In Senegal, religious leaders have gone on village-to-village pilgrimages to stop the practices. These steps at the local level are of utmost importance, because as has been concluded by the Special Rapporteur for Violence against Women, *'it is only with enthusiastic support from the local community that this practice can eventually be eliminated.'*[16]

Despite international norms and developments, the tension between universal human rights and cultural relativism negatively influence lives of many women throughout the globe. The situation is more complex because many women identify with their culture as their sense of dignity and self-respect is often linked with belonging to the community and they feel offended by outside criticism. Cultural markers and cultural identity that allow a group to stand united against the oppression and discrimination often entails restriction on women's rights. The issue of cultural relativism, cultural identity and respect should be taken sensitively when pushing for reforms. Therefore, women living in these communities should be leading the transformation. The international community should work closely with women from the religious and ethnic groups concerned, so that the changes may be made according to the vast majority of women who have lived in the discriminatory and oppressive environment.

Endnotes

[1] See Women's Human Rights Division of Human Rights Watch, at http://www.hrw.org/women/index.php

[2] Article 2, *United Nations Declaration on the Elimination of Violence against Women*.

[3] Quoted in M. Penn and R. Nardos, *Overcoming Violence against Women and Girls: The International Campaign to Eradicate a Worldwide Problem* (London: Rowman &Littlefield Publishers, 2003), 4.

[4] S. Armstrong, 'Honour's victims' in *Chatelaine* (March 2000), at http://tools.chatelaine.com/article.jsp?page=newsviews&cid=1536

[5] *News 24.com*, 'Honour Killing Still Rampant' (15 September 2003), at http://www.news24.com

[6] Gendercide Watch, *Case Study: 'Honour' Killings & Blood Feuds*, at http://www.gendercide.org/case_honour.html

[7] Amnesty International, *Pakistan: Honour Killing of Girls and Women*, ASA 33/018/1999 (1 September 1999), at

http://web.amnesty.org/library/index/ENGASA330181999

[8] See more about the work of Rana Husseini, at http://www.womensenews.org/article.cfm/dyn/aid/1321/context/jounalistofthemonth

[9] Women's eNews, at http://www.womensenews.org

[10] *Bangladesh International Community News* (October 1999), at http://womensissues.about.com/cs/acidattacks

[11] Penn and Nardos, *Overcoming Violence against Women and Girls*, 5.

[12] United Nations, *Cultural Practices in the Family that are Violent towards Women*, Report of the Special Rapporteur on Violence against Women, its Causes and Consequences, Ms. Radhika Coomaraswamy, UN Document E/CN.4/2002/83 (Geneva, 2002).

[13] See *Cairo Declaration for the Elimination of Female Genital Mutilation* (Cairo, 23 June 2003), at http://www. stopfgm.org/stopfgm/doc/EN/216.rtf

[14] The fact sheet relies on information based on the following sources: A. Rahman & N. Toubia, *Female Genital Mutilation: A Guide to Laws and Policies Worldwide* (London, New York: Zed Books, 2000). Ms. Rahman is the international programme director of the Center for Reproductive Rights and Ms. Toubia is the director of RAINBO.

[15] A Malian woman was jailed for eight years for circumcising 48 girls, following a trial in Paris. BBC Online Network, *Woman Jailed for 48 Circumcisions* (17 February 1999), at http://news.bbc.co.uk/1/hi/world/europe/281026.stm

[16] United Nations, *Cultural Practices in the Family that are Violent towards Women*.

Chapter 3

Gender-Based Violence and Poverty

'Study after study has shown that there is no effective development strategy in which women do not play a central role. When women are fully involved, the benefits can be seen immediately: families are healthier and better fed; their income, savings and reinvestment go up. And what is true of family is also true of communities and, in the long run, of whole countries.'

UN Secretary-General Kofi Annan, 8 March 2003

Women comprise more than two-thirds of the 2.5 billion people defined as 'poor,' that is those who are living on less than US$2 a day. However, poverty is not only a matter of lack of income. The Beijing Platform of Action (UN 1995) states: *'Poverty has various manifestations, including lack of food and productive resources sufficient to ensure a sustainable livelihood; hunger and malnutrition; ill health; limited or lack of access to education and other basic services; increasing morbidity and mortality from illness; homelessness and inadequate housing; unsafe environments; and social discrimination and exclusion. It is also characterised by lack of participation in decision-making and in civil, social and political life. It occurs in all countries — as mass poverty in many developing countries and as pockets of poverty in developed countries.'*[1] In all these manifestations of poverty, women tend to systematically fare worse than men. In some societies,

women and girls are often expected to eat the leftovers after the men and boys have finished eating. Most women do not have legal or traditional rights to land or other assets. They find it difficult to access loans or credit because they have no collateral. Moreover, women are less likely to have the resources needed for success in business including skills training, time, and information on markets. Hence, they are concentrated in low-return, insecure, informal occupations. Lacking alternatives, many women cannot leave abusive men because they are wholly dependent on them for their survival. In countries where people pay for healthcare, women are less likely to go to hospital or clinics when they are ill, and more likely to either treat themselves at home or go to traditional healers. Pregnancy and childbearing carry heavy risks for women who lack access to trained support. Women are also more likely to look after ill family members. Two-thirds of children not in

A malnourished Ethiopian woman sits with her child in a refugee camp in Wad Sharafin, Sudan where drought led to a famine that killed hundreds of thousands. The child died later that day.

ian casualties. Men traditionally do risky work, like mining or fire fighting, but increasingly women are also working with unsafe chemicals and technologies, in both factories and fields. Poor women are excluded for two reasons: poverty and gender. In most societies, women are grossly underrepresented in government. In many societies, women are also excluded or underrepresented from local decision-making bodies. Economic and financial policies are developed without recognising women's economic contributions in the unpaid and informal parts of the economy.

Over the years, the international development community has developed various approaches to address the socio-economic inequities between genders or, in other words, 'feminisation of poverty'. These approaches are embedded in and cannot be de-linked from the broader international discourse on development. However, while it is acknowledged that women's economic vulnerability contributes to overall powerlessness, analysis would indicate that it is far from clear that simply improving women's economic situation automatically and necessarily empowers them in other dimensions, including the physical dimension or the capability to protect themselves from violence. Some direct attempts to increase women's income levels, for instance through micro finance, have in fact attracted additional physical violence from men. Therefore, meeting women's basic needs is not enough. More crucially, there is a need for concurrent strategies that aim to challenge and transform the institutions and structures that systematically perpetuate asymmetries.

Persistent inequality between women and men and socio-economic roles

It is generally acknowledged that in no region of the developing and developed world are women equal to men in socio-economic rights. Gender gaps continue to persist in economic opportunities; in access, ownership and control of public and private resources (land, credit); and in economic decision-making power whether at the micro level (households), meso level (firms), macro level (national governments) and global level (international economic and financial institutions). The important question is why are women more vulnerable to poverty than men? A useful starting point for understanding the dissimilar socio-economic experiences of women and men are their differences in socio-economic roles as reflected in the sexual division of labour in societies and the time use for market and non-market activities. The labour division is based by longstanding imbalances in relations between women and men. Women generally have multiple and simultaneous roles that are largely devalued or uncompensated. Their activities are situated

school are girls. Many of them are at home doing housework and looking after other children. Parents may decide not to send girls to school because of fears for their physical safety on the journey to school, and even at school, where male teachers and pupils may sexually molest them. If a marriage breaks down, or a daughter displeases her parents, in most societies it is the woman who has to leave her home, because she has no rights of ownership regardless of the contribution she has made to the family. Female headed households are more likely to have sub-standard houses. Gender-based violence, including rape, makes moving around outside one's home perilous for women in all societies. Home is not a safe place either, since domestic violence is widespread, and often condoned by society. If war breaks out, adult men are the first to be called to fight, while women and children are more likely to be civil-

Box 3.1 : Some facts on women's status

In all manifestations of poverty, women tend to fare worse than men, as evidenced by statistics of UNDP (Women's World, 2000), United Nations' Statistics Division and UNIFEM (Statistics on Women and Development):

- 70 per cent of people in poverty, living on less than US$1 per day, are women.

- 66 per cent of the world's illiterate are women; of 140 million illiterate young people in the world, more than half (86 million) are young women.

- Women provide 70 per cent of the unpaid time spent in caring for family members. This unpaid work provided by women is estimated at US$11 trillion per year – one-third of the global GDP valued at US$33 trillion.

- Women own one per cent of the land in the world.

- Women's participation in managerial and administrative posts is around 33 per cent in the developed world, 15 per cent in Africa, and 13 per cent in Asia and the Pacific; in Africa and Asia-Pacific these percentages doubled in the last twenty years.

- There are only five women chief executives in the 'Fortune 500' corporations, the most valuable publicly owned companies in the United States.

- In Silicon Valley, for every 100 shares of stock options owned by a man, only one share is owned by a woman.

- Women's wages in industries and services are far less than men's wages in the same sector.

- Worldwide only about fourteen per cent of members of parliament are women.

- Seven per cent of the world's total cabinet ministers are women; women ministers remain concentrated in social areas (14 per cent) compared to legal (9.4 per cent), economic (4.1 per cent), political affairs (3.4 per cent), and the executive (3.9 per cent).

- In the United Nations system, women hold only 9 per cent of the top management jobs and 21 per cent of senior management positions, but 48 per cent of the junior professional civil service slots.

- In December 2003, out of over 180 countries only twelve were currently headed by women. Other women leaders in government include five vice presidents, four governor-generals, and four major opposition leaders. There are nine women ambassadors to the United Nations (representing Finland, Guinea, Jamaica, Kazakhstan, Kyrgyzstan, Liberia, Liechtenstein, Somalia, and Turkmenistan).

Sources:
UNIFEM Statistics on Women and Development, at
http://www.onlinewomeninpolitics.org/statistics.htm
UN Statistics Division, at
http://unstats.un.org/unsd/demographic/products/indwm/indwm2.htm

© *Giovanni Diffidenti, 1997*

A displaced woman cooks outside a train near Luena station in Angola, where more than a hundred had been based because of insecurity arising from civilian conflict.

developing world, women receive, on average, only 70 per cent of men's wages; and only a fifth of the wage disparity can be explained by differences in education and work.[2] Women face discrimination in job markets as they are often shunted into 'feminine' or low-skill and low-paid career tracks (for example, secretarial jobs). They are also largely represented in the informal sector where job insecurity, lack of labour rights and hazardous working conditions are the norm.

Studies show that women spend around two-thirds of their time on non-market work compared to less than a quarter for men.[3] Men could, in principle, do subsistence production, care and community work. However, these tasks are perceived by society to be mainly in the realm of women's responsibility. Thus, while women may provide care work willingly, it is also often extracted by social pressure or even by physical violence. Because most work

in both the productive and reproductive spheres while men's activities tend to be concentrated in the productive sphere. Where women are able to secure paid productive work for the market, they are generally underpaid relative to men given the same job and qualifications. In the

Chart 3.1:

Estimated annual income of women and men in selected countries in 2000 (in US$)

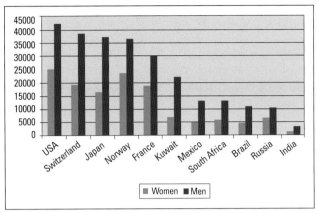

Source: UNDP, *Human Development Report 2002* (New York: UNDP, 2002), 222-25.

Chart 3.2:

Total work time for men and women (in minutes per day) in selected countries

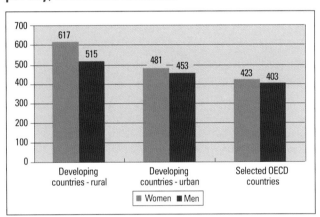

Source: UNDP, *Human Development Report 2004* (New York: UNDP, 2002), 233. Selected developing rural countries: Bangladesh, Guatemala, Kenya, Nepal, Philippines. Selected developing urban countries: Columbia, Indonesia, Kenya, Nepal, Venezuela. Selected OECD countries: Australia, Austria, Canada, Denmark, Finland, France, Germany, Hungary, Israel, Italy, Japan, Republic of Korea, Latvia, Netherlands, New Zealand, Norway, United Kingdom, United States.

in the social reproduction sphere is non-marketable, women's economic contribution remains largely unvalued, unrecognised and unpaid by the current economic system that values work according to its worth in the market. Care work is glaringly omitted in most – if not all – countries' gross national products. While the system of national accounts should in principle include production in households, this has not been done due in part to technical problems in measuring the value of non-market work, with its characteristics of multiplicity and simultaneity, and also due to lack of gender sensitivity and political will. For all of the above reasons women tend to have a weaker ability compared to men to generate income on a regular basis, making them more at risk, compared to men, of falling into poverty.

Vulnerability of Women Migrant Workers

Today women make up almost half of the 175 million migrants worldwide and according to some predictions the process of 'feminisation of migration' will continue with increased intensity. Such a trend demands that greater attention is given to the protection of women workers, as they are more prone to experiencing violence and discrimination than both male migrants and native-born women workers.

Women migrant workers are far from a homogenous group, although there are certain common characteristics that by now have been well established. A first profile is of the woman seeking a better, more autonomous and satisfying life, where she has greater control over her career and where she can empower herself with experiences that serve to build a more secure future. A second profile is of the obeying daughter who is sent abroad by her parents for the economic survival, if not prosperity, of the entire family. Such expectations are rooted in the cultural tradition whereby daughters are the breadwinners of the family and responsible for the livelihood of their aging parents. A third profile is of the woman accompanying her husband or male family member abroad, thereby making her a secondary dependent upon her husband or relatives. A fourth profile is of the girl or woman who is trafficked illegally to work abroad, very often in the sex industry. One out of every 35 persons worldwide is an international migrant, according to the Population Division of the United Nations. Based on the world population of 6.057 billion in 2000, migrants represent some 2.9 per cent of the total.[4] While the scale of migration is well-known, recent global data on female migration patterns is not widely available and although the United Nations published statistics in *The World's Women 2000: Trends and Statistics*, the data came from censuses conducted in

Table 3.1:

Female economic activity rate in 1980 and 2001 among potentially active women (aged 15-64) in percentage

Region	1980 (per cent of women in total labour force)	2001 (per cent of women in total labour force)
Middle East and Northern Africa	23.8	28.1
East Asia and Pacific	42.6	44.5
Latin America and the Caribbean	27.8	35.0
South Africa	42.0	42.0
Europe and Central Asia	46.7	46.3
Europe Economic and Monetary Union	36.4	41.3
World	39.1	40.7

Source: World Bank, *World Development Indicators 2002* (Washington D.C.: World Bank, 2002), 44.

1990. Today's estimates by the International Labour Organization, the International Organization for Migration and various other United Nations bodies, assess that women make up approximately 48 per cent of all international migrants (see table 3.3).

The origins and destinations of women migrant workers indicate that the main route leads from the developing world to the developed countries. According to UN estimates, in 1960, the number of women migrants in developed countries (48 per cent) did not differ much from that in developing countries (46 per cent). By 2000 female migrants constitute over 51 per cent of all migrants in the developed world while still accounting for 46 per cent in developing countries. The reasons for this augmentation are multiple. The demand for cheap labour for the domestic services in wealthy countries caused by large-scale entry of native women to professional careers; laws determining the admission of migrants as seen for instance in oil-rich countries of the Gulf; the status of women in both country of origin and destination; regulations on family reunification of legally admitted migrants; as well as social and economic conditions of countries - all this encourages women to seek work in economically developed countries. In the developing world men still tend to dominate the migrant flows, however, since the late 1970s, women's migration has been on the rise even there. Today major routes of women's migration create a broad network of countries of origin and destinations all over the world (see table 3.4).

Labour migrants decide to move to another country because of promises of a better economic situation and greater professional prospects. There are women for whom migration is a positive experience, both in the formal and informal sectors. While they might earn less than male migrants and be relegated to the non-regulated sectors of the economy, many women are able to improve the economic position of their family and boost their own status, thereby obtaining greater decision-making authority and independence within the family. An International Labour Organization report states that a female domestic worker in the United Arab Emirates can be paid between US$130 - US$200 monthly, which amounts to four times, ten times or in the case of an Indian foreign female worker, as much as 100 times the wages the women could earn in their home countries.[5] The recent trend in Africa shows a 'brain drain' pattern, suggesting that the more educated women are those leaving their countries in search of better economic and social conditions.

Poverty is a real push factor for women of all ages and as a result, those that do emigrate are often largely uneducated and unable to find proper employment opportunities abroad. Therefore, most female migrants end up working in the informal sector of the economy, which is not regulated and controlled and where, consequently, women are exposed to multiple hardships, notably forced labour, sexual exploitation, precarious working conditions and poorly paid work. In addition, the fact that women are also more prone to using unofficial and illegal channels of migration automatically places them in the informal sector of the labour market. Unfortunately, women migrants often accept the '3D jobs' – dirty, dangerous, degrading – because they have few viable alterna-

Table 3.2:

Gender and agriculture: Share of women in the agricultural labour force in 1950-2000, with the estimate for 2010 (in percentage)

Region	1950	1970	1990	2000	2010
Share of agricultural labour force in total labour force	89.6	84.2	75.6	70.6	65.2
Share of female labour force in total agricultural labour force	44.7	45.9	47.3	48.1	48.8
Share of female labour force in developing countries in the world	68.4	69.1	73.5	75.9	78.3
Share of females in agricultural population in developing countries in the world	81.3	90.3	94.5	96.1	97.1

Source: Food and Agricultural Organisation (FAO), *Gender Statistics and Maps*, at http://www.fao.org/gender/en/stats-e.htm

Note: The figures and estimates on the table above are drawn from the following FAO statistical studies:

FAO, Progamme for the World Census of Agriculture 2000, *Statistical Development Series*, No. 5 (Rome: FAO, 1995).

FAO, Conducting Agricultural Censuses and Surveys, *Statistical Development Series*, No. 6 (Rome: FAO, 1996).

FAO, Report on the 1990 World Census of Agriculture, International Comparison and Primary Results by Country (1986-1995), *Statistical Development Series*, No. 9 (Rome: FAO, 1997).

Table 3.3:

Percentage of female migrants among the total number of international migrants by major area in 1960-2000

Region	1960	1970	1980	1990	2000
World	46.6	47.2	47.4	47.9	48.8
More developed regions	47.9	48.2	49.4	50.8	50.9
Less developed regions	45.7	46.3	45.5	44.7	45.7
Europe	48.5	48	48.5	51.7	52.4
Northern America	49.8	51.1	52.6	51	51
Oceania	44.4	46.5	47.9	49.1	50.5
Northern Africa	49.5	47.7	45.8	44.9	42.8
Sub-Saharan Africa	40.6	42.1	43.8	46	47.2
Southern Asia	46.3	46.9	45.9	44.4	44.4
Eastern and South-eastern Asia	46.1	47.6	47	48.5	50.1
Western Asia	45.2	46.6	47.2	47.9	48.3
Caribbean	45.3	46.1	46.5	47.7	48.9
Latin America	44.7	46.9	48.4	50.2	50.5

Source: United Nations, *International Migration Report* (New York: United Nations, 2002), at http://www.un.org/esa/population/publications/ittmig2002/ittmigrep2002.htm

tives. Most women migrants find jobs in the domestic services, sweatshop manufacturing, 'entertainment' and sex industry.

Female migrant worker vulnerability

Forty-five years ago, there was no research being conducted on the gender aspect of migration as common belief had it that men were the primary migrants and that if women travelled, they would merely be accompanying their spouse or male family member. In spite of the recent interest of the international community and quite extensive research and data collection, policies of immigration and emigration continue to be gender insensitive, and newly established regulations often reproduce and reinforce already existing inequalities between men and women.

As women's vulnerabilities are numerous, they are best approached by looking at the various angles of the migration process. On the home front, women are vulnerable because they experience great family pressures. They also are led to believe that theexperiences of a migrant are only positive, as returning migrants often do not speak openly with their relatives and friends about the hardships they encountered. Women migrants in particular are less likely to reveal the true nature of their work out of sheer embarrassment or for fear of being chastened. Moreover, women returning home frequently enjoy a better hierarchical position within the family and local community and hence will chose to remain silent regarding the pain and suffering they experienced during their stay abroad. As a result, women who do decide to leave their countries of origin often depart with unrealistic expectations and perceptions, which ultimately makes it easier for them to be later abused and deceived.

The second stage of the migration process is that of the actual travel. The obvious challenge facing all women travelling to a new place, independently or through illegal means, is ensuring their own personal security. Sexual violence is an inherent danger facing women travellers and female migrants arriving in their countries of destination and they can be easy preys for local men. Women migrants may experience difficulties in communicating with local officials or feeling uncomfortable reporting an incident to the police, especially if they come from traditional conservative homes.

The third stage of migration is just as hazardous as the second. In comparison to male migrants or native women, women migrant workers tend to be much more vulnerable to discrimination, exploitation, abuse and further trafficking when they reach their destination country. Working mostly in the informal or even illegal labour sector, and being dependent largely on their employers for visa sponsorship, they are reluctant to turn to the police or trade unions for protection. Although some domestic workers are willing to speak publicly about their abuse after leaving their host families, while employed it is almost impossible to collect valid and representative data on their working conditions.

The fourth stage of the migration process is the return home and the reintegration into the family, which, after the period of independence, can be difficult. Problems can also arise if the migrant's experience proved disap-

© Reuters, Paolo Cocco, 2002

Illegal immigrants represent a third of the 50-70,000 prostitutes working in Italy. On the main highway in Rimini, prostituted women wait for customers under the cover of darkness.

pointing in the monetary gain for the family, thereby making it harder for the woman to be welcomed back into the community. Moreover, women may also find it more difficult to find a life partner because their stay abroad and work experience made them not only older, but more mature, better informed, resourceful and competent - the assets which in traditional communities do not make them desirable brides.

The issues of women migrants have emerged on the agenda of the international community only recently, therefore profound knowledge of all the incentives to cross borders to find better (or any) jobs, and of the factors creating the demand for their labour both in developed and developing countries, is still rather incomplete and fragmentary. What becomes increasingly evident is women's irreplaceable role in global economy and global transfers of information, capital and people. Women are emerging as crucial economic partners fully engaged in the current globalisation processes. Many women in poor countries accept job migration as a strategy of survival for themselves and their families. Women's (as well as men's) migration has also become a welcome source of income for many governments profiting from women's work and remittances. Unfortunately, migration is also the basis for the international infrastructure facilitating cross-border flows of people, including its illegal, yet highly profitable elements operating in human trafficking.

Women and girls are vulnerable at every stage of their migration, during the recruitment, the journey and crossing-borders, during the transit stay and working abroad, especially when they have to accept an irregular job or a work under unspecified conditions in non-regulated sectors. They are exposed to *'harassment, intimidation or threats to themselves and their families, economic and sexual exploitation, racial discrimination and xenophobia, poor working conditions, increased health risks and other forms of abuse, including trafficking into forced labour, debt bondage, involuntary servitude, and situations of captivity.'*[6] In some countries women working as maids or nannies are totally under the control of the employer, as corroborated by ILO reports from the Gulf countries where many women migrants from Asia work, not only in harsh conditions, but also in isolation from their relatives and compatriots.

In spite of the restrictions towards immigrants that some governments in developed countries have installed recently, the migration of women will continue and so will their discrimination and exploitation. To better protect them from all risks much more concern by the international community and more research and relevant data about their working conditions are needed.[7] It is crucial to raise awareness, promote advocacy and publicity based on the international human rights agenda and to improve existing international and national policies of emigration and immigration with more concern about the processes of 'feminisation of migration'. Creation and revision of the normative framework that could be used more effectively for protection of women represents another crucial condition for a more gender sensitive approach to the problem.

Women's Empowerment and Approaches within the International Development Discourse

Women's empowerment is often invoked in the development literature as the solution to women's poverty and subordination. But what does the concept mean? When women's empowerment was first used by women's organisations in the 1970s, it was intended to frame and advance the struggle for social justice and women's equality by reshaping economic, social and political structures at all levels.[8] It particularly underlined the importance of

women's agency and self-transformation. As Amartya Sen emphasises, women are not merely 'passive recipients of welfare-enhancing help, but are active agents of change - the dynamic promoters of social transformation.'[9] Within the orthodox development discourse of the 1990s, however, donor agencies and international organisations have tended to interpret women's empowerment as the enlargement of their sets of choices and improvement in their productivity levels in the context of weakening state

Mende Nazer was kidnapped as a child from her village in Sudan, sold into slavery, and held hostage in Khartoum and London. She has told her story in a memoir entitled 'Slave', and has asked for political asylum in Britain.

© Keystone, Camera Press, Amit Lennon, 2004

responsibility for macroeconomic decision-making and social support.[10]

There is broad agreement in the development literature that women's empowerment is multidimensional. It is comprised of cognitive, economic, political, psychological, and also physical components that interact with each other:

- The cognitive dimension requires women to have an understanding of the conditions and causes of their subordination at the various levels and entails making choices that challenge cultural expectations and norms.

- The economic dimension stresses the importance of women's access to, and control over, productive resources such as land and credit. While this may ensure a degree of financial independence, it is important to note that changes in the economic balance of power do

Box 3.2 : Domestic slavery of women migrants in Saudi Arabia

Nasiroh, an Indonesian woman, went to work in Saudi Arabia in 1993 where she was sexually abused by her employer, falsely accused of his murder and then tortured and sexually exploited by police officers during two years of incommunicado detention. Officials from her embassy did not visit her once. She told Amnesty International that her trial was so cursory that she did not know she had been convicted and she still has no idea for what 'crime' she was imprisoned for five years.

The problem of forced domestic labour is unfortunately not exclusive to the Arab World. Quite a number of cases have been made public in Africa and China. Furthermore, it is not a recent issue, throughout history rich families have often abused their privileges to get cheap help (slaves) in their households, abusing the poverty of others, be it in ancient kingdoms or in a colonial environment - and most often women were the victims.

However, women represent a third of nearly seven million of expatriates working temporarily in the kingdom of Saudi Arabia,

most of them coming from India, Bangladesh, the Philippines and Indonesia. In 2004, Human Rights Watch collected testimonies of labour exploitation, sexual abuse and other grave violations to which migrant women are exposed. Most of these migrant women, in regular and irregular status, work more than twelve hours daily, there is no social security, they are not entitled to take vacation, and they are prohibited from making phone calls to their families. They are forced to live in confinement or even total isolation, locked in overcrowded dormitories with little or no privacy and are not allowed to leave even in their free time. They are often provided with inadequate food. Shopping is always done in the company of the employers' family members, and women are forbidden to develop any contacts with other expatriates. The women's isolation is based upon the fact that they are never given official residency permits, which would be the only documents that enable expatriates to move around freely inside the kingdom. They can be sent home at any time, usually at great financial loss. These difficult, if not unbearable, labour conditions leave women migrants extremely vulnerable to sexual exploitation, rape, the possibility of contracting HIV/AIDS or other serious health problems, and unwanted pregnancy with grave consequences for the victims. Restrictions on abortion are in place; for instance a pregnant woman is not admitted to a hospital until she is accompanied by a man who admits paternity, or she is subject to intimidations by the rapists' side, or would be unable to cover medical costs – all of which drive pregnant women to seek help outside the hospital and therefore expose them to even greater health risks. Moreover, migrant women face imprisonment for becoming pregnant out of wedlock.

Auxiliary workers in hospitals, private households, cleaning companies or small workshops, women expatriates are excluded from domestic labour law which only increases their vulnerability. Their chances to lodge complaints while being in the kingdom are very slim and almost impossible after their return home. As these women are never reported in any official statistics, it is very difficult to track, contact and supply them with outside help.

Source:
Human Rights Watch, 'Bad Dreams: Exploitation and Abuse of Migrant Workers in Saudi Arabia', *Human Rights Watch Report*, Vol. 16, No. 5 (July 2004), at http://www.hrw.org/reports/2004/saudi0704/saudi0704.pdf

not automatically translate into changes in traditional gender roles and norms.

- The political dimension requires that women have the capability to analyse, organise and mobilise for social change.
- The psychological dimension refers to the belief that women can act at personal and societal levels to improve their individual realities and the societies they live in.
- The physical dimension emphasises women's control over their own body and sexuality and the ability to protect themselves against sexual violence.

International approaches to women in developing countries

Different analytical development frameworks tend to emphasise one or more or all of the dimensions of women's empowerment. These points of departure, however, cannot be isolated from shifts and movements in the international discourse on development. In the last three decades or so, international policy approaches to women in developing countries have evolved mainly within two agendas.

The Women in Development (WID) approach was developed in the context of structural adjustment policies, aimed at resolving budget deficits and promoting economic efficiency, imposed by the International Monetary Fund and the World Bank on borrowing countries as conditionality for financial aid and loans. Since the late 1980s there has been growing recognition of the heavy social costs of these policies, especially on women. International financial institutions have reacted to the criticism by putting poverty reduction at the top of its agenda. However, by continuing to focus on economic growth as central to poverty reduction, efforts under WID are directed at easing the symptoms rather than tackling the root causes of the problem of women's poverty and subordination. The WID approach aims to increase discussion and research on the role of women in development, as well as, institutionalise a concern for women's issues in governments and development agencies. Building on the perspective that women's poverty is rooted in their failure to participate in development, the WID approach believes that women's empowerment can be attained through income generating enterprises, heath care and other measures that enhance women's productivity.

The Gender and Development (GAD) agenda identifies unequal power relations between women and men. Therefore equity, not merely poverty reduction, is a key concern. It scrutinises social, political and economic structures at all levels based on gaps between women and men. Furthermore, it acknowledges that nothing less than a transformative change is needed for equality between women and men. Among others, the GAD approach aims to mainstream gender analysis in policy-making and programme planning.

Table 3.4:

Migration trends of female workers (most of them working in domestic jobs or in the sex industry)

Destination country/countries	Labour power source country/countries
Saudi Arabia	Indonesia, Sri Lanka, Philippines, India, Thailand
Kuwait	Sri Lanka
Western Europe	Columbia and Brazil; Russia, Ukraine
Italy	Philippines, Morocco, Ethiopia, Nigeria, Albania
Greece and Cyprus	Philippines, Sri Lanka, Somalia, Ethiopia, Poland, Albania, Bulgaria
Spain	Morocco, Dominican Republic, Peru, Guatemala
United States	Mexico, Central America, Philippines, Caribbean,
Canada	Central America, Sri Lanka, Philippines
Hong Kong	Philippines, Thailand
Singapore	Philippines, Sri Lanka
Malaysia	Philippines
Japan	Philippines
Thailand	Cambodia, Vietnam, Laos, China. Burma
Pakistan & India	Bangladesh
Turkey	Romania
Pakistan	India, Sri Lanka
Sri Lanka	India

Source: B. Ehrenreich and A.R. Hochschild (eds), *Global Woman: Nannies, Maids and Sex Workers in the New Economy* (London: Granta Book, 2003), 276-80.

Table 3.5:

Vulnerabilities at different stages of the migration process

Migration stage	Vulnerabilities faced by female migrant workers
Recruitment and pre-departure	Illegal recruitment and trafficking
	Excessive fees for placement and documents
	Cheating and extortion by agencies and brokers
	Non-existent jobs
	Inappropriate and expensive training programs
	Being locked up by recruiters, abuses in 'training camps'
	Not being sent abroad at all
	Falsification of worker's identity
	Lack of information on terms and conditions of employment
Journey	Expensive fares
	Unofficial transportation/smuggling
	Hazardous travel
	Victimisation in transit
Working and living abroad	Contract substitution or contract violations
	Dependent employment relationship
	Withholding of papers/documents
	Poor working and living conditions
	Health and safety risks and lack of societal protection
	Non-payment of or unauthorised deductions from wages
	Physical, psychological or sexual abuse or violence
	Limited freedom of movement
	Lack/absence of information, access to services and redress mechanisms
	No embassy or inadequate services provided by embassy
Termination of contract	Illegal termination
	Sudden, unjust termination
	No place to stay before being sent home
	Absence of complaint and redress procedure
Return and reintegration	No alternative source of income, difficulties of finding employment
	Extortion and overpricing of services by airport and customs personnel, money changers etc.
	Bankruptcy
	Family problems, adjustments
	Social reintegration difficulties, particularly for survivors of violence abroad
	Dangers of being re-trafficked

Source: International Labour Organization, *Preventing Discrimination, Exploitation and Abuse of Women Migrant Workers* (Geneva: ILO, 2003).

Especially since the 1990s, gender analysis has entered the thinking and operations of international development institutions and many governments so as to better understand the roots of women's poverty and subordination and from there, better define strategies to empower women, economically and in other dimensions. Miller and Razavi compare and contrast four paradigms of gender analysis that have framed development approaches to women in developing countries over the last decade based on a conceptualisation of gender, scope of institutional analysis, implications for development and issues of social change.[11] These are the Gender Roles Framework, the Triple Roles Framework, the Social Relations Framework and Feminist Economics approaches. The Gender Roles Framework (GRF), which stems from the early Women in Development approach elaborated by the US Agency for International Development (USAID), looks at access to and control over income and resources, highlighting the incentives and constraints under which women and men work in order to anticipate how projects will impact on productive and reproductive activities, as well as, responsibilities of other household members. Its approach to gender mainstreaming can be considered 'integrationist' rather than 'transformational'; viewing development as a process from which everyone can benefit. The GRF contends that for women to gain from development, projects must more adequately incorporate women and gender issues into development plans. It assumes, however, that women are a homogeneous and unchanging category, and thus fails to see how gender also intersects with class and ethnicity hierarchies in various circumstances.

The Triple Roles Framework (TRF) examines women's roles beyond the household to look at women's triple roles in production, reproduction and community management and the implications of these for their participation in development. The model distinguishes between practical and strategic needs. The former respond to immediate perceived necessities identified within a specific context such as inadequacies in living conditions, employment, heath care services, etc. These arise from the given division of labour in societies, hence, the division of labour, but women's subordinate position is not questioned. Meanwhile, strategic needs arise out of the unequal power relations between women and men, relating to the gender division of labour, power and control of resources. Meeting strategic needs through programmes intended to overcome systematic biases against women in culture and society would help women to achieve equality with men. However, the TRF focus on roles does not fully shed light on the nature of gender relations in society, barely touching on social relations through which resources, status and authority are produced. The institutions that perpetuate gender inequality, for example, markets and the state, are not scrutinised. Moreover, the distinction between practical and strategic needs takes an indirect look at the conflictual nature of gender relations.

The Social Relations Framework (SRF) is based on an analysis of the social relations within the family, community, state and market, thereby illuminating the streams through which gender and other inequalities are created and reproduced. It examines the social processes through which human needs are met, as well as the institutions, including development agencies, through which inequalities are constructed and reproduced. The SRF considers gender relations as a conflictual, as well as a collaborative process of bargaining and negotiation. By concentrating on gender roles and gender differences in access to and control over resources, it also provides a view of the web of relationships, including, class, ethnicity, age, religion, etc., in which gender is embedded. Women's subordination is located within the process of market-led production and distribution and it is argued that women are not left out of the development process, but are in fact integrated into that process, albeit on unequal terms. Finally, it looks at the infrastructure needed in order for women's empowerment to take place.

The body of work known as 'feminist economics' studies gender hierarchies in production and reproduction, looking especially at macroeconomic policy and legislative reform. Neo-classical feminist economics examines how gender biases undermine structural adjustment policies by causing a misallocation of resources between export and non-export sectors, preventing women from participating on equal terms in the production and sale of exports. Policy recommendations focus on improving women's ability to participate in different markets while assuming women's work in the social reproduction of

© Keystone, AP, Hasan Sarbakhshian, 2004

The political empowerment of women is key to development and social change, especially in post-conflict reconstruction such as here in Afghanistan.

the labour force will continue. Meanwhile, feminist critical economics argues that women's role in reproduction is not natural, but a function of power relations. It examines the link between economic and human resource indicators and the need to redefine efficiency to include unpaid resource use in social reproduction and maintenance of human resources. It looks at the politics of development and who controls it, underlining the role of women's constituencies in promoting gender aware development policy.

Micro credit programmes

Since the 1970s, micro credit programmes targeted at women borrowers have been employed by development agencies to address women's poverty based on the view that lack of economic dependence is central to women's powerlessness. Micro finance schemes are expected to help poor women in at least three ways. First, it provides independent sources of income, reducing women's economic dependency on their husbands and/or other male relatives and, thus, helping to enhance autonomy. Second, the sources of income together with exposure to new sets of ideas and social support should make these women more aware and more assertive of their rights. Finally, micro credit programmes – by enhancing control over resources – should increase women's prestige and status in the household, thereby promoting consultation between husband and wife in decision-making processes. However, have these expectations from micro finance been met? Many studies have been conducted on the Grameen Bank and other initiatives.[12] These show that micro credit schemes have, in many cases, contributed towards increasing women's income levels. In some cases, these programmes have also helped women to exert control over resources, resulting in improved perceptions of women's contribution to the household income and to family welfare, and thereby strengthening women's participation in decision-making in the household.

However, there is growing evidence that micro finance in and by itself is not the solution to the empowerment of

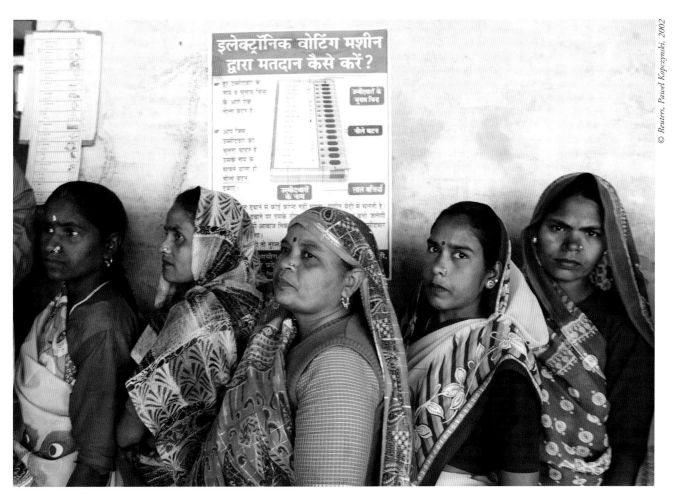

The voice of women in the political arena is one of the hallmarks of a society committed to equality. As Indian women wait in line to register their votes and make their voices heard they carry the hope of improving their lives and the society.

poor women.[13] Studies indicate that such programmes have not really benefited the poorest of poor women. Even in financially successful programmes, many problems remain. Women continue to be disadvantaged vis-à-vis men in terms of lack of access to complementary resources and infrastructural support (for example, land, literacy, skills and business training, childcare services, etc.). Because women continue to have responsibility for subsistence production and household care, the time and energy available for managing businesses remain limited. Women also face greater risk of losing control of their loans because they are sometimes culturally excluded from participating in markets in order to buy inputs and to sell their products. Furthermore, some women and their families have actually reported direct negative impacts from such schemes including the intensification of physical aggression from male relatives after taking out loans.

Linda Mayoux suggests several functional measures to make micro finance programmes more responsive to the goals of poverty reduction and women's empowerment.[14] These include the registration of assets used as collateral in women's names, the incorporation of clear strategies for women to graduate to bigger loans, and the provision of various loan options. Beyond these practical measures, some authors believe that the development community needs to begin with an understanding of the multidimensional nature of the poverty problem and empowerment in order to justify the diversion of funds to micro finance rather than to more ambitious development interventions.[15] Additionally, micro finance programmes have to be based on participatory processes for organisational learning and decision-making, which increase programme effectiveness and sustainability while at the same time being empowering. More critically, micro finance has to be linked to broader social, political and economic movements that challenge gender discrimination in all areas.

With the experience of structural adjustment in many developing countries, the link between micro projects and enterprises and the global economic environment began to be recognised. In an increasingly integrated global economy, small-scale income-generating enterprises financed with micro credit have become very much subject to fluctuations in the macro-economy and global markets. In the context of heightened trade and financial liberalisation, hard-earned gains from small-scale enterprises have often been unsustainable and tenuous as they are wiped out, for instance, by the influx of cheaper imports or financial crises. In the aftermath, poor women may be left even deeper in debt. In view thereof, many women's organisations believe that the economic agenda for women's empowerment has to shift from income generation initiatives to ensuring that women get on board the critical macroeconomic discussions that are impacting on their existence.

Gender sensitive budgeting

Recently, gender sensitive budgeting has attracted considerable attention, not only from local and international non-government organisations, but also from governments, international financial institutions and donor agencies. For many development actors, it has become one of the primary means of attaining gender equality.

Gender sensitive budgeting is about analysing fiscal budgets from a gender perspective and not about creating separate budgets for women and men. It is essentially a conceptual tool that reveals the different impacts of fiscal policies and budgets, including taxes and external debt, on women and men based on their different roles and therefore their different constraints and needs in society. At the same time, gender budgets can be used to critique the way policies and budgets are developed and serve as a platform for holding governments and policymakers accountable for their policies and commitments to gender equality. Glaring gaps often exist between the rhetoric of policy statements and the actual expenditures and measures to support these commitments. Therefore, in the end, the objective of gender sensitive budgeting is the reprioritisation of financial resources and economic decisions in line with commitments to gender equality. Gender budgeting involves five steps:

- Description of the situation of women and men, girls and boys, who are served by a particular sector or ministry.
- Examination of government policies and programmes in the sector, to see whether they address gender gaps.
- Examination of the budget to see whether sufficient money has been allocated to implement effectively the gender sensitive policies and programmes identified in step two.
- Monitoring whether the allocated money has been spent and who benefited from the money, for example, whether funding for health services reached women or men through clinics, hospitals and extension services, and whether these women and men were rich or poor, urban or rural.
- Going back to the first step and re-examine the situation, to see whether the budget and its associated programme have improved on what was initially described.

Gender budgets have been initiated in several countries (for example, Australia, South Africa, the Philippines, Tanzania, Barbados) to achieve a broader policy focus on gender issues and pro-poor needs. The current initiatives vary in terms of characteristics related to expenditure and revenue sides, levels of intervention, methods of analysis, and actors.

In the current development discourse where 'gender and development' and 'poverty reduction' are buzzwords, gender sensitive budgeting has become particularly popular especially with international financial institutions and donor institutions. Caglar warns that the very popularity of gender budgets should be taken with the proverbial grain of salt.[16] That is, the effectiveness of gender sensitive budgeting in promoting equity between women and men has to be evaluated more critically.

Notably, gender budgets fit into the Poverty Reduction Strategy Paper (PRSP) framework of the international financial institutions and donor agencies, since PRSP give direction to governments' development priorities and financial allocation decisions. However, the reprioritisation of financial resources does not necessarily entail a reprioritisation of macroeconomic goals. Therefore, the macroeconomic framework promoted by the international financial institutions and the World Trade Organization emphasising trade and financial liberalisation, deregulation and privatisation is not necessarily interrogated by the gender-budgeting exercise. The goal of economic growth continues to be the foremost priority while policies related to social justice are simply 'added on'. Thus, Caglar wonders whether gender sensitive budgeting has been reduced to a compensatory strategy in support of women's reproductive work.

Moreover, until now, the focus of gender sensitive budgeting efforts has been on the analysis of budgets using gendered lens rather than on actual implementation of gender sensitive budgets. Since implementation is a matter of political power and will, Caglar asks the following question: Is gender sensitive budgeting just an analytical tool with little or no political consequences? The experience of the Tanzania gender networking programme nonetheless provides an example of how its campaign for gender sensitive budgeting has managed to increase the space for women to play a more effective role in national and local decision-making processes, while at the same time exposing the constraints placed by the global economic framework imposed by the international financial institutions and the WTO on national governments. In some districts in Tanzania, the campaign has resulted in actual changes in district-level budgets. However, it remains doubtful as to whether the campaign has had national level impacts.

Gender and trade activism

In recognition of the overall failure of income-generating projects in transforming relations between women and men and the urgency of considering global and macro-

economic developments that are impacting tremendously on women's lives, many feminist economists and women's organisations are concentrating on research, literacy, networking and advocacy on gender and trade policymaking. These actions are founded on the view that gender is an important variable in trade policy formulation. Not only do trade policies impact differently on women and men because of their different roles, but unequal relations between women and men – in and by itself – have also

Girls in Kabul, Afghanistan reenter school after the fall of the Taliban regime, which had denied education to females.

been a driving force in the evolution of the international economy.[17]

Trade policies are the outcome of bilateral, regional and multilateral negotiations under the auspices of the World Trade Organization, which was inaugurated in 1995. While feminist economists have been at the forefront of the critique of structural adjustment policies since the 1980s, including policies promoting trade liberalisation, the issue of global trade is still relatively new to women's economic agenda. Particularly after the first ministerial meeting of the WTO in Singapore in 1996, women's organisations began to actively work towards bringing a feminist perspective into trade policy at various levels. These organisations are concerned about the undemocratic and non-transparent nature of WTO rules and procedures. They are also critical of the inequitable distribution of the benefits and costs of trade liberalisation among developed and developing countries, rich and poor, women and men.

Trade liberalisation has been associated with livelihood losses for women in the agricultural sector. While the hundreds of export processing zones located in Asia and Latin America have created more jobs for women, it has also disguised, maintained, exacerbated and created new forms of inequity between women and men. For instance, women's increased entry into the manufactur-

Table 3.6:

Women in decision-making positions in 1994 and 1998 (in percentage of total persons at ministerial or equivalent positions in the governments)

Region	Percentage of women 1994	Percentage of women 1998
East Asia and Pacific	5	–
Europe & Central Asia	3	7
Latin America & Caribbean	6	7
Middle East & N. Africa	2	2
South Asia	4	–
Sub-Saharan Africa	6	7
Europe: European Monetary Union countries	14	13
World	6	–

Source: World Bank, *World Development Indicators 2004* (New York: World Bank, 2004), 35.

Table 3.7:

Women in national parliaments worldwide in February 2005

Gender Representation in Parliaments	Absolute Figures	Percentage
Men	35,256	84.3
Women	6,564	15.7
Total MPs worldwide for which gender is known	41,820	100

Note: The total above, which is 41,820 MPs, represents the number of parliamentarians for which gender was communicated to the Inter-Parliamentary Union (IPU) by national parliaments. The overall total MPs worldwide that does not take into account gender categorisation is 42,832 MPs.

Source: Inter-Parliamentary Union, *Women in National Parliaments*, situation as of 28 February 2005 (Geneva: IPU, 2004), at http://www.ipu.org/wmn-e/world.htm

early phase of export-industrialisation. Women who are benefiting from jobs in export processing zones are typically young with at least secondary education and some skills, while those who have had no education and skills lose out. Women do not necessarily have control over their wages, and often work under hazardous conditions, in precarious jobs, with hardly any labour rights. Women continue to be responsible for domestic work, thus assuming a 'double work day'.

At present, several women's organisations and networks such as the International Gender and Trade Network and

Table 3.8:

Women in national parliaments in regions in February 2005 (in percentage)

Region	Single House or Lower House	Upper House or Senate	Both Houses combined
Nordic countries	39.9	–	39.9
Americas	18.7	18.5	18.6
Europe - OSCE member countries including Nordic countries	19.0	16.8	18.5
Europe - OSCE member countries excluding Nordic countries	16.9	16.8	16.9
Asia	15.0	13.5	14.9
Sub-Saharan Africa	14.9	14.0	14.8
Pacific	11.2	26.5	13.2
Arab States	6.7	5.6	6.5

Source: Inter-Parliamentary Union, *Women in National Parliaments*, situation as of 28 February 2005 (Geneva: IPU, 2004), at http://www.ipu.org/wmn-e/world.htm

ing industries has not necessarily been accompanied by a narrowing of the gender-based wage gap. Contrarily, some authors empirically associate trade liberalisation with greater gender-based wage disparity in Taiwan and South Korea – countries that achieved phenomenal growth rates in part by exploiting the wage differential between women and men.[18] Women's trade-related employment opportunities have largely been in less skill-intensive manufacturing industries such as garments and microchip assembly where there is limited scope for wage increases and skill upgrading (whereas men are often found in high-skill, technical, supervisory and management positions). Moreover, women are gradually squeezed out of the production force in favour of men as countries move on to the production of more technologically sophisticated and skill-intensive products such as cars. In short, women may gain only in the

the African Women's Economic Policy Network are mobilising women around practical needs such as decent employment, water, health and education that are impinged on by the General Agreement on Trade in Services and other agreements of the WTO. These organisations aim to show that trade liberalisation exploits women's paid and especially unpaid labour and hence the need to make visible the cost of social reproduction. These organisations are also stating that social justice – not least gender equality – and the realisation of human rights, including women's economic, social and cultural rights, should be the objective of global trade rather than economic growth per se. In this way, these organisations are questioning both the socially constructed and assigned gender roles and the orthodox macroeconomic model dominating economic policymaking today that is oppressive to many women.

Box 3.3: Rwanda's case – women's role in development

The 1994 genocide dramatically changed the social fabric of Rwanda - 70 per cent of the population were women who were called upon to play a vital role in the reconstruction process of the country. Women assumed new social and economic roles, and took on new responsibilities. The genocide forced women to think of themselves differently and in many cases to develop skills they would not otherwise have acquired. Backed by the spirit of local and international solidarity and mutual aid, women became organised into associations to improve their living conditions. As a direct consequence, a large number of women's associations were formed.

Rwandan women's associations worked towards the promotion of cultural tolerance and a peaceful mediation in the post-conflict environment with a view to lasting peace. As a woman from the Rwandan collective women's forum 'Pro-femme/Twese Hamwe' said: *'Our association, like many others, was created after the genocide. (…) After the 1994 war, these associations were set up, but they did not have the same guidelines. They were faced with the problem of the reconstruction of the country…. We came together and we were at loggerheads with each other. What did we do throughout our experience? We were lucky to succeed in doing something concrete. We had to participate in the reconstruction process of our country. We built 'peace villages', the first of which was called 'Nelson Mandela'. In these villages, we placed the orphans and people who lived in that region. There were all sorts of ethnic groups there, including survivors of the genocide and others who had fled from other regions. In the end, we managed to achieve good results because there was a lot of tolerance - people like coexisting peacefully. The Rwandan women were awarded the UNESCO prize for tolerance because of their positive action.'*

Recognising the specific achievements and skills of women, international and national actors provided them support and official means of empowerment. In the international level, the international community targeted development assistance to women and influenced national policies and programmes. An example of such co-operation has been the relationship between a development agency, the United Nations Development Programme (UNDP), and local women's associations. UNDP has been essential in providing knowledge on how to use the new dynamism of the recently formed women's associations, and sustained them through capacity building projects, micro-finance programmes and active support for national institution building with a specific view to safeguarding women's rights. For example, an important success of their collaboration was the advancement of property rights for women. Traditionally, Rwandan women could not inherit either land or property under customary laws. As a result, thousands of war widows and orphans did not have access to the houses and land essential for the livelihood of their families. In 1999, the new law on matrimonial property and succession ensured full access by women to their husbands' and parents' property. For the empowerment of women, the UNDP and the Inter Parliamentary Union (IPU) organised projects aimed at improving women's political participation and access to the polit-

ical sphere. Seminars and technical assistance for ensuring the gender sensitiveness of the new Rwandan Constitution, as well as workshops for women candidates running in the electoral campaign contributed to the empowerment of women in politics and decision-making on local and national level.

In the national level, the recognition of the inclusion of women in decision-making was linked to the fact that they were perceived as particularly victimised, more innocent of the genocide and also more trustworthy. According to the leaders of the Government of National Unity women's participation was essential for the democratisation of the country, which was deemed crucial for the reconciliation and prevention of future violence. The government was also aware of women's positive contribution to transition in countries like Uganda or South Africa. As a result, Rwanda's new constitution ratified in 2003, set aside 24 of 80 seats for women in the Chamber of Deputies, and called for a minimum of 30 per cent women in decision-making posts.

However, women stepped into the public sphere at the local level first. They have entered the political space in unprecedented numbers and have initiated policies and programmes addressing many of the root causes and effects of the genocide. They lobbied heavily, participated in drafting of the new constitution, developed voting guidelines that guaranteed seats to female candidates and pushed for the creation of a government ministry of women's affairs to promote policies in favour of women's interests. In the 1999 elections women won 13.7 per cent of the seats for the local councils, two years later they obtained 27 per cent of seats in the sector and district elections, and in the 2003 elections women won 48.8 per cent of the seats in the National Assembly. In addition, fifteen women were elected to non-reserved seats, making it a total of 39 women elected to the Chamber of Deputies. As for the Senate, the constitutional quota of 30 per cent was reached with six women elected out of 20 members. At the end of 2003, Rwanda's senate has elected the first female chief justice. In addition, 50 per cent of Rwanda's High Court judges were women.

The enormous success of women in 2003 elections has placed Rwanda at the top of the IPU world ranking of women in national parliaments. Rwandan women were enthusiastic about the political processes and keen to be party to them, and that there has been a general political recognition of the need to have women on board. For many Rwandans, the legitimacy of the new parliament hinged on an equal participation of men and women, both as voters and as candidates. In the words of Rwanda's president: 'The pillar of the new democratic order in Rwanda depended on many women winning the legislative seats, which is a good step towards development in the country.' However, the future challenge lies in translating women leadership positions into policies and steps empowering women at the grassroots level.

Sources:
Inter-Parliamentary Union, *Press Release No.176*, (Geneva: IPU, 22 October 2003).
Women Waging Peace Policy Commission, *Strengthening Governance: The Role of Women in Rwanda's Transition* (Hunt Alternatives Fund, September 2003).

Box 3.4: Roma women in Europe

The poorest among pariahs, deprived economically, despised, ostracised and politically neglected, their fundamental rights threatened, losing their for centuries preserved culture and not gaining much as a substitute – the Roma people or the Romani, more commonly known throughout history as the Gypsies. Over twelve million Roma currently live in Europe, the majority in the countries of the former Eastern bloc. The creation of ethnicity-based states have lead to even more isolation of the Roma, who have become outsiders to the ethnic majorities, and who are often deprived of their citizenship.

© ICRC, Boris Heger, 1999

A displaced Roma family from Kosovo living, like many others, under difficult conditions where food is scarce and rationed.

Roma women, firmly anchored in traditional patriarchal communities with strong family bounds, bear a double burden of abuse, criminalisation and marginalisation. Racism and poverty intersecting with a patriarchal community create a context, which is often a vicious circle of abuse, constructed by a long history of the Roma people's 'wandering life' and maintained by political negligence of local governments and authorities. Inability to participate in political structures that could change Roma women's lives, and poor access to social services such as health care, housing and education, in addition to discrimination and violence both from Roma and other men shortens Roma women's life span by as much as ten to eighteen years in comparison to the non-Roma female population in Europe.

In many European countries double standards are very much present in policies regarding the Roma. The police are abusive to Roma women in everyday situations and reluctant to intervene in domestic violence perpetrated on Roma women in their own communities. As reported by the Autonomous Women's Centre in Belgrade, the police usually do not prosecute rapes committed by Roma men on Roma women and girls.

Research on women in detention conducted in Spain showed that the percentage of imprisoned Roma women was as much as twenty times higher than in the general population. 60 per cent of the women were jailed for drug dealing, usually on a small scale, and the others mostly for theft or robbery, often also related to drug abuse. 60 per cent were repeat offenders, and 87 per cent had been held in custody until the trial because of their inability to apply for bail. Mistrust towards the Roma, is based on the myth that all Roma people are born criminals. Although the Roma are not involved in large-scale criminal activities, and the rate of criminality in their community is seemingly rooted in economic, social and educational

deprivation, rumours about them as a dangerous ethnic group has deepen the negative public opinion prevailing across Europe.

Forcible sterilisation of 110 Roma women in Slovakia in 2003 may be an extreme example of a flagrant violation of human rights. According to some reports, police officers threatened the Roma women with retaliation if they continued complaining. State officials also menaced Barbora Bukovská, Director of the Slovak human rights group 'Poradna', with a criminal investigation unless she handed over confidential research data, including the personal information on some of the complainants.

During the difficult times of war or armed conflict the vulnerability of unprotected groups increases. Such a situation was witnessed after the Kosovo war in March-June 1999 when thousands of Kosovo Roma became internally displaced persons in Serbia and Montenegro. The women, after being raped during the war, were denied medical assistance, even if pregnant or ill. Disturbing cases of racist violence occurred when thousands of Roma asylum returnees from Germany and Italy met a hostile welcome from the local authorities and inhabitants in Bosnia and Herzegovina, or when the Roma people were denied access to shelters during the bombing of Belgrade. Inevitably militarisation of societies in war expose Roma women to even more pressure, deprivation and abuse. Public aggressiveness of certain groups of the population, such as skinheads, tendencies of ethnic homogenisation, and trafficking in humans exist both in the East and the West. Roma women activists challenge problems on all levels. They meet with disapproval of their own communities where the traditional roles of mothers and wives do not allow them to express their opinion publicly. They address issues, which may be shocking to the majority of society. They have to overcome the Roma's own diverse cultural contexts rooted in varieties of Roma local habits, differences in social status and religion. Although not much valid and reliable information about the abuse of Roma women is available, common problems exist across Europe. Up until now no state has committed itself to the protection of Roma women's rights specifically, although social programmes and policies exist – at least officially if not in practise – in many European countries. The strongest promoters of the protection of their human rights are the Roma women themselves, as well as allied NGOs or individuals who have helped in highlighting the situation of the Roma women.

Faced with the patriarchal obstacles in their own communities, Roma women are breaking many taboos while dealing with such topics as domestic violence, the virginity cult and prostitution. It shows that Roma women can play an important mediating role in the Roma emancipation and integration into society, without losing their own ethnic identity. Generally speaking Roma women's testimonies and demands support the idea of social justice and human security across European countries.

Sources:

N. Bitu, The Situation of Roma/Gipsy Women in Europe, (Strasbourg: Council of Europe, 17 September 1999), at http://www.roma\mgsrom\doc99\MG-S-ROM (99) 9e
IRWN Charter, International Roma Women's Network / Roma, Sinti, Gypsies and Travelers Women in Europe (2002), at
http://www.advocacynet.org/pdf/resource/irwn_charter_eng.pdf
Centre for Reproductive Rights, Report on Sterilisation in Slovakia (2003), at
http://www.reproductiverights.org/pdf/bo_slov_part4.pdf
S. Savic, M. Aleksandrovic, S. Dimitrov and J. Jovanovic, 'Roma Women, Elderly Roma women in Vojvodina, Oral History', in Women's Studies and Research (Novi Sad: 2002).
Roma Women's Association of Romania (RWAR), at http://www.romawomen.org

Endnotes

1 United Nations, *The Beijing Platform for Action* (Beijing, China, 4-15 September 1995), at http://www.un.org/womenwatch/

2 World Bank, *Engendering Development Through Gender Equality in Rights, Resources and Voice* (Washington D.C.: World Bank, 2001).

3 UNIFEM, *Progress of Women Report* (New York: UNIFEM, 2000).

4 For more than 40 years, female migrant numbers have closely equalled male migrant figures. In 1960 there were 35 million female migrants and 40 million male migrants; by 2000, the gap between females and males remained about the same in spite of the total number of migrants more than doubling, with 85 million female migrants versus 90 million male migrants.

5 R. Sabban, 'Migrant Women in the United Arab Emirates: The Case of Female Domestic Workers', *Gender Promotion Programme Working Paper*, No. 10 (Geneva: ILO, 2002), at http://www.ilo.org/public/english/employment/gems/download/swmuae.pdf

6 ILO, *Preventing Discrimination, Exploitation, Abuse of Women Migrant Workers* (Geneva: ILO, 2004), at http://www.ilo.org/public/english/employment/gems/download/mbook1.pdf

7 For more information on the work of active organisations on this topic see 'Women migrants' rights' in the list of organisations dealing with women's rights in this volume.

8 For more information on women's associations see 'Development and empowerment of women' in the list of organisations dealing with women's rights in this volume.

9 A. Sen, *Development as Freedom* (New York: Anchor Books, 1999).

10 S. Bisnath, 'Globalisation, Poverty and Women's Empowerment', Paper presented at *the United Nations Division for the Advancement of Women Expert Group Meeting* (New Delhi, India, 26-29 November 2001).

11 C. Miller and S. Razavi, *Gender Analysis: Alternative Paradigms* (New York: UNDP, 1998).

12 The Grameen Bank is a successful system of loans and micro credits provided by banks and other donors to borrowers and small entrepreneurs, especially in developing countries, in order to fight poverty and support economic development.

13 UNIFEM, *Progress of Women Report*.

14 L. Mayoux, 'Questioning Virtuous Spirals: Micro-finance and Women's Empowerment in Africa', *Journal of International Development* (September 1999).

15 L. Mayoux, Learning for Empowerment Action through Participation, *Inception Report* (New Delhi, 2001).

16 G. Caglar et al., *Engendering Macroeconomic and Trade Policies*, Paper presented at the Summer School on Engendering Economic Policy in a Globalising World: Liberalisation, Services and Care Economies (Berlin, 21-26 June 2003).

17 S. Joekes, *A Gender Analytical Perspective on Trade and Sustainable Development* (New York: UNDP, 1999).

18 G. Berik et al., 'Does Trade Promote Gender Wage Equity? Evidence from East Asia', *CEPA Working Paper* (New York: The Levy Economics Institute, 2002); S. Seguino, 'The Effects of Structural Change and Economic Liberalisation on Gender Wage Differentials in South Korea and Taiwan,' *Cambridge Journal of Economics* (Oxford: Oxford University Press, 2000), 437-59.

Chapter 4

Domestic Violence: Violation of Women's Rights by their Intimate Partners

'At least one out of every three women has been beaten, coerced into sex, or otherwise abused in her lifetime, according to a study based on 50 surveys from around the world. Usually, the abuser is a member of her own family or someone known to her.

L. Heise, M. Ellsberg, M. Gottemoeller, 'Ending violence against women', 1999

Globally, the most common form of violence against women is violence perpetrated by a husband or other intimate male partner. Intimate partner violence (IPV) - often termed 'domestic violence' - takes a variety of forms, including physical violence, ranging from slaps, punches and kicks to assaults with a weapon and homicide, and sexual violence such as forced sex, or forced participation in degrading sexual acts. These are commonly accompanied by emotionally abusive behaviours including extreme jealousy, controlling behaviours such as preventing a woman from seeing her family and friends, constant belittlement, humiliation and intimidation; and economic restrictions, for instance preventing a woman from working, or confiscating her earnings.[1]

Global magnitude of intimate partner violence

Although it is widely recognised that IPV is widespread globally, accurately estimating its prevalence is difficult. Violence is a highly sensitive area that touches on fundamental issues of power, gender and sexuality. As a woman's partner commonly perpetrates violence, often within her home, it is frequently considered as 'private', lying out of the realm of public debate or exploration. Such factors have, until recently, resulted in violence against women remaining largely hidden and undocumented, particularly in developing countries.

Despite the hidden character of domestic violence there is a growing body of research. Well-designed population-based surveys from various parts of the world have found

| Domestic violence taking various forms of physical, mental or sexual abuse, is a worldwide phenomenon most often perpetrated by male partners.

Table 4.1:

Sexual violence against women by country

Percentage of adult women reporting sexual victimisation (attempted or complete forced sex) by an intimate partner: Selected population-based surveys conducted in 1989-2000

Country	Population	Year	Sample size	Attempted/completed forced sex (%)
Brazil	Sao Paulo	2000	941	10.1
Canada	National	1993	12,300	8.0
	Toronto	1991-92	420	15.3
Finland	National	1997-98	7,051	5.9
Japan	Yokohama	2000	1,287	6.2
Mexico	Durango	1996	384	42.0
Nicaragua	León	1993	360	21.7
Peru	Lima	2000	1,086	22.5
Sweden	Teg, Umeå	1991	251	7.5
Switzerland	National	1994-95	1,500	11.6
Thailand	Bangkok	2000	1,051	29.9
United States	National	1995-96	8,000	7.7
Zimbabwe	Midlands Province	1996	966	25.0

Source: Adapted from World Health Organization, *World Report on Violence and Health* (Geneva: WHO, 2002), 152.

that between 16 to over 50 per cent of women have been physically assaulted by an intimate partner. In North America, large national surveys conducted in Canada and the United States suggest that between 22 and 29 per cent of women have been physically assaulted by a partner. In Asia and the Western Pacific fourteen large population-based surveys found that between 8 and 45 per cent reported physical partner violence in their current relationship, and between 10 and 67 per cent had been physically assaulted by a partner. In Latin America and the Caribbean eight large population surveys suggest that between 10 and 28 per cent of women have been physically assaulted by a partner. In Europe, large surveys in the Netherlands, the Republic of Moldova, Switzerland, and one region of Turkey found prevalence rates of partner violence ranging from 14 to 58 per cent. In the Eastern Mediterranean large surveys in Egypt, Israel and the West Bank and Gaza Strip found that between 16 and 52 per cent have been assaulted by their partner in the previous twelve months. In sub-Saharan Africa surveys from Ethiopia, Kenya, Nigeria, South Africa and Zimbabwe found prevalence rates between 13 and 43 per cent.[2]

The wide variation in prevalence documented in different settings has to be interpreted with caution. The differences may not only result from differences in the levels of violence between settings, but also from differences in research methodology; definitions of violence; sampling techniques; interviewer training and skills; and cultural differences that affect a respondent's willingness to disclose their experiences. It is only recently that attempts to use standard definitions and survey methods across different studies have been made.[3] As the comparability of methods between studies increases, a more comprehensive understanding of the global burden of IPV will be obtained.

Research also highlights that many women are sexually assaulted by their partners, with some men using both physical and sexual violence to assert power and control their partners. In many settings sexual violence is common - in a household survey in one province in Zimbabwe, 26 per cent of married women reported being forced to have sex when they did not want to. When asked about the type of force used, 23 per cent reported physical force, 20 per cent reported that their partner shouted, 12 per cent reported being forced whilst they were asleep, and 6 per cent reported the use of threats.[4]

The consequences of intimate partner violence

In many countries, IPV is predominantly perceived as a legal issue. Yet, recent reviews highlight that IPV is an important cause of ill-health and death and is a risk factor for many health problems.

Box 4.1: Facts and figures on the magnitude of intimate partner violence

Information collected from recent studies and the media during the International Day of Violence Against Women in November-December 2003 – based mainly on reports of Amnesty International, Human Rights Watch, BBC News, and the Parliamentary Assembly of the Council of Europe – reveal an enormous scope and magnitude of violence committed against women in families and homes.

- Subjected to violence at home is/are:
  - One in six women in the Czech Republic.
  - One in five women in Switzerland.
  - One out of two women in India: according to a survey conducted in Delhi in 2003, during one year 217 women died from domestic violence in this city.
  - One in five women in Namibia.
  - Four out of five women in Pakistan.

- One in every four Russian families live in a cycle of domestic violence. An estimated 36,000 women in the Russian Federation suffer beatings from intimate partners every day. Every forty minutes a Russian woman's life is claimed by domestic violence.

- One in four adults experience domestic violence in Great Britain, the majority of them women. More than one in twenty crimes were classified as domestic violence by the British Crime Survey in 2000. Female homicide victims amounted to 92 cases. This means that one every four days or two women per week are murdered by their intimate partners.

- One in four women in Canada are reported to be victims in a key survey of over 12,000 Canadian women.

- In the US, 588,490 cases of intimate violence against female victims were reported in 2001 by the US Bureau of Justice Statistics. In the same year, a total of 1,247 women were murdered by their intimate partners. Criminal statistics show a high rate of female victims for sexual offences. According to the National Violence Against Women Survey in 2000 an approximate 300,000 intimate partner rapes occur each year against women eighteen years and older.

- Only after a number of assaults will women report to the authorities and still many of the crimes go unreported. The UK British Crime Survey in 2000 estimated it takes an average of 35 repeated incidents of assault before women chose to go to the police. Finally, only an estimated one out of three cases of domestic violence is actually reported.

- In 2002, the Council of Europe announced that violence against women was the major source of death and disability of women aged 16 to 44, causing more death and ill-health than cancer or traffic accidents.

- Studies in 2003 have demonstrated that even pregnant women are exposed to domestic violence. For example, an assessment in a hospital in the United Kingdom indicated that three per cent of 500 pregnant women experienced violence during their pregnancy. In Namibia this figure is six per cent of 1,500 women. In the US, an annual estimate totals 324,000 women experiencing intimate partner violence during their pregnancy.

- The family situation gravely deteriotes in cases of domestic violence especially affecting children. Studies in the United States suggest that between three to ten million children witness family violence per year. In a national survey with more than 6,000 families interviewed, 50 per cent of the men who frequently assaulted their wives also abused their children.

- In the Netherlands, a study in 1988 estimated one in six girls suffered sexual abuse before the age of sixteen with almost half of the abuse taking place within the core family.

- In certain situations women flee to refuge shelters, a phenomenon which has reached a significant level in Switzerland, where, in 2002, women and children stayed 55,459 nights in women's shelters. The overall cost to the economy was 400 million Swiss francs.

- In Austria, overnight stays totalled 96,535 in 1997.

- In the United States, where an estimated 1.3 million women are physically assaulted by an intimate partner annually, health costs of violence against women including intimate partner assault, rape and murder amount to US$5.8 billion. The sum covers direct medical health services, as well as, indirect costs of loss of productivity and wages. In the United Kingdom, a single town estimates the minimal cost of providing crisis services to women to be £7.5 million, an amount that merely covers limited provisional support to the women's children and none for the prevention of abuse.

- According to the National Survey on Demography and Health conducted in Columbia in 2002, 41 per cent of the surveyed women admitted that they had been physically assaulted by their partners. An earlier survey carried out by the Centre of Health and Gender Equality (CHANGE) for the John Hopkins University found that despite existing legislation on domestic violence, 40 per cent of Colombian women had been victims of domestic violence. 70 per cent of the cases of intimate partner violence in Colombia occur within married couples, women representing 91 per cent of those affected. According to the Forum on Intra-Family and Partner Violence organised by Profamilia, a leading Colombian organisation that conducts research on family issues, 69 per cent of the cases of domestic violence in Colombia's capital, Bogotá, have their origins in jealousy.

- According to a United Nations Development Fund for Women (UNIFEM) report, 45 nations have explicitly enacted laws against domestic violence, 21 others are drafting new laws and many have revised criminal legislation to include domestic violence. In addition, 118 states have drawn national plans of action for the implementation of their obligations under the Beijing Platform for Action.

Sources:
C. M. Rennison, *Crime Data Brief, Intimate Partner Violence 1993-2001* (Washington, 2003).
P. Tjaden and N. Thoennes, *Full Report of the Prevalence, Incidence, and Consequences of Violence Against Women, Findings from the National Violence Against Women Survey*, (Washington: US Department of Justice, 2000).
UNIFEM, *Not a Minute More! Ending Violence against Women* (New York: UNIFEM, 2003), 69, at http://www.unifem.org/filesconfirmed/207/312_book_complete_eng.pdf
Austrian Women's Shelter, Canadian Ministry of Supply and Services, US Centers for Disease Control and Prevention, US Department of Justice – Bureau of Justice Statistics, UK Home Office (British Criminal Statistics).
United Nations, *Mission to Colombia*, Addendum to the Report of the Special Rapporteur of the Commission on Human Rights on Violence Against Women, its Causes and Consequences, Ms. Radhika Coomaraswamy, UN Document E/CN.4/2002/83/add.3 (Geneva, 2002).
L. Creel with special reporting by S. Lovera and M. Ruiz, 'Domestic Violence: An ongoing Threat to Women in Latin America and the Caribbean', *Population Reference Bureau* (2000), at http://www.prb.org
Profamilia, at http://profamilia.org.co/profamilia/english/INDEX.HTM

Physical violence often causes serious or permanent injury, including broken bones and physical disfigurement from burns, bites, weapons or other objects. In the United States IPV is one of the most common causes of injury for women - several US studies of emergency care find that between 11 and 30 per cent of injured women were injured by their partner, and that these women are more likely to receive injuries to the head, face, neck, thorax, breasts and abdomen than other injured women.[5] Women who are physically abused also often have a range of less-defined complaints, including chronic headaches and abdominal and pelvic pain.

Chart 4.1:

Victims of various kinds of homicide by gender in the United States in 1976-2000 (in percentage)

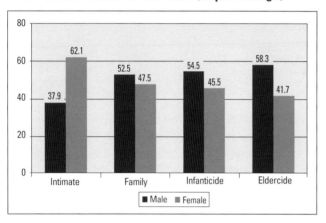

Note: Among all homicide victims, women are particularly at risk for intimate killings, sex-related homicides, and murder by arson or poison. Female victims are more likely to be killed by an intimate or family member than male victims, while male victims are more likely to be killed by acquaintances or strangers.
Source: US Department of Justice, Bureau of Justice Statistics, *Violent Crimes Rates by Gender of Victim,* at http://www.ojp.gov/bjs/glance/vsx2.htm

As well as injury, IPV also has substantial physical, psychological and reproductive health consequences. The fear and stress associated with IPV can result in less obvious, but chronic health problems, including chronic headaches or back pain, and recurring symptoms such as fainting or seizures. Women who have experienced partner violence also exhibit significantly more gastrointestinal symptoms and problems associated with chronic stress.[6]

Forced sex has a range of physical effects. Gynaecological problems include vaginal bleeding or infection, fibroids, and chronic pelvic pain. For example, a large United States population based study found that the odds of women reporting a gynaecological problem was three times greater for women who had experienced partner violence.[7]

Physical and sexual partner violence also lies behind unwanted pregnancies and sexually transmitted infections. Research in the United States and in developing countries has documented that violence by intimate

partners may substantially limit the degree to which women can refuse sex, control when sexual intercourse takes place, or insist on the use of condoms. Even when a man is not physically violent the fear of violence may greatly influence a woman's sexual and reproductive decision-making. The family planning literature documents how, in some settings, the fear of male violence greatly limits married women's ability to use contraception. Some women use contraceptives clandestinely, and risk violence if this is discovered. Likewise, the fear of violence is commonly cited by married women as a barrier to using condoms for HIV prevention.

The mental health consequences of partner violence include fear, anxiety, fatigue, depression and post-traumatic stress disorder (PTSD). It is likely that many of the gender differences in the incidence of depression around the world are attributable to the gender difference in intimate partner violence. PTSD as a consequence of intimate partner violence has been extensively studied in North America, with the prevalence among battered women being more than three times higher than among non-abused women.[8] Research from Canada suggests that, in addition to depression abused women have more problems with anxiety, insomnia, and social dysfunction.[9] In developing countries battered women often report mental health problems as a consequence of intimate partner violence. For instance, in Nicaragua 70 per cent of women seeking medical help after being abused by their partners suffer from emotional distress and similar findings are reported from Pakistan and Zimbabwe. Links have also been found between physical abuse and higher rates of psychiatric treatment, attempted suicide, and alcohol dependence.

Intimate partner violence also has fatal outcomes, partner homicide in North America is responsible for 40 to 60 per cent of female homicides. Data on homicide of women globally is sparse and warrants more research and surveillance. As well as homicide, mortality associated with domestic violence includes suicide. Suicidality has also been found to be associated with IPV in the United States, Scandinavia, and Papua New Guinea.

Intimate partner violence may put women at greater risk of HIV infection, and consequently premature mortality. In a recent study of HIV transmission between heterosexual couples in rural Uganda, women who reported being forced to have sex against their will in the previous year had an eight-fold increased risk of becoming HIV infected. In countries such as Namibia and South Africa, where HIV is widespread, the acceptability and legality of forced sex in marriage is now being challenged.

Intimate partner violence has other far-reaching consequences, for example, by limiting women's ability to work, participate in society, and potentially harming

Domestic violence against women often remains hidden in the privacy of the home. It is estimated that only a small fraction of female victims seek shelter or make their suffering public.

Violence during pregnancy has been associated with miscarriage, late entry into prenatal care, still birth, premature labour and birth, foetal injury, and low birth weight. The trauma may pose a threat to the health of the mother and foetus, which can result in death of either or both. Much research has explored whether IPV is a risk factor for low birth weight, and a recent analysis of fourteen published studies from North America and Europe showed significant association.[11] Little is known about the extent to which IPV is a risk factor for low birth weight in developing countries.

Intimate partner violence may also account for a large, but unrecognised proportion of maternal mortality. A

Chart 4.2:

Victims of homicide by circumstances and gender in the United States in 1976-2000 (in percentage)

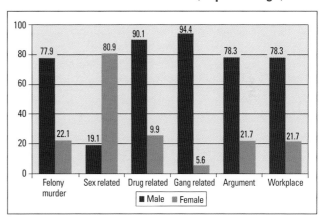

Source: US Department of Justice, Bureau of Justice Statistics, *Violent Crimes Rates by Gender of Victim*, at http://www.ojp.gov/bjs/glance/vsx2.htm
FBI, *Supplementary Homicide reports*, 1976-2000, quoted by the US Department of Justice, Bureau of Justice Statistics, at http://www.ojp.gov/bjs/homicide/gender.htm

their children. A woman experiencing abuse may have to sell assets to pay for things that her husband refuses to buy, to gain access to health and other services, or to support her family. Her work may be disrupted both through ill-health and injury, and as a result of her partner interfering at her workplace. Commonly, in abusive relationships, a woman may not be allowed to see her family and friends, or to participate fully in religious, development or community activities. Women and their children may also be forced to leave their homes when violence becomes severe.

Violence during pregnancy

Pregnancy is often viewed as a special time in a woman's life. However, research shows that pregnant women are often abused – with some violence continuing or increasing during pregnancy, and some starting during this time. A large review of United States studies found prevalence of abuse during pregnancy ranging from nine to twenty per cent, with the majority of studies documenting a range from four to eight per cent.[10] Population studies from Canada, Chile, Egypt and Nicaragua have found that six to fifteen per cent of pregnant women have been physically or sexually abused during pregnancy, usually by their partners.

study of 400 villages in Pune, India, found that sixteen per cent of all deaths during pregnancy resulted from partner violence.[12] Being killed by a partner has also been identified as an important cause of maternal deaths in Bangladesh and in the United States.

Individual factors associated with intimate partner violence

Most research on the causes of IPV has focused on investigating individual factors with the evidence coming primarily from the United States, and limited by the scope of factors explored. Possible male personal history risk factors include witnessing parental violence as a child, the ownership of weapons, the extreme use of alcohol or drugs, loss of status, and delinquent peer associations. A review of the social science literature on risk factors for physical IPV in North America has identified a number of demographic, personal history and personality factors linked to a man's likelihood of physically assaulting his partner. Among demographic factors, young age and low income were consistently found to be associated with an increased likelihood of a man physically assaulting his partner. More broadly across studies the relationship between physical assault and socio-economic status and educational level are not consistent. One longitudinal study in New Zealand found that family poverty in childhood and adolescence, low academic achievement and aggressive delinquency at age fifteen all strongly predicted men's physical abuse of partners at age twenty-one.[13]

Among personal history factors, growing up in a violent family has consistently been found to be a strong risk factor for men's aggression towards their partners. Research from thirteen industrialised and developing countries found higher rates of reported partner violence among women whose husbands had either been beaten as a child or had witnessed their mothers being beaten. However, not all boys who witness or suffer violence grow up to abuse their partners, and an important research question is to identify what influences whether boys grow up to perpetuate partner violence or not.

There is substantial evidence from a range of countries linking male alcohol use and/or heavy drinking with partner violence.[14] The evidence suggests that women

Shahnaz Bukhari (right), chief of the Progressive Women's Association, Pakistan, talks to Gul Marjan, whose husband allegedly tried to sever her hands with a butcher knife for her refusal to give up her job.

whose partners drink heavily are at a far greater risk of being physically assaulted by their partner. For example, in Canada women who lived with heavy drinkers were five times more likely to be assaulted by their partners than those who lived with non-drinkers. Although the

role of male use of alcohol as a risk factor for violence is commonly highlighted, the nature of the association is debated. Rather than alcohol use being a cause of violence, many believe that alcohol use increases the likelihood of violence by reducing a man's inhibitions and clouding his judgement.

Societal and community factors associated with intimate partner violence

There is limited evidence of the role played by different societal and community factors. A high socio-economic status has often been found to be protective – so that although women from all socio-economic status groups are vulnerable to partner violence, women from poorer households are the most vulnerable. In practise it is likely that a range of factors contribute to this, for example, for some men the stresses associated with poverty may result in frustration at their inability to provide for their families or financial stresses may fuel marital disagreements. There are also exceptions to this relationship – in Zimbabwe, for example, women of higher educational level were more at risk of sexual violence from their partners, perhaps because their partner felt that their status challenged their male authority.

An analysis of ethnographic data from ninety studies of societies with differing levels of violence suggests that wife beating occurs more often in societies where men have the economic and decision-making power in the household, where women do not have easy access to divorce, and where adults routinely resort to violence to resolve conflict.[15] Other factors hypothesised as potentially contributing to the risk of violence include societies where the notion of masculinity and being male is linked to dominance or toughness, where there are strong notions of male entitlement and ownership of women, and the physical chastisement of women is widely approved. Potential community characteristics may include the low social status of women, a lack of supportive services, high levels of unemployment, crime and male-on-male violence. Possible protective factors within the immediate social context may include the active involvement of women in groups that can support each other, communities where women can mobilise and control resources, or where they are able to maintain the custody of their children upon separation.

A greater understanding of the role played by these factors could provide important evidence on how to best prevent the violence. An ongoing multi-country study sponsored by the World Health Organization in seven countries (Bangladesh, Brazil, Japan, Namibia, Peru, Thailand and Tanzania) is collecting data on many of these factors, and may help substantially to improve our understanding.

Intimate partner violence on international and national agendas

Since 1993, there have been several initiatives developed by the international community that recognised violence against women as a violation of women's human rights. The first of these is the United Nations General Assembly Declaration on the Elimination of Violence Against Women, which was followed by the Conference on Human Rights in Vienna (1993) and the creation of the mandate of the Special Rapporteur on Violence Against Women (1994). It was also affirmed in the Fourth World Conference on Women in Beijing (1995). Unfortunately, in practice the level of international commitment to address violence against women is not reflected at the national level. In most countries the majority of activities have been spearheaded by women's organisations, with occasional funding from governments. Where governments are involved – as in Australia, Latin America, North America, Namibia, and many European countries – it has generally been in response to demands by civil society. A cornerstone of most national activity is the provision of hotlines, crisis-centres and shelters for women experiencing or fleeing intimate partner violence. These centres often provide support and individual counselling, programmes for children, assistance in dealing with social services and legal matters, and help in finding future employment. Women activists initially set up most of these centres, but they often go on to be run by professionals, and receive local and national government funding. More recently shelters and crisis centres have also been established in some developing countries. Alternative models have also been developed, including the provision of informal networks of 'safe houses' where women in danger can seek temporary shelter.

Legal responses

In the 1980s and 1990s many countries reformed laws relating to physical and sexual abuse by an intimate partner. The most common reforms involve criminalising physical and sexual violence by intimate partners, either through new laws on domestic violence, or by amending existing penal codes. To promote the wider adoption of domestic violence legislation the UN Special Rapporteur on Violence Against Women has developed a model legislation, which is to serve as a drafting guide to legislatures and organisations committed to lobbying legislatures for comprehensive legislation on domestic violence. There have also been initiatives to improve the implementation of new laws – with specialised domestic violence or family courts, specialised training of the police, court officials and advisers to support women. Many Latin American and some Asian countries have established police stations entirely staffed by women. However, evaluations suggest that although the presence of women increases the number of abused women coming forward, these may not always have specialised services, such as counselling. Moreover, not all female police officers are sympathetic to victims, and prevailing attitudes may result in the units and their staff being undervalued within police hierarchies.

A common problem when attempting to prosecute men for their violence is the onus on women to press charges, which often leads to withdrawal of charges. To address this policies have been introduced, in the United States and in other countries, that compel police officers to arrest perpetrators of IPV. However, there is mixed evidence from the United States about whether this reduces repeat assaults, with some suggestion that particularly in areas of concentrated poverty, perpetrators were more violent following an arrest than if they had simply received a warning. Alternative civil legal measures include protection orders, that may remove a man from his home and prohibit a man from contacting or abusing his partner. However, the evidence for their effectiveness is also mixed, and they seem to have little effect on men with serious criminal records.

Other legal responses include making it a legal requirement for men to seek counselling or to attend treatment programs for perpetrators. Treatment programmes generally use a group format to discuss gender roles, how to cope with stress and anger, and teach men to take responsibility for their actions. Although some evaluations suggest that the programmes do help men who complete the programme to become non-violent, they also highlight that many men do not attend the sessions, and that many drop out before completion. A review of existing evaluations suggests that perpetrator treatment programmes are most likely to work if non-attendance or breaches of the programme are penalised by the justice system, if programmes can sustain long-term participation, and enable men to discuss and acknowledge their behaviour.

The role of the health sector

In the past few years the World Health Organization, the American Medical Association, the International Federation of Obstetricians and Gynaecologists, the Royal College of Nursing and other professional medical bodies have made statements about the public health importance of violence against women. Several have developed guidelines on how health workers can better identify, support and refer victims of violence. The involvement of the health sector could potentially provide many opportunities since many women come into contact with health-care providers at some point in their lives. In practise however, in most countries, doctors and nurses rarely enquire about abuse or check for signs of violence. Several countries have incorporated guidelines to address domestic violence in their health sector policies, and countries such as Brazil, Ireland, Malaysia, Mexico, Nicaragua, the Philippines and South Africa have piloted projects to train health workers to identify and respond to abuse. An important aspect of this is to confront negative and judgmental attitudes and misconceptions about domestic violence. A number of programmes promote routine questioning of women attending specific health services about their experiences of violence. Although there is strong evidence that women do not mind being asked, there is less research on how this affects the services women receive, or their later risk or help-seeking behaviour.

Community activities

In many countries outreach workers are used to visit victims of violence in their homes, or provide abused women with information and advice. In many countries advocates help women who have been abused to negotiate the intricacies of the legal and welfare systems. For example, the Domestic Violence Matters Project in Islington in London places civilian advocates in local police stations, which contact all women who report partner violence to the police. An evaluation found that they increased the use of shelters, legal advice and support groups, and reduced the number of repeated calls to the police, and so may have reduced the reoccurrence of IPV.

At the community level, inter-agency forums are used to monitor and improve responses. These initiatives were originally piloted in the United States, but have been adopted in Canada, the UK, and parts of Latin America. Depending upon the setting, these councils may include representatives from the police, social and health services, as well as key women's organisations. In low income countries groups may include local political or religious leaders, community health workers, magistrates and representatives of women's groups. The limited numbers of evaluations conducted in industrialised countries have found improved rates of police prosecution and referral of men to treatment programmes. However, qualitative research also suggests that there is the danger that agencies focus primarily on the refuge and criminal justice system, and do not affect more widespread change.

Prevention activities

A range of communication campaigns has been used to raise awareness about partner violence, to challenge widely held attitudes and misconceptions, and to change behaviour. These include the Zero Tolerance Campaign in Glasgow and the United Nations Campaign 'A life free from violence, its our right'. A long-standing initiative is the annual Sixteen Days of Action Against Violence Against Women, running between 25 November and 10 December each year in many countries. A relatively new initiative is to incorporate prevention campaigns into a popular soap opera, including the successful example of the Soul City Project in South Africa (see box 4.3).

Although several violence prevention initiatives in industrialised countries target youth, very few focus on preventing dating and intimate partner violence. To date evidence of the effectiveness of such interventions come from North America, and primarily measure changes in knowledge and attitudes. However, one initiative that explored the effect of a school based intervention that covered the development of positive relationships, identifying abusive relationships, and how to seek help for eleven to seventeen year olds found a 60 per cent reduction in the self-reported perpetration of physical and sexual violence.[16] There is the potential to replicate such activities, incorporating issues of gender, power and consent into HIV and life skills programmes.

Conclusion

When dealing with the profound impact of intimate partner violence on women and their children, there is the danger of portraying women as victims, and men solely as perpetrators. Yet in the face of many barriers, women experiencing violence show great strengths and resourcefulness, and utilise a range of strategies trying to minimise the extent of violence or injury, to obtain support, and to end the violence. Likewise, there are many

For many women, comfort comes only at a place of refuge, such as a shelter for battered women.

© Network Photographers, Donna Ferrato, 2004

Box 4.2: Legal aspects of domestic violence in the Czech Republic

A tolerance towards intimate partner violence derives mainly from a generally low legal awareness in Czech society. Domestic violence has been considered a matter of private life rather than a criminal act, which only when achieving a certain intensity constitutes a criminal offence. Until recently, such attitudes have been reflected also within the enacted law considering domestic violence as an issue to be dealt with by the family and not to be interfered with by state authority.

Following extensive debates about the necessity of changing this approach, an amendment of the Penal Code concerning domestic violence as an individual criminal offence was enacted (effective since 1 June 2004). Before this amendment there were a number of provisions to prosecute violence, but no difference was made between various different forms of violent behaviour. The very specific nature of domestic violence was not taken into consideration, especially the fact that the perpetrator abuses the victim's emotional or material dependence upon him and therefore, is not able to defend herself effectively. Unfortunately, a large part of Czech society share this opinion based on the myths of 'victim's guilt' (victim-provoked violence), or on the belief that both the perpetrators and victims are criminals, psychopaths, or persons with intellectual or economic deficits.

The main feature of the new provision is that it covers violence 'behind closed doors', which does not only mean the home or household, but also hotels, weekend cottages, students dormitories, that is any place used for living. Another crucial innovation of the new provision is the fact that consent of the victim is no longer required in order to start prosecution. Moreover, there is criminal liability placed on persons knowing that domestic violence is taking place and failing to report it to the police. The new legal obligation to report domestic violence to the police aims to change the general ignorance towards domestic violence within Czech society.

While the police should guarantee the security of victims of domestic violence and prosecute the perpetrator, they often fail to fulfil their functions. Like the general public, police officers are influenced by the view that domestic violence is a private issue that should be solved within the family. Policemen without proper special training often contribute to secondary victimisation through, for example, belittlement, patronising or inattentive attitudes. Rather frequently they try to persuade victims to withdraw complaints. . At present, new training programmes for young police officers are taking place at police academies, as well as, sensitisation programmes managed by NGOs. Hopefully, they will improve the behaviour and attitudes of the police when encountering domestic violence.

The housing problem, from a civil law perspective, is among the most pressing issues to accompany domestic violence. While the highest occurrence of domestic violence is among spouses, victims of domestic violence have no legal means to prevent the perpetrators from sharing common housing facilities. Moreover, the exposure to violence may continue in the event of a divorce, especially due to circumstances forcing the victims of domestic violence to share housing with a violent ex-partner. Shared lease of housing facilities is not terminated as a result of divorce and the ex-partner is not always obliged to move out as it is preconditioned by the provision of alternative housing. Although this provision may rarely be considered realistic, the only solution remaining at the disposal of the victim is to take refuge along with the children. Furthermore, there are almost no municipal housing capacities available to the victims whose only chance is to benefit from the services of asylum facilities that sometimes - but nor regularly - provide such help. To make the reality for victims even more complicated, taking refuge may, depending on the category of the leasing contract, eventually be considered as 'abandoning the common household' so that the perpetrator may be declared, ad absurdum, as the only person entitled to benefit from the leased housing facility.

There is no single legal act providing for the protection against domestic violence in the Czech Republic. If the victim decides to use the civil judicial procedure to achieve protection, she carries the burden of proof. The instruments in this respect range from submitting an action, for which consideration may take several years, to demanding a preliminary ruling that is to be issued between one day to one week. Among other obstacles to effective protection are the lack of information on the part of the victims and the lack of the barrister's interest in representing victims of domestic violence, as dealing with domestic violence is neither lucrative nor prestigious. However, legal representation is essential since the judicial procedure is rather complicated as it regularly concerns several branches of law. Beyond the question of affordability a lack of qualified barristers is also an issue. The barrister's remuneration is frequently provided by women's organisations as many women suffering from domestic violence are financially dependent on the perpetrators of the violence. Apart from material concerns the civil procedure also means a high exposure to psychological and financial stress.

Finally, while the amendment of the Penal Code is an extremely positive development towards the elimination of domestic violence, it is just 'a first step'. Any amendment to a penal code cannot alone solve the problem of domestic violence. Interaction and co-operation with other branches of law, civil law in particular, as well as a change of approach by state authorities, the police in particular, and other professional groups (social workers, consultants, medical personnel, teachers, etc.) are necessary to succeed in the eradication of domestic violence.

Sources:
Profem, *Legal Aspects of Domestic Violence in the Czech Republic in 2002* (March 2002), at http://www.profem.cz
Miroslav Ruzicka, 'Domestic Violence – Inputs from Foreign Legislations, Proposal *de lege ferenda* for Penal Law', *Právník* (Prague, 2003).

A growing awareness of the character of intimate partner violence as an affront against women's human rights has mobilised many grassroots organisations, local media outlets and international agencies during the last decade. Many unique and creative initiatives have sought to address the roles of various actors in society, especially the role of men, and have denounced prevailing social attitudes which provoke violence. Many groups and associations have combined their efforts to raise public consciousness, reaching out to all communities, from the local to the global, and emphasising that everyone must be involved in combating this worldwide problem.

Soul City, South Africa

'Matlakala is home late and her family is already sitting at the dinner table having finished the meal. Thabang, her husband, yells at her and tells the children to go to their room. Then he loses his temper and starts beating her up. She breaks down, battered and unhappy. What is she to do?'

Matlakala lives in the fictional South African township Soul City. She is one of the main characters in the television series of the same name, broadcast in prime time on the country's largest television station, SABC. The first series was aired in 1994, and the seventh series is now being developed. Series Four included a strong story line on violence against women, covering domestic violence, AIDS, child abuse and rape, and promoted messages about the unacceptability of violence, and the role of families and communities in addressing violence. More broadly the series is careful to take into account gender issues, stresses the importance of the empowerment of women, takes care not to perpetuate gender stereotypes or objectify women, and includes male characters who are non-sexist and who communicate well with their partners. As well as being shown on television, the stories about Matlakala and the other people from Soul City also appear as newspaper strips, daily radio shows, and educational material for children and adults. Soul City is the most watched programme on South African television. For the last episode of Soul City 75 per cent of the population with access to a television turned it on. An evaluation of Series Four found increased awareness and knowledge of domestic violence, changed attitudes and norms, and a greater willingness to take appropriate action.

The Zero Tolerance Campaign, Glasgow

The Zero Tolerance Charitable Trust is an independent charity, which campaigns for the prevention of male violence against women and children. The Trust, which was established in 1995, works mainly in the UK and Europe, but also has links with organisations throughout the world. The first Zero Tolerance campaign was launched in Edinburgh in November 1992 by the Edinburgh District Council's Women's Committee. The campaign was prompted by a local survey by Edinburgh Council, which showed that violence against women was a priority issue for women in Edinburgh, and it was the first crime prevention campaign in Britain to tackle the issue of male violence against women and children. The original six-month campaign used four posters to raise the general public's awareness about the reality and prevalence of child sexual abuse, rape and sexual assault and domestic violence. Based on research and rooted in the experience of women and children, the posters used black and white photography and text to challenge existing attitudes. Using billboards,

mass distribution of posters and partnerships working with key organisations including the local press, the campaign generated overwhelming interest and support at a local and national level. The campaign was designed to run in four phases with separate poster executions. The first three posters tackled specific aspects of violence against women – with the third poster dealing with domestic violence and challenging the widely accepted myth that domestic violence only occurs in working-class households. In addition, this poster identified emotional and sexual abuse as forms of domestic violence. Partnerships with the local and national media proved a key component in the success of the first campaign and have been used in all subsequent campaigning. At the same time local events were organised. These included seminars for professionals working in key areas and debates, which the general public could attend.

Interest and demand for further Zero Tolerance campaigns gathered momentum and resulted in the establishment of the Zero Tolerance Charitable Trust in 1995. The Trust has gone on to develop further campaign packages, to commission research, to lobby the government, to establish an information database and develop education intervention and training programmes. The Excuses Campaign (1995–1996) directly challenged the excuses used by men to avoid taking responsibility for their violence. The Justice Campaign (1996–1997) raised awareness about the justice system's failure to deliver equality and justice to women and children experiencing violence. The Respect Campaign (1998-to date) highlights the issue of consent in personal relationships – challenging boys with the responsibility of ensuring consent in sexual relationships so that the onus does not continue to fall on girls, and to challenge girls by helping them to assert themselves in their personal relationships.

The Sixteen Days of Action Against Violence Against Women: 25 November - 10 December

Since 1999, over 1,000 individuals and organisations from more than 100 countries have sponsored activities in their communities during the Sixteen Days of Activism Against Gender Violence held every year from 25 November to 10 December. The dates are chosen symbolically to link violence against women – 25 November, as the International Day Against Violence Against Women - and human rights – 10 December, as the International Human Rights Day. By making this connection, communities worldwide call attention to the fact that violence against women is a violation of human rights.

The history of 25 November as a day to commemorate violence against women is derived from the story of three Latin American women whose courage became the symbol of resistance and resilience. As the 'Day to End Violence Against Women', it was first proclaimed in 1981 by the Latin American region in the *Feminist Encuentro* for Latin America and the Caribbean that took place in Colombia. These *Encuentros* are a biennial symposium of women's organisations in the region aimed at creating a forum for sharing information and experiences. The conferences denounced cases of gender-based violence such as sexual exploitation and rape, domestic violence and state condoned violence, for example, harassment and torture of women political activists. The day commemorates the assassination of the Mirabal sisters who fought against the dictatorial regime of

▶▶

Rafael Trujillo in the Dominican Republic in 1960. The three sisters, Patria, Minerva and Maria Teresa, together with their husbands, were important figures of the resistance and suffered persecution and repeated arbitrary detention. On 25 November 1960 the three women were killed by Trujillo's followers as they were on their way to visit their detained husbands. The apparent murder, staged as a car accident when the car and the bodies were found at the bottom of a cliff, spurred an uproar from the resistance movement, which spread to the whole nation scandalised by the demonstration of unacceptable violence. The following year, Trujillo's 30-year dictatorship was brought to an end, with the assassination of the Mirabal sisters as one of the powerful catalysts. Since then the sisters were considered national heroines, referred to as *'Inolvidables Mariposas'* or 'unforgettable butterflies' – eternal symbols for the fight for freedom. The actions and the fate of the Mirabal sisters had a far reaching effect regionally and globally. Not only have they become a source of inspiration, praised and remembered in literature, music and plays in their region, but their cause was also embraced the world over by the proclamation of 25 November as the International Day for the Elimination of Violence Against Women in 1999 by the United Nations. It is a day designated to commemorate their death and at the same time to reaffirm global commitment to end gender-based violence. UN General Assembly Resolution 54/134 emphasised the continuing violations of women's rights and the general failure in providing security to women, thus qualifying violence against women as a major obstacle to the achievement of UN's goals of equality, development and peace. As a result, it called for all governments, international organisations and NGOs to engage in a consciousness raising campaign on the problem of violence against women.

Over time the campaign has evolved and activities for the Sixteen Days of Action are conducted in many countries including Ireland, Malaysia, Zimbabwe, the United Kingdom and the United States. The first Sixteen Days Campaign in 1991 was co-ordinated by the Centre for Women's Global Leadership in the United States. In each country a range of events are used to highlight the prevalence of male violence, create awareness of this violence as a human rights issue, and promote women's leadership in addressing the problem (see also 'Domestic Violence' in the list of organisations dealing with women's rights in this volume).

men who are not violent to their partners. The challenge for concerned agencies and governments is to identify ways to support women in their bid to overcome violence, give a voice to men who reject violence, and to address the forces that help perpetuate intimate partner violence within society.

The interventions reviewed illustrate the complexity of mounting an effective response. Prevention initiatives focused on youth in combination with research and initiatives to address some of the root causes of violence are needed to reduce the scale of it. There is also much scope for early prevention – before violence becomes too entrenched within a relationship. At present we have limited evidence of how to effectively intervene at this time, but there is some indication that the health sector may provide important opportunities for early identification and referral.

The scale of the problem highlights the urgent need for expanded national and local level initiatives to prevent and respond to intimate partner violence. The women's movement has been at the forefront of initiating current activities – both launching and providing services, and pushing for policy and societal change. Future action must also draw upon this commitment and experience, and ensure that governments and society as a whole reject intimate partner violence and work towards its elimination.

Endnotes

1 C. Watts and C. Zimmerman, 'Violence against Women: Global Scope and Magnitude', *The Lancet*, No. 359 (London: The Lancet Publishing Group, April 2002), 1232-37.

2 E. G. Krug et al. (eds), *World Report on Violence and Health* (Geneva: World Health Organization, 2002), 87-113.

3 C. Garcia-Moreno, C. Watts, H. Jansen, M. Ellsberg, L. Heise, 'Responding to Violence against Women: A WHO Multi-country Study on Women's Health and Domestic Violence', *Health and Human Rights*, Vol. 6, No.2 (2003), 113-27.

4 C. Watts et al., 'Withholding of Sex and Forced Sex: Dimensions of Violence against Zimbabwean Women', *Reproductive Health Matters*, Vol. 6, No.12 (November 1998), 57-65.

5 J. K. McCauley et al., 'The "Battering Syndrome": Prevalence and Clinical Characteristics of Domestic Violence in Primary Care Internal Medicine Practices', *Annals of Internal Medicine*, Vol. 123, No. 10 (1995), 737-46.

6 J. L. Leserman et al., 'Selected Symptoms Associated with Sexual and Physical Abuse among Female Patients with Gastrointestinal Disorders: The impact on subsequent health care visits', *Psychological Medicine*, No. 28 (1998), 417-25.

7 McCauley et al., *The "battering syndrome"*.

8 J. M. Golding, 'Intimate Partner Violence as a Risk Factor for Mental Disorders: A Meta-Analysis', *Journal Family Violence*, Vol. 14, No. 2 (1999), 99-132; C. Silva et al., 'Symptoms of Post-traumatic Stress Disorder in Abused Women in a Primary Care Setting', *Journal Women's Health*, Vol. 6, No. 5 (1997), 543-52.

9 P. A. Ratner, 'The Incidence of Wife Abuse and Mental Health Status in Abused Wives in Edmonton, Alberta', *Canadian Journal of Public Health*, Vol. 84, No. 4 (1993), 246-49.

10 J. A. Gazmararian et al., 'Prevalence of Violence against Pregnant Women: A Review of the Literature', *JAMA*, Vol. 275, No.24 (1996), 1915-20.

11 C. C. Murphy et al., 'A Meta Analysis of Infant Birth Weight and Abuse during Pregnancy', *Canadian Medical Association Journal*, No. 164 (2001), 1567-72.

12 B. R. Gantra et al., 'Too Far, Too Little, Too Late: A Community Based Case-Control Study of Maternal Mortality in Rural West Maharashtra, India', *Bulletin of the World Health Organization*, No. 66 (1998), 643-51.

13 T. E. Moffitt and A. Caspi, *Findings about Partner Violence from the Dunedin Multi-disciplinary Health and Development Study, New Zealand* (Washington DC: National Institutes of Justice, 1999).

14 Krug et al. (eds), *World Report on Violence and Health*, 87-113.

15 D. Levinson, *Family Violence in Cross-cultural Perspective* (California: Sage, 1989).

16 V. A. Foshee et al., 'The Safe Dates Program: 1 Year Follow-Up Results', *American Journal of Public Health*, Vol. 90, No. 10 (2000), 1619-22.

Pervasive Forms of Violence in Prostitution: A Transgression against Human Dignity

'I met Shana when she was nineteen years old. She was an illiterate Nepali woman who possessed two valuable qualities: she was young and she was pretty. Her face earned her family the equivalent of fifty pounds when she was sold, aged twelve, to a brothel in India. It also earned her ten customers a day and HIV. She no longer works as a prostitute. This is not because she has been rescued from prostitution, or because she has found a happier livelihood, but because she is going to die.'

Louise Brown, *Sex Slaves, The Trafficking of Women in Asia*, 2000

Prostitution is a form of violation against a person's dignity. It is a source of pervasive forms of violence, especially to the women and children who represent the majority of exploited and abused. In the globalisation processes in the past decade, the magnitude of prostitution, a widespread practice in all regions of the world, has escalated. However, providing a general assessment and comparable statistics are difficult due to the clandestine nature of prostitution arising from the set up of the sex industry which is characterised by irregularity, criminalisation, non-documentation and stigmatisation. The sex industry covers street prostitution, massage brothels, escort services, strip clubs, lap dancing, phone sex, adult and child pornography, video and internet pornography, and prostitution tourism.[1] The prostitution market is fuelled by the demand that arises from locals and tourists alike. In Thailand alone, a country whose economy thrives on tourism, an unofficial estimate advanced the existence of two million prostitutes in 1993, making prostitution the 'largest commodity' for 450,000 Thai men daily and 5.4 million foreigners per year arriving in Thailand for sex tours. This figure shows a marked four times increase from the 400,000 existing prostitutes in the police figures in Thailand in 1974.[2] It is also a demand that leads to the migration and trafficking of women for prostitution. As much as the trade persists on

For many women, prostitution is an act of desperation and survival. Unable to find a job, Irene, 22-years-old and a mother of a three-year-old child, is forced into prostitution at a hotel room in Harare, Zimbabwe, where she earns around US$15-US$20 a day.

appearances, ethnicity and skin colour play an essential bargaining token. As an author stated, *'throughout history, women have been enslaved and prostituted based on race and ethnicity, as well as gender.'*[3] Particularly, of the recent estimates of 185 million international migrants globally, 50 per cent are women, all in search of better jobs with a majority ending up in the sex industry.[4] For example, in all European countries, there is evidence that show an increase in migrants in the sex industry. According to a study done by the TAMPEP project (Transnational AIDS/STD Prevention Among Migrant Prostitutes in Europe) in 1999, migrants among prostitute groups constitute 90 per cent in Italy, 85 per cent in Austria, 68 per cent in Holland, 45 per cent in Belgium and 25 per cent in Sweden and Norway. These figures show an increase from the study done in 1997.[5] Many of these women come from Central and Eastern Europe, which recorded 500,000 migrant prostituted women in European nations in 1998.[6] The problem is also widespread in Asia and Latin America, source countries for thousands of women in prostitution overseas. In 1996, the Dominican Republic with 50,000 migrants rated as the fourth highest source of migrant women in sex industries abroad following Thailand, Brazil and the Philippines.[7]

The prostitution industry and its internationalisation leads to profits of billions of dollars. According to the International Organization for Migration (IOM) the international commercial sex trade earns between 5–12 billions of US dollars in criminal profits.[8] Yet, not much emphasis has been placed on the costs to women's lives, specifically to their health and the broader negative consequences for gender equality and empowerment. Women in prostitution suffer deep and long lasting consequences from permanent exposure to diseases and psychological trauma, sexual exploitation including rapes and torture, slavery-like practices, and physical assault ranging from kicks to bodily abuse and murder. An author stated regarding the 1998 International Labour Organization's (ILO) report on the economic gains of the sex sector that *'the cost for women was conspicuously missing from the economic equation: no mention of the rapes, beatings, imprisonments, sexual abuse, servitude, illness, and the permanent destruction of millions of women's souls.'*[9] The intrinsic violence in prostitution represents enormous physical and psychological health costs. Noting that women are often subject to many injuries they also have a high probability of acquiring sexually transmitted diseases (STDs) including HIV/AIDS with many of their customers refusing to use condoms. In a Human Rights Watch report of Nepali women and girls in Indian brothels, it was estimated that 80 per cent of prostituted women suffered sexually transmitted diseases.[10] In addition, women suffer many cases of unwanted pregnancies, abortion, infertility and miscarriage and many of them also experience serious post-traumatic stress disorder (PTSD).[11] Interviews with women in prostitution show low self-esteem and profound self-loathing. A solution turned to by many is to slide into drug and alcohol abuse, and ultimately suicide. A study showed that 75 per cent of women in escort prostitution had tried to commit suicide.[12]

Root causes of prostitution

Many factors contribute to the universality and persistence of prostitution. Among these are the patriarchal system, resulting in deep gender inequality, destitution, homelessness, child abuse and trauma, erosion of traditional values through economic development and cultural changes, normalisation and promotion of prostitution in diverse cultures, racism, and the expansion of sex tourism.

Many men believe and act as if they have the right to control women's sexual behaviour and autonomy. The prostitution industry is based on this notion by turning women's lives into commodities. As Andrea Dworkin stated *the only thing of value a woman has is her so-called sexuality, which, along with her body, has been turned into a sellable commodity. Her so-called sexuality becomes the only thing that matters; her body becomes the only thing that anyone wants to buy.*'[13]

Many consider the prostitution industry as a legitimate or socially sanctioned license for violence and aggression. As John Stoltenberg stated, *'the practice of prostitution is a practice of sexual objectification of women. Every act of sexual objectifying occurs on a continuum of dehumanisation that promises male sexual violence at its far end.*'[14]

On the practical level, poverty and economic vulnerability are the main key factors that drive women into prostitution. Women's lower status in society, lower education and reduced work options expose them to exploitation. Women and girls are left with the sole responsibility of assuring their family's survival. Another important factor is the family environment to which personal security and homelessness are linked. Typically, young girls coming from abusive and dysfunctional families, which have ceased to provide protection of its members, are at great risk to fall into the hands of agents of prostitution. In many cases, the home is a place of insecurity from the girl child victim

of incest and beatings to the battered wife, pushing them to run away in the streets. Homelessness is an essential element that force women and girls into prostitution, as corroborated by a cross-national study with a sample of 475 women in prostitution of whom 72 per cent on average were currently or formerly homeless.[15] In the US, studies have showed that men and women who have been victims of child or adolescent sexual abuse are four times more likely to enter prostitution than non-victims.[16] It is generally estimated that 65 to 90 per cent of women in prostitution have suffered child abuse.[17]

Violence as an intrinsic feature of prostitution

Many studies have underlined the gravity of sexual and physical violence experienced by people working in prostitution. Among these crimes rape is specifically difficult to denounce and prove, generally viewed by society as part of the risks of the trade. The above mentioned cross-national study estimates that 62 per cent of prostituted persons have been raped and 73 per cent have undergone physical assault. In Glasgow, a study found that 361 prostituted women had been victims of violence ranging from name-calling, physical assault and murder. In Norway, interviews showed that 73 per cent of prostituted women suffered from physical assaults, rapes, captivity and death threats.[18]

Moreover, prostituted women exist in the margins of society making them expendable victims. They have been targeted by serial killers in some of the cruellest homicides. A report in Canada has shown that prostituted women and girls had a mortality rate forty times higher than the average.[19]

The perpetrators of violence against prostituted women range from the pimps and managers of prostitution houses, to the customers and law enforcement agents.

Table 5.1:
Violence in the lives of people in prostitution (in percentage)

	South Africa	Thailand	Turkey	USA	Zambia
Current or past homelessness	73	56	58	84	89
As a child, was hit or beaten by caregiver until injured or bruised	56	40	56	49	71
Sexual abuse as a child	66	48	34	57	84
Current physical health problem	46	71	60	50	76
Current alcohol problem	43	56	64	27	72
Current drug problem	49	39	46	75	16

Source: Farley, Baral, Kiremire and Sezgin, 'Prostitution in Five Countries: Violence and Post-Traumatic Stress Disorder', *Feminism & Psychology*, Vol. 8, No. 4 (1998).

Table 5.2:

Violence in prostitution (in percentage)

	South Africa	Thailand	Turkey	USA	Zambia
Physically threatened	75	47	90	100	93
Threatened with a weapon	68	39	68	78	86
Physically assaulted	66	55	80	82	82
Raped	57	57	50	68	78
Attempts to make them do what had been seen in pornographic videos/magazines	56	48	20	32	47
Forced to make pornography	40	47	–	49	47

Source: M. Farley, I. Baral, M. Kiremire and U. Sezgin, 'Prostitution in Five Countries: Violence and Post-Traumatic Stress Disorder', *Feminism & Psychology*, Vol. 8, No. 4 (1998).

A report by the Council for Prostitution Alternatives in 1991 affirmed that 78 per cent were raped an average of sixteen times a year by pimps and 33 times a year by customers.[20] It is not surprising that in Seattle in 1994, the Department of Housing in charge of domestic violence identified women in the sex industry as one of the three populations that required special services.[21]

In addition to the specific violence experienced by women in prostitution, they also undergo pervasive discrimination from the authorities and society in general. Law enforcement authorities such as the police often maltreat prostituted women. In many countries they are prone to arbitrary arrest, physical assault, and sexual harassment. In some cases, the police are part of the business, receiving bribe money and a sum for every transaction.

How it works

The development of the sex industry in different regions of the world occurred in phases. In Asia, the sex industry grew from three stages of development.[22] The first was during Asia's industrialisation and urbanisation after the Second World War, where there was a marked increase in men's earnings, which led to a higher demand for sexual services. The second development came after the establishment of military bases during the Cold War, specifically the Korean and Vietnam wars, where a new impetus on the demand side came from the military personnel deployed in the region. Alongside these bases, the red light district in the cities grew phenomenally, known as 'rest and recreation' facilities for military men. This was specifically the case for Korea, Thailand and the Philippines (see box 5.1). Recently, following geopolitical movements and the end of the Cold War, military bases gradually withdrew from the region. As a result, the third development arose from the replacement of the military clients by tourists – and the concept of 'sex tourism' became popular. In Thailand, this diversification was undertaken with the collusion of the government and the tourism industry where millions of tourists came for this purpose and where it has become one of the most important means of income for the government. The regulation of the sex industry undertaken in the 1980s in Europe led to the expansion of the trade. It resulted in the internationalisation of the demand reaching out to other parts of the world such as Southeast Asia, thus, establishing a complex structure where media, airlines, hotel chains, banks and international communication networks were involved with the tacit complicity of institutions and governments whose income grew dependent on the profits.

Prostitution is a complex business with the complicity of many actors, individuals, businessmen, politicians, corporations, organisations, NGOs and governmental institutions. Each has a specific profile in this intricate commercial web. The customers, the buyers of the product, have a key function in perpetuating the trade. They essentially provide a regular income to the pimps, managers and other business persons who keep the sex industry going. Male consumers of sexual services include men from all social classes, ethnic groups, educational backgrounds and religions. They are locals, tourists, military and policemen, men from white and blue-collar jobs etc. For example, in Asia, a study showed that the majority of consumers were locals, followed by tourists and lastly military men around the military base areas.[23]

Statistics show that 80 to 95 per cent of prostituted women are working directly under pimps.[24] Pimps operate within several layers of management, each with a specific profile and function, which together forms an intricate and interlinked web of manipulation. These layers are formed by the media, the business level pimps and the street level pimps.[25]

The media provide a powerful vehicle of ideas influencing people's attitudes and choices in society. They essentially construct a world of fantasies and promote stereotypes regarding gender identities and relations. For example, often they depict stereotypes of women as sex symbols and men as naturally violent characters. They create an ideal world of perfection, power and money with the necessary ingredient of sex and violence as the condition for success. These messages are embodied in advertising posters, newspapers, magazines, television shows and movies everywhere with two major results. First, ordinary people are left feeling second-rate compared to these characters. Second, it draws young, vulnerable people to seek fame and glory through the entertainment business only to be manipulated to enter the sex industry.

The second layer is represented by business level pimps who are responsible for putting up the infrastructure of the sex industry. They are either men or women who own bars, massage parlours, strip clubs, brothels, motels, 'casas' and other facilities used for the sex industry including the production of pornography and the set-up of adult video shops, sex shops and bookstores. These places may be legal or illegal, outwardly advertised or discreetly hidden away such as closed, exclusive sites, catering to specific types of clients, where only locals know the spot. They offer jobs to young people often deceitfully presented as legitimate work of entertainers, singers, dancers, waitresses and hostesses in order to lure and coerce them later on to provide sexual services. They also guarantee security and discretion to their customers. Business level pimps pose as legitimate businessmen, concealing their identity by acting through a corporation or subcontracting a third party who directly deals with the sex business. They have extensive contacts in the business community thereby drawing customers from the affluent parts of society such as famous people in show business, politicians, sportsmen and fellow businessmen. Usually, business level pimps are powerful entrepreneurs and respected social figures, often playing a role in local politics, providing funds to charities and joining respectful civic organisations.

The third layer is manned by street level pimps who are in charge of ensuring that the prostituted women are supplied to the business level pimps. Street level pimps are commonly small-timers who initially pose as friends, boyfriends, girlfriends, husbands and protectors to their victims. The street level pimps manipulate vulnerable women by emotional blackmail leading them to believe that they care for them to gain their confidence and trust. In the process, they use violence through physical assault, beatings, verbal abuse and sexual violence such as rape and other forms to threaten and force the women to work for them. They also supply them with drugs and alcohol to keep them doing the job. When fully under their control, the pimps collect money from the women, leaving the women with hardly anything.

The profile of a prostituted woman certainly varies in different places of the world where diverging conditions exist. Adolescent girls in Japan prostituting themselves willingly to get the newest designer clothes or electronic gadget, or educated women who have made an active choice to enter prostitution because of the advantages of earning well in a short time are a minority trend.[26] The majority of cases are women forced by several social and economic constraints to go into prostitution as a desperate means of survival. They cater to the ordinary and poorer men of society. For these women selling their bodies is not a positive choice, but rather a result of limited options. For example, in Asia, most of the women who find themselves in prostitution and the sex industry are those who were desperate to find a solution out of poverty, carrying the unique burden of the survival of the whole family and relatives. In general, around the world, the majority of prostituted persons are destitute women desperate to find jobs and who are dishonestly misled to the sex industry through false advertising and criminal networks. These are typically the women who have applied for occupations such as domestic helpers, waitresses, entertainers and singers in the big cities where wealthy families reside and elite clubs subsist. They paid large amounts of money for their travel often incurring a substantial amount of debt. However, upon arrival, they realise that the work they are asked to perform is different from what they have initially been told. They are transformed instead into sexual objects and forced to provide sexual services. Without money, they find themselves trapped in a well co-ordinated network of debt bondage, coercion and violence. According to estimates, trafficked women are sold into local prostitution networks for up to US$4,000-5,000. Many women are sold from one place to another, from the rural local recruiter, relative or neighbour to city brokers or trafficked across borders where they are purchased by brothel owners for exploitation. The women are later on forced to pay off this purchase money from their 'owners' through slavery-like practices which, according to one author, can be the *free "servicing" of up to 500 men, in 12-plus hour shifts, seven days a week'* before they can earn money.[27] In the poorest brothels, the conditions are deeply shocking. Women are locked up, repeatedly beaten up and raped until they have been 'conditioned' and 'trained'. The rooms are extremely dirty, women are provided with only two meals a day and are expected to service from two to forty clients a day.[28] The average age of entry of girls into the industry has been decreasing worldwide. In Asian countries as young as thirteen to fourteen year old girls have been recruited in prostitution with continually younger girls being exposed. A report by the Human Rights Watch Asia, 'Rape for Profit, Report on Trafficking of Nepali Girls and Women into India' in 1995, noted a drop in the average age of girls recruited into prostitution in Indian brothels, from fourteen to sixteen years old in the 1980s to ten to fourteen years old in the 1990s. This is a global phenomenon where similar cases have been reported in Brazil and Taiwan, in the latter with the use

A performer at the Thamel restaurant in Kathmandu, Nepal. While prostitution is illegal in the country, such a restaurant, which also operates as a massage parlor and disco club, serves as a front for prostitution businesses.

of hormones injections to accelerate physical development.[29] Young girls are preferred and virgins highly commended - young girls are known to be submissive, easy to manipulate and are believed not to be exposed to sexually transmitted diseases.

Why do these women stay with pimps, especially with abusers who pose as their boyfriends or husbands? According to studies, the answer is diagnosed as the Stockholm syndrome, which is the same manifestation for battered women. Women who are exploited in prostitution and who continue to live in an abusive relationship do so as a survival reaction. Shunned and marked for life, blamed as drug addicts, dismissed as an inevitability of social life, the prostituted women feel shut in with nowhere to go and no other option but to carry on the dismal life they have. In order to survive in their life and their relationship, they try to find meaning and justification for the violence by building a protective relationship with the abuser. The woman believes that if she continues to love him and continue to be loyal to him, he will change and eventually find the sympathy and kindness within himself to stop the abuse and love her back.[30]

In essence, the trade is a profitable business built on the exploitation of millions of women. Customers play an important part as they provide the money that keeps the trade running. Although one may believe that the person in prostitution receives money, in reality only a very small portion is left to this person, if at all any. According to the Human Rights Watch Report in India, when prostituted women have paid off their 'debt', they are then allowed to keep a third of the earnings, with one third going to the brothel owner, and another to local taxes.[31] Most, however, have their earnings confiscated by the agents for various reasons including 'safe-keeping'. The money is essentially extorted by the pimps and brothel owners who use it to purchase more women to be used in prostitution and for the violence and controlling mechanisms needed to force and keep them in the industry.

The agents, recruiters, pimps and brothel owners are undoubtedly the ones who make the highest profits, but the police, local crime rings and media also benefit from the industry. Society also plays a role in the perpetuation of the trade. Particularly, society's stigmatisation of prostituted women adds to their desperate and poor situation. Women in prostitution are often harshly looked down on and considered to be filth and dirt or discriminated against as criminals and considered undeserving of human treatment. The prostituted woman is often portrayed as the concrete manifestation of all that society regards as immoral with sexual relations, magnifying the evil side of the man, and exemplifying the corruption of the woman as the temptress. This leads to the conviction that prostituted women deserve to be punished, not only for what they do, but also for what they are.[32] Police, medical officers, lawyers, other authorities and everyday people conduct their profession and lives in complete discrimination and sometimes even with abuse and violence.

Women in prostitution are often dismissed as an inevitable consequence of society with unequal gender relations. In Asia, for example, both women and men consider the purchase of sex a natural part of men's needs.[33] The abuse and suffering of women in prostitution is dissolved into nothingness, and the 'profession', although considered and accepted by many as unavoidable, is scorned by society as dirty and evil. For the prostituted women there is no way out due to the shame, and even if they manage to return to their homes after the expiration of their visas, again they are socially stigmatised facing further disgrace and humiliation.

Although it is notoriously noted that rest and recreation (R&R) facilities for foreign troops, consisting of bars, night-clubs, karaoke bars and massage parlours serve as covering facilities for prostitution and other forms of sexual exploitation, it is difficult to make a direct connection between deployment of troops and prostitution publicly. These entertainment resorts are also used by local military and civilian men deployed in rural areas and not advertised or promoted as providers of sexual services. However, figures speak clearly that, for instance, prostitution in countries such as South Korea and the Philippines is aggravated by the presence of foreign armed forces. In South Korea, in the early 1990s, there were 18,000 registered 'club women' with an estimate of another 9,000 unregistered women, that is, women found outside the bars. In the Philippines, in the first quarter of 1990, within the two base lands alone, in the cities of Angeles and Olongapo, it was estimated that there were some 55,000 prostituted women - both licensed and unregistered and mostly underage. Today, without the physical presence of the bases, estimates of licensed women in entertainment establishments between the two cities are around 6,000 to 10,000, depending on the influx of local and foreign men. This does not include the streetwalkers whose number is difficult to ascertain because of the invisibility characterising the 'unlicensed' women, and their constant mobility. This figure is definitely conservative. Yet, when the troops arrive in the Philippine cities for their rest and recreation, establishment owners with the connivance of some local officials have been reported to frenziedly recruit women from many places – easily ballooning the numbers for a few nights.

The well-organised and profitable systems of prostitution has been changing the traditional cultures. Before the establishment of the foreign military bases, these communities basically wove their daily lives in the local tapestry of indigenous cultures. The arrival of a large number of foreign troops demanded the communities' lifestyles to be calibrated to the needs of the military. From sleepy towns, the base lands have become highly urbanised, setting up a particular militarised culture, and base lands, wherever they are, began to shape what has been termed militaristic sexuality. The paid sexual encounters between local women and soldiers brought about problems that merely heightened the traditional inequality between men and women.

In many cases, women in the prostitution industry, and not just in the area around military bases, are recruited when they are minors. The women that have been in prostitution from as young as thirteen are worn-out and weary by their early twenties. In South Korea, Okinawa and the Philippines, there is a common face of a woman in prostitution – she is very young, poor, often from a rural family, has a low education whose search for a decent job is a marginal possibility if not altogether impossible. She also has a background of abuse and violence during her childhood. In many instances, families and relatives rely on her income. There are many stories of women in prostitution who sent their siblings to school while they languished in the sex industry, unknown to their families. Often, she is recruited with deceit, told that she will be a dancer, without her knowing that the dancing is the aperitif to sexual offerings in prostitution. During recruitment the work is described as sitting down with customers, smiling a lot, and getting customers to buy them

drinks. Many women do not know exactly what 'entertainment' consist of, or what women are supposed to offer to the men to show their hospitality. It is true that not many women are brought into prostitution with a gun to their head or a knife pointed at their side. However, when the alternatives are to become a laundry woman, a domestic help or a casual factory worker where low wages, insecure tenure and sexual abuse or harassment is very likely, then the pathway to becoming an 'entertainer' is not exactly unappealing. Cynthia Enloe, on the background of case studies of Asian women during the economic boom of the 1980s, and 1990s, specifies four general conditions that promote organised prostitution:

- In spite of the fact that some women are joining the newly expanded middle-class the government and private entrepreneurs treat most of the female population as second-class citizens, a source of cheap labour power.

- The foreign government basing its troops on local land considers prostitution as a 'necessary evil' to keep up their male soldiers' morale.

- Local governments hosting those foreign troops are under the influence of their own military men, who prioritise 'national security' to human rights violations accompanying the prostitution.

- Tourism (including sex tourism) is considered by local and foreign investors as a fast road to development.

However, prostitution is based upon more deep and complex roots, such as racism, poverty, militarisation of societal life and patriarchy. The links between violence, sexism and racism have been demonstrated in the many stories of the women. In the Philippines, during the presence of the US military bases, a souvenir T-shirt sold like hotcakes in Olongapo City, it featured a cartoon drawing of a nearly naked image of a woman with the words, 'Little brown fucking machine powered by rice'. It is not just about prostitution and the buying of sex, it is also, and probably in a much more powerful manner, the way that clients, and presumably the public that bought the T-shirts, saw the women. They are commodities, machines that deserve no respect. The documentation of atrocities against women, and not only women in prostitution, in Okinawa, albeit incomplete, goes as far back as 1945. However, many cases go unreported. Women fear arrest and imprisonment especially in countries where prostitution is illegal, such as in Korea and the Philippines. Official reports of prostituted women murdered or missing are hard to come by. They are often regarded as dispensable and disposable commodities in a system where a 25-year old woman is regarded as on her road to retirement.

Another aggravating circumstance is the manner in which society at large looks at the issue of prostitution, and this is reflected in existing Philippine laws. Prostitution is viewed as an immoral act of promiscuous women selling sex. This is based on the assumption that women 'seduce' men, and that these women are social problems and must be held criminally responsible. Such a view is expressed in Article 202 of the Revised Penal Code (RPC). Under the Offences Against Decency and Good Customs, prostitutes are defined and identified as women, prescribing that they should be penalised as vagrants. The 'vagrancy law' requires evidence that women are (1) engaging in ▸▸

sexual intercourse or lascivious conduct; (2) having habitual conduct; (3) paid with money. Since these are difficult to establish, police authorities invoke other provisions of Article 202 on loitering on the basis of soliciting prostitution. Men on the other hand are not apprehended under this Article of the RPC. Article 341 of the RPC seeks to penalise individuals engaged in the business of prostitution under 'white slave trade'. This addresses pimping and profiting from prostitution and can also be invoked against patrons and customers. However, this provision of the law has never been enforced, since the Labour Code of the Philippines classifies women working in bars and similar establishments as legitimate workers. According to Article 138, *'any woman who is permitted or suffered to work, with or without compensation, in any night club, cocktail lounge, massage clinic, bar or similar establishment, under the effective control or supervision of the employer for a substantial period of time as determined by the Secretary of Labour, shall be considered as employee of such establishment for purposes of labour and social legislation.'* Just as Article 341 of the RPC, this provision of the Labour Code, particularly the 'substantial period' clause, has been implemented very rarely, and the prostitues never enjoy full employees' rights guaranteed to them by the law. These contradictions in local law are reflected in ambiguous attitudes of local governments, and authorities that are reluctant to criminalise the prostitution and the sex industry which are bringing substantial income to the country's economy. For instance, some reports from the Philippines indicate an alarming attitude and practices towards prostitution and trafficking of women by the local government and local police force, particularly those responsible for the protection of the base lands together with rest and recreation facilities. These undertakings have become opportunities for corruption, and very often 'lagay' (grease money) is used to avoid interrogation and detention, which the law imposes on those who organise and manage the sex industry.

Closure of the base lands does not necessarily mean the eradication of prostitution. In many parts of Asia, the troops have been followed by sex tourists, including in ever increasing numbers those who seek child victims.

Prostitution and the Law: Debates and Issues

The legal regime of prostitution worldwide is varied. There are currently three basic legal frameworks adopted by states in response to the problem of prostitution - prohibition, criminalisation and regulation.

Prohibition means that prostitution is illegal and those who sell sex and sometimes those who pay for it are penalised. Examples are the states of the Gulf and most of the USA. Criminalisation means that specific activities joined to prostitution, particularly activities leading to payment for sex, are illegal. For example, these activities include engaging people in the prostitution industry, assisting in the movement of prostituted persons in different countries, making a living off the earnings of prostituted persons, advertising, and soliciting for clients.[34] This legal practice is prevalent in Western Europe, India, Southeast Asia, Canada, Australia and the Pacific, and most of Latin America. Regulation means that the buying and selling of sex is legal and is controlled through various legal measures. For example, it is mandatory that prostituted persons get registered and go through regular health check-ups, the trade is restricted in specific zones, and a license is required for brothels. Examples of countries, which have opted for this regime, are the Netherlands and Germany (see box 5.2).

The variations in governmental policies and legal practices reflect the contentious issue about whether prostitution is the oldest form of exploitation that should be eradicated or an age old profession, which could be regulated eventually, but never uprooted? The debate takes two divergent positions, the abolitionists and the regulationists. The underlying elements that have launched the discussion are the elimination of stigmatisation of prostituted persons, their decriminalisation, and the reduction of harm and discrimination. However, the differences between the two positions lie in their interpretation of human rights and of the question of consent, as well as, the methods adopted and solutions suggested to efficiently confront the problems of the trade, particularly the violence experienced by the prostituted persons.

For abolitionists, prostitution is an act that reduces the dignity of the human person and therefore, in any form, constitutes a violation of fundamental human rights. The commodification and sexual objectification of the person in prostitution particularly leads to dehumanisation, alienation, abuse, exploitation and subjugation. Since the majority of persons in prostitution are women, for abolitionists, prostitution is a specific form of violence against women and studies corroborate the maltreatment, harassment, sexual violence, rape and murders suffered by women in prostitution. For this reason, prostitution and in general the sex industry, need to be abolished. Abolitionists advocate the decriminalisation of prostituted persons and the penalisation and prosecution of pimps and customers. The 1949 Convention for the Suppression of the Traffic in Persons and of the Exploitation of the Prostitution of Others follows the arguments of the abolitionists. Parties agreed to penalise any person who provides, lures, or escorts another person into prostitution even with the consent of that person. Penalisation also applies to any person who exploits another person for prostitution, keeps, manages or knowingly finances partially or entirely a brothel, or consciously rents a place for prostitution. Currently, the Convention has 22 signatories and 75 parties.

For abolitionists, the inherent violation of a person's humanity in prostitution causes the distinction between 'voluntary' or 'forced' prostitution irrelevant since according to them 'voluntary' prostitution does not exist. It is the lack of viable alternatives, the fact that women are not provided better choice, which drive them into prostitution. Surveys among law enforcement personnel and social workers in the US showed that 67 per cent of the former and 72 per cent of the latter conveyed the view that women had entered prostitution unwillingly.[35]

The abolitionists are against the transformation of the prostitution industry into a legitimate work sector. They resist the terms 'sex work' and 'sex worker' as politically loaded catchwords introduced in order to give legitimacy to women in prostitution, to liberate them from social ostracism and to disguise the women's abuse and exploitation.[36] According to abolitionists legalising the business would be to convert pimps, procurers and traffickers into legitimate business entrepreneurs, brothels and sex clubs into places where commercial sexual acts are authorised with minimum restraints, buyers of sexual services into accepted consumers of sex, and especially, would accept that women, children and male persons in prostitution are transformed into commodities.[37] As Melissa Farley underlined *decriminalising or legalising prostitution would normalise and regulate practices which are human rights violations, and which in any other context would be legally actionable (sexual harassment, physical assault, rape, captivity, economic coercion) or emotionally damaging (verbal abuse).'*[38]

Furthermore, the abolitionists state that legalisation leads to the expansion of the industry, increasing its profits and the demand, extending its activities especially the illegal and clandestine, instead of restraining it, and as a consequence intensifies violence and exploitation in prostitution. Several examples illustrate this fact such as the twenty per cent increase in the prostitution industry in the national economy of the Netherlands after the decriminalisation of brothels in 2000. In Switzerland, the number of prostitution houses doubled following partial legalisation, and nowadays the country has the highest density of brothels in Europe. Furthermore, legalisation fuels trafficking, as the cases in some regulationist countries such as the Netherlands and Germany indicate. 80 per cent of the prostituted persons in Dutch and German brothels were trafficked from abroad, mostly from South America, Central and Eastern European countries.[39] In addition, according to abolitionists, legalisation does neither lead to improved protection for women from violence nor does it promote their health or choice. The mandatory health check-ups on women are deemed to be discriminatory. Even with health controls, women are not protected from sexually transmitted diseases or HIV/AIDS, unless the customer – usually the major source of transmission – is targeted as well. It is practically impossible to sub-

© Reuters, Pilar Olivares, 2002

Sex tourism is increasing rapidly in the globalising world. In the historic central section of Lima, Peru, street prostitution is on the rise.

mit brothel's customers to health checks, as well as, to regulate effectively a condom strategy. All such preventive measures fail since the exchange of money for sexual services carry an implicit obligation to do whatever the customer demands, especially under threat and violence.

Finally, legalisation of the sex industry does not address the root causes, which initially drove women into prostitution, namely poverty, limited access to education and employment opportunities or traditional practices. Legitimising prostitution further provides governments with the excuse of not creating any other sustainable employment opportunities or educational programmes for women, thus condemning them to economic inequality.

The attempt to decriminalise and legitimise prostitution and the sex industry date back to the 1950s. It is important to note that the question of recognising the sex sector as a legitimate occupation does not apply to child prostitution, which is prohibited in all circumstances. The regulationist argument grew from criticisms on the ineffec-

Prostituted women stand behind windows waiting for customers in Amsterdam's Red Light district. In 1999, by a vote of 49 to 26, the Dutch Upper House approved a bill that made it legal to run a brothel.

In the Netherlands, the legislation for decriminalising prostitution was passed in 2000, which allowed brothels to operate under a license. The Netherlands' Ministry of Justice has formulated six major aims of this 'policy of tolerance':

1. Control and regulate the exploitation of prostitution.
2. Improve the prosecution of involuntary exploitation.
3. Protection of minors.
4. Protection of the position of prostitutes.
5. Combat the criminal affairs related to prostitution.
6. Combat the presence of illegal aliens in prostitution.

The law penalises for a maximum of six years a brothel owner who engages in forced prostitution, a trafficker who brings a person across borders for the purpose of prostitution (due to international treaties this is also applicable for voluntary prostitution), a brothel owner who organises the prostitution of a minor (under age eighteen) even if voluntary, a person who takes money from a prostitute who is forced, and a person who takes money from a minor prostitute. The law penalises for eight to ten years when the crime is perpetrated by two or more persons, when the minor is under sixteen years old, or when the crime results in bodily harm.

Source:
Mr. A. de Graaf Institute for Prostitution Issues, at http://www.mrgraaf.nl

tiveness of abolitionist laws, which failed to restrain the entry of women into the trade and prevent the violence and exploitation. In parallel the global alarm on the HIV/AIDS pandemic and the fear of its propagation through the sex industry propelled the issue in the debates for regulating the industry for reasons of occupational health and safety. Above all, the growing global economy has brought opportunities for substantial economic gains and a desire to boost the economy by legitimising the industry.

For regulationists the act of prostituting oneself is an affirmation of 'self-determination', that is to enable a woman to exercise control over her own body. They argue that it is a human right to dispose of one's body as one wishes and choose one's occupation freely, with no fear of criminalisation, discrimination or stigmatisation. According to advocates of legalisation, if sex work were viewed similarly to any other occupation, the prevailing attitude of the police, state or social officials, who portray prostituted people as victims, social undesirables or criminals would not only cease, but would also de-stigmatise these people who would be able to re-earn their deprived self-respect and dignity.

At the core of their argument is a sharp division between 'forced' and 'voluntary' prostitution. For advocates of legalisation, this distinction is important as not only do many prostituted women enter the sex sector in full consciousness of the nature of the trade, but also to define all people in prostitution as victims adds to the stigma.[40] According to a report written by the International Labour Organization (ILO) appealing for the economic recognition of the sex trade in 1998, a number of women with a privileged status, as well as those workers belonging to less advantaged social classes, prefer to work in the sex sector. Particularly, this conscious choice was made against working in sweatshops and factory lines, cleaning public toilets or working as clerks and secretaries. In many cases the sex industry is the only viable alternative for women from poor communities, who struggle with unemployment and family obligations or come from failed marriages. Allegedly, legalisation of prostitution will provide easier access to jobs, which offers them a higher income and flexible hours. Comparatively, studies show that women in prostitution can earn US$30 a customer while they are paid US$4 per day in factories. In Thailand, the earnings of those in the sex industry vary depending on the type and number of transactions they conduct, but according to relevant surveys the average monthly income is estimated around US$800 for all women, US$1,400 for massage parlour workers and US$240 for women in brothels. Similarly, in Indonesia the personal income of high-range sex workers can reach US$2,500 per month '*a level which far exceeds the earnings of middle-level civil servants and other occupations requiring a high level of education.*'[41] The sex industry provides many rural women with the necessary financial means to support their parents and relatives that live in poor areas. In Thailand, US$300 million earned by women in the sex industry is transferred annually to rural families, this astonishing sum exceeds the budgets of government-funded development programmes.[42]

Regulationists assert that society should enable voluntary prostitution to be executed under proper working conditions, regulated by the same rights as any worker and subdued to the scope of various international and national labour laws. Much of the violence and exploitation affecting women in prostitution is similar to the experience of those holding low status jobs.[43] Protection would thus be ensured by providing them with a legitimate worker status, including access to laws and legal redress. The legalisation would essentially transform them from living outside the law to being regulated by the law. If prostitution was legalised, abuse and violence, including trafficking, could be legally addressed and perpetrators prosecuted under the same conditions as all other occupations. Therefore, customers, pimps and even the policemen and other law enforcement personnel that abuses its authority would be discouraged from doing so if aware that they would be held accountable. What is more, prostitutes would be less restrained to report incidents of violence since they would know that they enjoy legal protection under equal terms with any other abuse occurring in a working environment. According to regulationists, the legalisation of the industry would render trafficking unnecessary, since people would migrate voluntarily to work in the sex sector without fear of prosecution. Advocates have coined the term 'sex workers' in order to take out the social stigmatisation of women in prostitution.

Box 5.3: Swedish law reform on prostitution

In 1998, the Swedish government submitted to the Parliament a bill on legislative provisions and measures to combat violence against women. One of the provisions of the law, which came into effect in January 1999 and has attracted much international attention, is the innovative approach to curbing prostitution by targeting the demand. The new law considers an offence the purchase or procurement of sex services against payment. The offence is punishable with fines and up to six months imprisonment. Therefore, the person who buys and not the one who sells the sexual service is penalised. The law clearly expresses Sweden's position on prostitution as an undesirable social phenomenon and an obstacle to the equality of women and men. Considered as the vulnerable partner in an exploitative and abusive relationship, the prostituted person is decriminalised. The law aims at encouraging prostituted persons to seek help and change their way of living. However, it emphasises that criminalisation of the customer cannot be sufficient in itself and can only partly contribute to the necessary broader social efforts of reducing prostitution. Several polls conducted in 2000 and 2001 demonstrate the public's support of the law (80 per cent). Several positive results have been observed such as a decline in street prostitution in the three years since the law entered into force, with the number of prostituted women reduced by 50 per cent and the number of buyers who have left public places ranging from 70 to 80 per cent. Evidence also showed that trafficking of women has declined within six months. What is more, the police reported that there are no indications that prostitution has gone underground or that prostitution in brothels or escort services has increased.

Sources:

J. G. Raymond, 'Ten Reasons for Not Legalizing Prostitution', *Journal of Trauma Practice*, No. 2 (2003), at http://action.web.ca/home/catw/readingroom.shtml?x=32972

The Ministry of Labour in Co-operation with the Ministry of Justice and the Ministry of Health and Social Affairs, Swedish Government Offices on Issues Related to Violence against Women, 1999 Swedish Law on Prostitution in Prostitution Research & Education, *Fact Sheet on Violence against Women* (Prostitution Research & Education, 2002), at http://www.prostitutionresearch.com/swedish.html

Furthermore, regulationists highlight the fact that legalisation would guarantee workers' social and labour rights, fair working conditions, access to social security and health services and protect them from exploitation and abuse during work. For example, many women providing sex services work under difficult conditions with long hours, low or no income and are subject to acts of violence and abuse. Recognition of the sex sector would give these women legal protection. By and large, exploitation and violation of labour rights could be effectively addressed through the existing national and international legal mechanisms. In addition, they would be able to organise in unions and civil society associations thus demanding better working conditions and fighting for their right to participate in decision-making that affect them. It would also enhance the working mobility of the prostitutes, as it would provide them with the opportunity to leave the sector if they wish to and seek occupation in other economic areas.

Last but not least, governmental recognition of the sex sector will confirm its significant contribution to fostering economic activity. The ILO report, which draws from studies in four countries – Indonesia, Malaysia, the Philippines and Thailand – recognises that the economic and social forces that have been driving the sex industry show no signs of slowing down. On the contrary their growth during the past decades has led to the sex industry becoming one major commercial sector contributing to employment and national income in the region.[44] It is, therefore, not surprising that the sex sector in the four countries accounts for two to fourteen per cent of the Gross Domestic Product (GDP) and the revenues sustain the livelihoods not only of the prostitutes, but also of millions of other workers that are directly or indirectly connected to the sex industry.[45] In addition, governmental authorities would benefit from the collection of substantial revenues through licensing fees and taxation of the establishment of the sex industry, such as bars, clubs, restaurants and hotels.

In sum, as legalisation of prostitution approaches reality one might ask if this would provide solutions to the deeper societal causes of the phenomenon. An alternative response is the action of many actors in society that are providing other legal reforms and choices for prostituted women and girls such as the innovative measures in Sweden targeting demand by penalising the purchasers of sexual services (see box 5.3). Many associations and support groups have also been established to help prostituted women and girls by providing counsel, education on women's rights and other services.[46] Indeed, a practice does not become right because it exists. The common point of departure for abolitionists and regulationists is the human rights concept, centred on enabling each person to live a life of dignity. The debate on prostitution should go beyond the simple views of voluntary or involuntary prostitution, it should concretely address the deeper economic and social problems that lead to it.

Endnotes

1 M. Farley, *Paper presented at the 11th International Congress on Women's Health Issues*, University of California College of Nursing (San Francisco, 28 January 2000).

2 K. Barry, *The Prostitution of Sexuality* (New York: University Press, 1995).

3 Barry, *The Prostitution of Sexuality*.

4 Forthcoming *IOM World Migration Report*.

5 L. M. Agustín, 'Working in the European Sex Industry: Migrant Possibilities', *OFRIM/Suplementos* (Spain, June 2000), at http://www.swimw.org/engverc.html

6 R. P. Paringaux, 'Prostitution Takes a Turn for the West', *Le Monde* (24 May 1998) cited in D. M. Hughes, L. J. Sporcic, N. Z. Mendelsohn, V. Chirgwin, *The Factbook on Global Sexual Exploitation* (Coalition Against Trafficking in Women, 1999), at http://www.uri.edu/artsci/wms/hughes/factbook.htm

7 IOM, *Trafficking in Women from the Dominican Republic for Sexual Exploitation* (June 1996) cited in Hughes et al., *The Factbook on Global Sexual Exploitation*.

8 A. E. Obando, *Migrant Sex Workers* (August 2003), at http://www.whrnet.org/docs/issue-migrantsexworkers.html#Facts

9 O. Wilson, 'Globalized Female Slavery', *Said It: Feminist News, Culture, Politics* (April 2000), at http://www.saidit.org

10 Human Rights Watch, *Rape for Profit, Report on Trafficking of Nepali Girls and Women into India* (New York: HRW, 1995), at http://www.hrw.org/reports/1995/India.htm

11 Studies carried out in five countries, South Africa, Thailand, Turkey, USA and Zambia, showed that from a sample of 475 people in prostitution, 67 per cent per cent suffered from PTSD. M. Farley, I. Baral, M. Kiremire, U. Sezgin, 'Prostitution in Five Countries: Violence and Posttraumatic Stress Disorder', *Feminism & Psychology*, Vol. 8, No. 4, (1998).

12 Letter from S. K. Hunter, *Council for Prostitution Alternatives* (6 January 1993) cited in P. Chesler in 'A Woman's Right to Self-Defense: The Case of Aileen Carol Wuornos', *Patriarchy: Notes of an Expert Witness* (Maine: Common Courage Press, 1994) compiled in M. Farley, *Prostitution: Factsheet on Human Rights Violations* (Prostitution Research & Education, 2000), at http://www.prostitutionresearch.com/factsheet.html

13 A. Dworkin, 'Prostitution and Male Supremacy', Speech delivered at the Symposium *Prostitution: From Academia to Activism* (Sponsored by the Michigan Journal of Gender and Law at the University of Michigan Law School, 31 October 1992).

14 J. Stoltenberg, *Refusing to Be a Man* (London: Fontana, 1990) cited in Farley, *Prostitution: Factsheet on Human Rights Violations*.

15 Farley et al., 'Prostitution in Five Countries'.

16 The Johns Hopkins University School of Public Health, 'Ending Violence against Women', Population Reports, Vol. XXVII, No. 4 (December 1999), at http://www.infoforhealth.org/pr/l11/violence.pdf

17 P. Murphy, *Making the Connections: Women, Work, and Abuse* (Florida: Paul M. Deutsch Press, 1993) cited in Farley, *Prostitution: Factsheet on Human Rights Violations*.

18 Farley et al., 'Prostitution in Five Countries'.

19 Canada Special Committee on Pornography and Prostitution, *Pornography and Prostitution in Canada* (1985) cited in Farley, *Prostitution: Factsheet on Human Rights Violations*.

20 S. K. Hunter, *Council for Prostitution Alternatives Annual Report* (Oregon, 1991) cited in. Farley, *Prostitution: Factsheet on Human Rights Violations*.

21 Seattle Department of Housing and Human Service, *Domestic Violence Community Advocacy Program Expansion* (1994) cited in Farley, *Prostitution: Factsheet on Human Rights Violations*.

22 L. Brown, *Sex Slaves: The Trafficking of Women in Asia* (London: Virago Press, 2000), 8-9.

23 Brown, *Sex Slaves*, 15.

24 Barry, *The Prostitution of Sexuality*.

25 J. Parker, *How Prostitution Works* (1998), at http://www.prostitutionresearch.com/parker-how.html

26 Brown, *Sex Slaves*, 22.

27 Wilson, 'Globalized Female Slavery'.

28 Human Rights Watch, *Rape for Profit*.

29 Coalition Against Trafficking in Women: Asia Pacific (CATW-AP), *Trafficking in Women and Prostitution in the Asia Pacific*, at http://www.catwinternational.org/fb/Asia_Pacific.html

30 D. Graham, Rawlings and Rigsby, *Loving to Survive: Sexual Terror, Men's Violence, and Women's Lives* (New York, New York University Press, 1994) cited in Farley, *Prostitution: Factsheet on Human Rights Violations*.

31 Human Rights Watch, *Rape for Profit*.

32 Dworkin, 'Prostitution and Male Supremacy'.

33 Brown, *Sex Slaves*, 32.

34 A. Otchet, 'Should Prostitution Be Legal?', *The UNESCO Courier* (Paris, December 1998), at http://www.unesco.org/courier/1998_12/uk/ethique/txt1.htm

35 J. G. Raymond, 'Ten Reasons for Not Legalizing Prostitution', *Journal of Trauma Practice*, No. 2, (2003), at http://action.web.ca/home/catw/readingroom.shtml?x=32972

36 J. G. Raymond, 'Prostitution as Violence against Women: NGO Stonewalling in Beijing and Elsewhere', *Women's Studies International Forum*, Vol. 21, No. 1 (1998).

37 Raymond, 'Ten Reasons for Not Legalizing Prostitution'.

38 Farley et. al., 'Prostitution in Five Countries'.

39 Raymond, 'Ten Reasons for Not Legalizing Prostitution'.

40 L. M. Agustín and J. Weldon, 'The Sex Sector: A Victory for Diversity', *Global Reproductive Rights Newsletter 66/67*, No. 2/3 (Amsterdam, 1999), at http://www.swimw.org/sexsector.html

41 World of Work, *Sex as a sector: Economic Incentives and Hardships Fuel Growth* (26 September-October 1998), at http://www.ilo.org/public/english/bureau/inf/magazine/26/sex.htm

42 Agustín and Weldon, 'The Sex Sector: A Victory for Diversity'.

43 J. Bindman, *Redefining Prostitution as Sex Work on the International Agenda* (UK: Anti-Slavery International, 1997), at http://www.walnet.org/csis/papers/redefining.html

44 Agustín and Weldon, 'The Sex Sector: A Victory for Diversity'.

45 In Thailand, during 1993-95, the estimated annual income from prostitution ranged between US$22.5 and US$27 billion, in Indonesia the income from the sex sector is between US$1.2 and US$3.3 billion per year. According to the same report, 0.25 to 1.5 per cent of the total female population of the region is engaged in prostitution and each sex job creates some seven other jobs (such as waitresses and security guards). The report further estimates that governmental recognition of the sex sector would improve the lives of 800,000 to one million people, who are paid for sexual services in the aforementioned countries. Agustín and Weldon, 'The Sex Sector: A Victory for Diversity'.

46 Some examples of associations that assist prostituted women and girls worldwide are the Prostitution Research and Education, at http://www.prostitutionresearch.com/c-escaping-rostitution.html, Sex Industry Survivors' Anonymous (US), at http://www.sexindustrysurvivors.com, Frauenbus Lysistrata (Switzerland), Bukal (Philippines), at http://avoca.vicnet.net.au/~win/bukal.htm, Foundation for Women (FFW) (Thailand), at http://www.humantrafficking.org/countries/eap/thailand/ngos/national/foundation_for_women.html, Casa Alianza (Costa Rica and Mexico), at http://www.casa-alianza.org, Sex Workers Outreach Project (SWOP), at http://www.swop-usa.org/, and the Coalition for the Rights of Sex Workers, at http://www.lacoalitionmontreal.com/eng_coalition.htm. For more information see the descriptive list of these organisations under 'Prostitution' in the list of organisations dealing with women's rights in this volume.

Chapter 6

Trafficking and Sexual Exploitation of Women: Global Trends and Responses

'When she was 27, Juree travelled from Nakhon Pathom to Japan, hoping to become a nanny. She was told by a friend, who paid her travelling expenses, that a good job awaited her. When she arrived, she discovered she was the 'property' of the money owner who had financed the trip. She was taken to sex venues and coerced into sex work. She was responsible for the debt from her travel as well as daily living expenses. She was assaulted and abused by the owner of the sex establishment, and threatened with death if she should try to run away. She was later sold on to another establishment. She later learned that she was HIV-positive, and was sent back to Thailand with neither savings nor benefits.'

Siriporn Skrobanek, Nattaya Boonpakdi and Chutima Janthakeero,
The Traffic in Women, Human Realities of the International Sex Trade, 1997

Efforts to combat trafficking in women have gained prominence on the international migration policy agenda over the past decade in response to the steady rise of the phenomenon. It has been reported that the volume of trafficking worldwide grew by almost 50 per cent from 1995 to 2000.[1] Trafficking has become a matter of concern for a number of sectors, from national administrations, international organisations, and actors in civil society, including non-governmental organisations (NGO). Its pervasive character is explained by the fact that trafficking in women is a multifaceted problem, which often involves human rights violations, sexual exploitation and forced labour, fosters conditions akin to slavery, and raises grave issues concerning women and children's rights. Despite the growing political will to combat human trafficking, a number of factors have contributed to stall progress. These include on the one hand causes of trafficking such as poverty, armed conflict and gender discrimination, which act as push factors in the countries of origin, and on the other hand the demand for cheap labour and sexual services in the countries of destination, which act as pull factors. Other challenges include the lack of adequate legislation, difficulties in gathering evidence to prosecute traffickers, poor data collection mechanisms and the impact of globalisation on employment and international migration.

Women wait to be questioned by the Philippine police inside a Manila compound raided for serving as an illegal human trafficking agency recruiting minors for Japan's entertainment industry.

Nisha, a survivor of prostitution in India, keeps watch at the Nepalese border for women being trafficked into India. She now works with NGOs and UNICEF helping to identify girls being forced into prostitution. There are an estimated 200,000 women from Nepal working as prostitutes in India.

Definition of trafficking

Until the signing in December 2000 of the Protocol to Prevent, Suppress and Punish Trafficking in Persons, Especially Women and Children (hereafter Trafficking Protocol), supplementing the UN Convention Against Transnational Organised Crime, there had been no internationally agreed definition of trafficking. The lack of a definition often led to trafficking being erroneously referred to as smuggling and vice versa, and when it involved women they were categorised as prostitutes, which led to the criminalisation of its victims. The Trafficking Protocol defines trafficking as follows:

"'Trafficking in persons" shall mean the recruitment, transportation, transfer, harbouring or receipt of persons, by means of the threat or use of force or other forms of coercion, of abduction, of fraud, of deception, of the abuse of power or of a position of vulnerability or of the giving or receiving of payments or benefits to achieve the consent of a person having control over another person, for the purpose of exploitation. [...]Exploitation shall include, at a minimum, the exploitation of the prostitution of others or other forms of sexual exploitation, forced labour or services, slavery or practices similar to slavery, servitude or the removal of organs.'

The Protocol also makes the issue of consent irrelevant, that is to say, for instance, that a person cannot consent to be trafficked for the purpose of sexual, or any other form of exploitation, consequently making the trafficker fully responsible for any subsequent abuse that occurs. Furthermore, the *'recruitment, transportation, transfer,*

harbouring or receipt of a child (any person under eighteen years of age) for the purpose of exploitation,' is classified as trafficking in persons even if this does not involve any of the means described above.[2]

By contrast, smuggling in persons is defined as *'the procurement, in order to obtain, directly or indirectly, a financial or other material benefit, of the illegal entry of a person into a state party of which the person is not a national or a permanent resident.'*[3]

Although some practitioners find these definitions impractical for operational purposes, it can clearly be deduced from the Trafficking Protocol that the process involves three fundamental phases of recruitment, transportation and the exploitation of one's labours or services, which helps to distinguish it from smuggling. The exploitation and coercion of a persons' labour, leading to the treatment of a person as a commodity, is a central element of trafficking, coupled with migration either within a country's borders or internationally. Thus, as described by Anti Slavery International, *'migration becomes trafficking when there is exploitation of a person akin to forced labour, slavery, or servitude.'*[4]

Trends and magnitude

Commonly perceived as a 'low risk, high profit' activity, the exploitation of trafficked individuals by transnational criminal networks is estimated to be worth between seven to ten billion dollars annually by the United Nations. Trafficking in human beings is very much an international phenomenon, which affects every region of the world for a multitude of purposes. Trafficking in women and girls is mainly for prostitution,[5] sexual exploitation, mail order brides, and domestic work, although trafficking may also affect men and boys, and involve other forms of forced labour such as agricultural, manufacturing and construction work. Trafficking routes are not only one-dimensional that is from the South to the North, but also exist between Southern countries, for instance from Brazil to Thailand and from Romania to Cambodia, and regionally from Mozambique to South Africa and Nepal to India.

The routes used by traffickers are complex and varied, and they are often quickly able to alter them in response to market demands or obstacles such as increased border control or the adoption of new legislation, all of which makes measures to combat it more difficult. For instance, while new legislation adopted in Sweden in 1999 to decriminalise prostitution, but more specifically to prosecute men who patronised prostitutes, had the desired effect of reducing the number of prostitutes in Sweden, the trade was simply diverted to neighbouring Finland, which saw an increase in trafficking.

Trafficking need not always involve the crossing of international borders. There are also reports of widespread internal trafficking in many regions across the world for prostitution, domestic work, forced marriages etc. Internal trafficking has been extensively reported in South-East Europe, West Africa, the Mekong sub-region of South East Asia and China. According to the United Nations Children's Fund (UNICEF), internal trafficking in China involves young boys, usually under the age of seven, for illegal adoption and girls for brides in villages where women are in short supply or dowries are too expensive. A 1997 report by the UN Special Rapporteur on Violence against Women suggested that between 30-90 per cent of marriages in some rural areas in China were a result of internal trafficking created by a shortage in women available for marriage.[6]

Box 6.1 : Some facts about the magnitude of trafficking

Because of its clandestine nature it is extremely difficult to accurately estimate the scale of international trafficking. Although existing estimates on the extent of trafficking are varied and divergent, they are able to give some indication of the magnitude of the problem.

- Although precise numbers of victims are impossible to assess, the International Organization for Migration (IOM) estimates that annually, some 500,000 to 700,000 women and children are trafficked worldwide by criminal networks - creating a new global slave trade that generates billions of Euros in criminal profits. Over 100,000 a year come from CEE and NIS countries. According to IOM's forthcoming *World Migration Report*, international migration is becoming increasingly feminised, with women comprising almost 50 per cent of the estimated 185 million international migrants worldwide.

- Figures by the United States Department of State from 2003 suggest that between 800,000-900,000 people are trafficked across international borders annually.

- United Nations Population Fund states that rough estimates suggest that between 700,000 to two million women are trafficked across international borders annually. Adding domestic trafficking would bring the total much higher, to perhaps four million persons per year.

- In South East Asia, conservative estimates suggest that between 200,000-225,000 women and children are trafficked annually. Girls as young as thirteen are trafficked as 'mail-order brides'.

- At the regional level, a European Commission study in 2001 estimated 120,000 people were trafficked into the European Union each year. The Organization for Security and Co-operation in Europe (OSCE) in June 2000 estimated that some 200,000 women and children from countries in Central and Eastern Europe (CEE), Russia and Commonwealth of Independent States (CIS - the former Soviet Union states) are trafficked primarily to other OSCE countries each year. Here the problem of trafficking in women for the purpose of sexual exploitation is particularly grave. Poverty, the lack of opportunities for women and the opening of borders are the primary factors contributing to the growth of trafficking in women from these countries to Western Europe. Recently, the European Commission raised concerns about a growing 'slave trade' among Eastern European female migrants - some 500,000 may have been forced into commercial sex.

- The Protocol to Prevent, Suppress and Punish Trafficking in Persons, Especially Women and Children, supplementing the United Nations Convention against Trafficking Organised Crime, which entered into force in 2003, currently has 117 signatories and 40 parties.

Sources:

US Department of State, *Trafficking in Persons Report* (Washington D.C., 2003).

European Commission, *Preventing and Combating Trafficking in Women: A Comprehensive European Strategy* (Brussels, 2001).

OSCE, *Press Release on Human Trafficking Meeting* (Vienna, 15 June 2000).

International Labour Organization, International Programme on the Elimination of Child Labour, *Every Child Counts: New Global Estimates on Child Labour* (Geneva, April 2002), at http://www.ilo.org

---

Causes of trafficking

Across the world it has been observed that more women today are migrating independently as principle breadwinners, both internally and internationally, for the purposes of employment. This phenomenon is often referred to as

the 'feminisation of migration', and recent reports reveal that almost half of the estimated 175 million migrants worldwide are believed to be women.[7] This trend is part of a larger process of globalisation and its resulting impact in facilitating international travel and communication. In terms of trafficking, processes of globalisation have become *'one of the most effective tools in globally linking the supply side with the demand side of trafficking.'*[8] Laden with foreign debt and rising unemployment the majority of countries in the South, it is argued, court global capital and *'pander to the demands of those who seek their services, especially by providing cheap labour and eagerly investing in leisure industries like tourism, which are widely associated with the recruitment of trafficked females for the sexual entertainment of foreigners.'*[9] Globalisation has also had the effect of 'feminising labour' by opening up avenues of employment abroad for unskilled women to become wage earners. Consequently, there has been an increase in the number of women from the South migrating to take up employment in richer countries, particularly as sex workers, mail order brides, in the domestic service or manufacturing industry. The fact that the majority of trafficked women come from poor countries is evidence of a link between trafficking and poverty.

This trafficking-poverty nexus is best illustrated by using experiences from Eastern Europe, particularly Moldova, Romania and Ukraine - countries with high poverty and unemployment levels, and also the main source countries of victims of trafficking intercepted in the Balkans. It is reported that up to 80 per cent of all prostitutes in Western Europe have been trafficked from Moldova, the poorest of the former Soviet Republics.[10] Despite the low official unemployment figures (two per cent), estimates from the Moldovan Ministry of Labour suggest that actual levels of unemployment stand at seventy-three per cent. According to the International Organization for Migration (IOM), up to one million Moldovans, out of a population of 4.5 million, are currently estimated to be living abroad, and this exodus is largely attributable to acute poverty and unemployment.[11] In a 2002 study, 90 per cent of youths surveyed in Moldova had close relatives or friends working abroad and in the absence of sustainable employment opportunities at home, nearly all were willing to migrate to Western Europe. It is important to emphasise that most of these potential migrants were looking for low skilled jobs such as domestic work, catering, and construction work, and not jobs in the sex industry.

The role played by restrictive immigration policies, enforced by major countries of destination, in encouraging human trafficking also needs to be highlighted. It has been observed in Europe, for instance, that stringent immigration policies applied by the EU member states, vis-à-vis countries in Central and Eastern Europe, coupled with the demand for labour in irregular sectors, have contributed to fuel incidents of human trafficking in the region. Recent interviews with trafficking victims suggest that nationals

from countries with automatic or facilitated access to the EU through temporary visa schemes, as in the case of the EU Accession Countries, are less likely to have been trafficked. Even when found working in the sex industry, *'such nationals are more likely to be doing so voluntarily, in control of their wages, freedom of movement and choice of work, and consequently not as victims of trafficking.'*[12]

Conversely, non-EU Accession Countries, such as Moldova, who face huge obstacles in obtaining visas to the EU, because of consular concerns over false documentation and the presumption that immigration conditions will be breached if granted entry, are forced to rely on middlemen in order to access the EU, thus making them vulnerable to exploitation at the hands of traffickers. The resulting effect of these hurdles to immigration has been to force potential migrants, and even genuine travellers, to resort to using middlemen for the sake of 'simplicity and reliability'. In the absence of legal channels of migration such middlemen become instrumental in facilitating international travel, through, for instance, the provision of false documentation, providing jobs in the irregular sector of the countries of destination, as well as financing international travel through the provision of credits. This over-dependency on intermediaries makes young women particularly vulnerable to being tricked into prostitution, and further exploitation through debt bondage, while their irregular status and the associated threat of deportation prevents them from seeking assistance or reporting their traffickers. For instance, the initial agreement to be smuggled and assisted in finding employment abroad may result in trafficking because of a deception about the nature of the work to be carried out in the country of destination. Offers of waitressing jobs can turn out to involve prostitution, or lead to incurring heavy debts, which makes the migrant dependent on the lender and subsequently being forced into sex work in order to service those debts.

National and international responses

Trafficking is by no means a modern day phenomenon and measures to prevent and combat the practice can be found, for instance, in earlier international legal instruments to abolish slavery, notably the 1926 Slavery Convention and the 1956 Supplementary Convention on the Abolition of Slavery, the Slave Trade, and Institutions and Practices Similar to Slavery. Other key human rights conventions that prohibit slavery and the exploitation of women and children include the International Covenant of Civil and Political Rights (ICCPR),[13] the Convention on the Elimination of All Forms of Discrimination against Women (CEDAW)[14] and the Convention on the Rights of the Child.[15]

The December 2000 Trafficking Protocol came about as a result of the general dissatisfaction expressed by UN organs, intergovernmental organisations, such as the IOM, and many NGOs with regard to the inadequacy of existing international instruments to combat trafficking and protect women from exploitation. This latest impetus to address trafficking is largely based on the three-pronged approach of 'prevention' of the act of trafficking, 'protection' of the victims of trafficking and the 'prosecution' of the perpetrators of trafficking, and many international, regional and national agencies have sought to incorporate this formula in their strategies to combat trafficking.

Within the UN, many agencies have become increasingly involved in issues relating to trafficking in women. Reports from the Working Group on Contemporary Forms of Slavery (established by the UN Economic and Social Council in 1974), the World Conferences on Women, and both the Special Rapporteurs on Violence Against Women and on the Human Rights of Migrants, have all been instrumental in highlighting violations committed against women during trafficking and providing recommendations to combat the practice. A recent development during the Commission on Human Rights in April 2004 led to the decision to appoint, for a period of three years, a Special Rapporteur on Trafficking in Persons, Especially in Women and Children, to respond effectively to reliable information on human rights violations with a view to protecting the human rights of actual or potential victims of trafficking. The International Labour Organization (ILO) has also adopted a number of conventions prohibiting forced labour and trafficking, especially relating to children, for example, Convention number 29 Concerning Forced or Compulsory Labour and Convention number 182, Concerning the Prohibition and Immediate Action for the Elimination of the Worst Forms of Child Labour. Other agencies that have taken anti-trafficking initiatives include the Office of the High Commissioner for Human Rights (OHCHR), the High Commissioner for Refugees (UNHCR) and UNICEF, all of which have made efforts to promote the human rights of those affected by trafficking, especially women and children.

Within its mandate as an organisation working to promote orderly and humane migration for the benefit of all migrants, the IOM has also worked with partners in the UN, national governments and NGOs to respond to some of the challenges presented by trafficking in women. Among others, its counter-trafficking initiatives have included capacity building measures, awareness raising, and conducting research to formulate policies that curtail migrant trafficking. Furthermore, IOM has implemented a number of counter trafficking projects in Asia, Central, Eastern and Western Europe, Latin America and Africa aimed at victim protection, assistance and return.

Several initiatives to combat trafficking have also been taken at regional level. Such regional efforts include the September 2002 EU conference on 'Preventing and

A young trafficking victim on the way to Benin was rescued at the border of Burkina Faso.

Combating Trafficking in Human Beings', which culminated in the Brussels Declaration on Preventing and Combating Trafficking in Human Beings. The Brussels meeting signifies one of the most far-reaching recent regional initiatives to address and combat the problem of human trafficking. The Declaration includes a set of policy recommendations for the EU in the area of trafficking in human beings and also makes provisions for the establishment of an Experts Group on Trafficking in Human Beings, a consultative body responsible for developing new EU trafficking policies, strategies and initiatives in the field of protection, prevention, law enforcement and judicial co-operation. The OSCE and the Council of Europe have also adopted comprehensive anti-trafficking programmes across Central and Eastern Europe. Other regional initiatives have included consultative processes such as the Puebla Process in the Americas and the Bali Process in Asia, both of which have been instrumental in co-ordinating regional approaches to combat trafficking at regional level. While in Africa, the Economic Community of West African States (ECOWAS) and South African Development Community (SADC) have also recently adopted mechanisms to combat trafficking.

Since the adoption in 2000 of the Trafficking Victims Protection Act (TVPA) by the United States, the US State Department has presented an annual evaluation of the performance of countries in combating trafficking, by placing them in three categories based on national legislation and measures to eliminate trafficking. While this annual Trafficking in Persons (TIP) report symbolises one of the most comprehensive international appraisals on national efforts to address trafficking in human beings it has also been criticised for some shortcomings, especially with regards to its methodology and its contents, not least from the countries most aggrieved.

NGOs, such as, the New York based organisation, Human Rights Watch, have also been extremely vocal in highlighting the governmental ambivalence to combating human trafficking, through, for example, paying lip-service to key international instruments to fight trafficking, while doing little at national level to implement the appropriate legislation. In light of such limited governmental action, it is important to emphasise the fundamental role played by NGOs not only in underlining legislative and policy deficiencies and publicising violations against trafficking victims, but also their work both at international and at grassroots level to provide vital services to support and protect victims of trafficking.

Some challenges to combating trafficking

Despite the growing political will to fight the scourge of human trafficking, a number of obstacles continue to present some difficult challenges. Until the past decade trafficking had been marginalised in international policy discourse, and the increasing priority awarded to it is often thwarted by the fact that it remains largely clandestine in nature. The lack of adequate and systematic data collection on trafficking, not only restricts our knowledge and understanding of its trends, but also limits the opportunities for taking appropriate policy action.

Another explanation for this scarcity of trafficking data can be attributed to the low priority awarded by authorities in many source and receiving countries to combating trafficking. Legislation on trafficking is often lacking, inadequate, or not implemented, making prosecution of traffickers very difficult and often impossible, and successful trafficking convictions may be difficult to acquire because they are usually dependant on victim testimony, which may be difficult to obtain due to, for instance, fear of reprisals.[16] Officials may consequently prefer not to prosecute traffickers at all because their efforts may not yield a conviction. The level of priority given by local enforcement agencies, therefore, has a significant impact on the availability of data on trafficking.

Box 6.2: Recommendations for further measures to combat trafficking

While recent initiatives to combat trafficking are to be commended, it is important to emphasise that genuine political will is vital if the problem is to be effectively tackled. As such, cosmetic ratifications of international anti-trafficking conventions by major source countries of trafficking in order to appease donors, without effective implementation will be a fruitless exercise. Source countries of trafficking should also be fully integrated in preventive efforts to combat trafficking, both at governmental level and with civil society. In countries of destination, the demand side of trafficking also needs serious attention in order to remove the incentive for traffickers to ply their trade. More importantly, the problem of human trafficking should be treated as a human rights crisis, which merits immediate action. It should be unacceptable that while efforts to abolish slavery can be traced as far back as the eighteenth century, modern slavery in the form of human trafficking is tolerated. Because trafficking disproportionately affects more women than men, gender-mainstreaming policies should form the basis of anti-trafficking strategies. In addition, long-term policies to combat trafficking will need to address the effects of poverty, which together with pervasive gender discrimination are major contributing factors, which spur trafficking on.

Prevention and prosecution
- Signing and ratifying the major international conventions that prohibit human trafficking and gender discrimination, particularly, the Protocol to Prevent, Suppress and Punish Trafficking in Persons, Especially Women and Children, supplementing the UN Convention Against Transnational Organised Crime.
- Implementing laws at national level that explicitly criminalise trafficking in human beings, but do not criminalise its victim.
- Awareness raising in countries of origin to prevent prospective migrants from falling into the hands of traffickers.
- Addressing the demand for labour in countries of destination by examining main 'pull factors', reducing the use of intermediaries and opening up more opportunities for legal and managed migration, for example, through the use of bilateral labour agreements, youth exchange programmes, trainee schemes etc.
- Long-term poverty alleviation strategies in countries of origin.

Addressing the root causes of trafficking including poverty and gender-based discrimination
- Improving opportunities for education for women, especially young girls, and providing skills and small enterprise support, for example, micro-credit schemes, business training etc.
- Tackling gender discrimination through legislation and informing women of their rights.
- Addressing the demand side of trafficking to combat the portrayal and perception of women as sex objects through awareness raising and re-education schemes.

Supporting trafficking victims
- Providing immediate assistance to trafficking victims in terms of protection from their exploiters (for example, safe houses), counselling, medical care, provisions for returning to their countries of origin or settling elsewhere as appropriate.
- In the long-term, assisting women in gaining vocational skills and educational qualifications that would help to improve their social status and break the poverty-trafficking nexus and prevent re-trafficking.

Need for better trafficking data
- Capacity building and providing technical support to countries most affected by trafficking, to enable them to collect accurate and regular data.
- Improving mechanisms for sharing available data on trafficking between concerned organisations.

Socio-economic roots of trafficking

The root causes of trafficking can mainly be attributed to economic and social inequalities and disadvantages that exist within and between countries. Extreme poverty, high rates of unemployment, discriminatory labour practices, gender-based violence, patriarchal societies, the breakdown of social or family networks all contribute to create a desperate desire for people to migrate in search of better lives, consequently making them vulnerable to exploitation by traffickers. This section examines in detail these cumulative challenges that contribute to the trafficking of women, and the effect of trafficking on its victims, especially with respect to the effects of HIV/AIDS, acquired through sexual exploitation and prostitution. Particular emphasis will be placed on the relationship between trafficking and poverty, conflict, and the impact of peacekeeping operations and the presence of armed forces on prostitution and local trafficking trends.

In what has been described as the feminisation of poverty, the above-listed socio-economic factors often tend to adversely affect women and young girls, thus creating push factors for migration. A recent publication by the Asian Development Bank (ADB) exploring the dynamics of trafficking in women and children in South Asia identifies poverty and gender discrimination as some of the main push factors that contribute to trafficking. The report states that *the necessity to meet basic needs, in combination with other factors is the most commonly identified motivation to migrate or to encourage a family member to leave.*' It continues by arguing that *there remains in South Asia extensive persistent poverty and the evidence that women are disproportionately excluded from development opportunities because of deep-rooted gender based discrimination.*'[17] Using examples from Bangladesh, India and Nepal, the report establishes a poverty-trafficking nexus. Among others, these countries have in common high incidences of poverty, a largely unskilled female workforce and widespread gender discrimination, especially with regards to social benefits. Three-fourths of India's women, for instance, are illiterate and an estimated 90 per cent of rural workers and 70 per cent of urban workers are unskilled. In 2001, 45 per cent of the Bangladeshi population lived under the poverty line, while Nepal ranks as one of the poorest countries in the world. As a result of such poverty, people are sometimes willing to place themselves or members of their family in difficult and dangerous situations in order to survive. Parents willingly accept offers of marriage or employment for payment, or hand over their daughters to family members, acquaintances or even strangers in the hope of giving them a better life and the prospect of receiving remittances to help other members of the family. Those most at risk of trafficking in these situations are children, those with no skills and those from economically and socially deprived backgrounds, which makes them vulnerable to sexual and labour exploitation. Experiences from other regions of the world, also reveal that where there is evidence of deep-rooted gender bias in society, families prefer to invest in the development of boys at the expense of girls, who are often left unschooled and sent off to work at a young age, which usually results in some form of exploitation.

Although numerous research studies have alluded to the relationship between trafficking and poverty it must, however, be emphasised that the link is a rather complex one, and trafficking is not necessarily always coterminous with poverty. Even though poverty is a significant contributing factor causing people to migrate in search of better lives, some financial capital, for instance, is necessary to facilitate international travel. Where trafficking is concerned, traffickers will also be looking for healthy individuals, with the potential of earning a reasonable income.

Numerous studies also demonstrate that trafficking and sexual slavery are intrinsically linked to conflict. An independent assessment in 2002 on the impact of armed conflict on women commissioned by the United Nations Development Fund for Women (UNIFEM) noted that *the breakdown of law and order, police functions and border controls during conflict, combined with globalisation's free markets and open borders have contributed to an environment in which trafficking of women has flourished.*'[18] Women and young girls in conflict-ridden countries, who suddenly find themselves as the sole breadwinners with the responsibility of taking care of their families, may be forced to work as prostitutes because poverty, related to the breakdown of social networks, does not afford them the opportunity to take up any other form of employment. In such environments, where the rule of law is absent, others may be either abducted or tricked into working in the sex industry. There are many examples from across the world demonstrating this.

Southeast Europe serves as a major source, transit and destination region of trafficking in women and girls for sexual exploitation, with complex routes, for instance, from Albania, through Eastern Europe and eventually into the European Union. The United Nations Mission to Bosnia and Herzegovina estimates that 60 per cent of all women trafficked through this region are aged between 19 and 24, and about 75 per cent leave home because of a false job offer.[19] A 2001 report on child trafficking in Albania stated that at least 60 per cent of the estimated 30,000 Albanians forced to work as prostitutes across Europe are children.[20] In most of these countries, trafficking thrives with the

Box 6.3 : Three interviews of trafficked women

Asia: Trafficked from Vietnam to Timor

In March 2003 the victim, H, seventeen years old, was approached by a female cousin, L, to work with her as a waitress in Timor. Her parents gave their consent, travel arrangements were made by L and appeared to have been paid for by the employer in Timor, including the procurement of a passport, relevant visas and air tickets.

H arrived in Timor, accompanied by L and one other female. H commenced work as a waitress at a restaurant, but reports that she was subsequently forced by her employer to have sex with him and then with other men. These men allegedly paid the employer for sex with her. It appears that one of them paid a large amount of money to spend a period of time exclusively with H. Some money was given by the client to H directly, but was taken 'for safe-keeping' by the employer's wife.

H claims that she told her employer that she wished to return home. He reportedly answered that she could leave once she paid him US$5,000. H had no money, as the employer withheld (by agreement) her monthly salary for working as a waitress, as reimbursement of the travelling expenses. Other than the money taken for safe-keeping by the employer's wife, H had not received any other money from the men with whom she was required to have sexual intercourse or otherwise spend time with.

H managed to escape from the restaurant to the house of a friend. H reports that on at least one occasion, men claiming to be her friends came to that place to look for her, but the landlady prevented them from entering. While at her friend's place she managed to contact a Vietnamese UN staff member and informed him of her situation and requested assistance.

The United Nations police interviewed the victim for several hours in the presence of the Human Rights Unit staff, and through an interpreter, she was able to tell her story.

Due to increasing concerns for H's safety, she was taken into secure accommodation. H was provided medical support and was examined by a clinical psychologist who found H to be in a stable psychological condition within a background of trauma related to her special condition.

The International Organization for Migration (IOM) has safely assisted in her return to her country and she is now living back with her family.

Latin America: Trafficked from the Dominican Republic to Argentina

C asked V, her neighbour, if she wanted to go to Argentina to work for K as a domestic servant, which would give her the possibility of studying and paying back her trip to Argentina. Her family accepted this offer because they thought this would be a chance for a better life, moreover, C was someone from the neighbourhood.

She left with K and another young girl called M and flew to Buenos Aires. When they arrived, K's husband and her son drove them to their home. They deprived V and M of their passports, identity cards and belongings. Two days later K drove them to a private apartment, which was managed by her daughter, and forced them into prostitution despite their refusal.

Later, they were moved to different private apartments, where the victims tried to escape, but were always caught. During those months, K denied V her freedom of movement and used physical violence to keep her quiet.

One day a man called T came and forced her to get into a car, threatening to kill her and to sell her to the countryside if she shouted or said anything. She was driven to a private apartment, where she had to be available to provide sexual services 24-hours a day, and had to be ready to leave the apartment at short notice. She worked there until the police raided the place.

K kept all the money the victim received, claiming that it was to repay the cost of her trip and her debt. She wants to return to her country to stay with her parents and to work and study. But V is afraid that by denouncing K, they may kill her or someone in her family, because she has 'friends' in her country. V returned to her home country and received reintegration assistance through a local NGO.

Eastern Europe : Trafficked from Romania to Bosnia

E met G in a discotheque in E's hometown. G proposed a well-paid job as a waitress in Montenegro. After three or four days she came to E's house and suggested that she leave on the same day. E asked if she was going alone, she replied that another girl would be travelling with her. E picked up some personal belongings and they went together by taxi to G's apartment. They stayed together for two days in her apartment.

One night G called a person who arrived the next morning. He told E and the other girl that they had to take a train to Timisoara. When they arrived, they stayed at an apartment for a couple of days. After two or three days, a bar owner called and said that they would have to go to Bosnia. The Romanian-Yugoslavian border was crossed legally. At the border, E was sold for US$600. In the beginning, E did not understand why there was an exchange of money, but later she realised that she had been sold. They continued the journey with the bar owner. After a long drive they arrived at another border. The bar owner told them that it was the Bosnian border. He also told them to say they were his friends and that the purpose of their travel was to visit his family. It was evening when they arrived at the border and they did not have any problems in crossing. They continued their trip until they arrived at a night-club.

She then realised what kind of work she would be doing. She was told that she had to strip, dance and provide sexual services to customers. The girls were told that they had to repay the money owed. She stayed in this bar for a couple of days and was then taken to a club where the working conditions were very bad. The girls were using cocaine and cannabis and she was supposed to do it as well. Since she refused, the owner took her to a room with a customer who raped her in front of a woman and two men. They paid for that. She was then taken back to the previous club. At this club she met a man, her client, who promised to help her. He paid US$150 to the owner (the price for one night) and he took her to a café bar. He asked her whether she would like to work there. She accepted and left the bar. E believes that the customer had to pay a certain amount for her, but she never saw any formal transaction. She worked in this bar as a waitress, but was forced to provide sexual services. E worked there until December 2001, when the International Police Task Force (IPTF) raided the bar and she asked for their assistance. The IPTF referred C to the IOM who provided return and reintegration assistance.

complicity of the police or border officials, who are willing to turn a blind eye for bribes. It has become increasingly apparent that trafficking in women represents an expanding area of transnational organised crime, where traffickers of drugs and arms have expanded their trade to include human trafficking.

In war-ravaged Sierra Leone, there were frequent reports of rebels abducting young girls to serve them at their camps, where they were regularly raped. Similarly in Uganda, the dissident group, the Lord's Resistance Army (LRA), has in its battle to overthrow the government severely persecuted the population in northern Uganda. Among some of its brutal acts is the abduction of thousands of children in this region to their camps in southern Sudan. Conservative estimates suggest that about 20,000 children have been abducted to date, although the rate of abductions dramatically escalated in 2002, following a military offensive by the government's army forces. An estimated 5,000 children have been abducted from their homes, schools and communities since June 2002, the highest increase in any year since the conflict began in 1986, and representing a sharp increase from the less than 100 children abducted in 2001. Girls are used as domestic labour, and at age fourteen or fifteen, many are forced into sexual slavery as 'wives' of LRA commanders and subject to rape, unwanted pregnancies, and the risk of sexually transmitted diseases, including HIV/AIDS, while boys as young as twelve are given arms training, forced to carry weapons and ammunition and in some cases, fight alongside LRA soldiers.[21]

It has also been reported that the arrival of peacekeeping personnel in conflict areas may also exacerbate trafficking in the region. Sexual exploitation and prostitution often increase with the arrival of well-paid personnel in countries where the local economy has been ruined by conflict and women have limited options for employment. The high incidence of trafficking in post-conflict areas in the Balkans, particularly Kosovo, Bosnia and Herzegovina and Macedonia have been partly attributed to the large international presence in these countries. Experiences in Goma and Kinshasa, in the Democratic Republic of Congo also reveal an increase in child and women prostitution after the arrival of peacekeepers. These reports have resulted in the UN Special Rapporteur on Violence against Women to call on the UN to take measures to prevent trafficking for sexual exploitation and punish its perpetrators. Efforts are also being made to bring a gender perspective into peacekeeping operations that is gender mainstreaming, with the aim of making male peacekeepers more reflective and responsible, broadening the repertoire of skills and styles available in missions to eventually, reducing conflict and confrontation and bolstering support for local women.[22]

A Chinese woman working as a prostitute in Hong Kong is arrested and will be returned to the mainland. According to Hong Kong police a powerful prostitution racket was responsible for trafficking sex workers from the mainland into Hong Kong.

Effects of trafficking

The effects of trafficking and sexual slavery on its victims are devastating. Young women and girls are often shunned by their families after their escape and stigmatised by society, leaving some with no choice other than returning to their abductors or continuing to work in the sex industry. In addition to the physical and psychological impacts of trafficking on its victims, there are also profound health risks, including infection with HIV, acquired through prostitution and sexual exploitation, which has an adverse effect on both the families and communities involved, and may indirectly encourage trafficking. Many researchers have established a link between child trafficking and HIV/AIDS, a growing cause of orphans especially in sub-Saharan Africa and in parts of Asia. In Asia, the WHO and UNAIDS reported in 1999 that some 140,000 children had been orphaned by AIDS, while Thailand's Ministry of Health and the Global Orphan Project estimate in Thailand that the virus may orphan half a million children by the time they reach adolescence. A 2003 report by the IOM on trafficking in South Africa highlighted the distressing effects of HIV/AIDS on children.[23] In Lesotho, children from rural areas, orphaned by AIDS and escaping domestic violence, are often drawn to the capital, Maseru. These street children are forcibly abducted and taken across the border to South Africa, where they are sexually assaulted. Others are also trafficked within the region by long distance truck drivers who use them as sex slaves on their journeys. The economic effect of HIV/AIDS on the families involved can be the loss of employment and subsequently a reduction in family income, which may result in children being taken out of school and into employment, consequently exposing them to the risk of trafficking. A recent Human Rights Watch report on child trafficking in Togo states that at least 95,000 children under the age of fifteen have lost a mother or both parents to AIDS in Togo.[24] A study in Togo's Maritime region by the World Bank and the NGO CARE further observed that children orphaned by AIDS, spent less time at school because of an inability to pay school fees, they were sometimes prohibited from attending public schools, and in some cases withdrew from school entirely.[25] These children, it was noted, became easy prey for child traffickers. According to a Togolese NGO working with trafficked children, those affected by AIDS are particularly vulnerable to trafficking when they are forced to earn money to care for a sick parent, or when children are forced to leave their community as a result of the stigma associated with having AIDS in the family, or after abandonment following the death of one or both parents.[26]

Conclusion

Successful approaches to combating trafficking will need to address the trafficking-poverty nexus, through long-term poverty alleviation policies, such as those embodied in the Millennium Development Goals, as well as policies to tackle gender discrimination in society and provide better opportunities for women to fully participate in the domestic labour market.[27] As part of any comprehensive strategy to combat trafficking, the demand side of trafficking also needs to be explored, not just in Western countries of destination, but also within the peacekeeping context and development context, in order to highlight the grave violations trafficking victims are subjected to and to raise awareness about women and children's rights. The connection between HIV/AIDS and trafficking also needs to be better addressed as the virus presents one of the greatest health risks to sex workers. Adequate medical care and counselling should be part of policies to assist and protect concerned victims, as well as measures to reduce the risk of HIV infection. Better support could also be provided for children orphaned by HIV/AIDS, for instance, through the provision of social care and encouraging them to stay at school or providing them with vocational training and skills. In this respect the potential impact of additional funding under the auspices of the Global Fund for AIDS, Tuberculoses and Malaria should be emphasised.

Just as the causes and effects of trafficking are interrelated, with significant implications on migration, human rights, health, development etc., so too should be the initiatives to combat the phenomenon. Increased co-operation among all concerned stakeholders, from actors in civil society, national governments, international and regional bodies should be encouraged with the aim of improving information gathering, complementing existing strategies and ensuring the overall effectiveness of anti-trafficking strategies.

Endnotes

1   'EU Toughens Line on Human Trafficking', *Financial Times* (19 March 2001).

2   Article 3, *UN Protocol to Prevent, Suppress and Punish Trafficking in Persons, Especially Women and Children* (December 2000).

3   Article 3, *UN Protocol Against Smuggling of Migrants by Land, Sea and Air* (December 2000).

4   E. Pearson, *Human Traffic Human Rights: Redefining Victim Protection* (Horsham: Anti-Slavery International, 2002).

5   Although this article refers to prostitution mainly in the context of trafficking that is involving an element of coercion, it is important to highlight that some women also work independently and voluntarily in the sex industry for purely economic reasons.

6   UNICEF, *Children on the Edge: Protecting Children from Sexual Exploitation and Trafficking in East Asia and the Pacific* (New York: UNICEF, 2001), at http://www.minori.it/cd/cd_lucca_2003/4/4.1.6_en.pdf

7   IOM, *World Migration Report* (Geneva, 2003).

8   V. Samarasinghe, 'Confronting Globalisation in Anti-Trafficking Strategies in Asia', *Brown Journal of World Affairs,* Volume X, Issue I (Providence: Brown University, Summer/Fall 2003), 93.

9   V. Samarasinghe, 'Confronting Globalisation in Anti-Trafficking Strategies in Asia', 94.

10 'Moldova Calls for France's Aid in Combating Prostitutes', *Agency France Press* (11 July 2001).

11 IOM, *Victims of Trafficking in the Balkans* (Geneva: IOM, 2001).

12 S. Scanlan, *Report on Trafficking in Moldova: Irregular Markets and Restrictive Migration Policies in Western Europe* (Geneva: ILO, May 2002).

13 'No one shall be held in slavery; slavery and the slave-trade in all their forms shall be prohibited. No one shall be held in servitude. No one shall be required to perform forced or compulsory labour.', Article 8, *International Covenant of Civil and Political Rights* (1966).

14 'States Parties shall take all appropriate measures, including legislation, to suppress all forms of traffic in women and exploitation of prostitution of women.', Article 6, *Convention on the Elimination of All Forms Discrimination against Women* (1979).

15 'States Parties shall take all appropriate legislative, administrative, social and educational measures to protect the child from all forms of physical or mental violence, injury or abuse, neglect or negligent treatment, maltreatment or exploitation, including sexual abuse, while in the care of

parent(s), legal guardian(s) or any other person who has the care of the child.', Article 19, *Convention on the Rights of the Child* (1989).

16 F. Laczko and M. Gramengna, 'Developing Better Indicators of Human Trafficking', *Brown Journal of World Affairs,* Volume X, Issue I (Providence: Brown University, Summer/Fall 2003), 93.

17 Asian Development Bank, *Combating Trafficking of Women and Children in South Asia: Regional Synthesis Paper for Bangladesh, India and Nepal* (Manila: ADB, April 2003).

18 E. Rehn and E. Johnson Sirleaf, *Women, War and Peace: The Independent Assessment on the Impact of Armed Conflict on Women and Women's Role in Peace-Building* (New York: UNIFEM, 2002), 12.

19 Rehn and Johnson Sirleaf, *Women, War and Peace: The Independent Assessment on the Impact of Armed Conflict on Women and Women's Role in Peace-Building*, 13.

20 Save the Children, *Report on Child Trafficking in Albania* (London: Save the Children, March 2001).

21 Human Rights Watch, *Stolen Children: Abduction and Recruitment in Northern Uganda* (New York: HRW, March 2003).

22 DPKO, Lessons Learned Unit, *Mainstreaming a Gender Perspective in Multidimensional Peace Operations*, (New York, July 2000), iii, cited in Rehn and Sirleaf, *Women, War and Peace: The Independent Assessment on the Impact of Armed Conflict on Women and Women's Role in Peace-Building*, 63.

23 IOM, *Seduction, Sale and Slavery: Trafficking in Women and Children for Sexual Exploitation in Southern Africa* (Geneva, May 2003).

24 WHO/UNAIDS, 'Togo, Epidemiological Fact Sheets on HIV/AIDS and Sexually Transmitted Infections', cited in Human Rights Watch, *Borderline Slavery: Child Trafficking in Togo* (New York: HRW, April 2003).

25 'Analyse de la Situation des Orphelins, Veuves et Familles Affectées du SIDA dans la Région Maritime en Vue de la Réalisation d'un Programme de Prise en Charge', *IDF/RIPPET Project* (Lomé: CARE/World Bank, 2001), 37, cited in WHO/UNAIDS, 'Togo, Epidemiological Fact Sheets on HIV/AIDS and Sexually Transmitted Infections'.

26 Togolese NGO, La Conscience, cited in WHO/UNAIDS, 'Togo, Epidemiological Fact Sheets on HIV/AIDS and Sexually Transmitted Infections'.

27 For more information on the work of associations on this topic see 'Trafficking of women' in the list of organisations dealing with women's rights in this volume.

Chapter 7

Violence against Women in Custody

'[R]ape of women in prisons, police custody or other detention facilities "not only is perpetrated... as a crime of opportunity but also is used as a method of torture."'

Dorothy Q. Thomas and Robin S. Levi, 'Common Abuses Against Women', in *Women and International Human Rights Law*, 1999

Custodial violence against women has been described as a 'particularly egregious violation of women's rights.'[1] Where persons are deprived of their liberty by virtue of any public authority or law, and from which situation they cannot voluntarily and freely leave, the state has a particular responsibility for the protection of the individual against any form of violence, inside and outside custody. Persons in any form of detention or imprisonment by the state retain the fundamental rights that are essentially guaranteed by international human rights law. This includes, primarily, the general prohibition of torture and ill-treatment. A woman deprived of liberty by the state, in addition, is not only protected by this general prohibition of torture and ill-treatment, but also by gender-specific standards of protection. The relevant specific treaties include the UN International Covenant on Civil and Political Rights, the UN Convention against Torture and other Cruel, Inhuman or Degrading Treatment or Punishment, and the UN Convention for the Elimination of All Forms of Discrimination against Women. Moreover, many soft-law standards aiming at establishing regimes that are not only humane, but actually prevent custodial violence have

been at the disposal of states and its law-enforcement and criminal justice agencies. Most notable among these soft-law standards are the UN Body of Principles for the Protection of All Persons under Any Form of Detention or Imprisonment, UN Standard Minimum Rules for the Treatment of Prisoners and the UN Basic Principle for the Treatment of Prisoners, which include a few, but significant, norms particular to the detention and imprisonment of women.

Particularly, with specific reference to the prohibition of violence against women, mention should be made of UN Declaration on the Elimination of Violence against Women and the Fourth World Conference on Women Beijing Declaration and Platform for Action. Guidance should likewise be taken from the General Comments issued respectively on Violence against women by the UN Committee for the Elimination of All Forms of Discrimination against Women (1992) and on Equality of Rights between Men and Women by the UN Human Rights Committee (2000), both of which contain language with respect to the protection of women against custodial violence. At the national level, protection guarantees extend to the protection of women in custody, as

Amanda is being detained at Bon Pastor women's prison in Bogotá, Colombia, for her involvement in the Colombia armed conflict.

expressed by constitutional prohibitions against torture and ill-treatment, coupled with the prohibition of discrimination on the basis of gender.

State custody can take the form of arrest, detention and imprisonment, as well as 'house arrests' and any limitations to liberty of movement. In certain countries, women are further subjected to 'protective custody' purportedly to shield women from external harm. Custody may occur at any stage of the legal proceedings and may, in fact, also be illegal according to international substantive and procedural standards. Custody, be it detention or imprisonment, may be held in diverse places including police stations, lock-ups, jails, public or privatised prisons, psychiatric or non-psychiatric hospitals, private or public houses or buildings used for such purposes, for example stadiums and make-shift camps. Detention or imprisonment may be at the hands of the police, other law enforcement officials, security forces, military or paramilitary forces.

Custodial violence against women is, first of all, greatly facilitated when the state's discriminatory laws and policies allows and targets women for custody based on their gender. In many countries around the world, discriminatory laws exist that make it easier to incarcerate women to impose harsher penalties on them because they are women. This usually takes two forms. First, so-called 'gender-blind' criminal justice, penal legislation and state practice in incarceration may result in the unjust application of the law, especially within a context where women continue to be deprived of basic rights and subjected to many forms of violence inside their homes and in the communities. Second, laws that are potentially or actually discriminatory are directed at detention or imprisonment of women alone. Unfortunately, many states around the world, regardless of their economic development and

forms of governance, violate the basic principle of non-discrimination with regard to the custody of women. This is undertaken not solely through negligence or non-compliance, but with active and direct participation in the perpetuation of violence against women in custody.

Women in custody, like men, are vulnerable to the abuse of the power that the custodial authorities wield. Extensive documentation of torture and ill-treatment of detainees and prisoners around the world have revealed a variety of techniques that are used in order to force information, confessions or for purposes of punishment, intimidation or coercion. Torture and ill-treatment are also inflicted due to discrimination based on gender, race and social class. Without any curbs to the power of custodial authorities over the detainees or prisoners, the risk of abuse increases. Moreover, with regard to women in custody, cases have demonstrated that the presence of male custodial authorities supervising or guarding women detainees and prisoners, or the housing of females in male facilities, increase the risk of gender-based custodial violence against women.

In custody, the nature of violence against women could, therefore, range from physical to psychological torture or ill-treatment and could extend to threatened or actual violence directed at their loved ones, particularly their children. In addition to the more 'political' or 'common' techniques of torture and ill-treatment, custodial violence of women is also expressed in acts of gender-based torture and ill-treatment including any abuse of personal dignity such as any form of sexual assault like rape. Cases of gender-based custodial violence against women have been researched and documented in practically all countries in the world with some forms being widespread and systematic in some. These acts include rape and other forms of sexual assault, touching, demeaning and sexually offensive language. In some states, 'virginity testing', defloration and forced impregnation or forced maternity have been recorded. In other states, abuse of reproductive capacity in enforcing state policies of population control take the form of forced abortion, forced sterilisation and forced miscarriages. Physical brutality against pregnant women in custody has similarly been documented, where pregnant women are not merely refused to be provided with the necessary amenities for a safe and decent pregnancy and delivery, but are actually abused and violated precisely because they are pregnant.

Gender-based forms of violence against women have been frequently referred to as sexual assault. A Minnesota Human Rights Centre project has defined sexual assault as *'non-consensual sexual contact that is often obtained through coercion or the use or threat of force as a deliberate act of gender-based violence and an expression of power, control and domination over another. [...]Coercion can cover a wide range of behaviours, including intimidation, manipulation, threats of negative treatment withholding a needed service or benefit, and blackmail.'* [2] In the context of state custody, therefore, where the power relations are so uneven and where women are at the hands of the custodial authorities, any sexual contact has to be presumed to be non-consensual.

Women who have suffered violence at the hands of custodial authorities who, instead of protecting them, inflict violence, further endure restraints in any attempts to bring complaints. Threats of retaliation through 'disciplinary' measures and curtailment of privileges, or filing cases against them, are usually levied against women who complain. Investigation procedures are usually not independent, gender sensitive or facilitated. Where complaints are duly investigated, many cases are not brought to trial due to insufficient evidence or a lack of political will to take the cases to court. In the handful of cases actually prosecuted and brought to conviction, the sentences imposed are weak and paltry compared to the violence inflicted.

Curbing custodial violence against women

Many of the recommendations that have been drawn up by United Nations bodies and experts, as well as international and national non-governmental organisations and women's groups point to one general, but essential, recommendation - the implementation of the relevant inter-

| *A woman in Phnom Penh, Cambodia received a life sentence after killing her husband's lover. Her daughter was born in prison.*

national human rights standards that prevent and protect custodial rights in general, and those that specifically pertain the problem of custodial violence against women. These minimum standards, found in international treaty and soft-law instruments provide guidelines that enhance the protection of women and men in custody, and that establish regimes that could actually minimise the instance of custodial violence against women. The protection of basic human rights is a prerequisite for respect of the dignity that is inherent even of women in custody. The fact that these persons are in state custody requires the actual implementation of these minimum standards.

With particular reference to custodial rights of women, the issue of discrimination based on gender, especially with regard to the rights to equality before the law and to equality of protection of law, is pertinent. As Amnesty International stated, measures *'will not eradicate torture of women unless discrimination on grounds of gender is addressed.'* [3] The protection afforded by international law and by national jurisdictions on, for example, the absolute prohibitions against torture and ill-treatment, could only be made a reality if discrimination based on gender is eradicated. Many action plans, therefore, provide for concurrent measures that aim to raise awareness of the unacceptability of any form of violence against women, and to build a consensus against discrimination at government, community and family levels. These measures should be placed within a context of fulfilling the basic respect for human rights of women in custody who are discriminated against not only on the basis that they are in custody, but also because they are women. Government policy should issue a categorical, public and sustained condemnation of custodial violence against women and, in the process, encourage the breakdown of legal and cultural structures that internalise discrimination against women. Moreover, state policy condemnation should be sustained with the recognition of the utility of international legal protective norms and guarantees, accompanied by the ratification of international treaties where this has not yet been done and co-operation with regional and international mechanisms.

The implementation by the executive agencies of existing international norms and guarantees is essential in the protection of women in any form of custody and in the operation of places of custody. Many of these minimum standards, such as only female guards supervising women in custody and male guards needing to be accompanied by female staff in places where women are detained or imprisoned, are clearly preventive in nature. Others are protective particularly where pregnant women and mothers with infants are concerned. The respect for the absolute prohibition of torture and ill-treatment and the minimum standards in places of detention should be considered part and parcel of the modernisation and professionalisation of any country's criminal justice system and its penal institutions.

The usefulness of sustained and effective training on existing international standards, coupled with appropriate gender-sensitivity training, has been recognised in some countries as directly contributory to the decrease of custodial violence. The need for this type of training is especially imperative for all state agents who are in direct contact with persons in custody at any stage of their detention and imprisonment. Particularly for custodial authorities, follow-up training is also useful in strengthening conformity with international standards of protection. In fact, such training is practically indispensable. It has been shown that where structural changes have been effected, for example when setting up of women's desks and shelters, the lack of effective training for law enforcement staff actually impedes effective dispensation of services and eventually discourages women from filing complaints.

Any structural reform should include adequate, but sustained efforts to prevent custodial violence against women. Some of these efforts should be directed at guaranteeing the rights of persons in detention, especially during the first part of their detention where the risk of torture and ill-treatment are relatively high. The European Committee for the Prevention of Torture has established that the guarantee of the minimum three rights that is to inform a close relative or third party of their situation, to request a medical examination by a doctor of her choice, and access to a lawyer of her choice, are effective guarantees to prevent such violations. In addition, one of the tools proven to be most effective in the prevention of torture and ill-treatment is the state's acceptance of regular visits to places of detention and to prisons undertaken by international, regional and national visiting mechanisms. Independent visiting mechanisms have proved to prevent torture and ill-treatment, and to enhance the transparency of the places of detention and prisons, leading to more constructive recommendations for improvement and a better use of resources, including tax money.

In addition, efforts to combat impunity of the perpetrators are necessary to break the cycle of custodial violence against women. The existence of accessible and non-threatening procedures for lodging complaints against alleged perpetrators should be part of the required and standard information provided to all detainees and prisoners. Investigations into allegations of custodial violence against women should be promptly undertaken by impartial bodies independent of the custodial authorities. Such investigations should be gender sensitive and follow effective investigative procedures and techniques such as those provided by the Istanbul Protocol.[4] The importance of competent medico-legal investigation and documentation has been emphasised over and over again. Training and close supervision in the implementation of investigative techniques is therefore part of the over-all programme to improve professional quality of investigation and prosecution.

The executive branch of government has one of the biggest roles to play in state action against custodial violence against women, particularly as it implements the laws, employs law enforcement and criminal justice personnel and operates the police detention centres, the jails and the prisons. Its policies and measures directly affect the persons in custody, and it is at the hands of the executive branch that custodial violence against women is usually inflicted. Government efforts at awareness-raising and information dissemination should, therefore, always be accompanied by programmes that aim, not only at attitudinal change, but structural reforms.

Legislation should be in accordance with the international prohibition of torture and ill-treatment, and of discrimination on the basis of gender, usually reflected in national constitutional provisions. The legislative branch, having the power to enact legislation, is indispensable in the review, revision and repeal of discriminatory laws that unjustly facilitate detention and imprisonment of women and that not only fail to provide protection against custodial violence against women, but actually sanction such custodial violence. Reviews should be undertaken periodically and the appropriate action taken as soon as possible. The enactment of progressive legislation should, furthermore, strive to expand protection. Parliaments have a leading role in the ratification of the relevant international human rights instruments. In order to ensure national implementation of international norms, parliamentary committees should exercise their parliamentary prerogatives in initiating inquiries in aid of legislation.

The establishment of adequate legal protection is a legislative priority. Certain legislation is already in place in a few jurisdictions. This takes the form of the complete prohibition and criminalisation of all acts of violence against women in custody, particularly gender-based violence including sexual assault and rape, between custodial authorities and detainees or prisoners. A further protection for women is the non-admission of 'consent' in sexual 'relationships' between a custodial authority and the person in custody. Another type of legal protection is the reversal of the burden of proof in allegations of non-consensual sexual relations in custody. Where the complainant alleges no consent in sexual relations between a custodial authority and a person in custody, the presumption is on the side of the complainant and the accused custodial authority is required to disprove the allegation of the non-existence of consent. Other best practices in legislation could be found in the provision of redress and rehabilitation of victims of custodial violence against women.

Last, but not the least, the legislature should ensure appropriate and adequate allocation of national resources towards the elimination of custodial violence against women. This includes support to women's shelters for victims, legal funding for cases alleging custodial violence and establishment of programmes and infrastructure in places of detention and prison to ensure prevention of custodial violence.

The judicial branch is indispensable in the fight against custodial violence. Until the necessary legal reforms are directly affected, there is much room for the use of judicial discretion as well as judicial activism that could actually curtail the implementation of discriminatory law and or minimise their consequences. Many national constitutions provide for the prohibition of torture and ill-treatment and the prohibition of discrimination on the basis of gender. The application of these national norms is essential to prevent custodial violence and protect women in custody.

Moreover, the judicial bench should strive to remain open to developments in the recognition of the discriminatory nature of custodial violence against women. An indispensable part in doing so is to incorporate international standards so that international norms can be implemented at the national level. The progressive interpretation of national laws in light of international legal developments is one of the most neglected areas in judicial activism. In addition, certain under-utilised judicial powers, such as issuing restraining orders, may actually prevent the discriminatory application of the laws. Another under-utilised judicial power that exists in many jurisdictions is the court's regular exercise of visits to places of detention and to prisons, which, if undertaken on a sustained basis and in an effective manner, could directly contribute to the prevention of custodial violence against women. Moreover, the courts should implement its independence from the executive and the legislative in ways that promote human rights, rather than curtail them.

Lastly, the judicial branch, composed as it is of judges who actually have the power to decide on the fate of persons, should be receptive to reforms that will enhance its effectiveness in the dispensation of justice in a non-discriminatory manner. Judicial consideration of cases on violence against women should avoid dealing with irrelevant issues such as the complainant's sexual history that obfuscate the facts of the incident that is the subject of the complaint or lead to biased decisions. The principles of gender-balance in the composition of the courts and its staff, and that of gender-sensitivity in the interpretation of the law, should be recognised as essential components in the non-discriminatory dispensation of justice. Courts should take the lead in affirming the need for competent investigations and capable prosecutions of custodial crimes against women. Courts should strive to apply the appropriate penalties commensurate to the violence inflicted against women in custody. The role of the judicial branch in combating impunity cannot be under-estimated.

Civil society organisations, in the forefront of the fight against custodial violence against women, need to be more supported and encouraged in their work, especially in the services that they provide, be it legal, social services or research and documentation. The state should not tolerate any violations of freedom of association of women's rights and prisoners' rights activists. In the conduct of their work, the advocacy and information campaigns of civil society organisations should be seen as enhancing over-all efforts to eliminate custodial violence. Civil organisations should strive to involve more men in over-all efforts to break the culture of discrimination against women and put to an end the cycle of violence and the impunity of perpetrators. Moreover, civil society organisations should not replace the work of the state, they should retain their independence and their vigilance with regard to state policies and practice. The regular monitoring of situations of women in custody, the services rendered and organising efforts for the empowerment of women and their families needs to be more focused and increased. International attention has drawn much-needed interest to the hitherto hidden issue of custodial violence against women. Its prevention and the protection of women in custody can only be achieved if states take their primary role seriously, if civil society organisations are allowed to work without fear and harassment and if women in custody are empowered by knowledge of their rights.

Maricopa County inmates prepare for chain gang duty in Arizona. The women are padlocked together at the ankle and marched off to be transported to their work site. The prisoners can volunteer for chain gang duty in lieu of lockdown, in which four prisoners are kept in an eight by twelve feet cell, twenty-three hours per day. To be allowed out of the cell, these inmates must agree to serve thirty days on the chain gang picking up trash, weeding and burying bodies.

Violence against women in detention is widespread in countries with weak legal protection of citizens and it reaches high levels especially in societies with deeply rooted inequality in gender relations, as corroborated by the following examples from the Philippines and Pakistan. However, the need for protection of women's rights is also fully applicable in affluent and democratic societies, as stressed by the UN Special Rapporteur on Violence against Women Radhika Coomaraswamy, whose report from the field mission to the United States in 1998 brought persuasive evidence that practice in the US prisons poses fundamental human rights questions.

The United States of America

The US is bound by an international legal framework that guarantees to prohibit torture and ill-treatment of prisoners and to provide protection from state violence. The country has ratified relevant international treaties including the UN Covenant on Civil and Political Rights, the UN Convention against Torture and other Cruel, Inhuman and Degrading Treatment or Punishment, and the UN International Convention on the Elimination of All Forms of Racial Discrimination. However, the US has not ratified the UN Convention on the Elimination of All Forms of Discrimination against Women, which provides guarantees for the protection of women in custody, including the right not to be subjected to gender-based violence. In addition, the US has not ratified any of the major regional human rights treaties provided by the Organisation of American States, including the Inter-American Convention to Prevent, Punish and Eradicate Violence against Women. Lastly, international soft-law standards, such as the UN Standard Minimum Rules for the Treatment of Prisoners, which contains important protection guarantees for women in custody, have not been systematically or consistently recognised or applied in US detention centres and prisons.

The constitutions and laws of the US and its states provide a wide range of protection for persons in custody, and all laws, practice and interpretation at federal, state and local government levels must comply with US Supreme Court interpretation. US Supreme Court decisions, as well as some state court decisions constitute a wide range of prisoners' rights to physical safety, medical care and procedural safeguards. However, in many prison practices, the US continues to provide a much lower legal protection for persons held in custody than that guaranteed by international standards, including protection against gender-based violence for women in custody.

As a federal political system, the federal government operates prisons primarily for convicted violators of federal crimes, while local governments operate jails where persons awaiting trials and minor offenders are detained. The US holds the largest number of prisoners compared to any country in the world with two million men and women behind bars in the country. In June 2003 the number of women under the jurisdiction of State or Federal prison authorities represented five per cent, which is lower than in other countries, but the population of women prisoners in the US is presently increasing at a higher rate than that of men. Statistics have also shown that the rate of imprisonment of black women is eight times, and that of Hispanic women four times higher than the rate of white women. The proportion of women put in prison for violent acts such as pre-meditated murders and kidnapping, large scale drug-dealing and white collar crimes is very small; the majority of the women are convicted for minor drug-related offences, usually as accessories to crimes committed by men, for example for carrying drugs or passing on messages to drug dealers. A number of convicted are substance-users. However, the inadequacy of community-based rehabilitation programmes has led to the tendency of inequality of sentencing, wealthier women substance-users are usually sent to private rehabilitation centres while poorer women are sent to prison.

Many studies have also concluded that women in general receive much harsher sentences than men since their minor participation in drug-related offences constrict the information that they can give; hence women are generally not in the position to assist the prosecution and make themselves eligible for more lenient sentences. Moreover, the legal system is not adequately able to take into account relevant gender-specific circumstances for purposes of mitigation of the penalty, such as a history of domestic violence from the partner-drug dealer or threats of loss of child custody, that lead a number of women to commit such crimes.

At least two-thirds of imprisoned women in the US is said to have experienced violence and abuse before they served their sentences. In recent years, US government investigations and non-governmental reports have observed that detention conditions in a number of jails and prisons not only amount to cruel and inhuman treatment and punishment, but also encourage violence against women in custody. These reports have documented detention conditions, which include an increasing over-crowding of women detention centres and prisons, inadequate access to health facilities and services and the use of prison restraints. Moreover, many cases of violations of fundamental human rights, including the right not to be subjected to ill-treatment and gender-specific violence, have been perceived as systematic, serious and prevalent in the prisons where they have been found. The UN Special Rapporteur on Violence Against Women has remarked that with the extraordinary diversity of conditions in US prisons, there is a glaring lack of minimum standards, both at policy and implementation levels, to prevent gender-specific violence against women, especially legally-sanctioned sexual harassment, where male guards monitor the female inmates in their cells, while dressing and undressing and while taking their showers. A US Justice Department report found that the surveillance employed by many guards goes beyond legitimate security needs. For instance, male guards are allowed to pat-frisk clothed women prisoners at any time and at any part of their bodies, the practice frequently including the genital area and the breasts. Statistics have revealed that while in custody, one out of five male inmates have suffered from forced sexual contact. Among female inmates, at least one out of four has been sexually assaulted.

Because of public campaigns in the US, more and more state laws now prohibit and criminalise sexual relations between persons in custody and correctional staff. As a recent result of public denunciation, US governmental investigations and congressional hearings, and reflecting the prevalence of the problem in US prisons, the US Congress unanimously passed in July 2003 the 'Prison Rape Elimination Act'. The new act, signed into law in September 2003, initiates a series of efforts to prevent and punish sexual assaults in US prisons and jails, provides funding for relevant programmes, and authorises the federal government to cut back prison funding for states that do not control sexual assaults against prisoners. It also sets up a federal body, the 'National Prison Rape Reduction Commission', that will spearhead a federal report on prison conditions in all fifty states in order to generate national standards to detect, prevent and punish prison rape.

The efforts so far made, at local, state and federal levels, by diverse government agencies and bodies, as well as with the campaigns and pressures from national and international NGOs, have led to limited and selective improvements in conditions and protection of women from gender-specific violence. However, a policy commitment and official condemnation of violence against women in custody should be accompanied by a resolve to effectively modernise its national standards on imprisonment. One essential condition in this regard is the effective implementation at local, state and federal levels, of at least the minimum standards for the protection of prisoners, and of women in custody, against state violence.

The Philippines

The Republic of the Philippines is one of the oldest democracies in the Asia-Pacific region, hosting a large vibrant civil society, a large government bureaucracy and a vocal and strident media and press. The Philippines has ratified all the major human rights instruments, including the UN Covenant on Civil and Political Rights and the respective Conventions against Torture and on Discrimination against Women that aim to protect persons from custodial violence and discrimination against women. However, despite the existence of fully functioning judicial, parliamentary and executive branches, the concrete implementation of such human rights standards remains one of the dismal failures of government.

One of these gross failures is, in the words of the UN Human Rights Committee (2003), 'the persistent and widespread use of torture and cruel, inhuman or degrading punishment of detainees by law enforcement officials.' Women in custody in the Philippines constitute one of the most vulnerable groups to torture, including rape and other forms of sexual abuse. National women's rights associations and international NGOs have documented numerous cases of violence of women in custody, mainly perpetrated by the police. A majority of these victims are sex workers, girl street children and suspected drug addicts who are often arrested under the so-called 'anti-vagrancy law'. Other women victims are usually suspected common criminals and alleged political dissidents.

From the time they are taken in police custody the women are subject to custodial violence. In addition to the 'typical' methods of torture and ill-treatment employed, such as severe beatings, placing of chilli peppers in detainees' eyes or genitals and induced suffocation, women suffer from rape and sexual assault in order to force

testimonies and for purposes of intimidation. The police have also been known to give promises of release if sexual favours are granted.

Human rights non-governmental organisations and women's shelter groups are increasingly documenting cases of violence against women in custody in the Philippines, providing social services to the women and campaigning on the issue in order to increase public awareness and create changes. Women's legal groups have criticised the 'anti-vagrancy law' as penalising the homeless, as discriminatory against the poor and discriminatory against women. In 2003, the UN Human Rights Committee had also expressed its concern that the 'vaguely worded anti-vagrancy law is used to arrest persons without warrant, especially prostitutes and street children.' This concern was further expressed within the committee's over-all observation that the continuation of the law and practice allowing for arrests without a warrant is open to abuse. The committee also pointed out that many of the reported sexual assaults are dismissed at the investigation stage for 'lack of evidence', since women are reluctant to talk about their experience because of the cultural shame and stigma attached to such violations. The possible incidence of HIV/AIDS heightens the reluctance to report rape and sexual assault. In cases where the female victim gets pregnant because of the rape, she suffers from further discrimination, fear and shame. Moreover, since abortion is deemed unconstitutional in the Philippines, she may resort to illegal abortion that can result in medical and further psychological complications.

Many recommendations by UN expert treaty-bodies and NGOs have been put forward to break the pattern of violence against women in custody in the Philippines. The majority of these recommendations has taken the form of the need for actual conformity of Philippine law and practice with international standards for the prevention and prohibition of acts of torture. Hope among women struggles to survive with efforts for much-needed reforms that answer the following imperatives:

- The absolute prohibition and criminalisation of torture and custodial violence against women, including all forms of sexual contact between law enforcement officials and detainees.

- The repeal of all laws related to arrests without a warrant, as well as, all discriminatory laws enabling arbitrary arrests of women.

- The strict implementation of norms provided by the UN Standard Minimum Rules for the Treatment of Prisoners relating to women in custody.

- The prompt, impartial and independent investigation (including correct medico-legal documentation) and prosecution of complaints of rape and sexual abuse against law enforcement officials, accompanied by effective protection, compensation and rehabilitation of complainants.

- Effective programmes towards gender-sensitivity and the abolition of legal and cultural discrimination against women.

Pakistan

Over the last many years, many human rights non-government organisations have issued credible documentation on the insufficient protection of women in Pakistan, the country that ratified its obligation to implement the provisions of the UN Convention on the Elimination of Discrimination against women 1996, and whose constitution guarantees the right to equality and non-discrimination on the basis of gender.

Discrimination and violence against women in Pakistan is deeply embedded in cultural attitudes and strongly reflected in legislation, practice and treatment of women in the homes, in the community, in state custody, as well as in the public domain. Domestic violence is rife, in many homes honour killings and other violence against women continue to be widely practised. In certain parts of the country, tribal councils have delivered judgements constituting women or girls as part of the 'compensation' packages for alleged crimes committed by third persons. Current legislation supporting these practices include the *Qisas* (retribution) and *Diyat* (compensation) ordinances that allow relatives to 'pardon' crimes of honour, usually perpetrated by the husbands or relatives, leaving totally unpunished the violence inflicted against women.

As part of this context of discrimination and violence against women in Pakistan, women in custody suffer what has been called as 'double jeopardy'. Human Rights Watch has estimated that between 50 to 80 per cent of female detainees are taken into state custody, equivalent to approximately 2,000 women detainees, and are in detention on the basis of the Hudood ordinances alone. These ordinances constitute a set of Islamic penal laws that criminalise rape, adultery and fornication. Women held in custody for allegedly violating these ordinances are those accused of adultery by their husbands or family members, or have tried to divorce their husbands and thus deemed to have violated family honour, or women and men who have married without the consent of their own families or in defiance of arranged marriages. Moreover, since the Hudood provides that the woman's testimony is equal only to half of a man's, rape victims who file complaints are often accused of adultery or illicit and immoral acts, and thus subject to the penalties of flogging or stoning, if the 'evidence' is not deemed sufficient. Since the required evidence of rape usually takes the form of testimonies from a number of men, most of the complaints of rape are not 'proven'. Other women vulnerable to state custody in Pakistan are Bangladeshi women trafficked into the country for prostitution. Abducted from their country of origin or tricked into domestic servitude or sexual slavery, these women are arrested by the police for violating either the Hudood ordinances or immigration laws. Government statements and some Islamic pronouncements have condemned these laws as unconstitutional or un-Islamic and a violation of the Koran, nevertheless the laws remain on the statute books and the practice continues.

While in custody, men and women have been subjected to various forms of torture and ill-treatment in the hands of the police in Pakistan. Documentation by Amnesty International has revealed that these include beating, kicking, electric shocks and hanging upside down. Women are subjected to gender-specific forms of torture and ill-treatment, such as sexual harassment, public

undressing and parading, as well as sexual assaults and rape. Human Rights Watch has approximated that more than 70 per cent of women in police custody experience some form of physical or sexual abuse from their jailers. Some of these women may be held in a police lock-up for days, beyond the 24-hour legal deadline for producing detainees before a magistrate. Overcrowding of jails, insufficient basic amenities, and sub-standard food have been found by human rights groups in many of the police detention lock-ups and jails. These physical conditions are compounded by the usual delays in investigations and trials, coupled by non-access to competent legal services by women detainees, who are often illiterate and unaware of their rights. Women held on minor or false charges are unable to post bail or probation facilities.

In the few cases where women are able to file complaints for custodial violence, alleged perpetrators often escape prosecution. Medical-legal documentation is often incompetent, biased and gender-insensitive. Some of these cases may eventually reach either the police disciplinary tribunals or the courts where the cases could either be dismissed for insufficient evidence under the Hudood laws, or be successfully prosecuted. Unfortunately, only a handful of the 'successful' cases are in existence, with the perpetrators usually obtaining minor sentences.

The inability of the government to effectively put in place legal and procedural safeguards and to adequately prosecute and punish perpetrators of violence against women in custody in Pakistan stands in sharp contrast with policy statements made by Pakistan's government leaders and representatives. This is compounded by a legal, political and cultural framework that is totally discriminatory against women and that actually actively promotes violence against women. Tribal councils, influential in many rural Pakistani regions, perpetrate discriminatory community attitudes sometimes in defiance of Pakistan's governmental structures. Persons in the law enforcement agencies and in the justice system are more often than not unaware of, ignore and abuse legal safeguards where they exist, as well as tolerate or promote violence against women. Legal, social and medical services, despite some governmental initiatives and non-governmental projects, remain inadequate to cover the wide scope of the problem.

Sources:

United Nations, *Report on the Mission to the USA*, Addendum to the Report of the Special Rapporteur of the Commission on Human Rights on Violence against Women, its Causes and Consequences, R. Coomaraswamy, UN Document E/CN.4/1999/68/Add.2 (Geneva, 1998).

U.S. Department of Justice, Bureau of Justice Statistics, at http://www.ojp.usdoj.gov/bjs/prisons.htm

United Nations Human Rights Committee, *Consideration of the Second Periodic Report of Philippines* (Geneva, 2003).

Amnesty International, at http://www.amnesty.org

Human Rights Watch, at http://www.hrw.org

Endnotes

1 United Nations, *Report of the Special Rapporteur of the Commission on Human Rights on Violence against Women, its Causes and Consequences*, R. Coomaraswamy, UN Document E/CN.4/1998/54 (Geneva, 1999).

2 Minnesota Human Rights Center, at http://www1.umn.edu/humanrts/hrcenter.htm

3 Amnesty International, *Broken Bodies, Shattered Minds: Torture and Ill-treatment of Women* (London: AI, 2000).

4 Office of the United Nations High Commissioner for Human Rights, *Istanbul Protocol: Manual on the Effective Investigation and Documentation of Torture and Other Cruel, Inhuman or Degrading Treatment or Punishment* (Geneva: OHCHR, 2001).

Key Reading Part I

Books

S. Altink, *Stolen Lives: Trading Women into Sex and Slavery* (London: Scarlet Press, 1995).

R. Anker, *Gender and Jobs: Sex Segregation of occupations in the World* (Geneva: International Labour Office, 1998).

R. Arditti, *Searching for Life: The Grandmothers of the Plaza de Mayo and the Disappeared Children of Argentina* (Berkeley: University of California, 1999).

A. E. Asghar (ed), *Islam, Women and Gender Justice* (New Delhi: Gyan Publishing, 2001).

Asian Development Bank, *Combating Trafficking of Women and Children in South Asia: Regional Synthesis Paper for Bangladesh, India and Nepal* (Manila: Asian Development Bank, April 2003).

Asian Development Bank, *Country and Programme Update, Bangladesh* (Manila: Asian Development Bank, 2001).

S. Bartky, *Femininity and Domination: Studies in the Phenomenology of Oppression* (New York: Routledge, 1990).

R. Bishop and L. Robinson, *Night Market: Sexual Cultures and the Thai Economic Miracle* (New York: Routledge, 1998).

A. Brooks, *Postfeminism: Feminism, Cultural Theory, and Cultural Forms* (London: Routledge, 1997).

L. Brown, *Sex Slaves: The Trafficking of Women in Asia* (London: Virago Press, 2000).

G. Buijs (ed), *Migrant Women: Crossing Boundaries and Changing Identities* (Oxford: Berg, 1993).

Canadian Ministry of Supply and Services, *The Violence against Women Survey* (Ottawa: Ministry of Supply and Services, 1993).

B. J. Carpenter, *Re-Thinking Prostitution: Feminism, Sex, and the Self* (New York: Peter Lang, 2000).

L. Cokorinos, *The Assault on Diversity: An Organized Challenge to Racial and Gender Justice* (Ranham: Lowman & Littlefield Publishers, 2003).

J. Connors, *Violence against Women in the Family* (Vienna: United Nations, 1989).

M. Davies (ed), *Women and Violence: Realities and Responses Worldwide* (New York and London: Zed Books, 1994).

N. J. Davis (ed), *Prostitution: An International Handbook on Trends, Problems, and Policies* (Westport: Greenwood Press, 1993).

R. P. Dobash and R. E. Dobash, *The Imprisonment of Women* (Oxford: Basil Blackwell, 1986).

N. Draijer, *Seksueel Misbruik van Meisjes door Verwanten* (*Sexual Abuse of Girls by Relatives*) (The Hague: Ministry of Social Affairs and Employment, 1988).

Economic and Social Research Council, *Taking Stock. What Do We Know about Interpersonal Violence?* (Egham: Royal Holloway University of London, 2002).

B. Ehrenreich and A. Russel (eds), *Global Woman: Nannies, Maids, and Sex Workers in the New Economy* (New York: Metropolitan Books, 2003).

C. Enloe, *The Morning After: Sexual Politics at the End of the Cold War* (Berkeley and Los Angeles: California University Press, 1993).

C. Enloe, *Bananas, Beaches and Bases: Making Feminist Sense of International Politics* (Berkley: California University Press, 2000).

C. Enloe, *Maneuvres: The International Politics of Militarizing Women's Lives* (Berkley: California University Press, 2000).

European Commission, *Preventing and Combating Trafficking in Women: A Comprehensive European Strategy* (Brussels: European Commission, 2001).

C. Galenkamp, *Protection from Sexual Exploitation and Abuse: Lessons Learned from Sierra Leone* (New York: United Nations Office for the Coordination of Humanitarian Affairs, 2003).

R. Hammer, *Antifeminism and Family Terrorism: A Critical Feminist Perspective* (Lanham: Rowman & Littlefield Publishers, 2002).

G. Hicks, *The Comfort Women: Japan's Brutal Regime of Enforced Prostitution in the Second World War* (New York: W.W. Norton, 1995).

International Organization for Migration, *Seduction, Sale and Slavery: Trafficking in Women and Children for Sexual Exploitation in Southern Africa* (Geneva: IOM, May 2003).

International Organization for Migration, *Trafficking in Women and Prostitution in the Baltic States: Social and Legal Aspects* (Geneva: IOM, 2001).

International Organization for Migration, *Victims of Trafficking in the Balkans* (Geneva: IOM, 2001).

International Organization for Migration, *World Migration Report* (Geneva: IOM, 2003).

J. James, *Resisting State Violence: Radicalism, Gender, and Race in U.S. Culture* (Minneapolis: University of Minnesota Press, 1996).

S. Joekes, *A Gender Analytical Perspective on Trade and Sustainable Development* (New York: UNDP, 1999).

A. Jones (ed), *Gendercide and Genocide* (Nashville: Vanderbilt University Press, 2003).

M. Karl, *Women and Empowerment: Participation and Decision-making* (London: Zed Books, 1995).

K. Kempadoo and J. Doezema (eds), *Global Sex Workers: Rights, Resistance, and Redefinition* (New York: Routledge, 1998).

E. Kofman, A. Phizacklea, P. Raghuram and R. Sales, *Gender and International Migration in Europe: Employment, Welfare and Politics* (New York and London: Routledge, 2000).

E. Krug, L. Dahlberg, J. Mercy, A. Zwi and R. Lozano (eds), *World Report on Violence and Health* (Geneva: WHO, 2002).

Kvinna till Kvinna, *Reaction and Revolt against Trafficking in Women and Girls* (Stockholm: Kvinna till Kvinna, 2003).

D. Levinson, *Family Violence in Cross-cultural Perspective* (Thousand Oaks: Sage Publications, 1989).

V. Malarek, *The Natasha: The New Global Sex Trade* (New York: Arcade Publishing, 2004).

L. Mayoux, *Women's Empowerment or the Feminisation of Debt? Towards a New Agenda in African Microfinance* (London: DFID, 2002).

C. Miller and S. Razavi, *Gender Analysis: Alternative Paradigms* (New York: UNDP, 1998).

C. Miller and S. Razavi, *From WID to GAD: Conceptual Shift in the Women and Development Discourse* (Geneva: UNRISD, 1995).

V. Miralao, C. O. Carlos and A. F. Santos, *Women Entertainers in Angeles and Olongapo,* A Survey Report (Quezon City: WEDPRO, 1990).

C. Moser, *Gender Planning and Development: Theory and Practice and Training* (London: Routledge, 1998).

P. Norris, *Rising Tide: Gender Equality and Cultural Change around the World* (Cambridge: Cambridge University Press, 2003).

E. Pearson, *Human Traffic, Human Rights: Redefining Victim Protection* (Horsham: Anti-Slavery International, 2002).

M. L. Penn and R. Nardos, *Overcoming Violence against Women and Girls* (Lanham: Rowman & Littlefield Publishers, 2003).

A. Rahman and N. Toubia, *Female Genital Mutilation: A Guide to Laws and Policies Worldwide* (London, New York: Zed Books, 2000).

S. Razavi and M. Molyneux, *Gender Justice, Development and Rights* (Oxford: Oxford University Press, 2002).

E. Rehn and E. Johnson Sirleaf, *Women, War and Peace: The Independent Assessment on the Impact of Armed Conflict on Women and Women's Role in Peace-Building* (New York: UNIFEM, 2002).

R. J. Rummel, *Death by Government* (Somerset: Transaction Publishers, 1994).

S. Scanlan, *Report on Trafficking in Moldova: Irregular Markets and Restrictive Migration Policies in Western Europe* (Geneva: ILO, May 2002).

M. Schuler, *Freedom from Violence: Women's Strategies from Around the World* (New York: UNIFEM, 1992).

M. Schuler and S. Kadirgamar-Rajasingham (eds), *Legal Literacy: A Tool for Women's Empowerment* (New York: Widbooks, 1992), at http://www.wld.org/ll.html

J. Seabrook, *Travels in the Skin Trade: Tourism and the Sex Industry* (Chicago: Pluto Press, 2001).

A. Sen, *Development as Freedom* (New York: Anchor Books, 1999).

M. Strauss, R. Gelles and C. Smith, *Physical Violence in American Families: Risk Factors and Adaptations to Violence in 8,145 Families* (New Brunswick: Transaction Publishers, 1990).

S. P. Sturdevant and B. Stoltzfus, *Let the Good Times Roll: Prostitution and the U.S. Military in Asia* (New York: The New Press, 1992).

J. G. Townsend, E. Zapata, J. Rowlands, P. Alberti and M. Mercado, *Women and Power: Fighting Patriarchies and Poverty* (London: Zed Books, 1999).

United Nations Children's Fund, *Children on the Edge: Protecting Children from Sexual Exploitation and Trafficking in East Asia and the Pacific* (New York: UNICEF, 2001).

United Nations Office of the Special Adviser for Gender Issues and Advancement of Women, *An Analysis of the Gender Content of Secretary-General's Reports to the Security Council* (New York: United Nations, 7 October 2003).

United Nations Office of the Special Advisor on Gender Issues and Advancement of Women, *Gender Mainstreaming; An Overview* (New York: United Nations, 2002) .

United States Department of State, *Trafficking in Persons Report* (Washington: Department of State, 2003).

D. A. Ward and G. G. Kassebaum, *Women in Prison: Sex and Social Structure* (Chicago: Aldine Publishing Company, 1964).

M. A. Warren, *Gendercide: The Implications of Sex Selection* (Totowa: Rowman & Littlefield, 1985).

World Bank, *Engendering Development: Through Gender Equality in Rights, Resources and Voice* (Oxford: Oxford University Press, 2002).

M. Zalewski, *Feminism after Postmodernism: Theorizing through Practice* (London and New York: Routledge, 2000).

Articles and papers

P. Adamson, 'Commentary: A Failure of Imagination' [on maternal mortality], *The Progress of Nations* (New York: UNICEF, 1996), at http://www.unicef.org/pon96/womfail.htm

L. M. Agustín and J. Weldon, 'The Sex Sector: A Victory for Diversity', *Women's Global Network for Reproductive Rights Newsletter,* 66/67, 2/3 (Amsterdam, 1999), at http://www.swimw.org/sexsector.html

H. Barrett, 'Women in Africa - The Neglected Dimension in Development', *Geography,* 80 (348) (1995).

B. Bergman and B. Brismar, 'Suicide attempts by battered wives', *Acta Psychiatrica Scandinavia* 83 (Oslo, 1991).

G. Berik, Y. van der Meulen Rodgers and J. Zveglich Jr., 'Does Trade Promote Gender Wage Equity? Evidence from East Asia', *CEPA Working Paper* (New York: The Levy Economics Institute, 2002).

S. Bisnath, 'Globalisation, Poverty and Women's Empowerment', Paper presented at the United Nations Division for the Advancement of Women Expert Group Meeting (New Delhi, India, 26-29 November 2001).

S. Bittle, 'When Protection is Punishment: Neo-Liberalism and Secure Care Approaches to Youth Prostitution', *Canadian Journal of Criminology* 44.3 (2002).

T. Branigan, 'Plight of London's Hidden Prostitutes Revealed', *The Guardian* (20 August 2004).

D. Budlender, 'Gender Budgets: What's in it for NGOs?', *Gender and Development,* Vol. 10 (Oxford: Oxfam, 2002).

C. Bunch, 'Making Common Cause: Diversity and Coalition', in L. Albrecht and R. M. Brewer (eds), *Bridges of Power: Women's Multicultural Alliances* (Philadelphia: New Society Publishers, 1990).

G. Caglar et al., 'Engendering Macroeconomic and Trade Policies', Paper presented at the Summer School on Engendering Economic Policy in a Globalising World: Liberalisation, Services and Care Economies (Berlin, 21-26 June 2003).

N. Cagatay, R. Lal, M. Keklik and J. Lang, 'Budgets as if People Mattered: Democratising Macroeconomic Policies', *SEPED Conference Paper Series 4* (New York: UNDP, May 2002).

J. C. Campbell, 'Health Consequences of Intimate Partner Violence', *The Lancet*, Vol. 359 (13 April 2002).

Center for Reproductive Law and Policy, 'Rape and Forced Pregnancy in War and Conflict Situation', *Reproductive Freedom and Human Rights* (1996), I-II.

D. A. Counts, 'Female Suicide and Wife Abuse in Cross Cultural Perspective', *Suicide Life Threatening Behaviour,* 17 (New York: Guilford Publications, 1987).

M. Farley, *Prostitution: Factsheet on Human Rights Violations* (Prostitution Research & Education, 4 February 2000), at http://www.prostitutionresearch.com/factsheet.html

F. F. Fikree and L. I. Bhatt, 'Domestic Violence and Health of Pakistani Women', *International Journal of Gynaecology and Obstetrics*, Vol. 65, No.2 (London: International Federation of Gynaecology and Obstetrics, 1999).

J. P. Flanzer, 'Alcohol and Other Drugs are Key Causal Agence of Violence', in R. J. Gelles and D. R. Loseke (eds), *Current Controversies on Family Violence* (Thousand Oaks: Sage Publications, 1993).

J. A. Gazmararian, R. Petersen et al., 'Violence and Reproductive Health: Current Knowledge and Future Research Directions', *Maternal and Child Health Journal*, Vol. 4, No. 2 (New York: Kluwer Academic Plenum Publishers, 2000).

R. J. Gelles, 'Alcohol and Other Drugs are Associated with Violence – They are not its Cause', in R. J. Gelles and D. R. Loseke (eds), *Current Controversies on Family Violence* (Thousand Oaks: Sage Publications, 1993).

C. Grown et al., 'Introduction', *World Development* 28, 7 (New York, 2000).

K. Hannah-Moffat, 'Neo-liberal Governance in Canadian Women's Prisons', *The British Journal of Criminology*, 40 (Oxford, 2000).

L. Heise, 'Violence against Women: Global Organising for Change', in Edleson and Eisikovits (eds), *Future Interventions with Battered Women and their Families* (Thousand Oaks: Sage Publications, 1996).

L. Heise, 'Violence Against Women: An Integrated, Ecological Framework', *Violence against Women*, 4(3) (June 1998).

L. Heise, M. Ellsberg, M. Gottemoeller, *Ending Violence against Women, Population Reports Series*, Vol. XXVII, No.4, Series L, No. 11 (Baltimore: John Hopkins University School of Public Health, September 1999).

S. Jacobs, R. Jacobson and J. Marchbank, *States of Conflict: Gender, Violence and Resistance* (London and New York: Zed Books, 2000).

J. Joachim, 'Shaping The Human Rights Agenda: The Case of Violence Against Women', in Edleson and Eisikovits (eds), *Future Interventions with Battered Women and their Families* (Thousand Oaks: Sage Publications, 2000).

N. Kabeer, 'The Conditions and Consequences of Choice: Reflections on the Measurement of Women's Empowerment', *Discussion Paper*, No. 108 (Geneva: UNRISD, 1999).

F. Khafagi, 'Breaking Cultural and Social Taboos: The Fight against Female Genital Mutilation in Egypt', *Development*, 44 (London: SAGE Publications, 2001).

G. Kirk, R. Cornwall and M. Okazawa-Rey, 'Women and the U.S. Military in East Asia', *Focus, Interhemispheric Resource Centre and Institute for Policy Studies,* Vol. 4, No.9 (March 1999).

F. Laczko and M. Gramengna, 'Developing Better Indicators of Human Trafficking', *Brown Journal of World Affairs*, Volume X, Issue I (Providence: Brown University, Summer/Fall 2003).

T. Maitse, 'Political Change, Rape and Pornography in Post-Apartheid South Africa', *Gender and Development,* Vol. 6, No. 3 (1998).

S. Mayhew and C. Watts, 'Global Rhetoric versus Local Realities: Linking Violence against Women and Reproductive Health', *Crossing Boundaries: Health Policy in a Globalising World* (Cambridge: Cambridge University Press, 2000).

F. T. McCarthy, 'In the Shadows: Trafficking in Women for the Sex Trade', *The Economist* (26 August 2000).

K. Monkman, 'Training for Change and Empowerment', in Nelly Stromquist et al. (eds), *Women in the Third World: An Encyclopaedia of Contemporary Issues* (New York: Garland, 1998).

C. Moore, 'Women and Domestic Violence: The Public Private Dichotomy in International Law', *The International Journal of Human Rights*, Vol. 7, No. 4 (London: Frank Cass Publishers, Winter 2003).

P. Norris and R. Inglehart, 'Cultural Obstacles to Equal Representation', *The Journal of Democracy*, 12 (3) (2001).

C. I. Nyamu, 'How Should Human Rights and Development Respond to Cultural Legitimization of Gender Hierarchy in Developing Countries?', *Harvard International Law Journal* (Cambridge, MA: Harvard Law School, 2000).

V. Ogenusanya, 'Peacekeeping programme at ACCORD', *ABANTU for Development, The Gender Implications of Peacekeeping and Reconstruction in Africa* (Mombassa: ABANTU Publications, May 2000).

L. O'Toole and J. Schiffman, 'The Roots of Male Violence against Women', in L. O'Toole and J. Schiffman (eds), *Gender Violence: Interdisciplinary Perspectives* (New York and London: New York University Press, 1997).

M. Quigley et al., 'Case-control Study of Risk Factors for Incidence HIV Infection in Rural Uganda', *Journal of Acquired Immune Deficiency Syndrome*, 5 (Philadelphia, 2000).

E. A. Ratcliff, 'The Price of Passion: Performances of Consumption and Desire in the Philippine Go-Go Bar', *Dissertation presented to the Faculty of the Graduate School of the University of Texas* (Austin, May 2003).

M. Rees, 'International Intervention in Bosnia-Herzegovina: The Cost of Ignoring Gender', in C. Cockburn and D. Zarkov (eds), *The Post War Moment: Militaries, Masculinities and International Peacekeeping* (London: Lawrence & Wishart, 2002).

A. Reiss and J. Roth (eds), *Understanding and Preventing Violence* (Washington, DC: National Academy Press, 1993).

M. Riley, 'Women's Economic Agenda in the 21st Century', *IGTN Occasional Paper Series on Gender, Trade and Development* (Washington, DC, 2001), at http://www.genderandtrade.net/PaperSeries/Women21st.pdf

L. F. de Rose et al., 'Does Female Disadvantage Mean Lower Access to Food?', *Population and Development Review*, Vol. 26, No. 3 (New York, September 2000).

R. Sabban, 'United Arab Emirates: Migrant Women in the United Arab Emirates – The Case of Female Domestic Workers', *GENPROM Working Paper*, No. 10 (Geneva, 2003).

V. Samarasinghe, 'Confronting Globalisation in Anti-Trafficking Strategies in Asia', *Brown Journal of World Affairs*, Volume X, Issue I (Providence: Brown University, Summer/Fall 2003).

S. Seguino, 'The Effects of Structural Change and Economic Liberalisation on Gender Wage Differentials in South Korea and Taiwan', *Cambridge Journal of Economics* (Oxford: Oxford University Press, 2000).

P. W. Sharps et al., 'The Role of Alcohol Use in Intimate Partner Femicide', *The American Journal on Addictions*, 10 (Philadelphia, 2001).

N. Stromquist, 'The Theoretical and Practical Bases for Empowerment', in Carolyn Medel-Anonuevo (ed), *Women, Education and Empowerment: Pathways Towards Autonomy* (Paris: UNESCO, 1995).

C. Watts et al., *WHO Multi-country Study on Women's Health and Domestic Violence* (Geneva: WHO, 2003).

C. Watts, C. Zimmerman, 'Violence against Women: Global Scope and Magnitude', *The Lancet*, 359 (London: The Lancet Publishing Group, 6 April 2002).

H. Zlotnik, *The Global Dimensions of Female Migration in Migration Information Source* (1 March 2003), at http://www.migrationinformation.org/Feature/display.cfm?ID=109

Documents and online reports

Amnesty International, '*Disappearances': Unresolved Cases Since the Early 1980s*, (London, 1997), at http://www.amnesty.org

Amnesty International, *Annual Report 2002* (London, 2002), at http://www.amnesty.org

Amnesty International, *Intolerable Killings: Ten Years of Abductions and Murders in Ciudad Juárez and Chihuahua* (London, 11 August 2003), at http://web.amnesty.org/aidoc/aidoc_pdf.nsf/Index/AMR410272003ENGLISH/$File/AMR4102703.pdf

Coalition Against Trafficking in Women, *The Factbook on Global Sexual Exploitation* (1999), at http://www.uri.edu/artsci/wms/hughes/factbook.htm

Derechos Humanos en Chile, *Under the Dictatorship,* at http://www.chip.cl/derechos/dictadura_eng.html

Global Campaign for Education, *A Fair Chance: Attaining Gender Equality in Basic Education by 2005* (April 2003), at http://www.campaignforeducation.org/_html/actionweek/downloads/AFairChanceFull Report.pdf

Human Rights Watch, *Borderline Slavery: Child Trafficking in Togo* (New York, April 2003).

Human Rights Watch, *Stolen Children: Abduction and Recruitment in Northern Uganda* (New York, March 2003).

Human Rights Watch, *Truth and Justice on Hold: The New State Commission on 'Disappearances'* (New York, December 2003), at http://www.hrw.org

Human Rights Watch, *We'll Kill You If You Cry: Sexual Violence in the Sierra Leone Conflict* (New York: Human Rights Watch, 2003).

International Labour Organization, *Every Child Counts: New Global Estimates on Child Labour* (Geneva, April 2002).

International Labour Organization, *Preventing Discrimination, Exploitation and Abuse of Women Migrant Workers: An Information Guide* (Geneva, 2003).

International Labour Organization, *Migrant Workers International Labour Conference*, 87th Session (Geneva, 1999).

International Organization for Migration, *World Migration Report 2003* (Geneva, 2003).

Network, *The United Nations Women's Newsletter*, Vol. 6, No. 4 (October - December 2002).

OXFAM, 'How Does Poverty Relate to Gender Inequality?' (Oxford, 2003), at http://www.oxfam.org.uk/what_we_do/issues/gender/poverty.htm

Physicians for Human Rights, *Maternal Mortality in Herat Province, Afghanistan: The Need to Protect Women's Rights* (September 2002), at http://www.phrusa.org/research/afghanistan/maternal_mortality.html

Program in Law and Public Affairs, *Princeton Principles on Universal Jurisdiction* (Princeton: Princeton University Press, 2001), at http://www.law.uc.edu/morgan2/newsdir/unive_jur.pdf

United Nations, *Violence against Women Perpetrated and/or Condoned by the State during Times of Armed Conflict (1997-2000),* Report of the Special Rapporteur of the Commission on Human Rights on Violence Against Women, its Causes and Consequence, Ms. Radhika Coomaraswamy, UN Document E/CN.4/2001/73 (Geneva, 2001).

United Nations, *Mission to Colombia*, Addendum to the Report of the Special Rapporteur of the Commission on Human Rights on Violence Against Women, its Causes and Consequences, Ms. Radhika Coomaraswamy, UN Document E/CN.4/2002/83/add.3 (Geneva, 2002).

United Nations, *A framework for model legislation on domestic violence*, Addendum to the Report of the Special Rapporteur of the Commission on Human Rights on Violence Against Women, its Causes and Consequences, Ms. Radhika Coomaraswamy, UN Document E/CN.4/1996/53/Add.2 (Geneva, 1996).

United Nations, Report of the Special Rapporteur of the Commission on Human Rights on Freedom of Religion or Belief, UN Document E/CN.4/2002/73 (Geneva, 2002).

United Nations, *Women and Health* (June 2000), at http://www.un.org/womenwatch/daw/followup/session/presskit/fs3.htm

United Nations, *The Beijing Declaration and Platform for Action* (Beijing, China, 4-15 September 1995).

United Nations, *Report of the United Nations Panel on Peacekeeping Operations (Brahimi Report)*, UN Document A/55/305 (New York, 2000), at http://www.un.org/peace/reports/peace_operations/report.htm

United Nations, *Security Council Resolution 1325: Women, Peace and Security* (New York, 2000), at http://www.un.org/events/res_1325e.pdf

United Nations Development Programme, *Human Development Report 1995* (New York, 1995).

United Nations Development Programme, *Human Development Report 2002* (New York, 2002) .

United Nations Development Fund for Women, *Not a Minute More! Ending Violence against Women* (New York, 2003), at http://www.unifem.org/filesconfirmed/207/312_book_complete_eng.pdf.

United Nations Development Fund for Women, *Progress of Women Report* (New York, 2000).

United Nations Development Fund for Women, *Progress of the World's Women 2002, Gender Equality and the Millennium Development Goals*, Vol. 2 (New York, 2003).

United Nations Economic and Social Council, *Civil and Political Rights, including the Questions of Disappearances and Summary Executions* (New York, January 2004), at http://www.un.org/esa/coordination/ecosoc/

United Nations Population Fund, *Reproductive Health Effects of Gender-based Violence* (New York, 1998), at http://www.unfpa.org/about/report/report98/ppgenderbased.htm

United Nations Office of Internal Oversight Services, *Investigation Into Sexual Exploitation of Refugees by Aid Workers in West Africa*, UN Document A/57/465 (New York, 11 October 2002), at http://www.un.org/Depts/oios/reports/a57_465.htm

United Nations Secretary-General's Bulletin, *Observance by United Nations Forces of International Humanitarian Law*, UN Document ST/SGB/1999/13 (New York, 6 August 1999), at http://www.un.org/peace/st_sgb_1999_13.pdf

United Nations Secretary-General's Bulletin, *Special Measures for Protection from Sexual Exploitation and Sexual Abuse* (New York, 9 October 2003).

World Bank, *A New Agenda for Women's Health and Nutrition* (Washington, DC,1994), at http://www.worldbank.org/html/extdr/hnp/health/newagenda/women.htm

World Health Organization, *Violence against Women*, WHO/FRH/WHD/97.8. (Geneva, 1997).

Websites

Amnesty International, at http://www.amnesty.org

Centre for Disease Control and Prevention, National Centre for Injury Prevention and Control, Costs of Intimate Partner Violence Against Women in the United States, at http://www.cdc.gov/ncipc/pub-res/ipv_cost/ipv.htm

Centre for Research on Violence against Women and Children, University of Western Ontario, at http://www.uwo.ca/violence/

Coalition against Trafficking in Women, at http://www.catwinternational.org Domestic Violence Institute, Northeastern University School of Law, at http://www.dvi.neu.edu/

Female Infanticide, at http://womensissues.about.com/cs/femaleinfanticide

Gendercide Watch, at http://www.gendercide.org

Gender Statistics Database, at http://www.unece.org/stats/gender/web/database.htm

Human Rights Library, University of Minnesota, at http://www1.umn.edu/humanrts/treaties.htm

Human Rights Watch, at http://www.hrw.org

International Committee of the Red Cross, at http://www.icrc.org

International Criminal Tribunal for Rwanda, at http://www.ictr.org

International Criminal Tribunal for the former Yugoslavia, at http://www.un.org/icty

International Federation of Red Cross and Red Crescent Societies, at http://www.ifrc.org

International Organization for Migration, at http://www.iom.int

Inter-Parliamentary Union, at http://www.ipu.org

Office of the United Nations High Commissioner for Human Rights, at http://www.unhchr.ch

OXFAM, at http://www.oxfam.org

Profemme Rwanda, at http://www.profemme.org.rw

Prostitution Awareness and Action Foundation of Edmonton (PAAFE), at http://www.paafe.org/index.htm

Prostitutes' Education Network, at http://www.bayswan.org/stats.html

Prostitution Research and Education, at http://www.prostitutionresearch.com

Sex Industry Survivors' Anonymous, at http://www.sexindustrysurvivors.com/splash.htm

Stop Female Genital Mutilation, at http://www.stopfgm.org

United Nations Children's Fund, at http://www.unicef.org

United Nations Development Fund for Women, at http://www.unifem.org

United Nations Development Programme, at http://www.undp.org

United Nations Educational, Scientific and Cultural Organization, at http://www.unesco.org

United Nations High Commissioner for Refugees, at http://www.unhcr.ch

United Nations Population Fund at http://www.unfpa.org

Women Aid International, at http://www.womenaid.org

WomenWatch, at http://www.un.org/womenwatch

Zero Tolerance, at http://www.zerotolerance.org.uk

PART II
WOMEN IN WAR
AND
ARMED CONFLICTS

Introduction

For people living in regions where peace has been preserved for half a century it is difficult to cope with the increasing evidence of the magnitude of violence women have suffered and are suffering when caught in wars and armed conflicts. One would believe that the activities of the international community, the development of international law and numerous peacekeeping missions would protect civilians living in areas of armed conflicts. Nothing is further from the truth. Armed conflicts, *coup d'états* and regime changes are a breeding ground for atrocities against women and other vulnerable groups of civilians such as children and elderly people. Moreover, wars and conflicts are prone to exacerbate existing inequalities and patterns of discrimination. Therefore, women who are exposed to discrimination in peacetime are victimised to an even greater extent during wartime since they bear the brunt of responsibility for caring for the family in situations where there is a general lack of survival commodities such as food, water and medication. Women face armed conflicts in a complex, multifaceted yet deeply individual way. Although the impact of armed conflict differs considerably between contexts, and between individual women within those contexts, it is possible to identify common themes – the outburst of sexual violence traumatising women and girls and contributing to the pandemic of HIV/AIDS; the extreme burden which war places on women left without protection and support of male family members; the necessity to take care of those dependent upon them; and finally the challenges that war brings to women who decide to take up arms and fight shoulder to shoulder with men. The following part of the book deals with these recurrent problems women face in the times of war and armed conflict.

Chapter 1

Vulnerability of Women

'Existing inequalities between women and men, and patterns of discrimination against women and girls, tend to be exacerbated in armed conflict. Women and girls become particularly vulnerable to sexual violence and exploitation. Women and children make up the majority of the world's refugees and internally displaced persons. [...] Some women may be forced to follow camps of armed forces, providing domestic services and/or being used as sexual slaves. But if women suffer the impact of conflict disproportionately, they are also the key to the solution of conflict. [...] The world can no longer afford to neglect the abuses to which women and girls are subjected in armed conflict and its aftermath, or to ignore the contributions that women make to the search for peace. It is time they are given the voice in formal peacebuilding and peacemaking processes that they deserve. Sustainable peace and security will not be achieved without their full and equal participation.'

Kofi Annan, UN Secretary-General's Statement to Security Council on Women, Peace and Security, Press Release, 2002

Vulnerability is most aptly assessed by reference to the exposure to risk and the capacity to cope with the stress, shock and trauma of warfare without sustaining long-term physical, emotional or economic damage.[1] Like men, women can be made vulnerable during armed conflict due to diminished access to basic means of survival – water, food, medical care, shelter – or because of violence or threats of violence. However, unlike men, certain groups of women may be *particularly* vulnerable in situations of armed conflict, such as pregnant women, nursing mothers or women head of households. Women are also susceptible to the marginal-isation, poverty and suffering engendered by armed conflict, especially when they are already victims of discrimination in peacetime. This discrimination may be a key determinant of a woman's capacity to cope with crisis, as it often pertains to her access to income, assets, resources, markets, information, education and social ties, as well as, to the expectations and obligations that may be incumbent upon her as a wife, mother or daughter.

The nature of women's vulnerability often lies in the fact that armed conflicts have evolved to the extent that the civilian population is totally caught up in the fighting. In the struggle to secure their own survival and that of their

South Vietnamese forces follow terrified children, including Kim Phuc (center), as they run after a Napalm attack. The girl had ripped off her burning clothes while fleeing.

families, women may be forced to take on new roles for which both they and their community are ill prepared. Such women may be vulnerable to attack or threats from members of their own family or community for not conforming to traditional roles, or may be targeted by the adversary in order to destroy or subvert these roles. Furthermore, during armed conflict women have been targeted by members of their own community for engaging in commercial activity in the public sphere, or for associating with men who are not from their community – actions which would not necessarily have been opposed prior to the hostilities. This phenomenon is particularly acute where an armed conflict has an ethnic dimension and a group is struggling to preserve its identity and traditions. In such situations, women have also been targeted for rape by armed forces or armed groups as a means of 'ethnic cleansing'. Ethnic cleansing through rape has two predominant dimensions. The first relates to the aim of impregnating women with a child supposedly having the nationality or ethnicity of the perpetrator. The second aims to 'cleanse' an area of its members of a certain ethnic group by forcing them to flee. Thus, it can be seen that while women are not necessarily and inevitably vulnerable, due to their resilience, capabilities and coping mechanisms, they do face particular risks in situations of armed conflict because of their status in society and their gender.

War forces women into unfamiliar roles and necessitates the strengthening of existing coping mechanisms and the development of new ones. This forces women to take on new roles in the family and the community, roles which often challenge and redefine the cultural and social perception of women and their former boundaries in society. For example, women may be forced to work outside the home, searching for a means to earn an income to support their family, and taking the main decisions for the household. Such roles, prior to the armed conflict, were the main preserve of men. This is aptly encapsulated in the words of a woman from El Salvador: *'Before the war women were not taken into consideration. Women were only working in the home. But, when war came, women came out of the house to demonstrate their capability. In part it was war which meant that women could be taken seriously and that they could do a lot of things. It made people realise that women are capable of changing our society.'*[2]

Changes in the gender roles can be seen as positive developments, yet it is important to recognise that this *'must be viewed through the lens of the loss, poverty and deprivation endemic to war, and the fact that in many societies women still only gain status (economic and social) through marriage. The lack of marriage possibilities (because of the lack of men, or social rejection of women because of a violation against them, or their role in the armed conflict) can have enormous implications for women.'*[3] It should also be recognised that many of these changes for women can be reversed once the armed conflict is over. Men return and expect to take up the roles that they held before or men do not return, but the community wants to 'revert to normality', which is often equated with the pre-war *status* quo regarding the expected roles of its members, particularly women. In such situations, women may be vulnerable to attack or threats from their own community, including acts of domestic violence, for not conforming to expected roles.

Although waging war is predominantly a male enterprise, and during wartime women are victimised in many ways, it does not mean that they are not able to take part in combat and to fight shoulder to shoulder with men, or to commit violent acts when such behaviour becomes part of war or post-war tactics.

A Palestinian women protests for her son's release from an Israeli prison.

Endnotes

[1] E. W. Jackson, *Coping and Vulnerability in Crisis: A Framework of Analysis and Response* (Tufts University, 1999).

[2] ICRC, *People on War RadioSeries: 'Women and War'* (March 2000).

[3] C. Lindsey, *Women Facing War: ICRC Study on the Impact of Armed Conflict on Women* (Geneva: ICRC, 2001), 31.

Chapter 2

Rape and Other Forms of Sexual Violence

'After my arrival in the concentration camp, they…raped me…in front of all the rest of the women…who were yelling and defending me, but they were beaten. The soldiers said "you will give birth to a Serbian child, we're doing that out of revenge"….'

Testimony of a Bosnian woman in Maria de Bruyn, *Violence, Pregnancy and Abortion*, 2003

A particular risk to the safety of women and girls in situations of armed conflict is the prevalence of sexual violence. It is insufficient to understand sexual violence solely in terms of rape. Sexual violence also encompasses forced prostitution, sexual slavery, forced impregnation, forced maternity, forced termination of pregnancy, forced sterilisation, indecent assault, trafficking, strip searches and inappropriate medical examinations. During the ICRC's People on War survey[1] undertaken in 1999, one in nine of all respondents reported that they knew someone who had been raped, and nearly as many reported that they knew someone who had been sexually assaulted. The answers of the women who took part in this survey were dominated by specific cases of rape or sexual violence experienced when their country was embroiled in armed conflict.

Recent conflicts have highlighted the systematic and specific targeting of women for sexual violence – in effect the use of rape as a method of warfare. Some organisations have frequently referred to rape in wartime as a 'weapon of war'. However, the use of this term requires some fine-tuning. The analogy between rape and a weapon is metaphorical, rather than precise. It is more precise to describe sexual violence as a method of warfare for two main reasons. Firstly, in grammatical terms, weapons are objects, whereas to rape or to starve is a course of action. Rape and starvation do not exist in the world as weapons, what does exist is rape and starvation as methods of warfare. Secondly, the technical understanding of a weapon is an instrument of combat used to inflict a wound, defined, under the auspices of pathology, as a 'breach or a disruption of the continuity of tissues'. Rape in wartime, however, is used for many reasons – to forcibly impregnate women for the purposes of altering the demographic composition of an area, to force a population to flee, to break the resistance of a person under interrogation and for many other reasons more complex than the direct infliction of a wound.

It remains difficult, however, to determine when sexual violence rises to the level of a method of warfare.[2] There

Torn between desperation and resilience - a survivor of sexual violence in Sierra Leone.

is a fine line between opportunistic rape that is not discouraged, and systematic, widespread rape aimed to achieve the objectives of the armed conflict. A particularly difficult case to define is the use of so-called 'comfort women' for the purpose of providing sexual services to armed forces. This could be seen as a provision of logistical support, part of remuneration and an incentive for continued participation in hostilities, albeit not a direct attack upon the adversary. This is particularly true when women have been brought into a country or area for this purpose, as was the case during Second World War (see Part IV, box 4.1). It is, however, necessary to emphasise that more important than the question of classification is the question of recognition of such acts as a violation against women and of the physical and psychological suffering endured as a result. Sexual violence has been used against women in wartime for many different reasons – as a form of torture, to inflict injury, to extract information, to degrade and intimidate, as a form of punishment for actual or alleged actions committed by the women or their family members, and to destroy the essence of a community. For example, women may be targeted for sexual violence in order to reach absent male relatives who may have fled or have joined the armed forces or an armed group. Targeting women in this way is a symbolic demonstration of the fact that men are not able to protect women - that 'dishonour' has been brought upon an entire family or community by virtue of the assault upon their women.

Two of the most frightening consequences of rape – which endure long after the initial violation has taken place – are the risks of pregnancy and sexually transmitted infections, including HIV/AIDS. The main risks associated with pregnancy for women stem from the physical and psychological trauma of carrying a child of their rapist, the fear of what members of their family and/or community will say and do when they find out, as well as, the physical concerns linked to being pregnant during an armed conflict when safety is precarious and resources are scarce. Sexually transmitted infections are also a risk, since in order to receive treatment the woman has to make something public that she may prefer to keep private. This is due to the fact that a woman who has suffered sexual violence may risk ostracism and reprisals from members of her family or the wider community, due to the perception that the woman has brought 'dishonour' upon her family. It is rarely acknowledged that the only person to be 'dishonoured' is the perpetrator of rape. A seldom-discussed issue linked to the rape of women concerns the fate of children born of sexual violence. This issue needs to be better taken into account, in order to provide appropriate assistance and protection for them.[3] What emerges from programmes that work with victims of sexual violence is that breaking down the taboos surrounding rape and sexual assault takes a long time.[4] It takes an equally long time to help women build up the confidence to talk, if they desire to do so, and to gain the confidence to seek help.

Table 2.1:

Estimated mortality caused by war-related injuries in 2000 sorted by gender and World Health Organization region (in absolute numbers in thousands and per 100,000 population)

Region	Men		Women	
	Absolute numbers in thousands	Cases per 100,000 population	Absolute numbers in thousands	Cases per 100,000 population
Africa	122	50.6	45	14.7
The Americas	2	0.4	<1	0.1
South-East Asia	49	6.6	14	2.2
Europe	30	7.0	6	1.5
Eastern Mediterranean	39	11.2	10	4.9
Western Pacific region	2	0.2	1	0.1
All WHO Regions*	233	7.8	77	2.6

* The World Health Organization (WHO) collects data on the number of deaths from various diseases, illnesses or injuries from about 100 countries all over the world, creating a database for its statistics included into WHO reports.

Source: Adapted from World Health Organization, *World Report on Violence and Health* (Geneva: WHO, 2002), 282-83.

Box 2.1: Sexual violence against women during wars and conflicts in Africa and on the territory of Former Yugoslavia

A woman mourns as skulls are collected and lined up in a church yard in order to count the number of people massacred during the war between Hutu and Tutsi in Rwanda.

In spite of widely reported sexual violence against women during recent wars there is an obvious lack of reliable data. Difficulties in providing quantified data on the magnitude of war rapes arise from the lack of reporting from victims who have either been murdered, or if they survived, are fearful of rejection by their families and society due to the profound pain and humiliation attached to rape. Immediately after the sexual assault the victims do not speak up due to fear of reprisals from their perpetrators, later on they do not want to be condemned and ostracised by their communities upon which they are fully dependent. In the same manner, there is the increasing reticence to report incidents of rape and sexual assault at the international level, since victims wish to get on with their lives and avoid reliving the shame and embarrassment of their experiences.

The occurrence of rape in the civil wars in Africa in the last decade is qualified as widespread and massive in scale. Few documented surveys exist that reveal the exact magnitude of sexual violence, yet estimates attempt to show its pervasiveness in conflicts in Africa. Recent findings at the end of the five-year armed conflict in Congo, starting in 1998, led to the discovery of thousands of women who had suffered brutal rapes and who recently moved forward to seek medical help. Some estimates revealed that for every three women survivor one suffered from rape. In Sierra Leone, the decade-long internal strife from 1991-2001 resulted in an approximate 50,000 to 64,000 incidents of war-related sexual violence against internally displaced women. Derived from the comprehensive population-based study under-

taken by the Physicians for Human Rights (PHR) in January 2002, these extrapolations were developed from the conclusion that of the 991 sample cases of female-headed households, nine per cent experienced sexual violence. Other important statistics in the study confirmed that 89 per cent of the cases of sexual violence were in the form of rape and one third of respondent women were gang-raped. The findings also led to some valuable information on the identity of perpetrators who have been recognised as rebels and armed forces with 53 per cent revealing 'face to face' contact with the Revolutionary United Front (RUF) rebel forces. In Rwanda, during the ethnic conflict that began in 1990 and culminated in the horrendous genocide in 1994, rape was committed on a massive scale. The total number of female rape victims, including those who perished and those who survived, totalled 250,000 to 500,000 – this number is based on extrapolations from statistics on pregnancies arising from rape. Studies have also shown that a majority of victims were between 16 and 26 years old although girls and women as young as two and as old as fifty have also suffered the abuse.

Most figures concerning the magnitude of rape and sexual assault during the Yugoslav wars of 1991–1995, even those quoted in official documents, are only a rough estimation of the real situation. For instance, estimates on the magnitude of rape and sexual assault during the wars in Croatia and Bosnia-Herzegovina vary from 10,000 to 60,000. To some extent medical data can help assess the number of rape victims. For instance, a UN medical team operating in former Yugoslavia during the early 1990s and investigating sexual violence among patients of six hospitals in Bosnia, Croatia and Serbia revealed that 119 pregnancies were associated to rape. Based on a medical estimate that 'a single act of unprotected intercourse will result in pregnancy between one and four per cent of the time' and assuming in the sample case from Bosnia, Croatia and Serbia that it is in the order of one per cent, then the 119 pregnancies represent a total of 11,900 rapes. A well documented study on the link between rape and ethnic cleansing was undertaken by the UN Commission of Experts between 1991 and 1993 establishing a database of tens of thousands of allegations of rape and sexual assault. In spite of all these and many other efforts, the chance that the true magnitude of rape and sexual assault will eventually be revealed is diminishing as time passes.

Sources:

B. Becirbasic and D. Secic, *Invisible Casualties of War* (Bosnian Institute, 18 November 2002), at http://www.bosnia.org.uk/news
Human Rights Watch, *Shattered Lives: Sexual Violence during the Rwandan Genocide and its Aftermath* (New York, September 1996), at http://www.hrw.org/reports/1996/Rwanda.htm
Physicians for Human Rights with the support of UNAMSIL, *War-Related Sexual Violence in Sierra Leone, A Population-Based Assessment, A Report* (Washington DC, January 2002), at http://www.phrusa.org/research/sierra_leone/report.html

Consequences of Rape for Women's Health and Well-being, Family and Society

In order to understand the consequences of war rape, it is essential to recognise that the victim's response is not to a single, isolated act of violation, occurring in a relatively sta-

ble society, with at least some access to medical, legal, communal and familial support. It is an act that is engulfed by social, cultural, domestic, physical and psychological repercussions. Violent social upheaval, genocide and ethnic cleansing form an all-encompassing environment that irrefutably shapes the response. In spite of the fact that war rape is notoriously frequent in many conflicts, there is little systematic research into the effects that such assaults

[...] that's something we don't talk about here. Only a handful of cases received publicity, the rest were hushed up. There are cases of girls going out and not coming home. A lot of young women are in prisons all over Russia. If they come home, they'd be better of shooting themselves. If anyone laid a hand on them, they'd be written off for good here in Chechnya. It's a kind of law. A sullied daughter is worse than a dead one to her father. It's a terrible disgrace. She'll never get married and no one will say a kind word to her, even though it's not her own fault she was dishonoured. So you see the war has dishonoured us too, not just our menfolk. But we don't go on about it the way they do. [...] Our men have lost what they consider the most important thing in life – their own dignity, which in our country is dependent to a certain extent on the ability to ensure their family's material security. They've been deprived of money and the opportunity to earn it. There is nothing worse for a Chechen man than to be poor or to do humiliating work to earn money. And for women, what counts most of all are their children. They are prepared to do anything to protect them. Even to humiliate themselves.

P. Procházková, The Aluminum Queen : The Russian–Chechen war through the eyes of women, 2003

Chechen women have been going through a double ordeal – as civilians they are exposed to human rights violations such as sexual assaults, forced disappearances, extrajudicial execution, widespread acts of torture, ill-treatment, and arbitrary detention committed by Russian troops. In addition, they are victims of continuing terrorist attacks against pro-Moscow Chechen officials and civil servants. In December 2003 at least 41 people were killed and another 155 injured in a commuter train explosion caused by a suicide bomber. According to 2002 unofficial estimates the number of killed civilian victims were 1,132 persons. Approximately 84,000 people are displaced in Ingushetia, most of them are women and children. These internally displaced people are being forced to return to Chechnya by various administrative obstacles, such as arbitrary deregistration resulting in their eviction from government-sponsored accommodation, arbitrary arrest and detention, interruption of infrastructure services, ill-treatment by policemen and Russian soldiers, operations intimidating displaced people in a numerous settlements and villages, or by obstruction of the building of alternative camps and shelters for displaced people. Moving displaced persons back into Chechnya would increase the opportunity to block outside scrutiny of human rights abuse.

It is almost impossible to obtain more precise and up-to-date figures on sexual assaults because of the absence of independent sources of information usually provided by international organisations and journalists, that are, in the Northern Caucuses, not allowed to visit the country and monitor the situation. In the spring 2003, the only international observers on the ground were three Council of Europe experts. Visits of the Special Rapporteur on Violence against Women and the UN Secretary-General's Special Representative on Displaced Persons have been repeatedly postponed, and the mandate of the OSCE Assistance Group of Chechnya has not been renewed by the Russian government. In 2000, Human Rights Watch began to collect information about sexual violence committed by Russian soldiers in areas of Russian-controlled Chechnya, and in 2002 the same organisation reported that the troops used rapes and sexual assaults during winter operations in 2001 as a means of intimidating civilians. Human Rights Watch researchers found that *'rapes occurred on the outskirts of villages, at checkpoints, and in detention centres. Fear of rape by Russian forces was pervasive, causing some*

families, particularly those with young women and girls, to flee and motivating desperate attempts to hide female family members.' A strong taboo in local culture against revealing instances of rape hamper any estimates of its real magnitude, but the very fact that the sexual violence was reported to outsiders suggest frequency of sexual abuse during the Chechen wars.

In April 2001, a joint Council of Europe/Russian Duma Working Group compiled a list of 358 criminal investigations into alleged abuses against civilians. However, only about twenty per cent of the cases were under active investigation and the authorities had suspended more than half of the total investigations. The criminal investigations did not include a single case of torture or ill-treatment and very few abuse cases ever advanced to the courts. Most of the perpetrators enjoy a high level of impunity as evidenced by the only case of a rape and murder charge against a Russian officer, Col. Yuri Budanov, that ended with his release of criminal responsibility based on psychiatric assessments. The UN Human Rights Committee remains concerned that the charges and sentences handed down do not appear to correspond with the gravity of the human rights violations. As stated in the Human Rights Watch Briefing Paper to the 59th Session of the UN Commission on Human Rights in 2003 *'[...] the human rights situation in Chechnya remains abysmal'.*

Chechen women sit in a cell at a detention camp in Chernokozovo, 40 km north-west of Grozny. It was alleged that such women have suffered violence to urge information about fellow-countrymen.

have on victims. While a diverse range of psychosocial projects in a variety of different places have been set up to respond to women's needs, few embrace a thorough knowledge of the particular context, the specific population, and even fewer are evaluated as to their efficacy. While study and evaluation may be difficult and hazardous, and considered something of a luxury in areas of acute crisis, many projects fall short of their most basic aims, leading to already scarce funding being wasted. Three aspects particularly pertinent to a conflict environment should be emphasised, namely, the context within which the rape occurs, that is the environment at the time and in the immediate aftermath of the rape, the post-conflict setting or 'recovery' environment, and the core perception associated with the rape itself, as experienced by the victim.

The context of rape and co-existing trauma

When rape occurs in the context of ethnic cleansing or invasion, the following situations frequently accompany it:

- Entire families are terrorised, and gang rape takes place in front of family members or in public. It has been estimated that 90 per cent of all war rape is gang rape.

- In detention centres, women are made available to soldiers and paramilitaries, where they are taken away to be raped and either killed or returned to the centre.

- In rape camps and brothels similar circumstances occur, but camps are more specifically organised for that purpose, and sexual torture is frequent. The larger the abusing group, the worse the torture and the greater probability of the victim being killed during or after the assault. In the Bosnian conflict women were forcibly impregnated to make 'Chetnik babies' and held until their pregnancy was too far advanced to have an abortion.[5]

Extreme abuse and humiliation frequently accompany rape. The victim is denied the option of keeping this trauma private – she must endure the pain and horror of her family, neighbours and community. When rape is accompanied by torture, victims must suffer and overcome severe physical injury. The nature of physical injury in ritual sexual torture (such as cutting off breasts) is an ever present, horrific reminder of the rape. The body is inescapable, and self-loathing and suicide are not uncommon responses.

In addition to the heinous experience of war rape, comes a daunting range of coexisting trauma that must also be endured in the context of violent social upheaval. Increasingly, conflicts are not played out on the battlefields, but in the heart of civil life at schools, hospitals, market places, and bread lines. Communities have been shattered, and families are torn apart by distance or death. Women are often the sole providers of food and shelter for extended families. They have experienced death, often multiple, of family members. Other family members are missing, some in concentration camps. As victims themselves they have experienced torture, death threats, deprivation and severe physical injury. Women have also witnessed atrocities committed against others. An increasing number of studies link witnessing atrocity to the highest incidence of pathology. Medical facilities range from non-existent to vastly inadequate. Often they must survive in an entirely unfamiliar environment, having lost all material possessions, their homes and birthplaces.

With respect to the post-conflict situation, or 'recovery' environment, a pervading misconception is that it is post-traumatic. In the context of war rape, the milieu is in fact the very antithesis of a recovery environment. Recent conflicts may give an erroneous message that warfare is automatically accompanied by a more or less planned scheme for humanitarian amelioration. Most wars are of a long genesis and a low intensity. They are accompanied by the chronic malfunction of state institutions and unremitting hardship for the vast majority of the population. It is thus a further misconception that displacement is of a temporary nature. Some three quarters of refugees are in asylum for more than five years.

Many of the traumatic circumstances that are experienced at the time of rape, continue for months and often years after the trauma. Women remain the sole providers, family members remain missing and medical facilities are little improved. In addition, there are the highly stressful aspects of refugee status to reckon with. These include the unfamiliar, often hostile environment, unemployment and acculturation. For displaced persons, the potential for human rights abuses is greater. The central role of tradition, community and a sense of continuity are disrupted or irreparably damaged. In recent years there has been a growing awareness and concern about the increase of family violence in post-conflict areas. Few post-conflict areas have a co-ordinated and comprehensive approach to the problem of family violence. The vast proportion of violence remains hidden and no communal support is available to victims.

Finally, in many instances, the post-conflict period is characterised by chronic insecurity for the victims. In Bosnia, numbers of individuals with questionable war records have assumed positions of authority. For those returning home, the risk of coming face to face with their attackers is a realistic fear. The nature of these stressors remains so severe, rendering the chances for recovery extremely grim, and attempts at intervention challenging. Attacks and reprisals on returning refugees are common in many areas, and can occur with impunity.

In an ironic twist of fate, victims of the Bosnian conflict had the additional burden of appearing as breaking news to the international community. The plight of tens of thousands of Bosnian women was splashed across newspapers and filled television screens. While such coverage did little to stem the tide of ethnic cleansing, it did bring an army of journalists, eager for stories and photographs. Their war rape became the most documented and investigated in history.

Core perceptions associated with rape

In war rape, the victims' core perceptions of the rape have far reaching consequences. Moreover, such perceptions can be significantly linked to the objectives of those who orchestrate, and those who commit the rape (not necessarily one and the same). The intentions of the perpetrators play an ominously predictive role. This demands an insight into the reasons for war rape that go beyond morale boosting and 'the spoils of war'. While certainly not the only explanation for war rape, rape as a tool of ethnic cleansing was particularly significant, and obvious, in conflicts such as Bosnia and Rwanda.

The aim in ethnic cleansing is the expulsion from a given territory under the threat of the destruction of a culture, or eradication of a people rather than the simple conquest by an army. Women are particularly vulnerable as an important tactical objective. Their significance in the structure of the family and the cultural role they play make them prime targets for such violence.

The pattern of rape is fairly consistent, with rape occurring both before fighting breaks out in a region involving small groups of soldiers or militia, and rape in conjunction with invasion of towns or villages. Rape camps in Bosnia estimate as many as 2,000 women were held, and as indicated above, the objectives of the rapist included forced pregnancies. Certain elements of rape are common, with a motive to humiliate and ensure a level of powerlessness and fear that will remain entrenched in the victim:

- Gang rapes - include the element of spectacle, with non-voluntary (family, other victims, local population), and voluntary (military and militia) spectators.

- Sexual torture – including rituals, mutilation and filming for pornography.

- Psychological torture – in the Bosnian context for example, women were forced to sing Serbian songs or say Christian prayers while being raped.

- Expressed motive of rape - rape occurring particularly in the phases of expulsion, accompanied by the expressed motive. Women were told that if they did not leave the soldiers would return the next day to rape again, to rape family members, and to kill them.

The aim to humiliate the victim is achieved when the victim feels isolated, fearing ostracism and stigmatisation. As a result, one is not looking only at multiple, severe and prolonged personal trauma, but trauma that impacts on the individuals' relationship with their community. Their own sanctity has been compromised by belonging to the group. Thus all avenues to recovery – self-esteem, a grounded sense of identity, family support, community help – are all to some degree damaged, and for some irrevocably destroyed.

Consequences for family and society

If victims feel isolated and ruptured from their social world, what then are the consequences of such violation on the family and community? Returning to the example of ethnic cleansing, they too are affected in ways orchestrated and predicted by the perpetrators. The circle of terror is extended as far as possible. Those who have not been raped have witnessed, and to witness is to bear testimony to the power of the invader, to the destruction of a multi-ethnic community, to the impossibility of return.

Raping women in a community can be seen as raping the body of the community, in so doing, undermining the entire fabric of that community. As a result, communities and families often respond by condemning the victims. There are accounts of women from a variety of regions testifying to expulsion and ostracism[6] when their rape became public knowledge. This is not specific to any particular religion or culture – diverse communities have demonstrated this. It has less to do with the mores of a particular society, but rather how a particular community will respond when under threat. Returning once more to the aims of the perpetrators, rape is intended to humiliate and punish the group by breaking down the national, religious and cultural identity. The physical abuse is often accompanied by attacks on religious facilities such as churches or mosques. To avoid shame and disgrace, their only choice is to flee

Ester Macauley was gang raped by militia fighters in Monrovia. In her refugee camp, there were 648 reported cases of women having been gang raped.

Box 2.3: War ends, sexual violence against women and girls continues

The human rights of women and girls continue to be violated in volatile post-war situations when security institutions are disorganised and unable to function properly. This continuation of rampant violence and discrimination of women and girls in post-conflict situations has some common features:

- The break-up of, or at least a disarray in, pre-war security institutions, especially the police who is unable to protect vulnerable groups of inhabitants against militia, rebels and their sympathisers.
- Low interest by governments in investigating and punishing perpetrators of violence.
- Reluctance of the international community to exert effective pressure on local governments to investigate and punish the perpetrators.
- Vulnerability of certain groups of inhabitants, such as female refugees and internally displaced women, to sexual violence.
- Gaps in local penal law, inefficient police provisions for filing and pursuing a complaint of sexual violence, poor preparedness of medical facilities to provide medical examinations and treatment.

In countries where women traditionally have been confined to home-making roles, sexual violence can be seen as the ultimate expression of an attempt to return gender relations to the pre-war situation. Such a situation was witnessed for instance in Liberia in 1999-2000, in post-war Kosovo, or more recently in Iraq under the Coalition Provisional Authority (CPA). In May and June 2003 Human Rights Watch conducted a survey in Baghdad both among women and girls who were abducted and raped and those who were in charge of protecting the population, as well as, medical practitioners and law enforcement authorities. The study revealed that the public security vacuum in Baghdad in the first few months after the end of the war heightened the vulnerability of women and girls to sexual violence. Prior to the war, the police usually received one rape complaint every three moths, but since the start of the war, several cases have been reported every week. Some of the cases involved girls under sixteen years of age. The final number of victims was estimated to be much higher, since only a small number of women's human rights violations had been reported and investigated.

Iraq, as well as the United States and other members of the CPA in post-war Iraq, is a state party to the Fourth Geneva Convention regulating the protection of civilians during war. Iraq also signed all the major international human rights treaties protecting the rights of women, such as the Convention on the Elimination of All Forms of Discrimination against Women (CEDAW). International law defines sexual violence as a grave violation of human rights. Moreover, rape and abduction are serious crimes under Iraqi law, punishable by lengthy prison sentences. However, there are obstacles that hamper the victims from obtaining justice.

For instance, provisions in the penal code gives a man the possibility to escape punishment for abduction by marrying the victim, and allow for significantly reduced sentences for so-called honour killings, rape and other cases of sexual violence. Thus, if victims do forward a complaint, they risk marriage to the perpetrator, where they would be exposed to further sexual and physical violence. Furthermore, the implementation of the law often leads to perpetrators' impunity, because of a widespread and deeply rooted opinion that women and girls are to blame for the violence, while perpetrators are treated leniently. If the victims inform their family about an attack, they risk a punishment for what is considered their transgression.

During the war and the occupation, according to the Human Rights Watch survey mentioned above, the magnitude of sexual violence sharply increased. Women and girls do not feel safe on Baghdad streets, and instead of going to schools and to work or of running their errands they prefer to stay in the relative safety of their homes.

Even if a victim of sexual violence is willing to report a sexual crime, there are other serious barriers in obtaining justice. Already at the level of police protocol, there are many obstacles to submitting a formal complaint. There are no female police officers in Iraq and male police officers, although they are concerned about women's safety, usually do not take the allegations seriously enough, prioritising other crimes frequently occurring in the post-war security vacuum. In addition, they share the commonly held opinion that it is primarily the victim who is to be blamed for sexual violence. Without a referral from the police, the victims cannot receive forensic examinations that would provide legal proof of sexual violence. According to the Human Rights Watch report, the police – who were in disarray, poorly managed, and understaffed – were reluctant to investigate sexual violence and abduction. Moreover, many hospitals and the forensic institutes are unable to operate 24-hours a day as they did before the war, thus preventing women from obtaining medical treatment and the forensic examinations necessary to document sexual violence in a timely manner.

Source:
Human Rights Watch, Climate of Fear: *Sexual Violence and Abduction of Women and Girls in Baghdad,* 15 (8) (E) (New York, July 2003), at http://www.hrw.org

---

their native surroundings. Entire communities move towards flight, further disintegrating community safeguards against rape. The agenda of the perpetrator is met. All of this is likely to heighten the perception that once women are raped, the well-being of the community is placed under threat. This may go some way to explain how those who are so evidently innocent victims are sacrificed for the sake of the community. In the same way that an individual may use denial to cope with an overwhelmingly destructive event, it is possible that a community chooses to use the same mechanism. The tacit message experienced by victims is to remain silent. For those who do not, the consequences range from a complete lack of understanding and support, to ostracism and even expulsion.

Psychological and psychiatric consequences

It is important to note that surrounded by such an array of shattering experiences, it becomes increasingly difficult to isolate the particular effects that 'belong' to the rape experience. The consequences of rape are inextricably linked to the consequences of a number of war and post-war experiences. Most information on the impact of war rape currently emanates from reports in clinical settings. Some of the most frequent psychological symptoms are anxiety, inner agitation, sleep disorders, nightmares, apathy, loss of self-confidence, and depression. In addition, denial is often used as a defence mechanism. More extreme defences are depersonalisation and numbing. There are also progressively more and more accounts of psychosis – argued also as a rigid defence against an impossible reality. Amongst war raped women, enforced pregnancy brings about the loss of vital instincts, sharply increasing the risk of suicide.

Although victims express feelings of panic, disgust and helplessness, these will not lead them to seek help. It is notably more often that physical symptoms are reported. These are largely psychosomatic, such as gastritis, serious headaches, permanent abdominal pain, palpitation of the heart, breathing disorders, paroxysms, paralysis and skin diseases.

Here it is important to acknowledge the influence of culture. There are distinct ways in which women from various cultures express their distress. In many cultures, distress is simply not described in psychological terms, but in physical ones. In a study of war rape of 107 Ugandan women, only two presented symptoms that could be classified as psychological, namely nightmares and loss of libido. All the others described their distress in physical symptoms such as headaches and chest pain, and gynaecological symptoms.[7] Such results are notably different from westernised women who admitted single rape episodes in peace time and who focus on – and seek help for – psychological distress. Commonly experienced reactions are shock, fear of injury or death, sense of loss of control, avoidance, feelings of shame, intrusive thoughts, and difficulty re-establishing intimate relationships. It is essential to recognise such differences in order to understand and respond to population groups where cultural influences are active.

With respect to the long-term effects, few longitudinal studies exist to examine the consequences of war rape over time. It is reasonable to assume, as with other forms of sexual abuse, that the effects are long lasting and complex. Moreover, future circumstances will play an important role in shaping the response. Here again, the prognosis is grim – for a clear majority, their environment will continue to be one of unmitigated stress. Understanding the consequences and designing and implementing appropriate responses to victims of war rape - particularly to those who remain in the conflict area – is an exploration in its early stages, and one which needs to be urgently highlighted and encouraged.

The International Criminal Tribunal for the Former Yugoslavia: The Impact of Witnessing on Rape Victims

Victims should be treated with compassion and respect for their dignity. They are entitled to access to the mechanisms of justice and to prompt redress […] for the harm that they have suffered.'

United Nations, *Declaration of Basic Principles of Justice for Victims of Crime and Abuse of Power*, UN Document A/40/53, 1985

With respect to justice, the identification and bringing to trial of offenders requires victims of human rights abuses to be witnesses. Systematic and widespread sexual abuse in the territory of the former Yugoslavia, and inclusion of rape as a crime against humanity in the Statute of the International Criminal Tribunal for the Former Yugoslavia (ICTY) has led the tribunal to seek victims of sexual abuse to bear witness in its proceedings.

While there is certainly recognition that the act of witnessing can be highly stressful and even traumatic, the exact nature of this impact is not fully understood, the precise ways to avoid such an impact are unclear and – given the legal restrictions – even feasible. In addition, there is a prevailing assumption that victims need to see their perpetrators punished, and that this is the key to being able to 'move forward'. Whereas victims may well benefit from seeing perpetrators brought to justice, to predict such far-reaching restoration is a tenuous assumption at best. Moreover, even if this were true in theory, the reality is that many witnesses will not see their perpetrators receiving the sentence they feel they deserve.

What then are the measures undertaken to ensure the protection and support of witnesses – particularly victims of sexual abuse? Are these measures adequate and effective and are there areas that require a greater awareness and further attention?

The ICTY Rules of Procedure and Evidence offer the following guarantees – protective measures and security arrangements, counselling and other appropriate assistance, in particular in cases of rape and sexual assault. All those who appear before the court and all others who may be at risk because of the testimony given by such witnesses are guaranteed assistance provided by the Victims and Witnesses Unit staffed with experts in trauma, particularly trauma related to crimes of sexual violence. The Unit assists victims with obtaining legal advice, with organising their legal representation, informing them of their rights, as well as in obtaining medical, psychological and other appropriate help. Furthermore,

Box 2.4: The Red Cross trains midwives to help rape victims

'It was the middle of the night and I was asleep. Suddenly I heard a noise. Our houses don't have any doors, so I got up to investigate. That's when a bright light was shone in my face, blinding me and preventing me from seeing my attackers. But I know there were two of them. For several weeks afterwards, it hurt to urinate but I was too ashamed to go and see a doctor.'

The woman speaking is a widow who was raped in a country in the Great Lakes region where many women are the victims of violence. The injury and suffering this causes women further aggravates their plight, as many are poverty-stricken widows and/or displaced persons. Many women have trouble speaking about violations of a sexual nature. It is essential that victims of sexual violence have access to appropriate and adequate health care, including pre and post-natal care for those who have become pregnant, and trauma counselling if they so choose. Women pregnant and babies born as a result of rape require appropriate medical care. The situation needs to be handled sensitively and confidentially to ensure that the women do not suffer further abuse or ostracism for having reported the violations – either from the perpetrators of the original violation or members of their family or community who perceive that they have been dishonoured because of the rape of the woman. Access to appropriate medical facilities is often particularly difficult in situations of armed conflict. Hospitals, medicines and medical staff may be difficult to access for security reasons, may no longer be functioning or may be in particularly short supply.

The ICRC recently carried out a broad survey of existing medical facilities in one country in the Great Lakes region and conducted various interviews with members of groups most concerned by the problem of sexual violence (women, young people and married men living in the affected neighbourhoods). It then set up a project designed to give the victims of sexual violence medical, as well as, psychological and social support. In conjunction with local associations, who provided the contacts, the public medical services, and the Ministry of Health, the project trained a group of traditional midwives from the affected areas. The training firstly focused on giving the midwives authority and recognition within their communities and secondly on enabling them to iden-

Women at a displacement camp in eastern Democratic Republic of Congo. As tens of thousands of women and young girls flee from the ravages of conflict, they are prone to rape and abuse by militia and renegade soldiers. Nearly all the crimes have gone unpunished.

tify the signs of sexual violence. This strengthened their role among women who would not otherwise – whether through shame, lack of resources or lack of information – receive the necessary care for the physical and psychological wounds they have suffered. A psychologist on the ICRC team, who played a key role in the project, emphasised that the midwives will learn, during their training, how to recognise women who have been the victims of violence and how to provide them with psychological support by actively listening to them. In turn, the victims will learn to trust and confide in the midwives. The midwives also serve as part of a chain of referral, referring victims to the appropriate medical structures for assistance.

---

the unit is responsible for providing administrative and technical assistance during all stages of the proceedings and thereafter, such as escorted travel, travel and medical insurance, comfortable and secure accommodation, childcare, and compensation for lost wages. This is a remarkably ambitious guarantee, and a considerable burden of responsibility on a unit that up until 2000 included but a handful of staff. The victims and witnesses section now has a team of forty, yet remain significantly stretched in both human and financial resources.

The protection measures referred to are not all clearly specified, which leaves support staff to define what these should be, *within* the restrictions of budget and number of staff available. When financial resources are insufficient, the same staff is responsible for seeking funding elsewhere. While there has been considerable support and interest

from the international community, it is pragmatic to recognise that donor interest will soon turn elsewhere.

The full ordeal of witnessing can be divided into three periods – pre-trial, trial and post-trial, thus affording an overview of services offered and particular challenges that arise from the witnessing experience.

The initial phase

An investigation team seeks out individuals who can act as witnesses. An interesting point to note here is that 81 per cent of witnesses have been male and 19 per cent female. Is this because of a predominance of male investigators? Could it result in fewer crimes involving female victims being investigated, are fewer females approached, or are they less willing to come forward when approached by males, particularly with respect to crimes of sexual vio-

The Bosnian Serb Dragoljub Kunarac is accused at the International War Crimes Tribunal for Former Yugoslavia in The Hague, Netherlands. He is charged with having raped, and having let his troops rape, Moslem women between April 1992 and February 1993 in the eastern Bosnian town of Foca.

lence? At one point, however, an all female team was established, and the number of female witnesses rose exponentially – indicating that the gender bias of the investigators played a significant role in such a large discrepancy. This team has subsequently been divided up among other investigative teams, so men continue to dominate as witnesses. The consequences of this discrepancy remain nebulous.

When a selected witness is reluctant to testify, a member of the support staff is dispatched to meet with this person, to discover the reasons for this reluctance, attempt to overcome these difficulties and persuade the individual to testify. Herein lies a dilemma for the support officer. They are under pressure from prosecutors to secure key witnesses, yet they also have a mandate to support the witness. This can be – and often is, a direct conflict of interests. Ultimately the person must give their full agreement to testify – so they cannot be brought against their will. While not coerced, they can be convinced to act against their better judgement – to agree in spite of being fearful or suspicious. In such cases the support officer is acutely aware that his or her influence may result in extreme emotional distress. Moreover, such discussions may in no way 'tamper with the evidence'. At all stages support staff must be acutely aware of what they may and may not discuss with witnesses – this can in some instances conflict with the needs of the witness.

Witnesses are sent a brochure with information on the place and procedure. Those with special needs are given extra assistance, such as escorted travel for vulnerable witnesses. An addition to the Victims and Witnesses Section is a field office in Sarajevo since the 59 per cent of witnesses are living in Bosnia and Herzegovina.[8] A protection officer and a support officer can meet some of the needs of wit-

nesses prior to their departure to The Hague. The majority of witnesses are from areas far outside of Sarajevo, so although this field office is a welcome development, most witnesses still receive information and support through brochure and telephone communication.

The trial phase

Measures undertaken to support and protect witnesses in this phase are also the most clearly defined and well established. With respect to protection of victims and witnesses, the Rules of Procedure and Evidence of ICTY allows for special measures to be applied for victims/witnesses of sexual violence, such as an exception to the principle of public hearings, conducting any part of the proceedings in camera or allowing the presentation of evidence by electronic or other special means. Certain measures may be ordered to prevent the disclosure of the identity or the location of a victim or a witness to the public or media. Such measures include *'expunging names and identifying information from the Chamber's public records; non-disclosure to public of any records identifying the victim; giving of testimony through image or voice altering devices or closed circuit television; and assignment of a pseudonym.* Appropriate measures can also be taken in order *'to facilitate the testimony of vulnerable victims and witnesses, such as one-way closed circuit television.'*[9]

In fact the majority of witnesses are heard in a public hearing. The protection measures referred to above - facial distortion, the use of pseudonym, voice distortion, and combinations of these measures – are used by 30 per cent of witnesses. Only one per cent of witnesses use a video link, and nine per cent of cases appear in closed sessions. The 'protection' referred to here is from the general public, not the accused. There has only been one instance where the accused was unable to see the witness; such cases are considered by some to be a violation of the rights of the accused, and cause much controversy. Contrary to what one might expect, many witnesses express the desire to come face to face with their adversary.

With respect to the psychological stresses of testifying, one can begin with those who go through all the hoops in preparation for trial, and then are not called to testify. This is likely to happen to one in ten witnesses, and most have great difficulty in accepting they have endured so much for nothing. Support staff must help these individuals accept this unforeseen turn of events. They may be encouraged to recognise that in spite of the fact that they have not been required to give testimony, they have nevertheless played an important role in the overall process. Most doubt such sentiments, and responses range from acute disappointment to feelings of betrayal.

Directly prior to testimony, witnesses must endure an unpredictable waiting time in an enclosed environment, with little sense of what will happen to them. The reactions to this are largely anticipatory anxiety, with both physical and emotional symptoms. Here the aim of support staff is to put them at ease, by giving them as much information as possible, as well as, practical attention if necessary from an attending nurse or psychologist.

Once in court the witness must undergo what can be a highly charged experience of seeing the accused and being present in the same room. For some this can be liberating – for example *'I didn't realise he was so small – at the time he seemed so big and powerful.'* For others it can be terrifying – to be in the same room means *'he can reach over and grab me, I can't possibly be safe.'* For many, however, the proceedings keep them focused and engaged in the task, and strong emotions will emerge later, when the same level of support network is no longer available.

The next hurdle is the recall of particularly traumatic memories. No matter how much care is taken to conduct proceedings with sensitivity, the fact remains that witnesses can be required to offer comprehensive and meticulous accounts of terrifying and humiliating events. In the months and years following such events, individuals have found ways to tolerate the recollection of these atrocities. Some of these ways include denial. As is often the case with missing persons, there is a refusal to accept that they will never return, and a staunch belief that they are 'out there somewhere', despite strong evidence to the contrary. There is also a conscious blocking out of the events and refusal to admit or talk about the experiences. The process of testifying systematically probes this veiled territory, unwittingly unravelling carefully constructed defences. Disclosure is an extremely precarious procedure, and can leave the victim exposed and defenceless.

Potentially the most exigent experience is that of cross-examination. Here is another example of how assurances to *facilitate the testimony of a traumatised person,* are in fact at cross-purposes with standard, and it can be argued, necessary court procedure. It is certainly in the interests of the defence to be, at best, meticulous in ensuring the information offered is accurate, and at worst, to cast doubt on the validity or legitimacy of the testimony, or even to question the integrity of the witness. The way in which this is accomplished may be less overtly aggressive or assertive when dealing with vulnerable witnesses, but the aims can be achieved nevertheless. Witnesses can be tremendously shaken by the process of cross-questioning, and left with the sense that no one believes their story. Once more it is up to the support staff to guide witnesses with information and feedback that may be helpful in mitigating the effects of cross-examination.

Post-trial phase

In an immediate post-trial stage, there is often a sense of euphoria. Witnesses have gone through an ordeal that many never imagined they could manage. There is a feel-ing of pride and accomplishment, and for some, happily, a sense of finality and closure. The heightened arousal is both emotional and physical – and is followed by exhaustion, the sustained stress having taken its toll.

This is an important moment of intervention by the support staff. Ideally they need to be available to take care of the potential fall-out from this emotional roller-coaster. More than that, they must undertake to help individuals integrate these experiences in a meaningful way. The way in which individuals navigate this process depends largely on whether or not their expectations have been met. Although there are a host of different private agendas, the following are the most common motives for testifying, namely, to speak for the dead; to tell the world the truth about what happened; to seek justice; and in the hope such crimes will not happen again.

Many victims experience some degree of 'survivor guilt' and feel one way to redeem themselves is to speak for the dead. For some this is symbolic, for others it is literally to appease the voices that are clamouring inside their head. The fact of giving evidence that leads to a conviction will go a considerable way to achieving this goal.

Ideally, witnessing may be the opportunity to tell the world the truth about what happened. Unfortunately, this often does not happen. The witness is there to give information that is required by the court. Lawyers may place great emphasis on some 'irrelevant' information – such as whether the witness sighted the accused on a particular day in a particular place – and prevent her from telling what actually occurred in that place. The courtroom is not a platform for the victim to tell her story, and being denied this can (re)create anger and disillusion.

Seeking justice is also a tenuous hope. This depends on whether or not the accused is convicted, what his sentence is, and what the victim feels his sentence should be, which is naturally highly subjective. Victims are often thoroughly distraught by sentences they perceive as light assuming there is any sentencing at all. To have endured so much, and to see the perpetrator getting off lightly is a heavy burden to bear, and makes moving forward very difficult.

To testify in the hope that such crimes will not happen again is a motivation that does not require any immediate feedback or 'proof'. Individuals who feel they have done something positive, are more likely to be able to move forward with a greater sense of optimism. Support staff have the substantial task of helping to establish a link between what is now over, belonging to the past and what the future holds. Unfortunately the opportunity to do so relies entirely on the amount of time available before the witness returns home, and on the number of new witnesses arriving and requiring attention (usually several groups arriving per week). The average witness can reasonably expect half an hour for such a 'debriefing'. While such a cursory intervention may offer useful food for thought for some, it cannot possibly hope to meet the needs of those who have found the process gruelling and struggle with how to move forward. If the ICTY is expected to provide thorough support for such vulnerable witnesses, there should be sufficient staff to do so. At present this is not the case.

The guarantee of protection and support weakens steadily as victims leave The Hague. The scrupulous and sophisticated protection measures during trial mask their identity to persons in the public gallery – an unlikely source of potential danger. Real risks of retribution or revenge are liable to take place in their hometowns. The absence of a person or persons from a village for the duration of a week precisely coinciding with the trial of a known war criminal makes their identity as witnesses common knowledge – particularly in close-knit communities. Here they can be exposed to acts of violence or harassment, and it is left to local police to respond. Unless witnesses can prove their lives are in danger, the ICTY does not intercede in any way. To date there are no records of witnesses actually being killed - unlike in Luanda, Angola where it is established that some genocide survivors were killed every week in an attempt to undermine the justice system.

Notably there is a considerable difference between what the protection unit considers mortal danger, and what witnesses perceive as such. For someone who has experienced torture and humiliation, stone throwing and verbal abuse can be a terrifying reminder and a life threatening experience. In fact, many of those indicted still wander around freely in the territories they claimed, confident their authorities will not attempt to find them and hand them over. Under these circumstances, victims require not only a guarantee of protection (whether it is from local police or ICTY protection unit), but also support for their emotional and physical needs. When responding to those who have returned, a further issue is raised - should those who have experienced sexual abuse and have been sought out to be witnesses for the ICTY receive support over and above victims of abuse who have not been summoned for the ICTY? Will such support alienate them from other members of the community?

Alongside the issue of protection is the impact that witnessing may have in the long-term. There are certainly those who experience negative consequences, and struggle to cope. The Victim and Witnesses Unit is currently establishing a network of organisations throughout the region that can provide more accessible, continuing assistance. In the context of a post-conflict setting, local institutions are quite often simply not equipped to deal with the problems faced by witnesses. The establishment of this network is in its very early stages, and time will tell as to whether this offers a satisfactory solution to the ongoing support of victims. The ICTY Rules of Procedure and Evidence are not particularly clear, perhaps intentionally, as to how and for how long witnesses will be protected and supported after their return home. It is clear, however, that resources necessary for any form of follow-up (considered desirable by those who are involved in the actual process of supporting victims) are simply not available.

Sexual Exploitation of Women and Girls by Peacekeepers: How to Curb the Dark Side of Peacekeeping

Abuse of human rights of local women, exploitation of prostitutes, both women and young girls – often based on the argument that such trade puts money in the pockets of the needy – can readily sap a mission's credibility. In addition, the belief by the population that peace personnel are corrupting or 'taking' local women can lead directly to their personal insecurity. In its most extreme form such behaviour can create an environment of impunity, a fear of harassment and assault and fear of those who came to bring peace.

Swedish National Defence College,
*Challenges of Peace Operations:
Into the 21ˢᵗ Century*, Concluding Report, 2002

The alarming news of the complicity of UN peacekeepers in sexual exploitation of women and girls in the recent years have led to co-ordinated efforts in the UN to respond adequately to the abuse. Several means have been implemented through increasing consciousness on gender issues by gender training, transparency and accountability, codes of conduct and the establishment of committees in charge of the elimination and prevention of sexual exploitation by humanitarian agents. An important revelation that placed these disturbing events on the international agenda was the release of the report entitled 'Sexual Violence and Exploitation: The Experience of Refugee Children in Liberia, Guinea and Sierra Leone' in February 2002 prepared by UN High Commissioner for Refugees and the British non-governmental organisation Save the Children. The report highlights cases of sexual abuse of women and children by humanitarian aid workers and individuals in positions of power. As such, it provoked an international outcry sparking a reaction in the international community to tackle the problem.

Sexual abuse of women and girls[10] by internationals who has come to provide humanitarian aid to war-torn regions is rooted in traditional attitudes both from the international community and local authorities. Furthermore, it is a consequence of everyday life with predominantly male troops concentrated in regions where recent wars have lead to a disintegration of traditional values. Due to high salaries in comparison to that of the local population, peacekeepers become a source of demand that fuels markets of trafficked persons in brothels and domestic labour. In numerous programmes dealing with trafficking in human beings, the problem of peacekeepers as an indirect and sometimes even a direct source of crime has been recognised. As indirect sources, local criminal circles use their expertise gained in trafficking drugs and arms to organise well controlled networks of trafficking women and girls for brothels targeting peacekeepers as clients. Methods used to confine women in Kosovo brothels do not differ very much from those used in the camps in the Bosnian war. It has been established that many Kosovo brothels were already opened before the arrival of the first peacekeepers, and that the criminal organisations behind the 'business' made use of the experience gained during IFOR and SFOR missions in Bosnia and Herzegovina.[11] As direct sources, in some cases peacekeepers have been implicated in trafficking through transporting victims and providing support to the contractors, as observed in peacekeeping missions in Bosnia and Herzegovina (SFOR), Kosovo (KFOR), Afghanistan (ISAF), East Timor (UNMISET), Sierra Leone (UNAMSIL), Democratic Republic of Congo (MONUC) and Ethiopia and Eritrea (UNMEE).

Gender training

The necessity of creating a level of awareness of the problem of sexual exploitation among peacekeepers and internationals have been advanced many times in UN and NGO studies.[12] One of the methods to achieve this goal is through a gender and culture-sensitive training, which needs to be taught to peacekeepers with the aim of making them aware of the cultural environment in the host country. This responsibility falls on different actors who each have an important role to play in different stages of the operation. First, as military and civilian peacekeepers are provided by various states, their training is primarily the prerogative of military and civilian departments of those states. Second, during the deployment of peacekeepers, the UN Department for Peacekeeping Operations (DPKO) takes charge of their training. In 2000, the DPKO Training and Evaluation Service developed a training module called 'Gender and Peacekeeping', adapted from the training package 'Gender and Peace Support Operations' produced by the Canadian Department of Foreign Affairs and International Trade (DFAIT) and the United Kingdom Department for International Development (DFID). The training module was tested in UNTAET, MONUC,

UNAMSIL and in UNMEE where it is now a compulsory part of the induction course for new peacekeepers who arrive in the mission. Furthermore, DPKO is developing a gender and peacekeeping field manual that would support the implementation of DPKO gender mainstreaming in peace support operations. It particularly provides middle military management with a set of tools for integrating a gender perspective in their daily activities. This manual would target mainly battalion commanders, military observers and staff officers and it will also be adjusted to be used by international civilian police and other staff in the mission.

These programmes compose materials developed by the DPKO for peacekeepers who are deployed in mission areas. However, in a latest development the importance of training prior to deployment has been emphasised. The DPKO is about to conduct pre-deployment training for peacekeepers who will be sent to the new peacekeeping mission in Liberia. For the first time, gender will be integrated into the pre-deployment training as part of a curriculum that encompasses other relevant skills needed for the mission. This initiative needs to be institutionalised and duplicated for other missions.

Finally, gender training does not solve all problems, but it ensures that common principles are internalised by all

© Keystone, EPA-Photo, EPA, Stephen Morrison, 2003

Peacekeeping troops and civilian staff serving in the Democratic Republic of Congo have been accused of rape and sexual exploitation of women and children. The UN faces one of the world's most neglected humanitarian violations and promises to act upon it.

involved. It further opens doors for a better understanding of the local reality in the mission countries. An essential factor for the success of gender training is its openness to a mixed audience of women and men including not only civilian police and military observers from the mission, but also representatives of the local population. The combination of actors brings an added-value as it triggers discussions on the differential impact of conflicts on women and men especially in the context of the host country. This lesson learned is highlighted by a Swedish project, which gathered together 230 organisations – think tanks, international organisations and NGOs from 50 countries in international seminars regarding peace support operations during five years starting in 1999. The conclusion of their report 'Challenges of Peace Operations: Into the 21st Century' produced in 2002 stressed the potential of training sessions in generating mutual trust between peacekeepers and the host country. It stated that *the outcome has been not only shared information, and a mutual appreciation of roles and responsibilities between the population and the military, but the beginning of the development of that essential trust between peacekeeper and civil society in the mission area.'*[13]

Codes of conduct

Another method used in preventing sexual exploitation of women and girls by peacekeepers is through the elaboration of codes of conduct. All UN staff including civilians, military and police, serving in a peace support operation are bound by UN rules and codes of conduct ensuring high standards of integrity and respect for the human rights of each and every person. The UN Charter under Art. 101 §3 underlines the criteria of integrity of its staff, which is reiterated in the UN Staff Regulations and Rules for civilian staff and Standards of Conduct for the International Civil Service adopted in 2001.[14] For peacekeepers, civilian and

© ICRC, Nick Danziger, 2001

Aminata still suffers from physical violence that she had to endure during the war in Sierra Leone.

military alike, the DPKO released the Guidelines and the Ten Rules of Code of Personal Conduct for Blue Helmets in 1997. The latter particularly prohibits *'indulging in immoral acts of sexual, physical or psychological abuse or exploitation of the local population or United Nations staff, especially women and children.'*[15] The DPKO also produced a UN Peacekeeping Handbook for Junior Ranks in 1997 wherein special conduct regarding gender issues were stipulated such as respect for human rights of women and children.

However, these UN codes of conduct and guidelines have limited authority in that they fall short of legal documents. The UN should have more room for applying sanctions than it currently has. As stipulated in the 1946 Convention on the Privileges and Rights of the United Nations, the status-of-forces agreements between the UN and the host country and the memorandum of understanding between the UN and the contributing state, UN staff benefit from immunities and privileges from legal processes and in case of a crime committed by a military peacekeeper, exclusive jurisdiction is granted to the contributing state. In cases of misconduct by military peacekeepers, the UN carry out investigations at mission level and sanctions can be applied by the force commander through internal disciplinary measures such as fines, detention and repatriation. The UN does not have authority to conduct criminal proceedings, as military peacekeepers are only accountable to their countries of origin. In many cases these countries have failed to prosecute where the conduct of their military officers were questioned. This highlights an important gap namely that in cases of criminal conduct, the importance of a balance between prevention strategies and legal redress is crucial. As stressed by Catherine Galenkamp in her report, *'all prevention and response initiatives must be balanced. Providing prevention in the form of training and awareness raising on sexual exploitation and abuse for beneficiaries without providing response methods for recourse and support systems, is as harmful as providing no systems at all.'*[16] In an attempt to bridge this lack of accountability field missions have responded in various ways. For instance, following reports of allegations of sexual abuse, the peacekeeping mission in Sierra Leone carried out its own investigation and strengthened existing preventive measures and training. In addition, it established the UNAMSIL Personnel Conduct Committee (UPCC), which receives allegations of misconduct by civilian and military peacekeepers and recommends investigations of reported cases. The mission further implements awareness programmes on the Code of Conduct for UN personnel, as well as training on child protection for incoming peacekeepers.

In parallel, some solutions have been advanced by the UN, which reflect a need to build bridges between peacekeepers and the local population to ensure that men and women of the host country have channels to communicate their concerns to the mission. For example, the DPKO has made the following recommendation of including community relations officers in peacekeeping missions whose duties would incorporate receiving grievances from the local population.[17] This idea is echoed in UNIFEM Independent Experts' Assessment that calls for the establishment of an ombudsperson in peacekeeping missions who would address cases of abuse by peacekeepers. However, to date, these recommendations have not been followed by action. Accountability and gender justice depends greatly on a gender sensitive leadership, which should create and promote a culture of gender awareness in the mission and show a determination in fighting against impunity. This factor has been highlighted in different international fora. In the NGO arena, the report of International Alert in 2002 stressed that a *'gender aware leadership is dependent on a person or persons in high-ranking decision-making positions, strategies and interventions.'*[18] A year after the UN Secretary-General officially underlined the issue of accountability of managers in the Bulletin on Special Measures for Protection from Sexual Exploitation and Sexual Abuse issued on 9 October 2003, which apply to all UN staff. He stated that *'the Head of Department, Office or Mission, as appropriate, shall be responsible for creating and maintaining an environment that prevents sexual exploitation and sexual abuse, and shall take appropriate measures for this purpose.'*[19]

Special committees

A last method used in responding to sexual violence by peacekeepers is through the examination by the international community of the responsibility of humanitarian institutions. Incidents of sexual abuse and exploitation by the humanitarian community reveal the failure of the responsible actors and institutions involved whose main work is to secure the protection and well-being of the society in need. A report from the UN Office for the Co-ordination of Humanitarian Affairs (OCHA) by Catherine Galenkamp revealed the range of humanitarian workers involved and the means they employed such as the trade of humanitarian goods for sexual services. She stated that *'much of the sexual abuse was perpetrated using the same goods and services meant for the beneficiaries as a means for bartering for sexual access. Employees from all levels working in all sectors of humanitarian aid were implicated, from NGO drivers, to child-care workers, to distribution staff. UN peacekeepers were accused of using money or food to procure sex from women and particularly underage children.'*[20] The humanitarian community responded to this failure by setting up a number of special co-ordination committees in charge of eradicating and preventing sexual exploitation by humanitarian workers.

The Inter-Agency Standing Committee Working Group, a humanitarian co-ordination body of the UN including other humanitarian organisations and NGOs,[21] established in March 2002 the Task Force on Protection from Sexual Exploitation and Abuse in Humanitarian Crises. It is mandated to '*make recommendations aiming to eliminate sexual abuse and exploitation by humanitarian personnel and the misuse of humanitarian assistance, within the overall objective of strengthening and enhancing the protection of and care of children and women in situations of humanitarian crisis and conflict.*' [22] Among the main areas of concern, the task force identified the need to establish a mechanism for protection against sexual abuse, as well as issues of gender and accountability.

In Sierra Leone, a Co-ordination Committee for Sexual Exploitation and Abuse was created in 2002 under the leadership of UN OCHA. The committee is an inter-agency body whose aim it is to examine methods of prevention of sexual abuse and the means for adequate response. In August 2002, a consultant was hired to work out of UN OCHA in Freetown as a co-ordinator of abuse and exploitation prevention. In the United Nations Interim Administration Mission in Kosovo (UNMIK), Regulation 2001/4 on the 'Prohibition of Trafficking in Persons in Kosovo' defines trafficking and related activities as criminal offences. Hence, any individual who knowingly asks a victim of trafficking for sexual services can be sentenced to jail from three months to five years; if the person providing sexual services is under eighteen, the penalty for the offender can be ten years of imprisonment. In October 2000, UNMIK police established five regional units that were tasked with gathering information on trafficking cases, thus facilitating the collection of evidence for prosecution in court.

Similarly, the UN Mission in Bosnia and Herzegovina (UNMIBH), particularly affected by this problem, established in 2001a 'Special Trafficking Operations Programme', called STOP, with the aim of addressing the growing number of reported cases of trafficking in women. The responsibilities of the STOP teams included, updating lists of suspected locations of trafficking victims; monitoring raids and inspections by local police; interviewing possible victims of trafficking to identify their status and provide assistance on their request. The European Union Police Mission took over the programme from UNMIBH when its mandate ended in December 2002.

The international community has elaborated multifaceted strategies to prevent and combat sexual violence and exploitation of women and girls by peacekeepers, underlining an international commitment for its eradication. The elaboration of codes of conduct, gender training in all phases of the mission and special committees monitoring abuse of women and girls have all been important initiatives in the struggle. Yet, many gaps remain. For example, the assessment of codes of conduct, the accountability of military peacekeepers under the sole jurisdiction of contributing states unwilling or incapable to provide justice, and the responsibility and implementation of training by all relevant actors.

Endnotes

1 The People on War survey was carried out in 1999 to mark the 50th Anniversary of the 1949 Geneva Conventions. The ICRC launched a consultation in seventeen countries, twelve of which had been or were at war, giving the general public the chance to express their opinions on war.

2 The confusion may stem in part from the lack of an unequivocal, widely accepted definition of 'method of warfare' in international law: see Major E. Harper, 'A Call for a Definition of Method of Warfare in Relation to the Chemical Weapons Convention', *Naval Law Review*, XLVIII (2001), 132.

3 C. Lindsey, *Women Facing War: ICRC Study on the Impact of Armed Conflict on Women* (Geneva: ICRC, 2001), 56.

4 For information on associations dealing with raped victims during armed conflict see 'Women and war', 'Sexual violence and armed conflict' and 'Gender justice' in the list of organisations dealing with women's rights in this volume.

5 Chetniks (āetnici) were members of a Serbian nationalist militia force, originally formed to fight against the Ottoman Empire. During the Second World War they became noted for their cruelty towards civilians while retaliating crimes committed against the Serbian population. During the Yugoslav Wars in 1991-95 some of Serbian armed forces boasted Chetnik insignia and committed crimes against non-Serbians, including ethnic cleansing and rape.

6 To ostracise a person means to avoid him/her intentionally or to prevent the person in taking part in activities of a group.

7 J. E. Giller, P. J. Bracken, & S. Kabaganda, *War, Women and Rape* (London: The Lancet Publishing Group, 1991), 337, 604.

8 Ten per cent of victims live in Serbia and Montenegro and six per cent in Croatia. The remaining 25 per cent are from countries outside the region.

9 Rule 75 of the ICTY Rules of Procedure and Evidence.

10 Although it is true that boys are also vulnerable to sexual exploitation and abuse, as seen in the context of Western Africa highlighted in the UNHCR/Save the Children's report.

11 J. Picarelli, 'Trafficking, Slavery and Peacekeeping: The Need for Comprehensive Training Program', *A Conference Report* (Turin: UNICRI and TraCCC, 2002), at http://www.unicri.it/TraCCCpercent20docs/Program.doc

12 For instance, in Amnesty International's 15-point program for Implementing Human Rights, the 'gender dimension' was included as point 12: *'Measures should be taken to guarantee consideration and respect for the particular needs of women in armed conflict situations. Peacekeeping personnel should receive information on local traditions and should respect the inherent rights and dignity of women at all times. Human rights components should include experts in the area of violence against women, including rape and sexual abuse'.*

13 Swedish National Defence College, *Challenges of Peace Operations: Into the 21st Century, Concluding Report 1997-2002* (Stockholm: Swedish National Defence College, 2002), 139.

14 The latter document replaced the 1954 'Report on Standards of Conduct in the International Civil Service' by the International Civil Service Advisory Board.

15 UN DPKO, *Ten Rules of Code of Personal Conduct for Blue Helmets*, Rule No. 4, at http://www.genderandpeacekeeping.org/resources/5_UN_Codes_of_Conduct.pdf

16 C. Galenkamp, *Protection from Sexual Exploitation and Abuse: Lessons Learned from Sierra Leone* (New York: OCHA, 2003), 9.

17 UN DPKO Lessons Learnt Unit, *Mainstreaming a Gender Perspective in Multidimensional Peace Operations* (New York: United Nations, July 2000), 16.

18 International Alert, *Annual Review 2002/2003* (London, 2003), 35, at http://www.international-alert.org/pdf/pubIA/annual_review_2002.pdf

19 United Nations, 'Special Measures for Protection from Sexual Exploitation and Sexual Abuse', *Secretary-General's Bulletin*, UN Document ST/SGB/2003/13 (New York, 9 October 2003), 2.

20 Galenkamp, *Protection from Sexual Exploitation and Abuse*, 9.

21 The IASC brings together UN organisations, the International Federation of Red Cross and Red Crescent Societies (IFRC), as well as three consortia of major NGOs, its mandate is to ensure a co-ordinated humanitarian response.

22 Inter-Agency Standing Committee Working Group, *IASC Task Force on Protection from Sexual Exploitation and Abuse in Humanitarian Crises: Report on the Activities of the Task Force*, 53rd Meeting (8-9 July 2003), 1.

Chapter 3

Torture of Women during Armed Conflicts

'At the end of June 2003, in the Saio district of Bunia, Ituri province, Democratic Republic of the Congo, a 45-year-old woman and her thirteen-year-old daughter were woken from sleep by a group of young militiamen who forced their way into the house. Once inside, they looted and destroyed property and accused the mother and daughter of hiding rival combatants. They then attempted to abduct the daughter. When the mother tried to intervene, both she and her daughter were brutally raped side-by-side by two of the militiamen.'

Amnesty International, Violence against Women in Armed Conflict, 2004

Over the span of many centuries, torture was widely practised and accepted. For over more than fifty years, the struggle against torture has been a central theme in the policies of the international community. Today, while it is unfortunately still a reality worldwide, torture is deemed, however, to be completely unacceptable and is regarded as an international crime. Torture is absolutely prohibited by international law, both customary and treaty law, including international legal instruments and regional treaties, and by many national constitutions.

The definition of torture most widely accepted is found in the United Nations Convention against Torture and Other Cruel, Degrading or Inhuman Treatment or Punishment, which is the most comprehensive international instrument prohibiting torture, laying down obligations for states parties. Torture, according to the Convention, is:

- An act of severe pain or suffering, physical or mental;
- That is intentionally inflicted on a person;

- For purposes such as obtaining confessions, punishment, intimidation or coercion, or any reason based on any kind of discrimination;
- Inflicted directly or condoned or tolerated by a public official or any person acting in an official capacity.[1]

The legal obligations in the absolute prohibition of torture can be found in convergence in both international human rights law (IHRL) and international humanitarian law (IHL). Other international legal regimes such as international criminal law and international refugee law reinforce this prohibition. In addition to the prohibition of torture, both IHRL and IHL provide specific obligations that aim to prevent the occurrence of torture, to repress the crime of torture and to provide redress for the victims of torture. These other specific obligations apply to states parties to the treaties and likewise to occupying forces and rebel groups within the context of armed conflict. The prohibition of torture has evolved into a peremptory norm of international law (*jus cogens*) that enjoys the highest legal rank and therefore prevails over international treaty and customary law and other laws.[2] As a consequence, the prohibition of torture is a non-derogable status prescribing that the act of torture cannot be justified under any circumstances or at any time, in both times of peace and of war. The protection of persons from torture, is a fundamental guarantee that states and, in the case of armed conflict, non-state actors such as rebel groups, are obliged to respect absolutely. No state or non-state actor may authorise, tolerate or condone torture, even in the most exceptional circumstances, including a state or a threat of war, the fight against terrorism, political instability or any public emergency.

The categorisation of an act as torture according to its definitional elements is important in order to distinguish torture from other acts such as cruel, inhuman or degrading treatment or punishment (so-called 'ill-treatment'). The distinction is necessary for purposes of establishing legal jurisdictions, especially where universal jurisdiction is being applied, as well as, specific state obligations on repression of the crime and reparations for the victims. However, the recognition of certain acts as amounting to torture has evolved over time as values emerge and as awareness is raised among policy makers and the public. This is particularly the situation with regard to borderline cases such as disappearances when it comes to the suffering of the relatives left behind, usually women. Moreover, rape and other gender-based violence are now accepted as acts that may amount to torture, and war crimes or crimes against humanity.

The degree of the suffering of the victim is an essential element distinguishing torture from ill-treatment. Some acts, such as conditions of detention, may qualify only in relation to other factors, for example, duration of time. However, given its subjective nature, the experience and degree of suffering may also depend on the personal characteristics of the torture victim, including gender and age, and conditions of vulnerability. The culture of the victim and specific contexts, such as armed conflict, may also be important factors in assessing whether the gravity of an act amounts to torture.

The purposive element in the definition of torture has attracted much attention in the consideration of torture based on gender. Much of the reason for the previous neglect of gender-based torture was the principal focus on the more 'traditional' purposes for torture that is obtaining confessions, punishment and intimidation or coercion, within a political context. The definition of torture, however, provides that it may also be perpetrated for any reason based on discrimination of any kind. In far-reaching international legal developments, the International Criminal Tribunals for former Yugoslavia and for Rwanda have developed a body of case law that underscores gender discrimination as relevant to the definition of torture and pronounces gender-based torture as one of its many forms. The Rome Statute establishing the International Criminal Court in 2002 has also contributed to these developments by recognising rape and other gender-based violence as constituting war crimes and crimes against humanity, including torture.

The prevention of torture assumes great importance because the harmful consequences of torture inflicted on the victim are irreparable. A distinct measure for torture prevention is for states, and non-state actors where applicable, to receive visits to places of detention by independent bodies such as the International Committee of the Red Cross, UN and other inter-governmental agencies, experts and even non-governmental organisations. These visits, as conducted by impartial and independent bodies, help to break down the isolation of the detainees from the rest of the world, to reinforce their protection from torture and ill-treatment and to eliminate the anonymity of detainees and the custodial officers.

The obligation to repress the act of torture lies not only in respecting the absolute prohibition of torture, but also in putting in place measures to ensure that such acts are punished if committed. States are obliged to search for persons alleged to have committed prohibited acts such as torture, to investigate, prosecute and punish them. Moreover, a

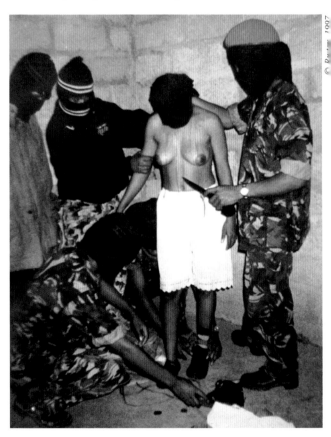

Above is a controversial photograph allegedly showing Indonesian soldiers torturing a Timorese woman, released by the Australia-East Timor Association. The photo was taken shortly after the East Timorese bishop Carlos Belo and exiled Timorese leader Jose Ramos Horta were jointly awarded the year 1996 Nobel peace prize.

state could be obliged to investigate, prosecute and punish a perpetrator of an act of torture in its own territory, even if the act of torture was committed elsewhere, under the principle of universal jurisdiction. Inversely, a state may be obliged to extradite an alleged perpetrator of an act of torture for prosecution in another state.

The obligation to provide reparation to victims has become of increasing significance as victims gain more confidence in telling their stories and in asserting their rights. If states fail to prevent or respond to violations of IHRL and IHL by repressing them, they are legally responsible for the act and its consequences. The forms of reparation may cover a wide range of measures such as compensation, restitution, rehabilitation, satisfaction and guarantees of non-repetition including public acknowledgement. With gender-based torture, especially rape, several decisions in the ICTY, as well as, in the European Court of Human Rights have recognised the gravity of the offence and the particular effects on the victims.

In spite of all this legal protection torture of women has increased in both quantity and gravity, both inside and outside the home, during armed conflict or during an escalation of hostilities. The main view throughout history that women are 'spoils of war' has consistently fuelled this vulnerability and has permitted the ensuing reluctance of authorities to take claims of violence seriously. Mass rape has even been viewed as part of military strategy. In innumerable cases of mutilation that accompany these acts, breasts were cut off, as in Liberia, while the women were forced to eat the lips, ears and noses that were cut off, as in Uganda. In short, in armed conflicts women are treated as non-humans. All of these patterns aim to reinforce the subordinate status of women in a society where women are not in the control of their destinies and their own bodies. This is illustrated by the use of rape and sexual slavery, as recorded in armed conflicts throughout history and until present times, either as a component of a widespread pattern or as individual cases. Now regarded as gender-based torture, these acts consist of some of the most ultimate forms of the subordination and control of women.

To reconsider gender-based torture according to its international legal definition gives a good illustration of the obstacles existing in the sphere of legal protection. The interpretation of the definition of torture, for example, has been much too biased in favour of other purposive elements, leaving on the wayside torture committed on the basis of discrimination. Documentation of cases of torture has, therefore, mainly focused on cases involving the extraction of confessions, for example, but did not include cases of torture based on discrimination of gender. Within the last decade, however, some efforts have been made to consciously document gender-based torture, since in recent international legal developments,

the interpretation of gender-discrimination as the basis for crimes of torture has been expounded on, including for purposes of persecution and humiliation.

Practically all forms of violence against women, be it rape and sexual assault, domestic violence, harassment and the like, are usually perceived to be within the 'private sphere' of society and are thus not part of the public domain. The link between these acts of violence against women and 'honour and chastity' intensifies this perception and mutely encourages the identification of victims as dishonoured and unchaste, thus discouraging revelation. Even protective legal instruments, such as the Geneva Conventions, identify acts of rape as crimes against 'honour'. Again, recent legal discourse has only started to disrupt this deceptive connection.

Moreover, although one of the 'traditional' purposes of torture is intimidation or harassment, this is all too often ignored or minimised because of the issue of consent, a perspective that inevitably works in favour of the perpetrator rather than of the victim. The prevalence of this attitude is linked to the false societal assumption that the victims may have had a part in the commission of the crimes. As one writer commented: *'Nobody asks a male torture victim whether he has consented to torture, but the issue of consent is always present when a women wants to reveal that she has been sexually abused.'*[3] It is only in cases of arbitrary detention where this assumption is usually not considered. This societal assumption of consent on the part of the woman explains why many victims retain feelings of guilt for the acts of violence perpetrated against them. Thus, the assertion that extreme forms of gender-based violence, such as rape and sexual slavery, could amount to torture, has only been recently understood. Among the many reasons for this is not only the heightened voice of the women's human rights movement and the victims, but also the official acknowledgement of the high costs of violence against women to society and to the women themselves. However, the journey for the full disclosure of the nature, circumstances and consequences of gender-based torture has only just begun.

Arbitrary detention of women during armed conflicts

The plight of women deprived of their liberty during wartime should not be overlooked simply because they are fewer in number in comparison to men. Of the women who are deprived of their liberty, very few are captured combatants. This is a reflection of the fact that women constitute a minority in the armed forces or in armed groups and that where women are enlisted they may not be allowed to operate in combat or on the front lines, hence they are less likely to be captured. The number of women held for other reasons than having been captured as combatants in armed conflict and internal strife - civilian internees, for example - is again small in comparison to men. This is due to several general factors - male civilians are far more likely to be perceived as combatants or potential combatants, and consequently to be detained or interned, than female civilians. Women may be less exposed to this sort of risk than men and, therefore, less likely to be detained.

Arbitrary detention could take the form of abduction, disappearance, slavery or continued detention without any legal basis. Arbitrary detention may be the starting point for many other atrocities, including torture and other forms of ill-treatment. The places of detention where women are kept may vary including 'safe houses', concentration camps, hospitals, prisons, football stadiums, school houses, and any other place of detention, official or unofficial, that may simply be available. Within this ambit, the vulnerability of women is increased manifold. In addition to the blatant injustice of the deprivation of liberty, the existence of unequal power relations between the captor and the person deprived of liberty, as well as, the patriarchal structure and values, force the latter into a subordinate status without any control of her destiny. Without the captor's respect and the implementation of the legal norms that are meant to protect persons deprived of liberty, the captive is at the total mercy and disposal of the captor. Without preventive safeguards in place, the abuse of this power is more or less guaranteed, resulting in a pattern of violations and abuses.

Women can be held as hostages against ransom, the surrender of family members or the release of persons from the enemy side. Women in arbitrary detention are more likely to undertake forced labour such as cooking, washing and menial tasks. Examples of forced labour have been cited from armed conflict situations in Uganda and Liberia during the 1990s. Forced labour cases have also been documented in Burma where women are kept for economic purposes. Women can also be held in arbitrary detention for alleged security reasons and can, therefore, be held as mere detainees or internees waiting for displacement or return. However, such cases of internment very rarely happen without the accompanying abuses. Aside from gender-based violence, women can also experience other types of atrocities such as beatings, being tied-up, strip-searches, and lock-ups. Some forms of detention may actually amount to sexual slavery. All of these take place within the legal ambit of 'arbitrary detention' from which women can only either escape, pay ransom for or be released at the behest of the powers keeping them, sometimes at the approach of impending defeat.

International humanitarian law clearly states that it is the responsibility of the detaining authorities to provide adequate material conditions such as food, water, sanitary and hygiene facilities, appropriate accommodation and clothing, adequate health and medical care. It is important to ascertain whether the places of detention are providing appropriate accommodation and material conditions of detention for pregnant women and nursing mothers, and whether these women face particular problems relating to their place of detention. For example, pregnant women and nursing mothers require a supplementary diet sufficient to maintain their own health and that of their babies.

In addition, women deprived of their liberty must have the possibility of maintaining regular contact with family members and of receiving regular family visits that respect both their privacy and dignity. International humanitarian law further provides that persons deprived of their liberty must be able to exercise their religious duties and religious practices.[4]

Endnotes

[1] *United Nations Convention against Torture and Other Cruel, Inhuman or Degrading Treatment or Punishment* (1984), Article 1.

[2] *Jus cogens* relates to the peremptory rules, which may not be altered by contracting parties. In international law, the topic is dealt with under Article 53 of the Vienna Convention on the Law of Treaties (1969), which states that *'a treaty is void of, at the time of its conclusion, if it conflicts with a peremptory norm of general international law'.* For the purposes of the present Convention, a peremptory norm of general international law is a norm accepted and recognised by the international community of states as a norm from which no derogation is permitted and which can be modified only by a subsequent norm of general law having the same character.

[3] L. T. Arcel, *Torture, Cruel, Inhuman and Degrading Treatment of Women: Psychological Consequences,* Paper presented at the International Symposium on Human Rights Protection and Anti-Torture in the 21st Century (Beijing, 26 June 2001).

[4] In situations of international armed conflicts, Articles 34–7, *Third Geneva Convention* and Articles 86 and 93, *Fourth Geneva Convention.* In relation to non-international armed conflicts, Article 5(1)(d), *Additional Protocol II.* In situations of non-international armed conflict, Article 4(1), *Additional Protocol II.*

Chapter 4

Female Combatants: Dilution of Gender Barriers in Times of War

'The qualities that are most important in all military jobs – things like integrity, moral courage, and determination – have nothing to do with gender.'

Etched on a glass panel on the upper terrace of the Women in Military Service for America Memorial in Washington, D.C.

In armed conflicts stereotypes of gender roles become more evident since men are expected to enter the armed forces, while women are supposed to provide for the non-fighting members of the family and for soldiers – whether it means to treat the wounded, or to take care of men's needs (including sexual ones). Briefly stated, men are soldiers while women are nurses, food and various service providers. As concerns atrocities men are stereotypically seen as aggressors and perpetrators of violence, while women are defenceless and passive victims. Consequently, men are bearers of nationalist and warmongering ideologies; women are peace advocates and peace negotiators. These gender norms – socially constructed and often manipulated by political ideologies – shape the behaviour of men and women to the needs of the war system. However, these gender roles can be exchangeable under the pressure of extreme circumstances. In many countries during the Second World War, women worked in munitions factories, support units or as joint reservist and many took part in the fighting as members of frontline units.[1] Since then, women are more and more frequently joining the armed forces, voluntarily and involuntarily, performing both support and combatant roles. Women have proven to be capable of actively supporting aggressive ideologies such as the Nazi parties before and during the Second World War, the communist parties in the Eastern Bloc during the Cold War, and nationalist movements after the disintegration of Tito's Yugoslavia. In the 1970s it was mostly Chilean middle-class women who gave massive support to Pinochet's regime; during the conflict in Northern Ireland, women were in rallies, mobs and demonstrations on both sides.

Women have been able to serve in oppressive and extermination institutions of totalitarian regimes, such as Nazi camps and Soviet gulags. The most outrageous photos of the recent 'Abu Ghraib scandal' were those of the US servicewomen posing over the naked bodies of Iraqi prisoners of war (see box 4.1). The 'Black Widows' of terrorist groups in Chechnya may be the most recent evidence of the interchangeability of gender roles.

© Keystone, AP Photo, Hasan Sarbakhshian, 2004

Armed veiled basijis, or women volunteers, attend a rally of 100,000 paramilitary forces in a show of strength in the southern suburbs of the Iranian capital Tehran.

There are not many armed forces worldwide where women are totally absent. They can be found in both regular/conventional and paramilitary forces. Especially in guerrilla forces, women are trained in the same way as men, and many of them become active frontline combatants. In addition, they have proved their extraordinary usefulness acting as couriers, spies and reconnaissance soldiers. Rather exceptionally are women promoted to higher commanding positions, prevailingly occupying auxiliary positions in logistics of armed forces, either regular or paramilitary. Most of the women work in medical, information, administrative or logistical jobs. Frequently, when opposition forces are fighting the ruling government, women's participation in 'rebel' forces has been encouraged for propaganda reasons – women combatants serve as a vivid example of the emancipating intentions of future political leaders. However, many of these intentions are often forgotten as corroborated by numerous examples of demobilisation processes in post-conflict situations (see Part III, Chapter 5). The presence of women in the conventional or non-conventional armed forces has never fundamentally changed their social position.[2]

In the 2003 Iraq conflict, about 14 per cent of US military personnel were women, making it the largest deployment of women to a combat theatre to date.[3] In 1975, the Tigrayan People's Liberation Forces (TPLF) were formed to fight for the liberation of Eritrea in Ethiopia, and women joined the army, underwent military training and fought shoulder to shoulder with men. Currently, it is estimated that a fifth of the Eritrean armed forces are women.[4] Women were engaged in the wars in Sierra Leone and in Rwanda, they fought in the guerrilla wars in the Philippines, and they were a part of the elite wing of the Liberation Tigers of Tamil Eelam (LTTE), the so-called the Black Tigers of Sri Lanka. In the Revolutionary Armed Forces of Colombia (FARC), Latin America's largest guerrilla army, women form at least one third of the personnel. Women fight in the opposition armed forces in India (Nagaland), Malaysia, Iraq, Turkey (South-Eastern Anatolia), Kosovo, Indonesia (Aceh), Guatemala, Salvador, Ecuador, and in many African armed conflicts - for instance in Burundi, Sudan, Somalia, and Sierra Leone.

Killing the enemy in combat is a vital element of military professionalism gained during military training, and women soldiers do not differ from men in their capability to learn the skill to kill. Moreover, in armed conflicts women have proved to be capable of the same cruelty and ruthlessness as their male counterparts, for example, in the case of the Rwandan wars, where women – both enlisted and civilians – took an active part in the genocide of the Tutsi in 1994.[5]

Female suicide bombers represent a relatively new and particularly abhorring chapter of women's direct engagement in violence. Generally, suicide attacks are used by small groups of terrorists in countries where relatively effective governments, able to prevent opposition groups taking over power, are present. In the nineties, suicide terrorism spread from Sri Lanka and Lebanon to Croatia, Turkey, Pakistan, Argentina, India, Panama, Algeria, Tanzania and Kenya. According to some experts, suicide terrorism is likely to become the main tool of terrorist groups in future. Currently, notable groups that execute suicide attacks are:

© Keystone FPA Nic Bothma 2003

Female guerrilla soldiers of the rebel group Movement for Democracy in Liberia (MODEL).

Al Qaeda, Tamil Tigers in Sri Lanka, Hamas, Hezbollah in Lebanon, Palestinian Islamic Jihadd, Al Aqsar Martyrs Brigade, Al Ansar Mujahidin in Chechnya, and the Kurdistan Worker's Party of Turkey (PKK).

There are women suicide bombers in the Tamil Tigers, in the Kurdish Workers Party and in the Chechen Al Aqsar Martyrs brigade. Although Palestinian women were fighting against Israelis during the past three decades, the first female suicide bomber appeared only in 2002 when a volunteer paramedic at an ambulance station in Ramallah detonated her explosives in a Jerusalem street, killing an 81-year-old man and injuring 100 other bystanders. The country with the highest frequency of female terrorists is Sri Lanka. Women, according to some estimates, have conducted 30 per cent of all suicide operations, including the assassination of the Indian Prime Minister Rajiv Ghandi in 1991. Recently there have been an increasing number of female suicide bombers in Muslim countries and communities.

In 2002, female bombers appeared within Chechnya's terrorist groups. In the seizure of the Moscow North-East theatre in October 2002, where 129 hostages and 41 Chechen guerrillas were killed, half of the terrorists were women. Additionally, Chechen women have taken part in another five terrorist attacks during the 2002-04 Chechen wars both in Russia and Chechnya. Two female suicide bombers blew themselves up at a rock festival outside Moscow, killing at least fifteen people and injuring more than 50 in October 2003. A 22-year-old woman attempted to enter a fashionable Moscow restaurant with explosives. She was stopped by security personnel, but a military officer died while dismantling the bomb. The so-called 'Black Widows' – Chechen female terrorists – are believed to have been behind the explosions that caused two Russian planes to simultaneously crash in 2004; in September 2004 they have taken part in the outrageous terrorist siege of the school in Beslan in Northern Ossetia, Russia. According to some reports, Chechen women fighting in guerrilla groups have killed almost 200 people and wounded several hundred more.[6]

Increasing deployment of women into terrorist groups can be explained by the fact that they are less suspicious in off-the-battlefield operations requiring infiltration, invisibility and deception. In traditional societies there is a hesitation to strip-search women, and a woman can successfully pretend to be pregnant and wear a suicide device beneath her clothes. Women's motives to join such an extreme form of terrorism may, however, be more complex, ranging from ideological reasons to anguish or revenge motives, and distress or despair reflecting their dismal personal situation all the way to strong societal and political pressure brought to bear on them.

Some of the terrorists who attacked a Moscow theatre in October 2002, were women.

Women in regular forces

Speaking about female combatants, servicewomen in regular forces cannot be omitted, since the numbers of female soldiers deployed to combat operations has been slowly, but steadily growing. There is one substantial difference between female guerrilla and paramilitary combatants and regular forces servicewomen deployed at the front lines. Usually, in guerrilla wars the possibility to deploy women to less dangerous, supportive positions does not exist, and women and men fight shoulder to shoulder even in ground combat, from which regular servicewomen in most armed forces are excluded. Experience from guerrilla armies has showed that women can perform successfully in combat operations, which is not so surprising considering women's participation in the Second World War. At that time many women were serving in non-combatant support arms and services, but some of them took active part in units experiencing front line fighting, for example, women in the Soviet Red Army. However, once the war was over the military reverted to using women primarily in support functions. The armed forces open their gates wide for women in times of war, or when there is a shortage of male recruits. The general processes of citizens' and

Box 4.1: International humanitarian law and Abu Ghraib

Lynndie England, a member of the US Military Police Company in one of the pictures from Abu Ghraib prison in Baghdad that shook the US and the world. She said in her public interview that her superiors gave her specific instructions on how to pose for the photos, which were part of so-called psychological operations.

In 2004 seven American soldiers, among them three service-women, were charged with assaulting Iraqi detainees in the prison of Abu Ghraib. The prominent participation of women in the abuse case made evident by the now notorious photos triggered consternation and public outrage in the US and all over the world. The fact that women were involved in this tragic incident - which contrasts so sharply with the values the United States stand for - was seen as particularly shocking. The soldiers involved were put on trial.

What happened in Abu Ghraib is, though, not linked to gender, but a breakdown in military discipline, training and education. The lessons of Abu Ghraib are clear: International law, in particular international humanitarian law, must be respected also in difficult circumstances.

Secondly, Abu Ghraib has clearly shown the additional dangers that can result from the growing phenomenon of private contrac-tors (both private military companies and private security com-panies). Such companies are increasingly employed all around the world by private business enterprises, governments, NGO's, international organisations, embassies, and private citizens.

Not every government activity can, though, be outsourced to the private sector. Where to draw the line is not easy to define. Clearly, prisoner interrogation should not be outsourced whereas testing candidates for a civilian job clearly can. Airlines should, obviously, be private businesses; but the setting of safety standards for air traffic should not be outsourced. There is – particularly in the age of globalisation – a clear need for a fun-damental debate on what can be privatised and what should not. There is a clear need to reinforce the law and to develop inter-national norms and standards in this area.

Third, there need to be international standards for the operation of private military and security companies. Most notably, every government should be obliged to have these companies register and obtain a license to operate. Depending on the type of activity, the issuing of licenses should be made subject to specific and – for armed and other critical mandates – ever more stringent obligations. These should include an obligation for transparency, clear training requirements (including, where indicated, the Geneva Conventions) and other key areas. The respect for these legal obligations should be controlled and imposed through a system of inspections and stiff sanctions in case of violations.

Finally, there needs to be a system of parliamentary oversight over such activities. It is not acceptable, if the state monopoly of legitimate force is to be preserved (one of the fundamental pillars of democracy, the rule of law, and human security) that significant elements of the security sector can escape civilian, parliamentary and hence democratic control.

The lessons of Abu Ghraib should give us pause for thought.

especially women's emancipation in western societies have sped up the process of integration. Not only have women actively demanded to be included in the forces, but more and more frequently they head for the positions primarily assigned to men, including those where the personnel is trained for combat deployment. Nevertheless, the com-batant status of women, that is their deployment in com-bat troops as front line soldiers, has continued to be one of the most controversial issues in the present debate about military recruitment and retention. In NATO's

armed forces only seven per cent of existing female soldiers hold positions in operational areas. Most servicewomen work in non-combat jobs in administration, personnel, medical or technical functions. In 1999, the European Court of Justice decided that it is up to national authori-ties to determine areas of exclusion of women from com-bat units. Therefore, in spite of the general trend of women occupying mostly non-combat positions in armed forces, there exist great variations even between NATO countries, as shown by Belgium, the Netherlands, Norway and Denmark where there are no job bans for service-women. Norway and Denmark have been most tolerant in opening their armed forces to women, who can join all combat functions. Norway was the first country to permit servicewomen aboard submarines, and as a logical consequence the Norwegian Navy had the first female submarine commander. In the British Armed Forces overall, 70 per cent of army posts are open for women, 73 per cent in the Naval Service and 96 per cent in the Royal Air Force. However, restrictions to women's employment on submarines and in special units still exist. A similar situation can be found in the American, Canadian and British armed forces where women serve in an increasing range of military jobs, including combat roles in some air forces and navies. However, their exclusion from the combat divisions of armies (infantry, armour, and artillery, special forces units), where they can occupy only administrative supporting roles, has been almost common for all of these armed forces, including the Israeli military where conscription is compulsory both for men and women. With the exception of Norway, submarine service also remains closed to women.

Canada and the UK are two particularly interesting cases in terms of gender occupational policies. Together with Germany after 2000, these countries have experienced rather strong external pressures to achieve gender equality in the services and to eliminate functional restrictions. These pressures, coming from broader society and particularly from civilian courts, reveal a new emergent trend in terms of civil-military relations, as well as a growing relevance of political factors in the definition of women's military roles. In Poland and Greece, women are by law excluded from any kind of combat functions; and only recently in Germany were women allowed to join forces other than the medical services.

Women's presence in major operations over the last half a century has contributed to the change of combat exclusion rules. About 7,500 American servicewomen, mostly

Chart 4.1:

Average occupational distribution of military personnel in thirteen NATO countries in 2000 (in percentage)

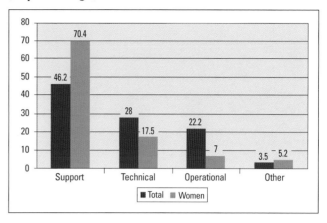

Chart 4.2:

Evolution of the percentage of women in NATO forces (1986/7-2000)

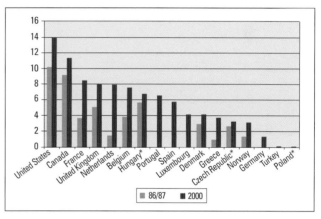

* Data for the first period refers to years 1990/2. The chart introduced numbers of women in the total active force, including conscripts.

Note: Both charts were kindly provided by Helena Carreiras.

Sources: Annual Report of the Committee of Women in the NATO Forces for 2004, at http://www.nato.int/ims/2004/win/stregnth.pdf

nurses, served in Southeast Asia during the Vietnam War. After the Gulf War, where 37,000 American and 1,100 English servicewomen were deployed, women were allowed to serve in combat missions in the US Army, the Navy and the Marine Corps. In 2000, more than 80 per cent of the total jobs, and over 95 per cent of all career fields in the US armed forces, were open to women. Their performance was highly appreciated by politicians, the command authorities, and the public at large, probably also due to the fact that during Operation Desert Storm there were only seven women killed in the line of duty (and two were taken as prisoners of war). The number of American women deployed in the 2003 war against Iraq, reaching some 10,000, far exceeds the numbers in Operation Desert Storm because women are now taking roles for which they had not been used before.

Female British troops of the NATO multinational force prepare to deploy for Macedonia.

In most NATO countries no formal legal restrictions exist with respect to the roles women can play in the armed forces. However, women do not appear in certain functions perhaps due to an unspoken, but quite prevalent, fear that their presence could affect the units' combat preparedness, or simply because they have not reached a considerable number of lower positions from which the best of them could be promoted to higher ranked combatant jobs. Quite often women do not wish to compete with men for the most demanding jobs, finding little attraction in military specialisations that combine the extremes of hardship in training with a high probability of getting killed in war.

The presence of women in regular forces and the gradual enlargement of positions they occupy have been both praised and disapproved. The arguments against women's inclusion into the military are found among conservative traditionalists, as well as, pacifist feminists. The former argue that job opportunities for women in the military inevitably results in a loss of combat capabilities, or that the inclusion is politically motivated without respecting the needs of the military organisation thus bringing more trouble than benefits.[7] There are also arguments about women's presence undermining the cohesion of previously all-male units, about sexual tensions between servicemen

and servicewomen, and about special logistics demands concerning hygiene and medical requirements. The expenditure of employing women in the forces is said to be higher due to lower retention rates stemming from motherhood. Any event that shakes public stereotypes of women's roles arouses a backlash of those opposing women's full integration into the armed forces. After the disclosure of the Abu Ghraib photos many commentators used the scandal to express their criticism against allegedly too liberal recruitment and retention policies of the US armed forces, specifically as they concern women.

Feminists' opposition to women's inclusions in the armed forces is based upon the notion that women's tasks are to build and maintain peace, not to fight war. Feminists point out the danger of militarisation of women and their lives, as well as, the danger of being exposed to violent behaviour from their male colleagues.[8] Those who support the full inclusion of women in the armed forces build their arguments on equal opportunity demands from which military organisations cannot be excluded. Denying that physical and psychological differences between the sexes could play any substantial role in women's military performance, they oppose the idea about the decline of combat preparedness of units where women work in tandem with men. There are also moderate experts arguing for the utilisation of women in the armed forces for limited jobs and positions, which corresponds more or less to the present situation in most countries, where servicewomen have accepted prevailingly supportive/auxiliary position within the armed forces.[9] The pro-inclusion experts also argue that although the modern military employs fewer service personnel, the army is increasingly regarded as an occupational career rather than a patriotic calling, usually ascribed to male professions.

The prevailing tendency to keep servicewomen away from combat roles is mostly justified by gender differences linked to physical strength and aggressiveness, raised in order to explain female inadequacies to attain performance standards. Moreover, the argument that women's presence undermines unit cohesion is seen as a pretext to exclude women from competition for much desired and much rewarded positions. In practice a gradualist approach has been the most common trend in current practice of armed forces personnel policies.

Nevertheless, in spite of strong opposition from experts and politicians, women will probably take over more and more roles in future forces, whether regular, paramilitary or guerrilla. The present trend to increase their representation in regular forces, and to include them gradually into roles until recently reserved exclusively for men, reflects both an objective demand for manpower and women's ability to meet the requirements of a military career.

Table 4.1:
Total strength of women in the NATO forces in 2004

Country	Percentage of women in total national force
Belgium	8.3
Bulgaria	4.2
Canada	12.3
Czech Republic	12.3
Denmark	5.0
France	12.8
Germany	5.2
Hungary	10.0
Greece	4.2
Italy	0.5
Latvia	13.5
Luxemburg	6.0
Netherlands	8.7
Norway	6.3
Poland	0.5
Portugal	8.4
Romania	4.0
Slovakia	6.1
Slovenia	19.2
Spain	10.5
Turkey	4.0
United Kingdom	8.8
United States	15.4

Source: Annual Report of the Committee of Women in the NATO Forces for 2004, at http://www.nato.int/ims/2004/win/03-index.htm

Endnotes

1 See F. Krill, 'The Protection of Women in International Humanitarian Law', *International Review of the Red Cross*, No. 249 (Geneva: ICRC, November-December 1985), 337.

2 See H. Afshar, 'Women and Wars. Some Trajectories towards a Feminist Peace', in H. Afshar and D. Eade (eds), *Development, Women, and War: Feminist Perspectives* (London: Oxfam, 2004).

3 S. Curphey, '1 in 7 US Military Personnel in Iraq is Female', *Women's E-news* (November 2003).

4 D. Hirst, 'Ethiopia: Human Waves Fall as War Aims Unfold', *The Guardian* (18 May 1999).

5 African Rights, *Rwanda – Not So Innocent: When Women Become Killers*, at http://www.unimondo.org/AfricanRights; and A. Golts, *The Moscow Times* (16 July 2003), at http://www.cdi.org/Russia/265-9.cfm

6 S. L. Myers, *Female Suicide Bombers Unnerve Russians* (August 2003), at http://www.peacewomen.org

7 M. Van Creveld, *Do Women Belong in the Front Line?* (London: Cassell, 2001), 25.

8 C. Enloe, *Does Khaki Become You? The Militarization of Women's Lives* (London: Pluto Press, 1989).

9 L. Miller, 'Feminism and the Exclusion of Army Women from Combat', *Gender Issues*, Vol. 16, No. 3 (1998), 33-64.

Chapter 5

Women and HIV/AIDS

'Violence against women is a challenge in itself, but comes with an added deadly dimension: the risk of HIV infection. Sexual violence increases women's vulnerability to the virus. All too frequently, the threat of violence forces women to have unprotected sex. Violence can also make it impossible for women to seek information, follow treatment or even raise the subject for discussion.'

Kofi Annan, United Nations Secretary-General, Message on the International Day for the Elimination of Violence Against Women, 25 November 2004

Sexual abuse and lawlessness in conflicts are major factors in the spread of HIV/AIDS principally affecting women and girls. Aside from the biological structure of women which makes the virus more easily transmitted from men to women, prevalent gender roles and prejudice in society considerably increases their vulnerability. Currently, there is no official control nor policy for carriers of the virus for men in the armed forces and peacekeeping operations. The armed conflicts in Africa and the infection rates of military men in the region are a case in point. In times of conflict or peace the virus has spread at alarming rates in the area.

In times of conflict

According to the Joint United Nations Programme on HIV/AIDS (UNAIDS), armed forces are at special risk of exposure to sexually transmitted diseases (STDs), including HIV. During times of peace, STD infection among military personnel is generally two to five times higher than in civilian populations, and in times of conflict the difference can be 50 times higher or more.[1] However, military forces rarely make public the rates of infection in their troops, making it impossible to assess the extent to which they are responsible for spreading the virus. Estimates on the prevalence of HIV infection in a number of African militaries are particularly high, most notably with 60 per cent of the military in Angola and the Democratic Republic of the Congo and 40 per cent in South Africa being HIV positive. Figures on the infection rates of various rebel groups and militias are unknown, although there is little doubt that they too are both vectors and victims of the HIV/AIDS epidemic.

Recently, the question of the role played by peacekeeping operations in transmitting HIV/AIDS has been raised. Former US ambassador Richard Holbrooke raised the issue at the UN Security Council in 2000, saying that *'it would be the cruellest of ironies, if people who had come to end a war were spreading an even more deadly disease.'*[2] A debate ensued as to whether or not the United Nations should require peacekeepers to be tested prior to and after

Florence, 35, lies in bed at home, east of Johannesburg. She is one of many victims of the AIDS epidemic that is forecasted to cripple South Africa's economy as millions die. One in every four South African women aged between 20 and 29 is HIV positive. In ten years time, South Africa's economy, the biggest in sub-Saharan Africa, is expected to be 17% smaller than it would have been without AIDS.

their deployment. The Director of the International Crisis Group's African program, Stephen Ellis, argues that *'this would permit individual soldiers to be aware of their health and encourage them to avoid spreading the disease or become infected. The testing should be matched with expanded education, counselling, and treatment for HIV positive soldiers.'*[3] However, the UN Department of Peacekeeping Operations (DPKO) argued that it cannot require any mandatory testing of military personnel, as those who serve for the UN have been determined by each contributing country.

What remains certain is that HIV/AIDS spreads during conflict like wildfire. The reasons for the substantial rise in infection rates are seen both in the lack of prevention and treatment programs, along with the use of infected blood during medical operations. Women who are infected with HIV/AIDS can also risk infecting their children either at birth or through breastfeeding. In conflict situations, women have no alternative but to breastfeed their infants, thereby increasing the chances of such transmission.

Unprotected sex is another major cause of the high infection rates, as neither civilians nor soldiers have recourse to proper forms of protection, especially given that contraceptives are not widely available, and even if so, many men would not accept them. Moreover, as conflicts tend to exacerbate poor living conditions, many women are driven to provide sexual services out of the sheer necessity to survive. These women are generally unable to negotiate safe sex with customers and the likelihood of unprotected sex ultimately leads to contracting the disease. A lack of good nutrients also hastens the development of AIDS

among HIV positive persons during conflict. Women are particularly affected as they usually receive less of the available food due to their lower status in society. Furthermore, women are under greater risk than men because biologically they are more vulnerable to infection. In fact, in the majority of cases where the transmission of the HIV virus is sexual, women's infection rates are greater than those of men. The systematic rape of tens and even hundreds of thousands of women by warring factions has dramatically increased the HIV infection rates in conflict zones, especially in Africa. The exposure of female refugees and internally displaced women to intense violence, sexual harassment and abuse makes them particularly vulnerable to HIV transmission. Moreover, they are often forced to provide sexual favours in order to obtain food and basic amenities.

Conflict also undermines the very fabric of society along with certain values that are upheld during peace times. Women from Sierra Leone and Rwanda have repeatedly alleged that long periods of conflict engender a culture of violence, as war erodes traditions that promote gender balance and respect. There is also the problem of fatalism among civilians and soldiers alike, who witness or partake in deaths of others during the midst of war. As one young Eritrean soldier explains, *'I have seen so many of my friends die at the front and I know that I might die as well. Why should I worry about a disease that would take years to kill me when I might die tomorrow?'*[4]

The African continent

Today, over one-quarter of the African continent is engaged in armed conflict. Most of the countries in Eastern and Southern Africa that have a history of recent conflict are also places where the pandemic is most severe. Coined by the International Crisis Group as 'Africa's deadly duo', HIV/AIDS and Africa's wars mutually reinforce each other and undermine efforts underway to establish development programs, thereby effectively crippling the entire continent.

The HIV/AIDS pandemic fosters insecurity and instability, resulting in conflict, leading to the breakdown of pre-established prevention and treatment programs and greatly increasing the infection rates among both soldiers and the civilian population. A major problem related to HIV/AIDS in Africa is the traditional approach of seeing the disease primarily as a health issue and not one of national security. HIV/AIDS is treated in the aftermath of conflict, not during it, thereby allowing HIV infections to go unchecked. Recent UNAIDS figures claim that AIDS is now the leading cause of death on the continent, a reason why it is imperative to address HIV/AIDS prevention and conflict prevention urgently and simultaneously.

Box 5.1: Armed conflict and HIV/AIDS: Rwanda

Petronille Mujawamariya, 30, was raped and infected with HIV during the Rwandan genocide.

Rwanda represents one of the most horrific examples of HIV/AIDS spreading in times of conflict, as sexual violence was rampant during the 1994 genocide and in its immediate aftermath. According to a UN report between 250,000 and 500,000 women were raped or gang raped during the genocide. While it is difficult to determine the exact transmission rate of HIV during the genocide due to the impossibility of ascertaining when a given individual was first exposed to the virus, it is certain that a large number of the victims were infected with the virus during the rape. The rate of HIV infection in Rwanda was extremely high already before the genocide - an estimated 25 per cent of the population and an estimated 35 per cent of the Rwandan army were HIV positive. Of the surviving women, 70 per cent are estimated to have been infected with HIV/AIDS. Amnesty International reported that most survivors of the Rwandan genocide still suffer from post-traumatic stress disorder, but have little hope of receiving adequate medical attention or care. Moreover, concern has also been expressed about the conduct of local associations set up to help people living with HIV/AIDS. Several of these associations have allegedly been discriminating against rape survivors in deciding who should receive anti-retroviral drugs.

Source:
Amnesty International, at http://www.amnesty.org

In times of peace

The AIDS epidemic is affecting women and girls in increasing numbers. Globally, just under half of all people living with HIV are female. In most regions, the proportion of women and girls living with HIV is continuing to grow, particularly in Eastern Europe, Asia and Latin America.

Women from Sub-Sahara Africa are most severely affected by AIDS also during peacetime. According to UNAIDS, three quarters of all women with HIV worldwide live in that region. More than one in five pregnant women are HIV-infected and the infection rate of women is at least 1.3 times greater than men in most countries of this region. Among young people aged 15-24 the ratio is the highest; women are found to be three times as likely to be HIV infected as their male counterparts.[5] These discrepancies have been attributed to several factors, such as the biological fact that HIV generally is more easily transmitted from men to women. In addition, sexual activity usually starts earlier for women, and young women tend to have sex with much older partners. However, HIV prevalence varies considerably across the African continent – ranging from less than one per cent in Mauritania to almost 40 per cent in Botswana and Swaziland.[6]

Research has confirmed a strong correlation between sexual and other forms of abuse against women and women's chances of being HIV infected.[7] A recent study conducted in South Africa confirmed a direct link between gender-based violence and increased spread of HIV. Women who are beaten or dominated by their partners are nearly 50 per cent more likely to become infected with HIV, compared with women who live in non-violent households. Researchers reported that abusive men are more likely to have HIV and impose risky sexual practices on partners. These statistics are all the more frightening when put into South Africa's context where a woman is raped every seventeen seconds.[8]

In addition, pervasive economic, social and legal discrimination contribute to the vulnerability of women towards HIV infection. According to the UN Development Program, cultural practices like early and forced marriages tend to deprive women of means by which to protect themselves from contracting the disease.

Violence against women is also a consequence of HIV/AIDS. When a woman discloses that she is HIV positive she may be abandoned by her husband because of the stigma that the disease brings on the family. Frequently, pregnant women are tested for HIV at prenatal clinics and, therefore, more likely to be diagnosed than their male partners. As a result, they are accused of being the source of HIV transmission and are often ostracised in their local communities. The fear of rejection, stigmatisation, violence and abuse prevents many women from

Kenyan prostitutes wait for blood tests and medical checkups at the Majengo clinic in the suburb of Nairobi. According to local health authorities 95 percent of the prostitutes in Majengo are HIV positive.

utilising HIV voluntary counselling and testing services, disclosing their HIV status, accessing HIV prevention programmes targeting pregnant women, mothers and their children, or engaging in safer sexual practices. HIV positive women who are either forced out of their homes or divorced then have to face the harsh reality and to engage in 'survival sex', that is sexual encounters in exchange for food, shelter, school fees or other goods. According to Rwandese government figures, an estimated 80 per cent of sex workers are infected with HIV.[9]

Furthermore, women suffer unequal access to health treatment, resulting in fewer HIV positive women being treated. Women may also be unable to access health services as their partners often control the household financial or transportation resources, as they cannot take time off work, or because they cannot leave their dependants to travel to a clinic or hospital.

Therefore, if HIV prevention activities are to succeed, they need to occur alongside other efforts that address and reduce violence against women and girls. Similarly, such programmes have to address the interconnection between gender and socio-economic inequality and vulnerability to HIV. Far more must be done to ensure sustainable livelihoods for women and girls, particularly those living in female headed households, if they are to be able to protect themselves against HIV infection and deal with its impact. Boosting women's economic opportunities and social power should be seen as part and parcel of potentially successful and sustainable AIDS strategies.

Box 5.2: Facts and figures of HIV/AIDS infection worldwide

According to the World Health Organization (WHO) and the Joint United Nations Programme on HIV/AIDS (UNAIDS), the number of people living with HIV rose in 2004 to its highest level ever with sub-Saharan Africa being by far the most affected region. Women and girls remain highly vulnerable to HIV infection representing an increasing proportion of people living with the virus. The data provided by the WHO/UNAIDS report are revealing:

- At the end of 2004, an estimated 39.4 million people worldwide – 37.2 million adults and 2.2 million children younger than fifteen years – were living with HIV/AIDS.

- An estimated 4.9 million new HIV infections occurred worldwide during 2004 – out of this 4.3 million were adults and 640,000 children under fifteen years.

- Worldwide, approximately 17.6 million women are HIV infected. Women and girls make up almost 57 per cent of adults living with HIV in sub-Saharan Africa (three quarters of all women with HIV worldwide), 36 per cent in Latin America and 34 per cent in Eastern Europe and Central Asia.

- In 2004 AIDS caused deaths of 3.1 million people, including 510,000 children under fifteen years.

Source:

UNAIDS/WHO, *AIDS Epidemic Update: December 2004* (Geneva: UNAIDS/WHO, 2004).

Table 5.1:

HIV statistics for women living with HIV/AIDS in some regions in 2004

Regions	Number of women (15-49) living with HIV	Percentage of adults (15-49) living with HIV who are women
Sub-Saharan Africa	13.3 million	57
South and South-East Asia	2.1 million	30
Latin America	610,000	36
Eastern Europe & Central Asia	490,000	34
North America	260,000	25
World	17.6 million	47

Source: Adapted from UNAIDS/WHO, *AIDS Epidemic Update: December 2004* (Geneva: UNAIDS/WHO, 2004), 5.

Endnotes

1 UNIFEM, Gender and AIDS, *HIV/AIDS, Women and War*, at http://www.genderandaids.org

2 Quoted in 'AIDS and Violent Conflict in Africa', *Special Report 75* (Washington: United States Institute of Peace, 2001).

3 International Crisis Group, *HIV/AIDS and War: Africa's Deadly Duo* (Brussels, 16 April 2004), at http://www.crisisweb.org

4 UNIFEM, Gender and AIDS, *HIV/AIDS, Women and War.*

5 UNAIDS/WHO, *AIDS Epidemic Update*: *December 2004* (Geneva: UNAIDS/WHO, 2004).

6 UNAIDS/WHO, *AIDS Epidemic Update*: *December 2003* (Geneva: UNAIDS/WHO, 2003).

7 *AIDS Epidemic Update: December 2004.*

8 Statement of Deputy Justice Minister of South Africa, Cheryl Gillwald, UCT Workshop on Gender and International Criminal Court (Pretoria, 1999).

9 Amnesty International, *Rwanda: 'Market for Death', Rape Survivors Living with HIV/AIDS in Rwanda* (London: AI, 6 April 2004), at http://www.amnesty.org

Key Reading Part II

Books

H. Afshar and D. Eade (eds), *Development, Women, and War: Feminist Perspectives* (Oxford: Oxfam, 2004).

B. Bedont, *International Criminal Justice: Implications for Peacekeeping* (Ottawa: Canadian Department of Foreign Affairs and International Trade, 2001).

M. de Bruyn, *Violence, Pregnancy and Abortion*, A review of worldwide data and recommendations for action (Ipas: USA: 2003)

M. Cooke, *Women and the War Story* (Berkeley: University of California Press, 1996).

M. Cook and A. Woollacott (eds), *Gendering War Talks* (Princeton: Princeton University Press, 1993).

C. Corrin (ed), *Women in a Violent World: Feminist Analyses and Resistance Across Europe* (Edinburgh: Edinburgh University Press, 1996).

A. Dworkin, *Scapegoat: The Jews, Israel, and Women's Liberation* (New York: Free Press, 2002).

C. Enloe, *Does Khaki Become You? The Militarization of Women's Lives* (London: Pluto Press, 1989).

C. Galenkamp, *Protection from Sexual Exploitation and Abuse: Lessons Learned from Sierra Leone* (New York: OCHA, 2003).

C. Giffard, *The Torture Reporting Handbook* (Colchester: University of Essex, 2000).

W. Giles and J. Hyndman, *Sites of Violence: Gender and Conflict Zones* (Berkeley: California University Press, 2004).

J. S. Goldstein, *War and Gender: How Gender Shapes the War System and Vice Versa* (Cambridge: Cambridge University Press, 2001).

M. Harrell and L. L. Miller, *New Opportunities for Military Women: Effects Upon Readiness, Cohesion, and Morale* (Santa Monica: RAND's National Defence Research Institute, 1997).

A. Helland, K. Daramé, A. Kristensen and I. Skjelsberg, *Women and Armed Conflicts* (Oslo: Norwegian Institute for International Affairs, 1999).

G. Hicks, *The Comfort Women: Sex Slaves and the Japanese Imperial Forces* (New York: W. W. Norton, 1995).

A. M. Hildson, *Madonnas and Martyrs: Militarism and Violence in the Philippines* (Sydney: Allen and Unwin, 1997).

M. Korac, *Linking Arms: Women and War in Post-Yugoslav States* (Uppsala: Life and Peace Institute, 1998).

K. Kumar (ed), *Women and Civil War: Impact, Organizations, and Action* (Boulder: Lynne Rienner Publishers, 2001).

R. Lentin (ed), *Gender and Catastrophe* (London: Zed Books, 1997).

C. Lindsey, *Women Facing War: ICRC Study on the Impact of Armed Conflict on Women* (Geneva: ICRC, 2001).

L. A. Lorentzen and J. Turpin (eds), *The Women and War Reader* (New York: New York University Press, 1998).

R. Manchanda (ed), *Women, War and Peace in South Asia: Beyond Victimhood to Agency* (Delhi: Sage, 2001).

C. Moser and F. Clark, *Victims, Perpetrators or Actors? Gender, Armed Conflict and Political Violence* (London: Zed Books, 2001).

F. Pickup, S. Williams, and C. Sweetman (eds), *Ending Violence Against Women: A Challenge for Development and Humanitarian Work* (Oxford: Oxfam, 2001).

P. Procházková, *The Aluminium Queen: The Russian–Chechen War through the Eyes of Women* (Prague: Lidové Noviny Publishing house, 2003).

Redress Trust, *A Sourcebook for Victims of Torture and Other Violations of Human Rights and International Humanitarian Law* (London: The Redress Trust, 2003).

I. L. Sajor (ed), *Common Grounds, Violence Against Women in War and Armed Conflict Situations* (Quezon City: Asian Centre for Women's Human Rights, 1998).

I. L. Sajor and M. Gomez (eds), *From the Depths of Silence: Voices of Women Survivors of War* (Quezon City: Asian Centre for Women's Human Rights, 2000).

S. Sharratt and E. Kaschak (eds), *Assault on the Soul: Women in the Former Yugoslavia* (Binghamton: Hawort Press, 1999).

A. Stiglmayer (ed), *Mass Rape: The War Against Women in Bosnia-Herzegovina* (Lincoln: University of Nebraska Press, 1994).

C. Sweetman (ed), *Gender, Development, and Humanitarian Work* (Oxford: Oxfam, 2001).

Y. Tanaka, *Japan's Comfort Women: The Military and Involuntary Prostitution during War and Occupation (Asia's Transformations)* (London: Routledge, 2002).

J. Turpin and L. Lorentzen (eds), *The Women and War Reader* (New York: New York University Press, 1998).

M. Turshen and C. Twagiramariya (eds), *What Women Do in Wartime: Gender and Conflict in Africa* (London: Zed Books, 1998).

M. Van Creveld, *Do Women Belong in the Front Line?* (London: Cassell, 2001).

J. Vickers, *Women and War* (London: Zed Books, 1993).

B. Victor, *Army of Roses: Inside the World of Palestinian Women Suicide Bombers* (New York: Rodale Books, 2003).

Voluntary Service Overseas, *Gendering AIDS: Women, Men, Empowerment, Mobilisation* (London: VSO, October 2003).

M. Waller and J. Rycenga (eds), *Frontline Feminism: Women, War and Resistance* (London: Routledge, 2000).

L. Wendland, *A Handbook on State Obligations under the United Nations Convention against Torture* (Geneva: APT, 2002).

Women in Black (eds), *Compilation of Information on Crimes of War against Women in ex-Yugoslavia - Actions and Initiatives in their Defence* (Montpellier: Women Living under Muslim Laws, 1994).

Y. Yoshiaki and S. O'Brien, *Comfort Women* (New York: Columbia University Press, 2002).

S. Zajovic (ed), *Women for Peace* (Belgrade: Women in Black, 1994).

Articles and papers

L. T. Arcel, 'Deliberate Sexual Torture of Women in War: The Case of Bosnia-Herzegovina', in A.Y. Shalev, R. Yehuda & A.C. McFarlane (eds), *International Handbook of Human Response to Trauma* (New York: Plenum Publishers, 2000).

L. T. Arcel, *Torture, Cruel, Inhuman and Degrading Treatment of Women: Psychological Consequences*, Paper presented at the International Symposium on Human Rights Protection and Anti-Torture in the 21st Century (Beijing, 26 June 2001).

J. A. Benjamin, *Women, War and HIV/AIDS: West Africa and the Great Lakes*, Paper presented at the World Bank, International Women's Day (Women's Commission for Refugee Women and Children, 8 March 2001).

U. Butalia, 'A Question of Silence: Partition, Women and the State', in R. Lentin (ed), *Gender and Catastrophe* (London & New York: Zed Books, 1997).

R. C. Carpenter, 'Surfacing Children: Limitation of Genocidal Rape Discourse', *Human Rights Quarterly*, Vol. 22, No. 2 (Baltimore: John Hopkins University Press, 2000).

R. Copelon, 'Surfacing Gender: Reconceptualizing Crimes against Women in Times of War', in L. A. Lorentzen and J. Turpin (eds), *The Women and War Reader* (New York: New York University Press, 1998).

C. Dandeker and M. W. Segal, 'Gender Integration in Armed Forces: Recent Policy Developments in the United Kingdom', *Armed Forces and Society* (San Marcos: Texas State University, Fall 1996).

A. Dworkin, 'The Women Suicide Bombers', *Feminista!*, Vol. 5, No. 1 (2002), at http://www.feminista.com/archives/v5n1/dworkin.html

J. Gardam, 'Women, Human Rights and International Humanitarian Law', *International Review of the Red Cross*, No. 324 (Geneva: ICRC, September 1998).

W. Kaelin, 'The Struggle against Torture', *International Review of the Red Cross*, No. 324 (Geneva: ICRC, 1998).

F. Krill, 'The Protection of Women in International Humanitarian Law', *International Review of the Red Cross*, No. 249 (Geneva: ICRC, November-December 1985).

G. Kümmel, 'Complete Access: Women in the Bundeswehr and Male Ambivalence', *Armed Forces and Society*, Vol. 28, No. 4 (San Marcos: Texas State University, Summer 2002).

G. Kümmel, 'When Boy Meets Girl: The "Feminization" of the Military: An Introduction Also to Be Read as a Postscript', *Current Sociology*, Vol. 50, No. 2 (Loughborough: Loughborough University, 2002).

H. Liebling, *Ugandan Women's Experiences of Violence, Rape and Torture during War in Lowero District: Implications for Health Policy, Welfare and Human Rights*, Paper presented to the 8th Interdisciplinary Congress on Women, Women's World 2002 (July 2002).

C. Lindsey, 'The Detention of Women in Wartime', *International Review of the Red Cross*, No. 842 (Geneva: ICRC, June 2001).

C. Lindsey, 'Women and War', *The International Review of the Red Cross*, No. 839 (Geneva: ICRC, September 2000).

G. Machel, 'Conflict Fuels HIV/AIDS Crisis', *HIV/AIDS Gender and Rights* (2004), at http://www.ipsnews.net/hivaids/section1_2.shtml

L. Miller, 'Feminism and the Exclusion of Army Women from Combat', *Gender Issues,* Vol. 16, No. 3 (1998).

S. L. Myers, *Female Suicide Bombers Unnerve Russians* (August 2003), at http://www.peacewomen.org

Norwegian Institute of International Affairs, *Women and Armed Conflict* (Oslo: Norwegian Institute of International Affairs, 1999).

M. Nuciari, 'That Long and Winding Road of Women in the Armed Forces: A Gaze From the Italian Perspective; and H. Carreiras, 'The Participation of Women in the Armed Forces. A Cross-National Comparison of Policies and Practices in NATO Countries', both in M. Vlachová, and L. Jelu‰oiã, *A Farewell to Peace Dividend? Military-Society Relations in Countries of Transition* (Baden-Baden: NOMOS, forthcoming 2005).

Pacific Women against Violence, 'Violence against East Timor Women', *Pacific Women's Network against Violence against Women*, Vol. 5, No.2/3 (2000).

S. Swiss and J. E. Giller, 'Rape as a Crime of War–A Medical Perspective', *Journal of the American Medical Association,* Vol. 270, No.5 (Chicago, 4 August 1993).

S. Swiss, P. J. Jennings, et al. 'Violence against Women during the Liberian Conflict (1989-1994)', *Journal of the American Medical Association,* Vol. 279, No. 8 (Chicago, 1998).

J. Ward, *'If Not Now When?', Addressing Gender-Based Violence in Refugee, Internally Displaced, and Post-Conflict Settings, A Global Overview* (New York: The Reproductive Health for Refugees Consortium, 2002), at http://www.rhrc.org

E. Wax, 'A Brutal Legacy of Congo War Extent of Violence against Women Surfaces as Fighting Recedes', *Washington Post Foreign Service* (25 October 2003), at http://www.washingtonpost.com/

Documents and on-line reports

African Rights, *Rwanda – Not So Innocent: When Women Become Killers,* at http://www.unimondo.org/AfricanRights

Amnesty International, *Rape and Sexual Abuse: Torture and Ill Treatment of Women in Detention* (New York, 1992).

Amnesty International, *Rwanda: 'Market for Death', Rape Survivors Living with HIV/AIDS in Rwanda* (London, 2004), at http://www.amnesty.org

Amnesty International, *Rwanda: Seven in Ten Genocide Survivors Living with HIV/AIDS,* News Release (London, 2004), at http://www.amnesty.org.uk/deliver/document/15298.html

Amnesty International, *Stop Violence against Women, Swaziland: Violence Fuels the HIV/AIDS Pandemic* (London, 2004), at http://www.amnesty.org

Commission Nationale de Lutte contre le SIDA, *Cadre Stratégique de la lutte contre le VIH/SIDA 2002-2006,* at http://www.cnlsburundi.org

Committee on Women in NATO Forces, *Annual Report of the Committee on Women in the NATO Forces* (Brussels: CWINF, 2000).

Department of Peacekeeping Operations Lessons Learned Unit, *Mainstreaming a Gender Perspective in Multidimensional Peace Operations* (New York: United Nations, July 2000).

Guidelines on International Protection: Gender Related Persecution with the Context of Article 1A(2) of the 1951 Convention and/or its 1967 Protocol relating to the Status of Refugees (2002).

Human Rights Watch, *Shattered Lives: Sexual Violence during the Rwandan Genocide and its Aftermath* (New York, September 1996), at http://www.hrw.org/reports/1996/Rwanda.htm.

Human Rights Watch, *We'll Kill You If You Cry: Sexual Violence in the Sierra Leone Conflict*, 15 (1) (A) (New York, 2003), at http://www.hrw.org

Human Rights Watch, *Women's Human Rights Step by Step, Women, Law and Development International*, Women's Rights Project (New York, 1997).

Human Rights Watch, *World Report 2001: Women's Human Rights–Women in Conflict and Refugees* (New York, 2001), at http://www.hrw.org/wr2k1/women/women3.html

Institute for Security Studies, *HIV/AIDS as a Security Risk* (Pretoria, 2003), at http://www.iss.co.za

Inter-Agency Standing Committee Working Group, *IASC Task Force on Protection from Sexual Exploitation and Abuse in Humanitarian Crises: Report on the Activities of the Task Force,* 53rd Meeting, IASC Task Force on Protection from Sexual Exploitation and Abuse in Humanitarian Crises: Report on the Activities of the Task Force (8-9 July 2003).

International Crisis Group, *HIV/AIDS and War: Africa's Deadly Duo* (Brussels, 16 April 2004), at http://www.crisisweb.org

Transcript of Oral Judgement delivered by the Judges of the Women's International War Crimes Tribunal on Japan's Military Sexual Slavery (The Hague, 4 December 2001).

UNAIDS, *Fact Sheet No. 2: HIV/AIDS and Conflict* (Copenhagen: UNAIDS Humanitarian Unit, August 2003).

UNAIDS/UNFPA/UNIFEM, *Women and HIV/AIDS: Confronting the Crisis* (New York/Geneva, 2004).

UNAIDS/WHO, *AIDS Epidemic Update: December 2004* (Geneva: UNAIDS/WHO, 2004).

UNIFEM, Gender and AIDS Organization, *HIV/AIDS, Women and War*, at http://www.genderandaids.org.

United Nations, *Beijing Declaration and Platform for Action* (Beijing, China, 4-15 September 1995).

United Nations, *CEDAW General Recommendation No. 19 Violence against Women*, UN Document A/47/38 (New York, 1992).

United Nations, *Gender-Based Violence, Relationship Power and Risk of HIV Infection in Women Attending Antenatal Clinics in South Africa* (Geneva, 2004), at http://www.unaids.org

United Nations, *International, Regional and National Developments in the Area of Violence against Women (1994-2003),* Report of the Special Rapporteur of the Commission on Human Rights on Violence Against Women, Its Causes and Consequence, Ms. Radhika Coomaraswamy, UN Document E/CN.4/2003/75 (Geneva, 2003).

United Nations, Office of Internal Oversight Services, *Investigation into Sexual Exploitation of Refugees by Aid Workers in West Africa*, UN Document A/57/465 (New York, 2002), at http://www.un.org/Depts/oios/reports/a57_465.htm

United Nations, *Report of the United Nations Panel on Peacekeeping Operations (Brahimi Report)*, UN Document A/55/305 (New York, 2000).

United Nations, *Report on the Situation of Human Rights in Rwanda*, Report of the Special Rapporteur of the Commission on Human Rights, Mr. R. Degni-Segui, UN Document E/CN.4/1996/68 (Geneva, 1996).

United Nations, 'Observance by United Nations Forces of International Humanitarian Law', *Secretary-General's Bulletin,* UN Document ST/SGB/1999/13 (New York, 6 August 1999).

United Nations, 'Special Measures for Protection from Sexual Exploitation and Sexual Abuse', *Secretary-General's Bulletin,* UN Document ST/SGB/2003/13 (New York, 2003).

United Nations, *CEDAW General Recommendation No. 19, Violence against Women*, UN Document A/47/38 (New York, 1992).

United Nations, *The Impact of Armed Conflict on Women and Girls*, Security Council Resolution S/RES/1325 (New York, 2000).

United Nations, *Violence against Women Perpetrated and/or Condoned by the State during Times of Armed Conflict (1997-2000),*

Report of the Special Rapporteur of the Commission on Human Rights on Violence Against Women, Its Causes and Consequence, Ms. Radhika Coomaraswamy, UN Document E/CN.4/2001/73 (Geneva, 2001).

United Nations, *Women, Peace and Security*, Report of the Secretary-General, UN Document S/2002/1154 (New York, 2002).

United Nations Development Fund for Women, Gender and AIDS Organization, *HIV/AIDS, Women and War*, at http://www.genderandaids.org.

United Nations Development Programme, *Gender Approaches in Conflict and Post-Conflict Situations* (New York: UNDP, 2002).

United Nations High Commissioner for Refugees, *Guidelines on the Protection of Refugee Women* (Geneva, 1991).

United Nations Development Programme, *Gender Approaches in Conflict and Post-Conflict Situations* (New York: UNDP, 2002).

United Nations High Commissioner of Refugees and NGO partners, *Protecting Refugees: A Field Guide for NGOs* (1999).

Union of the Women of Don Region, *Chechen women in the armed conflict of 1994-2000* (2000), at http://www.donwomen/novoch.ru

The United States Institute of Peace, 'AIDS and Violent Conflict in Africa', *Special Report 75* (Washington, 2001).

The Women's International War Crimes Tribunal 2000 for the Trial of Japanese Military Sexual Slavery, Summary of Findings and Preliminary Judgement (The Hague, 12 December 2000).

Women's Commission for Refugee Women and Children, *An Assessment of Ten Years of Implementation of UNHCR Policy on Refugee Women and Guidelines on Their Protection* (New York, 2002).

Websites

Amnesty International, at http://www.amnesty.org

Human Rights Watch, at http://www.hrw.org

International Committee of the Red Cross, at http://www.icrc.org

International Criminal Court, at http://www.icc-cpi.int/

International Criminal Tribunal for Rwanda, at http://www.ictr.org

International Criminal Tribunal for the Former Yugoslavia, at http://www.un.org/icty

International Federation of Red Cross and Red Crescent Societies, at http://www.ifrc.org

International Organization for Migration, at http://www.iom.int

Joint United Nations Programme on HIV/AIDS, at http://www.unaids.org

Peace Women, at http://www.peacewomen.org

Physicians for Human Rights, at http://www.phrusa.org

United Nations Children's Fund, at http://www.unicef.org

United Nations Development Fund for Women, at http://www.unifem.org

United Nations High Commissioner for Refugees, at http://www.unhcr.ch

United Nations Office of the High Commissioner for Human Rights, at http://www.unhchr.ch

United Nations Population Fund, at http://www.unfpa.org

Voluntary Service Overseas, at http://www.vso.org.uk

World Health Organization, at http://www.who.int

PART III

WOMEN

IN POST-CONFLICT

SITUATIONS

Introduction

The suffering of civilians does not end with a truce or a peace treaty and the victims' trauma does not disappear immediately with the end of conflict. Consequences of rape are aggravated by the fact that in volatile and grief-ridden post-conflict environments only rarely can the family and the community provide for any substantial help. There is a certain logic in the hostile behaviour of the families and communities, however, unjust it may be from the point of the innocent rape victim. Ostracism is the way in which the community protects its integrity and identity against systematic sexual violence, sacrificing innocent victims of sexual violence for the sake of the community's survival and well-being. The provision of psychological support and aid to victims of war atrocities, especially those who suffer from post-traumatic stress disorder, from outside the community can be risky, as indicated by the chapter dealing with issues of psychological interventions brought to the victims in regions with non-western cultures and survival traditions.

There is no social order without a properly functioning family, and if the war-torn society is to sustain and rebuild itself, the family must restore its main functions to be able to provide protection for its vulnerable members and to foster a sense of attachment, commitment, and direction to their younger members. Armed conflicts gravely affect all the main functions of the family and frequently this does not change for a long time after fighting ceases. It is mainly women who are confronted with the challenge to keep their families together and to assume a new role as breadwinners while maintaining at the same time their care-giving and provider functions. Thus, in addition to struggling for the survival of their families in an environment with limited basic resources, threatened by a high level of omnipresent violence, landmines scattered over the territory, and the concentration of small arms within the community, women have to cope with the stress of mourning or uncertainty about the destiny of their relatives who disappeared during wartime.

Women, who fled their homes to save their lives during the mayhem of war, experience the uneasy fate of war refugees and displaced persons. As they are deprived of the social protection of their native community they become more susceptible to further abuse, exploitation and gender-based violence while in refugee camps or during their return home.

In the majority of the wars that marked the latter half of the last century, women have struggled alongside men. Yet when conflicts come to an end, women's various contributions, as well as their needs in the reconstruction phase, have been almost entirely overlooked. It is argued that women who actively participated in combat fighting shoulder to shoulder with men have experienced the worst forms of violence, but like their male colleagues, they might be less affected than civilian population because they were physically and mentally better prepared for the atrocities.[1] However, in post-conflict situations former female combatants find themselves isolated from both their former co-fighters and their home communities. It is very difficult or even impossible for them to return to their previous roles as they no longer correspond to the traditional image of 'good' women. This is a very challenging situation to demobilisation programmes, which so far have not paid attention to the special needs of female combatants. The chapter on demobilisation, disarmament and reintegration (DDR) explains how these interlinked processes can be made more gender aware, how and why greater attention should be paid to women who have joined the forces as combatants and supporters, and how important it is to teach men who have embraced violence as a means to resolve conflict, a different approach in order to prevent a return to arms.

Peace can only come about through the transformation of violent societies, and it is gender awareness in the earliest post-conflict and transition periods that helps to decide whether peaceful development will become possible in the longer term. It is also a great chance for war-torn societies to make use of the enormous survival and transformation potential women have proved to possess in the difficult time of post-war reconstruction. Although mostly excluded from formal negotiations and political decision-making, women have demonstrated their ability to play an influential role through their work in grassroots organisations dealing with everyday problems of peace-building, challenging the authorities and demanding non-violent and non-discriminative solutions for the victims and all those whose security needs are neglected. To demonstrate this ability several examples of various activities of women's organisations and movements have been included in this third part of the book. These case studies show how effectively women can contribute to post-war reconciliation and justice, as well as, to building-up more stable and secure regimes in countries suffering from political turmoil.

They indicate women's ability to mobilise the public and the international community to protect those marginalised when priorities are set up by international aid providers and local governments. At the same time these case studies corroborate how strong and persistent pressure the representatives of newly established governments and local authorities are able to exert in order to return women to their pre-war positions and to preserve the discriminative gender relations.

Endnote

[1] L. Weisaeth, 'Psychiatric Problems in War' in L.T Arcel and G.T Simunkovic, *War Violence, Trauma and the Coping Process – Armed Conflict in Europe and Survivor Responses* (Copenhagen: RCT/IRCT/Institute of Clinical Psychology University of Copenhagen, 1998), 27.

Chapter 1

Psychosocial Interventions in Post-War Situations

'Many women described their lives as having been full of challenge, loss and suffering. However, they did not see themselves as victims, and resented pity. In most cases they have found ways to survive and to adapt, while protecting and supporting those close to them.'

S. J. Bowen, *Resilience and Health: Salvadoran Refugee Women in Manitoba*, Prairie Women's Health Centre of Excellence (PWHCE), Canada, 2005

In all war-affected communities people can be found who seem to have become even stronger through the horrors of the war. Research has tried to answer the question: what enables people to stay resilient in the face of such adverse circumstances? Resilience is defined as the capacity to do well when faced with difficult circumstances. This capability consists of two components: a) resistance against destruction, as the capacity to protect one's own integrity under pressure; and b) beyond mere resistance, the ability to construct a positive life in spite of difficult circumstances. Aaron Antonovsky introduced the 'sense of coherence' as a central construct that explains why resilient people pull through adversities and gain from challenges instead of succumbing to them. He defines the sense of coherence as *'a global orientation that expresses the extent to which one has a pervasive, enduring though dynamic, feeling of confidence that one's internal and external environment are predictable and that there is a high probability that things will work out as well as can reasonably be expected.'*[1]

Resilient people flourish in spite of conditions that impact negatively on the health, psychological growth and development, learning and occupational performance of most others. The following components have been found to promote the above-described attitude:

- The experience of empathy, care and respect for each other in the family.
- Living in an atmosphere of tolerance and acceptance of individual differences.
- Opportunities and obligations at an early age to participate in important decisions and activities and to assume responsibility for others.
- Acquisition of relevant knowledge to understand and deal with difficult situations.
- Training of useful skills.
- Successful application of knowledge and skills in daily life, including the management of difficult situations.
- Observation of good role models who cope successfully with difficulties and maintain an attitude of hope and purpose when facing adversities.

A young mother tries to leave Basra, Iraq, as fighting inside the city continues.

- Having access to systems of knowledge, ideologies or beliefs that give meaning to complex and difficult situations such as wars.[2]

Since women are at the heart of their families and communities, they deserve, particularly in post-war situations, special consideration in all efforts that support the reconstruction of communities after wars and projects should consider their specific needs. Especially in former Yugoslavia many lessons have been learnt from field experiences about what is needed to provide appropriate project assistance to affected populations so that they can recover from the many war-related stresses. The following aspects are usually emphasised:

- Develop real and well-defined project goals, based on good knowledge of the situation.

- Projects should include as many community members as possible.

- Create networks between institutions and people working towards the same goal(s) within the community.

- The family is the basic unit for all interventions, independent of a primary target population.

- Avoid medication and psychiatric stigmatisation of community members.

- Flexibility and long-term duration of projects according to the needs of the situation.

- Stable, reliable and trustworthy relationships between project teams and local population.

Elizabeth Jareg's pyramidal model of psychosocial interventions in post-conflict situations has found wide-spread recognition among professionals and agencies involved in post-war reconstruction projects.[3] She describes seven intervention levels.

Each lower level is assumed to have a broader rehabilitation impact on the affected population than the higher ones and it facilitates (and sometimes even enables) the efficiency of the latter. Again, in the attempt to rebuild societies after so much violence and destruction it is crucial to pay tribute to the significant role that women play on each of these intervention levels. **Political interventions** build the base of the pyramid. They have the deepest impact on the well-being of the largest number of family and community members. They may range from the international to the sub-national level. They aim at the prevention, modification or resolution of situations that are harmful and challenging to people's well-being, and restoring peace and normalcy. Political interventions may also contain information, advocacy and legal reform components. They are vitally necessary for general policy development and the preparation of large-scale structural interventions. Building partnerships is an essential element of political interventions. **Physical/survival interventions** build the second layer. They address the basic needs of populations in post-conflict situations. Supply of food, water, clothes, shelter, basic health care, protection from danger etc. are vital preconditions for the restoration of the psychosocial functioning of individuals, communities and societies.

Chart 1.1:

Elizabeth Jareg's pyramidal model of psychosocial interventions in post-conflict situations

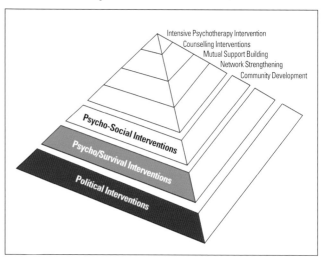

▌ *Thousands of ethnic Albanians were expelled from Kosovo by Serbian forces, with many women and children being separated from their families.*

Psychosocial interventions comprise five different intervention levels and include in ascending order community development, network strengthening, mutual support building, counselling and intensive psychotherapy interventions.

- ***Community development*** - general family and community-based psychosocial protection strategies are located on this intervention level. These strategies include the restoration of the social fabric of communities, their social, education and health services, as well as the psychosocial responsibilities of families. In the case of internally displaced and refugee populations, new, temporary communities have to be created through active participation and assignment of responsibilities to the people. Many psychosocial protection measures can in fact be executed by affected families and communities if they receive appropriate information, for example, on understanding and dealing with distress and the resulting psychological and social problems, the value of mutual support etc. Empowering people to take the reconstruction and development of their communities into their own hands and solve the problems that affect them, is a major avenue to reinstall their self-esteem. Besides, the restoration of normal family life and everyday routines is also known to increase families' and communities' resilience to stress.

The integration of targeted protection measures into education, social and health services - such integrated services are usually much more accepted by affected populations than highly specialised treatment centres.

The latter have often been found to lead to social labelling and discrimination of the users and usually they were only needed for a small minority of community members, while at the same being time rather cost-intensive.

- ***Network strengthening*** - helps to develop the capabilities of the affected populations to take charge of their own recovery and rehabilitation. This includes, among other factors, the reinforcement of existing formal and informal community and professional networks and the creation of the necessary new ones. Such networks can have all kinds of shapes. They may, for example, exist in the form of neighbourhood committees, youth and women groups, refugee councils, income generating initiatives, etc. Network strengthening also includes intensifying the links between existing education, social and health services, migrant and host communities. Networking brings those formal and informal community organisations together that may have similar goals, and whose joint potential is needed to achieve optimum efficiency of psychosocial interventions.

- ***Mutual support building*** - individuals, families and communities that face high risks and challenges usually have their own, culturally determined mechanisms of coping with stress and trauma and providing mutual support. This is often done in ritualised ways, like cleansing, healing and mourning rituals and ceremonies. It is important that psychosocial protection strategies acknowledge these idiosyncratic resources and promote opportunities for communities to practice

▌*Loss and sorrow – a displaced woman in Huambo, Angola.*

them. Such resources should particularly be drawn upon for community members who have experienced serious psychosocial harm. Sharing and processing distressing experiences in small groups in a culturally accepted way provides relief for each individual person and fosters healing from psychological wounds.

• ***Counselling interventions*** - community development and the promotion of networks and mutual support groups will offer sufficient psychosocial support for the majority of the population and enable people to cope with previous distressing, harmful high risks situations. In the course of applying psychosocial protection measures a limited number of community members will be identified who have gone through exceptionally distressing experiences, like multiple traumas, and who need to work through these experiences with more professional support. However, even here, paraprofessionals like teachers, social workers and nurses can do much of the work if they are properly trained, supervised and can fall back on a reliable personal support system.

• ***Intensive psychotherapy interventions*** - if measures on all other intervention levels work, the number of community members that require intensive psy-

chotherapy interventions and eventually medical support will be very limited. These specialised services should, as much as possible, be integrated into the normal life of communities and become part of other education, social and health services. They should also include an empowerment component and ensure that clients regain their full functioning as members of their community. Caution is suggested against premature diagnoses of psychiatric disorders in cultures that differ significantly from western cultures.

What is Post-Traumatic Stress Disorder and How Does It Affect Women Exposed to Violence?

The term trauma can be traced back to the Greek *traumatikos*, meaning wound or external bodily injury. The concept of trauma has been explained and understood in a variety of ways and often appears interchangeably with stress. Whereas stressful events challenge our ways of coping and adapting, traumatic stressors are events that violate our existing ways of understanding our reactions, our perceptions of other people's behaviour, and our framework for interacting with the world.[4] Moreover, a salient element of traumatic experiences is that they cannot be left behind in the past, and intrude pervasively in our daily lives. In the context of a post-conflict environment in particular, all trauma is confounded by exacerbating and chronic stressors.

The diagnosis of post-traumatic stress disorder (PTSD) requires exposure to an extreme stressor and a characteristic set of symptoms that have lasted for at least one month. There are three symptom groups:

• Re-experiencing the traumatic event, such as intrusive thoughts about the trauma, nightmares and flashbacks.

• Avoidance and emotional numbing, as indicated by extensive avoidance of activities, places, and thoughts related to the trauma.

• Difficulty sleeping, irritability or outbursts of anger, difficulty concentrating and hyper-vigilance.[5]

In surveying the clinical literature on PTSD affecting women, one is immediately confronted by a yawning discrepancy – most studies are performed in, and focus on North America, to a lesser degree Europe, and almost entirely exclude non-western countries. Yet, the vast proportion of wars and natural disasters occur in non-western or developing countries. All but two of the 127 wars since the Second World War have occurred in developing countries. In the period 1967-1991, an average of 117 million people living in developing countries

Box 1.1: The fate of female refugees in Former Yugoslavia

Ethnic Albanian refugees were forced to leave their homes in trains. Shortly before reaching the border from Kosovo to Macedonia, they were forced to walk.

A team of health professionals assisted refugees and internally displaced persons in former Yugoslavia over a period of three and a half years, from 1992 to 1995. Around three-quarters of this population were women. The health team found the following categories of those affected by the war:

- Refugees, who had not experienced physical or psychological torture, but were expelled from their homes - they were mostly well-adapted, although sometimes prone to mood changes, especially when their return was repeatedly postponed. Their adaptation was better in settlements in which they were able to organise their lives.
- Refugees who had experienced war, without having lost family members - they were irritable, their sleep was disturbed, and they had a tendency towards general projections, seeing their environment in the refugee camp inadequately hostile and threatening.
- Refugees who had lost family members showed signs of mourning - those who still did not know what had happened to their family members and had no information about their fate, had more problems, which made the mourning process more difficult.
- Demobilised soldiers with battlefield experience who had difficulties in adapting to a new life - they could not get used to the new circumstances and very often wanted to go back to their units.

- Persons that had experienced the destruction of their homes and/or had battlefield experience and spent several months in prison or detention camps - this group often showed all signs of developed post-traumatic stress disorder. Some of them had survived terrible torture, and showed fundamentally damaged self-respect and identity.

An analysis of the war-related experiences of a group of more than 2,000 Bosnian refugees and Croatian displaced persons in 1995 showed that around 60 per cent had experienced a direct combat situation and felt close to death, been without shelter for prolonged periods and suffered from severe shortages of food and water. Four out of ten had been forced to separate from their families and every third had witnessed the murder of a family member or of friends. Every fourth had been imprisoned and/or tortured and every fifth had suffered a serious injury. Rape or sexual abuse had taken place in almost six per cent of the cases. Bosnian refugees had on average experienced fifteen of such traumatic situations and internally displaced Croatians eight. Consequently, two thirds of this population suffered from clinical depression, 43.2 per cent from anxiety and 25 per cent from post-traumatic stress disorder. In a related study that was conducted by the International Rehabilitation Council for Torture Victims (IRCT) within the Danish psychosocial treatment program BOSWOFAM (Bosnian women and their families), among Bosnian women refugees in Croatia and among internally displaced Croatians, more than 1,500 interviewed women refugees described the following somatic and psychological problems.

Primarily somatic problems		Primarily psychological problems	
Inner restlessness	73.3	Thinking about worries and problems	93.3
Lack of energy	72.3	Private or professional problems	92.4
Inner tension	72.5	Fatigue with life	75.6
Shortage of breath	66.4	Fear	72.0
Exhaustion	64.4	A tendency to cry	66.4

Source:

L. T. Arcel and G. T. Simunkovic, *War Violence, Trauma and the Coping Process: Armed Conflict in Europe and Survivor Responses* (Copenhagen: RCT/IRCT/Institute of Clinical Psychology University of Copenhagen, 1998), 87.

were affected by disaster each year compared to approximately 700,000 in developed countries.[6]

Thus, the literature concerning prevalence of PTSD in women in the general population has little value in the context of this discussion, since the 'general population' is virtually all American, first world, developed, comparatively wealthy and comparatively free from disaster and war. An alternative avenue of exploration would be studies concerning refugees having experienced war and social upheaval. Once again, very little exists in the way of epidemiological studies on female refugees specifically. It does become apparent, however, that in populations

where traumatic events are extreme and of long duration, the incidence of PTSD is far higher compared to a 'general population'. In the area of sexual abuse, there is a more specific focus on women. As sexual abuse is a common experience among those in or emerging from war, it is pertinent to note that the incidence of PTSD is high and of long duration. However, one must bear in mind the extreme differences between a war and a civilian recovery environment. The relatively few clinical studies performed during conflict show evidence of high rates of PTSD, particularly for displaced persons and victims of sexual abuse.

Trauma – a trigger for a variety of psychiatric disorders

Post-traumatic stress disorder is in fact frequently accompanied by disorders such as major depression, an anxiety disorder or substance abuse. Studies indicate a prevalence of additional psychiatric disorders between 50 to 90 per cent. Clinical investigation with refugee survivors of massive trauma demonstrates that alongside PTSD, there can be changes in memory, consciousness, identity, personality and character. The most frequent additional disease reported is depression. Somatisation has been linked to trauma from the earliest of psychiatric studies, and is also very common amongst refugees and victims of extreme violence.[7]

Studies of battered women report pervasive suicidality. For those having endured war rape, particularly in impregnated women, the risk is high for attempted suicide. The fact that 'pure PTSD', uncomplicated by symptoms of other disorders is so uncommon, suggests that traumatic stress may precipitate a whole host of symptoms and conditions.

By far the most significant predictor of PTSD and depression is the amount of exposure to trauma. Other strong predictors are the nature of the traumatic stressor, prolonged traumatic experience such as captivity, and sexual abuse. Witnessing atrocity is closely linked to PTSD, as is participating in abuse, or atrocities. Being widowed has an associated risk for psychiatric disability, and there is general agreement across studies that women are at higher risk than men for PTSD.

Post-war factors

The expression of PTSD symptoms is extremely susceptible to ongoing environmental demands, particularly to events and situations that resemble the original traumatic experience. Prolonged uncertainty about asylum that many refugees have to face is a significant factor in the maintenance of PTSD symptoms along with financial stress and unemployment. Post-migratory stressors that predict PTSD are fears of being returned to the war environment, delays in processing asylum claims, poverty, isolation and family separation. Loss of social networks and family separation perpetuate psychiatric symptoms, particularly depression and PTSD.

Much research on the influence of personality traits, methods of coping and appraisal related to stress has been linked to acute stress rather than trauma. The sheer magnitude of some trauma events makes it hard to isolate and explore particular psychological variables. It is an area of research that is in urgent need of reappraisal. With respect to war populations and refugees, the emphasis in the literature is essentially of existing pathology. Yet, refugees present a pertinent example of the human capacity to survive despite the greatest of losses and assaults on human identity and dignity. We would be well advised to also focus on healthy refugees, exploring aspects of resilience, which are most certainly inherent in this remarkable group.

Varying perceptions of mental illnesses: Cultural context of PTSD

There is an ongoing debate surrounding the use of the PTSD concept in non-western or developing countries experiencing conflict. Critics assert that it is a western concept, and its diagnosis is not - or not always - applicable to certain population groups. Certainly the glaring imbalance referred to earlier, provides the basis for debate. Because of the increasing awareness of cross-cultural differences, there is now considerably more attention paid to these factors. However, modifications continue to be carried out in Euro-American countries, and largely on people in exile. Criticism remains levelled at a number of different areas that are potentially affected by what is seen as western ethnocentrism. Four arguments relevant to women in conflict and post-conflict situations are discussed. The first is the assumption that the experience and expression of trauma is universal, and more radically, the way in which western paradigms construe illness is in fact universal. The reality is that different cultures and societies have varying perceptions about mental illness. Mental disorders have personal meaning and social significance only within a cultural context. What constitutes psychological disturbance is the product of a particular culture at a particular point in time. The very assumption of 'mental disorder' as an identifiable domain of illness, evolved from a particular (western) cultural and historical tradition. The 'medicalisation' of experience – the increasing influence of medical explanations of behaviour and emotion – is another ubiquitous, more contemporary western tendency.

Not only are there differing perceptions of what constitutes mental illness, but also what constitutes mental health or well-being. Whereas western models locate the difficulty inside individuals, other systems seek to relate that individual's problem to others – or even the cosmology. Cambodian women in resettlement perceive that psychological well-being is largely a socially defined and socially constructed notion. Literature on war refugees begins to acknowledge that these people do well or not as a function of their capacity to rebuild their social world and cultural meaning systems. Certainly evidence across cultures from war rape victims shows a consistent aspiration to rebuild destroyed community infrastructures rather than enter into emotionally invasive psychotherapy programmes focusing on their rape trauma.

The most germane example of the 'medicalisation' of trauma is PTSD, and a number of questions are raised as to its clinical significance. To this end, critics have pointed out that two of the most common features of non-western traumatised populations are somatisation and dissociation.[8] This does not negate the validity of PTSD, but does strengthen the argument that cross-cultural differences in symptoms are present and need to be accounted for. South East Asian refugees, having experienced war-related trauma and displacement, display symptoms of western entities of PTSD and depression. Yet, they understand these symptoms within an animist and supernatural belief system. This makes them highly suspicious of western medicine, and the possibility of a western physician to ameliorate their suffering. As the above example suggests, this argument becomes particularly relevant when responding to victims.

The second argument concerns context, namely one cannot generalise from limited trauma to massive, enduring trauma. A trauma caused by common, unfortunate incidents (for example, traffic accidents) cannot be explained and treated in the same way as colossal atrocities such as the Holocaust. War is an utterly different social context to the one that applies, say, after a disaster in Britain, where survivors of a clear-cut event can recover in an intact and resourced society. Criteria for major depression exclude disturbances that are a normal reaction to the death of a loved one. However, how does one judge a 'normal' reaction to witnessing the death of a husband and two sons by shooting, the death of another child by

shelling, witnessing the death of a sibling by torture and witnessing the rape of a parent – and for that matter on a more existential level, but as shattering, the death of an entire way of life?

Certain aspects of traumatic experiences suffered by people in non-western cultures are not adequately encompassed by the PTSD construct, not because of a different culture, but because of the nature and extent of trauma. This concerns:

- Prolonged and repeated trauma. In many non-western countries this is the rule rather than the exception, so that even the PTSD criteria of experiencing 'an event outside the normal range of experience' is rendered somewhat ridiculous.[9]

- Acute traumatic episodes that can only be understood in a socio-political or multigenerational context. There are differences in responses noted when comparing genocidal rape in war with rape following a date with someone well known to the victim. Do they, however, generate a unique psychological expression? Much has been written on the latter, but very little on the former.

- Collective trauma as experienced by a whole community in the context of political repression, war or a natural disaster. The strong sense of community evidenced in non-western societies, compared to the often individualistic and subjective focus in western cultures must create significant differences in the psychological

Box 1.2: Difficulties in documentation

One of the greatest obstacles to understanding the effects and scope of war rape, is the difficulty in documentation. There are a number of reasons – many of which very shrewd – as to why the vast majority of those who survived atrocities of wars will not speak out:

- They (quite realistically) fear ostracism and stigmatisation.
- They fear retaliation by the perpetrators, either towards themselves, or more often towards remaining family in the region.
- They feel an all-consuming helplessness; that no one can help them now that they have been violated.
- They harbour extreme suspicion of authority – partially because displaced people and refugees are not always in possession of all required papers or residential permits.
- They experience insensitivity and egoistic motives from those persuading disclosure – many women have felt betrayed by those claiming a desire to help. These include journalists who have published photographs and names, women's groups wishing to sensitise the victims to the destructive patriarchal structures inherent in their society. Such feminist discourse is thoroughly lost on – or deeply offensive to – women who are freshly mourning their men, and longing for the stability and familiarity of the very patriarchal structures ultimately under criticism. Moreover, women deeply resent the insistence on

the part of psychosocial aid workers that the trauma of rape is paramount and must be dealt with. It overrides their own expressed desire to improve their disastrous living environment, and provide some security for their surviving children.

Data collection is very difficult because of the:

- Constant mobility of the population.
- Chaotic and primitive settings of help in displaced and refugee populations.
- Destroyed infrastructure and inadequate and untrained staffing of local social welfare and health services, making systematic investigation unfeasible.
- Ethical considerations of asking such traumatised people to disclose their experiences and feelings.
- In terms of forced pregnancy, documentation is even more difficult, since most women seek abortion. Even with pregnancies that were too late to be terminated, many women avoided medical assistance, as it would result in documented proof of rape. Data available on such pregnancies in the form of reports from women's clinics in different cities in Bosnia and Croatia, indicate the desire for abortion regardless of the stage of pregnancy, or abandoning the child in hospital immediately after birth.

impact and expression of such traumas. Collective and individual trauma are not, however, mutually exclusive, and will more than likely be experienced on communal, as well as, individual levels.

- Cumulative exposure to life events. Most studies focus on the relationship between a single life event and a subsequent psychological outcome. This unfortunately does not bear resemblance to real life experiences of many populations whose daily existence is characterised by unrelenting stress, if not trauma.

- Multiple refugee trauma. In addition to traumas experienced in home countries that include torture, starvation and witnessing killings, refugees must overcome problems of acculturation, racism, language, employment, housing and health. The process of rebuilding lives can prove to be as traumatic as the dislocation process from which they sought refuge.

The third argument proposes that when experience is 'medicalised', it is stripped of the social and political disposition. This means it ignores or downplays explanations of disorder at levels of social, political and economic functioning. As a consequence problems having their origins in, for example, poverty, discrimination and oppression, are treated medically. Many stress models currently in use are inappropriate for conceptualising politically induced violence and repression because they reduce social, political and historical problems to the individual level.

A final argument against the 'medicalisation' of experience is the objection to the inherent and often inappropriate imputation of a sick-role to war affected people *en masse* – the assumption that entire populations exposed to war are 'traumatised'. The main thrust of this argument is that suffering and trauma are not interchangeable; suffering is not *per se* pathology. This distortion may well not serve their interests in a struggle to rebuild meaningful lives. There is speculation that millions of dollars from donors have flowed to programmes whose impact has not been evaluated, and may even include negative effects on survivors' inner world and traditional coping strategies at the very moment when these are damaged and destabilised. Humanitarian organisations should go to where

© Keystone, EPA Photo, Kim Ludbrook, 2003

Social stigmatisation represents another layer of victimisation in the everyday lives of rape victims. Kema Jallah (left) and her friend Satta Lamie have both been repeatedly abused by soldiers during the conflict in Liberia.

the concerns of survivor groups direct them, towards their devastated communities and ways of life, and to address urgent questions about rights and justice.

These provoking criticisms of the largely western mental health community in no way diminish much of the essential work that has been performed in conflicts across the globe. They should, however, be viewed as necessary challenges, encouraging humility in the face of alternative cultural formulations of human distress.

Some recommendations in the treatment of PTSD

There is general agreement among mental health practitioners that a combination of medicine and psychotherapy will prove most effective in the treatment of PTSD. The vast majority of treatment outcome studies for PTSD have focused on cognitive-behavioural treatment programmes, their effectiveness in treating PTSD has consistently been demonstrated. These programmes include variants of exposure therapy, anxiety management and cognitive therapy.[10] The aim is to modify unrealistic assumptions (such as guilt), beliefs and automatic thoughts that lead to disturbing emotions and impaired functioning. Individuals are taught anxiety management through relaxation training, controlled breathing, positive imagery, and distraction techniques. In addition, the person is helped to confront specific situations, people, objects, memories or emotions that have become associated with the stressor and now evoke an unrealistic, intense fear. The suggested frequency of sessions is weekly to twice weekly, for the initial period, which is the first three months. Frequency of medication visits is weekly for the first month and every two weeks thereafter. The three main factors associated with successful therapy outcomes are patient perception of therapy as credible, high and regular attendance of therapy sessions, and most importantly, the absence of ongoing stress.[11]

The treatment described above is considered to be effective, given the appropriate, supportive environment. Anyone familiar with a conflict or post-conflict environment will recognise that few, if any of the necessary elements are present. All factors associated with successful therapy outcomes are challenged:

- Choice of medication is often very limited, and supply not necessarily consistent.

- The likelihood of a therapeutic setting being sufficiently staffed to attend to the numbers of PTSD patients individually and on a weekly basis is slim – particularly when rates in some populations are exceptionally high.

- Difficulties and expense in transport and familial responsibility (such as being the sole provider) may

well confound the possibility of attending on a regular basis. Many patients, particularly from rural areas, are unfamiliar and suspicious of seeking help in a therapeutic setting, and may well not perceive it as credible. Undoubtedly the absence of ongoing stress is a therapeutic demand that is virtually out of the question.

The nature and extent of therapy will thus largely depend on the resources available. Unfortunately under circumstances of social upheaval, staff are usually faced with a clinical overload, and the systematic documentation of therapeutic results does not take place. There is rarely the opportunity of publishing clinical findings that are so crucial to the improved understanding of trauma and its consequences. More funding should be directed towards such research, enabling professionals from different countries to contribute to this essential body of knowledge.

Although there is to date no well established, successful response to PTSD that can be implemented within the restraints of all conflict zones, the following are aspects of the conflict and post-conflict environment that may serve as guidelines about which practices should be avoided and which should be encouraged. Notably most points are pertinent to experiences of sexual abuse.

- Most women who have experienced sexual abuse refuse treatment. When women do seek help it is more often for physical ailments. A report from a psychiatric hospital in Croatia describes eighteen victims of sexual torture. All were diagnosed with PTSD, some suicidal, but came to seek assistance for forced pregnancy. All of the women refused any form of psychotherapy. This response is fairly consistent with reports from other psychosocial programmes.[12]

- Many displaced women have a rural background. Even aside from the aversion to therapy associated with rape victims, the social and cultural background thwarts participation in psychosocial programmes. Problems have always been solved within the extended family. In sharp contrast to the custom of particularly North Americans, the idea of expressing personal distress to a complete stranger is anathema to the majority of victims needing assistance.

- A number of harmful outcomes have been reported after rape victims were interviewed by medical personnel, including psychotic episodes and even suicide. In addition, some initiatives serve to drive the wedge even further between rape victims and their community by only offering assistance to rape victims.

- Many psychosocial programmes employ western models and staff – particularly in the initial phases. At the core of most therapy interventions is the understand-

Dr. Vivian Khamis investigated the impact of traumatic experiences on the lives of families after the first Palestinian uprising against the occupying Israeli force during the six years of Intifada (1987–1993). Based on the 1993 Palestinian Human Rights Information Centre Census, she allocated 900 Palestinian families who had sustained Intifada-related traumas. She found that 7 per cent of these had had a family member killed, 8per cent had one family member injured, 14.5 per cent had one family member imprisoned and 3.2 per cent had found their house demolished. The remaining 67.3 per cent had undergone more than one of these traumatic experiences.

Dr. Khamis found that around one third of the adult interviewees, of whom 51.4 per cent were men and 48.6 per cent women, showed a consequent history of post-traumatic stress disorder. If the trauma-related stress was very high, other mental health problems were also present. Such trauma-induced stress lasted in many cases for a long time. It had a serious impact on people's health, their work, their marriage and their family relationships. The experienced traumatic event(s) also led to serious role strains in the family. While many men experienced an inability to fulfil their traditional roles because of injury, disability or unemployment, the women, but also often older children, had to assume new and multiple roles. For women, the most obvious strains were increased role obligations in parenting, homemaking, income-generation, satisfying spousal needs and helping children with their schoolwork.

Source:
V. Khamis, *Political Violence and the Palestinian Family. Implications for Mental Health and Well-Being* (New York: Haworth Maltreatment and Trauma Press, 2000).

Daily life in the devastation of on-going conflict and violence in the West Bank city of Hebron.

ing that rape must be acknowledged and discussed. Given how fearful women are to speak about this, how many other traumas they need to deal with, and how little we know about the effects of war rape, one should seriously question whether this assumption can be made at all. Is giving voice to that experience therapeutic or iatrogenic – that is aggravated by the process of examination and 'treatment'? With increasing experience, more and more professionals in conflict zones are urging greater caution over encouraging victims to talk about rape if they are reluctant.

- There is a growing interest in the use of narrative techniques, and testimony methods. It is interesting to note that with the use of narratives, women freely describe experiencing other forms of violence, but frequently refer to their sexual trauma as if it had happened to someone else. Such storytelling can voice the 'unspeakable' without facing the consequences. However, considerable skill and care is required with regard to the implications of recounting such traumatic events. Regrettably such skilled staff is not always available.

- Survivors require an environment that feels safe and contains adequate social support. They must have a sense of control of when, where and if they talk about their traumatic experiences. Numerous occasions have been noted where women specifically asked for support in other areas, refusing support groups, individual and group psychotherapy focusing on rape. A number of positive outcomes could result from respecting these wishes. If women who had similar traumatic experiences were to form groups and tackle developmental projects, they would experience invaluable support from one another, begin to rebuild their community (an essential element in returning to a semblance of normality) and have a greater sense of agency and control over their situation.

- Programmes, often in the form of crisis intervention whose efficacy has yet to be proven, employ voluntary workers who are not trained mental health professionals. Their brief training cannot fully prepare them for the intensity of the torture experiences suffered by many women – consequently they are overwhelmed and unable to be of assistance.

- Funds that were forthcoming during an initial phase (crisis intervention, emergency rehabilitation) often dry up, resulting in the premature termination of programmes. Reliable, long-term projects often cannot elicit sufficient financial support. Programmes folding under financial strain create more problems than they solve, and interventions are more likely to succeed if there is no excessive dependence on imported expertise and support.

- Much of the language describing raped women, and the associations surrounding this issue, are far from helpful to the women.

There are constant references to them having 'lost their dignity', assumptions that these acts have completely destroyed them. Even the term 'victim' can have a negative association, and some prefer to use the term 'survivor'. It is true that there are many who have overcome these multiple atrocities. Many of them have shown tremendous dignity and courage. They are deeply offended by the assumption that they are 'sick' and in need of outside help. They are offered pity, when in fact many deserve admiration. The most exceptional stories are by no means those recounting the spectacular destruction of communities and individuals through such evil. Rather, they are accounts of women who continue to display an indomitable spirit and courage under such circumstances.

Given the wide domain of areas affected by multiple and prolonged trauma, the healing process should not only be dominated by health care professionals. In the absence of security, a home, family and community, which clinical interventions can begin to heal the destructive effects of war rape or torture? These limitations must be recognised; the responsibility of healing this group in the community lies far more broadly than with mental health professionals alone.

Endnotes

1 A. Antonovsky, *Health, Stress and Coping: New Perspectives on Mental and Physical Well-Being* (San Francisco: Jossey-Brass, 1979).

2 J. Salem-Pickartz, *Women and the Family: Sources of Preparedness and Resilience in the Face of Conflict and Terrorism.*. Presentation at the conference tThe Role of Women in Building Peace and Security (Beirut: MMM International, 16 – 17 October 2003).

3 J. Salem-Pickartz, *Psychosocial Programming for Children and Adolescents in Need of Special Protection* (Amman: UNICEF MENARO, 2001), 15.

4 A stressor is an event that is perceived as uncontrollable, unpredictable, challenging, and/or threatening.

5 Hyper-vigilance is an enhanced state of sensitivity accompanied by an exaggerated intensity of behaviours whose purpose it is to detect threats.

6 A. C. McFarlane and G. De Girolamo, 'The Nature of Traumatic Stressors and the Epidemiology of Post Traumatic Reactions', in B. A. van der Kolk, A. C. McFarlane and L. Weisaeth (eds), *Traumatic Stress* (New York: The Guilford Press, 1996), 129-154.

7 Somatisation is a syndrome marked by the chronic experience of unpleasant or painful physical symptoms for which no organic cause can be found.

8 Dissociation is a process of the splitting off of clusters of mental contents from conscious awareness, a mechanism central to hysterical conversion and dissociative disorders; the separation of an idea from its emotional significance and effect as seen in the inappropriate affect effect of schizophrenic patients.

9 American Psychiatric Association, DSM-IV, *Diagnostic and Statistical Manual of Mental Disorders* (Washington DC: APA, 1994).

10 Cognitive-behavioural therapy is a treatment based upon changing negative schemata that influence a person to construe life in a depressing way. It focuses on changing negative patterns of thinking and on solving concrete problems through brief sessions in which a therapist helps a client challenge negative thoughts, consider alternative perspectives, and take effective actions.

11 E. Foa, 'Psychosocial Treatment of PTSD in Expert Consensus Treatment Guidelines for Post Traumatic Stress Disorder', *Journal of Clinical Psychiatry*, 60 (1999), 43-8.

12 D. Kozaric-Kovacic, V. Folnegovic-Smalc and J. Skrinjaric, 'Systematic Raping of Women in Croatia and Bosnia and Herzegovina: A Preliminary Psychiatric Report', *Croatian Medical Journal*, 34 (1993), 86-7.

Chapter 2

Women in Flight

'I was an organizer and educator of peasant groups in Magdalena Medio, the heart of the oilfields in northern Colombia. I was in the office when a videotape was delivered to me. I saw on the tape a colleague of mine being tortured and killed. The message was clear: If I continued with my activities, I'd be next. I ran to the police and asked for their protection but they told me there was nothing they could do. I was afraid for my own life, and for my co-workers. I fled to Bogotá.'

Maria, a community organiser, in E. Rehn and E. J. Sirleaf, *Women, War, Peace*, 2002

Women and children comprise approximately 80 per cent of the world's 34.8 million uprooted people – refugees and internally displaced persons (IDPs). Refugees are those who have crossed an international border, while IDPs remain within their country of origin. Although numerous provisions of international and national law, legal standards and policies exist to protect refugees, these often go unheeded. Moreover, internally displaced persons, including women and children, lack any specific legally binding instrument for their protection and may only benefit from some provisions of human rights and humanitarian treaties and other general international standards. For women and girls in particular, the gap between laws and standards on the one hand – and practice on the other – continues to threaten their lives and, in doing so, the safety and security of their families and communities. While over the last decade, increased attention has been paid to the situation of refugee and internally displaced women, more must be done to ensure that this awareness translates into concrete action that improves the lives of these women and their families.

Causes of flight

The causes of flight are many and rooted in the atrocities civilians are exposed to during political turmoil, wars and armed conflicts - human rights abuses, including gender-based violence, ethnic violence discrimination, and the fear of persecution. The breakdown of state and family/communal authority and the accompanying loss of protection add to a person's insecurity and spur flight. Many refugee advocates maintain that flight must be seen in the broad context of a range of international issues such as good governance, sustainable development, trade, and peace and security issues.[1] They argue that the key to understanding the causes of flight, and thereby the solutions to ending it, is within this broader context. An understanding of the consequences of flight can lead to the means by which to prevent further flight, and perhaps one day break the cycle of insecurity and violence that

A Palestinian mother tries to escape an Israeli missile attack in Gaza City.

affects millions of refugee women and girls in conflicts worldwide.

During armed conflict, women become more vulnerable as societies break down and their traditional protections – family, community, local authority – disappear. They may feel their only chance for security is to seek safe haven elsewhere. They could also be escaping a trauma, such as rape or forced marriage. Flight can be spurred by a distortion of traditional practices brought about by conflict often manifested in the treatment of girls and women. In order to retain a measure of stability and familiarity during chaotic times, societies often stress traditional activities as a perceived means to protect cultural heritage. During the war in Sierra Leone, there was evidence of an increase in the number of girls undergoing traditional rites of passage, as in secret Banda societies, involving female circumcision among a wider range of girls and women than before the conflict. Communities may reintroduce or extend these practices as a means to preserve tradition in the face of threats to survival of the clan or ethnic group.

The poverty and insecurity brought on by war can also increase tendencies towards forced marriage of girls at earlier ages as a way to ensure the protection of daughters in a family that already has difficulty supporting its children. For example, Afghanistan has had a history of arranged marriage. As twenty years of war challenged the ability of Afghans to survive, parents or guardians often chose, as a survival tactic, to force the girls in their care to marry at younger ages so that they would have a male protector. Hence lessening the demands placed on the those family members who are responsible for providing food, shelter and other needs. In some societies, it is traditional for parents during peacetime to send one or two of their

children to stay with relatives or close friends who are wealthier and in a better position to give the child a quality education and opportunities for skills building and employment. If and when conflict breaks out, such 'foster care' situations can become exploitative – the caretaker may treat the child as a second-class family member and subject them to child labour, or other activities that put them at risk of abuse.

For refugee women and girls, the violence that causes them to flee their homes or countries is only the beginning. Leaving their homes, villages or countries is a gamble because the destination – whether refugee camps or urban areas, abandoned homes or the homes of friends or family – can put women at greater risk of gender-based violence, abduction, exploitation, poverty and illness. As they attempt to cross a border or move from an unsafe location, refugee women and girls may be victimised by army or rebel groups, border guards or even the local community. Women who lose their male head of household or other male family members can be specifically targeted for abuse because there is no male protector. Therefore, flight does not necessarily bring immediate security. Displaced women and their families must often move repeatedly to find adequate protection. As a result, they often experience multiple displacements and a downward spiral of insecurity and poverty. New threats to their safety emerge. It is a cycle that is difficult to escape and leads to an even greater need for protection. In Colombia, internally displaced women who manage to escape the brutality of paramilitary and guerrilla groups can be found living in the slums of Bogotá. As they can find jobs only in the unofficial, unregulated sector, most of them become domestic workers, likely to experience economic and physical exploitation. Moreover, since the government of Colombia is trying to discourage the internally displaced persons from

Chart 2.1 : Trends in the number of refugees and other persons of UNHCR concern in the last two decades (1980-2002)

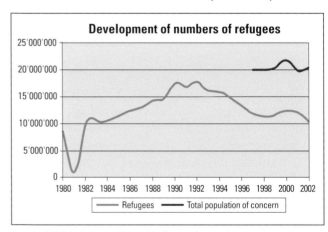

Source : UNHCR, *Refugees by Numbers* (2003), at http://www.unhcr.org/

moving to the slum areas, internally displaced women do not dare to seek legal and adequate protection. Women's choices as to when and how to flee may also be limited because they often lack the essentials for mobility such as documentation, (identification cards, passports, birth certificates), funds for transportation, basic literacy, and access to information. The lack of control over when and how they flee makes women more vulnerable to abuse and exploitation.

Too often women are not able to provide an elementary level of security and safety for themselves and their children. Even those responsible for helping women in flight – including UN agencies, local assistance and human rights groups – may not perceive supporting women as a priority in their work. The rights of refugee women and girls can be a low priority for host governments, as they are generally unwanted in the countries to which they have fled. Internally displaced women are frequently not protected by their own governments that are too often reluctant to recognise their situation and may also be fuelling repression. Humanitarian actors usually face difficulties when accessing internally displaced populations or receiving information about their condition. The assistance provided to IDPs by the United Nations High Commissioner for Refugees (UNHCR) is also limited.[2]

Protection gaps while displaced

When refugee and internally displaced women and girls arrive at a destination, they continue to remain at risk of abuse, exploitation, violence and abduction. In Nepal, Bhutanese women who escaped the threat of violence by armed combatants were abused or threatened with violence in the refugee camps to which they fled.[3] Domestic violence can also increase. Burundian women who fled their country for safety in Tanzania in the late 1990s, for example, were found to face an increase of domestic violence once in the camps. The special pressures, uncertainties, and indignities associated with flight combined with the housing, security,

Basic supplies are scarce in the Chechen refugee camps in Ingushetia, Russia, especially when the government fails to provide official recognition and support.

food, and other problems, which people tend to face in the camps can exacerbate already frayed domestic situations and men's feeling of powerlessness.[4]

Women refugees who move to urban areas of host countries are at particular risk because the UNHCR, gives limited assistance to these populations. Although they should be protected under the national laws of the host country and under international law, including conventions to which the host country is a state party, refugees in urban settings are very often discriminated against and abused by the local population. In addition, the host country's institutions, courts, police, and local human rights organisations often do not see refugees as a priority, or are reluctant to support them, for fear of the country becoming a 'magnet' for refugees. They also do not want to be seen as putting refugees' needs above those of their own citizens.

Refugee women and girls can face different forms of abuse than men and boys. In Pakistan, while the government detains and deports mainly Afghan men and boys because they are more mobile in urban areas and accessible to the

---

Box 2.1 : Existing international instruments on the protection of female refugees and internally displaced women and girls

Existing legislation constitute a relatively solid base for the protection of women refugees and internally displaced persons, under the condition that conventions and laws are incorporated into national law and implemented properly:
- Universal Declaration of Human Rights (1948).
- International Covenant on Civil and Political Rights (1966).
- Convention Relating to the Status of Refugees (1951), and its Protocol (1967).
- Four Geneva Conventions (1949), and the two Additional Protocols (1977).
- Convention on Consent to Marriage, Minimum Age for Marriage and Registration of Marriages (1962).

- Declaration on the Protection of Women and Children in Emergency and Armed Conflict (1974).
- Convention on the Elimination of All Forms of Discrimination against Women (1979).
- UNHCR Policy on Refugee Women 1990.
- Guidelines on the Protection of Refugee Women 1991 (UNHCR).
- Sexual Violence against Refugees, Guidelines on Prevention and Response, UNHCR (1995, revised in 2003 to include returnees and internally displaced persons).
- Refugee Children, Guidelines on Protection and Care (UNHCR, 1994).
- Guiding Principles on Internal Displacement (UN, 1998).
- Five Commitments to Refugee Women (UNHCR, December 2001).

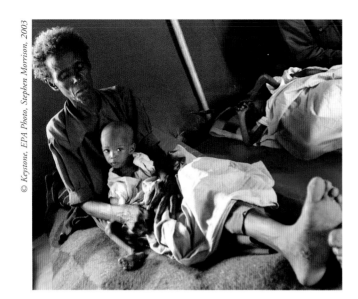

A refugee woman's status in her community makes it difficult to survive. This Ethiopian mother and child rest at a UNICEF-feeding center.

Pakistani authorities, women are less likely to be detained or deported. Afghan women heads of household and their children living in urban areas, however, can be exploited by local property owners, especially when they are too poor to pay rent. For example, Afghan women living in Peshawar described how their community representative, an Afghan, was forcing them, or their children, to have sex or transport drugs in exchange for living rent free. The women said that the Pakistani authorities were not only aware of, but also involved in the criminal activity. The women were too afraid to approach the Pakistani police, due to the threat of detention or deportation.[5] In these situations, women have little or no recourse and few options for assistance.

Internally displaced women face many of the same problems as refugee women, as governments are often unwilling to provide services or protection because the women are from a particular social or ethnic group, or are not perceived as a priority for support. They can be seen as liabilities and easy

to ignore. The government of Sierra Leone, for example, has classified internally displaced persons living in Grafton Camp, near the capital city Freetown, as 'homeless', thereby relieving the government of its responsibility to assist this population. The camp residents are overwhelmingly women heads of household and their children. Because the camp population has been classified as 'homeless' and not internally displaced, they do not fall under the budgets or programmes run by the government, or international humanitarian assistance agencies.

Barriers in protection of refugee women

To address more precisely the protection and needs of refugee women, the United Nations High Commissioner for Refugees introduced its 1990 Policy on Refugee Women and the 1991 Guidelines on the Protection of Refugee Women. However, although the guidelines include many important recommendations and have succeeded in raising awareness among UNHCR staff and other humanitarian assistance agencies of the protection concerns of refugee women, major challenges remain in the implementation of these tools.

While the guidelines include recommendations on camp design and stress the importance of women's participation in

Table 2.1:

Estimated number of persons who fall under the mandate of the UNHCR in January 2004 (in absolute numbers)

Region	Refugees & Others
Asia	9,378,917
Africa	4,593,199
Europe	4,403,921
Northern America	1,061,199
Latin America and Caribbean	1,050,288
Oceania	69,206
TOTAL	20,556,781

Notes:

The table above includes refugees and internally displaced and other persons of UNHCR concern. The term 'refugees' in the UNHCR is used to indicate the refugee status of persons according to the 1951 Convention Relating to the Status of Refugees or its 1967 Protocol, or the 1969 Convention Governing the Specific Aspects of Refugee Problems in Africa by the Organisation of African Unity (OAU), or the UNHCR Statute. The internally displaced and other persons of UNHCR concern are those who do not fall into the category of refugees but who are in need of humanitarian aid, i.e. asylum-seekers, recently returned refugees, and other stateless and war-affected populations. The number of all uprooted persons in theat present world is about 35 million which is- higher than the estimates given by the UNHCR due to persons who do not belong to the two categories of UNHCR concern.

Source: UNHCR Statistics, *The Refugee Story in Statistics,* at http://www.unhcr.ch/cgi-bin/texis/vtx/statistics

Table 2.2:

Structure of refugees according to the UNHCR categories in January 2004 (in absolute numbers)

Refugees	Asylum-seekers	Returned refugees	Internally displaced	Stateless and various	TOTAL
10,389,700	1,014,400	2,425,000	5,777,200	950,800	20,556,700

Source: UNHCR/Governments, Compiled by UNHCR, Population Data Unit/PGDS.

Chart 2.2: Female refugees per region in 2000 (in percentage)

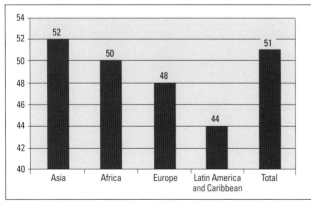

Region	Percentage
Asia	52
Africa	50
Europe	48
Latin America and Caribbean	44
Total	51

Source: UNHCR, *Women, Children and Older Refugees* (July 2001), at http://www.unhcr.org

Thousands of women seeking shelter at a camp for internally displaced people in Darfur, Sudan. It is estimated that one million fled the violence in the country during 2004.

camp decision-making to promote the safety of refugee women and girls, too often the guidance goes unheeded. In a series of interviews in Pakistan, for instance, Afghan refugee women said they were not consulted when a UNHCR implementing partner built baths in a refugee camp. A survey of Afghan refugee women there found that they refused to use the baths, which were along the perimeter of the camp, because they were afraid of attacks and harassment.[6]

Although the guidelines also provide that women's needs and participation must be considered in resource distribution, unequal allocation of resources remains a problem in many camps. In too many cases, food and other assistance is given only to the male head of household or a male family member. A refugee woman's culture or status in her community may make it difficult for her to demand her equal share. In addition, she may not have access to UNHCR to voice her concerns. In an interview, a UNHCR staff person described an instance where newly arriving refugees gathered at a refugee camp while tent distribution was underway. As men competed for the limited supply, a UNHCR member of staff noticed a group of veiled women sitting quietly nearby. The staff person learned that they were widows who had not been included in the tent distribution.[7]

This problem is compounded when women are not given their own documentation and, therefore, are unable to directly access the assistance and services they need. Without their own identification, they cannot receive goods and have to rely on the male head of household or other benefactors to provide for their families. Refugee women have described serious difficulties accessing resources such as fuel and food aid because it was delivered in their communities without their participation. UNHCR quotes a refugee woman as stating: '*We are second-class citizens when it comes to food, water and shelter distribution. We remain the world's invisible refugees.*'[8] The 1991 guidelines have helped increase awareness of this problem among UNHCR staff, implementing partners and the displaced populations, but more still needs to be done.

Part of the problem is the failure of those on the ground to recognise the vital link between protection and assistance. The traditional focus on legal protection such as *non-refoulement* and separation of civilians and combatants is now expanding to include physical protection. The latter includes ensuring equal access to quality humanitarian assistance and services, such as food aid, education, shelter materials and skills training. This broader definition of protection

A protest against forced repatriation in a refugee camp at the Thai-Cambodian border. People are wary due to the experience of previous refugees who were resettled in Cambodia near mined areas or close to Khmer Rouge-controlled territory.

more clearly outlines the link between the two, however, humanitarian assistance and human rights groups have not yet fully embraced and implemented protection strategies to encompass this wider context and ensure that it is a programme priority. The following example underscores the failure to recognise the vital connection between protection and assistance – and how this failure can lead to increased abuse of women. Marie, a Congolese refugee, was living in Lusaka, Zambia, with her children. As the head of her household, she was struggling to provide her family with food and shelter, and went to a non-governmental organisation (NGO) for assistance. The NGO staff said she was getting pregnant too often; she confessed that she had to trade sex in order to survive. UNHCR and NGO staff discussed her case and determined that her problem was that she had too many children, therefore she should stop having them. They failed to recognise her situation as a protection problem, that is, lack of food/assistance was forcing her to turn to prostitution. She had requested assistance with food and shelter, and explained that her circumstances were dire, yet the protection risks she faced were not considered.[9] Widespread recognition of this link would go a long way to ensure the safety of refugee women and girls.

Staff of UNHCR and other agencies are not necessarily aware of how to implement programmes effectively and they may have difficulty understanding how to put guidelines into practice. For example, a UNHCR staff member in Ethiopia was preparing for a large influx of Ethiopian refugees returning from Sudan. The Ethiopian refugees had been living in Sudan for many years, and while in exile, followed a system of separate education for girls and boys. The staff member was concerned that the returning refugees would not send their daughters to school because most of the classes in the Ethiopian community were now co-educational. If the education demands had been considered earlier in the planning phase of the return, UNHCR could have initiated an awareness campaign encouraging co-education in the refugee camp before the families returned home. In another example, a UNHCR officer was trying to protect a woman from extremely violent domestic abuse. However, it was not clear how to do so, since sending the woman to a shelter would mean separating her from her children and possibly jeopardising her ability to obtain custody of the children in case the community or authorities perceived her as abandoning them.[10]

The lack of female staff in UNHCR and other agencies is another obstacle to protecting women from violence. Because women refugees are more likely to share protection problems with other women, their presence in the field would improve the ability to obtain information about the issues refugee women and girls face, and the best way to address them. The recruitment, hiring and training of more women by UNHCR, international and local NGOs and governments would likely increase the reporting of and response to protection problems. In 2004, UNHCR announced a pilot project to mainstream gender and age in its operations. This presents an opportunity to move forward to protect the rights of women and children.

In addition, staff attitudes may be a barrier. Whether a refugee, local hire or expatriate, each may have different attitudes as to whether they should be promoting equal status for women, as well as equal access to resources. An understanding that abuses such as rape and domestic violence must not only be investigated, but also dealt with and prevented, must be reached. This understanding must also be attained by UNHCR staff, governments and implementing partners to ensure that combating violence against refugee and internally displaced women and girls is a priority.

Return home

The precarious situation of refugee and displaced women does not necessarily improve once conflict has ended and the displaced return home. Many examples exist of gender-based violence increasing in post-conflict situations, particularly when demobilised men are not fully integrated into the community and feel powerless. In Bosnia, for example, the incidence of alcohol abuse among men increased, as did

A Sudanese refugee after she and her family reached the safety of Bahai on the Chad border. In Darfur, tens of thousands have been killed and millions have been driven from their homes.

An estimated 1.2 million Azerbaijanis were forced out of their homes during the 1988-94 ethnic conflict. Today, thousands still live in abandoned railway cars, mud-brick houses and tents.

domestic violence. In addition, although the war has officially ended, an unstable government may be unable to protect its citizens, as can be seen in present-day Iraq and Afghanistan. Or, there may be a lack of commitment by the community or civil forces because violence against women is not seen as a crime worth preventing or punishing.

Refugee or internally displaced women who want to return home may be unable or unwilling to do so for several reasons. Some may feel their safety would still be in jeopardy if they returned. Many Afghan refugee women, for example, remain in dismal conditions in refugee settlements in Pakistan because they fear continued insecurity in their homeland.[11] Lack of ownership or access to property, including land and housing, may also be an obstacle. Inheritance laws and practices in many countries do not allow a woman to inherit land, therefore, a widow might have nothing to return to. Women may also be prevented from returning by the closing of a border, if they lack proper identification needed to cross the border, or if there is a risk of being abducted and trafficked en route.

Some women may have no choice but to face potential risks. In families with a male head of household, men often make the decision whether or not to return, they may not consider the potential risks to the women and girls in their family, or may not consider these dangers sufficient reasons to delay return. Assistance agencies may also play a role, too often such agencies do not investigate the protection risks to women and girls in the return process and therefore families, including female headed households, may be unwittingly placing themselves in danger. Yet, the refugee experience can be beneficial for women as they gain skills and other forms of empowerment. In one example, Guatemalan women in refugee camps in Mexico in the 1980s and 1990s were trained by the UN and women's organisations on their rights and how to address gender discrimination. The attitudes of these women, who had previously been confined to the home, were altered as they began to recognise the bene-

fits of literacy, education and skills building. There is evidence that the younger generations who lived in the camps, as well as the mothers, are pushing for greater educational opportunities. In a similar fashion, doors were opened for women refugees from El Salvador who had been living in refugee camps in Honduras. These refugee women, whose roles had been limited to domestic work and gardening, learnt to read and gained non-traditional skills in basic health care and family planning. In many cases, returnee women contribute to reconstruction because they have higher levels of education and skills, such as Afghan girls and women who were educated during their stay in Pakistani refugee camps. They are also able to promote change in their native communities by becoming role models. Jamila Akberzai and Partawmina Hashemee are directors of the Afghan Women Welfare Department and the Afghan Women's Resource Centre, respectively, with offices in Afghanistan and Pakistan. Refugees for more than fifteen years, they are creating opportunities for other refugee and returnee women. Their organisations provide literacy training, health information, and skills building, to Afghan refugee women in Pakistan and returnees in Afghanistan. The organisations are expanding in Afghanistan and, as a result, contributing to the country's reconstruction.

For women who are unable to return to their home country due to continued persecution, but cannot remain in the first country of asylum for the same reason, resettlement is an option. To be processed while in flight is very difficult, as women first need to access the agency charged with the screening. This may involve paying for transportation to get to the office and the risk of being seen by the people who are persecuting her. Screening an asylum case can take several months or years until a decision is made, which can increase the trauma on the asylum seeker.

Moreover, many refugee-receiving countries are increasing barriers to the movement of asylum seekers, so women and others are turning to illegal means to get to the asylum country. On arrival, countries often put asylum seekers in detention for an indefinite period of time, which puts refugee women at risk. The Women's Commission for Refugee Women and Children in 2000 documented, for example, widespread sexual, physical, emotional and verbal abuse of women in detention by officers at a detention centre in the United States.[12] Sexual abuses ranging from rape to sexual molestation and harassment were perpetrated repeatedly by US immigration and naturalisation services officers. Women who co-operated in sexual activities were made false promises of release from detention. Threats of deportation, transfer to county jails, or even death were levelled at women who dared to resist. Physical and emotional abuses included demanding Muslim women to remove their veils, in violation of their religion, not providing adequate food, and verbal abuse of women of particular nationalities.

Violence against refugee and IDP women resulting from armed conflict will not abate until international assistance groups, governments and the UN make its prevention a priority. Instruments such as UNHCR guidelines are important tools in addressing this issue, but there are gaps in their implementation. Another key issue is ensuring that refugee women are involved in all the decisions that affect their lives. Participation promotes protection, either through local groups or individual women. These women have a strong voice; the international community must learn to listen. Local women's groups are key to changing attitudes towards women in communities and to creating more opportunities for women, which is the first step in ending the often prevailing indifference toward the violence refugee and IDP women face.

Legal and Other Instruments for the Protection of Female Refugees and Internally Displaced Women

Refugees

The core international legally binding instruments concerning the protection of refugees are the 1951 Convention Relating to the Status of Refugees and its 1967 Protocol. Today, there are a total of 145 state parties to one or both of these instruments.

© Reuters, Andrea Comas, 2003

In the Sahara desert 200,000 Saharawi refugees, 80 percent being women and children, struggle for survival. Women play a central role in creating a new life, actively developing health systems, education, resource distribution and participating in politics.

According to the 1951 convention, a refugee is a person who is outside his or her country, who has a well-founded fear of persecution based on race, religion, nationality, membership of a particular social group or political opinion, and whom the state is unwilling or unable to protect. The 1951 convention contained a geographical and time limitation, protecting mainly European refugees in the aftermath of the Second World War, but the 1967 protocol expanded the scope of the convention, as the problem of displacement spread throughout the world. In addition to the 1951 convention and its 1967 protocol, the rights of refugee women are also spelled out in other international instruments, including human rights and humanitarian treaties (see box 2.1). While every state may not be a state party of these instruments, they provide a framework of international law standards that supports protection and assistance activities related to refugee women.

The Convention Relating to the Status of Refugees does not specifically identify gender as one of the basis of persecution, which makes the presentation of claims based on gender particularly complex and challenging. Gender refugee and asylum claims have been adjudicated under the political opinion category and membership of a particular social group.

In many conflict settings, women have difficulty accessing refugee determination systems. Barriers they face include ambiguity in the way in which gender related persecution is addressed during status determinations; failure to provide gender or age sensitive interviews; and cultural considerations that make it difficult to discuss such abuses.

Gender related persecution may involve inhuman treatment for violating social norms; sexual violence; harmful traditional practices, such as female genital mutilation; the imposition of coercive and intrusive methods of birth control; and severe cases of domestic violence, where state authorities are unable or unwilling to provide protection to the person(s) concerned. As part of a refugee status determination, decision-makers may consider whether a woman could have remained safely in, or could return to some part of her own country, rather than seeking asylum in another country. This is referred to as an 'internal flight alternative'. If a decision-maker finds that a woman has an internal flight alternative, then the fear of persecution may not be well-founded.

There is wide acceptance of the legal analysis, which considers women as part of a 'particular social group' for purposes of status determination, but there is less agreement on how far that argument should go. For example, domestic violence is one of the leading causes of injury to women worldwide, but whether women who suffer from domestic violence should be able to access international legal protection is far from settled. In order to demonstrate unwillingness or inability to protect, a woman must present her situation to the authorities and risk retribution from her abusers if the state authorities are unwilling to protect her or be able to demonstrate a pattern of inaction by the state to similar situations.

For women who have fled their country of origin because of generalised violence, but cannot articulate a claim of persecution, there are limited legal protections. Many women become separated from their male members during flight and find themselves unaccompanied in a host country. When they have lost their traditional protectors, they are more vulnerable to human rights abuses and may even face persecution in their host country, but may still not qualify for refugee status. To qualify, women must be found to have a well-founded fear of persecution in their *home* country, a requirement that does not allow for the processing of women who have protection concerns in their *host* country. Many women in this situation are caught in a limbo. They cannot return to their country of origin because of ongoing armed conflict and face persecution in their country of first asylum, but do not qualify for third country resettlement because their protection problems are in their host country and not their home country.

Aside from substantive legal issues facing women asylum seekers, there are also procedural issues that can significantly impact upon a woman's claim. A woman asylum seeker may not always be given a separate interview if she is accompanied by her spouse; she may be reluctant to speak freely in front of male interviewers, either because of cultural mores or past experiences; and she may feel embarrassed or humiliated when relating information about sexual assaults she has had to endure. It is essential to use female staff when trying to elicit information from female refugees.

In a recent assessment of the implementation of the Guidelines on the Protection of Refugee Women, adopted by the UNHCR in 1991, the Women's Commission for Refugee Women and Children made several recommendations to UNHCR, including the strengthening of the Offices of the Senior Co-ordinator for Women and the Senior Co-ordinator for Children.[13] The rationale for this recommendation was to ensure accountability for the enforcement of UNHCR's internal guidelines. Unfortunately, this recommendation was not followed. In fact, in 2003 UNHCR announced the elimination of both of these offices because of budget concerns and a desire to mainstream their functions. The impact of this policy change is uncertain. It is imperative for refugee women advocates to closely monitor how UNHCR manages the enforcement of its protection guidelines in the absence of the Offices of the Senior Co-ordinator for Women and the Senior Co-ordinator for Children. Key to this is ensuring that the guidelines are implemented and monitored by

Box 2.2: Colombia's internally displaced women

For more than forty years Colombians have been involved in war waged by the armed forces, communist guerrillas, right-wing paramilitary groups, and the drug cartels. The majority of the conflict's victims are innocent civilians who are either killed by one of the warring factions, or affected indirectly - uprooted, forcibly displaced or have their livelihoods destroyed. Internally displaced women are among the most affected victims of Colombia's ongoing internal conflict belonging to a large list of unacknowledged victims of a conflict that has claimed millions of lives and caused grievances to many more.

Displacement in Colombia has not followed a consistent pattern, as the conditions that have prompted people to flee have changed dramatically during the evolution of the conflict. Today, a complex set of factors has forced people to move to less isolated, and what people believe to be more secure, regions of the country. According to CODHES, Consultoria para los Derechos Humanos y el Desplazamiento, a leading Colombian humanitarian NGO, an estimated three million people have been internally displaced since 1985. Most of the internally displaced persons migrate to large cities, or cities near the areas of expulsion where they confront the difficulties of urban life and the increasing rejection from its inhabitants, who distrust them and regard them as intruders. Women endure particular suffering due to the changing economic and domestic conditions that result from displacement and from the new demands imposed on them by the transformation of traditional gender roles.

Although there is an estimated two million internally displaced persons in the country, precise statistics do not reflect the total number of people who have moved as a consequence of fighting. Although refugee legislation states that governments have the obligation to register every internally displaced person, in Colombia, official authorities refuse to do so unless identification papers are presented at the moment of registration, since basic personal documents are one of the requirements to obtain emergency aid. Without the basic documents the displaced persons have no proof of land or property ownership, are unable to vote, drive, work in the formal sector, receive hospital treatment, move from region to region, they cannot leave the country, or even send their children to public schools.

Women account for the largest percentage of internally displaced people. According to data obtained by the Global Internally Displaced Persons Project from 2003, women and children make up 73 per cent of the displaced population in Colombia. Internally displaced women are often discriminated against on racial, ethnic, or economic grounds. A large number of internally displaced women have Afro-Caribbean or indigenous origins, groups that are the object of most victimisation in Colombia. As a large number of men fall victim to rural war waged by diverse armed actors, a significant number of internally displaced women in Colombia are widows or single mothers. CODHES estimates that between 25 per cent, in the rural areas, and 49 per cent, in the urban settings, of displaced women are heads of household. Women most commonly flee as a result of increased general violence, the killing of their husband or relatives, or the imposition of threats on their lives. Paramilitary groups, as well as guerrillas, use rape as a weapon of war, and often punish women for the alleged offences committed by their brothers, fathers or husbands.

Internally displaced women often face radical changes in their traditional social and gender roles as they have to assume responsibilities that in the past belonged exclusively to men. Facing the necessity of protecting and feeding their families, many displaced women do not have other possibilities but to work as maids and servants, traditionally exploited, regarded with disdain, and often exposed to sexual and economic abuse by their employers. The cases of women who engage as prostitutes in order to sustain their families are not rare.

Internally displaced women are victims of numerous health dangers. They have very limited access to insufficient, highly bureaucratic and corrupted health services. Although they are more likely to become victims of sexual assault and abuse, they face special difficulties in access to reproductive health care, which is not included in the assistance given to internally displaced persons by the government, thus for instance emergency contraception is not available to them. According to the Women's Commission for Refugee Women and Children, 'internally displaced persons, particularly women and girls, experience horrendous reproductive health problems in Colombia. Gender-based violence, including rape followed by murder, sexual slavery, forced contraception and abortions is extensive and largely unaddressed by state authorities.'

Sources:

Brookings-Cuny, Internal Displacement in the Americas: Some Distinctive Features, *Occasional paper* (May 2001), at http://www.disasterinfo.net/desplazados/informes/brooking/informe2001julio.htm

Global IDP Project/Norwegian Refugee Council, *Profile on Internal Displacement: Colombia*, compilation of the information available in the Global IDP database of the Norwegian Refugee Council (Geneva, 14 May 2003), at http://www.idpprojetc.org

Women's Commission for Refugee Women and Children, *Displaced and Desperate: Assessment of reproductive health for Colombia's internally displaced persons*, Executive Summary (2003), at http://www.womenscommission.org

UNHCR to ensure maximum impact, particularly during the onset of a humanitarian emergency.

Internally displaced persons

Internally displaced persons (IDPs) may have fled for similar reasons as refugees, but remain within their own territory and thus are still subject to the laws of that state. There is no specific international treaty, or any lead agency protecting the rights of the internally displaced. In 1992, the UN Secretary-General appointed a Representative on Internally Displaced Persons, who has undertaken initiatives to raise the visibility and focus on internal displacement. In 1998, the representative presented the Guiding Principles on Internal Displacement, which was the first attempt to articulate the rights and guarantees relevant in all phases of displacement. This non-binding document brings together the various forms of protection to internally displaced persons by joining existing rules of international humanitarian law, human rights law and refugee law. The challenge in enforcing these guidelines is that frequently it is the state that is either the agent of persecution or tolerating the persecution of its own citizens and may not welcome an international presence to monitor the situation. Examples of internally displaced populations with limited access to the outside world for assistance include Iraqis under the rule of Saddam Hussein, Afghans during the rule of the Taliban and North Koreans under the dictatorship of Kim Jung Il.

Internally displaced women face additional protection challenges and often have less legal protection. In societies where the international community has difficulty accessing internally displaced populations, many women face institutionalised discrimination from their own government, which makes them even more vulnerable. For example, the Taliban prohibited girls from going to school, severely restricted women's ability to work and limited their mobility. The limited access of the international community combined with these restrictions left women with very few options. Similarly, Iraqi women during the reign of Saddam Hussein could not leave the country, unless they were accompanied by a close male relative. This mobility restriction limited a woman's ability to flee to bordering countries, such as Jordan, to seek asylum. To overcome this restriction many women used informal networks, such as smugglers, and became more vulnerable to traffickers willing to capitalise on their desperate need to leave the country.

Another dynamic of providing protection and assistance to internally displaced persons is to do so without limiting their ability to cross borders and seek asylum. During a humanitarian emergency there is a tendency for border countries to try and minimise refugee flows by providing cross border assistance to communities that allow them to stay in their country of origin. This strategy has had mixed results. Sometimes these 'safe' areas will the targets of external attack, local military forces will continue to operate from these areas or groups that control the area will restrict civilians' freedom of movement by not allowing them to leave.

Table 2.3:

Estimated number of internally displaced persons (end of 2003)

Region	Number of countries of refuge	IDPs (in millions)
Africa	20	12.7
Asia-Pacific	11	3.6
Americas	4	3.3
Europe	12	3.0
Middle East	5	2.0
Global	52	24.6

Source: The Global IDP Project, *Internal Displacement: A Global Overview of Trends and Developments in 2003*, at http://www.idpproject.org/global_overview.htm

Although gender is not specifically referenced in the 1951 convention definition, it is widely accepted that the definition covers gender-related claims. As a result, many would argue there is no need to add gender as an additional basis for a refugee claim to the 1951 convention. The risks of opening the 1951 convention for amendment could result in losing ground in other areas. Also, there is nothing to prevent state parties to the 1951 convention from making their national laws more protective and adding gender as a specific category.

As international humanitarian and human rights law evolves, one of its biggest challenges may be to develop legally binding provisions protecting internally displaced persons in order to contribute to a strategy of meaningful protection and assistance to these uprooted people.

Endnotes

1 J. Milner, G. Loescher, 'New Safety or Old Danger? UN "Protection Areas" for Refugees', *Open Democracy* (13 February 2003).

2 UNHCR assists several million, but not all of the estimated 20-25 million internally displaced persons worldwide during humanitarian crises. There is ongoing international debate on how to increase the protection of IDPs.

3 Human Rights Watch, *Trapped by Inequality: Bhutanese Refugee Women in Nepal* (September 2003).

4 Human Rights Watch, *Seeking Protection: Addressing Sexual and Domestic Violence in Tanzania's Refugee Camps* (October 2000).

5 Women's Commission for Refugee Women and Children, Interviews with Afghan refugee women in Peshawar, Pakistan (October 2003).

6 Women's Commission for Refugee Women and Children, 'We Simply Do not Want to Die', Assessment of Protection Concerns and Case Studies of Afghan Women in New Shamshatoo Refugee Camp, Pakistan (December 2001).

7 M. Diaz, *Panel Presentation, Global Consultations on International Protection*, Panel Presentation, (May 2002).

8 UNHCR, 'Women Seeking a Better Deal', *Refugees Magazine*, Issue 126 (April 2002).

9 Women's Commission for Refugee Women and Children, *UNHCR Policy on Refugee Women and Guidelines on Their Protection: An Assessment of Ten Years of Implementation* (May 2002).

10 Example from Women's Commission for Refugee Women and Children, mMission to Ethiopia (March 2001).

11 Women's Commission for Refugee Women and Children, Interviews with Afghan refugee women, Peshawar, Pakistan (October 2003).

12 Women's Commission for Refugee Women and Children, *Behind Closed Doors: Abuse of Refugee Women at the Krome Detention Centre* (October 2000).

13 Women's Commission for Refugee Women and Children has been founded in 1989 as an independent affiliate of the International Rescue Committee, a world leading NGO in relief and protection of people in disaster and post-conflict situations.

Chapter 3

Women in Mourning

'I went through the book of belongings of those found dead, one photograph after another, and I prayed to God not to recognise anything, even though I wanted to know at least something – to end this uncertainty. As long as I can, I will fight for the truth about where my husband is and where my children are. I live on their memories. I have their voices in my head.'

From ICRC/Urban Films film production, '*Women Facing War*', October 2001

A long-neglected aspect of the impact armed conflict has on women relates to the loss of family members. Families are often separated when they flee or when men are conscripted, detained, or disappear, and their relatives are not informed of their whereabouts. Family separation, for example, the systematic separation of civilian men and boys from their female relatives, is also used as a method of warfare.

The impact of missing family members on women should not be underestimated. To give two examples, in Bosnia-Herzegovina 92 per cent of persons missing in relation to the armed conflict are men; in relation to the armed conflict in Kosovo this figure is 90 per cent.[1] The majority of these missing men were not members of the armed forces or armed groups, but civilians. This is a key determinant of women's experience of war. Imagine losing all the male members of your family between the ages of 15 and 65 years either because they have been detained as a perceived threat, or because they have been arrested and there is no trace of what happened to them. This has an enormous impact on how women experience armed conflict – the loss of loved ones (husbands, fathers, sons,

brothers), the loss of protection – in many communities women are largely afforded protection by the presence of their men – the loss of a breadwinner and head of household. The reality for women who survive armed conflict cannot be detached from the reality of armed conflict for men, as they are part of the same families and communities.

Not knowing the fate of relatives and unable to bury loved ones is a trauma and a terrible burden for the survivors of an armed conflict. The effects on their ability to cope and the chances of reconciliation between communities are enormous. Additional Protocol I to the Geneva Conventions, which expressly recognises the right of families to know the fate of their relatives provides that *the activities of the [...] Parties to the conflict [with regard to missing and dead persons] shall be prompted mainly by the right of families to know the fate of their relatives.*[2] International humanitarian law seeks to maintain and restore family unity in a number of ways. First, by preventing the separation of family members against their will;[3] and second, in situations where families are separated due to internment, displacement or the participa-

A woman mourns at the burial of 282 Bosnian Muslims who had been killed by Bosnian Serb forces in Srebrenica in 1995. The burial was part of a memorial ceremony to mark the Srebrenica massacre.

tion of certain family members in the hostilities, it requires the adoption of measures that will facilitate reunification. These measures are mainly a matter of ensuring that a person's identity is registered in order to prevent disappearances and to trace and reunite dispersed family members. Particular attention in this regard is given to children.[4] Finally, if separation has occurred, international humanitarian law lays down measures aimed at facilitating the re-establishment of family ties and the reunification of dispersed families.[5]

Family members separated by armed conflict need to be reunited as soon as security conditions permit or at the end of hostilities. In some cases, family members need to be reunited on a priority basis because of their precarious situation, such as unaccompanied children, mothers separated from their babies, elderly persons living alone and other persons whose security is particularly threatened. Children are especially vulnerable when they have been separated from their families and depend on themselves, the goodwill of neighbours or third persons for their support. This can cause immense mental stress and anguish for their mothers as well.

Family members separated by armed conflict need to be able to search for information on the fate of relatives with whom they have lost contact - whether they are missing, detained, sick or wounded soldiers, or civilians caught up in the conflict.[6] This problem may be remedied for many families at the end of hostilities when family members return, or when contact is re-established through, for example, the exchange of family news via 'Red Cross Messages' organised by the International Committee of Red Cross (ICRC). The ICRC visits persons deprived of their liberty, persons displaced or otherwise separated due to armed conflict or internal strife, with the aim of re-establishing family contact.

Widowhood often changes the social and economic roles of women in the household and community, and the structure of the family thus having an impact not only on women, but also on society in general. However first of all, widowhood can affect the physical safety, identity and mobility of women, the access to basic goods and services necessary for their rights to inheritance, land and property.

The impact of widowhood differs between cultures and religions. In some communities a widow is responsible for her late husband's dependants, in others she is taken in by his family. Cultural practices may demand that widows are taken in by extended family members, but poverty or reduced resources as a result of war may mean that extended family members are not able to meet this obligation. Social traditions may be abandoned by families so overburdened by economic hardship due to war that they can no longer cope, and women can be left entirely without any help of their community. The situation can become desperate for those women who have to assume responsibility for dependent family members. The death of the main breadwinner can cause a breakdown in the family's division of labour because women take over roles traditionally carried out only by men. Women can face particular difficulties when they become heads of households if they do not have an adequate educational background or are prevented from obtaining further education; this can, for example, restrict their capacity to find work. Moreover, in countries where use or ownership of land is regulated by customary laws or cultural barriers, women are often denied the right to own land and personal property. Where armed conflict has led to the destruction of traditional coping mechanisms this may lead to widows becoming homeless and unable to support themselves and their dependants.[7]

There are large numbers of widows in many countries who have suffered armed conflicts. All too frequently, the parties to an armed conflict do little to determine the fate of missing persons. Women face many constraints when searching for information about missing relatives, since

A woman passes a blackboard of missing children in Bong Mine, Liberia. As a result of the war many families have been separated. The ICRC has set up networks to reunite parents and children, many of which are displaced in Sierra Leone and Guinea refugee camps.

not only financial, cultural, traditional and social barriers, but also safety concerns often restrict their access to the authorities, political representatives and the military. As a result, many women form or join groups, such as family associations, to exert pressure on the authorities for news of their relatives and to ensure that they are not forgotten. Many women are organised into networks to support each other and to fight for recognition of their loss and status. In some cases it is widowhood that can stimulate changes of women's roles and patterns of behaviour, as it happened after the Indian-Pakistan war in 1999.

Changing Ancient Societal Patterns: The Widows of the Kargil War

According to the 1991 census, there are 33 million widows in India, which means that in every fourth household in India there is a widow. 50 per cent of Indian widows are over the age of fifty. Only a very small minority of widows could claim to be comfortable, secure and well looked after. The mortality rate for widows of a shocking 85 per cent higher than for married women is the result of the many deprivations that a widow faces. Once a

woman ceases to be wife, especially if she is childless, she ceases to be a 'person', neither daughter nor daughter-in-law. A 1994 survey revealed that although 88 per cent of widows remain in their deceased husband's village, less than three per cent are allowed to stay in the same house. The others are either abandoned, often by their own sons to appropriate their father's property, or sent back to their parents' houses. Widows have severe restrictions on food habits, dress and re-marriage. They are forbidden to attend socio-religious functions, they are culturally isolated, and separated from worldly affairs and pleasures.

After the Indian-Pakistan war in 1999, called the Kargil War after the main town of the district where the war was fought, the Government of India for the first time gave a huge amount of money as compensation to every dead soldier's family. Each dead body was sent to the respective villages, and each fallen soldier received a state funeral, which was attended by thousands of villagers including several ministers and Maharajas. Not only did the government provide huge financial compensation and other benefits to widows, but also, according to a governmental provision, the money and the material aid were given directly to the widows. Each widow received between

A Bosnian Muslim woman mourns her loved ones, who went missing or were killed in Srebrenica. Almost 90 per cent of the victims remain unidentified.

US$50,000 to US$60,000 from the central government, state government and other agencies. This is unprecedented in independent India and it makes the Kargil widows very unique and special. A study conducted in 2001 highlighted several ways in which the Kargil war widows felt that entitlements to the financial package had improved their lives, including greater economic security, opportunity to improve housing conditions, ability to send children to school, increase in self-confidence, very positive effect on their status in the family and society, new role of empowerment, and, new role in decision-making processes.[8]

The immediate gain of huge sums of money, house, petrol pump, land and numerous other facilities has had a positive effect on widow status in the family and society. However, their experiences suggest that the money they received led to problems of money management, proper guidance and gainful investment. The tradition of control over women by a leading man of the family who owns her power to invest in financial matters, together with a very low level of their education, played an important role in their ability to cope with the unexpected burden of responsibility. The experiences of the widows are very telling. The widows expressed both hope of a new life and at the same time fears whether they will be able to cope with it: *Suddenly my decision-making power has come to light, my in-laws are asking me for every detail, I feel so happy and satisfied. Now I know I am very*

important, since I have lots of money, how much I do not know.' […] 'I cannot leave my in-laws since they are keeping the records of the financial matters, I cannot handle the work all by myself.' […] 'I need somebody who would explain [to] me my financial position so that I know where I stand. I have got a lot of money but I do not understand much.' […] 'When I became a widow, I was very scared, as I knew the status of widows in society. But over-night my status has gone up. They asked my opinion about everything, which was not there when my husband was alive, because without my signature money cannot come to the household.'

Almost all the women interviewed realised the value of education: *'Now I understand the need for education, if I had been educated, I would have led an independent life.'[…]'Now I want to read and write, so that I know what I am signing and for what purpose the money is being spent. I want to be free from the clutches of my in-laws and parents, but without education I cannot do anything. I do not even know how to sign.'*

The Kargil war widows are young and most of them are illiterate and can barely sign their names. They have only been seen as daughters, wives and mothers with the normative rules of conduct, but not as individuals with rights of their own. The actions of the central and state government to full pension and other financial benefits are highly empowering experiences. The introduction of a huge sum of money as compensation to the Kargil war widows delivered directly in their name created a new social situation in a rural region with strict social norms, strong family, governed by patriarchy, low education of women, and custom of levirate (getting married with the younger brother of the dead husband). Governmental financial benefits gave the Kargil war widows the chance to gain more self-confidence and to increase their status in the family and society. Indian rural women are less educated, less visible in the authority structure, and suffer more the effect of customs and patriarchal norms and values. A majority of women are still not enjoying the rights and opportunities guaranteed to them by the constitution. Child marriages are continuing. The new life situation of the Kargil war widows may stimulate a change of the entire dynamics of rural families in the region, and may serve as an example for Indian women in general. Their case also shows the necessity to combine any financial aid to rural women with awareness-raising campaigns, adult education programmes and counselling.

Endnotes

1 Based on the number of tracing requests received from family members by the ICRC.

2 Article 32, *Additional Protocol I to the Fourth Geneva Convention.*

3 Article 27, *Fourth Geneva Convention*, Article 49, *Fourth Geneva Convention.*

4 See, e.g. Article 78(3), *Additional Protocol I to the Fourth Geneva Convention.*

5 See, e.g. Article 26, *Fourth Geneva Convention*; Article 74, *Additional Protocol I.*

6 This search may be carried out privately or through a humanitarian organisation, such as the ICRC and/or the National Red Cross or Red Crescent Society.

7 In Rwanda, the law was altered in the aftermath of the genocide to protect the matrimonial property and succession rights of widows and orphaned girls.

8 The study was based mainly upon first hand data, collected via unstructured interviews, during which every woman interviewed was asked to narrate the incidents of her life, her own feelings and reactions on the death of her husband. Besides the interviews case-studies and observation were used. The sample of respondents encompasses almost all the Kargil widows (450 respondents).

Chapter 4

Designed to Kill and Maim: The Effect of Landmines and Other Explosive Remnants of War on Women

'On 4 December 1995, my mother and I left our house in order to go visit my aunt in her house. She lived in a place which was a front line for a long time. To reach her house we had to cross some agricultural fields where some bushes had grown. While I along with my mother were crossing the bushy fields, I saw something which encouraged me to take it. I didn't know it was a mine field, suddenly, a loud sound of an explosion took place. I started to cry, immediately, my mother rushed to me to take me out of the spot, but unfortunately she also stepped on another anti-personnel mine which was also laid there.'

Testimony of Shabnam, eleven-year-old girl, Afghanistan

Anti-personnel landmines were first employed on a large scale during the First World War. As military technology progressed, anti-personnel landmines were developed as a weapon in its own right leading to widespread use during the Second World War and subsequently. Landmines were initially used for defensive and tactical purposes. As wars evolved, and partly due to their low cost, mines became the weapon of choice for internal conflicts. Consequently, mines were not only used against military targets, but also against civilian populations, as a way to harass and terrorise them, prevent their movements, or block vital access to water points, land or infrastructure. The new types of conflicts also saw the emergence of home-made devices, as well as the development of more sophisticated mines, including plastic mines difficult to detect.

Landmines and other explosive remnants of war (ERW), in particular unexploded ordnance (UXO), remain long after the fighting has finished and continue to claim victims in an indiscriminate manner. While during a conflict, most victims are generally military, this trend changes at the end of the hostilities and civilians become the group most affected. The appalling humanitarian costs of anti-personnel mines, therefore far outweigh their limited military utility.

Mines and ERW may kill or cause horrific injuries resulting in the loss of limbs, hearing, and eyesight or in a permanent

❚ *Latifa survived a landmine and continues with her daily chores with the help of a friend, in Kabul, Afghanistan.*

disability having a dramatic impact on individuals both at physical and psychological level. After an accident, earning an income, being accepted within the family and society and carrying out daily activities will become a struggle for the victims. The survivors may be unable to cope with the emotional strain and physical pain in countries where psychological support is not available. If the head of household is involved in the accident, the whole family will suffer the loss of income. Moreover, the costs of the medical treatment and rehabilitation services put an additional burden on the victim and its family.

Landmines and ERW can bar access to farmland, irrigation channels, roads, power plants and other infrastructure, obstructing reconstruction and development activities. In addition, they can place an additional burden on the health care system of the country due to the increased need of medical treatment, surgery, blood banks and rehabilitation.

The Landmine Monitor 2002 estimated that millions of mines and UXO are scattered over 80 countries in Africa, Asia, Europe, the Middle East and the Americas. In addition, eleven other areas, which are not internationally recognised states, are affected by landmines and UXO. In 2003, there were fifteen countries still actively producing anti-personnel mines, Burma, China, Cuba, Egypt, India, Iran, Iraq, Nepal, North Korea, South Korea, Pakistan, Russia, Singapore, United States and Vietnam, and six countries were using anti-personnel mines, namely India, Iraq,

Burma, Nepal, Pakistan and Russia. The United Nations suggested that while anti-personnel mines are relatively cheap as they cost between US$3 and US$30 each, the expenses of de-mining ranges between US$300 and US$1,000, making clearance interventions an expensive operation.

According to the statistics of the International Committee of the Red Cross (ICRC), the average cost of an artificial leg is between US$800 and US$4,000. A child who sustained an amputation as a result of a mine accident will have to replace the artificial leg every six months. Assuming a child was injured at ten and that he/she will live another 50 years, the disabled person will need 25 prosthesis during the lifetime at a total cost of between US$20,000 and US$100,000. An adult will have to change it every three years. Presently, only ten per cent of landmine victims can afford health care.

The response to the worldwide problem of landmines

Landmines have only been highlighted as a cause of humanitarian tragedy at the end of the 1980s, following an increasing number of civilian victims, the medical staff of NGOs and international organisations working in mine-affected countries. The first 'mine action' programmes were developed in Afghanistan (1988-89) and Cambodia (1991-93) as a result of political events, which triggered the return of refugees and internally displaced people into affected areas.

During the 1990s a strong international humanitarian mine action-movement against landmines developed focusing in improving efficiency and credibility. The extensive lobbying of governments and the public advocacy of the International Campaign to Ban Landmines, as well as the unprecedented awareness-raising campaign of the International Committee of the Red Cross, significantly contributed to the ban of on the production and use of land-mines resulting in in the Anti-Personnel Mine Ban Convention in 1997. However, while the situation has improved, the world is still not free of landmines today. Both the causes and effects of the landmine crisis still need to be addressed by stopping mine laying,

The International Campaign to Ban Landmines (ICBL) was initiated and led by Jody Williams. In 1997 she was awarded the Nobel Peace Prize for her work.

production and stockpiling;, clearing mined areas; and helping landmine survivors.

The International Committee of the Red Cross (ICRC) provides assistance to landmines victims (first aid, surgery, blood banks, rehabilitation etc.) and implements mine risk education programmes.

The Geneva International Centre for Humanitarian De-mining (GICHD) is an independent and impartial foundation working for the reduction of the humanitarian impact of remnants of war by providing operational assistance, creating and sharing knowledge, and supporting instruments of international law. GICHD supports Humanitarian Mine Action through operational assistance and research, and the implementation of the Anti-Personnel Mine Ban Convention. In 12001, state parties to the Ottawa Convention mandated the GICHD to establish an Implementation Support Unit to deal with the issues related to the convention.

The International Campaign to Ban Landmines (ICBL), a global network of organisations working to eradicate anti-personnel mines, was founded in 1991. The campaign calls for an international ban on the use, production, stockpiling, and transfer of anti-personnel landmines, and for increased international resources for humanitarian mine clearance and mine victim assistance programmes. In recognition of its achievements ICBL was awarded the Nobel Peace Prize in 1997, together with its then co-ordinator, Jody Williams. Today the network represents over 1,100 organisations in over 60 countries, which work locally, nationally, regionally, and internationally to ban anti-personnel landmines.

The rate of deaths and injuries suddenly created a consciousness of the problem and subsequently raised the interest of media, donors and international humanitarian organisations. People needed to be warned and informed, and the threat itself, the landmines, had to be located and removed. During the 1990s, similar responses were organised in other contexts where peace agreements occurred (Mozambique, Angola), where new conflicts had taken place (Balkans, South and North Caucasus, Iraq, Central Asia etc.) or where former or latent conflicts had left countries with the lethal dangers of landmines and unexploded ordnance (Asia, the Middle East region, South and Central Americas, Africa). Humanitarian mine action became more co-ordinated and less fragmented, therefore establishing the credibility of the main actors and hence donor recognition followed. Other ERW became progressively included into mine action programmes as part of the efforts to decrease the threat of unexploded munitions.

Mine action involves activities, which aim at reducing the social, economic and environmental impact of mines and unexploded ordnance. It comprises five complementary groups of activities - UXO and mine risk education, human-

itarian de-mining (mine and UXO survey), mapping, marking and clearance, victim assistance including rehabilitation and reintegration, stockpile destruction and advocacy. As it is impossible to clear all mines before people return to their areas or before they resume their daily activities after the immediate end of hostilities, it is essential to inform the population and integrate de-mining activities with other post-conflict interventions. An integrated mine action approach can take place only if the concerned actors – national authorities, NGOs, the United Nations, the ICRC and other international organisations – are involved. They all have a specific role contributing to threat reduction.

In the middle of the1990s, the International Campaign to Ban Landmines (ICBL), a coalition of NGOs, came together to inform public opinion and to lobby governments to achieve a ban on the production and use of land-mines. The ICRC initiated its own unprecedented public campaign with the same goal. Both campaigns led to the adoption in 1997 of the Convention on the Prohibition of the Use, Stockpiling, Production and Transfer of Anti-personnel Mines and Their Destruction (Ottawa Treaty). The treaty prohibits the development, production, stockpiling,

▍ *Two young women try on their new protheses in Luanda, Angola.*

▍ *Landmine awareness and education are key strategies to curb land-mine accidents. The International Committee of the Red Cross distributes brochures on mine awareness to women in Kabul, Afghanistan.*

transfer and use of the anti-personnel mines in all circumstances. It obliges each state party to clear all anti-personnel mines already in the ground within a set deadline and it calls upon all countries to do their utmost to ensure the care, rehabilitation and reintegration of mine victims. Significantly, for the first time ever a weapon in widespread use has been prohibited under international humanitarian law.

Similarly the concerns about the humanitarian impact caused by explosive remnants of war were raised and lead to the negotiation and adoption of Protocol V to the 1980 UN Convention on Certain Conventional Weapons (CCW) in 2003. The protocol makes state parties responsible for clearance of all explosive remnants of war in the territory under their control and also for warnings, risk education, and other measures to protect the civilian population. Although this new instrument represents a significant development and should be useful in reinforcing the necessity and urgency of cleaning up the detritus of war, it falls far short of what is needed.

Women victims of landmines

In general, 80 to 90 per cent of landmine victims are male, while less than 10 per cent are female. There are exceptions to this general trend, such as in Angola where 23 per cent of the victims were women out of the 3,000 total number of victims reported between 1998 and 2002. In general 50 per cent of all male and female casualties are adults between 19 and 35 years of age. Children generally account for between 15 and 30 per cent of the victims and boys are usually more at risk than girls, since they are also more inclined to tamper with mines than their female peers. Exceptions to this general trend can be found, for example, in Afghanistan where half of the victims are children because of the high number of UXO and the lack of places where children can play safely. Mine accidents, however, affect the whole family, whoever is the victim.

According to interviews the ICRC conducted in Chechen refugee camps in Ingushetia in July 2000, women did not practice risky behaviour, and if so, it was usually because they were not aware of the danger. For them, the mines were an additional problem to what they have already been through - destroyed houses, killed relatives, and survival. However, mines still represented an obvious burden on their lives and on the lives of their family members, especially children. The ICRC report conducted in Angola in early 2003 stressed that mines affected women's struggle for survival on a daily basis by impeding wood collection, access to rivers, and other activities with regard to farming the land.

Becoming a mine victim can have a dramatic impact on a woman and her family. A girl injured by a mine may have little chance of getting married, a disabled woman may be

Table 4.1:

Landmine victims by age group in Bosnia-Herzegovina (in percentage)

	1996	1997	1998	1999	2000	2001	2002
Children less than 1 up to 18	24.0	19.0	14.7	20.0	29.0	13.7	26.0
Adults from 19 to 39	40.0	40.6	37.5	41.0	40.0	41.0	36.0
Adults from 40 to 60	25.0	28.9	29.5	26.3	24.0	26.4	30.5
Elderly people over 60	6.5	6.8	11.4	10.5	7.0	8.0	6.9
Age unknown	4.5	4.4	6.7	2.0	0.0	10.3	0.0

Table 4.2:

Landmine victims by gender in Bosnia-Herzegovina (in percentage)

	1992	1993	1994	1995	1996	1997	1998	1999	2000	2001	2002
Men	95.2	93.7	96.3	96.4	90.3	90.3	90.6	93.7	91.0	87.4	90.2
Women	4.8	6.3	3.7	3.6	9.7	9.7	9.4	6.3	9.0	12.6	9.8

Source:

Data from Bosnia and Herzegovina collected by the International Committee of the Red Cross in 1992–2002.

Box 4.2: Women de-miners in Cambodia: Chan Sovannarorn's story

Chan Sovannarorn, 24 years old, lives in a village called Rumchek, 237 kilometres to the north of Cambodia's capital, Phnom Penh. Her father died in 1984 after stepping on a landmine about one kilometre from Rumchek. He was travelling to the forest to look for vines and resin. *'I shook with fright after hearing about my father. My mother and I went straight to the spot when we were told,'* said Sovannarorn, *'but luckily we met him on the way because one of his friends had moved him to the ox-cart path. My mother and I cried and cried when we saw him covered by blood. I remember that one of his legs had blown up, about ten centimetres below the knee, and the other was completely lacerated. A day later he died at Rovieng district hospital.'*

There was heavy fighting in the area in the 1980s between the Khmer Rouge and Cambodian government troops. During the fighting, a military camp was established in the centre of the village by government troops. Anti-personnel blast mines and fragmentation mines were laid around this camp, especially on the access roads inside the village, around big trees, and around water sources. The people of Rumchek fled their homes to live at Rovieng village, about eighteen kilometres to the north-east where the conditions were safer. They returned back to the village in late 1996, after the fighting had stopped completely. In 1993 when Sovannarorn was fourteen years old, her mother died from malaria. At that time, she was in grade four of Rovieng primary school. Since her mother passed away, Sovannarorn was not able to continue her study, and was asked to live with her aunt. Every day she had to work as a labourer in the rice field, or pick crops of soybeans, black pepper, or chilli. She received 3,000 riels (US$0.75) per day.

An assessment conducted by Mines Advisory Group (MAG) in August 2002 identified eight minefields, covering 37 hectares, located in and around Rumchek village. The minefields prevent people from building houses, planting vegetables or crops and also make road access difficult. The people feel afraid for their lives.

Chan Sovannarorn is one of 25 women currently attending the basic de-miners training in Preah Vihear province. *'I am very happy now because I have an opportunity to join the basic de-miners training, conducted by MAG. I concentrate very hard because I do not want to fail at the end of the course,'* Sovannarorn said. *'If I have money I will help my aunt to buy cows or buffaloes in order to support her farming. At the moment, only my uncle in-law is responsible for my family consisting of six people including me.'*

After completion of the training, these new de-miners will join with a number of experienced MAG de-mining teams, before regrouping into MAG's first ever all female de-mining team by the end of the year. MAG is the only mine action agency in Cambodia to employ women in technical roles - currently twenty per cent of de-miners are female. MAG is striving to increase this percentage, with a particular emphasis on women from mine-affected communities such as Sovannarorn.

The story was written by Prak Sary, MAG Regional Manager, Preah Vihear Region, Cambodia, at http://www.mag.org.uk/magtest/cambodia/cam01a.htm

Female de-miners, mostly widows or amputees, hired by an NGO for mine action located in Battambang, Cambodia.

---

abandoned by her husband, as in some societies, disability lowers women's social status. Women's role as children's care-taker is also affected by mine accidents, because women must continue to take care of their families even if suffering from pain and trauma. Knowing that their environment is mine-affected is a constant burden for women worrying about their families. Coping with a mine injury in a post-conflict situation with displacement, limited resources, post-traumatic disorders, widowhood or loss of a child represents an additional burden.

Women's contribution to mine risk education

Women play an important role in the Mine Risk Education (MRE) programmes because they can deliver mine aware-ness messages to their families and communities. Mine action organisations have recruited both men and women as MRE teachers, but in certain contexts such as Kosovo and Afghanistan, it was essential to have mainly female teachers in order to specifically target women from affected communities.

In the middle of the1990s, in Cambodia, women were recruited as de-miners for the first time by the Mines Advisory Group (MAG), an international NGO for mine action. As heads of household or breadwinners, women were extremely motivated to take on such an activity, which was going to contribute to make their community and family safer. Other clearance organisations followed this model and women de-miners were recruited and trained in Bosnia-Herzegovina, Kosovo and other countries contaminated with mines and explosive remnants of war. Expatriate de-miners have often highlighted that clearance tasks were gen-erally performed very well by women who showed more commitment and were more meticulous and conscientious than men.

Chapter 5

Disarmament, Demobilisation and Reintegration Processes: Where Do Women Stand?

'The terrible irony is that women and girls are not invisible to armed groups, who see them as essential, accessible – and often expendable – military assets. Yet having survived the devastating experiences of war as combatants, sexual captives or military "wives" and slave or willing labourers in the conflict period, these women and girls often become invisible when DDR planning begins.'

UNIFEM, Getting it Right, Doing it Right:
Gender and Disarmament, Demobilisation and Reintegration, 2004

Countries that are emerging from violent conflict are often seen as a potential site of positive change, even for women. Some theorists argue that war and the aftermath of war can present opportunities to influence social and political structures which, in peacetime, were beyond women's purview.[1] In this vein, Matthias Stiefel writes: *'Gender roles and social values [are] deeply affected by the experience of wars [so that] the reconfiguration of gender roles and positions is an integral part of the challenge of reconstruction.*[2]

However, women's participation in war-related work can also be overlooked or hidden away because stereotypical notions of gender appropriate labour are often re-mobilised after war when a society strives to return to

'normal'. This is why women frequently lose political ground after the conflict ends. Despite their active engagement in all aspects of social life in times of conflict, when post-war reconstruction processes such as the appointment of transitional governments begin, women do not often gain positions of political leadership. Since DDR processes are typically agreed upon during the course of peace negotiations, and women representatives do not sufficiently participate in negotiations, women's view are often overlooked during the planning of DDR operations. The problem is compounded because women are not only under-represented in national structures, but also in international policy and structures. The fact that women leaders have been excluded from the planning of many DDR processes is a fault, which must be squarely laid at the feet of gender-blind governments and gender-blind donor agencies.

A disarmament, demobilisation and reintegration process is normally agreed on at formal peace talks. It is a continuum that can only be effective if it has been incorporated into a form of peace agreement. The voluntary surrender of small arms and light weapons (SALW) is often an essential qualification for a combatant or group of combatants to be included in a DDR process. However, ex-soldiers can feel unsafe without their weapons for a number of complex reasons and may therefore be reluctant to surrender all of their arms. They may hand in their second or third-best weapon and hide the others, which means that many weapons do not get collected. The disarmament that takes place, as part of a DDR process should, therefore, be understood as only one aspect of SALW collection in a post-conflict environment. Longer term types of SALW control interventions are required after the end of the DDR process, which are comparable to the kind of SALW control programmes that need to be put in place in countries that are awash with SALW, but have not experienced a full-scale war. Because of the breadth and severity of their impact, and the danger they pose when peace is fragile, a reduction in the number of SALW that circulate before, during and after a conflict is a vital accompaniment to reconstruction efforts. The proliferation of SALW undermines the rule of law, fuels crime and instability, exacerbates tensions, negates security confidence building measures, and acts as an obstacle to social and economic development.

The impacts of these problems differ for women and men. While women have been excluded from the DDR process because they do not have a weapon to hand in or cannot pass a test by which they have to prove familiarity in handling a gun in order to proceed to demobilisation, men have traditionally been associated with the use, ownership and promotion of small arms. Therefore, they are injured and killed by guns in far larger numbers than women. However, the security implications of prolific weapons can also be significant for women and must therefore be considered during the planning phase of a SALW control intervention. When SALW flow freely into communities and are not removed after the armed conflict ends, women run the risk not only of facing lethal domestic violence, but also become more vulnerable while managing their daily workload. Women are burdened with caring for those who have been injured or disabled by gunfire, and often have the sole responsibility for economically supporting the family unit.

When weapons remain in communities after the onset of peace, large numbers of men continue to abuse them. Women are inevitably caught up in this violence.

Because of the weapons left in circulation after conflict, crime takes on an added danger. Women are raped at gunpoint, children are killed in gang crossfire or 'playing' with SALW, and homes are robbed by armed thieves. Humanitarian staff or women from the local community may launch SALW awareness campaigns as a means to urge authorities to take more responsibility for SALW control. There are many examples of women organising awareness campaigns, and they have taken the lead in Cambodia, South Africa, Brazil and the United States of America. In the Democratic Republic of the Congo, women demanded effective SALW control measures on International Women's Day 2001 because they understood it as a first step towards peace. Liberian women participated actively in a weapons collection and destruction campaign before the elections in 1997 and they are significant supporters of the disarmament processes undertaken there since 2003.

It is important to stress, however, that SALW collection and destruction is a dangerous and highly technical procedure. It should never be undertaken by civilians because they do not have the expertise to handle weapons and especially ammunition (unexploded ordnance or UXO) safely. The successful inclusion of women in SALW control interventions relies, therefore, on a combination of education and a careful process of trust building between them and members of the security forces. Women most affected by

Combatants in the Catatumbo Mountains, Colombia, are provided lectures on humanitarian law by the ICRC.

guns often have the best ideas about incentives to support the removal of SALW from the community and, working alongside trained personnel, can play a significant role in convincing people to surrender their weapons. UNDP's 'Weapons for Development' collection programme in Albania owes a measure of its success to the participation of women who, supported by UNIFEM, were trained in aspects of SALW control measures and then sent out to support SALW awareness in their communities during the SALW amnesty and collection process. In Gramsch women went door to door preaching the danger of SALW under the slogan, 'a gun less, a chance more!' In Elbasan, where the authorities collected 2,332 weapons and 1,801 tons of ammunition, and in Diber, where 2,407 weapons and 855 tons of ammunition were handed in, women played a significant role, particularly in influencing family members to voluntarily surrender their illegal weapons.

However, it should not be taken for granted that women automatically oppose prolific SALW. Like men, they need to be educated and encouraged to seek other alternatives to achieve an improvement in human security and safety. In the district of Tirana, women's associations distributed questionnaires on the issue of micro-disarmament, which offered an insight into the complexity of women's responses to weapons. *While filling out the questionnaire we talked to many women,'* one of the organisers said. *'They spoke about anxiety about the arms they had in their houses. The general feeling was that the arms are a great danger for every family. There were some women who considered arms as necessary for defence because of the weak police force. If the state would better defend people and help them feel safe, then arms would not be needed in the home.'*[3]

As these examples show, there are many aspects to a micro-disarmament process. The media, the schools and society in general can play an important role in supporting SALW awareness campaigns by advocating that weapons do not necessarily provide security. Throughout the Albanian SALW collection process the media played a significant role. In Rio de Janeiro, Brazil, a popular soap opera has taken on the problem of the effects of uncontrolled SALW on people's lives. Operation Essential Harvest, a NATO mission to disarm ethnic Albanian groups in Macedonia, was supported by public service announcements on television and radio, many of which focused on women and home safety. Such initiatives bring the conversation about ridding a society of weapons into the home – a place where, as many women have publicly stated, weapons have no place.

However carefully the process of disarmament is undertaken and monitored, it will only remove a portion of a community's arms. In situations where they fear reprisals, or doubt that the conflict has truly come to an end or in any other way question their personal security, people will not easily give up what they imagine is a source of protec-

A female combatant from LURD (Liberians United for Reconciliation and Democracy) breastfeeds her baby while waiting to be disarmed by UN peacekeepers in Liberia.

tion. The identification and collection of weapons caches is, therefore, a project that must continue for long periods after official DDR processes have come to an end. A conscious strategy of disarmament should be to engage with both women and men on the subject of small arms, but this is complicated by women's often paradoxical relationship with such weapons. While it is true that their proliferation makes women's safety much more precarious, it cannot be assumed that women will not participate in the smuggling and storage of small arms and ammunition. In Sierra Leone, for example, women were very active movers of light weapons.[4] In the liberation struggles in Namibia, South Africa and Zimbabwe, while relatively few women formally entered the armed struggle, large numbers were engaged in supporting the conflicts by other means such as arms smuggling.[5] During the conflict, the ownership and usage of arms was perceived as a legitimate means of supporting a political cause. As a result, *laissez-faire* attitudes to weapons became normalised. In South Africa today, the price for casual attitudes to gun ownership is being paid in a spate of armed banditry, as well as accidental deaths from gunshots, the latter often involving children.

Civil society has increasingly rallied and supported the global effort to reduce the proliferation of small arms and light weapons in Sierra Leone.

Women all too rarely make a significant contribution to the politics that end war. This was also the case when peace agreements were signed in Sierra Leone (the Lomé Accord of 1999). Women, who had for decades been excluded from, yet exploited by the country's increasingly corrupt and militarised governments, were barely represented in negotiations. As a result, they did not benefit from, or participate at all, in the planning and execution of the DDR process.

Sierra Leonean women, horrified by the worsening violence perpetuated by the governmental and opposition forces, had begun to organise for peace already since 1994, lobbying the government, the opposition Revolutionary United Front (RUF) and the Armed Forces Revolutionary Council (AFRC), as well as the international community. Despite their efforts, no women were present at the first peace talks in 1996, which led to the abortive Abidjan Peace Accord.

Undeterred, Sierra Leonean women continued their campaign, working not only at home, but also towards creating a women's peace network in the entire sub-region and establishing solidarity with women in the similarly war-torn neighbour, Liberia. Their campaigning paid off in the sense that, by the time of the Lomé Peace Accord three years later, two women representatives had been included in the negotiating team (although they were not invited to sign the accord). In addition, there were some parts of the accord, which aimed at recognising both women's specific needs and their capacity to promote long-term peace. However, the final version of the accord was stereotypical in its understanding of women's experience of armed violence. In the end, it made no space for women who were not only victims, but also combatants or otherwise involved with fighting forces, even though it was well known that particularly for the RUF rural women were essential, accessible – and expendable – military

assets. Some have estimated that there were as many as 10,000 women associated with the rebel forces. While a handful held leadership positions, it is believed that an appalling 9,500 of these women were abducted or 'donated' to the fighters by family members. In other words, even though the accord was centrally concerned with DDR, about twelve per cent of all fighters and military supporters were simply ignored. Furthermore, no women (civilian or military) formed part of the Commission for the Consolidation of Peace under which the National Commission on DDR fell. No women work in decision-making positions on the National Commission for Reconstruction, Resettlement and Rehabilitation, the ceasefire monitoring committees, or on the disarmament sensitisation committee. Moreover, women are not being well served by the transitional justice mechanisms that have been put in place. There is only one female Sierra Leonean Commissioner in the country's Truth and Reconciliation Commission and no female Sierra Leonean judge in the Special Court.

The blame must squarely be laid at the door of the government and international agencies. The harsh truth in DDR operations, as in most national projects, is that the poorer and more marginal a woman is, the smaller her chance of benefiting. In Sierra Leone, a country whose literacy rates are one of the lowest in the world, only an estimated seventeen per cent of all women can claim literacy, with the lowest rates in the rural areas. Furthermore the majority of women, both volunteers and those abducted into the RUF, were rural dwellers, the poorest of poor in Sierra Leonean society.

Yet the Sierra Leone DDR process has been regarded by many as the most successful such exercise to date, in particular because of the attention it paid to child soldiers – or, to be specific, boys who had been forced into fighting. It has become increasingly clear in the period following the DDR process, however, that from the perspective of many thousands of women – and especially from the perspective of girls, whose plight simply did not come to the proper attention of social planners – it was not substantially different from anything that had gone before. Observers and analysts who support women's rights have been highly critical of its failure to satisfactorily address women's issues and are urging that significant lessons should be learned from its shortcomings.

Sources:

S. Anderlini, *Women at the Peace Table: Making a Difference* (New York: UNIFEM, 2000).

K. A. Bah, Rural Women and Girls in the War in Sierra Leone, *Occasional Paper* (Conciliation Resources, 2003), at http://www.c-r.org/pubs/occ-papers/khadija.shtml

J. Ginifer, 'Re-integration of Ex-combatants', in M. Malan (et al.), *Sierra Leone: Building the Road to Recovery,* Monograph 80 (Pretoria: Institute of Security Studies, 2003).

The demobilisation and reintegration of women combatants

Programmes to meet the needs of combatants must be put into place as quickly as possible after the formal cessation of hostilities, because the presence of armed and experienced fighters is a tremendous threat to the continuation of peace. Nevertheless, DDR planners should not lose sight of how demobilisation, disarmament and reintegration interact with other social reformations after war. To improve the chances that this interaction will be peaceful and constructive, DDR needs to be understood as a comprehensive process through which to promote social transformation, not only as a 'quick and dirty' means to reduce the number of armed fighters after war.

A female soldier from the Sierra Leone Army in the Benguema training camp.

Carefully implemented, the gender aware approach to demilitarisation called for in Resolution 1325 will benefit both male and female ex-fighters because it can help to promote several changes in the ways in which combatants' needs are managed after war. The first is immediate and practical, in that the establishment of a course of action, which highlights the requirements of women, as well as men, will contribute to the fairer demobilisation of all soldiers and support workers. Secondly, in the longer term, gender awareness during the demobilisation process can play an important role in promoting the recognition that gender roles are dynamic and thus present a potential site for change. Thirdly, gender aware DDR is vital for successful reintegration because the gendered impacts of wars do not end when conflict comes to an end. Those who are traumatised by war and then demobilised with inadequate psychosocial care frequently carry on the fight inside their own homes, turning the violence they have witnessed or perpetrated inwards and expressing their rage and pain in attacks on those who are nearest to them. The lethality of this domestic violence is heightened because of the large numbers of small arms and light weapons that continue to circulate after wars end.

The intention of demobilisation is to downsize, or where possible, completely disband armed forces (government and irregular/guerrilla), both to reduce the number of members of the armed forces and to help prevent a spill-over of trained combatants into neighbouring conflicts where they might work as mercenaries. This is typically achieved by assembling combatants, quartering and disarming them, and usually offering them some form of compensation and other assistance to encourage their transition back to civilian life. The primary intent of demobilisation is to remove combatants from their fighting roles as quickly as possible. Most programmes aim to equip ex-combatants with new skills and assist their reintegration

into civilian economic and social processes. Although initially an expensive process, in the long-term, demobilisation facilitates the re-direction of economic resources once used for the maintenance of war into development initiatives.[6]

With growing experience of demobilisation, there has been a considerable refinement in the ways in which combatants are thought about. The differences between participants in guerrilla movements and conscripts to a national army have long been highlighted, and demobilisation planners are committed to the development of support systems to deal with combatants from different groups. The developers of most contemporary operations are increasingly careful to differentiate between combatants on the basis of gender and age and to emphasise different physical and psychological needs. Increasingly, they reflect on the special challenges presented by child soldiers, including girls, a field where the need for gender awareness has also become more and more obvious.[7]

After the adoption of Resolution 1325, and women's continued activism to promote their contribution to peace-building, women and girl soldiers are officially on the agenda of demobilisation planning. There are, however, still some significant oversights concerning the 'special needs' of female ex-combatants, and this places a heavy burden on women in the post-conflict period. The first challenge women face is that they present an embarrassment (even if it is unspoken) to their communities after war. After wars end, societies often make a significant effort to forget how gender identities were challenged. In Zimbabwe, popular images of the liberation war reinforced the belief that women had made their greatest contribution as wives and mothers. In Nicaragua, Eritrea and Sierra Leone, women who challenged the re-imposition of patriarchal authority were vilified, and those who had seen active combat became objects of shame.[8] In Namibia, ex-combatant Teckla Shikola observed: *'No one mentions the contributions women made during the struggle. That's true all over the world. You never find an appreciation of what women did. Men appreciate women who cook for them, and they respect women who fought the war with them, but after independence, they don't really consider women as part of the liberation movement.'*[9]

Even formal attempts to record the hidden suffering of a persecuted community can leave women out. In Central America, and again, in South Africa during the hearings of the Truth and Reconciliation Commission (TRC), women only spoke out about what had happened to their male partners and family members. In South Africa, it was not until a group of feminist activists challenged the commission to hold private hearings for women that their stories began to emerge.[10]

The exclusion of women soldiers from decision-making positions is a particularly important problem when

Among micro disarmament policies, the exchange of development aid for weapons held by civilians in post-conflict areas is becoming increasingly popular with donors. Although such policies are often aimed at men, who generally tend to hold the weapons, UNIDIR's field research in Mali in March 2003 found that successful projects tend to involve the avid participation of the entire community that is, of both men and women.

In Mali, women played an indispensable part in securing a favourable climate for handing over weapons. In the face of violence, women served to persuade men as their wives, sisters, mothers and in-laws to give up their weapons. They organised inter-community meetings, involved the media, visited cantonment areas, and persuaded male family members to hand over their weapons. In a certain village, an elder woman told the UNIDIR research team that she had threatened her young male family members by saying that she would go naked in public unless they handed over their weapons. Women played a major role in the early process of peacebuilding, and the male community members highly appreciated their contribution.

Women also tend to maintain a holistic view of the goal of weapons collection. In Mali, both men and women agreed that the final goal of weapons collection is to eradicate poverty and bring peace to the community. However, when asked to elaborate on this thought, men and women reacted differently. For women, the aim of weapons collection programmes was to bring reconciliation among the various ethnic factions in the community, resumption of free transportation, and provision of opportunities for young men. Male community members tended to focus on reducing the number of weapons in circulation. While men could identify correctly the most effective procedures for collecting weapons, women emphasised that the ultimate purpose of collecting weapons is peacebuilding in the community.

Women in Mali proved also to be capable of identifying effective aid incentives for weapons collection projects. When asked how to judge the success of weapons collection projects, men focused on such material factors as the number of weapons collected and destroyed, and the reduction of gun-related crime and injuries. They also identified the building of roads and bridges as appropriate incentives for handing over weapons. Compared to men, women stressed the need to address the root causes of violent conflict. Moreover, women deemed projects such as provision of water wells, grain mills and cereal banks, that is the projects that provide basic needs for daily lives such as water and food, as the best sort of incentives to be provided in exchange for weapons. Women also explained that effective weapons for development projects should be linked to the underlying causes of small arms and light weapons problems. Especially, they emphasised the importance of job creation for young men in economically marginalised communities. This suggests that involving women in project design and evaluation can help donors in the selection of incentives for weapons collection programmes. In order to make weapons collection projects cost effective, it might be worth to reconsider providing a big one-time incentive such as the construction of roads and bridges. Such infrastructure could be most suitably offered at the national rather than at the community level.

From the Mali experience it would seem that men and women contribute to each stage of a weapons collection process in a complementary manner. Gender consideration in programmes of weapons collection seems then a matter of pragmatics. Involving both men and women in the design, implementation, monitoring and evaluation is key for effective projects. But how can the contribution of women in this respect be maximised?

First and foremost, the international assistance community should make sure that women are involved in the decision-making process. Although there is a desire to involve them, they are often left aside when projects are implemented, because they are more tied to their housework. In Mali, once weapons collection began, women's role in the process decreased. Therefore, the international community needs to pay more attention to maintaining women's participation throughout the implementation of such projects.

One way to encourage women's participation would be to incorporate participatory monitoring and evaluation techniques into weapons collection programmes. These methods, long practised in the fields of health and development, have the potential to facilitate communication among the actual beneficiaries of the projects. The techniques involve group discussion and visual aids such as flow charts, to enable as many members of the community as possible to participate. It is important to pay attention even to meeting times. In Mali, urban women had less difficulty in participating in disarmament processes than rural women who generally tend to have less spare time that can be devoted to meetings. In this case, holding a meeting late in the afternoon (after daytime errands, before the preparation of dinner), for example, might allow more women to participate.

When women are involved, their 'heterogeneousness' should not be overlooked. In Mali, women are altogether narrowly defined as wives and mothers. However, if they are unmarried, or do not fit in the social strata, they might be excluded from consideration, even by fellow women. An illustrative example is female ex-combatants. During its field research, the UNIDIR team came upon a few female ex-combatants in a community. When the research team asked to involve them in an ex-combatants' discussion group, the male members of the group refused, because 'they were women'. Likewise, when women were asked to integrate the female ex-combatants in their discussion group, they too declined, because 'those women were fighters, not civilians'. Participatory monitoring and evaluation techniques are strong tools to involve various beneficiaries in aid programmes. However, one still needs to be sensitive to local conditions and to refine methodologies according to local context, in order to make all voices heard.

Sources:

E. F. Barth, *Peace as Disappointment, The Reintegration of Female Soldiers in Post-conflict Societies: A Comparative Study from Africa* (Oslo: PRIO, 2002).

B. Byrne et al., Gender, Conflict and Development: Case Studies: Cambodia, Rwanda, Kosova, Somalia, Algeria, Guatemala and Eritrea, *BRIDGE Report* (Brighton: Institute of Development Studies, 1996).

K. Kingma, 'Assessing Demobilisation: Conceptual Issues', in K. Kingma (ed), *Demobilisation in Sub-Saharan Africa: The Development and Security Impacts* (London and New York: Macmillan Press Ltd, 2000), 23-44.

attempts are made to demilitarise a society, because women who have seen active combat are likely to be even more marginalised than other women in the society under reconstruction. While men fulfil the conditions of masculinity by being violent to support a cause, women fighters do not occupy a position that can be easily reconciled with predominant patriarchal ideologies. Militarised women are posed with a unique set of challenges in the demobilisation phase and afterwards. Unlike male combatants, they are refused promotion or expelled from the army altogether, excluded from new political structures, refused access to re-training or land, overlooked in veteran's organisations, and regarded with fear and suspicion when they attempt to return to the lives they lived before war broke out.[11] Their experiences prove that, even though some of the normally accepted ideas about 'womanly' behaviour might be suspended during wartime, women who contradict the stereotype of appropriate female behaviour through active participation in the violence of war 'are often regarded as more deviant or unnatural than men'.[12] To address the challenges faced by women combatants after war, demobilisation planning has, therefore, to recognise the different needs of fighters of both sexes, and not assume that one plan of action will be suitable for all ex-combatants.

It is also important to remember that not all women who participate in war do so as fighters. In planning DDR processes, programme designers and implementers must not only address the needs of women ex-combatants, but also of those women who played other support roles, for instance as porters, cooks, or 'wives' (which should include those abducted and widowed) of combatants. Women and girls associated with fighting forces are not always officially married to male fighters, and they might therefore be difficult to identify and are also in other ways especially vulnerable.

A valuable lesson can be learnt from agencies specialising in assisting refugees and internally displaced persons. They have learned that women are far more likely to speak to women support workers, especially when intimate health care issues must be discussed. This knowledge should also be applied to women associated with fighting forces, because if they do not feel safe or welcomed in a DDR process, they are likely to 'self-demobilise' – in other words, to disappear from view without taking advantage of any of the opportunities of demobilisation. While some may argue that women should be allowed to choose not to be formally demobilised, this is a self-destructive option because it excludes them both from immediate benefits such as medical care and re-training and from longer term gains such as re-employment in alternative security forces, greater political participation and access to economic alternatives. Their capacity for self-reintegration is likely to be very limited, resulting in homelessness, isolation, and

exclusion from safe paid work. To avoid this situation, training must be put in place for women field workers whose role will be to interview women combatants and other participants in order to identify who should be included in DDR processes.

Although the primary intent of demobilisation is to remove combatants from their fighting roles as quickly as possible it is, even in the planning stages, imperative to think about how returning ex-soldiers will be received by the civilian community. From the perspective of this receiving community, it can seem that DDR 'rewards' people who supported or committed atrocities. Civilians often express resentment that they are expected to re-embrace those who have wronged them, and they often feel excluded from the plans that are developed to reintegrate ex-combatants and those who worked with them. In other words, for reintegration to succeed, women ex-combatants, as well as, women in receiving communities need support. Programme planners should take into account that women who have been associated with fighting forces may have very different needs, and want to make different choices, in the post-conflict period than other women. While some may wish to return to their original homes, others may choose to follow male partners to a new geographical location. Some women may be abandoned by departing soldiers. Some may choose to remain behind in a new place when their male partners return to their places of origin.

Because the period of rehabilitation and reintegration will be long, if is it not well planned, it is more likely that ex-combatants will not reintegrate and that divisions between them and the receiving community will widen as time passes. Recognising this danger from the outset is an imperative part of ensuring long-term stability and peace-building. Without considering how communities of soldiers interact with communities of civilians, DDR as a peacekeeping measure is likely to fail in the long run. From the perspective of those who return, a specific challenge for planners may be to address the fact that life in the armed forces was relatively egalitarian. Reintegrating into a society with rigidly gendered social structures will put enormous stress on women who have been accustomed to freer modes of behaviour and fairer divisions of labour. The attitudes of these women after the conflict ends may lead to social stigmatisation from communities who resent, do not understand, or do not wish to change to accommodate this freedom. Often it is the women in the receiving community who will be the harshest judges of the women who return, so careful attention has to be paid to building bridges and networks between the women of these very different groups.

Women are also likely to suffer particular stigmatisation as war widows, or as 'fallen' women who are bearers of 'fatherless' or 'ethnically different' children, for whom they may be expected to take sole responsibility. Such community isolation is especially dangerous in places where child soldiering is common. It may end up perpetuating cycles of violence because children who live on the margins of society are more vulnerable to recruitment and abduction into armed forces than those who feel they are full participants in the communities where they live.

Gender differences impact on people's ability to adjust to post-war conditions, both materially and psychologically, so that the adequate demobilisation of combatants requires an approach which is sensitive to the different challenges faced by women and men in the post-war era. Social transformation after war implies far more than the disbanding of militarised structures. Developing the means to support women's access to social, cultural and political representation, as well as changing attitudes to land access and developing a heightened awareness of levels of violence against women in a post-conflict society, are also essential parts of the process of conversion.

To move into successful long-term peacebuilding processes, narrow social constructs of masculinity and femininity need to be consciously addressed. Demobilisation and reintegration processes form only one part of the broader task of demilitarising society, but they present an opportunity to do more than manage the transition of personnel into non-combatant roles after war. Demobilisation and reintegration, and the longer term challenges of disarmament, can also become part of the broader movement for social change after war.

Endnotes

1   The experience of South African women, who are rare in having successfully influenced the drafting of a gender aware constitution after the apartheid war ended, suggests, however, that it is only in the presence of an active women's movement that positive developments are possible after conflict (see V. Farr, *A Chanting Foreign and Familiar: The Production and Publishing of Women's Collective Life Writing in South Africa*, unpublished Ph.D. thesis (Toronto: York University, 2002).

2   B. Sorensen (ed), *Women and Post-conflict Reconstruction. Issues and Sources*, 9. (Geneva: UNRISD, 1998), II.

3   UNIFEM Portal on Women, Peace and Security, at www.women warpeace.org/issues/smallarms/docs/salw-chapter.doc

4   B. Mansaray, 'Women Against Weapons: A Leading Role for Women in Disarmament', in A. Ayissi and R. E. Poulton (eds), *Bound to Co-operate: Conflict, Peace and People in Sierra Leone* (Geneva: UNIDIR, 2000), 139-58.

5   J. Goldstein, *War and Gender* (Cambridge and New York: Cambridge University Press, 2001), 82.

6   K. Kingma, 'Assessing Demobilisation: Conceptual Issues', in K. Kingma (ed), *Demobilisation in Sub-Saharan Africa: The Development and Security Impacts* (London and New York: Macmillan Press Ltd, 2000), 23-44. Also, K. Kingma, 'The Role of Demobilisation in the Peace and Development Process in Sub-Saharan Africa: Conditions for Success', *African Security Review*, 5 (1996), 33-42.

7   S. McKay and D. Mazurana, *Where Are The Girls? Girls fighting forces in Northern Uganda, Sierra Leone and Mozambique: Their lives during and after war* (Rights and Democracy: Montreal, 2004). See also the findings of the International Conference on War-affected Children held in Canada in September 2000, at http://www.waraffectedchildren.gc.ca/menu-e.asp

8   F. Barth, *Peace as Disappointment. The Reintegration of Female Soldiers in Post-conflict Societies: A Comparative Study from Africa* (Oslo: PRIO, 2002). Also, B. Mansaray, Women Against Weapons: A Leading Role for Women in Disarmament.

9   T. Shikola, 'We left Our Shoes Behind', in M. Turshen and C. Twagiramariya (eds), *What Women Do in Wartime: Gender and Conflict in Africa* (London and New York: Zed Books, 1998), 150-62.

10   See also the special issue of the South African feminist journal *AGENDA* 43 (2000) and *Canadian Women Studies* 19 (4) and 22 (3), which focus on women's experiences in the aftermath of war.

11   Barth, *Peace as Disappointment*, also, Shikola, *We Left Our Shoes Behind*.

12   B. Byrne et al., 'Gender, Conflict and Development: Case Studies: Cambodia, Rwanda, Kosovo, Somalia, Algeria, Guatemala and Eritrea', *BRIDGE Report* (Brighton: Institute of Development Studies, 1996).

Chapter 6

Women and Men Combating Violence: Examples

'Women have been both peacemakers and peace preventers and the range of their attitudes and responses has been as wide and varied as that of men. [...] They have provided some of the vital tools which the whole society needs in order to build peace - it now remains to be seen how good women and men will be at using them.'

Valerie Morgan, Northern Ireland, October 1995

Transitional Justice, Reconciliation and the Role of Women

'There is no handy roadmap for reconciliation. There is no short cut or simple prescription for healing the wounds and divisions of a society in the aftermath of sustained violence. Creating trust and understanding between former enemies is a supremely difficult challenge. It is, however, an essential one to address in the process of building a lasting peace. Examining the painful past, acknowledging it and understanding it, and above all transcending it together, is the best way to guarantee that it does not – and cannot – happen again. As our experience in South Africa has taught us, each society must discover its own route to reconciliation. Reconciliation cannot be imposed from outside, nor can someone else's map get us to our destination: it must be our own solution. This involves a very long and painful journey, addressing the pain and suffering of the victims, understanding the motivations of offenders, bringing together estranged communities, trying to find a path to justice, truth and, ultimately, peace. Faced with each new instance of violent conflict, new solutions must be devised that are appropriate to the particular context, history and culture in question.'

Desmond Tutu, Archbishop Emeritus
D. Bloomfield, T. Bames and L. Huyse,
Reconciliation After Violent Conflict, A Handbook

These thoughtful words of Archbishop Tutu define the very essence of the worldwide efforts to deal with the consequences of repression and often horrific crimes against humanity, even genocide so as to 'find a path to justice', but also to prevent the repetition of cycles of violence. Women have been prominent in anti-war movements and pacifist circles throughout history, even when the wars they opposed were widely considered holy, as in the Middle Ages.[1] More recently, women maintained a significant presence in both nineteenth and twentieth century pacifist and anti-war movements. Two thousand women held an anti-war conference at The Hague in 1915, in the midst of the First World War. The still active Women's International League for Peace and Freedom (WILPF) was created as a result of this gathering. One of the conference participants Rosika Schwimmer, a peace activist from Hungary, voiced her belief that the building of peace depends on how the war was ended. Military settlements dictated by the militarists would carry the seeds of future conflicts. Unfortunately, this prediction proved to be prophetic in many instances that followed, including the majority of most recent wars. The famous writer Virginia Woolf was convinced that violence and militarism were strongly linked to men since they were in charge of what she named the 'military industrial complex'. She believed that women have a potential to change the situation because they remain outside of traditional structures. Woolf was not opposing working with men towards the same objectives, but advocated that women should act in their own way. This is exactly how most of the well-known women peace activists' initiatives and networks have been organised in their resistance against wars.

The growing concern for human rights during the last two decades of the twentieth century resulted in a mounting consensus to confront the legacies of rights abuses in the periods of transition, following wars and repressive, authoritarian regimes, in a comprehensive way. *'A wide range of initiatives has been put in place to address the accountability challenges that emerge at the point of transition and the diversity and richness of these initiatives is impressive. This growing area of developing mechanisms to address past crimes at a point of transition is often referred to as "transitional justice". […] The field of transitional justice is self-consciously interdisciplinary and nationally driven, while also grounded in comparative international experiences. As these issues gain increasing attention, one can see almost daily new challenges and unique contexts in which justice policies must be crafted, as well as new and creative ideas on how to best respond. Both national and international civil society organisations, plus the broader international community, have a critical role in advancing these developments.'* [2]

Criminal justice remains the most important pillar of transitional justice. However, after a violent conflict or a long lasting repressive regime there may be thousands of perpetrators that should be put on trial and many more victims that demand justice and some form of reparation. Even well developed judicial systems would have enormous difficulties to face such a task. Most of the transition countries are either inheriting a society without the rule of law, or with weak institutional infrastructure, including judiciary. The images of overcrowded jails in Rwanda where

tens of thousands of alleged perpetrators were waiting for trials were the most worrisome confirmation of this enormous problem. The International Criminal Tribunal for Rwanda and the International Criminal Tribunal for former Yugoslavia succeeded in achieving important breakthroughs, such as trials against the highest political representatives of countries involved in violent conflicts, and the first conviction where rape had been qualified as war crime. These tribunals in the context of a growing awareness about the importance of transitional justice also contributed to the establishment of the International Criminal Court, endorsed by more than 60 countries, unfortunately not yet by the most influential such as the United States, Russia, and China. Although, international courts cannot, and should not, substitute national criminal procedures, they remain new, crucial instruments of transitional justice.

As Priscilla Hayner from the International Centre for Transitional Justice argues, the concept of justice *'cannot fully be captured simply by identifying the wrongdoers, taking them to court, and sentencing them to serve time in jail. We must ask: what form of justice is due to the victims of the crimes, especially those who suffered severe physical or psychological injury, or whose economic means have been severely disrupted, such as through the loss of a breadwinner? What would be an appropriate form of justice for whole communities that have suffered or been completely destroyed?'* [3] We must also ask how to help citizens of a region or an entire country to face the recent past, to acknowledge that many members of their communities and often on their behalf participated in horrific crimes? How to establish the truth, how to avoid the long lasting denials that characterises even the search for the truth about the Holocaust, the best documented genocide in history? Importantly, Jan Gross's investigative research about mass atrocities against Jews committed by their Polish neighbours,[4] published almost 60 years after they were committed, was still met with denial by many Poles.

The tendency to deny is present in most societies faced with similar histories. This has been the case in Japan, South Africa, Chile, Argentina, former Yugoslavia and numerous other countries. For example, after the massacre in Srebrenica most of the Serbian population refused to believe what had happened. Women in Black and many other NGOs organised public debates and protests devoted to Srebrenica, books about the war crimes were published, conferences organised about truth, responsibility and reconciliation after regime change with the participation of high ranking politicians, independent media broadcast the first films about Srebrenica even while Milosevic was still in power, and the International Criminal Tribunal for the former Yugoslavia processed dozens of perpetrators. Denial started to decrease in September 2003 during the most

Palestinian women, with their hands symbolically chained, at a demonstration demanding freedom for Palestinian prisoners jailed in Israeli prisons in the West Bank city of Nablus.

famous talk show in the country, called the 'Impression of the Week'. This show broadcast the message of a Bosnian Muslim mother from the site of a memorial service in Srebrenica, who explained that her husband and son were killed, as were two sons of a Serb mother from Visegrad, whom she met recently. She asked for justice regardless of the nationality of the perpetrators in order to achieve reconciliation.

The notable involvement of women in peace movements on all sides during the last Balkan wars was one of the more conspicuous features of the conflict.[5] The peace movements in the countries of the former Yugoslavia had a crucial impact on the development of new women's movements in the Balkans. Anti-war activities generated a whole range of women's NGOs that cover a wide variety of initiatives from crisis centres helping victims of war-related and domestic violence, information and research centres, non-violent conflict resolution training, to local and regional networks of anti-war activists such as the Women in Black. It is important to stress that almost all grassroots women's initiatives, even those devoted to academic work, such as centres for women's studies, have been part of anti-war activities. The latter were, in addition to being among the first civic, non-governmental academic institutions, also the first academic institutions dealing with women rights, human and minority rights, peace studies and transitional justice. Women's NGOs were the pillar of humanitarian work as well, including supporting large numbers of refugees and displaced persons. They did not stop co-operating across borders even when the conflicts were at their peak, risking being labelled 'traitors' or a 'fifth column'.

Twelve years after the wars in the former Yugoslavia started, there are still thousands of women living in refugee camps, and many have to take care of their children under these appalling conditions. It must also be stressed that women led many of the most important and courageous human rights organisations in the region during the last decade. Their work greatly contributed to the fact that for the first time in history rape was acknowledged as a war crime, and that the first suspects for this crime have been convicted at the International Criminal Tribunal for former Yugoslavia in The Hague.

The role of women in building an open, civil society and their potential in the reconstruction of the Balkan countries deserves serious attention. Women's NGOs mushroomed during the last decade. This was women's way of finding a new sense of identity beyond ethnicity, and of surviving the inhuman conditions their societies faced. Foreign donors, international women's foundations and

NGOs rushed to support them. The question we must confront in the post-war period is whether the energy and commitment will survive when the war is over, as these countries enter the process of transition to more stable, functional societies? What will be the role of women in post-war reconstruction? How can women contribute to the new security architecture of the region if gender issues are left out of the mainstream economy and politics? Are women's NGOs strong enough to articulate a necessary gender perspective during the transition process? Is there a political will both within these countries and in the international community to support such a perspective?

These questions are complex and difficult, as was evident during the transitions in East and Central Europe and in the countries of the former Soviet Union. The political transition in the post-communist period has often been understood as a return to the values of the past, patriarchy included. The introduction of market economy left many without jobs, and the majority of the unemployed were women. Social policy and social institutions collapsed. At a women's conference in Berlin in November 1990 women from East Germany, many of who played a major role in the pro-democracy movement, spoke about their desperate economic and political situation in the new environment. Some of them publicly wondered whether they were wrong when they joined the resistance movement against com-

munism. This happened only a year after the most exciting moment of their lives - the fall of the Berlin Wall. In Romania, in the December 2000 election, urban youth and women made up the majority of those who voted for Vadim Tudor, an extreme nationalist. This was, according to most analysts, the direct result of a very difficult and ill-conceptualised transition. When political change is not accompanied by social policies aimed at vulnerable groups of the population, women and youth often pay a harsh price. In searching for a way out the response may be a (re)turn to anti-reformist, or even chauvinist-populist demagogues.

Another impressive case of women peace activism is to be found in the Middle East. In the midst of a long lasting, from time to time very violent conflict, women have succeeded in developing a whole range of non-violent, politically very articulate responses. In fact since the formation of Women in Black in 1988, women have been the most vibrant, daring, and progressive part of the Israeli peace movement. Before anyone else, they advocated a two-state solution, sharing Jerusalem as the capital of both states, and creative solutions to the refugee issue. They engaged in a dialogue with Palestinian women; broke through the closure to bring food, medicine, and a message of coexistence; paid condolence calls to the families of victims on both sides; and spoke out in a clear, daring voice against

© Vesna Pavlovic, 1994

Women in Black is one of the most daring movements to resist war and build tolerance and understanding. They support the creation of conditions for reconciliation and lasting peace. Women in Black demonstrators protest the Balkan wars in Novi Sad City Square, Serbia and Montenegro.

the very idea to resolve this multi-faceted and immensely difficult conflict by military means. They had a partner in implementing 'people-to-people' projects, namely Palestinian women committed to peace.

In 1989, a meeting was convened in Brussels between prominent Israeli and Palestinian women peace activists. The meeting initiated an on-going dialogue that in 1994 resulted in the establishment of the Jerusalem Link comprising two women's organisations – Bat Shalom on the Israeli side, and the Jerusalem Centre for Women on the Palestinian side. The two organisations shared a set of political principles, which made it possible to build an understanding between them about coexistence and joint activities. When the second Intifada broke out many believed that it marked the death of such efforts. Palestinian NGOs decided to halt their joint projects with the Israeli side, particularly the 'people to people' projects and any programme, which contained an approach of 'normalisation'.[6] Although there have been an almost complete break in people-to-people communication the women did not give up. In late September 2000, nine Israeli women's peace organisations formed the Coalition of Women for Peace and launched a series of non-violent actions, some of them involving civil disobedience. Bat Shalom, the women's peace group committed to end the occupation and the establishment of a Palestinian state, was among them. This group and a few others maintained communication all along. This is why it was possible to return to mass actions such as the march in December 2001, when 5,000 Israeli and Palestinian women marched together from the Israeli to the Palestinian side of Jerusalem under the twin banners, 'The Occupation is Killing Us All' and 'We Refuse to be Enemies'.[7]

There are still many who wonder whether this type of non-violent resistance can bring real results in severe, protracted conflicts such as in the Middle East. The results of the Four Mothers Movement, a group of four women, whose sons were serving in the Israeli army, could provide an answer. This group was founded in 1997 and it sought to mobilise the Israeli public to demand that Israel withdraw from Lebanon, based on the argument that its prolonged presence there serves no security purposes, but jeopardises the lives of soldiers. Although it was faced with scorn from senior military officers the small demonstrations and silent vigils of mothers appealed to the Israeli public. *They demanded - and were accorded - meetings with the highest government officials, whose inadequate answers were then magnified through the well-run media work of this group. The "authentic", mother-oriented nature of this movement, and its dissociation from partisan politics, struck an empathetic nerve among the Israeli public. The deaths of Israeli soldiers were on the increase in Lebanon, and the message of the Four Mothers fell on attentive ears, feeding public dismay over the seemingly endless body bags. Within three years of the start of the movement, the Israeli army withdrew from Lebanon.'*[8]

Although the Balkan and Middle East women peace activists live and struggle in very different circumstances they proved that genuine peace efforts reach out to a worldwide community. The Women in Black movement, which started in Israel in 1988, when a group of women dressed in black held silent vigils at the central square in Jerusalem and throughout the country demanding the end of hostilities, was embraced by women in Serbia in 1991. From these two places it spread all over the world. When eight Danish and Norwegian parliamentarians (four men and four women) nominated them for the Nobel Peace Prize in 2001 they emphasised that these women succeeded not only to endure for more than a decade in their resistance to war, but consequently rejected hostile enemy images of their neighbours and reached out to the 'other' in order to build the preconditions for a lasting peace and reconciliation. Women in Black have proved to have the potential of spreading to many countries. Their calm and dignified, but still visual and telling way of protesting has inspired peace activists in many countries. They became a global grassroots network of women who carry the potential to influence global civil society in the making.

The Balkan and Middle East women's peace movements are outstanding examples of women's peace activism, but are by no means the only ones. From the anti-war movement in the United States, which, in fact, ended the war in Vietnam to the courageous effort of Russian and Chechen women to stop this ongoing bloody conflict, women have been a central pillar of every single peace and non-violent movement around the globe. Although the United Nations Security Council Resolution 1325, adopted in October 2000, recognises the key role that women play in conflict transformation and holding communities together in times of crisis, and commits the UN to address the gender dimensions of conflict and include women in formal peace negotiations and processes, there is still a long way to go until their real potential as peacemakers will be fully recognised. The first necessary step is to broaden the understanding about the civil and political value of women peace activism, to include them in peace negotiations and to secure their presence and influence during post-conflict reconstruction.

The story of victimisation of women is very well known. In the context of transitional justice and reconciliation it is of utmost importance that offences against them are recognised and punished, children who are a result of rape must be given full rights, and women provided with the necessary post-trauma treatment and economic assistance.

Turkish protesters run from tear gas in Istanbul, Turkey, during a demonstration to mark Women's Day.

Since in most of these countries patriarchy is still very strong, special attention has to be paid to inheritance laws and practices, since war widows or female children may be dispossessed. The stories of women in resistance against abuses of rights, against political, ethnic, racial and religious fundamentalism are, unfortunately, less known. How many reporters wrote about women who organised underground schools for girls under Taliban rule, risking their lives to prevent women from falling into the darkness of ignorance? How many news channels reported about Women in Black, as an 'international peace network', and as a 'means and formula for action'? Although the Mothers of Plaza de Mayo, a group of Argentinean women who became a symbol of human rights activism and courage in Argentina, is better known, the question of how many understood their role in bringing down the junta and leading the struggle for justice is still valid. '*Dressed in black, they have been demonstrating for years every Thursday at 3:30 in the afternoon, in the famous Plaza de Mayo in Buenos Aires, demanding to know the fates of their loved ones. Marching around the statue of liberty, in front of the presidential palace, they used to tie white handkerchiefs imprinted with names of disappeared sons and daughters, around their heads, and carry signs emblazoned with photographs of those about whose destinies they sought information. The Mothers' use of the imagery of Christian motherhood made them particularly effective against the professedly Catholic military regime.*'[9] Several of them, including their founder, Azucenab Villaflor de Vicenti, disappeared as a result of their protests.

Women have struggled for justice by participating in public debates about crimes committed both against women and men, by testifying publicly and behind close doors, sometimes risking further stigmatisation, by participating in memory writing projects, by their own investigative reporting, by being outstanding members of truth and reconciliation commissions in South Africa, Argentina, Peru, Sierra Leone, in fact, in most of truth and reconciliation commissions around the globe. With the help of international human rights organisations a Women's Task Force on the TRC and Special Court has been established in Sierra Leone. This task force consults regularly with the Special Court and TRC to create an enabling environment that will encourage the participation of women at all levels of both these institutions. The Women's Task Force, with direct support from International Human Rights Law Group, has also successfully pushed for the creation of a special unit to investigate gender specific war crimes during the country's decade long civil war.[10]

Women activists in close coalition with all those who care for a better, more just and less violent world must do everything possible to raise awareness about gender related crimes, but also to continue their resistance against circumstances in which those crimes are committed, and to be active in drafting a new human security agenda. To achieve their most precious goals, women activists must enter into the political processes, to make their voices heard loud and clear where the most important decisions are made.

Box 6.1 : Women in Black

Women in Black is a loose network of women worldwide committed to peace and actively opposed to war and other forms of violence. It is not an organisation, but a means of mobilisation and a formula for action. By demonstrating together, Women in Black networks share a sense of solidarity and purpose as women and can encourage and lend support to other women around the world who are often closer to the violence. They also try to educate, inform and influence public opinion so as to make war an unthinkable option.

Women in Black vigils were started in Israel in 1988 by women protesting against Israel's occupation of the West Bank and Gaza, demanding peace between Israel and the Palestinians. Italian women supporters of the Israeli women brought the idea back to Italy, where Women in Black mobilisations have occurred in many cities. Contacts between Italian women and the Yugoslav women led to a similar reaction. Women in Black vigils have been held in Republic Square, Belgrade, opposing the Serbian regime's involvement in aggression.

It is impossible to know how many women there are who identify with Women in Black, how many groups or mailing lists exist, or how many actions have been held. Certainly it has become a worldwide movement. Women in Black conferences and encounters have been held in Jerusalem and Novi Sad (Yugoslavia) since 1994. A Women in Black vigil was held in Beijing at the time of the 1995 UN Conference on Women. An exhibition in 1996 was held in New York of photos of Women in Black actions around the world. In 2001 Women in Black were nominated for the Nobel Peace Prize by Danish and Norwegian parliamentarians.

Source : Women in Black, at http://www.womeninblack.net

Economic crises, political upheaval, social discrimination, personal loss, none of these predicaments have discouraged women from maintaining a sense of justice and equality. On the contrary, these hardships have strengthened women's ability to overcome difficulties, and often encouraged them to establish organisations that seek to bring back their dignity. Particularly, in traditionally patriarchal and macho societies such as those in Latin American, women's efforts to promote peace gain even greater significance.

Women's response to conflict has been characterised by establishing pacifist movements or organisations that deal with a diverse array of issues from taking care of people's basic needs, such as food and shelter, to confronting authoritarian regimes in their plea to find the whereabouts of the *desaparecidos*, or missing, those men and women who were, and today still are, abducted by regimes for politically motivated reasons. Women from the most diverse backgrounds, literate and uneducated, married or single mothers, politicians or peasants have participated in the establishment of organisations that have allowed them to express their opinion on such key issues. At the same time, these movements can be seen as a medium through which women attempt to find, or assert their identity, and try to position themselves in a very much male-dominated society. Despite their traditionally subjugated position, Latin American women have, in the last century, become increasingly aware of their power to mobilise and steer the interest of national, as well as international audiences.

Elisabeth J. Friedman rightly illustrates this point: *'Women's movements in Latin America have a rich history and a vibrant presence. The movements are notable for the diversity of their actors, including autonomous feminists and party leaders, workers and peasants, heterosexuals and lesbians, rich and poor, Afro-Latin and indigenous women. As a result of this diversity, women in the region have not held a single set of shared interests, nor relied on one organisational model. Because gender is crosscut by other social relations of power, such as race and class, and all are mediated by particular socio-political and economic contexts,* *differently situated women have had very different experiences of the intensity or centrality of gender relations in their lives. As a result, women's movements in the region have addressed a wide range of interests, using a wide variety of structures – including, of course, alliances around particular issues.'*

One of the most well-known women's movements in the world is the Argentinean *Asociación de Madres de la Plaza de Mayo*, created in 1997 by fourteen women committed to the search for their missing children. This movement has set an example to millions of women in Latin America and abroad, partly because it has touched one of the most sensitive issues in a woman's life, motherhood; and partly as a result of its success in obtaining the attention of those they wanted to target, namely the Argentinean regime, as well as the international community.

The activities of the association began when a group of women whose children had been kidnapped refused to accept the official response to their queries and complaints. Thus, each Thursday afternoon the mothers appeared at Plaza de Mayo wearing kerchiefs, embroidered with the names of their missing relatives and the dates of their disappearances. In a tight circle, the group walked around the monuments at the centre of the square in absolute silence. Although, the group did not succeed in their immediate objective of obtaining precise information on the whereabouts of the missing, they did succeed in re-creating a civil society consciousness in Argentina. Moreover, they demonstrated that not only had society a right to express itself, but also that women could fulfil their role as citizens by being actively engaged in political issues. The symbolic significance of the movement is of greatest importance. The mothers stood in clear defiance to an authoritarian and bloody regime that left thousands of people dead or disappeared.

Sources:

Asociación de Madres de la Plaza de Mayo, at http://www.madres.org

Women Waging Peace, *Examples of Women Peace-builders (Colombia) and Background* (2003), at http://www.womenwagingpeace.net/content/conflict_areas/colombia.asp

The Madres de la Plaza de Mayo march through the streets in Buenos Aires. They carry posters of the thousands who have been reported missing during the 1976-1983 military dictatorship in Argentina.

Women's Inclusion in Peace and Security Processes Building: An NGO Campaign to Engage the UN Security Council

The global campaign 'Women Building Peace: From the Village Council to the Negotiating Table' was launched by International Alert in 1999 with support from over 200 organisations around the world.[11] The campaign aimed to encourage the United Nations system, particularly the Security Council, and the European Parliament to develop a political framework demonstrating their commitment to women's inclusion in all aspects of peace processes. Simultaneously, in collaboration with the United Nations Fund for Women (UNIFEM), the campaign sought to highlight women's positive role and to validate their peacebuilding initiatives through the launch and delivery of the first ever Millennium Peace Prize for Women.

With widespread support from local, national and international agencies and together with other critical actors such as like-minded NGOs, UN agencies and sympathetic governments, the campaign contributed to the unanimous adoption of Security Council Resolution 1325 on Women, Peace and Security (October 2000). During the same period, the campaign supported a resolution adopted by the European Parliament on the Gender Aspects of Conflict Prevention (November 2000).

In recognition of women's concerns, an international conference on 'Women, Violent Conflict and Peace-Building: Global Perspectives' was organised early in May 1999, by International Alert, the Centre for Defence Studies at King's College, and the Council for the Advancement of Arab British Understanding (CAABU). This conference brought together women from various conflict and post-conflict contexts with participants, chosen from organisations with a focus on women, to share their experiences of armed conflict and their peace-building agency. Citing the wealth of the existing international frameworks, women discussed and assessed existing international mechanisms for their advancement and empowerment and reflected on the degree to which these mechanisms have been interpreted and entrenched into national laws. The conference participants unanimously agreed on the need for a global campaign that is a rallying point for the mobilisation of women's demands and a focus for highlighting women's concerns on the international stage. The women agreed on five concise demands that they wanted the international community to address in order to demonstrate accountability and compliance with the norms that have been developed: 1) Include women in peace negotiations as decision-makers. 2) Put women at the heart of reconstruction and reconciliation. 3) Strengthen the protection and participation of female refugees, internally displaced and other war affected women. 4) End impunity and ensure redress for crimes committed against women. 5) Provide women's peacebuilding organisations with sufficient and sustainable resources.

Late in May 1999, International Alert launched the Women Building Peace campaign at the Hague Appeal for Peace Centennial conference. According to the organisers, this was the largest international peace conference in history with representatives from NGOs, policy makers, heads of state and even royalty from the Middle East in attendance.[12] It presented an ideal forum for launching the initiative with Queen Noor of Jordan publicly endorsing the campaign. The launch provided an opportunity to disseminate an interactive CD-ROM on Women, Conflict and Peace and facilitate workshops on cross-cutting issues such as the protection of women's human rights in conflict and post-conflict situations.[13]

The Women Building Peace campaign had four strategic objectives:

- Policy impact - securing a policy instrument from the Security Council providing a political framework for integrating women's perspectives on peace and security issues into peace processes and a similar instrument from the European Union Council of Ministers or the European Parliament.

- Participation and partnership - creating a loose coalition of women's organisations from all regions working collaboratively to highlight the campaign's five demands and an international advisory committee to provide guidance.

- Peace prize - launching of the first Millennium Peace Prize for women with UNIFEM to promote and highlight women's peacebuilding agency and positive contribution to conflict prevention and transformation.

- Popular education - creation of a number of user friendly products that would convey the campaign's messages and that would secure buy-in and legitimacy from women's organisations around the world.

The primary aim of the campaign was to engage the Security Council to adopt a resolution that would incorporate the women's five demands and that would require members of the Security Council, other member states of the United Nations and the international community generally to implement it in a gender sensitive and gender aware manner. It was hoped that such a policy device would energise all relevant stakeholders to examine and incorporate the needs of women into their own national policies, programming and practice. The Security Council was identified as the key target for the

Women and children were important actors in the protest demanding peace talks in Colombia during the three decade war which has claimed 35,000 civilian lives.

campaign because its primary function is the maintenance of peace and security. Moreover, the Security Council was gradually expanding its mandate, as evidenced by their thematic debates on such issues as the Protection of Civilians, Children and Armed Conflict and the HIV/AIDS epidemic. At the same time, the UN system was preparing for a review of the Beijing Platform for Action. This was, therefore, an opportune time to highlight the issues of women, peace and security and project them onto the global agenda.

However, there were a number of challenges. The Security Council meeting was to be held in October 2000 and to secure a resolution within twelve months was a substantial challenge. International Alert's campaign staff was acutely aware that momentous policy initiatives such as the adoption of a Security Council resolution are not achievable by any one organisation working unilaterally. Rather, successful global advocacy initiatives require tight multi-level collaboration and strategic alliances. In order to secure a resolution, ensure widespread and representative support for the initiative, and to shape and impact policy at the global level, the International Alert led campaign needed to work closely with a number of key stakeholders, particularly in New York.

The Women Building Peace campaign employed a variety of tactics to achieve its goals. These included policy dialogues, local and global campaigning, policy research resulting in targeted policy recommendations, awareness-raising, resource sharing and strategic use of leverage. A widespread and supportive base among local and international women's groups was created through a series of systematic consultations with women's organisations around the world. These meetings proved to be extremely useful with the consultations in the regions providing a contextual focus, while the New York and European meetings contributed to the refinement of the cross-cutting themes, adding the global perspective that would appeal to the international community. On the broader global front, the campaign mobilised grassroots NGOs with a focus on women and peacebuilding to advocate at the local, regional and national level. These were kept abreast of the campaign's progress through a quarterly newsletter, listservs[14] and periodic teleconferences. The review of the progress made by governments towards the implementation of the Beijing Platform for Action that took place in New York in June 2000 (Women 2000: Gender Equality, Development and Peace for the Twenty-First Century, or so called Bejing+5) provided an opportunity for the creation of a loose NGO caucus (the NGO Working Group on Women, Peace and Security) and the articulation of a shared resolve to work together to lobby for the adoption of a resolution with the critical support of UN agencies and key Security Council member states. The campaign staff, with the NGO working group lobbied the Permanent Mission of Namibia, then presiding over the Security Council to put the issue of Women, Peace and Security on the Security Council's agenda for October 2000. With the support of UNIFEM and the Namibians the resolution, previously drafted by the NGOWG, was redrafted with wording acceptable to the member states and was presented to the Security Council members on 24 October 2000 for discussion and debate. Women representatives from conflict countries, Guatemala, Zambia, Somalia, and Sierra Leone, participated in an open debate at the Security Council in order to provide testimony about the experiences of women and girls in conflict and post-conflict contexts and outline peacebuilding efforts of women worldwide. The draft resolution was unanimously adopted by the UN Security Council on 31 October 2000. Subsequent debates on Women, Peace and Security have taken place at the Security Council as part of the resolution's anniversary event in following years.

To demonstrate grassroots support, the campaign organised a global petition, addressed to the UN Secretary-General, calling for the implementation of the women's five demands. The petition proved an enormous success with over 100,000 signatures collected and formally presented to Angela King, the Special Adviser to the UN on Gender Issues and Advancement of Women (OSAGI) on International Women's Day 2001.[15] This generated increased visibility and support for women and enhanced the campaign's legitimacy and credibility in policy-making circles.

Achievements of the campaign

The results of the campaign have been multifarious, ranging from the unanimous endorsement of Resolution 1325 to an increased profile for the organisation, its global issues department and the issues at large, as well as many further opportunities for engagement with women's organisations and other groups in regions throughout the globe.

The joint Millennium Peace Prize for Women has enhanced women's visibility. Collaboration with UNIFEM, respected individuals from different communities on the process of the prize and its delivery to women and women's organisations from the Asia-Pacific, South America, the Great Lakes of Africa, South Asia and West Africa have raised the profile of both individual women and their organisations and have accorded them a degree of protection from victimisation and harassment by different belligerent actors in their political contexts.

The work with the UN, and particularly with EU member states, significantly assisted the passing of the European Parliament Resolution on Gender Aspects of Conflict Resolution and Peacebuilding in November 2000.[16] The campaign has given new hope, and new opportunities to those many women who wish to have their voices heard in the urgent task of peacebuilding that so many communities are still facing. However, while Resolution 1325 is undeniably an asset for women, more needs to be done to translate the policy into practice. The international community has indicated political will to provide a political framework for women's engagement in peace processes and to mainstream their perspectives into emerging policy. What is still missing, however, is the institutionalisation of that policy so that it becomes routine in implementation and reporting procedure. What is needed is a system-wide plan for implementation of all its aspects. Demands and expectations of member states need to be accompanied by clear guidelines as to what will happen if they fail to carry out the expected duties. Without this the policy will remain largely rhetoric.

Box 6.3: South Africa: The principle of inclusion

The first women political body within the African National Congress (ANC), the Bantu Women's League, was founded already in 1931. However, it took two decades fighting against the restrictive passes for black women before women's political potential had been recognised by the male leadership of the ANC and the first women joined executive bodies. The anti-apartheid struggle brought together women from across the social and racial spectrum and the tradition of local activism became a good training ground for their inclusion into politics. As Cheryl Carolus, former South African High Commissioner in London stated, *'we were not going to allow ourselves to be treated badly, after we had made equal contributions and sacrifices to the struggle for liberation.'*

In the years leading up to the 1994 elections, women activists formed the influential National Women's Coalition that cut across racial, social and political lines. Having observed other women's liberation movements fall by the wayside when the peace talks began in other countries, the South African women were determined to secure their place in the official negotiating teams. Realising that they had a historic opportunity to contribute to reconciliation through participating in drafting the new constitution, the coalition mobilised broad political support including South African women's organisations on grassroots level and began to advocate for women's inclusion into negotiation teams to reach a more proportional political representation.

Women successfully fought for participatory mechanisms in the constitution to ensure that the government would not neglect their needs. For instance, the constitution guarantees the right of women to inherit and own land, which enable sustainability of female heads of households in rural areas. Female parliamentarians played a major role in creating a primary health care system accessible to all women and children. Furthermore, they initiated special aid projects for single mothers and other groups at risk, they improved women's access to small business and financing opportunities and introduced laws and policy programmes to deal with 'women issues' such as marriage and divorce, and elimination of domestic violence and sexual assault.

The drafting of the constitution was a critical step for South African women in the struggle against discrimination. It provided a lifetime opportunity to establish a system of laws that would influence the process of women's emancipation and enable them to advocate for the human rights of other vulnerable groups of the population. The work of the coalition also opened a door to women's participation in power and decision-making structures. The adoption of a quota system proved to be highly effective and resulted in 25 per cent representation of women in parliament, and fair representation across all levels of government, which makes the South African political system one of the most democratic on the continent. The public, sceptical at the beginning of the process, has become more positive about the process of women's empowerment. Today, if women are not part of an important political body or activity, the governmental officials are immediately queried by the media and non-governmental organisations as to the reasons for this exclusion. These achievements are the result of women's capability of self-organisation within political parties, as well as on a multi-party level and their ability to effectively co-operate with civil society, especially with women's NGOs. Though South Africa is still a country with many societal problems, nevertheless, there is a broadly shared opinion that the economic, political and social progress recently made is also to be ascribed to the fact that women were given the opportunity to contribute to development.

Women's achievements in South Africa are:

- Women occupy 30 per cent of the seats in parliament.
- Women occupy twenty per cent of the seats in the nine provincial legislatures.
- Women occupy eighteen per cent of the seats in local municipalities.
- There are nine female ministers and eight female deputy ministers.
- Women account for almost seven per cent of directors on boards of South African companies.
- There have been a large number of female nominees in the information technology sector for the African Achiever Awards in 2002.

Sources:

S. N. Anderlini, *Women at the Peace Table – Making a difference* (New York: UNIFEM, 2000)

Business Day Newspaper (8 August 2002), at http://www.bday.co.za

Box 6.4 : Women as advocates of non-violence in Africa

The Bangwe project is a unique new initiative aimed at drawing on ancient mediation tools of the communities in the Great Lakes sub-region of Africa. Officially created in 1998, the project emerged from a partnership between women NGOs holding observatory status at the United Nations and several local grass-roots organisations. In spite of a strongly patriarchal society, local tradition ascribes the role of conflict arbitrators in families and village communities to women. This project wants to utilise that tradition and to bring women, mostly from Rwanda, the Democratic Republic of Congo and Burundi, together in order to make use of their negotiating abilities in the peace processes in the region.

The idea of 'bangwe' arises from a societal custom in the Great Lakes area. It can be illustrated by the example of a village in Burundi where female family relatives habitually mediated between two warring brothers who became embroiled in a land property clash. Women have the right to stand between the disputing brothers shouting 'bangwe', stopping the fight and forcing the men to resolve the dispute peacefully. This traditional mechanism of conciliation has become the basis of the Bangwe project, funded mainly by the Swiss association Femmes Pour la Paix and benefiting from the generous donations of several anonymous donors, as well as from contributions from Geneva communes.

The primary purpose of the Bangwe project is to create a network of women from Burundi, the Democratic Republic of Congo and Rwanda to exchange their experience in peace ne-gotiating and mediating. The project seeks to bring together women who wish both to express their opinion on the current sit-uation in the Great Lakes and to act as a cohesive group, in the hope that together they will be able to contribute to building l-asting peace in their respective countries.

The project also promotes awareness programmes of ancestral practices of non-violent resolutions to conflicts wherein the broad discussion about traditional peace mediation elucidates the positive role women can play as moderators and effective decision-makers. Such discussions empower national and sub-regional grassroots organisations and associations in exerting influence on governmental policies, mainly by moral pressure based upon traditional tools of communication. Another impor-tant objective of the project is to create a strong women's move-ment for peace and non-violence in the Great Lakes region.

To ensure the success, a support committee has been estab-lished in Geneva. This committee consists of international NGO representatives and members of Swiss associations. Confe-rences, seminars, and training sessions are organised annually, most often taking place during the session of the United Nations Commission on Human Rights wherein prominent female spokespersons from each of the three countries are invited to attend. Moreover, the support committee organises a sub-regional conference and multiple training sessions in Africa, in close collaboration with the local network of Bangwe. Since 1998, this committee has become an umbrella body for various women organisations in Burundi and Rwanda and in certain regions of the Democratic Republic of Congo, most notably in Bukavu, Goma and Kisangani.

In the Rwandan districts of Gisenyi and Ruhengeri, for example, a project aimed at the young generation has been launched, where songs in kinyarwanda, special verbal artistic forms pro-moting peace and non-violence, are elaborated by young people and presented to their contemporaries in youth clubs. Burundi's national committee organised a writing contest among second-ary school girls in the provinces of Bujumbura. In their essays - the best of which were awarded - the contestants wrote about heroes and heroines who had risked their lives to save others during times of local conflicts. The lessons learnt from the Bangwe project was presented at workshops in Goma, the Democratic Republic of Congo, and later on at the all-African conference on 'African Principles of Resolution of Conflicts and Reconciliation', which took place in Addis-Ababa in 1999.

Yet, the most important programme of Bangwe to date has been the organisation of sub-regional meetings for training and exchange of experience for women from the three countries of the Great Lakes region. These meetings have taken place in Bujumbura (December 2000), Kigali (December 2001), and Goma (December 2002). All these conferences shared the common theme of 'Women, Peace and Non-Violence' and enabled women of neighbouring countries to exchange their experiences on peace initiatives and solving problems of violence in everyday life. A call to governments and the international community was also made to put more effort into regional peacebuilding. The programme of action for Bangwe, adopted during the last work-shop held in Goma in October 2002, established a biennial inter-national conference that would create larger networks and touch on more diverse fields of peacebuilding, such as reconcil-iation and trauma healing. The Bangwe initiative is a project with a recognised potential not only for the Great Lakes communities, but also within the whole international community.

Working with Women through the Troubles in Northern Ireland

Women have experienced the roller-coaster of political violence and political developments that have impacted on society in Northern Ireland since 1969. Over this period the victims of the Troubles who were killed have been overwhelmingly male – 3,279 (91.1 per cent), compared to 322 women. The vast majority of those who died were young. Women suffered from the impact of the violence as mothers, wives, daughters, lovers and sis-ters, although in a relatively small number of cases they were also combatants, prisoners and targeted victims. In addition to those that died, there were an estimated 40,000 that were injured, a substantial number out of a population of 1.6 million. Since much of the bombing in the early years of the Troubles was indiscriminate in nature, women became both victims and survivors. Yet, despite their experiences of violence and political divi-sion, few women were elected as political representatives, even since 1996, which marked the constitutional phase of the staggering peace process.[17]

As in every other society in conflict women were to be found on every side of the political equation – Loyalist and Republican, Nationalist and Unionist. In 1996 the Northern Ireland Women's Coalition was set up to offer a niche political voice to those women who tended towards a feminist perspective that favoured cross-community

During the riots in Northern Ireland, women crossed the lines from Catholic to Protestant areas under armoured protection in order to take their children to school.

aggravated crime wave rather than a politically motivated war, the victims could not be acknowledged as victims of war.[19] This situation created a continuing obstruction of anger and hurt among many victims.

Then there were those women who remained virtually unaffected by the Troubles. Living in comfortable middle-class areas that were merely disturbed by the incessant drone of army helicopters or the distant echo of a bomb-blast. For them the violence was an inconvenience, but one that could be lived with by adopting an attitude of disengagement. Yet even in these areas the pulse of a divided rather than a shared identity beat strong. Voting patterns established that people from a Catholic background were Nationalists, and those from a Protestant background were Unionists. Religion, political allegiance and cultural identity were all marshalled to re-enforce division.

Community action during the troubles

One of the strong movements to emerge during the years of the conflict was the community-based movement. Deprived local communities engaged in various forms of collective self-help in an effort to highlight their problems and to improve their conditions. Women were at the forefront of this movement. Set up in 1979 as an independent donor for community development, the Community Foundation for Northern Ireland also played a major role in supporting this movement. The foundation provided financial assistance to community groups that worked both within, and between, communities. Many of these communities were single identity in nature, reflecting the residential segregation of working-class Catholics and Protestants in urban areas of Northern Ireland. The Community Foundation funded work within these single identity communities, but also actively promoted opportunities to bring people together around shared concerns across the community divide.

Although the Northern Ireland Women's Rights Movement was set up in 1975, it was the 1980's that saw women in local communities actively organising in local women's groups, and in some cases establishing women's centres. The latter offered childcare facilities, advice and support, as well as second-chance educational opportunities for women. The local women's groups talked about poverty, childcare issues and the 'bread and butter' topics of day-to-day survival. In 1981, the Community Foundation provided funding for a Women's Information Day initiative, which brought together women from all the local women's groups and centres across Belfast, to meet for one morning every month to discuss shared issues of concern. The information day was regularly attended by over 200 women, meeting in alternative Catholic and Protestant communities. While few contentious political issues were on the agenda for these

mobilisation. The coalition managed to get elected to the peace talks, and continued to have elected representatives until the November 2003 election.[18] The establishment of a women's political party was historic, and sent a shock through the political system that had been overwhelmingly male in composition and attitude.

However, apart from the diversity of political perspective and allegiance, many women from urban, working-class or disadvantaged rural areas, shared the experience of sheer survival or living 'from minute to minute' during the years of the violence. Whether Republican or Loyalist theirs was a story of social and economic struggle, balancing the pressure of visits to see a son or a husband in jail, with the demands of caring for children, while at times being drawn into street protests and confrontation with the security forces. For other women – the relatives of the many civilians or security force members killed or injured in the Troubles – there was the gall of inadequate support, little monetary compensation and even less recognition. Because of the British government's depiction of the Troubles as an meetings, stereotypes were challenged, and women exchanged political views and experiences informally on the fringes of the meeting. The Women's Information Day continued to be held during the darkest of days in Belfast and the women are still meeting.

The main lessons emerging from the work undertaken with, and by, women during the years of violence was the need to respect the diversity of political perspectives of the women involved. Political proselytising through community action had a limited impact and often alienated the target audience. Nevertheless, bringing women out of single identity communities to meet with women who shared many of the same concerns and experiences could, and did, challenge perceptions. Furthermore, working within communities to build women's confidence through discussion groups and educational courses helped to build a basis for cross-community engagement.

The other important achievement of community-based work with women was to provide them with a means of making their voice heard. A range of Northern Ireland women's conferences also ensured that these voices would be listened to.[20] The concerns expressed did not all centre on the political situation, but also spoke about domestic violence in the home; the lack of affordable childcare; women's health issues; and the economic inequalities that women experienced. On a more positive level, local women's groups produced books of their own poetry; they effectively lobbied for more progressive divorce legislation; and they set up training and personal development initiatives. Much of this work may have been ignored by local politicians and the media, but it is clear that women were the leaven in many deprived communities during the decades of the conflict. They continue in this role.

Addressing the demands of peacebuilding

With the advent of the peace process in the autumn of 1994, the opportunities to build peace became more accessible. Again, women activists came together to explore the potential that had been opened up by the new political context. The Northern Ireland Women's Coalition was to be born out of these discussions, but so too were many other organisations. Funded by the Community Foundation for Northern Ireland, a 'Women into Politics' training course was devised to promote the effective political involvement of women in whatever political party they related to. The availability of funds from the European Union also encouraged women to undertake a range of cross-community (and cross-border with the Republic of Ireland) contact programmes. The Community Foundation for Northern Ireland became one of the delivery mechanisms for the major European PEACE Programme funding.[21]

Alongside local community-based projects, the period opened up by the paramilitary ceasefires demanded consideration of how work could be undertaken to facilitate the reintegration of politically motivated ex-prisoners, of which there had been some 25,000, and to address the needs of the victims and survivors of the Troubles. The European Union funding enabled the Community Foundation for Northern Ireland to work with both these groups. The first Republican Ex-Prisoners' Centre was set up by a woman, Caral Ni Chuilin, who had been a prisoner herself. She identified the psychological and material difficulties experienced by ex-prisoners and their families, particularly where the period of imprisonment had been long-term. Over the period 1996-2003, some 60 self-help ex-prisoner groups came into operation in both Loyalist and Republican areas. They largely reflected specific political and/or paramilitary allegiances. Work undertaken included counselling, education and training, advice and support, as well as political discussion related to the ongoing peace process. Over a period of years the Community Foundation for Northern Ireland brought together these ex-prisoner groups on a cross-community basis.

The work in support of the victims and survivors of the Troubles in Northern Ireland was even more difficult. The hurt and resentment of being treated as an uncomfortable set of statistics for three decades made collective action amongst victims difficult and contentious. Again, a wide range of political opinions was reflected in the large number of different self-help groups that emerged. While sharing certain common concerns, many of the victims' groups were so politically at odds with each other, that it was difficult to organise gatherings where all felt comfortable. As with so many community-based initiatives, the initial work around victims' concerns had been pioneered by women, but as the political edge of this work became more pronounced in the post-Good Friday Agreement period (post-April 1998), men became the more visible spokespeople in this area. True to its ethos of inclusion and cross-community effort, the Community Foundation for Northern Ireland funded a range of individual victims' self-help groups, but also created opportunities for the various groups to meet together.

Ironically the difficulties in pursuing a cross-community agenda became increasingly difficult in the post-agreement period. The stark reality of political change challenged people who had become almost comfortable with managing 'an acceptable level of violence'. The management of political change was not an art that was well developed in a Northern Ireland that was rooted in the call of 'What we have we hold'. The politics of fear was kept well honed by those political leaders that were opposed to the politically inclusive power-sharing concept that lay at the heart of the Good Friday Agreement. Political instability was augmented by a long list of unresolved contentious issues including the decommissioning of paramilitary weapons; the new nature of policing; demilitarisation by the British government; and the human rights and equality agenda. Street violence became a depressingly common feature at the so-called interface areas – those single identity communities that were divided by a 'peace wall' or barrier to prevent inter-communal attacks. Very often the physical existence of a flash point attracted protagonists, who lived in other hinterland communities, into the contested area. Since much of the violence tended to take place over the summer period, the Community Foundation for Northern Ireland responded in 2001 with the establishment of a Summer Interface Crisis Fund. This grant-making programme made available small amounts of money for community groups to develop diversionary programmes for young people who might otherwise become caught up in the interface violence. The foundation had also been involved over many years in working with community groups to hold local festivals as a positive focus for community spirit. One interesting initiative to address the challenges of interface conflict is the Springfield Inter-Community Development Project, which brings together community activists and ex-prisoners from both sides of the long Springfield 'peace wall', to exchange information, dispel rumours, and negotiate political accommodations. The activists meet on a regular basis, and keep in touch through a mobile phone network in an attempt to prevent sectarian attacks.

From its experience over recent years, the Community Foundation has concluded that peacebuilding is long-term in nature, and is inextricably linked with developments in the macro political process. It is virtually impossible to expect local community activists to engage in peacebuilding initiatives at community level when their political representatives are not only at odds with one another, but can even be exacerbating fears. Where peacebuilding approaches do take place, then there needs to be support, resources and information available. Money is important, but so too are skills and expertise. The Community Foundation for Northern Ireland has found that the sharing of experience with activists drawn from other divided societies is of particular value. Considering the lessons learned in South Africa, the Middle East or Central America can open up the neutral space required to encourage local activists in Northern Ireland to engage in discussion about the challenges and opportunities of their own peacebuilding processes. The Community

Foundation has benefited from a partnership with the Project on Justice in Times of Transition (Harvard University, US), in undertaking this work.

Concluding comment

Women in Northern Ireland have lived in an insecure society – although the adverse impact of that insecurity has been experienced in a concentrated form by those women who live in poorer areas and communities that have suffered disproportionately from the violence. This may well be the reason why the multiplicity of local, self-help initiatives has been developed in these communities. Women have been at the forefront of these developments, particularly when the work required was voluntary in nature. The concerns that drove them were related to the well-being and life opportunities of their families, as well as political motivations. In many cases, the motivation was purely related to family and local community needs.

Increasingly, however, it is becoming clear to women that they have to engage with policymakers and the political system if local needs are to be registered and responded to. There is only so much that can be achieved at community level. The Northern Ireland Women's Coalition emerged out of this realisation, but so too did the more active engagement of women in other political parties and in campaigning groups. The current uncertainty of the peace process in Northern Ireland means that women are keeping their options of organising and influence open. There is no one single approach.

The role of the Community Foundation for Northern Ireland in this situation is to provide financial support for the range of strategies identified by women in disadvantaged areas. The foundation cannot support political parties, but it has a clear social justice agenda, which offers support for lobbying and campaigning. The foundation has always been at the cutting edge, as a donor, to work in support of women who are crafting a vision of peaceful progress both for themselves and their shared society.

Gender Equality and the Union of the Committees of Soldiers' Mothers of Russia

In the modern era, there are two approaches for women non-governmental organisations (NGOs) to advance gender equality. The first strategy, used by the majority of these advocacy groups, is to protect the rights of women by raising public awareness and fighting for a change in legislation. Activities and programmes orchestrated by this type of NGO are diverse by nature, but in general all of them are aimed at both strengthening the social and political role of women and diminishing gender discrimination.

The second approach, embraced by the Union of Committees of Soldiers' Mothers in Russia, known otherwise as Soldiers' Mothers, consists in challenging the current gender roles through involvement in military and security debates of the government. Since the very beginning, Soldiers' Mothers has positioned itself as an equal partner of the state, thereby demanding equal participation rights in the decision-making process of the military. This strategy has permitted them not to be seen as a socially discriminated gender group fighting for their own rights. It enabled them to act as an organised and respected segment of civic society, capable of pushing for socio-political changes in a strategically important part of the country's development.

This strategy has brought important results. In 1989, Soldiers' Mothers succeeded in changing state regulation with regards to conscription, thereby allowing approximately 200,000 students, who had previously been forced to join the armed forces after their first academic year, to return to their respective schools and colleges. In 1990, a Russian presidential decree was signed, effectively implementing the proposals made by Soldiers' Mothers on the democratisation of the military service. During the same year, Soldiers' Mothers held their first forum, during which the NGO publicly announced the strategic goals for their human rights agenda under the heading 'What kind of the armed forces do we need: mothers against violence.'

The collapse of the Soviet Union engulfed the Russian armed forces in a deep crisis, precipitating a tremendous increase in the number of human rights violations in the country. There are currently about 300 Soldiers' Mothers committees working in various cities, towns and villages across the country to protect people whose rights have been violated during and after military service. In Russia, taking into consideration the burdensome heritage of Soviet militarisation, this issue involves millions of victims from every strata of society. The committees are responsible for collecting individual complaints of human rights violations in the military sphere, which they later use as evidence to strengthen their propositions for effective ways of remedying the situation. The strategic goals of Soldiers' Mothers in this area are the advancement of democratic military reform and the abolishment of compulsory conscription.

When the first Chechen war began in 1994, the Soldiers' Mothers Committee was the very first NGO in Russia to make an official anti-war statement. Soldiers' Mothers demanded immediate withdrawal of the armed forces from Chechnya and declared the war illegitimate, illegal and criminal. Soldiers' Mothers worked on multiple fronts. In the conflict zone, it fought to protect human rights of peaceful civilians, participated in the exchanges of prisoners of war and organised quests for missing sons on Chechen territory. Simultaneously, it organised a nationwide anti-war campaign. Soldiers' Mothers also protected soldiers who refused to participate in the unlawful activities of state and military bodies, and attended to prisoners of war and their relatives. After the first war Soldiers' Mothers proposed in the *Duma* an amnesty for acts committed during the conflict on both sides – Chechen fighters as well as the federal Russian military. In effect, they became the centre of all anti-war activities in Russia. The Soldiers' Mothers' peaceful work was supported by other NGOs and democratic governments abroad, ultimately leading to four international awards and a nomination for the Nobel Peace Prize in 1996.

After President Putin's ascension to power in 1999, public attention to the situation in Chechnya noticeably decreased as a result of the tightening of state control over information. The federal power proceeded to use terrorist attacks in Russia to mask its political failures in bringing about a resolution to the Chechen crisis, benefiting at the same time from the fact that the Russian public attitude tended to support official governmental policy. Thus the work of Soldiers' Mothers has remained an important source of influence on the consciousness of Russian society.

Eventually, the Union of the Committees of Soldiers' Mothers grew to be the largest women's NGO in Russia, capable of influencing state policy in the military sphere. Although the state and military bodies were not always willing to agree to all of the NGO's proposals, they nevertheless realised the impossibility of ignoring the demands or of downplaying the results achieved. In fact, during the recent all-Russian Civic Forums held in 2000 and 2003, Soldiers' Mothers was invited as the main negotiator between the state and those elements of civil society dealing with military policy and defence reform.

The position of Soldiers' Mothers as a serious partner in the decision-making process proved to be one of the most effective ways to advance gender equality. It has heavily influenced state policy in the most sensitive sphere - national security - constituting the most important mechanism of civilian control over security structures. The state and military bodies cannot publicly deny the relevance of human rights protection, which forms the basis of the work of Soldiers' Mothers, especially with regard to the fact that Russia has not carried out institutional changes to that effect. Currently the organisation, in co-operation with military bodies, solves more than 20,000 individual complaints of human rights violations annually, struggling to gain amnesty for the 40,000 soldiers, who had deserted their military units to escape grave bullying (torture, beatings and hunger). It would be no exaggeration to say that soldiers turn to the organisation, individually or collectively, in order to save their lives and health. Moreover, it has advocated for legislative changes in order to finance the search for the soldiers who disappeared in Chechnya, to exhume bodies and ensure a dignified burial for the deceased.

The indisputable right of mothers to protect their sons against violence constitutes the main factor of the organisation's success. Soldiers' Mothers has been systematic and consistent in their efforts, exclusively using non-violent methods to foster respect for human rights. The fact that the military has recognised the organisation as an important actor in human rights protection renders it possible to work effectively and make a difference in the lives of civilians and soldiers alike. A third factor of its success, is the objective character of the information accumulated during the course of the organisation's activities. Soldiers' Mothers is now considered a pioneer and champion of human rights activities in Russia, despite numerous legal and illegal obstacles and the absence of supporting materials from both Russian official authorities and business circles.

Box 6.5: Women's inclusion in the Macedonian peacebuilding process

Throughout the turbulent years of ethno-nationalist conflicts in Yugoslavia, Macedonia was deemed a 'success story' on at least two occasions. This country not only peacefully obtained its independence from the Yugoslav Federation, but it also became the only former republic to avoid the bloody pattern of state-building that characterised the other nations in the region. In the period 1991-2001 the country was known as an 'oasis of peace' in the Balkans, having gone through an upward process of power transition and multi-ethnic democracy-building. Moreover, Macedonia is the only country to have benefited from a United Nations mission of preventive deployment that later became a model of preventive peacekeeping. The outbreak of violence in early 2001 called for a sudden and completely different agenda, moving Macedonia along from successful conflict prevention to the stage of successful conflict management and post-conflict peacebuilding. After the adoption of the Ohrid Framework Agreement in August 2001 that effectively ended the six-month long conflict, Macedonia was once again seen as a good case study of post-conflict peacebuilding.

Given its heritage as a republic of the former Yugoslavia, Macedonia does not generally differ much from the other republics, especially when dealing with the issue of women's emancipation. Although the communist regime recognised women's participation in the guerrilla movement and state-building during the Second World War, statements about women's emancipation and equality were more declaratory in nature than substantive. Nevertheless, the overall perception of existing gender equality, nurtured through the media and education, made it possible for women to *feel* emancipated and politically empowered. Such sentiment proved to be a significant capital for future feminist and peace movements. Yet, as the peacefulness of the Yugoslav society was to a great extent chimerical, the same applied to female emancipation.

Macedonia lagged behind the progressive trends of the authentic feminist movement that took place in the more developed republics of Croatia, Slovenia and Serbia in the 1970s and 1980s. The relative passivity of women – or better, their limited activism channelled exclusively through communist women's organisations – had deep roots in the underdevelopment of Macedonian society. Since the two major ethnic groups were always living next to each other and never with each other, also gender relations differed significantly between the two ethnic communities. Although both of them can be considered traditional and male dominated, the patriarchy is more rigid among the Albanians. This can also explain the fact that recently Macedonia has seen an emergence of ethnically divided women's organisations. Given the opposing views and attitudes of the major parties involved, there was hardly ever an unanimous stance on actions relating to peace protests and marches organised as conflicts loomed all over Yugoslavia. In fact, it is likely that there was more solidarity with other women's organisations and actions all over Yugoslavia than within the Macedonian society.

The first women's peace actions took place on the eve of the bloody Yugoslav disintegration and were organised by the Union of Women's Organisations of Macedonia (*Sojuz na organizaciite na zemite vo Makedonija*, SOZM). This 'umbrella' organisation intended to overcome societal fragmentation and co-ordinate various efforts, but it has never managed to fully promote unity and action. In addition to SOZM, there was also the Union of Albanian Women, as well as women's organisations of Roma, Turks, Vlachs, and other ethnicities. Contributions to the Yugoslav peace activities came mainly from the women around SOZM, with the exception of the demands made to recall the Yugoslav People Army's conscripts of Macedonian origin to their mother-republic, there were no other women-led activities.

For a decade, the activities of civil society aimed at building a democratic multi-ethnic and multicultural society. It appeared as if the 'good and peace loving' people of Macedonia did not need any intensive peace-oriented activism. Women lobbied mainly for greater inclusion in politics and for the introduction of a 'gender quota system' in both political parties and parliament. The best example of such work is the Macedonian Women's Lobby founded in March 2000, which is part of the regional Gender Task Force initiative of the Stability Pact. On a grassroots level, ANTIKO, a women's multi-ethnic network was established in 1999 to facilitate women's empowerment in local communities. The approaching conflict of 2001 made their work both difficult and crucial.

At first glance, there is an indisputable demarcation between the male (former and current) combatants and women peacemakers, which have resulted in downplaying women's direct involvement in the conflict. However, it appears that women in Macedonia took a leading role in the post-conflict peacebuilding process, particularly in the UN-sponsored action for disarmament of small arms and light weapons. There are numerous examples of female politicians, peace activists and NGO leaders directly involved with state organisations and civil society networks promoting the peace process and raising self-awareness about the seriousness of peacebuilding. Yet the reasons explaining such high level of female participation in post-conflict peacebuilding are unclear. One may wonder whether the participation has been truly effective or if it serves only as an 'alibi' for the democratisation process, with no substantial changes in gender relations and women's inclusion in public life.

One of the most astonishing phenomena in the conflict's aftermath was related to the appointment of a woman scholar and feminist as the vice-president of a new political party (DUI, *Demokratska Unija za Integracija*, Democratic Union for Integration) supported by former Albanian rebels against the state. Dr. Teuta Arifi's career was based on activities in conflict prevention and peaceful conflict resolution. Her appointment to the top leadership of a party composed primarily of former combatants came, therefore, as a surprise. Nevertheless, her case suggests that women in Macedonia can use their intellectual and political capital to influence the peace process. Currently, there are no legal constraints for women's inclusion in political structures and a number of significant political posts is held by women (Ministry of Foreign Affairs, Ministry of European Integration, vice-speaker of the parliament, members of the parliament, etc.). Yet women still remain a small minority in the system of decision-making.

The improved gender participation in the post-conflict period is more related to civil society engagement. One should, however, bear in mind that civil society is taken as a milieu that provides alternative forms of social and political engagement or more correctly, compensates for the lack of political influence. Nevertheless, this general weakness could be taken as a great opportunity, given the fact that the 'peace process' orchestrated by local politicians and the international community usually overlooks micro-societal level of peacebuilding, including women's voices. Currently, Macedonia has a significant number of women organisations, dealing with a number of trendy issues such as empowerment, child care, domestic violence, human trafficking and disarmament. The action platforms follow the classical *cliché* of protests and marches, media campaigns, seminars, and training. Women's organisations also continue to suffer from ethnic division, lack of co-ordination and funds. Moreover, women's peacebuilding activities receive too little political recognition to be taken seriously or treated as partners; they become popular only if endorsed by the international community. This situation is far from a network of multi-ethnic grassroots organisations able to exert influence on politics and society at large.

There is a pressing need to build coalitions across the divided ethnic communities. Women's organisations have the potential to build such bridges because of their apparent distance from both militant activities and non-transparent politics. However, well-educated and publicly engaged women cannot speak on behalf of the whole society that remains deeply troubled by poverty, unemployment, underdevelopment and post-conflict traumas. As inspirational the positive examples of women human rights and peace activists, intellectuals and politicians might be, they remain inadequate unless such examples are followed by 'ordinary' mothers, who in turn speak to their sons about *peace* rather than the *heroism of war*.

Women in Post-War Iraq and Afghanistan: Two Views on Post-Conflict Interim Governance Structures

Women's issues affect not only women; they have profound implications for all humankind [...] We, as a world community, cannot even begin to tackle the array of problems and challenges confronting us without the full and equal participation of women in all aspects of life.

Former US Secretary of State Colin L. Powell

Women's citizenship in Iraq and Afghanistan: An optimistic perspective

International Women's Day is an annual opportunity for the world to take stock of the advancement of human rights for women throughout the world. On 8 March 2004, it was evident that the winds of change were blowing in the right direction for women from Morocco to Iraq and to Afghanistan. In Morocco, the passage of a new Family Code was a milestone in the legal history of women in the Middle East. The many changes include according women marital property rights and granting both spouses equal authority in the family. In Iraq and Afghanistan, women are asserting their right to participate in the political arena. When, in February, the Iraqi Governing Council threatened to impose Shari'a law, a diverse array of women took to the streets to protest. Asked why they were protesting, one woman firmly stated, *'We didn't wait all these years without the most basic rights to be denied now.'* Afghan women, who comprise over 40 per cent of the registered voters, are also determined to insert their voices into the political process. This was evident in the women's turnout for the presidential elections in October 2004. Ensuring that women have equal opportunities for political participation and economic advancement is at the core of building a civil, law-abiding society and is an indispensable prerequisite for a true democracy and a peaceful, prosperous world. The words of the King of Morocco, as he signed into law the new Family Code, captured the imperative of enshrining women's rights in all spheres of life: *'How can a society advance when the rights of women are squandered and they are subjected to injustice, violence, and marginalisation?'*

The world has come together to recognise the value of women taking their full places in society, politics and economy. In December 2003, the United Nations General

Assembly adopted a landmark resolution on women and political participation, sponsored by the United States and 110 other member states. The resolution calls on countries to ensure that women are able to exercise their rights, associate freely, express their views publicly and openly debate political policy on equal terms with men.

Our commitment to secure the full inclusion of women in the reconstruction of their countries illustrates the conviction that peace cannot succeed unless men and women are equally important components of the reconstruction process. The United States has taken a leadership role in translating the idea of equality for women into concrete action by investing in a diverse range of initiatives aimed at increasing women's political participation and economic opportunities, improving access to education and health, and the promotion of women into leadership positions in civil society, with a special emphasis on women in Afghanistan and Iraq.

Afghanistan

Women in Afghanistan have achieved remarkable results since the fall of the Taliban in 2001. Under the Taliban, they were denied the right to attend school or to hold jobs. The restrictions on the movement of women kept many of them virtual prisoners in their homes. The conditions imposed by the Taliban were especially hard on widows. Without a male provider, women found it difficult to obtain the basic necessities of life.

Currently, Afghan women are taking the initiative to reclaim the variety of roles that they once filled. The determination of women to reclaim their rights as full citizens was evident in the drafting of the new constitution. The women of Afghanistan are justifiably proud that they participated extensively in the process, openly questioning the leadership when they felt that key issues were not being addressed. Women hold almost twenty per cent of the 500 seats in the constitutional *Loya Jirga*. Two of the nine members of the Constitutional Drafting Committee and seven of the 35 members of the Constitutional Review Commission were women.

Approved by the constitutional *Loya Jirga* on 5 January 2004, the constitution affords all *'citizens of Afghanistan – men and women – equal rights and duties before the law.'* The constitution reserves 25 per cent of its seats in the lower house and 17 per cent in the upper house of parliament for women. Afghan women now have the right to vote and run for office – one woman ran for president. Implementing the constitution is one of many challenges ahead for women and Afghanistan. However, what is more important is that Afghan women very much need and want the knowledge and skills to run for political office, improve the quality of health care and education for their families, tackle legal

reforms, and create economic opportunities. While the public sector plays a critical role in mobilising resources and people, the United States recognises the valuable skills that the private sector can contribute to Afghanistan. For this reason, the United States has instituted the US-Afghan Women's Council to bring together Americans and Afghans to undertake projects that meet the needs that Afghan women have identified as most crucial.

Reflective of the broad-based approach that the United States has taken, the US-Afghan Women's Council is implementing a variety of projects, including educational and literacy programmes, job skills training, microfinance, and leadership capacity building. Women's resource centres are the locus of many of these activities and a good example of how public and private sectors can work together. The US-Afghan Women's Council, the US Agency for International Development, and AOL/Time Warner are helping to build women's resource centres throughout Afghanistan.

Among the other needs that Afghan women have identified is training for judges. They recognise that judges will play a key role in ensuring that equal rights become a reality for Afghan women. With a grant from the Department of State and private support from the US-Afghan Women's Council, the International Association of Women Judges trained a group of Afghan women judges in international and family law.

Years of conflict and deprivation have left Afghanistan with the second highest maternal mortality rate in the world and millions of children without adequate education. In the short term, the United States has put a priority on rebuilding health clinics and schools, training midwives and teachers, and providing supplies, such as textbooks and medical equipment. In the longer-term, however, the goal is to build the capacity of the Afghans to sustain these positive changes. In 2004, approximately 4.8 million children were in school, of whom 40 per cent were girls. Basic health services, in 2004, were available to more than 2.5 million people in 21 provinces; 90 per cent of the recipients were women and children.

In working with Iraqis in the transition to a self-sustaining democracy, the United States has carried over some of the lessons learned in Afghanistan. As in Afghanistan, building public-private partnerships and engaging Iraqi women in identifying needs and designing initiatives are the cornerstones of US support for Iraqi women.

Iraq

Life for women and men under Saddam Hussein was a living nightmare. Iraqi women were brutally suppressed under his regime. Women were singled out as victims of torture and other human rights abuses. Rape was used to intimidate, blackmail, and force confessions from

After decades of repression and exclusion from the political, economic and social life of their countries, women in Iraq and Afghanistan have finally the opportunity to make their voices heard, notably through their participation in interim state bodies. The US administration actively supports the representation of Iraqi and Afghan women in governmental bodies and underlines the importance of their inclusion in the political process from the early stages of state-building.

Iraq

US government officials (President Bush, Vice President Cheney, National Security Adviser Rice, members of Congress, US State officials, etc.) have met and continue to meet with Iraqi women in the US and Iraq.

Under Secretary of State for Global Affairs Paula Dobriansky travelled to Iraq, and together with Ambassador Bremer, participated in the conference 'Voice of Women Iraq' held on 9 July 2003.

The country's draft constitution includes a provision calling for 25 per cent representation for women in the future government.

Three women were appointed by the US to the Iraqi Governing Council:

    Sondul Chapouk

    Raja Habibal-Khuzaai

    Aquila al-Hashimi – assassinated on 25 September 2004, and subsequently replaced by Salama al-Khufaji.

One woman was appointed to the Iraqi cabinet:

    Nesreen Mustafa Sidiq Berwan, Minister for Public Works.

Women in the new Council of Ministers:

    Sawson Ali Magid Al-Sharifi, Minister of Agriculture.

    Pascale Isho Warda, Minister of Displacement and Migration.

    Mishkat Moumin, Minister of Environment.

    Leyla Abdul Latif, Minister of Labour and Social Affairs.

    Nasreen Mustapha Berari, Minister of Public Works.

    Narmin Othman, Minister of State for Women.

Afghanistan

The United Nations Talks in Bonn resulted in the establishment of the Afghan Interim Authority (AIA). Five women participated in these talks: Rona Mansuri (full delegate of the Rome process); Sima Wali (full delegate of the Rome process); Amena Afzali (full delegate of the Northern Alliance/United Front); Seddiqa Balkhi (adviser to the Cyprus Group); Fatana Gilani (adviser to the Peshawar Group).

The Bonn Agreement, signed on 5 December 2001, set up the Afghan Interim Authority consisting of an Interim Administration, a Special Independent Commission for the Convening of the Emergency *Loya Jirga* (a traditional assembly of elders) and a Supreme Court of Afghanistan. The interim administration is composed *'with due regard to the ethnic, geographic and religious composition of Afghanistan and to the importance of the participation of women'* (Bonn Agreement) and includes two ministries headed by women. The interim authority is comprised of 30 members; 28 men and two women: Habiba Sarabi, Minister of Women's Affairs and Vice-Chair; and Suhaila Seddiq, Minister of Public Health.

In January 2002, the Special Independent Commission for the Convening of the Emergency *Loya Jirga* (Grand Council), was appointed, including three women among its 21 members: Mahbooba Hoquqmal (Vice-Chair), Humaira Nematy, Soraya Parlika.

There was a peaceful transfer of power from the Afghan Interim Authority to the Transitional Islamic State of Afghanistan (TISA) during the 2002 Emergency *Loya Jirga*. President Karzai selected a cabinet of five vice presidents and 30 ministers. A constitutional *Loya Jirga* was held in December and a new constitution approved in January 2004. Unlike the November 2003 draft of the constitution, which made no specific mention of women's rights, the final version includes a clause on equal rights between men and women stating that *'any kind of discrimination and privileges between the citizens of Afghanistan are prohibited. The citizens of Afghanistan – whether man or woman – have equal rights and duties before the law.'* Out of the 502 delegates (representing the 32 provinces of the country) responsible for debating the draft constitution, 64 women delegates were elected while President Hamid Karzai appointed 25 (out of a total of 50), bringing the count up to 89 women at the constitutional *Loya Jirga*.

While Afghan women and advocates of women's rights were pleased by the final version of the constitution, they nevertheless warn that rhetoric does not mirror the reality of the country. In fact, during meetings of the Drafting Committee of the Constitutional Commission, a few women delegates complained of harassment and death threats.

Currently, there are several women holding cabinet positions, notably the two ministers of Health and Women's Affairs. There is also a chairwoman for the Afghan Independent Human Rights Commission. During 2003, 45 women leaders across the country also met up and devised the Afghan Women's Bill of Rights, a document demanding equal treatment while specifically outlining the challenges remaining for the country.

Sources:

F. C. Smith, Senior Adviser from the Office of National Security Affairs at the Coalition Provisional Authority.

Women Waging Peace, *Afghan Constitution a Partial Victory for Women* (14 January 2004), at http://www.womenwagingpeace.net/content/articles/0382a.html

US Department of State, Bureau of Democracy, Human Rights and Labour Country Reports on South Asia, at http://www.state.gov/g/drl/rls/hrrpt/2003/c11114.htm

Human Rights Watch, *Between Hope and Fear: Intimidation and Attacks against Women in Public Life in Afghanistan*, A Human Rights Watch Briefing Paper, (October 2004), at http://hrw.org/backgrounder/asia/afghanistan1004/1.htm

Afghan Independent Human Rights Commission, at http://www.aihrc.org.af

detained family members. Saddam Hussein introduced Article 111 into the Iraqi Penal Code, legalising honour killings of female relatives by men who believed that their families' honour had been violated. Deprivation permeated all aspects of peoples' lives. For example, the unwillingness of the government to invest in education resulted in deplorably low literacy rates for women. According to the United Nations, women's literacy in 2002 had plummeted to 23 per cent, the lowest level in the entire Arab world. The United States has strongly supported Iraqi women's participation in the political, economic, and social reconstruction of their country, allocating US$27 million to projects that specifically help women. Iraqi women are working with the United States to develop diverse programmes, from literacy, computer and vocational training to educating women about their rights. Women's self-help and vocational centres are springing up across Iraq, from Karbala to Kirkuk, and micro-credit facilities and workshops are helping aspiring Iraqi businesswomen. Some of these funds are also improving women's access to quality health care, including maternal and child health.

Responding to the needs of Iraqi women, US support for Iraqi reconstruction entails many facets. In March 2004, Secretary of State Colin Powell announced a new Iraqi Women's Democracy Initiative and the US-Iraq Women's Network. To be effective participants in the political process, the Democracy Initiative will support a range of workshops for Iraqi women. Some of the skills that these workshops will focus on are public speaking, political advocacy and building political constituencies and legislative coalitions. Because women who have a stake in the economy have a more vested interest in the political process, the Democracy Initiative will also allocate resources to women entrepreneurs. As Iraqi women begin to initiate projects, the US-Iraq Women's Network will serve as a forum for sharing information and resources.

With the world's attention focused on Iraq's historic transition to a self-standing democracy, the rights and status of women in society and governance have been important issues in the constitutional debate. Leaders from around the world have emphasised that the role of women in Iraq must not be neglected in the context of the country's emerging political structure. The challenges of ensuring full and fair representation and equal rights for women have been many. However, these challenges have, in fact, mobilised Iraqi women to assert their rights and make their voices heard. Currently, there are three women among the 25 members of the Iraqi Governing Council and women occupy six of the 37 seats on the Baghdad City Council. The United States continues to encourage and work for greater representation for women in Iraq's emerging political institutions.

Iraqi women are already taking advantage of their new freedoms. During the framing of the Transitional Administrative Law, the Iraqi Governing Council threatened to impose Shari'a law. In response, Iraqi women took to the streets to speak publicly, many for the first time, after decades of oppression. In al-Fardous Square, more then 200 women marched for greater rights, chanting, 'Yes for equality, yes, for freedom'. They were supported and applauded by a group of Iraqi men. One man observed that, 'This is the first time women have demonstrated freely in Iraq.'

The benefits of women's activism are evident. On 8 March 2004, the Iraqi Governing Council signed the Transitional Administrative Law, a historic document that guarantees the basic rights of all Iraqis, men and women, including freedoms of worship, expression and association. It sets important precedents for a new Iraqi constitution. It protects unions and political parties and outlaws discrimination based on gender, ethnic class and religion. The law provides that the electoral system should aim to ensure that women constitute not less than 25 per cent of the Transitional National Assembly. This interim constitution is unprecedented in the region for its forward-thinking and progressive support of fundamental rights for all Iraqis, especially women.

These are extraordinary and historic times, especially for women. No society can prosper when half of its population is not allowed to contribute to its progress. Educated and empowered women are vital to democracy - and important for the development of all countries. As President Bush said in his first State of the Union Address, *'America will always stand firm for the non-negotiable demands of human dignity, the rule of law, limits on the power of state, respect for women, private property, free speech, equal justice, and religious tolerance.'* These values are a vital part of our humanity, and their scope includes all women and men. The United States will continue to work with the peoples of the world to advance the rights of women.

A critical perspective on inclusion of women: The case of Iraq

'A democracy that does not include 50 per cent of the population is no democracy.'

From an open letter to President George W. Bush
and Prime Minister Blair
from the Women Peacemakers Program (WPP).

'Women's vision for their societies often differ from men's because they understand clearly the impact of distorted priorities on their families and communities. The vision of many women is one of inclusion not exclusion, peace not conflict, integrity not corruption, and consensus not imposition.'

Ellen Johnson-Sirleaf,
Presidential Candidate, Liberia, 1997.

Despite an avalanche of international resolutions, conferences and public statements, male leaders continue to overlook or deliberately exclude women from peace negotiations and mediation, from post-conflict reconstruction planning and policy-making, and from interim and transition governing councils at local and national levels.

Largely, men appoint men to power, who in turn design governance, judicial, electoral and power systems that entrench male incumbency. In the aftermath of dictatorship and conflict, everyone talks about human rights and democracy, but women find themselves having to fight hard for any voice at all. At the time of the Kosovo crisis, Tony Blair repeatedly stated that the NATO bombing in Serbia and Kosovo was for democracy and human rights. Apparently this did not apply to Balkan women. Within weeks of the British Prime Minister's statement, the men at the top of the United Nations Mission in Kosovo appointed an interim government with seventeen members. All seventeen were men.

The international community seems to regard religious tolerance, market capitalism, and rule of law as a necessary and desirable break with custom and tradition. However, when it concerns women's human rights, including the right to participate equally in the governance of their community and nation, political leaders and civil servants in the international community collude with local self-appointed spokesmen and warlords from the conflict region to block women's human rights. Men in every culture, whether mullahs, military or government minister, do not view the introduction of computers and the internet and mobile phones as an objectionable break with custom and tradition. Yet, when it concerns women's human rights, international politicians and diplomats back off and hide behind the excuse of *'we must not upset cultural sensitivities', 'there are more important issues to address',* or *'it's not part of the culture and anyway women here are not interested in taking part in politics.'* Diplomats, politicians, senior civil servants, military officers and warlords are always the first people involved in peace processes. The majority of these are men, men who have worked their way laboriously up through traditional male hierarchies. Almost none have had gender awareness experience or training. Their perception of women in post-war situations is as eternal victims, needing band-aid and baby food. They have never looked at the world's women as potential leaders who could be the key to bringing about a peaceful, democratic and prosperous post-conflict society.

There is a further extremely serious consequence of the lack of women in top posts in post-conflict recovery programmes, namely the likelihood that – as in many private sector corporations – when a woman gets near the senior level she might find herself the sole female in committees and discussion groups of ten or twenty men. There are many anecdotal reports from international missions of men driven to bunch up against a sole woman, irrespective of her experience, knowledge and valid suggestions. To overcome this appalling level of sex-discrimination, the UN Security Council unanimously passed Resolution

1325 in October 2000. Nevertheless, as seen in the post-conflict recovery of Sierra Leone, Afghanistan and Iraq, all of which have flared up since the enthusiastic passage of the UN Security Council and EU resolutions, a pattern has emerged where a fig-leaf in the form of two or three women at the highest levels of government has become the norm. In Sierra Leone, the British Department for International Development even went as far as funding and empowering 150 Paramount Chiefs all except three or four were men.

In Iraq, after years of sharing equally with men in the horrors, torture and wars of a brutal dictatorship, Iraqi women told the author how deeply they fear they will end up yet again living under a distorted legal system and a constitution, which denies them their basic human rights. They say they have good reason to be concerned. In the early and critical aftermath of the fall of the Saddam regime, despite an intensive lobbying campaign directed at the American and British governments – and the public exhortations of President Bush and Prime Minister Blair - just like their sisters in Afghanistan and Timor, Iraqi women have in no sense been included as equal partners. In mid-December 2002, the US State Department and British Foreign Office helped facilitate a gathering of the Iraqi opposition in London. The Follow-up Co-ordinating Committee (FCC), which was formed at the end of the conference, comprised three women and sixty-two men. At subsequent opposition gatherings women continued to be marginalised. In February 2003 at the meeting in Salahaddin, Iraqi Kurdistan, the final conference statement did not make a single reference to the future of women in Iraq, or any reference to their rights.

Iraq's women, both those who remained in Iraq and Iraqi women living in exile after their families fled Saddam's brutal regime, have a great deal to contribute to peacebuilding and decision-making processes in shaping a peaceful, prosperous and democratic Iraq. Iraqi women were famously advanced compared to most other countries in

© Reuters, Carlos Barria, 2003

▌ *In Chile women protested heavily against the war in Iraq.*

Box 6.7: Obstacles to the inclusion of women in post-conflict governance, democratisation and peacebuilding processes

Post-conflict reconstruction and democratisation provide crucial opportunities in redressing women's discriminated status in society. The equal participation of women in rebuilding their communities through access to peace processes and governance structures have been recognised in many international documents such as the Windhoek Declaration and the landmark United Nations Security Council Resolution 1325 in 2000. Yet these achievements remain on paper as the following obstacles persist which lead to the consistent exclusion of women.

- The gender blindness of many politicians and diplomats to the inclusion of women at any important level of governance further reinforced by the prominence of military leaders and rebel leaders, and often further reinforced by religious and traditional leaders who want to grab or retain power.

- Lack of access to people in power: The prospective role of women as mediators in trying to facilitate communication between warring groups is often ignored in official peace mediating initiatives as well as in post-conflict reconstruction processes, planning and consultations.

- Lack of equal participation: Women lack equal access to participation in all levels of the democratisation processes. This starts with the choice of who sits on the mediating and negotiating teams and with the appointment of interim and transition governing bodies. This also includes staffing of senior personnel posts for peace operations.

- Trivialisation: When they get access, women's suggestions are often not taken seriously enough to be implemented by politicians and ministers.

- Lack of gender aware men (and women) appointed to top posts in peacebuilding missions.

- Lack of gender balance in appointment of personnel to senior posts in peace operation missions – the vast majority of top posts are held by men.

- Communication gap between the formal and informal sector, and a constant mismatch between the formal and informal sectors, which results in the role of women being seriously overlooked. Leaders in the formal sector are mostly male. Many female leaders are to be found in the informal sector (see chart 6.1).

Chart 6.1: Men and women in post-conflict reconstruction – division of labour and power

Key actors in a post-conflict situation - 1
Source: Lesley Abdela 2003

- Politicians (international and local)
- Combatants and war lords (including terrorists and freedom fighters)
- Senior Diplomats, Heads of Missions
- Military – NATO (e.g. ECOWAS or UN)
- International organisations (UN, EU, UNHCR, OSCE)
- Community leaders and religious leaders
- Private sector enterprise – legitimate and illegitimate (crimminal/mafia)
- Police
- Paramilitary

Mostly male or male led

Key actors in a post-conflict situation - 2
Source: Lesley Abdela 2003

- Indigenous civilian population
- Governmental organisations (e.g. SIDA, DFID)
- Hundreds of international NGOs
- Indigenous/local NGOs
- Small private sector enterprises
- Journalists/Reporters/Media anchors
- Humanitarian aid and development organisations

Women and men

Key actors in a post-conflict situation - 3
Source: Lesley Abdela 2003

- Refugees and Internatinally displaced people
- Windows (new heads of households)
- Lone parents
- Potential peace promoters among the community
- Women's NGO Leaders and activists
- Editors of women's media (e.g. magazines, radio and TV programmes)

Mostly women (approx. 89%)

the region. Despite adverse circumstances under the Baathist regime since the early 1990s, many Iraqi women are well educated. They are doctors, engineers, scientists, lawyers, pharmacists and teachers. A number of Iraqi women exiles became leaders of women's organisations campaigning for human rights, democracy and peace. Iraq's women have a history of activity in politics and public life. In 1948, Iraq was one of the first countries in the Middle East to have a female judge. In 1958 Iraq had one of the first female government ministers in the region.

Alarmed by the ominous and clearly discernible pattern of women's *post-bellum* exclusion, Iraqi women's groups started to lobby for a significant presence of women in the new governmental structures. They held meetings, appeared in the international media, and sent letters to the leaders of the international community. In March 2003, Kurdish Women Action against Honour Killing, a group founded in 2000 by Dr Nazand Begikhani, an expert reporter to several British legal bodies on women's human rights violations in the Middle East, sent an open letter to UN Secretary-General, Kofi Annan, to President George W. Bush, and to the European Union. The letter stated: 'Our principal concerns are the future of Iraq under a new regime and the nature of the governmental institutions that will replace the present ones. We are very worried that women may not be properly represented in these institutions. The Iraqi opposition groups ignore the voice of Iraqi women who campaign for women's rights and who work towards a true civil society founded upon justice and equality. If there is to be any hope of securing for Iraq in the post-Saddam era a democratic federal system based on pluralism, justice and gender equality, women must be full participants in the process, not mere spectators. We therefore demand that women be granted their rightful place in the future governmental structure of Iraq.'

A group of Iraqi women exiles met with British Prime Minister Tony Blair. The meeting was front-page news in the British media and prominent on television and radio. Later in March 2003, in London, a small group of exile Iraqi women peace and human rights campaigners issued a statement saying they wanted appointed positions at all levels of the interim government - national, regional and local - to include at least 40 per cent women and they wanted a new constitution for Iraq to be constructed by a gender balanced team. Any new constitution might otherwise discriminate against women and would certainly exclude women's perceptions of the future of Iraq.

There is a precedent. The negotiating team, which drew up the post-apartheid South African constitution was 50 per cent female. Former South African High Commissioner to London Cheryl Carolus believed this remarkable gender balance was fundamental to an outcome acceptable to 26 different political parties, a constitution 'united in our diversity'. The Iraqi women drew up a list with names of Iraqi women exiles who would be qualified to serve on interim governing councils. They also pointed out there were other women inside Iraq who would also be qualified. The list was widely circulated to UK and US government foreign service and defence departments. Iraqi women exiles attended a series of meetings with British ministers and the Foreign Office. International women's organisations also lobbied on behalf of Iraqi women. The Women Peacemakers Programme (WPP), a programme which works internationally to empower women in peacebuilding skills, sent an open letter to President Bush and Prime Minister Blair stating: 'Any arguments that there is no tradition in Iraq of women's political participation have no basis in fact. Arguments that women's political participation may somehow be un-Islamic are equally baseless, given the declarations of progressive imams and Islamic scholars worldwide. In order to support democracy in Iraq, we urge you, in any Iraqi advisory bodies that may be formed towards the goal of planning a new government, to include a minimum of 30 per cent of Iraqi women. This figure should be the minimum for all posts in any transitional government, including posts which may be involved in issues of public security, oil and industry, finance and banking, and the development of democratisation initiatives.'

In April a conference co-sponsored by Women Waging Peace and the Woodrow Wilson International Centre for Scholars brought together 26 women leaders from Iraq and more than 60 US policymakers from the US State Department, the US Agency for International Development, the US Defence Department and other agencies. Conference participants urged the US reconstruction leadership in Iraq to ensure that no less than 30 per cent of all governing organisations be made up of women.

Despite all this global activity, on the ground in Iraq the infamous and familiar parallel universe was developing. When international men arrive in a disorganised and confused post-conflict situation, they negotiate with the first individual 'spokespeople' to come across on their radar screens. The first people they encounter are mostly warlords, mafia, prominent nomenclature from the previous regime or religious leaders. Many are more interested in grabbing swag and political (and physical) muscle than in concepts of universal human rights and democracy. Moreover, in aftermath of war, for a variety of reasons men are far more able and ready than women to make contact with the internationals. In Iraq the surge of looting and violence on the streets, and an ominous return of 'Islamic' extremism and violence, forced women to stay inside. Coalition military officers referred to the few women they saw scuttling along the dangerous streets dressed in their long abbeys as 'BMOs' (Black Moving Objects). The military consulted religious leaders and tribal chiefs, but overlooked prominent women and women community leaders. Senior international men are not very willing to seriously listen to women in the local population. Far from treating local women as equals, with the exception of a few individuals, local women in general are treated as an underclass. Senior men in the international community recruit women as language assistants and secretaries, but not as leaders in any numbers.

In April 2003, concerned at the exclusion of women, Iraqi women activists flew to Washington. The Washington File press service reported: 'Iraqi women, who constitute at least 55 per cent of their country's population, want a voice in its rebirth following the fall of Saddam's regime. This message was strongly conveyed by Iraqi women in their 23 April meetings at the State Department with Secretary of State Colin Powell and Under Secretary of State for Global Affairs

Paula Dobriansky. Rend Rahim Francke, the Executive Director of the Iraq Foundation, spoke of the challenge Iraqi women face in trying to gain political participation. Francke and fellow visitor Zainab Al-Suwaij had gone to the 15 April meeting in Ur, outside Nasiriyah, to take part in the first meeting of Iraqis to discuss their future government after the fall of the Baath regime. They were dismayed to discover that, even though more than half of Iraq's population are female, only four out of the 80 delegates to Ur were women.'

In late April 2003, the Centre for the Democratic Control of the Armed Forces hosted a meeting in Geneva. Twenty women with international conflict experience met as an advisory board on women and war. Krishna Ahooja Patel, President of the Women's International League for Peace and Freedom, has spent 25 years working inside the UN system. She summed up our frustration when she said: *'UN Resolution 1325 was passed in 2000 stating clearly that women must be included in all aspects of peacemaking and peacebuilding discussions. It didn't happen in Afghanistan and so far it doesn't look as though it is being implemented in Iraq. Why, why, why?'*

L. Paul Bremer, the US administrator in Iraq, acted as midwife to an interim government consisting of 22 men and three women. Bremer's interim governing council contained more than seven men to every woman. Bremer claimed the new Iraqi governing council was representative of a complete cross-section of the community. An estimated 55 per cent of Iraq's 24 million people are female. A council truly representative of Iraqi diversity would result in fourteen women and eleven men. Does any of this matter? Will a cabinet largely composed of men pay full heed to the needs of women? History suggests the answer is no. However, even beyond the needs of women, Iraq is facing enormous challenges and its leadership should be drawn from across the entire pool of talent, from women and men, not just from half the talent pool.

In September 2003, the author of this article was recruited by the Research Training Institute of North Carolina to travel to Al Hillah in south-central Iraq to work on the local government programme. The task was to help develop civil society by working with newly formed women's associations and human rights organisations. The CPA team had already started to renovate buildings for women's centres, and the first centre opened in Al Hillah on the first week of October. In September and October the present author ran fifteen democracy workshops in the towns of Hillah, Diwaniya, and Kerbala, eleven of the workshops were with women's associations. Along with the need for security, medicines in hospitals and text books in schools, the first issue raised by each group of women was their passionate desire for equal participation of women and men on any council or committee set up to discuss Iraq's constitution. They wanted to be certain that women's human rights are properly enshrined. In October the author attended The Heartland of Iraq Women's Conference at the University of Babylon, hosted by the Women's Association of Babylon, The Iraq Foundation and The Women for a Free Iraq. Some 200 women came to the conference from across Iraq – Kurds, Shia, Sunni, etc. Paul Bremer attended the final day's session and listened to the key issues raised by the Iraqi women. The women loudly called for at least 40 per cent women on any council or committee drawing up the constitution and at least 35 to 40 per cent women in parliament and at ministerial level in any future Iraqi government.

The women's message is clear. The key questions are: Have lessons from other conflicts been learned about the exclusion of women? Will heed be paid to such lessons learned? Will action be taken by Iraqi and coalition men in power to include women as equal partners in developing the future society in Iraq?

Endnotes

1 P. A. Throop, *Women Loom Large in the Medieval Opposition to the Crusades, Criticism of the Crusade: A Study of Public Opinion and Crusade Propaganda* (Amsterdam: N.V. Swets & Zeitlinger, 1940).

2 P. Hayner, 'Justice in Transition: Challenges and Opportunities', *Presentation to the 55th Annual DPI/NGO Conference Rebuilding Societies Emerging from Conflict: A Shared Responsibility* (New York, 9-11 September 2002).

3 Hayner, 'Justice in Transition: Challenges and Opportunities'.

4 J. T Gross, *Neighbours: the Destruction of the Jewish Community at Jewabne, Poland* (Princeton: Princeton University Press, 2001).

5 S. Licht and S. Drakulic, 'When the Word for Peacenik was Women: War and Gender in the Former Yugoslavia', in M. Spencer (ed), *Women in Post-Communism*, Volume 2 (Greenwich, Connecticut: JAI Press, 1996), 111-39.

6 D. Wurfel, 'Israel/Palestine, The Peace Movement Endures Crisis', *Peace Magazine* (April-June 2003).

7 G. Svirsky, *Non-violence in the Israeli Women's Peace Movement* (Düsseldorf, Germany), at http://www.diak.org

8 G. Svirsky, *Non-violence in the Israeli Women's Peace Movement*.

9 See Mothers of Plaza de Mayo, at http://www.madres.org/

10 See International Human Rights Law Group, at http://www.hrlawgroup.org/

11 International Alert is an international non-governmental organisation based in London and dedicated to the non-violent, prevention, management and transformation of violent conflict. IA works at national, regional, and global levels in order to enhance the capacity of individuals, peace networks, constituencies and organisations to build sustainable peace. For fFurther information is available, at http://www.international-alert.org.

12 The Hague Appeal for Peace is an international network of peace and justice organisations that has produced 50 recommendations for the global promotion of peace,. Further information is available at http://www.haguepeace.org/.

13 Subsequent launches occurred at several international fora, including the 1999 Association of Women in Development Annual Conference, Virginia, USA, the regional preparatory conferences for the Beijing+5 Review organised in 1999 and 2000 in Bangkok, Addis Ababa and Geneva, and in the Finnish Parliament and numerous meetings in the United Kingdom. Additionally, the 43rd session of the Commission for the Status of Women (CSW) and the International Women's Day celebrations in 1999 provided further opportunities to launch the initiative. This consisted of round table discussions and high profile speakers such as Dr. Noeleen Heyzer (UNIFEM), along with representatives of well-known NGOs e.g. Femmes Africa Solidarite (Geneva) and support from the Women's Desk of the Netherlands Ministry of Foreign Affairs.

14 A listserv is a communication tool that offers the opportunity to post suggestions or questions to a large number of people at the same time. When e-mail is addressed to a LISTSERV mailing list, it is automatically broadcast to everyone on the list.

15 Leitana Nehan, the conflict and development agency from Bougainville, presented the signatures to the Secretary-General's Representative during the International Women's Day celebrations on 8 March 2000.

16 European Parliament Resolution on Gender Aspects on Conflict Resolution INI/2000/2025, at http://www.cities-localgovernments.org/uclg/web/wldmdocument.asp?id=19

17 The Peace Process commenced with the declaration of Republican and Loyalist paramilitary ceasefires in autumn 1994. Elections were held in spring 1996 to the Peace Talks, chaired by US Senator George Mitchell, that later resulted in the Good Friday Agreement (Spring 1998).

18 For further information on the Northern Ireland Women's Coalition see M. McWilliams and A. Kilmurray, 'Athena on the Loose: The Origins of the Northern Ireland Women's Coalition', *Irish Journal of Feminist Studies 2* (1) (Summer 1997), 1-21.

19 The first government initiative to recognise the needs of victims was the establishment of the Bloomfield Commission in 1997. For further information see M. Smyth and F. M. Therese, *Personal Accounts from Northern Ireland's Troubles: Public Chaos, Private Loss* (London: Pluto Press, 2000).

20 M. McWilliams, 'Struggling for Peace and Justice: Reflections on Women's Activism in Northern Ireland', *Journal of Women's History 6* (4) and 7 (1) (Winter-Spring 1995), 13-39.

21 See publications from the Community Foundation for Northern Ireland, including Taking Calculated Risks for PEACE (2003) and related publications on work with the Women's Sector; Politically Motivated Ex-Prisoners and Victims/Survivors of the Troubles.

Key Reading Part III

Books

S. N. Anderlini, *Women at the Peace Table: Making a Difference* (New York: UNIFEM, 2000).

P. Athavale, *Hindu Widow* (New Delhi: Reliance Publishing House, 1986).

E. F. Barth, *Peace as Disappointment. The Reintegration of Female Soldiers in Post-Conflict Societies: A Comparative Study from Africa* (Oslo: PRIO, 2002).

J. Benjamin, K. Fancy, *The Gender Dimension of Internal Displacement* (New York: Women's Commission for Refugee Women and Children, UNICEF, 1998).

A. Boraine and R. Scheffer (eds), *Dealing with the Past, Truth and Reconciliation in South Africa* (Cape Town: IDASA, 1994).

I. Bottigliero, *120 Million Landmines Deployed Worldwide: Act or Fiction?* (Geneva: Pro-Victimis, 2000).

E. Boulding, *Culture of Peace: The Hidden Side of History* (New York: Syracuse University Press, 2000).

I. Breines, D. Gierycz and B. Reardon (eds), *Towards a Women's Agenda for a Culture of Peace* (Paris: UNESCO, 1999).

B. Byrne et al., *Gender, Conflict and Development: Case Studies: Cambodia, Rwanda, Kosova, Somalia, Algeria, Guatemala and Eritrea*, BRIDGE Report (Brighton: Institute of Development Studies, 1996).

A. Callamard, *Investigating Women's Human Rights Violations in Armed Conflicts* (Rights and Democracy, 2001).

Cambridge Women Peace Collective (eds), *My Country is the Whole World: An Anthology of Women's Work on Peace and War* (London: Pandora, 1984).

Canadian International Development Agency, *Gender Equality and Peacebuilding: A Draft of Operational Framework* (Ottawa: CIDA, 1998).

C. Cockburn, *The Space Between Us: Negotiating Gender and National Identities in Conflict* (London: Zed Books, 1998).

C. Cockburn and D. Zarkov, *The Postwar Moment: Militaries, Masculinities and International Peacekeeping* (London: Lawrence & Wishart, 2002).

R. Cohen and F. M. Deng, *Masses in Flight: The Global Crisis of Internal Displacement* (New York: UNHRC, 1998).

M. Croll, *Counting the Human Cost* (Geneva: Small Arms Survey, 2002).

P. Dandavate, K. Ranjana and J. Verghese, *Widows, Abandoned and Destitute Women in India* (New Delhi: Radiant Publishers, 1989).

J. El-Bushra, A. El-Karib, and A. Hadjipateras, *Gender-sensitive Programme Design and Planning in Conflict-affected Situations* (London: Accord, 2002).

D. Elson and H. Keklik, *Progress of the World's Women 2002* (New York: UNIFEM, 2002).

V. Farr and G. Kiflemariam (eds), *Gender Perspectives on Small Arms and Light Weapons: Regional and International Concerns* (Bonn: Bonn International Centre for Conversion, 2002).

T. Fitzsimmons, *Beyond the Barricades: Women, Civil Society, and Participation after Democratization in Latin America* (Hamden: Garland Science, 2000).

R. Gellately and B. Kiernan (eds), *The Specter of Genocide: Mass Murder in Historical Perspective* (Cambridge: Cambridge University Press, 2003).

Geneva International Centre for Humanitarian Demining, *A Guide to Mine Action* (Geneva: GICHD, September 2003).

Geneva International Centre for Humanitarian Demining, *Explosive Remnants of War, A Threat Analysis* (Geneva: GICHD, 2002).

K. Grieg, *War Children of the World* (Bergen: War and Children Identity Project, 2001).

M. Guzman Bouvard, *Revolutionizing Motherhood: The Mothers of the Plaza De Mayo* (Wilmington: Scholarly Resources, 2002).

P. B. Hayner, *Unspeakable Truth–Confronting State Terror and Atrocity* (London: Routledge, 2000).

J. L. Herman, *Trauma and Recovery* (New York: Basic Books, 1992).

C. Hesse and R. Post (eds), *Human Rights in Political Transitions: Gettysburg to Bosnia* (Zone Books, 1997).

C. Horwood, *Humanitarian Mine Action: The First Decade of a New Sector in Humanitarian Aid, Relief and Rehabilitation Network* (London: Humanitarian Peace Network, March 2000).

International Committee of the Red Cross, *Anti-personnel Mines – Friend or Foe? A Study of the Military Use and Effectiveness of Anti-personnel Mines* (Geneva: ICRC, 1996).

International Committee of the Red Cross, *Arms Availability and the Situation of Civilians in Armed Conflict* (Geneva: ICRC, June 1999).

International Committee of the Red Cross, *Banning Anti-Personnel Mines: The Ottawa Treaty Explained* (Geneva: ICRC, 1998).

S. Jacobs, R. Jacobson, and J. Marchbank (eds), *States of Conflict: Gender, Violence and Resistance* (London: Zed Books, 2000).

K. Kingma (ed), *Demobilization in Sub-Saharan Africa: The Development and Security Impacts* (London and New York: Macmillan Press Ltd, 2000).

A. Krog, *Country of my Skull: Guilt, Sorrow, and the Limits of Forgiveness in the New South Africa* (New York: Random House, 1999).

Landmine Action, *Explosive Remnants of War, Unexploded Ordnance and Post-Conflict Communities* (London, March 2002).

S. Macdonald et al. (eds), *Images of Women in Peace and War: Cross-cultural and Historical Perspectives* (Houndmills: Macmillan Press, 1987).

A. J. Marsella, M. J. Friedman, E. T. Gerrity, R. M. Scurfield (eds), *Ethnocultural Aspects of Post-traumatic Stress Disorder* (Washington DC: American Medical Psychological Association, 1994).

S. F. Martin, *Refugee Women* (London and New Jersey: Zed Books, 1991).

D. Mazurana and K. Carlson, *From Combat to Community: Women and Girls of Sierra Leone* (Washington: Women Waging Peace, 2004).

S. McKay and D. Mazurana, *Where Are The Girls? Girls in Fighting Forces in Northern Uganda, Sierra Leone and Mozambique: Their Lives during and after War* (New York: United Nations, 2004).

S. Meitjes, A. Pillay, and M. Turshen (eds), *The Aftermath in Post-conflict Transformation* (London: Zed Books, 2002).

M. Minow, *Between Vengeance and Forgiveness: Facing History after Genocide and Mass Violence* (Boston: Beacon Press, 1998).

C. Moser and F. Clark (eds), *Victims, Perpetrators or Actors? Gender, Armed Conflict and Political Violence* (London: Zed Books, 2001).

V. Nikolic-Ristanovic (ed), *Women, Violence and War: Wartime Victimization of Refugees in the Balkans* (Budapest: Central European University Press, 2000).

L. Parmar, *Kargil War Widows* (Jaipur: Rajasthan Patrika, 2003).

V. S. Peterson and A. S. Runyan, *Global Gender Issues* (Boulder: Westview Press, 1999).

E. Rehn and E. Johnson Sirleaf, *Women, War, Peace: The Independent Assessment on the Impact of Armed Conflict on Women and Women's Role in Peace-Building* (New York: UNIFEM, 2002).

R. Roach Pierson (ed), *Women and Peace: Theoretical, Historical and Practical Perspectives* (London and New York: Croom Helm, 1987).

D. E. Russell, *Lives of Courage: Women for a New South Africa* (New York: Basic Books, 1989).

R. Sachdev, *Women in White* (New Delhi: Humanscape, 2000).

United Nations Development Programme, *Gender Approaches in Conflict and Post-conflict Situations* (New York: UNDP, 2002).

United Nations DPKO, *Disarmament, Demobilization, Demobilisation and Reintegration of Ex-Combatants in a Peacekeeping Environment: Principles and Guidelines* (New York: United Nations Department of Peacekeeping Operations/Lessons Learned Unit, 2000).

United Nations Educational, Scientific and Cultural Organization, *Women Say No to War* (Paris: UNESCO, 1999).

H. Wiberg (ed), *Peace and War: Social and Cultural Aspects* (Warsaw: BEL CORP for UNESCO and the Centre for Peace and Conflict Research in Copenhagen, 1995).

Articles and papers

L. T. Arcel, 'Sexual Torture of Women as a Weapon of War: The Case of Bosnia-Herzegovina', in L. T. Arcel and G. T. Simunkovic, *War Violence, Trauma and the Coping Process: Armed Conflict in Europe and Survivor Responses* (Copenhagen: RCT/IRCT/Institute of Clinical Psychology, University of Copenhagen, 1998).

C. Cockburn, *Gender, Armed Conflict and Political Violence*, Background Paper (The World Bank: Washington DC, 1999), at http://www.asylumsupport.info/publications/worldbank/gender.pdf

R. Cohen, 'Protecting Internally Displaced Women and Children', *Rights Have No Borders: Worldwide Internal Displacement*, Global IDP Survey (Oslo: Norwegian Refugee Council, 1998).

P. Collett, 'Afghan Women in the Peace Process', in Loretzen and Turpin (eds), *The Women and War Reader* (New York and London: New York University Press, 1998).

V. Farr, 'Men, Women and Guns: Understanding How Gender Ideologies Support Small Arms and Light Weapons Proliferation', *BICC Conversion Survey 2003: Global Disarmament, Demilitarisation and Demobilisation* (Baden-Baden: Nomos Verlagsgesellschaft, 2003).

E. B. Foa, 'Psychosocial Treatment of PTSD in Expert Consensus Treatment Guidelines for Post-Traumatic Stress Disorder', *Journal of Clinical Psychiatry*, 60 (Memphis, 1999).

J. E. Giller, P. J. Bracken and S. Kabaganda, 'War, Women and Rape', *The Lancet*, 337 (London: The Lancet Publishing Group, 1991).

D. Kozaric-Kovacic, V. Folnegovic-Smalc and J. Skrinjaric, 'Systematic Raping of Women in Croatia and Bosnia and Herzegovina: A Preliminary Psychiatric Report', *Croatian Medical Journal*, 34 (Zagreb: Medicinska naklada, 1993).

B. Mansaray, 'Women Against Weapons: A Leading Role for Women in Disarmament', in A. Ayissi and R. E. Poulton (eds), *Bound to Cooperate: Conflict, Peace and People in Sierra Leone* (Geneva: UNIDIR, 2000).

D. R. Marshall, 'Women in War and Peace – Grassroots Peace-building', *Peaceworks* 34 (Washington DC: USIP, August 2000), at http://www. usip.org/pubs/peaceworks

D. Mazurana, S. McKay, K. Carlson and J. Kasper, 'Girls in Fighting Forces and Groups: Their Recruitment, Participation, Demobilisation, and Reintegration', *Peace and Conflict: Journal of Peace Psychology*, Vol. 8, No. 2 (2002).

A. C. McFarlane and G. De Girolamo, 'The Nature of Traumatic Stressors and the Epidemiology of Post-Traumatic Reactions', in B. A. van der Kolk, A. C. McFarlane and L. Weisaeth (eds), *Traumatic Stress* (New York: The Guilford Press, 1996).

A. Naik, 'Protecting Children from the Protectors: Lessons from West Africa', *Forced Migration Review*, No. 15 (Oxford, October 2002), at http://www.fmreview.org/FMRpdfs/FMR15/fmr15.7.pdf

A. Naik, 'UN Investigation into Sexual Exploitation by Aid Workers: Justice Has Not Been Done', *Forced Migration Review*, No. 16 (Oxford, January 2003), at http://www.fmreview.org/FMRpdfs/FMR16/fmr16.15.pdf

A. Naik, 'West Africa Scandal Points to Need for Humanitarian Watchdog', *Humanitarian Exchange*, No. 24 (London, July 2003), at http://www.odihpn.org/report.asp?ID=2561

OECD, *Gender and Post-conflict Reconstruction: Lessons Learned from Afghanistan*, Joint workshop of the UN Inter-Agency Network of Women and Gender Equality and the OECD-DAC Network on Gender Equality (Paris: OECD, 10-11 July 2003).

S. Reynolds, 'Deterring and Preventing Rape and Sexual Slavery During Periods of Armed Conflicts', *Law and Inequality*, Vol. 16, No. 2 (Minneapolis: University of Minnesota, 1998).

M. Schmuki, 'Human Rights: Setting the Stage for Protecting Refugee Women', *Refugee: Canada's Periodical on Refugees*, Vol. 17, No. 1 (1998).

T. Shikola, 'We Left Our Shoes Behind', in M. Turshen and C. Twagiramariya (eds), *What Women Do in Wartime: Gender and Conflict in Africa* (London and New York: Zed Books, 1998).

B. Sorensen, Women and Post-Conflict Reconstruction: Issues and Sources, *Occasional Paper*, No. 3 (New York: UNRISD and War-torn Societies Project, 1998).

D. A. Summerfield, 'A critique of seven assumptions behind psychological trauma programmes in war-affected areas', *Social Science & Medicine*, Vol. 48 (1999).

L. Vincent, 'Engendering Peace in Africa: A Critical Inquiry into Some Current Thinking on the Role of African Women in Peace-building', *Africa Journal in Conflict Resolution*, No. 1 (Umhlanga Rocks, 2001).

T. Wallace, 'Refugee Women: Their Perspective and Our Responses', in H. O'Connell (ed), *Women and Conflict*, Oxfam Focus on Gender, Vol. 1, No. 1 (Oxford: Oxfam, 1993).

N. de Watteville, 'Addressing Gender Issues in Demobilisation and Reintegration Programs' (New York: UNDP, 2002), at http://www.undp.org/erd/ddr/index.htm

Documents and online reports

ICRC, 'Women with Missing Loved Ones – Emotional Distress and Economic Hardship', *ICRC Press Release* (6 March 2003), at http://www.icrc.org

International Campaign to Ban Landmines, *Landmine Monitor Report 2002* (2002), at http://www.icbl.org

Truth and Reconciliation Commission Final Report, *Special Hearing: Women*, Vol.4, Chapter 10 (1998), at http:/www.polity.org.za/commissions/trc/1998

United Nations, *Mission to Colombia*, Addendum to the Report of the Special Rapporteur of the Commission on Human Rights on Violence Against Women, its Causes and Consequences, Ms. Radhika Coomaraswamy, UN Document E/CN.4/2002/83/add.3 (Geneva, 2002).

United Nations, *Report of the Secretary-General on Women, Peace and Security*, UN Document S/2002/1154 (New York, 16 October 2002).

United Nations, *Beijing Declaration and Platform for Action* (Beijing, China, 4-15 September 1995).

United Nations, *Windhoek Declaration* (2000), at http://www.reliefweb.int/library/GHARkit/FilesFeb2001/windhoek_declaration.htm

United Nations High Commissioner for Refugees, *Agenda for Protection* (Geneva: UNHCR, 2002).

Women's Commission for Refugee Women and Children, *Displaced and Desperate: Assessment of Reproductive Health for Colombia's Internally Displaced Persons, Executive Summary* (New York, 2003), at http://www.womenscommission.org

Websites

Bonn International Centre for Conversion, at http://www.bicc.de

Campaign Against Arms Trade, at http://www.caat.org.uk

Geneva International Centre on Humanitarian Demining, at http://www.gichd.ch

Handicap International, at http://www.handicap-international.org

International Action Network on Small Arms, at http://www.iansa.org

International Campaign to Ban Landmines, at http://www.icbl.org

International Committee of the Red Cross, at http://www.icrc.org

International Federation of Red Cross and Red Crescent Societies, at http://www.ifrc.org

International Mine Action Standards, at http://www.mineactionstandards.org

International Organization for Migration, at http://www.iom.int

International Rehabilitation Council for Torture Victims, at http://www.irct.org/usr/irct/home.nsf

Landmine Survivors Network, at http://www.landminesurvivors.org

Mine Action, at http://www.mag.org.uk

Palestinian Human Rights Information Centre, at http://www.baraka.org/phric.htm

Project on Justice in Times of Transition, at http://www.ksg.harvard.edu/justiceproject

Small Arms Survey, at http://www.smallarmssurvey.org

South East Europe Clearinghouse for the Control of Small Arms and Light Weapons, at http://www.seesac.org

United Nations Children's Fund, at http://www.unicef.org/smallarms

United Nations Department of Disarmament Affairs, at http://www.disarmament2.un.org/gender/note3.htm

United Nations Development Fund for Women, at http://www.unifem.org

United Nations E-Mine, at http://www.mineaction.org

United Nations High Commissioner for Refugees, at http://www.unhcr.ch

United Nations Institute for Disarmament Research, at http://www.unidir.org

United Nations Office of the High Commissioner for Human Rights, at http://www.unhchr.ch

United Nations Populations Fund, at http://www.unfpa.org

US Agency for International Development, at http://www.usaid.gov/regions/afr/conflictweb/demob_bib.html

World Bank, at http://www.worldbank.org

PART IV

STRATEGIES

AND

SOLUTIONS

Introduction

The concluding part of this book should facilitate the reader's orientation in the thicket of laws, norms and documents providing information on strategies and solutions in eradicating violence against women brought by the human rights agenda, feminist studies and international humanitarian law. It deals with two crucial concepts of the women's movement namely women's human rights and gender mainstreaming.

Many hopes were pinned to the latter. Gender mainstreaming has become the most debated tool of empowering women in present academic debate. Viewing peace support operations (PSOs) through a gender lens leads to the question as to how to integrate women in the institutions and processes of these missions. The examples from different regions where peace support operations have been implemented indicate the complexity of the ongoing uneasy process of inclusion of gender issues in the missions' mandates, into their practical activities and personnel policies.

A seemingly simple idea that the rights of women are indivisible from human rights, enshrined in the Declaration of Human Rights and fully developed in the Vienna Declaration in 1993, has had a great impact on international documents, laws, judicial judgements and practical measures. The establishment of the international criminal tribunals of Rwanda and of the former Yugoslavia, and the adoption of the Statute of the International Criminal Court in 1998 can be considered a result of the reinforced protection of women's rights. The UN Security Council Resolution 1325 represents a present culmination of the struggle to protect women in wars and armed conflict, and unlike most resolutions, it has become a central document for organisations and individuals who know and quote its clauses and expect its full implementation. The last part of this book elucidates the ways in which the resolution works, providing a number of operational mandates, as well as, a political framework that women can use for advocating, lobbying, and negotiating with state bodies and demanding political accountability.

Chapter 1

Violence against Women from the Perspective of the Human Rights Agenda

'The human rights of women and of the girl-child are an inalienable, integral and indivisible part of universal human rights. The full and equal participation of women in political, civil, economic, social and cultural life, at the national, regional and international levels, and the eradication of all forms of discrimination on grounds of sex are priority objectives of the international community.'

Vienna Declaration and Programme of Action, World Conference on Human Rights, 1993

The struggle for women's equal rights is not a recent phenomenon, being at the core of the women's movement dating back from the beginning of the nineteenth century. As a reaction to the proclamation of the principle of *universal* individual rights in the American and French Revolution in the late eighteenth century, the Declaration of the Rights of *Man* and Citizen, the women's movement questioned its validity in a deeply gender unequal society where its application to women was illusionary.[1] Since then the movement has strived to effect change by demanding the revision of the unequal power relations between women and men through the legal recognition of women's rights. In international law it is only in the second half of the twentieth century that the formulation of women's rights truly developed in conjunction with the expansion of human rights norms.[2] Since 1945 women's human rights

standards have increasingly been formally articulated in the international arena where states decide jointly to elaborate legally binding conventions and political standards for the international community. The United Nations (UN) has been a key actor and a vital forum in this endeavour, not only drawing together a majority of states (having 191 members in 2005), but also providing a space for civil society through the growing participation of non-governmental organisations (NGOs). The latter are an essential avenue for the expression of women's voices, bringing women's rights onto the international agenda and, most importantly, playing a crucial role in monitoring the implementation of state commitments.[3] Since the UN's inception, the respect for and promotion of human rights have been a central tenet of its goals for international peace and security, and economic and social cooperation. Thus, the equality of women and men in their rights and fundamental freedoms was enshrined in its preamble and purposes. However, since 1975 – conscious of the fact that the secondary status of women arises from deep-seated social inequalities in the political, economic and cultural fields and hinders women's full participation in society, thus impeding the pursuit of the organisation's goals – the UN undertook a holistic approach in addressing women's rights in three interlinked concepts of equality, development and peace.[4] Formulated in the first UN World Conference on Women in Mexico in 1975, and resulting in the UN Decade for Women (1975-1985), this strategy has continued to be the framework for progress and assessment in subsequent international conferences on women held in Copenhagen in 1980, Nairobi in 1985, Beijing in 1995, and UN evaluations in New York for Beijing + 5 in 2000 and Beijing + 10 in 2005.

In thirty years of its commitment to the status of women, the essential contribution of the United Nations is the elaboration of an international human rights legal framework promoting and protecting the equal rights of women and providing international recognition of these rights. The evolution of the UN's normative work began with the creation of specific legal instruments in certain areas such as political and social rights in the 1950s-1960s, which later developed into the establishment of a more comprehensive convention in the 1980s aimed at eliminating all forms of discrimination against women. It culminated in the 1990s by tackling violence against women as a pervasive obstacle in the realisation of women's rights.

Since the late 1940s, the UN has established human rights instruments that stipulated the respect and enjoyment of human rights without discrimination based on gender. This principle was enshrined in the International Bill of Human Rights (IBHR), composed of the Universal Declaration of Human Rights (UDHR) in 1948, the International Covenant on Economic, Social and Cultural Rights (ICESCR), and the International Covenant on Civil and Political Rights (ICCPR), both in 1966.

This principle of non-discrimination was further developed in the 1950s-60s in a number of legal documents affirming women's equal rights in specific political, social and economic aspects of their lives. For example, in 1954, the Convention on the Political Rights of Women was approved, affirming the right of women to vote and to hold public office. In addition, education rights of women were affirmed by the adoption of the Convention against Discrimination in Education in 1962, which stipulates a free and compulsory primary education and

access to secondary and higher education. With regard to economic rights, the International Labour Organization (ILO) has built up a set of standards since 1919 regulating women's working conditions such as the guarantee of equal wages, protection from night work and harmful substances, and the safeguard of maternity benefits.[5] Women's rights within the family were also guaranteed through the Convention on the Nationality of Married Women in 1958 and the Convention on Consent to Marriage, Minimum Age and Registration of Marriages in 1962. Furthermore, women were protected from particular forms of exploitation such as slavery and prostitution in the Convention for the Suppression of the Traffic in Persons and of the Exploitation of the Prostitution of Others in 1949.

In the 1970s, these rights of women, which until then were dispersed in different general conventions, were brought together and acknowledged in a single comprehensive document that aimed to cover all aspects of discrimination in women's lives. The adoption of the Convention on the Elimination of All Forms of Discrimination against Women (CEDAW) in 1979 by the UN General Assembly, commonly referred to as the international bill of women's rights, was acclaimed as a milestone.[6] It called on states to acknowledge the economic and social contribution of women in society and denounced discrimination against women as a barrier to their full participation in the development of the family and the larger community.[7] The most wide-ranging of all legal documents on women, the convention covered the eradication of discrimination in political life, education, employment, access to financial credit, health, family, marriage and other aspects of economic and social life. It also advocated for changing cultural norms and stereotypes that maintained women's inferiority and included measures to suppress prostitution and the traffic of women. The convention was commended as an important development in the human rights framework that not only reaffirms and summarises the standards and principles declared in other general human rights conventions, but also adds new dimensions and principles.[8] Discrimination against women was defined as '*any distinction, exclusion or restriction made on the basis of sex, which has the effect or purpose of impairing or nullifying the recognition, enjoyment or exercise by women, irrespective of their marital status, on a basis of equality of men and women, of human rights and fundamental freedoms in the political, economic, social, cultural, civil or any other field.*' Accordingly, state parties have committed to implement standards embodied in the CEDAW by adjusting their legislation or enacting new law, and they are furthermore obliged to carry out temporary affirmative action in order to accelerate equality between women and men in society.

The Head of the Swiss Federal Department of Foreign Affairs, Mrs. Micheline Calmy-Rey, led an initiative in the 60th session of the Commission of Human Rights, 2004 focusing on violence against women. Together with twenty women leaders they adopted a united stand on fighting all forms of abuse and exploitation of women and urged states to ratify and implement international standards such as the CEDAW and the Beijing Platform for Action.

In 1999 an optional protocol was adopted enabling an individual communication procedure whereby persons under jurisdiction of state parties may submit a complaint of an alleged violation of the convention to the committee charged with monitoring CEDAW's implementation by its state parties.

In the 1980s, the international community had accumulated an impressive set of normative documents reducing *de jure* discrimination, or discrimination before the law, yet inequality in society persisted. Consequently international strategies targeted ways and means to remove *de facto* discrimination, or discrimination in practices and thus emphasised the need to change socially constructed gender stereotypes that continued to devalue women. The Nairobi Forward Looking Strategies (FLS), agreed to by UN member states during the world conference to review the achievements of the UN Decade for Women, affirmed that equality is both a goal and a means whereby women are not only granted legal equality but also equal responsibilities and opportunities to enjoy their rights and to develop their potential talents and skills.[9] The FLS called for equality rights for example in marriage and divorce; the affirmation of women's autonomy and power through property rights, equal involvement in development and promotion of women to positions of power; recognition of women's unpaid work in the home through its inclusion in national accounting and the sharing of domestic responsibilities; and finally, the promotion of women's paid work through equal employment opportunities. It outlined a detailed recommendation for

governments calling on them to establish, modify and enforce a wide-ranging legal base for the equality of women and men combined with the concrete provision of facilities for education, health, employment opportunities and services.

The 1990s set further landmark achievements in women's rights with the unprecedented international declaration that these rights were human rights. The Vienna World Conference on Human Rights in 1993 proclaimed that women's rights were an 'inalienable, integral and indivisible part of universal human rights', including economic, political, civil, social and cultural rights.[10] The symbolic and practical outcome of this affirmation is the full integration of women's rights as an essential part of human rights mechanisms. This means that not only do human rights standards have to take into account the differential impact of human rights abuses on women but also that women are provided with a framework and vocabulary to articulate the violence they experience such as the qualification of rape and domestic violence as torture.[11] In addition, states have a responsibility to protect and ensure these rights and are held accountable for their inaction.

This decade also marked a global awareness that violence against women in multiple forms remain a severe impediment to the realisation of women's rights. Thus a broadened concept of women's rights focused on violence against women, and UN-sponsored human rights conferences and resolutions responded to this by condemning violence against women and elaborating international measures for protection. The Committee that monitors CEDAW has expressed in its General Recommendation No. 19 in 1992 an official interpretation of violence against women as a form of discrimination – defining it as 'violence directed against a woman because she is a woman or that affects women disproportionately.' State parties to the convention were urged to include manifestations of violence against women in their reports, as well as to implement measures for the prevention of, protection from and punishment of such acts. The Committee further stated that violence against women may breach international law whether the state is party to the convention or not, and whether or not the act is perpetrated by authorities or private persons. In 1993 the UN General Assembly adopted the Declaration on the Elimination of Violence against Women (DEVAW). It encompassed a wide-ranging definition of violence against women, which included all public and private forms of violence as *'any act [...] that results in, or is likely to result in, physical, sexual or psychological harm or suffering to women, including threats of such acts, coercion or arbitrary deprivation of liberty, whether occurring in public or in private life.'* [12] Most importantly, the scope of the forms of violence became more specific without being an exhaustive list. It encompassed violence in the family such as battery,

Delegates from 189 countries participated in unprecedented numbers in the Fourth UN Conference on Women in Beijing, 1995. The groundbreaking Declaration and Platform for Action was adopted, placing the struggle against violence against women as one of the priorities of the international community.

sexual abuse, dowry-related violence, marital rape, female genital mutilation and other harmful traditional practices, non-spousal violence and violence related to exploitation. Violence occurring in the community was also targeted such as rape, sexual abuse, sexual harassment and intimidation at work or educational institutions, trafficking and forced prostitution. Finally, it also included violence perpetrated or condoned by the state. DEVAW further emphasised the duty of states to prevent, investigate and punish such crimes through *due diligence* and to avoid re-victimisation through gender-sensitive laws and enforcement procedures. In 1994, the Commission on Human Rights designated a mandate of the Special Rapporteur on Violence against Women in order to study the roots and consequences of violence against women, collect information from governments, intergovernmental and non-governmental organisations and prepare recommendations and measures to be executed at all levels. The commission adopted several resolutions condemning violence against women and encouraging gender equality from 1995 including integrating the rights of women into the human rights mechanisms of the United Nations and denouncing trafficking in women and girls.

In 1995, the World Conference on Women held in Beijing further underlined a major human rights accomplishment for women in setting the global agenda, evoked by an author as *'the convergence of political and legal processes to underscore, on a global scale, the centrality of human rights to the struggle for equality.'* [13] As a call to action, then UN Secretary-General Boutros-Boutros

Ghali stated that equality remained elusive as discrimination continued. Believing that the basis for change was at hand, he appealed to states for their determined commitment in making equality a reality.[14] Building on the Nairobi Forward Looking Strategies, the conference adopted a comprehensive programme entitled the Beijing Platform for Action, which gave priority to twelve critical areas: poverty, education, health, violence against women, armed conflict, economic structures, power sharing and decision-making, mechanisms to promote the advancement of women, human rights, the media, the environment, and the girl-child. It brought to the fore previously taboo subjects such as domestic and sexual abuse, rape, forced pregnancy, sexual slavery, the role of degrading or pornographic materials in acts of violence against women, sexuality rights, and discrimination based on sexual orientation. The Beijing document provided a global framework for gender equality and empowerment of women requiring states, international organisations and NGOs to mainstream gender in all their policies and programmes. With regard to violence against women three strategic objectives were adopted: to undertake integrated measures in its prevention and elimination; to study the causes and consequences of violence and the effectiveness of preventive measures; and to eliminate trafficking in women and to assist victims. States engaged to implement international human rights norms and instruments relating to violence against women, to review legislation that focuses on prevention and prosecution of offenders; to protect women; and to provide access to just and effective remedies. The conference was attended by around 8,000 NGO and media representatives witnessing the act of commitment of 189 governments to the Platform's implementation, which was hailed as a major achievement.[15]

Marking the gravity of the problem in 1999, the General Assembly proclaimed 25 November as the International Day for the Eradication of Violence against Women, commemorating those who have suffered or are suffering from violence and representing a time for the international community to assess progress and reaffirm commitments to eliminate gender-based violence. In the Millenium Declaration in 2000, states further explicitly pledged to combat all forms of violence against women and to implement the CEDAW as part of their global vision for the new millenium, in which they also recognised gender equality and women's empowerment as key aspects to poverty eradication and to the true achievement of sustainable development.[16] Furthermore, a move towards the end of impunity for crimes of gender-based violence was underscored by the international recognition of rape and sexual violence as crimes against humanity, war crimes and as acts of genocide in the ad hoc international criminal tribunals of the former Yugoslavia and Rwanda and the Statute of the International Criminal Court (ICC).

The current UN High Commissioner for Human Rights, Louise Arbour, former chief prosecutor for the ad-hoc criminal tribunals in Rwanda and Yugoslavia. The Office of the High Commissioner continues its work in protecting and promoting women's rights, with a particular focus on peace and security issues.

At the turn of the century new issues emerged that gravely undermined the enjoyment of women's rights such as an unprecedented amount of trafficking of women and children, the intersection of women's rights violations with the HIV/AIDS pandemic, gender dimensions of armed conflict and the role of women in peace and security, the feminisation of poverty, women's reproductive rights, and the gendered impact of environmental degradation.

Due to globalisation, trafficking in persons has dramatically increased in the last decade, with women and children as primary victims. In response to this challenge, the UN General Assembly adopted the Protocol to Prevent, Suppress and Punish Trafficking in Persons, Especially Women and Children, supplementing the UN Convention against Transnational Organised Crime in 2000. The problem remained high on the agenda with the Secretary-General highlighting it as a priority challenge for human rights in his 2003 Report on the Implementation of the UN Millennium Declaration. Qualified by acting High Commissioner Bertrand Ramcharan as 'the negation of every basic human right', the 60th session of the Commission of Human Rights in 2004 adopted a resolution on the elimination of trafficking in persons especially women and children. The Commission on Human Rights further decided to establish in 2004 a mandate of the Special Rapporteur on Trafficking in Persons, Especially in Women and Children, to focus on the study on the human rights protection of victims.

The evolution and widening scope of women's rights, especially in the eradication of violence against women, have led to an increased level of expectation. In this context, the years 2000 and 2005 represented a stocktaking of the international community in the implementation of the Beijing Platform for Action. The most significant outcome for both Beijing + 5 and Beijing + 10 review processes is the complete and unconditional reaffirmation of the commitments made ten years ago.[17] The 49th session of the Commission on the Status of Women hosted the Beijing + 10 event which provided an opportunity to launch a broad debate critically evaluating the accomplishments of governments and highlighting the obstacles that hinder implementation of the existing international legal measures and conventions on women's rights. Based on a questionnaire, responded to by 134 member states and an observer state, the recorded achievements are improvements in education, poverty reduction, women's health and social and legal status, and the participation and political representation of women.[18] Progress has also been noted on capacity building, training and gender-disaggregated data collection. Fighting violence against women has become a key priority in most countries, which seek to combat this plague through comprehensive approaches of legislative changes, action plans, support measures for victims, awareness-raising, education and sensitisation measures, training, and the prosecution, punishment and rehabilitation of offenders. Most importantly, the role of men and boys in preventing violence has been increasingly addressed. Governments also adopted several strategies on the national, regional and international levels to fight trafficking in women.

Among the obstacles to women's rights, states have indicated low participation at the decision-making levels, the persistence of stereotypical attitudes and discriminatory practices, and occupational segregation. Violence against women, specifically domestic violence, remains prevalent in all countries, with concerns for particular forms deriving from harmful traditional practices in the African region. In Asia, Latin America and Africa women are disproportionately affected by high poverty levels and obstacles to access to health exemplified by high maternal mortality rates. Trafficking and a high prevalence of HIV/AIDS have been noted for countries in Africa, Latin America and Central and Eastern Europe. In addition, in many countries, discriminatory legislation still exists preventing women's full enjoyment of political, civil, economic and social rights. Finally, many states recognised a gap in the implementation of policies and legislation once enacted due to lack of understanding of the concept of gender equality and the strategy of gender mainstreaming, vague or deficient guidelines, poor capacity and knowledge, and over-burdened national mechanisms which most often lack the ability to influence policy.

Looking back, the struggle for equality in women's rights has come a long way. Yet, as the recent assessments show, despite the achievements at the international level there has been little progress on country implementation of women's rights. This was underlined by Radhika Coomaraswamy, former Special Rapporteur on Violence against Women, who emphasised that '*the international community has made great strides in setting standards and elaborating a legal framework for the promotion and protection of women from violence. While at the normative level the needs of women are generally adequately addressed, the challenge lies in ensuring respect for and effective implementation of existing law and standards.'* [19] This challenge continues today. New, innovative suggestions such as the development of comparable indicators to measure gender justice and state accountability by the current Special Rapporteur on Violence against Women, Yakin Ertürk, provides a path for future work.[20] It remains that not only

is there a gap between policy and practice but that also public attitudes and mindsets have not followed the same pace of change as the legal and institutional structures. Undeniably however, women's rights standards are today explicitly drawn in international human rights law. These are valuable standards to be used by all – as guidelines for governments and international institutions, or instruments for the civil society to lobby and press governments on their commitments, and as a tool for change in the larger society.

Box 1.1: Landmark international legal instruments and documents concerning women's rights

Women's rights have been progressively codified into the international human rights, humanitarian, refugee and criminal law instruments. These have been supplemented by political declarations and global action plans that provide guidelines for implementation. The following list contains the most important developments on women's rights in legal and political documents, both international and regional.

Legal documents

1927 Slavery Convention
1945 Charter of the United Nations
1948 Universal Declaration of Human Rights
1949 Four Geneva Conventions
  (I) Convention for the Amelioration of the Condition of the Wounded and Sick in Armed Forces in the Field
  (II) Convention for the Amelioration of the Condition of Wounded, Sick and Shipwrecked Members of Armed Forces at Sea
  (III) Convention relative to the Treatment of Prisoners of War
  (IV) Convention relative to the Protection of Civilian Persons in Time of War
1951 Convention on the Status of Refugees
1951 Convention for the Suppression of the Traffic in Persons and of the Exploitation of the Prostitution of Others
1951 Convention on the Prevention and Punishment of the Crime of Genocide
1953 Protocol Amending the Slavery Convention
1954 Convention on the Political Rights of Women
1957 Supplementary Convention on the Abolition of Slavery, the Slave Trade, and Institutions and Practices Similar to Slavery
1958 Convention on the Nationality of Married Women
1962 Convention on Consent to Marriage, Minimum Age and Registration of Marriage
1962 UNESCO Convention against Discrimination in Education
1966 International Covenant on Economic, Social and Cultural Rights
1966 International Covenant on Civil and Political Rights
1977 Additional Protocols of the Geneva Conventions
  (I) Protocol Relating to the Protection of Victims of International Armed Conflicts
  (II) Protocol Relating to the Protection of Victims of Non-International Armed Conflicts
1979 Convention on the Elimination of All Forms of Discrimination against Women
1985 Convention against Torture and Other Cruel, Inhuman or Degrading Treatment or Punishment
1989 Convention on the Rights of the Child

1990 International Convention on the Protection of the Rights of All Migrant Workers and Members of their Families
1991 Inter-American Convention on the Nationality of Women
1991 Inter-American Convention on the Granting of Political Rights to Women
1991 Inter-American Convention on the Granting of Civil Rights to Women
1993 Statute of the International Criminal Tribunal for the Former Yugoslavia
1994 Inter-American Convention on the Prevention, Punishment and Eradication of Violence against Women
1994 Statute of the International Criminal Tribunal for Rwanda
1998 Rome Statute of the International Criminal Court
1998 First war crimes judgment citing guilt on grounds of rape, International Criminal Tribunal for the former Yugoslavia
1999 Optional Protocol to the Convention on the Elimination of All Forms of Discrimination against Women
2000 Protocol to Prevent, Suppress and Punish Trafficking in Persons, especially Women and Children, supplementing the UN Convention against Transnational Organised Crime
2003 Protocol to the African Charter on Human and Peoples' Rights on the Rights of Women in Africa

Political documents

1974 Declaration on the Protection of Women and Children in Emergency and Armed Conflict
1975 First UN International Women's Conference – Mexico
1980 Second International Women's Conference – Copenhagen
1984 Cartagena Declaration on Refugees
1985 Third UN International Women's Conference, Forward Looking Strategy for the Advancement of Women – Nairobi
1993 UN General Assembly Declaration on the Elimination of Violence against Women
1993 World Conference on Human Rights, Vienna Declaration – Vienna
1994 International Conference on Population and Development – Cairo
1995 UNHCR Policy for the Protection of Refugees (revised 1997)
1995 Fourth UN Conference on Women, Declaration & Platform for Action – Beijing
2000 UN General Assembly Outcome Document on Follow-up to the Platform for Action
2000 UN Millennium Declaration
2000 UN Security Council Resolution 1325 on Women, Peace and Security
2000 Windhoek Declaration

Endnotes

1 Emphasis added, see Olympe de Gouge, *The Rights of Women* (1791) and Mary Wollstonecraft, *Vindication of the Rights of Woman* (1792).

2 Some precedents for norms of equality of women and men are mentioned in the Charter of the League of Nations and the interwar period in international organisations such as the International Labour Organization and the Organization of American States. See M. Rendel, 'New Alternatives for Old Challenges', in F. Tabak (ed), *New Alternatives for Old Challenges: Women's Rights* (Spain: IISL ONATI, 1997), 25-27.

3 There are many NGOs advocating women's rights in various fields. See the list of selected organisations dealing with women's rights in this volume.

4 The inter-relations of these concepts are underscored by the fact that persisting gender inequality and discrimination impede the realisation of peace and development can only begin if there is a peaceful environment.

5 For instance the ILO elaborated the *Maternity Protection Convention* (No. 3) (1919) (revised No. 103, 1952) *Convention No. 45 Concerning the Employment of Women on Underground Work in Mines of All Kinds* (1937), *ILO Night Work (Women) Convention* (revised 1948), *Protocol of 1990 to the Night Work (Women) Convention* (revised 1948), *ILO Equal Remuneration Convention* (1951) and *ILO Workers with Family Responsibilities Convention* (1981).

6 CEDAW was preceded by the UN Declaration on the Elimination of Discrimination against Women in 1967. CEDAW, being a legal instrument, goes beyond the Declaration as it contains enforcement provisions.

7 M. Rendel, 'New Alternatives for Old Challenges', 33.

8 J. Symonides and V. Volodin, *Human Rights of Women: A Collection of International and Regional Normative Instruments* (Paris: UNESCO, 1999), xi.

9 The Nairobi conference was attended by 157 countries and 300 NGOs. F. Verucci, 'Women's Rights in International Conventions, Their Integration into Human Rights Mechanisms', in F. Tabak (ed), *New Alternatives for Old Challenges*, 48.

10 United Nations, *Vienna Declaration and Programme of Action* (part I, § 18), UN Document A/CONF.157/24 (Part I), chap. III) (Vienna, 25 June 1993). The Vienna Conference was attended by 171 countries and 2000 NGOs. F. Verucci, 'Women's Rights in International Conventions', 49.

11 C. Bunch and S. Frost, 'Women's Human Rights: An Introduction', in *Routledge International Encyclopedia of Women: Global Women's Issues and Knowledge* (Routledge, 2000)

12 *United Nations Declaration on the Elimination of Violence Against Women* (New York, 1993), Art. 1; see also Art. 2 for the scope of various forms of violence, at http://www.womenwarpeace.org/issues/violence.htm.

13 K. Timothy and M. Freeman, *International Women's Rights Action Watch: The CEDAW Convention and the Beijing Platform for Action: Reinforcing the Promise of the Rights Framework* (University of Minnesota, 2000).

14 UN Press Release, *Secretary-General's Statement to Fourth World Conference on Women*, WOM/BEI/8 (3 September 1995).

15 UN Press Release, *Declaration and Platform for Action Break New Ground in International Efforts for Advancement of Women to Year 2000*, WOM/BEI/40 (15 September 1995).

16 United Nations, *Millenium Declaration*, A/RES/55/22 (18 September 2000). Although the third goal of the Millenium Development Goals (MDG) specifically targets equality and empowerment of women, it has been progressively accepted that the incorporation of gender perspectives in all the goals is essential since gender equality is a prerequisite for their achievement.

17 The twenty-third special session of the UN General Assembly entitled 'Women 2000: Gender equality, development and peace for the twenty-first century' adopted an outcome document on 'Further actions and initiatives to implement the Beijing Declaration and Platform for Action'. It called on all governments to treat all forms of violence against women as criminal offences.

18 Report of the Secretary-General, *Review of the implementation of the Beijing Platform for Action and the outcome documents of the special session of the General Assembly entitled 'Women 2000: Gender equality, development and peace for the twenty-first century'*, Commission on the Status of Women, 49th session, E/CN.6/2005/2 (28 February – 11 March 2005), 7, 15-21.

19 United Nations, *International, Regional and National Developments in the Area of Violence against Women*, Report of the Special Rapporteur on Violence against Women, its Causes and Consequences, R. Coomaraswamy, Addendum 1, UN Document E/CN.4/2003/75 (Geneva, 2003).

20 United Nations, *Towards an Effective Implementation of International Norms to End Violence against Women*, Report of the Special Rapporteur on Violence against Women, its Causes and Consequences, Yakin Erturk, UN Document E/CN.4/2004/66 (Geneva, 2004).

Chapter 2

Feminist Approaches to Gender-Based Violence

'I want to share that even with all the problems, women's vision, presence and struggle are very important because they are crucial to finding our voice and making it heard. We have to mourn women's deaths, rape and slavery. For this reason and for our desire to live, we have to be there, even in the spaces they don't invite us to and convince society in some way that without our presence and proposals things are not complete.'

Sandra Morán, Guatemalan political activist, artist and member of the follow-up team of Sector de Mujeres, in *Women's Human Rights Net*

As mentioned above, the human rights framework has provided a useful entry point and tool for the implementation of several feminist approaches. By identifying gender-based violence and advocating its removal from the private sphere and the public sphere, and by acknowledging that it is central in all political, social and economic life, it has been possible to elevate the issue and bring it close to the fore of international attention. What is more, this strategy also serves, to some extent, to neutralise the power of the male over the female in what have been unequal power relations. This approach has not only drawn global attention to a global issue, it has galvanised action in varying degrees at national level by eliciting the commitment of states to certain norms and standards, thereby providing legitimacy for local action and efforts to address gender-based violence. The human rights approach has evolved over time and it is undoubtedly the most crucial strategy used by feminists. Initial focus was placed on general universal human rights principles, which implied the protection of all human beings from all forms of discrimination and maltreatment without specific pronouncements

on the human rights of women. This has gradually evolved to include explicit reference and acknowledgement of gender discrimination. A pattern of violence against women was identified and efforts have been made to address this within a human rights framework.

The human rights instruments dealing with women's issues have played important roles in the response to gender-based violence, providing useful entry points for feminists and activists. By arguing that the 'private is public', feminists have sought to demystify the notion that violence against women conducted in the home or family, that is domestic violence, is a private issue. They have used these human rights instruments to challenge abusive behaviour and to hold states accountable for the protection of women and the promotion of their equality. Feminists argue that human rights are non-divisible and non-negotiable and thus, women should own their bodies and be entitled to make decisions concerning themselves, or, at worst, be consulted and not treated as minors or juveniles.

The setting of standards through the establishment of normative frameworks is only one aspect of the strategy to

Switzerland did not grant women the right to vote on the national level until 1971. The last canton to grant women the right to vote at the local level did not do so until 1990.

address gender-based violence. However, it is an important one, which provides legitimacy for all other forms of action that ultimately can lead to culture and attitudinal change among various actors, including the social and political institutions that support this practice. Moreover, it has provided the space for the flourishing of various feminist approaches and activities, which are geared toward reversing the trend of abuse of women by making gender-based violence a public issue.

Gender mainstreaming and affirmative action

The formal mainstreaming of gender is another feminist approach, which has pushed for gender to be discussed by all and not to be seen as an issue that falls only within the domain of women. Since the 1990s there has been an explosion of Ministries of Gender or Women, particularly in the aftermath of the UN Fourth Conference on Women in Beijing. Affirmative action has also been a feminist approach. It is often assumed that increased representation of women in public office, particularly in senior political and decision-making positions will achieve a corresponding increase in political and social action to combat gender-based violence and other forms of discrimination against women.

However, increased representation and numbers is not a guarantee that political action in support of women will increase as women in senior political positions are not necessarily always sensitive to the issues and herein lies an apparent tension between the arguments for gender mainstreaming and gender balance. Supporters of affirmative action believe that at the very least, the presence of more women in political office will make it harder to ignore women and the issues of concern to women. Some countries have taken steps to ensure an increase in the political representation of women in politics. For example, in Rwanda, 49 per cent of parliamentarians are women, the country almost reaching parity of men and women; in

South Africa, the African National Congress (ANC) has a policy of 35 per cent female representation in politics, aiming at 50 per cent female representation. Furthermore, efforts are constantly made to move boundaries as women continue to seek greater representation not just in political leadership, but also in leadership of communities of faith.

These approaches of gender mainstreaming and gender balance are not mutually exclusive. The mainstreaming of gender is in itself a strategy that can ultimately bring about greater representation of women in politics and decision-making positions. Mainstreaming allows for sensitisation across the board and serves to generate a multiplier effect in the effort to address gender discrimination. As discussed further below, another feminist strategy has been training of women in leadership positions, as well as, training of young women for leadership. The combination of this and gender mainstreaming should ultimately bring about gender balance in ways that will achieve positive results for women, rather than a mere increase in numbers without corresponding action.

Research and writing

Feminist writers as well as other writers have conducted extensive research and written on the issue of gender-based violence. Research and written work in this area have focused on several elements. One element is the need to challenge existing notions and definitions of violence. In Africa, women researchers are working to develop theories that challenge traditional roles without antagonising useful

Table 2.1:

Women's political participation in March 2004: Seats in national parliaments held by women (percentage of total)

Country	Percentage of women seating in parliaments
Rwanda	48.8
Sweden	45.3
Denmark	38.0
Finland	37.5
Netherlands	36.7
Norway	36.4
Cuba	36.0
Belgium	35.3
Costa Rica	35.1
Austria	30.6
Germany	28.3
Spain	28.3
Switzerland	25.0
Uganda	24.7
Canada	20.6
United Kingdom	17.9
United States	14.3
France	12.2
New Zealand	12.2
Italy	11.5

Source: UNDP, Human Development Report 2004 (New York: UNDP, 2004), 234-37.

Gertrude Mongella, Member of the Tanzanian Parliament, has been elected the first President of the new Pan-African Parliament in 2004. She is admired internationally for organising the UN Conference for Women in Beijing and for participating in numerous other campaigns for women's rights.

local norms and values. This has entailed, for example, an examination of systems that protected women in traditional African cultures, where there have been taboos around spousal battery and institutionalised child abuse. Similarly, theologians have looked at religious writing through feminist lenses, arguing that all world religions condemn the abuse of women. Oral histories are written to document the achievements of and gains made by women without going back to the drawing board. The feminist agenda requires recording oral history, researching feminist angles and female friendly frameworks. Additionally, some writers have focused on the development of training modules and courses – an equally important factor that will be useful in the sensitisation of a cross-section of actors as well as the education of a future generation and ultimately serve to broaden the constituency of actors working to reverse a pattern of abuse against women.

Education and training

Only through training and continuous sensitisation can the constituencies of actors working to address the issue of gender-based violence be broadened and a multiplier effect achieved. Emphasis has been placed on educating and sensitising society about gender, the rights of women and the need to combat violence against women. This has entailed challenging age-old myths in some societies, which serve to perpetuate violence against women. For example, the rule of thumb in some communities is that beating a woman proves manhood; and that females are the property of the father and will only be released into the hands of the next male, even where this male happens to be an abusive spouse.

One of the methods supported by feminists is the monitoring of school curricula to ensure that they include gender sensitive content. There has also been a campaign for same access to education for boys and girls, so that girls are better skilled and have alternatives, so that they, for example, are able to leave abusive situations. Academic institutions and institutions of higher learning in some countries have equal rights offices to monitor gender bias. This is the case for example in Switzerland, Germany and Sweden, where *crèches* were initiated for female students with children, to enable them to study. Efforts to sensitise public officials on this issue are also continuing in many parts of the world. In several parts of Africa, non-governmental organisations have led the effort to make parliamentarians and other public departments more receptive to gender sensitive approaches. For example, Ugandan police has a central task force for domestic violence. Kenyan Women' Lawyers Association trained and sensitised police on violence against women. Hospitals have trained their staff and social workers to deal with women who are victims of domestic violence.

Law and institutional reform

Passing laws, which protect victims and punish perpetrators, is an approach that is considered critical to success in the campaign to reverse the pattern of violence against women. National laws around domestic violence have been challenged with varying degrees of success in many countries. A lot of work is done with the police to sensitise them to gender-based violence and abuse. We have witnessed modifications in discriminatory laws and practices as seen, for example, in the State of New Jersey and several other states in the US, whereby if the police are called in cases of domestic violence the perpetrator will be arrested even if the woman does not press charges. A woman can take legal steps if she is not provided with the name and contact address of a shelter for abused women. The establishment of these shelters in part a result of campaigns by feminists in the 1970s. Although women's shelters offer refuge for the woman if she leaves her violent environment, some states are pursuing the alternative of enforcing the removal of the man, as opposed to the

A woman attends an educational center in Kabul, Afghanistan. A national campaign to boost girls' education in Afghanistan was launched in 2005. According to reports by UNICEF and the World Bank, 60 per cent of girls under eleven are still not attending school, and girls represent only 35 per cent of those enrolled.

woman. This will ensure that women do not suffer doubly, as women and children are often forced to disrupt their lives and go into hiding from abusive spouses. Other strategies are sought to ensure protection for the victims rather than their abusers. Similarly, laws have been passed against sexual harassment in many countries. Perpetrators of rape are now accountable, and the act of rape in situations of war has now been declared a crime of war. Additionally, feminist activists continue to challenge such myths that women are to blame for rape because of how they are dressed or how they behave.

Notwithstanding some of the tangible progress that has been realised in the area of law and institutional reform, much remains to be done and these practices are not yet widespread in many countries. Thus, activists and feminists continue to campaign for greater legal protection for women, to ensure that there are judicial consequences for perpetrators and those who abuse the laws that protect women. For example, they argue that jail sentences for perpetrators of violence against women are often milder when compared to sentences for other felonies and that there should be efficient court systems to deal seriously with the issue. Governments are urged to recognise the systematic use of violence against women as a strategy of war as seen, for example, in Bosnia and Algeria, and thus ensure adequate measures to protect victims and punish perpetrators; and where relevant, women should be allowed independent asylum status.

Addressing traditional rituals and negative perceptions

In order to eradicate harmful practices such as female genital mutilation (FGM), alternative forms of rituals are being proposed in some cases, so that the tradition of initiating girls into adulthood can still continue without the accompanying act of FGM. This has been possible in communities where the main argument advanced for continuing with FGM is the need to uphold the tradition of initiation for girls, for example in Kenya and Ghana. Similarly sensitisation campaigns are carried out in several places to address negative perceptions of girls and women, such as initially blaming women for HIV/AIDS. The Indian women's movement in Southern India has exposed the caste system especially of the *Dalits* (the untouchable). The movement generated by these groups has increased sensitisation among them and others and this sensitisation came mainly through feminist theology. The struggle for freedom and safety from abuse is in the feminist movement. The feminist movement has unified the *Dalits* with

Political empowerment of women is vital for equal gender policies and gender equality. Herero women queue to vote at a polling station in Windhoek, Namibia.

© Reuters, Sven Torfinn, 1999

other women's movements in India, using diversity and solidarity as a means of changing perceptions.

Feminists have also sought to challenge what is described as the 'feminising of poverty', arguing that women are disproportionately affected in the distribution of resources worldwide. It is estimated that while women do 90 per cent of the work, only a third of all world resources go to women. The feminist approach seeks to promote the understanding that the full participation of women and girls is crucial for the full development of a society.

Part of the feminist approach has been to challenge uncontrolled, widespread pornography, including child pornography and negative images of women. Feminist thought has also encouraged the medical world to revisit other issues including contraception and the use of extremely harmful drugs, such as pills, which might result in women giving birth to handicapped children. On contraception, they argue that women have the right to make decisions concerning their own bodies as well as a right to safe medical attention. In a gradually expanding literature on sexual and reproductive sex, feminists and other writers have drawn attention to these issues among many others.[1]

Ultimately, feminist approaches have converged with other approaches and collectively, they have moved the agenda of women forward although a lot of work remains to be done. It has also become apparent that no one approach is a panacea in the effort to confront gender-based violence. It must be a multi-disciplinary approach and a collective effort at all levels from the local to the national, regional and international levels.

Endnote

1 See D. Cornell (ed), *Feminism and Pornography* (Oxford: Oxford University Press, 2000), G. Dines, R. Jensen and A. Russo (eds), *Pornography: The Production and Consumption of Inequality* (London: Routledge, 1998). See also R. Weitz, *The Politics of Women's Bodies: Sexuality, Appearance, & Behavior* (Oxford: Oxford University Press, 2002), J. Price and M. Shildrick (eds), *Feminist Theory and the Body: A Reader* (London: Routledge, 1999).

Chapter 3

Gender Mainstreaming of Peace Support Operations

'Women's presence [in peacekeeping missions] improves access and support for local women; it makes male peacekeepers more reflective and responsible; and it broadens the repertoire of skills and styles available within the mission, often with the effect of reducing conflict and confrontation. Gender mainstreaming is not just fair, it is beneficial.'

UN Department of Peacekeeping Operations, *Mainstreaming a Gender Perspective in Multidimensional Peace Operations*, 2000

The first UN peacekeepers performed narrowly defined military and technical tasks such as supervising and verifying ceasefires or troop withdrawals, collecting weapons surrendered by demobilised soldiers or patrolling demilitarised zones. Contemporary peacekeepers, in contrast, tackle much more diverse tasks, many of them of a humanitarian nature. They oversaw the transition to independence in Namibia (UNTAG), organised elections in Cambodia (UNTAC), monitored human rights in El Salvador (ONUSAL), facilitated the delivery of humanitarian aid in Bosnia and Herzegovina (UNPROFOR), rebuilt essential infrastructure in Kosovo (UNMIK) and even took over all governmental functions in conflict-ravaged East Timor (UNTAET). In present-day peacekeeping operations, an ever-increasing number of civilian specialists work alongside soldiers, policemen and military observers. A 1960s Blue Helmet visiting the headquarters of a modern peacekeeping operation would experience a veritable culture shock, discovering not only offices labelled 'Force Commander' or 'Situation Centre',

but also doors leading to a Humanitarian Affairs Department, Child Protection Section, Human Rights Unit and Gender Office.

The multidimensional tasks of today's peacekeeping missions are rooted firstly in the 'anarchic' nature of many modern conflicts, where an apocalyptic worst-case scenario might feature uncontrolled and unstructured gangs roaming territories whose governmental systems have collapsed, fighting each other as much as their opponents and the civilian population, and where the driving force is a desire to get rich rather than a thirst for political power. Secondly, the United Nations have realised that rebuilding societies emerging from complex conflicts requires much wider efforts than patrolling a buffer zone for a year and hoping that tempers will cool down in the meantime. The face of modern warfare is not only burned-out tanks and fallen soldiers on the battlefield, but also smuggling of diamonds, drugged child soldiers, starvation of civilians, mass rape and genocide. The conflicts in the Balkans and the Great Lakes region have proven that a sustainable peace requires much more than disarming and supervising soldiers. It needs a multi-faceted response that addresses all sectors of society, not only the military, but also the civilian population, the justice and political system, the economy and educational infrastructure.

As soon as the international community moved beyond a strictly military agenda it was realised that the stakeholders in the peace process consisted of more than male, able-bodied soldiers. Men and women of all ages and educational or professional backgrounds emerged as conflict victims, recipients of humanitarian aid and potential partners in reconstruction efforts. With the emergence of 'civilian peacekeeping', which was more human rights-oriented than military in nature, civil society groups in post-conflict societies started claiming a role in the reconciliation processes and working hand in hand with UN peacekeepers. Women's groups made some of the most vocal claims for better protection, political recognition and an enhanced role in peacebuilding.

The call for women's integration in security decision-making is reflected in a global consensus since 1995 with the Beijing Declaration and Plan of Action from the Fourth World Conference on Women, reiterated by the Agreed Outcomes on Women and Armed Conflict by the Commission on the Status of Women in 1998, accentuated by the Windhoek Declaration and Namibia Plan of Action in 2000 and finally rendered official in the watershed UN Security Council Resolution 1325 on Women, Peace and Security of the same year and further underlined in 2002 Security Council Open Session. Resolution 1325 particularly recognises the importance of the inclusion of women and gender issues in the structures of peacekeeping and peacebuilding in post-conflict regions. It calls on all main stakeholders to integrate a gender perspective in training for peacekeepers, to take action in the protection of women; and to support local women's peace initiatives.

These constant and reinforced declarations were generated by an international awareness that women's specific experience of war, whether as peace actors or victims, provide them with a knowledge base that can only be taken into account adequately by involving women as active and equal partners in peace operations. The UN's policy of gender mainstreaming, defined by the ECOSOC in 1997, provided a framework for integration of gender issues in the concept, design and implementation of peace support operations. This policy is based upon a general conviction that peacekeepers should understand the gender dimensions of post-conflict reconstruction in countries where they serve in order to be able to respond to the specific needs of local populations, and to acknowledge the lives of both men and women, their different needs, interests, priorities as well as to understand how power is shared and used within the communities.

Integrating a gender perspective in peace support operations

The UN's policy stipulates gender mainstreaming as *'the process of assessing the implications for women and men of any planned action, including legislation, policies or programmes, in all areas and at all levels. It is a strategy for making women's as well as men's concerns and experiences an integral dimension of the design, implementation, monitoring and evaluation of policies, and programmes in all political, economic and societal spheres so that women and men benefit equally and inequality is not perpetuated. The ultimate goal is to achieve gender equality.'* [1]

Peace support operations (PSOs) are complex as they include many actors – military and civilians alike and a broad variety of activities. Many organisations are involved in establishing peace support operations – such as the United Nations, the African Union, the OSCE, the European Union and NATO. In this chapter, PSOs are examined from the point of view of the UN. PSO activities range from observer missions, peacekeeping operations, peace enforcement operations, diplomatic

© Keystone, AP Photo, Hidajet Delic, 2003

As the peacekeeping duties in Bosnia were transferred from the United Nations to the European Union, police forces became an integral part of the mission.

activities, peacemaking and peacebuilding, as well as humanitarian assistance, good offices, fact-finding and electoral assistance. The differences of these activities lie in the mandate and type of mission.[2]

Developing a gender perspective in peace support operations is an important challenge that needs to be met. Several approaches to reach this objective can be outlined. The first approach involves the inclusion of gender mainstreaming tools directly into the missions' mandate, which establishes the type and range of activities of the mission. Gender issues should be included in the mandate of a peacekeeping operation as much as humanitarian aid, child protection, political analysis, and military concerns or human rights issues. A lack of concrete directives in the mandate will lead to random implementation of gender issues depending on the importance attributed to them by the head and staff of the mission. Until now, although mandates of peacekeeping operations make reference to the impact of violence on women and girls, none has included a commitment to gender equality as part of a mission's mandate. However, it is interesting to note that currently a few resolutions, for example concerning the Democratic Republic of Congo and the Ivory Coast, are emphasising the importance of integrating a gender perspective in peacekeeping operations, using Resolution 1325 as a framework for action.[3]

The second approach deals with the integration of a gender dimension to all substantial activities of a mission. In the initial phase, it is essential to address gender concerns in needs assessments, planning of a peacekeeping operation and policy development. During the mission, gender perspectives should be incorporated in the instruments used to support the implementation of operations on the ground, such as guidelines and codes of conduct. In the end, the extent to which the gender dimension was integrated throughout the mission must be included in the monitoring and reporting system. It is of utmost importance to integrate gender perspectives in the reports of the UN Secretary-General to the Security Council with the aim of better understanding the different impact of armed conflicts on men and women. These reports should help to better target the missions' programmes and activities by providing a clear picture of the reality in the field. The present practice is far from satisfactory. The UN Office of the Special Adviser on Gender Issues and the Advancement of Women (OSAGI) undertook a study of 264 Secretary-General's reports to the Security Council for the period between January 2000 and September 2003. The aim of the study was to analyse to what extent the reports included gender perspectives, as required by different official documents, particularly the Resolution 1325 (2000). The analysis revealed that 18 per cent of the reports make multiple references to gender concerns, 15 per cent make minimal reference and 67 per cent of the reports make no or only one mention of women or gender issues. The vast majority of the reports citing gender concerns mention the impact of conflict on women and girls, primarily as victims – not as potential dynamic actors in reconciliation, peacebuilding or post-conflict reconstruction.[4]

A third approach to gender mainstreaming lies in dispatching experts on gender issues to missions. Over the past three years, staff working exclusively on gender issues have been assigned to five peacekeeping missions, either as gender advisers or through a human rights entry point such as the United Nations Mission in Sierra

Box 3.1 : Women in peacekeeping operations (PKO)

The UN Resolution 1325 from 2000 declared the necessity to increase women's representation in decision-making and to expand their roles in peace and security issues. Today women constitute approximately a quarter of the total professional personnel in peacekeeping operations (27.5 per cent in July 2004). In PKO five per cent of total staff are civilian policewomen, and about one percent of the total military personnel deployed in international operations are women. Recently, several United Nations member states reported on national initiatives to improve representation of uniformed women (serving both in armed and police forces) in international peace operations (France, Spain, United Kingdom, Australia, Argentina, Malawi, Switzerland). A senior Australian policewoman served as the UN Police Commissioner in Timor-Leste from June 2003 to May 2004.

Civilians (both men and women) in the positions of gender advisers, senior gender advisers and gender focal points are working in Afghanistan, Burundi, Côte d'Ivoire, Democratic Republic of Congo, Haiti, Kosovo, Liberia, Sierra Leone, Sudan, Timor-Leste, Western Sahara, Ethiopia-Eritrea and Georgia. Two out of 27 peace operations are headed by women: the Special Representatives of the Secretary-General to the United Nations Observer Mission in Georgia (UNOMIG) and the United Nations Operation in Burundi (ONUB). There are three women Deputy Special Representatives of the Secretary-General in peacekeeping operations: the United Nations Verification Mission in Guatemala (MINUGUA), the United Nations Mission in Afghanistan (UNAMA), and in the United Observer Mission in Georgia (UNOMIG). Currently, out of 27 operations, two are headed by women - ONUB in Burundi and UNOMIG in Georgia. Three women serve as deputy Special Representatives in the UN Verification Missions in Guatemala (MINUGUA), in Afghanistan and Burundi.

Sources:
UN statistics, at http://www.un.org/womenwatch/osagi/fpgenderbalancestats.htm
United Nations, *Women and Peace and Security*, Report of the Secretary-General, October 2004 (S/2004/814), at http://www. un.org/womenwatch/osagi/wps/sg2004.htm

Leone (UNAMSIL). In general, beyond the specificity of each mandate, gender advisers are responsible for incorporating gender concerns in all the activities of the mission, conducting awareness raising and training on these issues to all staff, including military and civilian personnel at all levels, and to some extent initiating empowerment of local women in view of their inclusion in the peace process and assisting in launching national mechanisms for gender concerns.

Several examples of the work and accomplishments of gender advisers can be cited for illustration. For instance, in the United Nations Organisation Mission in the Democratic Republic of Congo (MONUC), the senior gender adviser developed a two-pronged strategy to ensure that a gender perspective is integrated into the mission's policies and programmes; and to interface with civil society organisations, especially women's groups.[5] In the United Nations Transitional Administration in East Timor (UNTAET),[6] the Gender Unit assisted the East Timorese Women's Network in implementing the Beijing Platform for Action, which emphasised the major issues of concern for Timorese women that needed to be addressed at that time by the transitional administration and the succeeding government. As regards the current United Nations Mission of Support in East Timor (UNMISET), the gender adviser participates in mission-funded programmes for radio and television that address issues such as the campaign on domestic violence. In Sierra Leone, the gender adviser was placed in the Human Rights Unit through an agreement between the UN Department of Peacekeeping Operations (UNDPKO) and the Office of the High Commissioner for Human Rights (OHCHR). The gender adviser created a Women's Task Force of the Truth and Reconciliation Commission to give particular attention to gender-based violence during armed conflict. She also undertook research on war-related sexual abuses, together with an NGO, with a focus on the promotion and protection of women's rights in post-conflict societies.

However, despite the importance of the functions carried out by gender advisers in the field some institutional problems arise regarding their work. To date, gender advisers have regrettably been working without a budget and proper backup from headquarters, thus lacking clarity about their own mandate and feeling isolated without proper and official communication channels. As underlined in the United Nations Development Fund for Women (UNIFEM) Independent Experts' Assessment, *'so far, the range of responsibilities given to gender advisers appears to exceed both their authority and their limited resources. […] Aside from needing adequate staff, gender units need a strategy and plan of action that comes from the highest level, indicating a serious commitment to integrating gender issues in all activities of the mission.'*[7]

© Keystone, EPA Photo, AFPI, Issouf Sanogo, 2001

In some cultures it is impossible for a woman to talk to men about sexual violence. Therefore it is essential to have women peacekeepers and medical personnel. Pakistani UN soldiers of MINUSIL operate a free-treatment hospital in Kailahun, Sierra Leone.

The Department of Peacekeeping Operations' Best Practices Unit is the focal point for gender mainstreaming in peace support operations. Yet, it has neither had the capacity, nor the resources to provide adequate support to the field in the past years. The situation is, however, about to change with the creation of a full-time position for a permanent gender adviser at the DPKO, which was approved by the General Assembly in July 2003.[8] The adviser's responsibilities include, advising the DPKO leadership on gender mainstreaming in peacekeeping operations, co-ordinating gender-related activities in the mission, providing backstopping and policy guidance to the gender advisers in the field as well as liaising with other UN departments and local state and non-state authorities and agencies.

Women peacekeepers:
Do women make a difference?

The added value of women's presence is twofold. First, the presence of an international team of men and women from different cultural backgrounds, working together, sets a positive example for the local population. Good practice of high level female participation was found in the United Nations Transitional Assistance Group in Namibia (UNTAG), as reported by Louise Olsson who described the experience of a female UN peacekeeper on *'how the local population at first tended to project their own gender assumptions on her, believing her to be the secretary of her male colleague rather than his equal. But this changed as the staff member and her male colleague worked together and the population could see that she too had authority and was treated as an equal.'*[9]

Second, evidence shows that female peacekeepers improve access to local populations and enhance the confidence building process between the mission and local communities. In a post-conflict environment, the role of civilian police is crucial in creating an environment where local women feel sufficiently safe to participate in the reconstruction process of their own society. Civilian police play an important role in strengthening the rule of law, training and rebuilding local police forces, restoring an accountable justice system, as well as combating trafficking of women and girls. In environments where local women have been victims of sexual violence perpetrated by militia or military groups, women may be more comfortable talking to other women than to men in uniform. As a Congolese woman confided to the UNIFEM Independent Experts, *'in my culture, it is not common to talk about sex with men, let alone strange men [...] many of the women who were raped like I was can identify the attackers, but it is difficult to report them to the police. We can talk to you because you are women like us. But we can't talk about these things with men. If only we had a female police in MONUC to whom we can report these horrible things that happened to us.'* [10]

Recruitment of women as peacekeepers has, however, produced a debate, which explores the traditional identity and role of women in society. On the one hand, recruiting more women based on the stereotypical assumption that they would be more effective peacebuilders because they are 'naturally' nurturers and care givers would be a big mistake. The 'maternal thinking' ideology tends to keep women in the private realm where working on conflict resolution is just another extension of their domestic chores to which they will return at the end of their mission. On the other hand, refusing to acknowledge women's roles in peace and security on the grounds that they are not capable or interested, is not only a case of social injustice, but also counter-productive in the current multidimensional missions that involve human rights, good governance, gender issues and police training which require a diversity of skills, backgrounds and exposures. The changing nature of peace support operations from traditional military activities to multidimensional aspects including police functions, establishment of rule of law and state administrative structures, monitoring of human rights, and delivering humanitarian aid, provide broader avenues for the participation of women in peacekeeping. There is a need to challenge the limited role of women in peacekeeping missions, which tend to concentrate solely on specific women's issues. Women should be recognised as equals for decision-making positions, the patriarchal division of labour should not be replicated in conflict management by assigning women to the periphery of political and decision-making action. [11]

However, progress in recruiting women in peace operations is slow and recruiting more women as peacekeepers in the ranks of the military and civilian police remains one of the greatest challenges of today's peacekeeping missions (see box 3.1). For the past few years, the DPKO has encouraged contributing countries that provide military contingents and civilian police for the missions to promote the recruitment of women. For instance, the DPKO Civilian Police Division is currently implementing a policy that requires contributing countries to systematically recruit ten per cent female police officers out of the total number of police officers who will be deployed in a peacekeeping mission.

However, difficulties in recruiting women are underscored by the fact that the contributing country retains the final decision in the selection of the people it sends on mission. In addition, societies very often put pressure on women to conform to the traditional division of labour, thus placing women in the dilemma of having to choose between family and mission. Women police officers are less likely to request postings with the UN Civilian Police because of their role as mothers and carers and the length of time required away from their families.

Only a critical mass of women in the ranks of peacekeepers has a chance to break the masculine dynamics of current peacekeeping missions and the 'boys will be boys' mentality that perpetuates stereotype attitudes towards women, which very often lead to cases of sexual abuse and exploitation. It is important to make peacekeepers understand that their own attitude can contribute to insecurity. Although it is difficult to measure the success of a peacekeeping mission, Dyan Mazurana strongly emphasises that 'success' means *'the ability of the operation to meet its mandate, contribute to peaceful resolutions of external disputes, promote human rights education, provide assistance in enabling civil society to develop, and empower the local community in ways that help them reconstruct their lives and society.'* [12] This can only be achieved in a mission that has integrated a gender dimension in its daily endeavours.

As peace support operations extended their mandates in the last decade to cover humanitarian needs, they have become instrumental in post-conflict reconstruction and the establishment of democratic governance structures. In undertaking this challenge the differential impact of armed conflicts on women and girls need to be addressed, inevitably leading to the absolute necessity for the participation of women and gender mainstreaming in all phases of peace support operations. The following field experiences from East Timor, Congo and the UNITAR training programme show the successful incorporation of the gender perspective in these missions as well as their impact in redressing gender discrimination in society, empowering local women and raising gender awareness.

East Timor/Timor-Leste: UNTAET

The United Nations Transitional Administration in East Timor (UNTAET), deployed in 1999 is known to be the first to establish a well-functioning and successful gender affairs unit. Already in the planning phase the integration of gender issues were raised and a prior analysis of the gender situation in East Timor was conducted. It was revealed that aside from specific gender-based violence suffered by women during the conflicts, deep cultural inequalities exist between women and men in East Timor wherein women lack full access to resources, decision-making levels in politics and economic development. As a result, UNTAET's mandate explicitly acknowledged the needs of women by stressing the violence they suffered and their widespread displacement. Furthermore, it expressly identified the inclusion of personnel with appropriate knowledge in gender-related provisions of international humanitarian, human rights and refugee law.[13] This provision in the mandate consequently led to the creation of a Gender Affairs Unit (GAU) in the planning stage of the mission, which was given the task of establishing gender concerns in the design, implementation, monitoring and assessment of the mission.

Under the leadership of UNTAET's Special Representative of the Secretary-General, the late Sergio Viera de Mello, much publicised support to gender mainstreaming was given through public speeches and dialogues with high level personalities, political parties and consultative groups. This was further underlined by UNTAET's media network via newspapers, television and radio programmes and advertisements.

The Gender Affairs Unit (GAU) was established in the Governance and Public Administration section, which was in charge of setting up judicial reform and legal training, civilian police, social services such as health, education, culture, social and labour systems and infrastructure. Therefore, within this framework, it began to address local women to involve them in the process of establishing local governance structures. The implementation of gender concerns was underlined by two key strategies.

The first strategy was UNTAET's dynamic assistance and support in including women in East Timor's governmental and administrative composition. It accomplished an exemplary participation of women in the first elections of the East Timor parliament in 2001, the Constituent Assembly, tasked to draw up the constitution of the independent East Timor. UNTAET established quotas, provided media support to women, created networks among women's organisations and advocated the inclusion of women's concerns in party dialogues. Together with the United Nations Development Fund for Women (UNIFEM) it organised workshops and training sessions on political and technical skills for potential women candidates to the elections of the Constituent Assembly. These efforts have led to women representing 27 per cent of the total seats – considered a critical mass and one of the highest in Asia-Pacific. The new elected executive government in 2001 included two appointed women to the ministerial portfolios of Justice and Finance, one as Vice-minister for Internal Administration, two advisers in the Office of the Chief Minister, one for the Promotion of Equality and the other for Human Rights. The critical participation of women in politics led to the inclusion of women's rights in the constitution of East Timor promulgated in 2001 where equality between men and women in all aspects of life and non-discrimination on the grounds of gender were incorporated.

The second strategy was the fight against domestic violence. Together with the United Nations Population Fund (UNFPA), a two-year major campaign on domestic violence was launched. The incidence of domestic violence has reached a menacing magnitude due to the culture of violence and militarism engendered by the long-lasting civil wars. The campaign involved raising public awareness through the media and training journalists, legal counsellors and police staff.

A special police unit called the Vulnerable People's Unit was created and staffed by women to undertake cases of gender-related crimes. In addition, a police officer was appointed a gender focal point at each district police. In the end, women made up over 30 per cent of the East Timor police service. These achievements meaningfully created an environment of safety for women to report their grievances. In June 2003, a female UN Police Commissioner was appointed in the succeeding UN Mission of Support in East Timor (UNMISET), representing the first woman to lead a UN police force.

Democratic Republic of Congo: The Office of Gender Affairs in MONUC

The Office for Gender Affairs (OGA) for the United Nations Organisation Mission in the Democratic Republic of Congo (MONUC) was operational in mid-March 2002. OGA consists of a senior gender adviser, a gender affairs officer, two United Nations volunteers, one local administrative assistant and one local secretary. The senior gender adviser is accountable to the Special Representative of the Secretary-General. It is extremely important for the OGA to be located at the top management level to be taken seriously and have enough authority to carry out its mandate. The OGA has a twofold strategy. Within the mission, it raises awareness on gender and builds the capacity of UN mission staff, international and national, and mainstreams gender into their work. Using Resolution 1325 (2000) and MONUC's Resolution 1445 (2002), it disseminates information on gender issues throughout the mission, to the military, civilian police, and national and international staff with the aim of promoting a better understanding of the nature of gender mainstreaming. The OGA had to put special efforts into integrating a gender perspective in the disarmament, demobilisation, and reintegration programmes of the mission; the OGA has ascertained the level of preparedness of transit centres set up for the demobilisation of

A French soldier searches a woman for weapons in Bunia, Congo. Having women in a peacekeeping contingent allows them to effectively search women without offending them and their traditions.

former combatants. The OGA has been very concerned with the situation of the so-called Congolese 'wives' of foreign soldiers who withdrew from the Democratic Republic of Congo after an occupation of several years. When the Ugandan soldiers were ordered to go back home, they received instructions to leave behind 'wives' and children. A large number of these 'wives' and children have been spotted in Gbadolite, in northern Congo, where they live in harsh conditions, with the sole assistance of a local NGO.

All new peacekeepers receive training on gender issues as part of their induction course when they arrive in the mission. The training revolves around explaining the roles of men and women in post-conflict situations, and gender and power, that is emphasising that women bear the brunt of the conflict and may have to exchange sex for food in order to feed extended families. A context-specific Code of Conduct is distributed to peacekeepers during the session. One innovation was the introduction by the OGA of a gender sensitive checklist to assist military observers in their monitoring functions so that they see women as untapped sources of information. Very often peacekeepers will talk to male leaders of the community who hold the official power at local level, thus overlooking women's groups that are less visible.

In Resolution 1493 (2003), the Security Council, reaffirms the importance of a gender perspective in peacekeeping operations in accordance with Resolution 1325 and, for the first time, calls on MONUC to increase the deployment of women as military observers as well as in other capacities. This is very timely. At the beginning of August 2003, there were only 114 female military personnel in MONUC, out of a total of 17,500 (including military observers and contingents) and only three female police officers out of a total of 90. Although the percentage of international women heads of units and sections has increased, women mostly fill administrative positions at the lowest level.

Outside the mission, the Office of Gender Affairs is to facilitate the involvement of local women, groups and networks in the peace process including reconstruction, reconciliation and rehabilitation and other processes leading to a sustainable peace.

As part of its outreach activities, the OGA has supported the involvement of Congolese women in the peace process and the Inter-Congolese Dialogue. Although the OGA functions without a proper budget, it is trying to find creative ways of working on capacity-building with local groups of women through constant interaction with women, consultations, meetings, field trips, organisation of debates around Resolution 1325, and distribution of relevant documentation that help women build up their own advocacy strategy. Congolese women have been very active in the promotion of peace in their country. They requested their participation in the official peace talks and the integration of gender issues on the agenda of the negotiations, and they demonstrated their preparedness to participate in the creation of a transitional government. They have used MONUC's *Radio Okapi* to explain to the general public the importance of having women involved in post-conflict reconstruction and disseminate information on the different stages of the peace process.

By the end of 2003, despite all their efforts, the participation of Congolese women in the transitional government is minimal with only seven per cent representation. Although Article 51 of the Transitional Constitution states that women have a right to significant representation in national, provincial and local institutions, there is a gap between the political level and the status of women in Congolese society. Although Congolese women are present in the transitional government and vigilant about the promotion of their rights, they will have to mobilise to a greater extent for the next elections, which are expected to be held in 2005. They will have to launch a nation-wide campaign to reach out to rural women in remote areas, inform women about their rights, promote female candidates, and formulate a platform for political action.

The Office of Gender Affairs is also raising concerns about the situation of widespread sexual violence against women in eastern DRC. A recent survey conducted by a local NGO[14] in the district of Kabinda showed that a large number of young women suffered from post-traumatic stress disorder following multiple rapes by armed groups. Elsewhere in the country similar stories are heard, emphasising the urgent need for protection of women and girls against sexual violence. Initiatives are taken by local NGOs like the Centre Olame in Bukavu that provides health assistance and counselling to rape victims. These initiatives need to be strengthened and supported by the international community because they are rooted in the reality of the conflict and are working on a confidence-building process with the victims on a daily basis. The NGO workers know the needs of the local population, but lack resources for a sustainable action. The issue of sexual violence has to be tackled so that Congolese women will be able to participate in the different stages of the reconstruction process of their society and not marginalised and ostracised because they have been sexually abused.

The OGA will remain committed to its mandate and hopes to get more staff and resources in the near future to be able to open a branch in eastern DRC, thus strengthening its out reach activities and further promoting the need for integrating a gender perspective within the mission.

UNITAR's training programme:
An eye-opener that may change the face
of peace support operations

One of the actions that the UN Security Council in Resolution 1325 called for was gender training, not only for soldiers and

Training on the special needs of women and children during peace support operations is important in the success of peacebuilding and reconstruction.

police serving in UN peacekeeping operations, but also for their civilian staff – human rights and humanitarian experts, personnel managers, logisticians, administrative and support staff. UNITAR, the Geneva-based United Nations Institute for Training and Research, prides itself on a flexible, efficient, needs-based, down-to-earth and hands-on approach to training. It identifies problems and designs solutions to address these problems through training and fills training gaps not yet covered by other providers. Peacekeeping training by the United Nations and by UN member states is a classic case because it has, for many years, focused on soldiers and civilian police, neglecting the ever-growing number of civilian staff. To address this deficiency, and in close co-operation with the UN Department of Peacekeeping Operations, a UNITAR training programme was developed as an open-ended initiative to make peacekeeping operations more sensitive towards the needs of women and children and, ultimately, more efficient and successful in fulfilling their mandates. In the first three years of its existence, UNITAR has organised sixteen training events for peacekeeping operations in Bosnia and Herzegovina, Congo (DRC), East Timor, Eritrea, Ethiopia and Kosovo. The programme is funded by the Geneva Centre for Security Policy[15] and Ted Turner's United Nations Foundation.

In an acknowledgement of the work conditions of peacekeepers, programme implementation takes the form of short (normally three-day), intensive training seminars that are held in the mission area of peacekeeping operations. The seminars are highly participatory, with group exercises, discussions and a focus on 'learning from each other'. They are, therefore, limited to 30 participants, but it has become standard practice to organise several identical seminars in a row to train a higher number of peacekeeping staff and keep the costs per participant low. If a peacekeeping operation comprises a Civilian Training Cell, Gender Office or Child Protection Unit, staff from these departments will work closely with UNITAR in designing and implementing the training events. The seminars are advertised to all civilian staff members and most are heavily oversubscribed. UNITAR emphasises that its seminars provide sensitisation on topics that are relevant to all staff – men and women, junior and high-level staff, persons who work directly on gender or child protection, but also (or perhaps particularly) all others. UNITAR advocates mixed audiences of expatriates and locally hired personnel since these two staff categories work alongside each other in peacekeeping operations, but are often trained in separate groups. Some non-peacekeepers who work for other UN agencies, for NGOs or for governmental institutions in the target country are also normally invited to attend the seminar. Separate, short 'wrap-up briefings' are often organised for the senior leadership of the peacekeeping operation, who have the ultimate authority to make gender and child sensitive decisions. These briefings summarise the seminars' main messages, reflect on participants' feedback, offer further opportunities to exchange views and generate recommendations for concrete action.

Each seminar includes an introduction to the situation of women and children in conflict and post-conflict situations, analyses applicable law and describes relevant activities of the UN and other stakeholders. UNITAR adapts the curriculum to each new mission so that it is tailored to the target country and reflects the reality on the ground. Evidently, particular attention is paid to gender and child sensitive policies of peacekeeping operations and their activities that affect women and children. UNITAR does not shy away from using the seminars to make concrete recommendations for a mission's work or to call upon UN staff to behave in a gender sensitive way. The typical three days are filled with individual sessions that address a certain topic and can last from half an hour to half a day. If UN agencies, NGOs or inter-governmental organisations with gender or child protection mandates are active in the mission area, UNITAR makes every effort to involve them. Often these agencies and their staff will take over responsibility for a certain topic while other training modules are taught by experts flown in by UNITAR. Co-ordinating lecturers from all over the world to converge on a particular training event is never an easy task, and especially the enthusiastic, but overworked humanitarian staff in a hectic peacekeeping environment frequently falls victim to the phenomenon of 'having bitten off more than they can chew', but the mixture of local and foreign trainers is a factor that greatly contributes to the success, practical relevance and well-functioning cross-fertilisation of this programme.

Some gender experts have expressed conceptual reservations against lumping women and children together, fearing that this is an old-fashioned approach that would indirectly reinforce stereotypes about two social groups that 'belong together', with women reduced to their traditional role – raising children. Others objected to the term 'special needs', warning that this might support the image that women are victims who need assistance, ignoring the multifaceted roles that women play in situations of conflict. UNITAR felt, however, that its approach reflected the reality in the United Nations and increased the likelihood of its training programme to become acceptable and successful. Firstly, whether one likes it or not, throughout the UN system women and children are still often seen as one vulnerable group. Secondly, both women and children have remained invisible to peacekeeping planners and peacekeepers for far too long. While there is now a forceful drive to mainstream gender throughout all aspects of UN's work, the organisation is still a long way from mainstreaming the concerns of children in all its activities. The widespread view prevails that UNICEF cares for children and thus no other part of the UN system needs to worry about them. Thirdly, one must recognise that women and children are two

groups of persons who do need particular humanitarian protection in times of conflict, very often simultaneously. This view may be simplistic, but even those peacekeepers who have never had a minute of gender or child protection training can easily understand and sympathise with it. Lastly, and perhaps most importantly, the curriculum of UNITAR's training seminars tirelessly promotes the message that the role of women and children in a society is precisely something that must change and evolve, and that women (and even children, to a certain extent) are not only passive aid recipients, but must be empowered, that is be encouraged and taught to play an active role in the political, reconstruction and peacebuilding process in post-conflict environments.

Each seminar closes with an evaluation session and participants also complete a detailed questionnaire. Genuine gender or child protection experts sometimes find the seminars too broad and basic, but appreciate them as a refresher course and often take an active role by sharing their own knowledge and experiences with their fellow participants. Peacekeepers with little pre-existing knowledge in the field (the vast majority of the audience), however, praise how useful the seminars are in familiarising them with a new subject, often describing them as a veritable eye-opener. Participants regularly state that with their newly acquired knowledge and awareness they would henceforth be able to fulfil their professional tasks in a more gender and child sensitive manner, without requiring additional time or resources. Notwithstanding the inevitable traditionalist who still views peacekeeping as a frontier-watching job for men in uniforms and blue helmets, acceptance of the UNITAR seminars as a timely and useful initiative is almost universal. Participants regularly recommend that such training ought to be provided to all staff (civilian and military) working in peacekeeping operations, ideally immediately after the person's arrival in the mission, and that states should include gender and child protection in their curricula of national pre-deployment training. UNITAR hopes that as trained participants move on to other missions and as the information disseminated in the seminars trickles down to other staff the growing recognition that UN peace operations must put women and children on their agenda will change the reality of peacekeeping in the decades to come.

Endnotes

1 The United Nations Economic and Social Council (ECOSOC) Agreed Conclusions 1997/2. A further explanation of gender mainstreaming is formulated by the Office of the Special Adviser on Gender Issues and Advancement of Women (OSAGI). *'Mainstreaming situates gender equality issues at the centre of policy decisions, medium term plans, programme budgets, and institutional structures and processes. Mainstreaming entails bringing the perceptions, experience, knowledge and interests of women as well as men to bear on policy-making, planning and decision-making.'* OSAGI, *Gender Mainstreaming; An Overview* (New York: United Nations, 2002), at http://www.un.org/womenwatch/osagi/pdf/factsheet1.pdf, 1.

2 For instance, on one hand, a peacekeeping operation is agreed upon by parties to the conflict and carried out under the UN Charter, Chapter VI concerning peaceful settlements of disputes. A multinational military, police, civilian personnel and humanitarian actors who execute or monitor the execution of agreements on the management of conflicts (such as a ceasefire) and their resolution and/or guard the distribution of humanitarian relief play an important part in it. On the other hand, peace enforcement operations are executed under Chapter VII of the UN Charter, related to the actions with respect to threats to the peace, breaches of the peace, and acts of aggression. It involves coercive actions in order to bring an end to the conflict. Lastly, recent multidimensional operations have involved a greater expansion of activities to include nation building missions such as taking charge of the transitional administration of a country, monitoring human rights, developing institutions to guarantee the rule of law and democracy building.

3 United Nations, *Security Counsel Resolution on the Democratic Republic of Congo*, UN Document S/RES/1493/2003 (28 July 2003) and *Security Counsel Resolution on the Democratic Republic of Congo*, UN Document S/RES/1445/2002 (4 December 2003); *Security Counsel Resolution on the Côte d'Ivoire*, UN Document S/RES/1479/2003 (13 May 2003).

4 Office of the Special Adviser for Gender Issues and Advancement of Women, *An analysis of the Gender Content of Secretary-General's Reports to the Security Council* (January 2000 – September 2003) (7 October 2003), 1.

5 See 'Democratic Republic of Congo: The Office of Gender Affairs in MONUC' in box 3.2 Gender Mainstreaming: Experience from the field.

6 UNTAET was established in 1999 to assist East Timor in its transition to independence; it was phased down in 2002 and replaced by UNMISET to ensure political stability through the post-independence phase.

7 E. Rehn and E. Johnson Sirleaf, *Women War Peace: The Independent Assessment on the Impact of Armed Conflict on Women and Women's Role in Peace-Building* (New York: UNIFEM, 2002), 68.

8 In August 2004, Comfort Lamptey, former Senior Gender Adviser of the UN Human Rights Commission, was appointed for the position.

9 L. Olsson, 'Gender Mainstreaming in Practice: The United Nations Transitional Assistance Group in Namibia', in L. Olsson and T. L. Tryggestad, *Women and International Peacekeeping* (London: Frank Cass Publishers, 2001), 103.

10 E. Rehn and E. Johnson Sirleaf, *Women War Peace*, 70.

11 V. Ogenusanya, 'Peacekeeping Programme at ACCORD', *ABANTU for Development, The Gender Implications of Peacekeeping and Reconstruction in Africa* (Mombassa: ABANTU Publications, May 2000),17.

12 D. Mazurana, 'International Peacekeeping Operations: To Neglect Gender is to Risk Peacekeeping Failure', in C. Cokburn and D. Zarkov (eds), *The Post War Moment: Militaries, Masculinities and International Peacekeeping* (London: Lawrence & Wishart, 2002), 41-50.

13 United Nations, *Security Counsel Resolution on East Timor*, UN Document S/RES/1272/1999 (25 October 1999).

14 MONUC, 'Gender: Le lourd héritage des viols après la guerre', *MONUC Bulletin No. 84* (9 October 2003), 17.

15 Geneva Centre for Security Policy (GCSP) is an international foundation created under the framework of Swiss participation in the Partnership for Peace.

Chapter 4

Legal Protection of Women

'Pak Yong Sim was taken at the age of 17, from a village in North Korea and brought to Pyong Yang. Then she was transported to Nanjing in China, then to Shanghai. She travelled with the troops all the way to Singapore and then to Burma where she stayed in a comfort station in the mountains of Burma for two years. She was forced to have an abortion and she was never thereafter able to have children. She was released from the prisoner of war camp in 1946 and finally returned home. She served seven years as a comfort woman.'

Indai Sajor, Speech in the Asia Pacific War Conference in Vancouver, 2003

Laws are a collection of rules imposed by authority and agreed to by society to allow freedom while enforcing order. Essentially positive in society, they can also be the source of discrimination against women. For example, women may be prevented from legally owning or inheriting property, opening bank accounts, conducting business or even driving. Women may have to give up their nationality upon marriage or lose custody of their children upon divorce. They may be punished - even killed - with impunity for real or perceived sexual impropriety. A woman's word may carry less weight than a man's in a court of law and women may find it difficult or impossible to obtain legal redress for violence committed against them. The limitations to full citizenship that they sometimes face (for example, the need for male endorsement to transact business) increase their insecurity and make them vulnerable to abuse.

Of the international instruments aimed specifically towards the protection of women, reference must be made to the International Convention on the Elimination of Discrimination against Women (CEDAW), which includes gender-based violence, in its definition of discrimination.[1] At regional level, the Inter-American Convention on the Prevention, Punishment and Eradication of Violence against Women prohibits *'conduct, based on gender, which causes [...] physical, sexual or psychological harm or suffering to women.'* [2] Among the soft-law instruments, the most notable is the UN Declaration on the Elimination of Violence against Women, which brings together all prohibitions against the personal integrity of women in peace and in armed conflict.

International human rights law prohibits torture and ill-treatment, as well as arbitrary detention both of men and women, in particular through the International Covenant

Women stand up for their rights. Aung San Suu Kyi was awarded the Nobel Peace Prize in 1991 for her nonviolent resistance for democracy and human rights in Myanmar. In Asia and the world over she has become a symbol of the struggle for freedom from violence and oppression.

redress for violations of the law and it reinforces their right to participate in processes that ensure peace and security when countries emerging from conflict revise their existing constitutions.

International humanitarian law is the body of law that applies in times of armed conflict and protects persons not or no longer taking an active part in hostilities and regulates means and methods of warfare. These rules protect both women and men, either as combatants (through limitations on the means and methods of warfare), or persons *hors de combat* (captured combatants including the sick and wounded), or as civilians. One of the most fundamental principles of international humanitarian law requires that parties to an armed conflict must distinguish between civilians and combatants at all times and must not direct attacks against civilians and civilian objects.

The principal instruments of international humanitarian law today are the four Geneva Conventions of 1949 and their two Additional Protocols of 1977. The first Additional Protocol is applicable in situations of international armed conflict, and the second in non-international armed conflicts. There are also numerous conventions restricting or prohibiting the use of specific weapons, for example, the 1997 Convention on the Prohibition of the Use, Stockpiling, Production and Transfer of Anti-Personnel Mines and on their Destruction.[4]

International humanitarian law is binding on states and armed opposition groups, as well as troops participating in multilateral peacekeeping and peace enforcement operations if they take part in hostilities.

International humanitarian law provides women with a 'two-tiered' legal protection regime. Women are afforded both *general* protection on the same basis as men, and *special* protection reflecting their particular needs. These specific provisions for women aim to provide protection with regard to their particular medical and physiological needs, which are often - but not always – related to their childbearing role and considerations of privacy. Further, women are accorded protection against sexual violence, which is categorically prohibited in all its forms.

Other bodies of law may also be applicable in situations of armed conflict, principally human rights law, refugee law and national law. These bodies of law may offer important complementary protection. Thus, for instance, the law, which applies to all persons prescribes that the commission of torture cannot be justified at any time, including in armed conflict, or under any circumstances, including under superior orders.[5]

In addition to the existence of rules and the need to respect them, mechanisms for enforcing rights and redressing violations are also of crucial importance. In this respect, recent developments, both at the national and international level,

on Civil and Political Rights. In addition, many soft-law standards exist to prevent torture and ill-treatment, and minimise arbitrary arrest and detention.[3] International refugee law, by laying down the principle of *non-refoulement* in the 1951 Refugee Convention relating to the status of refugees, reinforces the protection of refugees against torture by preventing states from sending persons to a place where they are at risk. The convention of the Organisation of African Unity, as well as, the Cartegena Declaration have broadened the scope of *non-refoulement* to persons fleeing a country's occupation, internal conflict and large-scale violations of human rights. In numerous applications for asylum, torture as a legitimate reason for seeking asylum has included gender-based torture as persecution aimed specifically at women. Moreover, the Convention against Torture (1987) enshrines the principle that a state cannot send a person to a country where that person may be subjected to torture.

In situations of and after conflict, the law protects women against the effects of hostilities and a wide range of atrocities committed by belligerents, it guarantees them in the prosecution of those responsible for war crimes are a very important step forward in the fight against impunity, not only because the perpetrators are actually brought to justice, but also because of the general deterrent effect it is hoped such developments will have.

It was the Second World War, which brought a realisation that appalling atrocities against women should never again be permitted. Yet, it took several decades before the experience of female victims had been recognised in international criminal tribunals. In 1946, the International Military Tribunal of Nuremberg and the International Military Tribunal of the Far East located in Tokyo were established to try German and Japanese government officials for violations of international law committed during the war. The charters of the tribunals established jurisdiction on crimes against peace, war crimes and crimes against humanity. The Allied Control Council Law No. 10 (CCL10) signed by the US, USSR, UK and France in 1945, which provided the legal basis to prosecute individual war criminals in Germany, specifically listed rape under Article 2 as a crime against humanity. Yet, neither the Nuremberg nor the Tokyo Charter explicitly mentioned any form of gender-based crime within their jurisdiction despite evident cases of rape and sexual violence perpetrated during the war.[6] Some argue that the definition of crimes under Article 6 of the Nuremberg Charter used an expansive language enough for gender-based violence to be inferred, however, these broad terms did not lead to any prosecution or charges built on gender-based violence. As a result, the experience of the post-Second World War tribunals were meagre in advancing justice for female victims of violence as they formally failed to account for rape and sexual violence and to provide redress.

In the 1990s, conflicts erupted within fragile states, among ethnic and national rivalries with the particular use of rape and other forms of gender-based violence as a war strategy. The use of rape has been transformed from the traditional view of a collateral and inevitable excess of war to a public and political affair. Acting under Chapter VII of the UN Charter with respect to threats to peace and security, the UN Security Council's Resolution 808 (1993) and Resolution 955 (1994) established ad-hoc International Criminal Tribunals for the former Yugoslavia (ICTY) and Rwanda (ICTR) respectively. In terms of recognition of gender-based crimes, progress has been achieved in these tribunals as the statutes of the ICTY in Article 5 and ICTR in Article 3 specifically enumerated rape as a crime against humanity. The ICTR under Article 2 prosecuted serious violations of common Article 3 of the Geneva Conventions, which protected civilians not taking part in the conflict. It specifically mentioned sexual violence as *'outrages upon personal dignity, in particular humiliating and degrading treatment,*

© Keystone, EPA Photo ANP Pool, Ed Oudenaarden, 2001

Carla del Ponte, the Chief Prosecutor for the International Criminal Tribunal of Rwanda and former Yugoslavia, has become a symbol of justice for the victims of war. Her unwavering determination for enforcing the rule of law has shed hope for ending impunity.

rape, enforced prostitution and any form of indecent assault.' The ICTY defined rape according to the so-called 'Foca indictment', which was the first to prosecute rape as torture and to consider other forms of sexual violence such as forced nudity and sexual enslavement as inhuman treatment. In Foca, a village in south-eastern Bosnia and Herzegovina, which in April 1992 was taken over by Serb forces, Muslim and Croat inhabitants were arrested, killed and beaten. Women were subjected to torture, rape and detained in houses that served as brothels for soldiers.

The ICTR essentially recognised rape and sexual violence as an instrument of genocide. The first prosecution of this type was that of Jean-Paul Akayesu, the mayor of Taba commune in Rwanda where in 1994 Tutsis were killed and women subjected to sexual violence. The trial chamber stated *'with regard to … rape and sexual violence, the chamber wishes to underscore that they constitute genocide if committed with the specific intent to destroy, in whole or in part, a particular group, targeted as such. These rapes resulted in physical and psychological destruction of Tutsi women, their families and their communities. Sexual violence was a step in the process of destruction of the Tutsi group – destruction of the spirit, of the will to live, and of life itself.'*[7]

The statutes and jurisprudence of the two *ad hoc* tribunals have been very important in developing the law protecting women in situations of armed conflict, particularly with regard to sexual violence. The use of sexual violence in wartime – whether used as a method of warfare or for any other reason – is now recognised as a serious violation of international humanitarian law.[8] Having laws and holding perpetrators accountable for their violation is a fundamental part of what makes societies function. This is as important in times of war as in times of peace.

These past experiences have led to the landmark establishment of the International Criminal Court (ICC) on 17 July 1998 in Rome by 160 nations, its statute entered into force on 1 July 2002. On 11 March 2003, eighteen judges, seven women and eleven men were elected and took the oath. The event was hailed a watershed for the universality of human rights with the global recognition of women as full subjects of human rights in international criminal justice. Certainly, the above precedents contributed to the increased international awareness of the linkage between gender-based violence and international peace and security, leading to the ground-breaking codification in the ICC Statute of rape and other forms of sexual violence among international crimes. The ICC possesses jurisdiction on all persons aged eighteen and above and holds them criminally liable without distinction in their capacity as government officials, whether head of state or government or a member of parliament.[9] Furthermore, military commanders and superiors are held legally accountable for criminal offences perpetrated by forces under their effective command or authority and control.

The International Criminal Court marks an important achievement in integrating gender concerns in international justice through numerous provisions. First, gender balance was recognised for judges within Article 36 (8) that requires *'fair representation of female and male judges'* who possess *'legal expertise on specific issues, including but not limited to, violence against women and children.'* These conditions also apply to the staff of the Office of the Prosecutor and the Registry. In addition, based on the experience of the ICTY and ICTR, the ICC has included gender sensitive procedures to ensure that victims are protected and treated correctly. For example, a Victims and Witnesses Unit was established within the registry, which applies protective measures and security arrangements, including counselling and other appropriate assistance. It particularly includes staff with expertise in trauma, including trauma related to crimes of sexual violence. During the trial, victims and witnesses to crimes involving sexual violence are particularly guaranteed protection, for example, they are allowed to give testimony in a courtroom closed to the public.

The legal protection of women is a central goal of human development as affirmed by the Millennium Development Goals set by 189 governments at the United Nations Millennium Summit at the dawn of the new century. Comprehensively considered, the above described legal framework offers adequate protection to women in peacetime, as well as in times of armed conflict, if only it is duly applied. With the protection afforded to women in conflict by humanitarian law and the additional coverage offered by international human rights law, international refugee law, and international criminal law, it might seem as if the issue is settled. However, despite recent signs of progress, rape 'remains a war crime which is difficult to condemn', and there are a number of challenges to women's realisation of their rights. These include harmonisation of international law with local law, the conflict of international law with social and cultural norms, lack of political will to apply international law and, more importantly, the ignorance of women about their rights, particularly in poor urban and rural areas. In order to have an empowering impact, the appropriate laws should be accompanied by activities to enhance women's legal literacy and effective participation in decision-making. Hopefully, with these current legal developments, not only will the gravity and type of atrocities employed in future conflicts, as well as the means and methods of conflicts be impacted, but also impunity for gender-based violence should significantly diminish.

The case of the former 'comfort women' in Asia during the Second World War continues to haunt the international community for its failure to give proper attention to their demands for justice and accountability from the Japanese government. Civil society has taken on the issues and organised a war crimes tribunal that was established in Tokyo in December 2000 and uniquely addressed state and individual accountability under international and humanitarian law. However, the application of almost all the legal principles from the judgements of the tribunal go beyond the cases of the 'comfort women' and can also be extended to women victims of war in the former Yugoslavia, Rwanda, East Timor, Columbia, Sierra Leone, Liberia, South Africa, Vietnam, Cambodia, Iraq and Afghanistan whose search for justice continues to this day. It is for this reason that we have much to learn from the Tokyo Tribunal judgement and the implementation of its recommendations.

The Women's International War Crimes Tribunal for the Trial of Japan's Military Sexual Slavery was held in Tokyo from 8-10 December 2000 and handed down its judgement in the Hague on 4 December 2001. The tribunal heard the testimonies of survivors, experts, perpetrators and the legal arguments of the prosecutors. It took a decade to organise the tribunal with ground work in twenty nations across five continents. Around nine countries from the Asia Pacific region, as well as the Netherlands took centre stage, representing more than 200,000 women who were sexually violated. It was the first time that an international war crimes tribunal was organised to specifically hear cases of sexual slavery and sexual violence perpetrated against women. It was organised as an addendum to the International Military Tribunal of the Far East in 1946, as the latter failed to prosecute the cases of the former 'comfort women.'

The organisers were motivated by the conviction that the failures of the state or obscure accountability for such crimes against humanity must not be allowed to silence the voices of survivors. It was established to redress the historic tendency to trivialise crimes against women, particularly sexual crimes. 64 survivors from the victimised countries of North and South of Korea, the Philippines, Indonesia, China, Taiwan, East Timor, and the Netherlands attended the proceedings seeking justice, so long denied them. The tribunal heard the testimonies of 'comfort women', legal experts, psychologists, historians, and two former Japanese Imperial Army soldiers who are members of an anti-war organisation and who testified to the existence of the comfort station system and admitted their personal participation in rapes.

Voluminous evidence were presented by the victimised countries, which included historical documents and facts, soldiers' memoirs, pictures of former comfort stations and women 'working' in them, Japanese Imperial Army documents on the rules and obligations of these stations, officials' statements and results of historical research. It was an overwhelming presentation of ten years of hard work and commitment by the advocates, activists, lawyers and the survivors. The testimonies of the 'comfort women' accused not only the conduct of Japan during wartime, but also its failure to accept responsibility after the Second World War ended. Women's stories confirmed that the policy of sexual slavery in comfort stations violated international and humanitarian law and women's human rights.

Survivors of sexual slavery, perpetrated by the Japanese Army during the Second World War. The courage of such survivors to end their silence has mobilised Korean and other Asian women to seek justice, a necessary step to rebuild their lives.

The stories of the 'comfort women' substantiated that their enslavement was a systematic, orchestrated policy, emanating from the highest level of the Japanese government and that Japan's crimes against them did not end with the dissolution of the comfort station system, but continue today in the form of Japanese denials and evasion of responsibility. The women demanded that Japanese responsibility did not rest only with the government or the military of the time, but also extended to the Japanese citizens who condoned, and later ignored, their sexual oppression.

To come forward after more than five decades of silence to demand recognition and justice cost the 'comfort women' a great personal sacrifice. In many cases, it was the first time that their families had heard about the fate of these women, and they had mixed emotions of anger and shame. Many of the women lived alone in isolation and poverty, some of them longing to forget the past. However, their courage changed the profile of the international human rights movement's understanding of sexual slavery and violence against women in war.

The tribunal's judgement recommended that the government of Japan fully acknowledges its responsibility for the establishment of the 'comfort system', and that it issues a full and frank apology to the victims and survivors, as well as compensate them properly. Moreover, the government was recommended to establish a mechanism for the thorough investigation into the system of military sexual slavery and allow for public access and historical preservation of materials, and consider the establishment of a truth and reconciliation commission that would create a historical record of the gender-based crimes committed during the war, transition, occupation and colonisation. Furthermore, the government should recognise and honour the victims and survivors through the creation of memorials, museums and libraries dedicated to their memory.

It was the case of the 'comfort women' that brought the language of 'sexual slavery' to the halls of the United Nations, during the UN Commission on Human Rights in Geneva in 1993. UN Special Rapporteur on Violence against Women, Rhadika Coomaraswamy, in her report to UN Commission on Human Rights strongly asserts that no treaty - such as those negotiated between Japan and the victimised countries at the end of the war - can be viewed as a compensation to the former 'comfort women', who were victims of sexual slavery, a crime totally disregarding human rights.

The Tokyo Tribunal's judgement in 2000 is an important legal document, but more significantly it gave a sense of justice to the 'comfort women' who survived the ordeal. Many of them will not ever know that finally the crimes committed against them have been acknowledged by the international community. The judgement is a living document that will guide the struggle against impunity of sexual violence and slavery making states and non-state actors responsible for their crimes during wartime.

Sources:

The Women's International War Crimes Tribunal 2000 for the Trial of Japanese Military Sexual Slavery, *Summary of Findings and Preliminary Judgement* (12 December 2000).

Transcript of Oral Judgement, delivered by the Judges of the Women's International War Crimes Tribunal on Japan's Military Sexual Slavery (The Hague, Netherlands, 4 December 2001).

Yoshimi, Yoshiaki, *Comfort Women: Sexual Slavery in the Japanese Military During World War II* (Columbia: Columbia University Press, 2001).

Endnotes

1 Committee of the Convention on the Elimination of All Forms of Discrimination against Women, *General Recommendation No. 19* (1992).

2 Inter-American Commission on Women, *Inter-American Convention on the Prevention, Punishment and Eradication of Violence against Women* (Belém do Pará: IACVAW, 1994), at http://www.oas.org/cim/English/Convention%20Violence%20Against%20Women.htm

3 See United Nations, *The Protection of All Persons under any Form of Detention or Imprisonment,* UN Document 43/173, (December 1988).

4 *Convention on the Prohibition of the Use, Stockpiling, Production and Transfer of Anti-Personnel Mines and on their Destruction* (1997); *Convention on Certain Conventional Weapons* (1980).

5 Aside from being prohibited by the International Covenant on Civil and Political Rights, the UN Convention against Torture sets out state obligations to prohibit, prevent, repress and redress torture. Regional human rights treaties also prescribe its prohibition, namely the European Convention for the Protection of Human Rights and Fundamental Freedoms, the American Convention on Human Rights, and the African Convention on Human and Peoples' Rights. Other instruments worth mentioning are the European Convention for the Prevention of Torture and Inhuman or Degrading Treatment or Punishment and the Inter-American Convention to Prevent and Punish Torture and the Inter-American Convention on the Forced Disappearance of Persons.

6 For example there were 200,000 'comfort women' detained in rape camps by the Japanese army (see box 4.1).

7 International Criminal Tribunal for Rwanda, *Prosecutor v. Akayesu,* Judgement, Case No. ICTR-96-4-T, §731-732 (2 September 1998), at http://www.ictr.org/default.htm

8 ICRC, *Mémorandum sur les Violations Commis au Cours du Conflit Armé dans l'ex-Yougoslavie* (3 December 1992).

9 *International Criminal Court Statute,* Art. 26, Exclusion of jurisdiction over persons under eighteen; Art. 27, Irrelevance of official capacity.

Chapter 5

The UN Security Council Resolution 1325: A Watershed in the History of Women's Defence of Peace

'Resolution 1325 holds a promise to women across the globe that their rights will be protected and that barriers to their equal participation and full involvement in the maintenance and promotion of sustainable peace will be removed. We must uphold this promise. To achieve the goals set out in the resolution, political will, concerted action and accountability on the part of the entire international community, are required.'

UN Secretary-General Kofi Annan,
Report of the Secretary-General on Women, Peace and Security, 2004

On 31 October 2000, the Security Council unanimously adopted the landmark Resolution 1325 calling for the active participation of women in the processes of peacemaking and peacebuilding worldwide. This resolution was the culminating point of a long journey undertaken by women's organisations, NGOs and the United Nations system.[1] This resolution focuses on the impact of conflict on women, but specifically on women in the situation of war rather than peace. The most important outcome of the resolution is that its operative paragraph urges governments to include women in the peace process as happened recently and most importantly in Iraq, Afghanistan, Sri Lanka and Sierra Leone. According to this resolution member states, UN agencies and others, must act to ensure that gender issues are accounted for in all aspects of conflict prevention, peacekeeping and post-conflict reconstruction. If fully implemented, this resolution would place women at the centre of peace and security matters in all countries. Unlike some recent UN Security Council resolutions, this resolution is likely to have a far-reaching influence on the political participation of women for a long time to come. After years of efforts by a few committed NGOs including the Women's International League for Peace and Freedom (WILPF),[2] this resolution has suddenly given rise to a proliferation of discussions among policymakers, and has become a focus of seminars and conferences across many regions. Women are slowly recognising that

Shirin Ebadi was awarded the Nobel Peace Prize in 2003 for her courage in fighting for democracy and human rights. As an activist and the first female judge in Iran she has led numerous reforms in family law, inheritance legislation and criminal justice.

the contents of Resolution 1325 cannot easily be ignored by governments while conflicts and violence among countries and communities increase at a rapid rate.

There exists a vast literature on women's link to the peace process in various documents and treaties since the establishment of the United Nations in 1945.[3] For more than half a century, equality between men and women has been recognised and affirmed by the United Nations Charter (26 June 1945) and Article 25 of the Universal Declaration of Human Rights (10 December 1948). In that period of history very few women participated at the highest level of decision-making nationally or internationally. For this reason it is all the more noteworthy that the United States' first lady at the time, Eleanor Roosevelt, championed the cause of women during and after the Second World War. However, it is less well known that during the negotiations preceding the adoption of the Universal Declaration on Human Rights, it was the woman delegate from India who put forward an amendment to Article 25, adding another dimension to the list on equality of rights. To different forms of discrimination such as ethnic origin, colour, religion, and belief, the term sex was included.

For a long time the United Nations recommendations, decisions and standards assumed that roles, needs and concerns of both men and women were similar or the same and there was no differential impact in the development process based on gender. In the 1960s when the decolonisation process continued in the UN Trusteeship Council, the equality of rights between men and women became a controversial issue in international discussions and national campaigns. The first resolution specifically protecting women and children in emergency and armed conflict was adopted by the General Assembly on 16 December 1966 and its operative paragraphs (4 and 6) recognised women as victims that need to be protected and helped rather than participants in negotiating their own security. In the struggle for peace, national liberation and independence, women made enormous contributions and sacrifices in countries that were colonised even when equality of rights between women and men was not on the agenda of international conferences or the General Assembly. A large network of formations, groups and organisations were slowly and surreptitiously evolving to promote the concept of equality to persuade governments that women in the economy and society should not be seen only as beneficiaries, but as agents of development and peace. The newly independent countries recognised and incorporated equality clauses in their constitutions.

In 1972, an NGO, the World Council of Churches, proposed the idea of declaring an International Women's Day. This proposal culminated in the preparations and holding of the first UN World Conference on Women in Mexico in 1975. During the preparations of this conference, the background document presented to the world leaders, added to the concept of equality the words 'and their contribution to development and peace'. Equality, development and peace thus became the three core themes of the decade for women. One of the core points made in that document, later discussed by representatives of several countries, recognised that women play multiple roles as peacemakers in the family, community, nation and the world. More importantly, among other recommendations, the Mexico Plan of Action called for greater representation of women in international fora that included peace and security issues. The turning point occurred when the General Assembly adopted the Convention on the Elimination of All Forms of Discrimination against Women (CEDAW) on 18 December 1979. Ten years later in 1989, after the Second Conference on Women took up its substantive issue to raise the status of women in economic and political life, a strong link was made to peace in the debates. The final report entitled Copenhagen Programme of Action established a rationale between the achievement of peace and women's participation at decision-making levels. However, the plan provided conceptual links between political and economic life and between peace and women's rights.

Between 1982 and 1985, women's movements in several countries followed up and campaigned on the issues of equality, development and peace separately and together concluding that they were interdependent. National seminars in Asia and Africa linked the three concepts and women's networks gained new insights on the core themes of the UN Decade for Women, namely 'equality, development and peace'. It was not until the third UN World Conference on Women in Nairobi (15-16 July 1985) that a collective plan of action for women at the political levels of decision-making was debated, in which many more governments took part and arrived at a consensus on the contribution of women to the world economy. This involved political controversy in negotiating and re-negotiating the eleven paragraphs of the Nairobi Forward Looking Strategies, which were specifically concerned with women and peace. It may be recalled that there was a serious ideological competition between the two super powers on the different roles women played in socialist and capitalist countries. The UN negotiations on the final document were triangular among the spokespersons of the countries of the developing world, the centrally planned economies and the free market economies. These complex, ideologically charged negotiations took place over a period of two years in Geneva and New York. Several times as the Cold War escalated and the question of peace remained an ideological issue between the 'free world' and the socialist world, research on women and peace became marginalised in the UN system of agencies and organisations. However, the Copenhagen Plan of Action concluded that peace and women's rights 'were interdependent'.

In the 1990s, when the series of UN conferences on children, environment, and human rights were planned, it became clearer that women continued to suffer disproportionately as victims of violence in all conflicts among nations, ethnic groups, civil wars and in their own households. This global problem was reflected in the UN Declaration to Eliminate Violence against Women based on research and analysis of a large number of countries across different regions. About the same time, the Vienna Program of Action adopted after the World Conference on Human Rights on 12 July 1993, specifically addressed the *'situation of women in armed conflict including systematic rape that occurs as an integral part of these conflicts since wars began.'* Two years later, it was the Fourth World Conference on Women in Beijing (4-15 September 1995), which picked up the political complex issue of linking women with peace initiatives once again, but this time raised it to the higher level of the advancement of women. The Beijing Platform for Action recognised the

Kenyan environmentalist Wangari Maathai was awarded the Nobel Peace Prize in 2004 for sustainable development, gender equality, democracy and peace. Her Green Belt Movement has mobilised women in planting 30 million trees in the past 30 years, a successful strategy for empowerment and development at the grassroots level.

leading role that women have played and continue to play in the international peace movement. For the first time, a sub-chapter of the Beijing Platform for Action listed specific strategies to increase women's participation at all political levels including in governments and international institutions. The main strategy included reducing excessive military expenditure, promoting non-violent conflict resolution, fostering a culture of peace and providing assistance and training to refugees and displaced women.

After the Beijing conference, which empowered women in political and economic life in 1995, the disastrous war in Bosnia once again proved that systematic rape was a weapon of war. Powerful evidence gathered by a large number of women's organisations and the European Union Women's lobby provided empirical evidence to support legal change in international law. Later, it was the war in Kosovo that further gave dramatic evidence of mass rape as an international crime, the reality of which continued to be ignored by international conventions, especially by the lack of an explicit reference from the existing 1949 Geneva Conventions. An enormous struggle of lobbying by women's organisations made it possible for the Statute of the International Criminal Court to incorporate a specific clause defining rape as a weapon of war and an international crime against humanity.

During the 42nd Session of the UN Commission on the Status of Women in 1998, it was becoming obvious that specific and special political action needed to be taken by governments to address the needs of women during armed conflict.[4] The report of this session remained on the shelf for a long time due to lack of co-ordination among UN agencies and organisations.[5] When the Security Council adopted a resolution on the protection of Civilians in Armed Conflict (17 September 1999), its operative paragraph for the first time urged governments to implement a gender perspective on humanitarian assistance. The intensity and degree of violence against women meant that they continued to be seen as a population in need of protection, but not as active agents who were capable of direct involvement in the discussions on peace and security wherever conflicts occurred. Women's organisations worldwide continued to lobby for greater visibility of women and raised issues such as systematic sexual slavery by the Japanese military in the Second World War and systematic rape during the genocide in Rwanda. It was a remarkable achievement for the struggle of women's organisations that the Rome Statute of the International Criminal Court under the guidance of the Women's Caucus for Gender Justice (now called Women's Initiatives for Gender Justice) included these issues in the definitions of crimes against humanity.

Despite these achievements, when a comprehensive review on UN peacekeeping was incorporated in the Windhoek Declaration, considered by the General Assembly on 3 May 2000, once again women's contribution to peace was ignored as an international issue. During the proceedings, in statements made by several governments, it became obvious that women were being deprived of the possibility of playing a legitimate role in the peace process and the peacekeeping efforts of the United Nations system. Whatever subject was discussed whether operations, mandates, leadership, planning, recruitment or training, the role of women was visibly missing in the discussions, gender was mentioned only in a marginal way without context. The Windhoek Declaration could be considered a turning point in women's struggle to become an integral part of peacebuilding and peacekeeping. The declaration persuaded women's organisations, NGOs and some sympathetic governments to consider a new strategy to promote the inclusion and participation of women in UN peace operations.[6]

The diplomats from Namibia were particularly sensitive to the point that the document on peacekeeping operations, the Windhoek Declaration, was negotiated in their country where years of armed conflict made it politically essential for women to be involved at all levels of government. As a result, of campaigning and lobbying internationally, a working group on women and peace was established in New York. The members of this group included Amnesty International, the Hague Appeal for Peace, the Women's Commission for Refugee Women and Children, International Alert and Women's International League for Peace and Freedom. Their concerted efforts finally succeeded, for the first time, in lobbying for an open session of the Security Council on women, peace and security. In October 2000, when Namibia was elected as the Security Council President, the United Nations Development Fund for Women (UNIFEM) put forward the draft of the now famous Resolution 1325. Its objective was clear, women should participate at all negotiating levels whenever the protection of women and girls during armed conflict is determined, debated and decided. The last paragraph of the resolution notes that the UN Security Council will 'remain actively seized of the matter'. This means that the issue will not be dropped from the Security Council agendas in the near future. What an achievement by the civil society!

Implementation of the resolution: Different UN practices

Since the adoption of the resolution in October 2000, a number of political initiatives have been taken by women's organisations to analyse its operative paragraphs and adopt strategies based on different realities where the conflicts originate. In 2002, a WILPF project on Peace Women, after extensive research, profiled over 52 initiatives worldwide that are currently organised by women on conflict prevention, peacebuilding, refugees, reconstruction, rehabilitation, disarmament, demobilisation,

Irene Khan, Amnesty International Secretary General, is promoting Amnesty's campaign to stop violence against women.

transitional justice, HIV/AIDS in the context of war, peace education and violence against women.[7] These initiatives taken by UN, NGOs and women's organisations need to be closely analysed and followed to acquire a new understanding and political insight into the scope and significance of the resolution in conflict zones. This would contribute towards drafting a new strategy to ensure that women are present in the peace processes at the highest political level with top representatives of governments.

For illustrative purposes some initiatives have been selected below, which reflect different approaches towards involving women by the United Nations, governments and civil society.

The UN system:
Organisations and agencies

There are two important implications of Security Council Resolution 1325. The first relates to the statistical increase of women in existing UN institutions and field operations. This is an integral part of formulating additional rules within the UN system to include the gender dimension. Increasing the number of women at all levels of decision-making, particularly the top jobs relates to the prevention, management and resolution of conflicts at national, regional and international levels of decision-making. This policy action includes the appointment of more women at higher levels such as special representatives and in field based operations among military observers and civilian police.

It is not surprising that Resolution 1325 has been tested in the two most recent international conflicts, Afghanistan and Iraq. It is the continuing process of peacebuilding and reconstruction that makes Iraq an important case study on women's involvement. The first politically significant Security Council Resolution 1483, adopted in May 2003, urges the Iraqi people to form *a representative government based on the rule of law that affords equal rights and justice to all Iraqi citizens without regard to ethnicity, religion or gender.'* Before the Iraq resolution was adopted, four women participated in the negotiations that were held in Bonn and were nominated as members of the interim government in Afghanistan, 2002. Similarly in Southern Iraq, two women were selected to represent different women's organisations in talks leading to the reconstruction of Basra. When the members of the governing council were selected in Iraq, four women were named in May 2003 and that makes the practical implication of the resolution even more complex. The requirement to include women's groups in actual peace processes, currently undertaken by different groups of countries, is linked to a very significant paragraph of the resolution, which makes it obligatory on governments to involve women when political negotiations and the peace process

In her capacity as Director of UNICEF, Carol Bellamy was a keynote speaker at the 6th International Security Forum in Montreux, Switzerland. She promoted a world 'fit for children'.

is being launched by different bilateral entities and not multilateral mechanisms through the UN system. The low number of representation of women in Afghanistan was highly criticised by several women's organisations. However, the fact that women were nominated was considered to be a positive step towards advancing the implementation of Resolution 1325.

The UN Secretary-General's report on Women, Peace and Security (October 2002)

This report[8] has spelled out the different steps that need to be taken by governments in order to *protect* women during conflicts. The preliminary findings of the report were supported by global studies on the impact of armed conflict on women and girls, the role of women in peacebuilding and the gender dimension of peace processes and conflict resolution. What is the status of peacekeeping missions and their efforts to include women in the peacebuilding process? This subject area has not been adequately researched and there are very few general conclusions to be drawn from the existing data. The importance of involving women in peacekeeping missions is to ensure that all civilian personnel receive similar training and that the awareness on HIV/AIDS is included in the training before the military and civilian police is employed in a country. The Secretary-General has emphasised that Iraqi women were *'a powerful force for peace, reconstruction and stability, who should be empowered and ensured the opportunity of playing the rightful political and economic role.'* This report was prepared by the late UN Special Representative to Iraq, Mr. Sergio Vieira de Mello, who developed contacts with a wide variety of Iraqi leaders, especially with Iraqi women.

United Nations Development Fund for Women

UNIFEM is the lead agency, which has published a report on the impact of conflict and war on women and children taking into account a number of countries and working in partnership with local NGOs and women's organisations. In a series of interviews in selected countries where women were victims of extreme violence, the experts recorded their experiences and learnt first hand the real problems at ground level. This report consolidates an enormous amount of material from which some very novel and important recommendations for policy action are made. The extreme suffering of women and children during conflict and often the lack of timely humanitarian assistance raise political issues which need to be picked up by policy or legislation in the country concerned. The role of the international humanitarian agencies is also crucial at different stages of the conflict. The International Labour Organization (ILO) and the International Committee of the Red Cross have also undertaken surveys and studies on the impact of conflict on women and the need for humanitarian assistance in crises.

Steps taken by different authorities

The European Parliament organised a public hearing on Iraq, the aim of which was to invite Iraqi women representatives to the European Commission and the UN to support the need for involving women in the reconstruction of the country. On 1 October 2003, in this hearing, the UN Security Council Resolution 1325 was discussed in detail and the necessity for women in Iraq to have equal access and opportunities to rebuild their country was emphasised.

Palestinian Women's Affairs Minister Zahira Kamal, right, and Israeli former Knesset member Naomi Chazan, left, were awarded the 2005 Prize for Freedom and Human Rights. They have been instrumental in building bridges for peace through dialogue and reconciliation via women's voices.

Occupying Authority in Iraq: During the transitional period when a 24 member governing council was formed in Iraq, the US-led coalition leaders announced that three of the members of the council would be women from diverse ethnic and religious backgrounds. An Iraqi women's conference held on 8 July 2003 consisting of social activists, lawyers and physicians, discussed different aspects of the future Iraqi constitution and gender mainstreaming.

Ghana Peace Talks: During the Accra Peace Talks on Liberia held in Ghana, a significant statement was made by women under the title 'the Golden Tulip Declaration'. This declaration, adopted on 15 August 2003, stated that women should be included in all the existing and proposed institutions, executive, legislative and judiciary, and within all structures involved in the process of peacebuilding. The declaration specifically underlined that there should be greater participation of women in peacekeeping missions as well as in the disarmament, demobilisation and reintegration processes. It was suggested that women leaders who were observers at the talks should be made full delegates and that there should be 50 per cent representation of women in the transitional leadership or government.

Initiatives by the Civil Society: A remarkable number of meetings, seminars and conferences have been recently organised on the role of women in post-conflict Iraq. From all over the world, women's organisations have sent messages to women in Iraq regarding the vital role women should play in rebuilding their country. For example, a statement by the NGO Working Group on Women, Peace and Security, a coalition that monitors Resolution 1325 advocated women's equal participation in peacebuilding and reconstruction on 20 May 2003. Another organisation called Women for Women International circulated pages from the diaries of its President, Zainab Salbi, based on interviews with Iraqi women and men documenting war casualties, the impact of religious extremism and the presence of the American military. She also presented her testimony before the US Senate, which addressed a number of issues including the point that women should be considered core participants in the reconstruction process and included in all governmental and non-governmental sectors.

The Woodrow Wilson International Centre on Conflict Prevention organised a meeting in Washington on 21 April 2003 for two days, which included US policy makers, international and national NGOs to discuss the role of Iraqi women in the transition from war to peaceful reconstruction. The finding and conclusions of the April meeting has been distributed to various women's organisations and NGOs nationally and internationally. Its main focus is on winning the peace and enhancing women's role in the reconstruction of the country ravaged by war.

The International Women's Commission (IWC) consists of various NGOs including Women's Centre for Women's

Aid in Counselling and Bat Shalom. They have collaborated on an initiative to address the historical absence of women from formal negotiations and to ensure women's active participation in the Israel-Palestinian peace processes. Their basic aim is to be recognised by the UN, EU, US and Russia quartet in order to reframe the divisive issues, sustain political will and popular support for negotiations in order to build bridges between antagonistic sides to move towards sustainable peace.

A communiqué was published by the Niger Delta Consultative Meeting (7-12 August 2000) held under the auspices of International Alert. The communiqué spells out the harmful practices conducted by the multinationals in the exploration of oil and the subsequent devastation on the environment, which has totally destroyed their livelihood. Their communities are suffering from the consequences of leakage of the crude oil, which has devastated their daily lives.

Box 5.1 : A global coalition of women defending peace

Suzanne Mubarak, left, President of the Women's International Peace Movement and First Lady of Egypt, hosted the international conference Women Defending Peace, together with the Head of the Swiss Federal Department of Foreign Affairs, Micheline Calmy-Rey.

In 2004 a global coalition was born from the international conference 'Women Defending Peace' co-chaired by Suzanne Mubarak, President of The Suzanne Mubarak Women's International Peace Movement, and Micheline Calmy-Rey, Federal Councillor, Head of the Federal Department of Foreign Affairs of Switzerland. The conference was held from 22-24 November 2004 at the ILO headquarters in Geneva, Switzerland. Women and men from all over the world contributed to this unique event, which was attended by some 500 representatives of non-governmental organisations, Nobel Peace Prize laureates, academics, jurists, and representatives of international organisations and governments.

The purpose of the conference was to provide a forum for the free exchange of experiences and information among participants representing different cultures and religions, and yet who all share a common goal: finding ways and means of enhancing peace – and strengthening women's roles in security processes. Not only were best practices highlighted but also a wide range of efforts in overcoming obstacles were shared such as mobilisation through social movements, reforming political processes, or economic reconstruction. The conference enabled the building of alliances for consolidated and strategic action among participants to be taken on specific priority issues. For this purpose a three-fold aim of the Global Coalition – Women Defending Peace were detailed in its Action Plan:

- Involve women systematically in all stages of conflict prevention, peace making, peace building and peace keeping, including decision making at all levels;

- Reject violence in all its forms and promote peace, where peace is more than the absence of war, but is a state of equal rights, rule of law, mutual trust, participation, involvement and well –being of all; and

- Protect women and children, especially girls, in times of war, occupation and conflict against all forms of violence and exploitation.

The Coalition invites women's groups and other organisations, as well as individual women and men, to combine their respective skills, capacities, best practices, lessons learned and resources to achieve those goals.

Sources:
Extract from the official *Conference Report on Women Defending Peace*, 2004 *International Conference Women Defending Peace*, Official documents and speeches at http://www.dcaf.ch/wdp

---

Political implications of the resolution

The emergence of Resolution 1325 at the highest level of the UN is the culmination of several years of protest and planning by women's organisations in several countries that continually attacked the political vacuum at leadership level. Official recognition and acceptance of women as heads of state, such as president or prime minister, has been slow since the 1970s. The first breakthrough occurred in Sri Lanka when a woman prime minister was elected through the democratic process. Member states of the United Nations have elected 27 out of 190 women as heads of state. In 2001, the number of women heads of state, increased to 29, but it is worth remembering that in a 1995 UN photo, taken before the Beijing Conference, there were only ten female faces at the international meeting. As a result of Resolution 1325 issues relating to women in war zones are receiving attention at the highest levels, but the lack of institutional infrastructure to consult women at the local and international level among women's and NGO's groups has become a political obstacle. There are gaps and weaknesses in the resolution, which need to be closely analysed in the UN system and incorporated in the mainstreaming efforts of its various agencies and organisations. For example, for effective implementation and monitoring, the mandates of all peacekeeping and peace support operations should be amended to include protection of women and consultation with them. There is also an urgent need to appoint senior gender advisers who have decision-making powers and who can be part of field operations and fact-finding missions. There needs to be, in addition, mechanisms of accountability for peacekeepers who violate and exploit

local populations particularly women. In addition, a database of experienced women peacemakers need to be constructed in order to bring their voices and experiences from the field to the United Nations. There are three types of actions that remain at the level of the UN, governments and NGOs. The Secretary-General should be requested to consult with an NGO advisory committee in the process of drafting a report. The advisory committee needs to undertake a global consultation with women's groups to analyse their views and projections. The NGOs need to continue to monitor the implementation of this resolution at national and international levels in order to advocate stronger action for peacebuilding.

Box 5.2 : The European Union combating gender-based violence

© Keystone, EPA, Georg Lisonski, 2004

Former Austrian Minister of Foreign Affairs, Benita Ferrero-Waldner, is the current EU Commissioner of External Relations and Neighbourhood Policy. The fight for women's rights has always been high on her agenda and she continues the EU's commitment to improve women's status in society.

The first resolution of the European Parliament on violence against women, dating back to June 1986, deals with trade in women, domestic violence, sexual harassment, prostitution, and pornography. In April 1989, a resolution on prostitution and trafficking in human beings was adopted in the plenary, followed, in September 1993, by a resolution on trade in women. Following the UN Beijing Platform of Action in September 1997, the European Parliament, in close co-operation with the European Women's Lobby (EWL), addressed the issue of domestic violence and asked the European Commission to organise a

campaign for zero tolerance of violence against women and asked the member states to criminalise it in their national laws. In the same year, while reporting to the European Commission on trafficking in women for sexual exploitation, the European Parliament suggested several measures including the creation of an assistance system for victims, awareness raising campaigns in non-EU countries, and common actions of member states aimed at implementing the international commitments made at the ministerial conference in The Hague in April 1997. In that report it was also suggested to consider the suspension of any EU bilateral agreements with those non-EU countries, which would not be amenable to measures against trafficking. Recently it has been recommended to the European Council and the European Commission that a clause in trade agreements should be included providing sanctions in cases of serious and repeated violations of women's rights.

Already in 1997 an EU policy to stop trafficking in women called the 'STOP Programme' was established to support research, data collection and training, but its scope was rather limited. Therefore, the European Commission proposed another programme, the 'DAPHNE Initiative', which provides help to non-governmental assistance programmes for victims. In 2000 trafficking in human beings was defined by EU law as a crime, and a violation of fundamental human rights. Trafficking in human beings is prohibited by the Charter of Fundamental Rights of the European Union and there is an increasing recognition among the member states that trafficking is not a separate issue, but a cross-national crime linked to a wide scope of illegal activities by numerous actors operating in various states. Moreover, it requires a variety of measures in order to be combated, including emphatic legal protection to all individuals, the criminalisation of sexual violence in all its forms, law enforcement and judicial co-operation, working out preventive measures, as well as steps to ensure adequate protection of and assistance to the victims. The European Commission has been pushing for the adaptation of national criminal laws and procedures in member states. It has presented the European Council with two legislative proposals on common definitions and penalties and on criminal procedures of the member states. The EU Council of Ministers adopted a framework decision on ▶▶

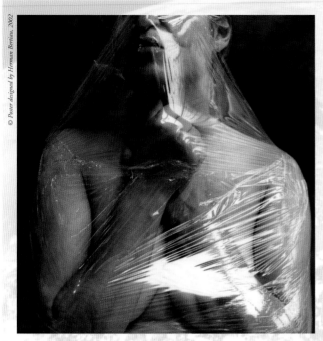

Between 1999 and 2002 the European Commission conducted a campaign to raise awareness on violence against women. The campaign accentuated domestic violence as the most widespread form of violence against women.

Furthermore, the reports submitted to the EU bodies dealt with female genital mutilation, promotion of women's rights in the Mediterranean countries, and with gender aspects of prevention and resolution of armed conflicts. The importance of the role of women in conflict resolution began to be sensitised in the European Parliament and the European Commission during wars in former Yugoslavia. The reports of women raped and sexually abused have raised the question of how to avoid such crimes in future. The most concrete achievement is represented by the support the EU has given to the Rome Statute and the International Criminal Court. The EU also contributed to an alternative negotiation process started by groups of prominent Israeli and Palestinian women. In some other countries torn by recent conflicts efforts have been made to put in place a gender responsive framework. In Afghanistan, for instance, a gender adviser has been deployed since the initial assessment mission in 2002, and certain funds have been allotted to women's empowerment projects.

Despite all the efforts in last two decades the struggle against gender-based violence has not yet been fully 'institutionalised' within the EU system, and resources have been too modest to confront the problems seriously. Sexual violence, domestic violence, and trafficking for sexual exploitation are all on the increase in Europe. The numerous tools and measures described above have been too marginal, often too partial and the responsibilities of them scattered through the different EU departments. In many cases, violence has failed to be fully recognised as 'gender specific', which in practice makes prevention or redress more difficult. The Beijing Platform of Action from 1995 recognises that violence against women, wherever it takes place, is produced by the imbalance in the power relationship between women and men, this idea has been repeated many times including in several EU political declarations and documents. Yet, true progress in redressing violations of women's rights has still to be made.

Sources:
Commission Communication to the Council and the European Parliament on Trafficking in Women for the Purpose of Sexual Exploitation (COM(96)0567 - CA-0638/96).
AGIS Program, at http://europa.eu.int/comm/justice_home/funding/agis/funding_agis_en.htm
DAPHNE II Program, at http://europa.eu.int/comm/justice_home/funding/daphne/funding_daphne_en.htm

combating trafficking in human beings in July 2002 and a resolution for initiatives to fight trafficking of women in particular was passed in November that same year. In September 2002 an expert group on trafficking in human beings was set up. Two new programmes were developed in order to raise more funds:

- AGIS, which replaces the STOP Programme, is aimed at better evaluating existing policies, and exchanging good practices in order to improve co-operation between the EU member states and candidate countries to combat human trafficking.

- DAPHNE II, for 2004-2008, was established to prevent and combat violence against children, young people and women and to protect victims and groups at risk.

Endnotes

1 See list of organisations dealing with women's rights in this volume for some selected organisations active in women's role in building sustainable peace under categories 'Women and War/Armed Conflict', 'Human Rights', and 'Peacebuilding and Peacemaking' etc.

2 The Peace Women Project originated in the UN New York WILPF Office. Its former Director, Felicity Hill, and her team researched the subject and placed it on the international agenda.

3 The information on the historical background on Resolution 1325 has been summarised from Sara Poehlman-Doumbouya (WILPF consultant to the Peacewomen Project), WILPF, *Women and Peace in United Nations Documents: An Analysis* (New York: 2002).

4 See United Nations, *Nairobi Forward Looking Strategies* (New York: UN, 1985).

5 K. Annan, *The Causes of Conflict and the Promotion of Durable Peace and Sustainable Development in Africa* (New York: UN, 1998).

6 See United Nations, Panel on UN Peace Operations, UN Document A/55/305-S/2000/809 (New York: UN, 21 August 2000).

7 WILPF, *Initiative to Address Women's Active Participation in Post-conflict Reconstruction in Iraq*, at http://www.peacewomen.org/resources/Initiativeslist.html

8 Report s/2002/1154, at http://www.un.org/womenwatch/osagi/wps/sg2002.htm

Key Reading Part IV

Books

K. Annan, *The Causes of Conflict and the Promotion of Durable Peace and Sustainable Development in Africa* (New York: United Nations Department of Public Information, 1998).

K. D. Askin, *War Crimes against Women: Prosecution in International War Crimes Tribunals* (The Hague: M. Nijhoff, 1997).

B. Bedont, *International Criminal Justice: Implications for Peacekeeping* (Ottawa: Canadian Department of Foreign Affairs and International Trade, 2001).

A. Callamard, *Investigating Women's Human Rights Violations in Armed Conflicts* (London: Amnesty International, 2001).

International Alert, *Gender Mainstreaming in Peace Support Operations: Moving beyond Rhetoric to Practice* (London: IA, 2002).

A. Lyth, *Getting it Right: A Gender Approach to UNMIK Administration in Kosovo* (Stockholm: Kvinna till Kvinna, 2001).

D. Mazurana and E. Piza Lopez, *Gender Mainstreaming in Peace Support Operations: Moving beyond Rhetoric to Practice* (London: International Alert, 2002).

E. Rehn and E. Johnson Sirleaf, *Women, War and Peace: The Independent Assessment on the Impact of Armed Conflict on Women and Women's Role in Peace-Building* (New York: UNIFEM, 2002).

M. Schuler and S. Kadirgamar-Rajasingham (eds), *Legal Literacy: A Tool for Women's Empowerment* (New York: Widbooks, 1992), at http://www.wld.org/ll.html

J. A. Tickner, *Gender in International Relations: Feminist Perspectives on Achieving Global Security* (New York: Columbia University Press, 1992).

United Nations, *Women, Peace and Security* (New York: United Nations, 2002).

United Nations Department of Peacekeeping Operations, *Mainstreaming a Gender Perspective in Multidimensional Peace Operations* (New York: UNDPKO, 2000).

United Nations Development Programme, *Human Development Report 2002* (New York: UNDP, 2002).

United Nations Office of the Special Adviser for Gender Issues and Advancement of Women, *An Analysis of the Gender Content of Secretary-General's Reports to the Security Council* (New York: United Nations, 7 October 2003).

United Nations Office of the Special Adviser on Gender Issues and Advancement of Women, *Gender Mainstreaming: An Overview* (New York: United Nations, 2002).

Articles and papers

G. DeGroot, 'A Few Good Women: Gender Stereotypes, the Military and Peacekeeping', in L. Olsson and T. L. Tryggestad, *Women and International Peacekeeping* (London: Frank Cass, 2001).

O. Louise, 'Gender Mainstreaming in Practice: the United Nations Transitional Assistance Group in Namibia', in L. Olsson and T. L. Tryggestad (eds), *Women and International Peacekeeping* (London: Frank Cass, 2001).

D. Mazurana, 'International Peacekeeping Operations: to Neglect Gender Is to Risk Peacekeeping Failure', in C. Cokburn and D. Zarkov (eds), *The Post-war Moment: Militaries, Masculinities and International Peacekeeping* (London: Lawrence & Wishart, 2002).

M. McKenna, 'Sins of the Peacekeepers', *Sunday Herald* (11 July 2002), at http://www.sundayherald.com/25914

Network, *The UN Women's Newsletter*, Vol. 6, No. 4 (October, November, December 2002).

C. N. Niarchos, 'Women, War and Rape: Challenges Facing the International Tribunal for the Former Yugoslavia', *Human Rights Quarterly*, 17 (Baltimore: John Hopkins University Press, 1995).

V. Ogenusanya, 'Peacekeeping Programme at ACCORD', *ABANTU for Development: The Gender Implications of Peacekeeping and Re-construction in Africa* (Mombassa: ABANTU Publications, May 2000).

J. Peck, 'The U.N. and the Laws of War: How Can the World's Peacekeepers be Held Accountable?', *Syracuse Journal of International Law*, Vol. 21(1995).

Programme in Law and Public Affairs, *Princeton Principles on Universal Jurisdiction* (Princeton: Princeton University Press, 2001), at http://www.law.uc.edu/morgan2/newsdir/unive_jur.pdf

M. Rees, 'International Intervention in Bosnia-Herzegovina: the Cost of Ignoring Gender', in C. Cockburn and D. Zarkov (eds), *The Post-War Moment: Militaries, Masculinities and International Peacekeeping* (London: Lawrence & Wishart, 2002).

B. Sorensen, *Women and Post-conflict Reconstruction: Issues and Sources*, WSP Occasional Paper No. 3 (June 1998), at http://www.wsp-international.org/op3/op3-04.htm

Swedish National Defence College, 'Gender Perspectives in Effective Peace Operations', in *Challenges of Peace Operations: Into the 21st Century: Concluding Report 1997-2002* (Stockholm: Swedish National Defence College, 2002).

S. Whittington, 'Gender and Peacekeeping: The United Nations Transitional Administration in East Timor (UNTAET)', *Signs: Journal of Women in Culture and Society*, Vol. 28, No. 4 (Chicago: University of Chicago Press, Summer 2003).

S. Whitworth, 'Gender, Race and the Politics of Peacekeeping', in E. Moxon-Browne (ed), *A Future for Peacekeeping?* (New York: Saint Martin's Press, 1998).

Documents and online reports

Amnesty International, *Human Rights Are Women's Rights* (London, 1995).

Centre for the Study of Human Rights, *Women and Human Rights: The Basic Documents* (New York: Columbia University, 1996), at http://www.un.org/Docs/journal/asp/ws.asp?m=S2003/715

International Alert, *Gender Mainstreaming in Peace Support Operations: Moving beyond Rhetoric to Practice* (London, July 2002).

International Criminal Tribunal for Rwanda, *Prosecutor v. Akayesu*, Judgment of the Trial Chamber, Case No. ICTR- 96-4-T (2 September 1998), at http://www.ictr.org

International Criminal Tribunal for the former Yugoslavia, *Prosecutor v. Kunarac* et al, Judgment of the Trial Chamber, Case No. IT-96-23-T & IT-96-23/1-T, at http://www.un.org/icty

United Nations, *Protocol to Prevent, Suppress and Punish Trafficking in Persons, Especially Women and Children, Supplementing the United Nations Convention Against Transnational Organised Crime* (2000), at www.odccp.org/crime_cicp_documentation.html

United Nations, *Report of the United Nations Panel on Peacekeeping Operations (Brahimi Report)*, UN Document A/55/305 (October 2000).

United Nations, *The Beijing Declaration and Platform for Action* (Beijing, China, 4-15 September 1995), at http://www.un.org/womenwatch/daw/beijing/platform/declar.htm

United Nations, *UN Security Council Resolution 1325: Women, Peace and Security* (2000), at http://www.un.org/events/res_1325e.pdf

United Nations, *Violence against Women Perpetrated and/or Condoned by the State during Times of Armed Conflict (1997-2000),* Report of the Special Rapporteur of the Commission on Human Rights on Violence Against Women, Its Causes and Consequence, Ms. Radhika Coomaraswamy, UN Document E/CN.4/2001/73 (2001).

United Nations Development Fund for Women, *Gender Equality and the Millennium Development Goals,* Progress of the World's Women 2002, Vol. 2 (New York, 2003).

UN Secretary-General's Bulletin, *Observance by United Nations Forces of International Humanitarian Law,* UN Document ST/SGB/1999/13 (6 August 1999), at http://www.un.org/peace/st_sgb_1999_13.pdf

Websites

Centre Olame, at http://www.rodhecic.org

European Union, at http://europa.eu.int

International Committee of the Red Cross, at http://www.icrc.org

International Labour Organization, at http://www.ilo.org

United Nations Development Fund for Women, at http://www.unifem.org

United Nations Division for Women, at http://www.un.org/womenwatch/daw

United Nations Institute for Training and Research, at http://www.unitar.org

United Nations Inter-Agency Network on Women and Gender Equality (IANWGE), http://www.un.org/womenwatch/

United Nations Mission in the Democratic Republic of Congo, at http://www.monuc.org

United Nations Mission of Support in East Timor, at http://www.un.org/Depts/dpko/missions/unmiset/

United Nations Population Fund, at http://www.unfpa.org

United Nations Transitional Administration in East Timor, at http://www.un.org/peace/etimor/etimor.htm

Women for Women International, at http://www.womenforwomen.org

Women's Initiatives for Gender Justice (formerly Women's Caucus for Gender Justice), at http://www.iccwomen.org

Women's International League for Peace and Freedom, at http://www.wilpf.int.ch

Working Group on Women, Peace and Security, at http://www.peacewomen.org/un/ngo/wg.html

CONCLUSIONS

AND

RECOMMENDATIONS

Conclusions and Recommendations

Combating violence against women has a long history. The protection of women from systemic violence has been on the agenda of one of the oldest world movements - female emancipation - since its dawn at the turn of the eighteenth century. In the twentieth century, after the conception of the United Nations, violence against women has largely been framed as anti-discrimination claims pointing out that basic human rights - the right to education, labour and political participation - were equal and indivisible. However, to recognise the struggle against violence as a political issue, violence as an obstacle to economic and social development, and women's safety as a human right, has been a long, uneasy and winding process. Although issues of gender-based violence have been included on the agendas of all world conferences on women, an international document devoted exclusively to the issue, the UN Declaration on the Elimination of Violence against Women, declaring gender-based violence unacceptable regardless if it occurs in private or public, and whether committed by state or non-state actors, was not adopted until 1993. It was the UN Security Council Resolution 1325 on Women, Peace and Security, a binding document, adopted in 2000 that enabled all actors to take actions within their responsibility and capability and to lay a solid legal basis for women's inclusion in all the phases of peace processes and protection against violence, specifically in times of war and armed conflict.

It is undeniable that profound and positive changes in the status and roles of women have occurred in the last 50 years. Women have entered the labour market in great numbers gaining unprecedented economic decision-making power. Women have been major actors in the rise of civil society throughout the world, stimulating a gender sensitive approach to the resolution of all vital economic, political and social processes. There is a relatively well-developed legal framework delineating standards and norms of unacceptable behaviour that has contributed to practical steps in bringing to justice the perpetrators of violence against women, for example through the *ad-hoc* International Criminal Tribunals for Rwanda and former Yugoslavia. There are worldwide campaigns, such as the International Day for the Elimination of Violence against Women commemorated annually all over the world, or the long-lasting campaign launched in 2003 by Amnesty International called 'Stop Violence against Women!' Most of the internationally renowned NGOs operating in the field of human rights protection monitor gender issues reporting numerous cases of women's rights violations. Within expert circles and academia violence against women has been recognised as a systemic and structural principle of existing gender relations, and within international organisations it has been declared as one of the main obstacles to development and progress. Due to such a broad and diversified monitoring, public awareness of the issues of gender-based violence has increased significantly during the last two decades.

However, monitoring, examining and reporting cases of violence is not enough. This publication pervasively corroborates that despite much progress, despite a relatively broad body of international laws, violence against women and girls continues to be universal in occurrence and multiple in forms. The spread of HIV/AIDS, especially in Sub-Saharan Africa and its devastating consequences to women, maternal mortality in the developing world, feminisation of poverty, poor access of girls to education, and trafficking in women worldwide - are topics that certainly will remain on the agenda for the next years to come. In some cases violence is exacerbated by global processes in communication and labour migration, which enable criminal gangs to create new forms of abuse and exploitation of women, particularly in connection with the impoverishment of rural regions in the developing world. One example can be mentioned, namely the gruesome trade of body organs and tissues. Research conducted in several countries over the past five years indicate that the transfers flow mainly from those disadvantaged by their economic status, race and sex, that is from impoverished, African, Asian, Middle Eastern or Latin American women to rich white men.

Sudan is a party to several core human rights treaties, including the legally binding International Covenant on Civil and Political Rights (ICCPR). Moreover, Sudan signed the Rome Statute of the International Criminal Court declaring systematic and widespread rape as a war crime and crime against humanity. Nevertheless, in Sudan's western region, Darfur, hundreds of women were raped in 2003-2004 during armed militia attacks on villages. Women who sought refuge in urban centres in the region were at continued risk of sexual attacks as the refugee camps came under the control of the militia. Investigation into these crimes will be difficult due to the unwillingness of the victims to reveal their 'shame' and the poor co-operation of local authorities in bringing the perpetrators to justice. How familiar all these facts sound! East Timor, Rwanda, the Democratic Republic of Congo, Sierra Leone, Guatemala, Bosnia … The picture is strikingly similar. In Darfur once again women's bodies became a tactic of war used to humiliate the enemy's community, ethnicity, religion - to break their resolution and strength. The atrocities in Darfur corroborate that in spite of all progress achieved in the protection of civilians against war atrocities, there is no firm guarantee that in future conflicts women and children will not again become deliberate targets of violence.

Most of the information in this book clearly shows the necessity to continue the struggle to curb gender-based violence. Ratification of international instruments linked to the protection of women's human rights, such as the Optional Protocol of CEDAW, the International Covenant on Economic, Social and Cultural Rights, the Rome Statute of the ICC, the ICCPR, and special documents on migration, by all states has become a priority goal of international community. There is a need to enhance the process of monitoring by gaining more reliable and valid national data and information, especially from the developing world. During the next five years the achievements of women's movements in practice and theory will be broadly evaluated within the international community, and the implementation of the basic documents into national legislation critically reviewed.

Presumably, the attention of the international community will continue to focus on the sphere of private life, on families and local communities, where all too often physical, sexual and psychological violence against women occurs. Strong resistance, due to a widespread and deeply embedded conviction that violence in the private sphere is of less gravity, is to be expected. There is a broad debate whether the principle of universality of human/women's rights should not be considered an outcome of a highly individualistic Western culture neglecting the importance of community-oriented standards of non-Western societies. The motives behind many national governments' resistance to implement international conventions will have to be put under new scrutiny to suggest remedies that will treat the economic and social roots of violence perpetrated in the name of customary laws, religious practices or traditional ceremonies.

One of the main goals of this publication was to illustrate that women worldwide have learnt how to demonstrate and use their potential in protecting themselves and other vulnerable groups. It was grassroots organisations that contributed to the sensitisation of violence against civilians during armed conflicts and their aftermath. Unsurprisingly, the impetus to apply a gender sensitive approach to many of the crucial problems came from the non-governmental level. Publishing reports about rape, sexual abuse, and the situation of women in refugee camps, as well as famine, malnutrition and homelessness among women in war-torn countries, these NGOs have given a true estimate of the implementation of relevant international laws and recommendations. During the last twenty years the international community began to recognise - at least on a declarative level - the value and strength of women's organisations devoted to the eradication of violence against women. The NGOs, including charitable associations and feminist academic institutions, are now seen as actors capable of enriching the activities of the international community, bringing critical views and standpoints to the table, and being able to shed light on numerous problems that otherwise would have been left unnoticed. Their voices must not be silenced or marginalised because they express the need to save lives of millions of people that become the most frequent victims of political measures taken in the name of global security or 'holy war'. They express the possibility of non-violent solutions to the present world's problems.

Amid these organisations and groups there is a growing concern about the tendency towards political doctrines that can negatively influence chances for peace and downplay all non-violent approaches. The militarism, as accentuated by feminists, seeking a single-minded global security, reinforces the patriarchal discriminative features of gender relations and the recurrence of violence against women and girls. Malfunctioning and low accountability of state institutions responsible for the protection of citizens, blindness of the law, unwillingness of governmental and parliamentarian authorities to implement international law, and marginalisation of human rights violations, all reduce the possibilities of bringing perpetrators to justice.

As accentuated many times in this book, those are gender relations that are at the roots of structural violence against women. The years ahead should re-establish discourse on these relations in all agendas dealing with violence against women, whether from the point of view of development, social justice, peace and conflict resolution or human rights. At the same time they hold the promise of becoming an important period, if not even a watershed in the combat against gender-based violence. The wide set of Beijing +10 activities and the preparation for the fifth world conference on women, proposed for the end of this decade, represent remarkable opportunities to collect more information, to debate broadly the contested issues and to act collectively and individually, using the vast spectrum of actors and time-tested instruments. The lessons of the past decades of combating violence against women have proved that only persistent effort on a broad front by various actors can bring results in combating violence against the defenceless and the vulnerable. We hope this publication is able to make a humble contribution to this combat by increasing awareness among those who feel the need to be primed about what is increasingly more and more difficult to neglect and disregard.

Recommendations

1. Prevention

1.1 Prevention through awareness-raising and training

a) *Increased awareness-raising on the rights of women and gender-based crimes*

Deeply entrenched social beliefs regarding the identity and role of women in society constitute a strong barrier to the full enjoyment of women's rights. Such conventional knowledge lacks an understanding of the rights of women and what constitutes a violation of these rights. Therefore it is important to increase awareness about the different gender relations, the rights of women and most

importantly the nature of sexual violence, in all its forms, as a crime in society. This awareness raising should be taken up in systematic and comprehensive programmes in the education system – including police and military academies, the working environment, media, justice, health and social systems, as well as, civil society. Since parents have a key role to play in teaching mutual respect among girls and boys at an early stage, they should be educated about their responsibilities in bringing up children in a non-violent environment, to not discriminate against girls and inculcate values based on the respect of equal rights. The media has a significant part to play in promoting well-balanced representations of women and men, as well as, eliminating images that depict violence. Ideally, this responsibility should be regulated by professional media guidelines and codes of conduct. Specific education and training should also be given to law enforcement personnel and actors in justice, health and social systems regarding the causes and consequences of violence against women and how best to prevent them. Furthermore, general campaigns should be organised to reach out to the local level as well as national, regional and international communities on the nature of violence against women.

b) *Effective training for all actors in society*

In order to formulate adequate and comprehensive responses to the problem of gender-based violence, authoritative agents, for example, public officials, the police, prison officials and security forces, as well as actors from the medical, judicial, social and educational fields need to be sensitised through training about the nature of gender-based violence. These individuals would also benefit from being kept abreast of the existence and nature of all humanitarian and human rights laws, which are related to such crimes. Training materials and guidelines at the communal, national, regional and international levels, for all actors involved, should be developed in the protection of women and girls from violence. In addition, such materials outlining their rights and specific needs in various contexts such as crimes perpetrated in war, domestic violence, trafficking and other forms of violence against women and girls should be produced. Furthermore, women and girls in general, as well as victims or potential victims should be informed about their rights and how to better protect themselves from violence.

1.2 Prevention through research

a) *Effective collection of gender-disaggregated data*

Reliable data is imperative in order to formulate adequate responses and strategies. Over the past decade, various studies and strategies in international *fora* have initiated research on data and statistics concerning the status of women. Programmes run by the United Nations and reporting mechanisms have been important catalysts for forcing governments to provide progress evaluations on the state of their female population. However, deficiencies still exist in the systematic collection of 'gender-disaggregated' data especially on violence against women. Therefore, the collection of data and statistics concerning all forms of violence against women and girls should be promoted and an efficient data collection methodology should be devised. All actors involved such as medical staff and law enforcement agents, especially the police, should all be made aware of the nature of violence against women as crimes and specific procedures must be drawn up in order to maintain a reliable record.

b) *Furthering research on causes,
consequences and solutions*

The current body of knowledge on violence against women is limited due to several barriers. First of all, in general, such crimes are still treated as taboo, thus restricting access to victims and preventing a deeper analysis of the problem. Most often, these crimes are sealed in silence, which leads to a lack of necessary data. In addition, the place of women in society tends to be relegated to the private sphere, which is an excuse used by many government officials not to deal with such matters. However, these obstacles need to be surmounted. Research on the root causes and consequences of violence against women in the economic, political, cultural and social fields needs to be undertaken to understand the nature and scope of the problem. Targeted studies on the needs and methods to advise and rehabilitate perpetrators should also be undertaken in an effort to prevent any re-occurrence of violence. For an effective response mechanism, current solutions and adopted measures ought to be continually assessed both in terms of their effectiveness and success. In addition, in order to formulate better policies and programmes, further research should be carried out on the impact of war on women, considering the physical, psychological, economic and social aspects. Finally, there is also a need for research to be conducted on the role of women in the prevention of war, conflict resolution and reconstruction. It is essential that research from universities, institutes and NGO grassroots organisations be collected as a valuable resource in the formulation of government policies.

c) *Effective monitoring and assessment*

The elimination of gender-based violence and discrimination against women in accordance with various international conventions need to be assessed through monitoring committees. For this, it is essential that global indicators are agreed upon internationally to enable assessment of violence against women. Relevant institutions both at international and national levels, should incorporate efficient follow-up mechanisms such as the incorporation of the status of women and progress on the attainment of women's rights in reporting mechanisms at the topmost level.

2. Protection

2.1 Protection through law

a) *Universal ratification of international instruments on
international human rights and humanitarian issues*

At the international level, an important legal framework drawn from international conventions on human rights and humanitarian law exists, and this framework provides protection for women from violence and prohibits any prejudice against women's rights. These instruments are essential as they establish common standards and norms. Accession to these instruments and their implementation mark the commitment of states to improving the status of women. Furthermore, reporting mechanisms provide monitoring of the implementation of these standards. It is, therefore, essential that these instruments are ratified by all states and that they are implemented adequately.

b) *Effective implementation of legal reform
and improvement of access to justice*

National legislation, starting from the constitution, should assure women's rights. In this context, it is crucial to criminalise violence against women in all its forms, including domestic violence and traditional practices harmful to women. Laws that punish official agents that is the police, security forces and any other state officials who become engaged in any form of violence against women in carrying out their duties, should be reinforced. Women and girl victims should be provided with adequate access to legal remedies including the provision of gender sensitive justice, compensation and indemnities.

c) *End impunity by ensuring adequate punishment
of perpetrators*

The criminalisation of all forms of gender-based violence through legal reform will acquire meaning only if these are appropriately implemented. As such states have a responsibility to punish all criminals including military and public officials. States should strengthen co-operation in extraditing perpetrators. In addition, states should refrain from referring to traditional or religious practices to avoid their duties. It is essential that penal, civil, labour and administrative sanctions for all perpetrators are strengthened in order to ensure compliance and make it clearly understood that no one can avoid responsibility for such acts and that these acts will not be tolerated in society.

2.2 Protection through institutions

a) Strengthening of institutional mechanisms for protection : Co-ordinated approach

The problem of gender-based violence is wide in scope in terms of the actors and institutions involved. The response therefore requires a multidisciplinary approach engaging institutions from the political, justice, health, labour, media, education, social and security systems at all levels. An effective response is assured through the co-ordinated institutionalisation of gender perspectives and protective mechanisms against gender-based violence in all these sectors. Training alone is not enough as its impact diminishes as time passes. For a longer-term commitment, it is essential that institutions are able to adapt dynamic and visible gender policies and strategies aimed at changing the institutional culture. This change requires mainstreaming a dynamic policy and strategy in gender issues, which should be reflected in the institution and its programmes and particularly in the set up and design, goals, leadership, implementation and evaluation. The change should bring about a transformation in cultural prejudices and beliefs. For example, in considering the security sector, an important strategy would be to create institutional mechanisms that enable women and girls to report or testify against gender-based violence in a secure environment. For this, it is crucial that women are involved in security sector institutions and programmes, such as the police and the military, and are integrated in their transformation and reform. For instance, some states have set up women-only police stations, which is to be encouraged and could be further improved by providing services such as legal advice and counselling. An alternative solution is a unit at each police station that is staffed by women who are responsible for receiving complaints about gender-based crimes.

The justice system should also be made sensitive to the special needs of victims of gender-based violence, in terms of investigative procedures and providing testimonies. The number of female judges, prosecutors and investigators should be increased so as to ensure balance and equality.

In addition, any investigations of gender-based crimes also require an appropriate reaction by the medical field – as the provision of evidence by means of medical analysis is significant in such crimes. Doctors and other paramedical actors should establish specific procedures that neither discriminate against female victims nor perpetuate cultural prejudices.

The co-operation and partnership between state institutions and non-governmental organisations, as well as, support for anti-violence networks should be promoted.

Finally, gender mainstreaming in institutions at all levels should be accompanied by efficient follow-up mechanisms that illustrate progress.

b) Allocation of proper budget

For institutions to reflect gender perspectives and establish proper response mechanisms, it requires the government to allot sufficient funds and financial support for the long-term. Without proper funding, programmes become inadequate, reflecting staff shortages and will inevitably be limited in their ability to provide assistance and protection mechanisms.

c) Establishment of shelters and support mechanisms

Women and girls suffering from gender-based violence need to have a safe place to go. This is especially true for victims of domestic violence for whom their own home has ceased to be a safe haven. Governments need to put up shelters and assistance hotlines and offer support for victims, which should include medical, psychological, social and legal services for women and affected family members.

d) Protection of women in armed conflict

The experience from recent wars and conflicts has enabled the formulation of appropriate measures of how to protect women in extreme situations. Among them, the prosecution of all criminals guilty of gender-based violence during war is a priority, as is the provision of legal redress, and compensation or indemnity for the victims. Offering assistance to victims - legal, social, medical help as well as guaranteeing their personal safety and paying special attention to the specific needs of women during wartime that is delivering food, water, sanitation and health, etc. – is also extremely important. The complex situation during war and its aftermath needs an integrated effort by the local and international community, especially engaging women in all phases of peace negotiations and the reconstruction process. It is also desirable to increase the participation of women in peace support operations at the decision-making level, as well as, in all phases of the mission.

3. Empowerment

3.1 Empowerment through education and labour

In many cultures, the subordinate status of the female gender and socially attributed stereotyped roles often lead to the exclusion of girls and women from education and formal labour systems, in particular at the top levels. Although numerous official documents and human rights conventions have enshrined the right to education, including free and compulsory elementary education, and the right to work encompassing the right to receive wages commensurate to a standard of living, progress in this area is very slow.

Education and labour systems are key areas for the empowerment of women and girls, which reduce their vulnerability to several forms of gender-based violence such as trafficking. It is therefore crucial to identify all persisting barriers to the education of girls and women and their access to formal labour systems. Furthermore, all ministries of education have a key role to play in transforming established social perceptions of the inferiority or superiority of either gender and their stereotyped roles through education curricula.

3.2 Empowerment of women through their participation in decision-making

Studies have shown that the lives of women and girls are favourably influenced by changes in policies, which are enabled when there is a critical mass of women in public life. The achievement of a critical mass is in the order of 30 per cent of public positions in decision-making levels. There are several ways to reach these goals such as the establishment of a quota system. However, the integration of women should not just be an exercise in establishing a tally, but a real commitment to engaging women by providing assistance and training to potential female candidates and providing them with access to all decision-making level positions including the ministries of defence and ministries of foreign affairs. The knowledge and practical know-how in conflict resolution and security issues that women possess are valuable resources that need to be tapped. Many female grassroots organisations and national, regional or international women's NGOs have been engaged in conflict prevention, peacebuilding and reconstruction. However, women's efforts have so often been relegated to the informal channels. For peace agreements to have a lasting and sustainable effect, all sectors of society, including women's associations, need to be involved. In this respect, the official participation of women should be recognised and implemented in preventive diplomacy, peace negotiations and all phases of formal mediation, peacekeeping operations, peacebuilding and post-conflict reconstruction. Most importantly women should be engaged in decision-making in sectors involved with peace and security at the national, regional and international levels. Input by women is necessary in the design, implementation and assessment of solutions and remedies on peace and security so as to ensure a balanced and equal output that responds to the grievances of all involved.

The experience of the ad-hoc International Criminal Tribunals in the 1990s illustrated that the presence of women judges led to a breakthrough in criminalising gender-based violence during wars. That women participate on an equal basis to men as judges, prosecutors and investigators in truth and reconciliation bodies and national and international courts is essential as it provides greater sensitivity to gender-based crimes and enhances gender justice. The presence of female judges or investigators leads to an atmosphere of increased confidence for women victims for whom re-telling the abuse is a very difficult and traumatic experience.

Abbreviations

AFRC	Armed Forces Revolutionary Council
AIDS	Acquired Immune Deficiency Syndrome
ANC	African National Congress
BCPR	Bureau for Crisis Prevention and Recovery
CCSEA	Co-ordination Committee for Sexual Exploitation and Abuse
CCW	Convention on Certain Conventional Weapons
CDA	Conflict Related Development Analysis
CPA	Coalition Provisional Authority
DDR	Disarmament, Demobilisation and Reintegration
DDRR	Disarmament, Demobilisation, Reintegration and Repatriation
DFAIT	Department of Foreign Affairs and International Trade (Canada)
DFID	Department of Foreign and International Development (United Kingdom)
ECOSOC	Economic and Social Council
ECOWAS	Economic Community of West African States
ECSC	European Coal and Steel Community
EEC	European Economic Community
EP	European Parliament
ERW	Explosive Remnants of War
EU	European Union
EWL	European Women's Lobby
EWPM	Early Warning and Preventive Measures
FARC	Revolutionary Armed Forces of Colombia
FCC	Follow-up Co-ordinating Committee
FGM	Female Genital Mutilation
FLS	Forward Looking Strategies (Nairobi)
GAD	Gender and development
GAM	Gerakan Aceh Merdeka (Free Aceh Movement)
GAU	Gender Affairs Unit
GC	(Four) Geneva Conventions (of 1949)
GPA	Governance and Public Administration
GRF	Gender Roles Framework
HIV	Human Immunodeficiency Virus
IA	International Alert
IASC	Inter-Agency Standing Committee
ICBL	International Campaign to Ban Landmines
ICC	International Criminal Court
ICCPR	International Covenant on Civil and Political Rights
ICRC	International Committee of the Red Cross
ICTR	International Criminal Tribunal for Rwanda
ICTY	International Criminal Tribunal for the former Yugoslavia
IFIs	International Financial Institutions
IHL	International Humanitarian Law
IHRL	International Human Rights Law
ILO	International Labour Organization
IMT	International Military Tribunal of Nuremberg
IMTFE	International Military Tribunal of the Far East
IOM	International Organization for Migration
IPTF	International Police Task Force
IPU	Inter-Parliamentary Union
IPV	Intimate partner violence
ISAF	International Security Assistance Force (Afghanistan)
KFOR	Kosovo Force
LBW	Low birth weight
LRA	Lord's Resistance Army (Uganda)
LTTE	Liberation Tigers of Tamil Eelam
MDGs	Millennium Development Goals
MLSA	Military Logistical Support Agreement (USA/Philippines)
MONUC	United Nations Organisation Mission in the Democratic Republic of Congo
MRE	Mine Risk Education
NAD	Nanggroe Aceh Darussalam
NATO	North Atlantic Treaty Organization
NCDDR	National Commission on DDR
NCRRR	National Commission for Reconstruction, Resettlement and Rehabilitation
NEPAD	New Partnership for Africa
NGO	Non-Governmental Organisation
NGOWG	NGO Working Group on Women, Peace and Security
OAS	Organization of American States
OAU	Organization of African Unity
ODIHR	Office for Democratic Institutions and Human Rights
OGA	Office for Gender Affairs
OHCHR	Office of the High Commissioner for Human Rights
ONUSAL	United Nations Observer Mission in El Salvador
OSAGI	The United Nations Office of the Special Adviser on Gender Issues and the Advancement of Women
OSCE	Organization for Security and Co-operation in Europe
PRSP	Poverty Reduction Strategy Paper
PSO	Peace support operations
PTDS	Post-traumatic stress disorder

RAF	Royal Air Force		UNICEF	United Nations Children's Fund
RCM	Red Cross Messages		UNIFEM	United Nations Development Fund for Women
RUF	Revolutionary United Front		UNITAR	United Nations Institute for Training and Research
SADC	South African Development Community		UNMAS	United Nations Mine Action Service
SALW	Small Arms and Light Weapons		UNMEE	United Nations Mission in Ethiopia and Eritrea
SCR	Security Council Resolution		UNMIBH	United Nations Mission in Bosnia and Herzegovina
SEESAC	South East Europe Clearinghouse for the Control of Small Arms and Light Weapons		UNMIG	United Nations Mission in Georgia
			UNMIK	United Nations Interim Administration Mission in Kosovo
SFOR	Stabilisation Force in Bosnia and Herzegovina			
SIDA	Swedish International Development Agency		UNMIL	United Nations Mission in Liberia
SLA	Sierra Leone Army		UNMISET	United Nations Mission of Support in East Timor
SOZM	Union of Women's Organisations of Macedonia (*Sojuz na organizacite na zenite vo Makedonija*)		UNOCHA	United Nations Office for the Co-ordination of Humanitarian Affairs
SRF	Social Relations Framework		UNPROFOR	United Nations Protection Force
SRSG	Special Representative of the Secretary General		UNSC	United Nations Security Council
STOP	Special Trafficking Operations Programme		UNTAC	United Nations Transitional Authority in Cambodia
TGNP	Tanzania Gender Networking Programme		UNTAET	United Nations Transnational Administration in East Timor
TIP	Trafficking in Persons			
TPLF	Tigrayan People's Liberation		UNTAG	United Nations Transition Assistance Group
TRC	Truth and Reconciliation Commission		UPCC	UNAMSIL Personal Conduct Committee
TRF	Triple Roles Framework		USFJ	United States Forces in Japan
TVPA	Trafficking Victims Protection Act		USSR	Union of Soviet Socialist Republics
UCSMR	Union of Committees of Soldier's Mothers in Russia		UXO	Unexploded Ordnance
UN	United Nations		VFA	Visiting Forces Agreement (USA/Philippines)
UNAIDS	The Joint United Nations Programme on HIV/AIDS		WEDPRO	Women's Education, Development, Productivity and Research, Inc. (NGO)
UNAMSIL	United Nations Organisation Mission in Sierra Leone			
UNDAF	United Nations Development Assistance Framework		WFP	World Food Programme
UNDDA	United Nations Department of Disarmament Affairs		WGDD	Women, Gender and Development Directorate
UNDP	United Nations Development Programme		WHO	World Health Organization
UNDPKO	United Nations Department of Peace-Keeping Operations		WID	Women in development
			WILPF	Women's International League for Peace and Freedom
UNDW	United Nations Decade for Women		WPA	Mexico World Plan of Action
UNFPA	United Nations Population Fund		WPP	Women Peacemakers Programme
UNHCR	United Nations High Commissioner for Refugees		WTO	World Trade Organization

Glossary

Acid attacks - punishment received by women from men who throw acid on the woman to disfigure her. The most common reasons are refusal of marriage, denial of sex or rejection of romance. Most attacks are directed at the face in order to permanently scar the victim and destroy her physical appearance; often the victim is left blinded.

Affirmative action - a set of public policies, measures and initiatives designed to help eliminate past and present discrimination based on race, colour, religion, sex, or national origin. Introduction of quotas (mandatory percentage of representation) in public positions, for example parliament, in order to achieve equitable representation of women is one measure of affirmative action.

Arbitrary detention - the deprivation of a person's liberty without any legal basis or after an unfair trial by means of confinement in jail, detention centre, psychiatric facility etc.

Blue Helmets Code of Conduct - ten point guidelines for UN civilian and military peacekeepers. The guidelines ensure high standards of integrity, respect of the laws and culture of the country, and respect of human rights. It specifically prohibits immoral acts of sexual, physical or psychological abuse or exploitation of the local population or UN staff, especially women and children.

Bride burnings - a murder arranged by a husband to look like an accident, frequently the bursting of a kitchen stove, when he feels that the obligatory marriage dowry is not adequate. In India, thousands of women are killed in bride burnings. Only a small percentage of the perpetrators are brought to justice.

Child soldier - a person less than eighteen years of age recruited to serve in government armed forces, guerrilla groups or armed militias. While most child soldiers are aged between fifteen and eighteen, many are recruited from the age of ten and sometimes even younger. In many countries, both girls and boys are used as soldiers; girls are at particular risk of rape, sexual harassment and abuse.

Comfort women - a term that comes from the English translation of the Japanese '*jūgun ianfu*' (military comfort women) referring to young females of various ethnic and national backgrounds who were abducted and forced into sexual slavery by Japanese troops during the Second World War.

Commission on the Status of Women (CSW) was established as a functional commission of the Economic and Social Council by Council Resolution 11(II) on 21 June 1946 to prepare recommendations and reports to the council on the promotion of women's rights in political, economic, civil, social and educational fields. In 1996, through Resolution 2001/4, the commission expanded its work from 2002-2006 to provide the framework for assessment of progress achieved after the *Fourth World Conference on Women in Beijing* and to strengthen the implementation of the *Beijing Platform for Action*.

Convention against Discrimination in Education (14 December 1960) was adopted by the General Conference of UNESCO, which met in Paris from 14 November to 15 December 1960. It recognises the right to education as a vital element of the development of human personality. It calls on the state parties to provide free and compulsory primary education and to adopt all the necessary measures to eliminate any form of discrimination in education and ensure equal access for all.

Convention on Consent to Marriage, Minimum Age for Marriage and Registration of Marriages (9 December 1964) establishes the right of both women and men of full age, irrespective of race, nationality or religion to marry with their free will. It underlines that no marriage shall be legally entered into without the complete and free consent of both parties. State parties further agreed to eliminate practices of child marriages and the betrothal of young girls before the age of puberty.

Convention on the Nationality of Married Women (11 August 1958) establishes that neither the celebration nor the dissolution of a marriage between one of its contracting state's nationals and an alien, nor the change of nationality by the husband during marriage, shall automatically affect the nationality of the wife. It also guarantees that the alien wife of one of its contracting state's nationals may, at her request, acquire the nationality of her husband through specially privileged naturalisation procedures.

Convention on the Political Rights of Women (7 July 1954) recognises the right of women to vote and be eligible for election in all public functions and publicly elected bodies without any discrimination.

Crime against humanity - an act of persecution against a group reaching a very grave level so as to necessitate punishment under international law. A crime against humanity is characterised by intentional, widespread and systematic acts directed towards the civilian population. The term originated in the 1907 Hague Convention Preamble, which codified the customary law of armed conflict. The Nuremberg International Military Tribunal (1945) stated that crimes against humanity included: murder, extermination, enslavement, deportation, and other inhumane acts committed against civilian populations, before or during the war; or persecutions on political, racial or religious grounds in execution of or in connection with any crime within the jurisdiction of the tribunal, whether or not in violation of the domestic law of the country where perpetrated. The International Criminal Tribunal of former Yugoslavia and the International Criminal Tribunal of Rwanda expanded this list by adding rape and torture. The statute of the International Criminal Court added crimes of enforced disappearance of persons and apartheid.

Cultural relativism - a notion opposing the principle of universality of human rights. It has been used to justify violations of human rights by invoking cultural traditions and customs. In the context of women' rights, this notion was meant to serve as a justification of women's inferior position in society and their limitations or as a justification of violations of their human rights.

Declaration on Protection of Women and Children in Emergency and Armed Conflict was proclaimed by General Assembly Resolution 3318 (XXIX) on 14 December 1974. It calls for the prohibition of persecution, torture, punitive measures, degrading treatment and violence, especially against women and children and for full abidance by all states to the Geneva Protocol of 1925 and the Geneva Conventions of 1949, and other instruments of international law relating to respect for human rights in armed conflicts.

Declaration on the Participation of Women in Promoting International Peace and Co-operation was adopted by the General Assembly through Resolution 37/63 on 3 December 1982 reaffirming the need for women's equal participation with men in the economic, political, social, and cultural sphere towards achieving international peace and co-operation and eradicating all forms of racism and racial discrimination. It further urged for women's increased participation in positions in governmental and non-governmental institutions, as well as diplomatic and UN agencies.

Disarmament, Demobilisation and Reintegration (DDR) - a specific process during peacemaking and peacebuilding in the post-conflict period. Disarmament is the collection, control and disposal of small arms, ammunition, explosives and light and heavy weapons in the possession of combatants and civilian population within a conflict zone. Demobilisation is the process by which combating forces disband their military structures or downsize and combatants progressively return to civilian life. Reintegration is the process, which permits ex-combatants and their families to economically and socially adapt to a productive civilian life.

Domestic violence - see Intimate partner violence.

Dowry killing - the homicide of women whose dowry, the payment in cash or/and in kind by the bride's family to the bridegroom's family along with the giving away of the bride in marriage, was not considered sufficient by her husband or in-laws. Most of these incidents are reported as accidental burns in the kitchen or disguised as suicide.

Empowerment of women - the power to think and act freely, exercise choice and to fulfil one's complete potential. Strategies for women's empowerment encompass social, economic and political dimensions and requires a transformation of power relations. For example, in the area of women's political empowerment, women both empower themselves and are empowered. This relates both to individual (such as increasing individual civic competencies) and collective empowerment (such as networking). Empowerment also involves creating a conducive environment so that women can use these competencies to address the fundamental problems of society together with their male counterparts.

Enforced disappearance - the arrest, detention or abduction of persons by, or with the authorisation, support or acquiescence of, a state or a political organisation, followed by a refusal to acknowledge the deprivation of freedom or to give information on the fate or whereabouts of those persons, with the intention of removing them from the protection of the law for a prolonged period of time.

Ethnic cleansing - the organised attempt by one racial or political group to completely remove from a country or area anyone who belongs to a different racial group by using violence and often murder. Women's specific reproductive role in society cause them to be targets in such conflicts for various forms of violence such as rape, sexual violence or forced sterilisation, the aim of which is to force the ethnic group to flee or to affect its ethnical composition.

European Committee for Prevention of Torture (CPT) - a preventive mechanism, which examines, by means of visits, the treatment of persons deprived of their liberty with a view to strengthening their protection from torture and inhuman or degrading treatment or punishment within the state parties of the European Convention for the Prevention of Torture and Inhuman or Degrading Treatment or Punishment.

Explosive remnants of war (ERW) includes all types of explosive weapons except anti-personnel and anti-vehicle mines (unexploded ordnance contaminating the ground, abandoned munitions and fighting vehicles, small arms and light weapons), which remain dispersed in the country after armed conflict. Their presence is recognised as a threat to the security and livelihood of civilian communities as they cause deaths and injuries through numerous accidents.

Female foeticide - the sex-specific abortion of female foetuses. See also Female infanticide.

Female genital mutilation - the removal of part, or all, of the female genitalia leading to long-term harmful physical and psychological effects. The most severe form is circumcision. This customary practice is widespread in Africa and in some countries in the Middle East. It also occurs, mainly among immigrant communities, in parts of Asia and the Pacific, North and Latin America and Europe.

Female infanticide - the deliberate killing of female infants soon after birth due to the preference for male babies and the low value associated with the birth of females in certain cultures. The practice has its roots in traditional customs and remains a critical concern in a number of countries today, notably China and India.

Feminism - a set of social theories and political practices that generally involves a critique of gender inequality and more specifically, advances the promotion of women's rights and interests. Feminism is critical of past and current social relations and is primarily motivated and informed by the experience of women.

First World Conference on Women (Mexico, 19 June-2 July 1975) / World Conference of the International Women's Year - was convened in 1975 to coincide with the International Women's Year, observed to remind the international community that discrimination against women is a constant problem. It adopted the World Plan of Action whose main targets were equal access for women to education, employment, political participation, health services, housing, nutrition and family planning.

Forced impregnation - a form of gender-based violence in armed conflicts where women are sexually abused and forced to become pregnant with the intent to affect the ethnic composition of the population. Under certain conditions it may constitute a crime against humanity. See also Crime against humanity. See also Ethnic cleansing.

Forced labour - work under the menace of penalties/punishment such as physical harm or other constraints. This is often the case for women who have been recruited with the promise of jobs as dancers, waitresses, housemaids etc., but are instead forced to provide sexual services and work in prostitution. Coercion may include debt bondage, confiscation of identity documents or the threat of other reprisals.

Forced marriage - a union concluded without the free and full consent of the persons involved. International law not only prohibits forced marriage, but also considers any marriage that is forced upon a girl or woman by her family or guardians, a practice similar to slavery as stipulated in the 1956 Supplementary Convention on the Abolition of Slavery, the Slave Trade and Institutions and Practices Similar to Slavery. In the context of armed conflict, women and girls are often abducted and coerced to become wives of rebels or soldiers.

Forced prostitution - an engagement in one or more acts of a sexual nature by force or threat of force or coercion, as for example fear of violence, duress, detention, psychological oppression or abuse of power. Under certain conditions it may constitute a crime against humanity. See also Crime against humanity.

Forced sterilisation - when a person is deprived of his or her biological reproductive capacity with no medical justification or hospital treatment and without his or her genuine consent. It is used particularly in the context of ethnic conflicts in order to change the ethnic composition of the population. Under certain conditions it may constitute a crime against humanity. See also Crime against humanity.

Fourth World Conference on Women (Beijing, 4-15 September 1995) - one of a series of UN World Conferences on Women within the context of UN's efforts in improving women's status. It adopted the *Beijing Declaration* and the *Platform for Action*, which call for the protection and promotion of women's human rights and the intensification of efforts for the achievement of gender equality. Twelve areas of concern were identified where state and international community action is required: poverty, access to education, provision of health care, elimination of violence against women, women in armed conflict, access to resources, women in decision-making policies, empowerment, lack of respect for human rights of women, stereotyping of women, environment and the girl child.

Gender - refers to the economic, social and cultural attributes and opportunities associated with being male or female in a particular point of time in society. Gender roles are not fixed, they are socially constructed and vary widely within and between cultures. They also vary according to social factors such as age, race, ethnicity, class and marital status.

Gender-based crime - a serious offence committed because of gender or on the basis of gender, most of which are illustrated by various forms of sexual violence but not only. Women and girls are more vulnerable to such crimes than men and boys. Recognition and criminalisation of gender-based crimes are hampered by social stigma, cultural attitudes and stereotypes resulting in deficient laws and enforcement mechanisms. In international law, traditionally marginalised as a natural consequence of war, recent developments in the 1990s resulted in the codification of gender-based crimes in the International Criminal Tribunals of Yugoslavia and Rwanda and finally in the International Criminal Court (ICC), an important step towards ending impunity. These crimes are enumerated in the ICC Statute as a crime against humanity and a war crime (international or non-international armed conflict). These include rape, sexual slavery, enforced prostitution, forced pregnancy, enforced sterilisation and any other form of sexual violence also constituting a serious violation of the Geneva Conventions (regarding war crimes) or other forms of sexual violence of comparable gravity (regarding crimes against humanity). In addition, two other gender-specific crimes have been enumerated under crimes against humanity, the crime of persecution against any identifiable group or collectivity on the grounds of gender, and the crime of 'enslavement'. See also Crime against humanity, War crime, Slavery.

Gender-based violence - violence rooted in prescribed behaviours, norms and attitudes based upon gender and sexuality. It particularly reflects unequal power relations between men and women in society. It takes various forms including physical, sexual and psychological violence. See also Violence against women.

Gendercide - a pattern of human behaviour, enduring over time, that leads to large scale, disproportionate extermination of persons of a particular gender. The term, which is sex neutral, recognises the way gender roles play a part in this act.

Gender-disaggregated data - information and statistics collected, analysed and presented based on gender. Gender statistics are designed to illustrate the conditions of women and men in order to generate awareness of the situation, guide policy, mobilise action and monitor progress towards improvement. There is however, a lack of systematic collection of gender-disaggregated data and many national and international institutions are currently making efforts to remedy this deficiency.

Gender equality - the equal treatment of women and men in laws and policies, and their equal access to resources and services within families, communities and society at large. Achieving gender equality signifies that a person's rights or opportunities do not depend on being female or male. For women, it requires that their views, interests and needs shape community decisions as much as men's.

Gender mainstreaming - a global strategy for promoting gender equality, and for ensuring that attention to the gender perspective becomes an integral part of interventions in all areas of social development. Gender mainstreaming was introduced in one of the strategic objectives in the Platform of Action at the UN Fourth World Conference on Women in Beijing (1995). Mainstreaming includes gender-specific activities and affirmative action whenever women or men are in particularly disadvantageous positions.

Gender-sensitive budgets - focus on gender awareness and mainstreaming in planning and budgeting at national and local levels. They analyse the involvement and participation of different stakeholders, monitor government expenditure and delivery of public services and taxation, and analyse allocation of resources from a gender perspective.

Genocide - the deliberate killing of a national, ethnic, racial or religious group which aims at the group's physical destruction. There are various acts that qualify as genocide such as inflicting serious physical or mental harm to members of the group, preventing births and forcibly transferring children to another group. Recently, it has been recognised that under certain circumstances acts of rape, sexual slavery or other sexual violence may constitute a crime of genocide. Women, due to their reproductive role in society, have been particularly targeted for such crimes. Ethnic conflicts in the early 1990s in Rwanda and former Yugoslavia where the experience of Tutsi and Bosnian women as victims of heinous crimes are examples of genocide and genocide propaganda. Genocide is prohibited under international law and constitutes a crime against humanity. See also Crime against humanity.

Girl child - a female child from zero to eighteen years of age. In many countries the girl child is still discriminated from the earliest stages of life, through her childhood and into adulthood. The reasons for the discrepancy include harmful attitudes and practices, such as female genital mutilation, son preference, early marriage, sexual exploitation, sexual abuse, discrimination in food allocation, education and health care. As a result, fewer girls than boys survive into adulthood.

Global Campaign for Education (GCE) - promotes education as a basic human right, and mobilises public pressure on governments and the international community to fulfil their commitment for free, compulsory public basic education for all, especially women, children and all deprived sections of society. The GCE is based on the implementation of the Education for All Goals and Strategies, a Platform for Action adopted in 2000 by 185 governments in Dakar, with special reference to achieving gender equality in education by the year 2015.

Honour killing - a customary practice where male family members kill female relatives in the name of family 'honour' for sexual activity outside marriage, either suspected or forced, even when they have been victims of rape. Often, young teenage boys are chosen to perform the crime because their sentences are generally lighter than those for adults. The practice is deeply rooted in patriarchal/tribal traditions where males are looked upon by society as the sole protector of females and by this duty confer on him, he has complete control of the female. In general, females are viewed as inferior, likened to a commodity. In case the man's protection is violated through the perceived immoral behaviour of the woman, the man loses his honour in society as it is interpreted as a failure either to protect the woman adequately or to educate her properly. These crimes are widespread all over the world although it is prevalent in countries such as Pakistan, Bangladesh, Turkey, Jordan, Syria, Egypt and other Mediterranean and Gulf countries. Some cases have also been reported in India, Brazil, Ecuador, Israel, Italy, Sweden, United Kingdom etc.

Human security - a specific approach of security from the perspective of the individual. It encompasses freedom from pervasive threats to one's rights, safety and life. The key values in the fulfilment of human security are economic development, social justice, environmental protection, democratisation, disarmament, and respect for human rights and rule of law. A gender perspective of human security entails a more nuanced understanding of how women in a given society experience insecurity and risks, for example by being subject to specific forms of violence or as a result of discrimination in access to education, land, credits etc.

Ill-treatment - often used to include cruel, inhuman or degrading treatment. Ill-treatment falls below that of an act of torture. Ill-treatment may include the actions of state authorities (i.e. police or prison staff) conducting psychological harassment or degradation of a person's dignity. The state not only has the duty to refrain from conduct amounting to ill-treatment, but also includes the duty to ensure, by taking positive steps, that ill-treatment is not inflicted upon others.

Impunity - is an exemption from legal punishment or loss. Worldwide many perpetrators of various forms of crimes of violence against women such as rape, sexual exploitation in wartime, domestic violence etc. are not adequately sanctioned by the legal system either by lack of recognition of the act as a crime or by insufficient application procedures. As a result many criminals freely walk away from these crimes.

Inter-American Convention to Prevent, Punish and Eradicate Violence against Women (Belém do Pará, Brazil, 9 June 1994) - was adopted by the Organisation of American States. It reaffirms women's human rights, prohibits all forms of violence against women in the public and private sphere and stipulates that state parties will pursue policies to prevent, punish and eliminate such violence. It also established a mechanism of protection according to which any individual or group of individuals or non-governmental entity recognised by any member state of the organisation can lodge complaints of violations of the convention with the Inter-American Commission on Human Rights.

Internally displaced person - are persons or groups of persons who have been forced to flee their homes, due to armed conflict, situations of generalised violence, violations of human rights or natural or human-made disasters, and who have not crossed an internationally recognised state border. A majority of world's internally displaced persons are women and children.

International Conference on Population and Development (Cairo, 5-13 September 1994) - recognised the importance of women's empowerment in achieving development, which was highlighted in the Programme of Action adopted by the conference. The programme underscores the internal linkages between population and development and focuses on meeting the needs of individual women and men, rather than on achieving demographic targets. The conference called for the enhancement of women's access to education, development and decision-making processes, the eradication of gender-based violence and protection of women's reproductive rights within the context of its action on family planning. Assessment of achievements, identification of problems and challenges ahead, were the main areas of the review process of the conference on its tenth anniversary in 2004.

International Covenant of Economic, Social and Cultural Rights - was adopted by General Assembly Resolution 2200A (XXI) on 16 December 1966. It is the principle human rights instrument guaranteeing full enjoyment of economic, social and cultural rights equally to women and men. These include the right to work, to social security, to adequate standard of living, to health, to education and to cultural life.

International Day for the Elimination of Violence against Women (25 November) - originates from the story of three women, the Mirabal Sisters (Minerva, Patria and Maria Teresa), who represented, as political activists, a strong symbol of resistance against Dominican Republic's dictator, Rafael Trujillo (1930 to 1961). The assassination of the sisters on 25 November 1960 spurred popular indignation and became one of the catalysts in bringing the dictatorship to an end. Since then, their activism came to symbolise female victimisation and resistance worldwide. In commemoration of this event, the United Nations designated 25 November as the International Day for the Elimination of Violence against Women through General Assembly Resolution 54/134 on 17 December 1999.

Intimate partner violence - actual or threatened physical or sexual violence or psychological and emotional abuse directed towards a spouse, ex-spouse, current or former boyfriend or girlfriend/dating partner. Intimate partners may be heterosexual or of the same sex. Abuse may include threats, harm, injury, intimidation, harassment, control, economic restrictions, or damage to living beings or property. Intimate partner violence can be a single incident, ranging in intensity from harassment to homicide. Most often it is a systematic pattern of abuse that escalates over time in frequency and severity. Worldwide, most victims of intimate partner violence are women.

Jus cogens - are the most important norms of international law of an absolutely binding nature, expressing in the normative sphere the fundamental values of the international community as a whole. These are non-derogable rights as they cannot be limited or suspended under any circumstances or at any time. Examples of *jus cogens* are the prohibition of the threat or use of force in international relations, as well as, the prohibition of torture and prohibition of slavery.

Machismo - refers to social norms, attitudes and characteristics of men denoting excessive masculinity such as a cult of virility. It is characterised by hostility in male to male relationships and arrogance and sexual violence in male to female relationships. It holds an extreme conservative view of gender roles such as complete domination of wife and children, a right to have sexual relations with any woman the man wants and the right to dominate women at all levels – sexual, procreation, work and relational. The term is derived from Hispanic culture although the control and power of men in Muslim culture and the refusal of the Catholic Church to admit women in priesthood and papal positions are also referred to as machismo.

Maternal mortality - the number of maternal deaths resulting from complications of pregnancy and childbirth in a given population.

Micro-disarmament - the collection, control and disposal of small arms, ammunition, explosives, light and heavy weapons in the possession of combatants and the civilian population. It includes the development of responsible weapons and ammunition management programmes.

Militarism - a political orientation of a set of people or a government to maintain a strong military force and to be prepared to use it aggressively to defend or promote national interests.

Militarisation - a process in which military ideology, principles and patterns of behaviour acquire a major influence on the political, economic, social and external developments of a society. The process results in increased violence in society, especially violence against women and girls.

Millennium Developments Goals (MDGs) - a gradual compilation of goals from international conferences in the 1990s and later assembled and became known as International Development Goals. By 2015 all UN member states pledged to eradicate extreme poverty and hunger; achieve universal primary education; promote gender equality and empower women; reduce child mortality; improve maternal health; combat HIV/AIDS, malaria and other diseases; ensure environmental sustainability; and develop a global partnership for development. For the realisation of the goals, 18 targets and 48 indicators have been identified. In September 2000 the UN unanimously adopted the *Millennium Declaration* and the General Assembly recognised the MDGs as part of the road map for the implementation of the declaration.

Misogyny - an attitude that describes hatred towards women.

Montreal Massacre (6 December 1989) - refers to the tragic event of the death of fourteen young female engineering students murdered at the Montreal University by a gunman who called them 'feminists'.

Non-refoulement (principle of) - the prohibition to expel or return ('*refouler*' in French) a refugee in any manner whatsoever to the country where his life or freedom would be threatened due to his race, religion, nationality, membership to a particular social group or political opinion. However, the right of *non-refoulement* can not be claimed by someone who is considered a risk to the security of the country, or who has been convicted of a particularly serious crime.

Paedophilia - a sexual attraction or perversion in an adult towards children, usually under the age of thirteen. Paedophilia is a synonym for the sexual abuse of children. Because this is usually understood as a psychiatric description, law enforcement agents often employ a broader definition of paedophilia to include adults who have a sexual attraction for persons legally considered children.

Patriarchy - comes from Greek (*patria* means family and *archy* means rule) and is a family, government or society controlled by senior men. In general the term is often used to mean societal control by men. In feminist theories it has been employed to mean a gender hierarchy in which men dominate women.

Peacekeeping operations (PKO) - non-combat military operations undertaken by outside forces with the consent of all major belligerent parties designed to monitor and facilitate the implementation of an existing truce or peace agreement in support of diplomatic efforts to reach a political settlement. These cover peacekeeping forces, observer missions and mixed operations.

Peace support operations (PSO) - operations and activities of civil and military organisations deployed to restore peace and/or relieve human suffering. It includes preventive deployments, peacekeeping and peace enforcement operations, diplomatic activities such as preventive diplomacy, peacemaking and peacebuilding, as well as humanitarian assistance, good offices, fact-finding and electoral assistance.

Plan of Action for the Elimination of Harmful Traditional Practices Affecting the Health of Women and Children - was adopted by the Sub-Commission on Prevention of Discrimination and Protection of Minorities in its Resolution 1994/30 on 26 August 1994 calling for national and international action including legislative measures prohibiting traditional practices affecting the health of women and children, especially female genital mutilation.

Post-traumatic stress disorder (PTSD) - a recurrent emotional reaction that can occur following a traumatic event which happened in a person's life or to a friend or family member of that person. Rape and physical assault have been identified among the most common causes for PTSD of women.

Prostitution - part of the commercial sex industry which includes street prostitution, massage brothels, escort services, call-out services, strip clubs, lap-dancing, phone sex, adult and child pornography, video and internet pornography, and prostitution tourism. Most women who are in prostitution for longer than a few months drift among these various permutations of the commercial sex industry.

Protocol to Prevent, Suppress and Punish Trafficking in Persons, Especially Women and Children, supplementing the United Nations Convention against Transnational Organised Crime - was adopted by General Assembly Resolution 55/25 on 8 January 2001 and requests the state parties to approve legislative measures establishing trafficking in persons as a criminal offence. It applies to the prevention, investigation and prosecution of crimes of trafficking in persons of transnational nature where an organised criminal group is involved.

Racism - discriminatory or abusive behaviour towards members of another race. It is based on the prejudice that members of one race are intrinsically superior to members of other races.

Refugee - a person outside of his or her country of nationality who is unable or unwilling to return because of persecution or a well-founded fear of persecution on account of race, religion, nationality, membership in a particular social group, or political opinion.

Reproductive rights - based on the recognition of the basic right of all couples and individuals to decide freely and responsibly the number, spacing and timing of their children and to have the information and means to do so, and the right to attain the highest standard of sexual and reproductive health. They also include the right of all to make decisions concerning reproduction free of discrimination, coercion and violence.

Rest and recreation facilities (R&R) - are, in the context of military deployment, services for foreign troops which consist of bars and night-clubs, but in reality, operate as covering facilities for prostitution and other forms of sexual exploitation.

Safe houses - facilities where women and children in danger, particularly from domestic violence, can seek temporary refuge.

Sati - the Hindu practice through which widows are voluntarily or forcibly burned alive on their husband's funeral pyre. It has been mainly reported from India, where it was banned in 1829 and again in 1956 after a resurgence. The idea justifying *sati* is that women only have worth in relation to men.

Second World Conference on Women (Copenhagen, 14 - 30 July 1980)/ World Conference of the United Nations Decade for Women: Equality, Development and Peace - called to appraise the progress achieved since the First World Conference on Women in Mexico City in 1975 and recognised that significant steps had been made, especially with the adoption by the UN General Assembly of the *Convention on the Elimination of All Forms of Discrimination against Women* in 1979. It emphasised, however, certain areas of concern: access to education, employment opportunities and adequate health care services. The conference adopted the Programme of Action for the Second Half of the UN Decade for Women, which called for stronger national measures to ensure women's economic and political rights.

Security Council Resolution 1325 on Women, Peace and Security - was adopted on 31 October 2000 as a landmark resolution addressing a number of areas linking women, peace and security. It recognises the importance of maintaining a gender perspective in all facets of peacekeeping operations; urges for intensification of women's participation in prevention, management and resolution of conflict; calls upon all parties to respect and protect women's and girls' rights in armed conflict taking into account their special needs.

Security Sector Reform (SSR) - a term used to describe the transformation of the security system, which includes all the actors, their roles, responsibilities and actions. The aim is to work together to manage and operate the system in a manner that is more consistent with democratic norms and principles of good governance, and thus contribute to a well-functioning security framework.

Sexism - discriminatory or abusive behaviour towards members of the opposite sex.

Sexual assault - a non-consensual sexual contact that is often obtained through coercion or the use or threat of force, as an expression of power, control and domination over another person. Coercion can cover a wide range of behaviours, including intimidation, manipulation, threats of negative treatment, and blackmail.

Sexual exploitation - the participation by a person in prostitution, sexual servitude, or the production of pornographic materials as a result of being subjected to a threat, deception, coercion, abduction, force, abuse of authority, debt bondage or fraud. In the case of persons under the age of eighteen, sexual exploitation means the mere participation in prostitution, sexual servitude or the production of pornographic materials.

Sexual harassment - unwanted and offensive sexual advances, sexual favours and other sexual behaviour either verbal or physical in the workplace when acquiescence to such acts is aimed at explicitly or implicitly affecting an individual's continued employment, promotion or satisfactory job assessment or creates a hostile environment. The victim and the harasser may be a woman or a man. Most often it happens in hierarchical positions with the harasser being the victim's supervisor. Other examples of sexual harassment are offensive language, humiliating sexual inquiries and vulgarities, sexually offensive signs, cartoons, literature or photographs displayed in public etc.

Sexual slavery - a status or condition of a person over whom any or all of the powers attached to the right of ownership are exercised, including sexual access through rape or other forms of sexual violence. Sexual slavery also encompasses situations where women and girls are forced into marriage, domestic servitude and forced labour that involves forced sexual activity, as well as forced prostitution. Slavery is prohibited by international law in all circumstances and constitutes an international crime. The 'comfort stations' that were maintained by the Japanese military during the Second World War and the 'rape camps' that have been documented in the former Yugoslavia are examples of sexual slavery.

Sexual violence - any violence, physical or psychological, carried out through sexual means or by targeting sexuality. It includes rape, forcing a person to strip naked in public, forcing two victims to perform sexual acts together or harm one another in a sexual manner, mutilating a person's genitals or a woman's breasts, and sexual slavery. Such acts are often intended to inflict severe humiliation on the victims and to intimidate the larger community particularly in the context of armed conflict.

Sexually transmitted diseases (STDs) - include any disease that is communicated primarily or exclusively through intimate sexual contact. Commonly transmitted STDs include chlamydia, gonorrhoea, syphilis, genital herpes, and HIV infection. STDs are a common cause of infertility.

Sixteen Days of Action against Violence Against Women (25 November – 10 December) - a campaign raising awareness worldwide to end gender-based violence starting from 25 November, International Day on the Elimination of Violence against Women and ending on 10 December, International Human Rights Day. It started in 1991 when activists chose the dates to symbolically link violence against women and human rights, thus emphasising that such violence is a violation of human rights. The sixteen-day campaign has been used to create a global movement to raise awareness, address policy and legal issues, educate the public, campaign for the protection of survivors of violence, lobby the government, provide a forum, and call for action to all actors involved i.e. police, social workers, medical workers etc. The movement grew in 2004 to over one thousand organisations in 130 countries.

Slavery - the status or condition of a person over whom any or all of the powers attached to the right of ownership are exercised. Slavery is prohibited by international law and qualifies, under specific conditions, as a crime against humanity. An enslaved person is usually forced to work, is controlled, dehumanised, treated as a commodity, bought and sold as 'property' and physically constrained or restricted in his/her movement. Contemporary forms of slavery include, for example, forced labour, certain forms of child labour, commercial sexual exploitation of children, trafficking and forced and early marriages. See also Crime against humanity, Forced labour, Trafficking in persons, Forced marriage.

Small arms and light weapons (SALW) - deadly conventional munitions and explosives that can be carried by an individual combatant or a light vehicle. Small arms are weapons aimed at personal use and light weapons are those used by a small group of persons. In general, they do not require a substantial logistic and maintenance capability. Small arms include, for example, revolvers, self-loading pistols, rifles and carbines, sub-machine-guns, light machine guns, and assault rifles. Light weapons consist of heavy machine guns, hand-held, under-barrel and mounted grenade launchers, portable anti-aircraft guns, portable launchers of anti-tank missile and rocket systems etc. SALW also include ammunition and explosives such as cartridges, shells and missiles for light weapons, anti-personnel and anti-tank grenades, and landmines.

Smuggling in persons - the procurement, in order to obtain, directly or indirectly, a financial or other material benefit, of the illegal entry of a person into a foreign country.

Stove death - the punishment of a wife by setting her ablaze, often disguised by the perpetrator as a suicide. It has been reported mainly in Pakistan. Causes vary, but the main reasons are failure to give birth to a son, the desire to marry a second wife without having the financial means to support the first, and long-running animosity with mothers-in-law.

Third World Conference on Women (Nairobi, 15-26 July 1985) / World Conference to Review and Appraise the Achievements of the UN Decade for Women - reviewed and evaluated the progress achieved and the obstacles encountered in attaining the goals of the UN Decade for Women: Equality, Development and Peace and the sub-theme: Employment, Health and Education, taking into account the guidelines set at *the* First World Conference on Women in Mexico City (1975) and the Second World Conference on Women in Copenhagen (1980). It adopted the Nairobi Forward-looking Strategies for the Advancement of Women, which called for equal social, economic and political rights for men and women and the elimination of all forms of discrimination against women.

Torture - an act of severe physical or mental pain intentionally inflicted on a person, by a public official (or tolerated by), for the purpose of obtaining information or confession, punishment or intimidation. Torture is prohibited by international law in all circumstances. Recent developments of international humanitarian law have recognised sexual violence in armed conflict as a form of torture.

Trafficking in persons - the movement of persons under the threat of violence or other form of coercion for the purpose of exploitation. Trafficking includes the recruitment, transportation, transfer, harbouring or receipt of persons. The exploitation includes sexual exploitation, prostitution, forced labour, slavery and slavery-like practices, servitude or the removal of organs. The consent of the victim is irrelevant if received under threat or as a result of payments or benefits given to the victim in order to achieve such consent. Most victims of trafficking are women and children. New forms of trafficking include mail order bride industries and sex tourism. See also Sexual exploitation, Prostitution, Forced labour, Sexual slavery, Slavery.

UN Basic Principles for the Treatment of Prisoners - was adopted and proclaimed by General Assembly Resolution 45/111on 14 December 1990. It sets out rules for the non-discriminatory treatment of prisoners with respect to their human dignity and ensures protection of their human rights and fundamental freedoms under the Universal Declaration of Human Rights, except for the necessary limitations due to incarceration.

UN Body of Principles for the Protection of All Persons under any Form of Detention or Imprisonment - adopted by General Assembly Resolution 43/173 on 9 December 1988. It stipulates the right to humane treatment of every person in detention or imprisonment and strictly forbids any form of torture or degrading punishment under any circumstances. It also calls on states to legally prohibit any act contrary to the rights and duties established in the document.

UN Convention against Torture and Other Cruel, Inhuman or Degrading Treatment or Punishment (CAT) - adopted by General Assembly Resolution 39/46 of 10 December 1984. It prohibits torture, cruel, inhuman or degrading treatment or punishment under all circumstances. It established the Committee against Torture to monitor implementation of the provisions of the convention by its states parties.

UN Convention on the Elimination of All Forms of Discrimination against Women (CEDAW) - adopted by General Assembly Resolution 34/180 on 18 December 1979. It is the main international legal instrument protecting women's rights, often referred to as the international bill of rights for women. It requests states to ensure the full development and advancement of women and to guarantee them equality in the enjoyment and exercise of all human rights and fundamental freedoms. In practice, it essentially calls for the incorporation of the principle of equality in the legal system including the abolition of discriminatory laws; the establishment of public institutions for the efficient protection of women against discrimination and the elimination of all acts of discrimination against women by individuals, organisations and enterprises. It established the Committee on the Elimination of Discrimination against Women to monitor implementation of the convention's provisions and to consider complaints of individuals. The Optional Protocol to the CEDAW, adopted in 1999, enables individual complaints.

UN Declaration on the Elimination of Violence against Women (DEVAW) - adopted by General Assembly resolution 48/104 of 20 December 1993. It recognises that violence against women is an obstacle to the full achievement of equality, development and peace in society. It provides an important definition of violence against women stressing the roles of different actors such as the individual, the community and the state. It stipulates that states should pursue by all appropriate means and without delay a policy of eliminating violence against women. States are further called to condemn violence against women and avoid invoking any custom, tradition or religious consideration to forestall their obligations with respect to its elimination.

UN Human Rights Committee (HRC) - the monitoring body, established by the International Covenant on Civil and Political Rights, charged with consideration of the reports of its state parties and of complaints of individuals on alleged violations of the rights stipulated in the covenant by states parties to its Optional Protocol. See also UN International Covenant on Civil and Political Rights.

UN Inter-agency Campaign on Women's Human Rights in Latin America and the Caribbean: 'A Life Free of Violence: It's Our *Right*' - comprises eight UN agencies (UNIFEM, UNDP, UNFPA, UNICEF, UNHCR, UNHCHR, UNAIDS, ECLAC) and various national organisations in Latin America, which co-operate for combating violence against women and girls. The campaign raises awareness for women's rights, supports public and private programmes for the elimination of gender-based violence and encourages change in states' legislation towards gender equality.

UN International Covenant on Civil and Political Rights (ICCPR) - adopted by General Assembly Resolution 2200A (XXI) on 16 December 1966. It is the main human rights instrument protecting civil and political rights. It also established the Human Rights Committee. It explicitly guarantees equality of men and women in the enjoyment of all civil and political rights. See also Human Rights Committee.

UN Millennium Declaration - unanimously adopted by 150 heads of state at the conclusion of the UN Millennium Summit on 8 September 2000 in New York. Six priority areas were agreed: peace, security and disarmament; development and poverty eradication; protection of the environment; good governance, democracy and human rights; protection of the vulnerable; and strengthening the United Nations. See also Millennium Development Goals.

UN Special Rapporteur on Violence against Women, Its Causes and Its Consequences - the mandate created by the UN Commission on Human Rights to collect and analyse comprehensive data concerning violence against women and to recommend measures aimed at eliminating this violence at international, national and regional levels. The first Special Rapporteur, Ms. Radhika Coomaraswamy (Sri Lanka), was appointed in 1994 and succeeded by Ms. Yakin Ertürk (Turkey) in 2003. See also World Conference on Human Rights (Vienna, 14-25 June 1993).

UN Standard Minimum Rules for the Treatment of Prisoners (the Standard Minimum Rules) - a document adopted by the First United Nations Congress on the Prevention of Crime and the Treatment of Offenders held in Geneva in 1955 and approved by the Economic and Social Council by its Resolution 663 C (XXIV) on 31 July 1957 and Resolution 2076 (LXII) on 13 May 1977. The document represents a comprehensive guideline as to how governments may comply with their international legal obligations concerning the treatment of prisoners. It also contains important provisions regarding treatment of women prisoners.

Unexploded ordnance (UXOs) - explosive weapons except landmines, which remain non-discharged either by malfunction or design and left dispersed in an area or country after an armed conflict. UXOs have an enduring impact in many post-conflict communities.

United Nations Conference on Human Settlements - known as Habitat II or the 'City Summit', was held in Istanbul in 1996 to address the issue of socially and environmentally sustainable cities, in particular adequate shelter for all and sustainable human settlements development in an urbanising world. It adopted the Habitat Agenda and Istanbul Declaration. The Habitat Agenda contains commitments to the goal of gender equality in human settlements development.

United Nations Decade for Women: Equality, Development and Peace (1976-1985) - was proclaimed by General Assembly Resolution 3520 (XXX) on 15 December 1975 on the occasion of the first world conference on women held in Mexico in 1975. During the decade, the UN addressed women's marginalisation and empowerment in the areas of equality, development and peace. Numerous results were achieved such as the adoption of conventions and declarations enshrining equal rights of women in society and in all aspects of their life; integration of women and their needs in development mechanisms; and the recognition of women as equal partners in all processes of society including national and international decisions on peace and security. The decade was marked by two other world conferences on women held in Copenhagen in 1980 and in Nairobi in 1985. These conferences served to assess achievements and map out priority issues for the road ahead. See also the First, Second, and Third UN World Conferences respectively held in Mexico (1975), Copenhagen (1980), and Nairobi (1985).

Universal Declaration of Human Rights (UDHR) - drafted by the Commission on Human Rights and adopted on

10 December 1948. It is the core international human rights instrument setting forth the basic inalienable rights and fundamental freedoms of each and every person. The UDHR together with the International Covenant on Civil and Political Rights and the International Covenant on Economic, Social and Cultural Rights form the international bill of human rights. See also International Covenant on Civil and Political Rights and the International Covenant on Economic, Social and Cultural Rights.

Violence against women (VAW) - any act or threat of gender-based violence that results in, or is likely to result in physical, sexual or psychological harm or suffering to women, including coercion or arbitrary deprivation of liberty, whether occurring in public or in private life. This includes physical, sexual and psychological violence such as wife beating, burning and acid throwing, sexual abuse including rape and incest by family members, female genital mutilation, female foeticide and infanticide, and emotional abuse such as coercion and abusive language. VAW does not only occur in the family and in the general community, but is sometimes also condoned or perpetuated by the state through a variety of policies and actions.

Virgin myth - a false belief that sex with a virgin will cure sexually transmitted diseases, in particular that it may cleanse a person of HIV/AIDS. Even very young girls and infants have been sexually abused for this purpose. Prevalence of the virgin myth has been reported in some African countries, particularly in South Africa.

War crime - a punishable misconduct under international law for violations of the laws of war by individuals, groups, military or civilians. The laws of war identifies the conduct and responsibilities of belligerent nations, neutral nations and individuals engaged in warfare, in relation to each other and protected persons, usually civilians. The laws of war are codified primarily in the Geneva Conventions (1949 and 1977 Protocols) and Hague Conventions (1899 and 1907), which are obligatory to state parties. These aim to reduce the damage caused by war by protecting both combatants and non-combatants from unnecessary suffering; safeguarding certain fundamental human rights of prisoners of war, the wounded and sick and civilians; and facilitating the return to peace. Examples of war crimes include mistreatment of prisoners of war, mass murder, genocide and the use of inhumane weapons. Certain types of gender-based crimes such as rape, sexual slavery, enforced prostitution, forced pregnancy, enforced sterilisation and any other form of sexual violence have been considered a serious violation of the Geneva Conventions. War crimes have been defined and prosecuted by international tribunals such as Nuremberg, Tokyo, ICTY, ICTR and the ICC.

Windhoek Declaration and Namibia Plan of Action on 'Mainstreaming a Gender Perspective in Multidimensional Peace Support Operations' (Namibia, 31 May 2000) - adopted at a seminar organised by the Lessons Learned Unit of the UN Department of Peacekeeping Operations in Namibia on 29-31 May 2000. The declaration emphasised the lack of effective participation of women in multidimensional peace support operations (PSO) nationally and internationally. It advocated for the equal role of women and men as partners and beneficiaries in all aspects of the peace process, from peacekeeping, reconciliation and peacebuilding, to an equal part in the political, economic and social development of the country. The seminar recommended the Namibia Plan of Action that raised practical ways of mainstreaming gender in PSOs. These include equal access of women in negotiations, incorporation of gender mainstreaming in the mandate and budget, respect of women's rights and needs in the training of personnel, access to leadership and decision-making positions, institution of gender units and advisers and establishment of efficient and regular monitoring and accountability mechanisms.

Women 2000: Gender Equality, Development and Peace for the 21st century (New York, 5-9 June 2000) - the 23rd special session of the General Assembly called together to review progress in the implementation of the Nairobi Forward-looking Strategies for the Advancement of Women and the Beijing Declaration and Platform for Action. It adopted a Political Declaration and Outcome Document entitled 'Further Actions and Initiatives to Implement the Beijing Declaration and Platform for Action', which reaffirmed the importance of gender mainstreaming and recognised the need to ensure women's advancement by focusing on their basic needs through a holistic approach based on equal rights and partnerships.

Women Building Peace Campaign - launched in 1999 by women from conflict areas with the purpose of ensuring women's equal access to political, economic and social resources and strengthening their role in peacebuilding, reconstruction and reconciliation.

World Conference on Human Rights (Vienna, 14-25 June 1993) - an international conference that examined the link between the right to development and democracy, as well as political, social and economic rights and evaluated the effectiveness of the UN mechanisms on the advancement and protection of human rights. It took historic action in promoting women's rights by affirming that the human rights of women and the girl-child are an inalienable, integral and indivisible part of universal human rights. It further asserted the equal participation of women in political, civil, economic, social and cultural life at all levels and the elimination of all forms of discrimination based on gender. It also supported the creation of a new mechanism, the Special Rapporteur on Violence against Women. See also Special Rapporteur on Violence against Women.

World Summit for Social Development (Copenhagen, 5-12 March 1995) - a worldwide conference that pledged to make the elimination of poverty, full employment and the fostering of social integration, principal objectives of development. It adopted the Copenhagen Declaration, and the Programme of Action, which recognised that gender equality and women's empowerment are both objectives and sources of development.

Zero Tolerance Campaigns - a set of campaigns launched by the Zero Tolerance Charitable Trust towards the prevention of male violence against women and children. The first campaign was held in Edinburgh in 1992.

Bibliography

Books

H. Afshar (ed), *Women and Empowerment* (London: Routledge, 1997).

H. Afshar and D. Eade (eds), *Development, Women and War: Feminist Perspectives* (Oxford: OXFAM, 2004).

S. Altink, *Stolen Lives: Trading Women into Sex and Slavery* (London: Scarlet Press, 1995).

S. Anderlini, *Women and the Peace Table: Making a Difference* (New York: UNIFEM, 2000).

K. Annan, *Women, Peace and Security* (New York: UN Publications, 2002).

R. Appleyard and J. Salt (eds), *Perspectives on Trafficking of Migrants*, Offprint of International Migration, Vol. 38, No. 3, Special Issue 1/2000 (New York and Geneva: UN and IOM, 2000).

K. Askin, *War Crimes Against Women: Prosecution in International War Crimes Tribunals* (The Hague: M. Nijhoff, 1997).

K. Askin and D. M. Koenig, *Women and International Human Rights Law*, Vol. 1-3 (New York: Transnational Publishers Inc., 1999).

P. Bart and E. Geil Moran (eds), *Violence against Women: The Bloody Footprints* (California: Sage, 1993).

E. Bell, *Emerging Issues in Gender and Development: An Overview*, BRIDGE Report No 58 (November 2000).

D. Bloomfield, T. Bames and L. Huyse, *Reconciliation After Violent Conflict, A Handbook* (Stockholm: Institute for Democracy and Electoral Assistance, 2003).

K. Booth and S. Smith (eds), *International Theory Today* (Cambridge: Polity Press, 1995).

M. Braig and S. Wölte (eds), *Common Ground or Mutual Exclusion? Women's Movements and International Relations* (London: Zed Books, 2002).

S. Brownmiller, *Against Our Will Men: Women and Rape* (New York: Ballantine Books, 1975).

D. Budlender and G. Hewitt (eds), *Gender Budgets Make More Cents: Country Studies and Good Practices* (London: The Commonwealth Secretariat, 2002).

D. Budlender et al., *Gender Budgets Make Cents: Understanding Gender Responsive Budgets* (London: The Commonwealth Secretariat, 2002).

C. Burack and J. J. Josephson (eds), *Fundamental Differences: Feminists Talk Back to Social Conservatives* (Lanham: Rowman & Littlefield Publishers, 2003).

M. Buvinic, A. Morrison and M. Shifter, *Violence in Latin America and the Caribbean: A Framework for Action* (Washington DC: Inter-American Development Bank), at http://www.iadb.org/sds/doc/1073eng.pdf

R. Carillo, *Battered Dreams: Violence Against Women as an Obstacle for Development* (New York: UNIFEM, 1992).

C. Cockburn and R. Stakic-Domuz, *The Space between Us: Negotiating Gender and National Identities in Conflict* (London: Zed Books, 1999).

R. Cook (ed), *Human Rights of Women, National and International Perspectives* (Philadelphia: University of Pennsylvania, 1994).

M. Cooke and A. Woollacott (eds), *Gendering War Talk* (New Jersey: Princeton University Press, 1993).

M. van Creveld, *Men Women & War: Do Women Belong in the Front Line?* (London: Cassell & Co, 2001).

M. Davies (ed), *Women and Violence: Realities and Responses Worldwide* (London: Zed Books, 1994).

R. E. Dobash and R. Dobash, *Violence against Wives* (London: Open Books, 1979).

B. Ehrenreich and A. Hochschild (eds), *Global Woman: Nannies, Maids and Sex Workers in the New Economy* (London: Granta Publications, 2003).

J. Elshtain and S. Tobias (eds), *Women, Militarism and War: Essays in History, Politics and Social Theory* (Boston: Rowman and Littlefield, 1990).

C. Enloe, *Bananas, Beaches and Bases: Making Feminist Sense of International Politics* (Berkley: University of California Press, 1989).

C. Enloe, *Does Khaki Become You? The Militarization of Women's Lives* (London: Pandora Press, 1988).

C. Enloe, *Manoeuvres: The International Politics of Militarizing Women's Lives* (Berkley and London: University of California Press, 2000).

L. Fairstein, *Sexual Violence: Our War against Rape* (New York: William Morrow and Co., 1993).

M. Fitzduff and C. Church, *NGOs at the Table: Strategies for Influencing Policies in Areas of Conflict* (Lanham: Rowman & Littlefield Publishers, 2004).

M. French, *The War against Women* (New York: Ballanatine, 1992).

A. Gnanadason, M. Kanyoro, L. McSpadeen (eds), *Women, Violence and Non-Violent Change* (Geneva: WCC Publications, 1996).

J. S. Goldstein, *War and Gender: How Gender Shapes the War System and Vice Versa* (Cambridge: Cambridge University Press, 2001).

F. Halliday, *Rethinking International Relations* (Basingtoke: Macmillan, 1994).

R. Hammer, *Antifeminism and Family Terrorism: A Critical Feminist Perspective* (Boston: Rowman & Littlefield Publishers, 2002).

L. Heise, M. Ellsberg and M. Gottemoeller, *Ending Violence against Women: Population Reports L (11)* (Baltimore: Johns Hopkins University, School of Public Health, Population Information Program, 1999), at http://www.infoforhealth.org/pr/l11edsum.shtml

A. Helland, K. Daramé, A. Kristensen, I. Skjelsberg, *Women and Armed Conflicts* (Oslo: Norwegian Institute for International Affairs, 1999).

R. Inglehart and P. Norris, *Rising Tide: Gender Equality and Cultural Change around the World* (Cambridge: Cambridge University Press, 2003).

IOM, *Victims of Trafficking in the Balkans* (Slovak Republic: IOM, 2001).

R. Jahal, *The Elusive Agenda: Mainstreaming Women in Development* (London: Zed Books, 1995).

E. King and A. Mason, *Engendering Development: Through Gender Equality in Rights, Resources, and Voice* (New York and Oxford: Oxford University Press, 2001).

D. Kyle and R. Koslowski (eds.), *Global Human Smuggling: Comparative Perspectives* (Baltimore: Johns Hopkins University Press, 2001).

F. Laczko, I. Stacher and A. K. von Koppenfels (eds), *New Challenges for Migration Policy in Central and Eastern Europe* (The Hague: IOM and ICMPD, 2002).

La Strada, *Trafficking in Women in Post-communist Countries of Central and Eastern Europe* (Prague: La Strada Centre for Gender Studies, 1997).

G. Lerner, *The Creation of Patriarchy* (Oxford: Oxford University Press, 1986).

C. Lindsey, *Women Facing War* (Geneva: ICRC, 2001).

M. K. Meyer and E. Prügl (eds), *Gender Politics in Global Governance* (Boulder, CO: Rowman & Littlefield, 1999).

A. Morrison and L. Biehl (eds), *Too Close to Home: Domestic Violence in the Americas* (Washington DC: Inter-American Development Bank and Johns Hopkins University Press, 1999).

M. Niederhauser and S. Wehrli, *Sécurité 2002: Points de Vues Féminins et Masculins: Analyse des Opinions en Matière de Politique Étrangère, de Politique de Sécurité et de Politique de Défense du Point de Vue des Deux Sexes* (Bern: Direction de la Politique de Sécurité, 2002).

L. Olsson and T. L. Tryggestad (eds), *Women and International Peacekeeping,* (London: Frank Cass, 2001).

A. O'Neill-Richard, *International Trafficking in Women to the United States: A Contemporary Manifestation of Slavery and Organized Crime* (United States: Center for the Study of Intelligence, 1999).

Open Society Institute, *Bending the Bow: Targeting Women's Human Rights and Opportunities* (New York: Open Society Institute, Network Women's Program, 2002).

E. Pearson, *Human Traffic Human Rights: Redefining Victim Protection* (London: Anti-Slavery International, 2002).

M. Penn and R. Nardos, *Overcoming Violence against Women and Girls: The International Campaign to Eradicate a Worldwide Problem* (Boston: Rowman & Littlefield Publishers, 2003).

J. Peters and A. Wolper, *Women's Rights Human Rights: international feminist perspectives* (London: Routledge, 1995)

V. S. Peterson (ed), *Gendered States: Feminist (Re)Visions of International Relations Theory* (Boulder CO: Lynne Rienner, 1992).

J. Pettman, *Worlding Women: A Feminist International Politics* (London: Routledge, 1996).

P. Procházková, *The Aluminum Queen: The Russian – Chechen War through the Eyes of Women* (Prague: NLN, s.r.o., 2002).

S. Rai and G. Lievesley, *Women and the State International Perspectives* (London: Taylor & Francis, 1996).

B. Reardon, *Women and Peace – Feminist Visions of Global Security* (Albany: State University of New York Press, 1993).

E. Rehn and E. Johnson Sirleaf, *Women, War and Peace: The Independent Assessment on the Impact of Armed Conflict on Women and Women's Role in Peace-Building* (New York: UNIFEM, 2002).

I. Sajor (ed), *Our Common Grounds: Violence Against Women in War and Armed Conflict Situations* (Quezon City: Asian Center for Women's Human Rights, 1998).

V. Shiva, *Staying Alive: Women, Ecology and Development* (London: Zed Books, 1989).

I. Skjelsbaek and D. Smith (eds), *Gender, Peace and Conflict* (Oslo and London: PRIO International Peace Research Institute and SAGE Publications, 2001).

S. Skrobanek et al., *The Traffic in Women: Human Realities of the International Sex Trade* (London: Zed Books), 1997.

B. Sorensen, *Women and Post-Conflict Reconstruction: Issues and Sources* (Geneva: UNRISD and PSIS, 1998).

A. Stiglmayer (ed), *Mass Rape: The War against Women in Bosnia-Herzegovina* (Lincoln: University of Nebraska Press, 1994).

N. Stromquist (ed), *Women in the Third World: An Encyclopaedia of Contemporary Issues* (New York: Garland Publishing, 1998).

A. Suki et al., *Global Feminist Politics: Identities in a Changing World* (London and New York: Routledge, 2000).

J. Symonides and V. Volodin, *Human Rights of Women: A Collection of International and Regional Normative Instruments* (Paris: UNESCO, 1999).

T. Terriff, S. Croft, L. James and P. M. Morgan (eds), *Security Studies Today* (London: Polity Press, 1999).

J. Tickner, *Gender in International relations: Feminist Perspectives on Achieving Global Security* (New York: Columbia University Press, 1992).

J. G. Towsend, E. Zapata, J. Rowlands, P. Alberti and M. Mercado, *Women and Power: Fighting Patriarchies and Poverty* (London: Zed Books, 1999).

M. Turshen and C. Twagiramariya (eds), *What Women Do in Wartime. Gender and Conflict in Africa* (London and New York: Zed Books, 1998).

UNICEF, *Trafficking in Human Being in Southeastern Europe* (Belgrade: UNICEF, OHCHR, ODIHR, 2002).

J. Vickers, *Women and War* (London: Zed Books, 1993).

L. Welchmann (ed), *Women's Rights and Islamic Family Law* (London: Zed Books, 2004).

C. Wichterich, *The Globalized Woman: Reports from a Future of Inequality* (London: Zed Books, 2000).

P. Williams (ed.), *Illegal Immigration and Commercial Sex: The New Slave Trade* (London: Frank Cass), 1999.

V. Wolf, *A Room of One's Own/Three Guineas* (London: Penguin Books, 1993).

M. Zalewski, *Feminism after Postmodernism: Theorising through Practice* (London: Routledge, 2000).

Reports

Amnesty International, *Bosnia-Herzegovina, Rape and Sexual Abuse by Armed Forces*, (January 1993).

Amnesty International, *Human Rights Are Women's Rights* (New York, 1995).

Amnesty International, *'Not Part of My Sentence' Violations of the Human Rights of Women in Custody* (USA: Amnesty International, 1999).

Amnesty International, *Women in the Front Line* (March 1991).

Commission on Human Security, *Human Security Now* (New York: Commission on Human Security, 2003).

R. Coomaraswamy, *Further Promotion and Encouragement of Human Rights and Fundamental Freedoms, Including the Question of the Programme and Methods of Work of the Commission Alternative Approaches and Ways and Means within the United Nations System for Improving the Effective Enjoyment of Human Rights and Fundamental Freedoms*, UN Document E/CN.4/1996/53/Add.1 (4 January 1996).

R. Coomaraswamy, *Integration of the Human Rights of Women and the Gender Perspective: Violence against Women*, Report of the Special Rapporteur on Violence Against Women, Its Causes And Consequences, submitted for the 59th Session of the Commission on Human Rights, UN Document E/CN.4/2003/75/Add.1 (27 February 2003).

R. Coomaraswamy, Report A/CONF.189/PC.3/5, World Conference against Racism, Racial Discrimination, Xenophobia and Related Intolerance, Preparatory Committee (27 July 2001).

Department for International Development (DFID), *Breaking the Barriers: Women and the Elimination of World Poverty* (London: DFID, 1998).

Development Assistance Committee (DAC), *DAC Guidelines on Gender Equality and Women's Empowerment in Development Co-operation* (Paris: OECD, 1998), at http://www.oecd.org/dac/htm/pubs/p-gender.htm

D. Elson and H. Keklik, *The Progress of the World's Women 2002 Vol. 2, Gender Equality and the Millennium Development Goals*, (New York: UN Publications, 2002).

European Union, *Trafficking in Women, the Misery behind the Fantasy: From Poverty to Sex Slavery, A Comprehensive European Strategy*, at http://europa.eu.int/comm/employment_social/equ_opp/index_en.htm

Human Rights Watch, *Crime or Custom? Violence Against Women in Pakistan* (USA: HRW, 1999).

Human Rights Watch, *Shattered Lives: Sexual Violence during the Rwandan Genocide and its Aftermath* (USA: HRW, 1996).

Human Rights Watch, *The War within the War: Sexual Violence against Women and Girls in Eastern Congo* (New York: HRW, 2002).

International Alert, *Gender Mainstreaming in Peace Support Operations: Moving Beyond Rhetoric to Practice* (London: International Alert, 2002).

International Organization for Migration (IOM), 'Trafficking in Migrants', *Quarterly Bulletins*, No. 23 (April 2001), Special Issue, No. 25 (Spring 2002).

E. Krug, L. Dahlberg, J. Mery, A. Zwi and R. Lozano, *World Report on Violence and Health* (Geneva: WHO, 2002).

Norwegian Institute of International Affairs (NUPI) and FAFO (Institute for Applied Social Science), *Gendering Human Security: From Marginalisation to the Integration of Women in Peace-Building*, Recommendations for policy and practice from the NUPI-FAFO Forum on Gender Relations in Post-Conflict Transitions (Oslo: NUPI and FAFO, 2001).

S. Schmeidl and E. Piza-Lopez, *Gender and Conflict Early Warning: A Framework for Action* (London: International Alert and Swiss Peace Foundation, 2002).

United Nations, *Final Report of the Commission of Experts on the former Yugoslavia*, UN Document S/1994/674 (27 May 1994).

United Nations, *Mainstreaming a Gender Perspective in Multi-dimensional Peace Operations* (New York: UN Department of Peacekeeping Operations Lessons Learned Unit, 2000).

United Nations Children's Fund, *Women in Transition, Regional Monitoring Report No. 6 of the MONEE* (Central and Eastern Europe in Transition: Public Policy and Social conditions) Project (Florence: UNICEF, 1999).

United Nations Development Programme, *Human Development Report 2002: Deepening Democracy in a Fragmented World* (New York and Oxford: Oxford University Press, 2002).

United Nations Development Programme, *Human Development Report 2004: Cultural Liberty in Today's Diverse World* (New York: UNDP, 2004).

United Nations Fund for Women, *Getting it Right, Doing it Right: Gender and Disarmament, Demobilisation and Reintegration* (New York: UNIFEM, 2004)

United Nations Institute for Disarmament Research, *Women, Men, Peace and Security,* Disarmament Forum, Issue 4, Special Issue for the third anniversary of UN Security Council Resolution 1325 (2003).

United Nations Population Fund, *The State of World Population* (New York: UNFPA, 2000), at http://www.unfpa.org/swp/2000/english/index.html

M. Waring, G. Greenwood and C. Pintat, *Politics: Women's Insight*, IPU Reports and Documents No. 36 (Geneva: IPU, 2000).

World Bank, *World Development Indicators 2002* (Washington DC: World Bank, 2002).

World Bank, *World Development Report 2004* (Washington DC: World Bank, 2004).

Articles, papers, journals

R. Anker, 'Theories of Occupational Segregation by Sex: An Overview', *International Labour Review*, Vol. 136, No. 3 (1997).

E. F. Barth, *Peace as Disappointment: The Reintegration of Female Soldiers in Post-Conflict Societies: A Comparative Study from Africa*, PRIO Report 3/2002 (Oslo: PRIO, 2002).

C. Benninger-Budel and J. Bourke-Martignoni, *Violence Against Women: 10 Reports/Year 2002* (Geneva: OMCT, 2003).

T. Bouta and G. Frerks, *Women's Roles in Conflict Prevention, Conflict Resolution and Post-Conflict Reconstruction: Literature Review and Institutional Analysis*, Occasional Paper (The Hague: The Clingendael Institute, 2002).

S. J. Bowen, *Resilience and Health: Salvadoran Refugee Women in Manitoba*, (Canada: PWHCE Prairie Women's Health Centre of Excellence, 2005)

M. de Bruyn, *Violence, Pregnancy and Abortion, Issues of Women's Rights and Public Health*, A Review of Worldwide Data and Recommendations for Action (USA: IPAS, 2003)

C. Burke, *Women and Militarism* (Geneva: WILPF, 1994).

B. Byrne, *Gender, Conflict and Development, Volume 1: Overview*, BRIDGE Report 34 (Sussex: BRIDGE, 1995).

B. Byrne, R. Marcus and T. Powers-Stevens, *Gender, Conflict and Development. Volume 2: Case Studies Cambodia, Rwanda, Kosova, Somalia, Algeria, Guatemala and Eritrea*, BRIDGE Report 35 (Sussex: BRIDGE, 1995).

Center for Women's Global Leadership (CWGL), *16 Days of Activism Against Gender Violence, November 25 – December 10, 2003, Violence Against Women Violates Human Rights: Maintaining the Momentum Ten Years After Vienna (1993-2003)* (CWGL, 2003).

C. Chinkin, 'Rape and Sexual Abuse of Women in International Law', *EJIL,* 5 (1994).

R. Copelon, 'Gender Crimes as War Crimes: Integrating Crimes against Women into International Criminal Law', *McGill Law Journal* (2000).

L. Heise, J Pitanguy and A. Germain, *Violence against Women: The Hidden Health Burden*, World Bank Discussion Paper 255 (1994).

B. Hernández-Truyol, 'Sex, Culture, and Rights: A Re/conceptualization of Violence for the Twenty First Century', *Albany Law Review,* 60 (1997).

D. M. Hughes, 'The Internet and Sex Industries: Partners in Global Sexual Exploitation', *Technology and Society Magazine* (Spring 2000).

D. M. Hughes, *The 'Natasha' Trade: Transnational Sex Trafficking* (National Institute of Justice, January 2001).

A. Jones, 'Case Study: Female Infanticide', *Gendercide Watch* (2000), at http://www.gendercide.org/case_infanticide.html

L. Kelly and L. Regan, 'Stopping Traffic: Exploring the Extent of, and Response to, Trafficking in Women for Sexual Exploitation in the UK', *Police Research Series*, Paper 125 (London: Home Office, Policing and Reducing Crime Unit, 2000).

V. Morgan, 'Peacemakers? Peacekeepers? Women in Northern Ireland 1969-1995', *Occasional Paper 3* (Londonderry: INCORE, 1996).

P. Norris and R. Inglehart, 'Cultural Barriers to Women's Leadership: A Worldwide Comparison', *Journal of Democracy* (21 March 2003).

R. Seifert, *War and Rape, Analytical Approaches* (Geneva: WILPF, 1992).

A. Sen, 'Many Faces of Gender Inequality', *The Frontline,* Vol. 18, Issue 22 (27 October-9 November 2001).

A. Sen, 'More than 100 Million Women are Missing', *New York Review of Books* (December 1992).

A. Sen, 'Women's Survival as a Development Problem', *Bulletin of the American Academy of Arts and Sciences,* 43 (1989).

S. Shermann, *State of the World's Mothers 2002, Mothers and Children in War & Conflict* (USA: International Save the Children Alliance, 2002), at http://www.savethechildren.org/publications/sowm2002.pdf

I. Skjelsbaek, *Gendered Battlefields: A Gender Analysis of Peace and Conflict*, PRIO Report 6/97 (Oslo: PRIO, 1997).

V. von Struensee, 'Globalized, Wired, Sex Trafficking in Women and Children', *Murdoch University Electronic Journal of Law* Vol. 7, No. 2 (June 2000).

Swiss Peace Foundation, *War against Women: The Impact of Violence on Gender Relations,* Working Paper, Report of the 6th Annual Conference, 17-18 September 1995 (Bern: Swiss Peace Foundation, 1995).

M. Vlachová and L. Biason, 'Violence against Women as a Challenge for Security Sector Governance', in H. Hänggi and T. H. Winkler (eds), *Challenges of Security Sector Governance* (Geneva: DCAF in LIT Verlag Münster, 2003).

Speeches, presentations

K. Annan, *UN Secretary-General's Statement to Security Council on Women, Peace and Security* (2002).

D. M. Hughes, 'The 2002 Trafficking in Persons Report: Lost Opportunity for Progress', *Foreign Government Complicity in Human Trafficking: A Review of the State Department's 2002 Trafficking in Persons Report*, Presentation on US House Committee on International Relations (Washington DC, 19 June 2002).

I. Sajor, 'The Women's International War Crimes Tribunal On Japan's Military Sexual Slavery: A Historical Landmark in Ending Impunity', *Conference on Preventing Crimes Against Humanity: Lessons from the Asia Pacific War (1931-1945)* (University of British Columbia, Vancouver, Canada, March 21-22, 2003).

Statistics

D. Elson and H. Keklik, *The Progress of the World's Women 2002 Vol. 2, Gender Equality and the Millennium Development Goals* (New York: UN Publications, 2002).

ILO, *Yearbook of Labour Statistics* (Geneva: ILO, 2000).

UN, *The World's Women, Trends and Statistics 1970-1990* (New York: UN Publications, 1991).

Women's Indicators and Statistics Database Version 4 (New York: United Nations Statistical Division, 2000).

World Bank, *World Development Indicators 2002* (New York: The World Bank, 2002).

News, press releases

K. Annan, *UN Secretary-General Message on International Women's Day,* Press Release (8 March 2003).

Amnesty International, 'Broken Bodies, Shattered Minds – The Torture of Women Worldwide', *Amnesty International News Release* (6 March 2001).

International documents

Beijing Declaration and Platform for Action, adopted in the Fourth World Conference on Women (Beijing, 1-15 September 1995), at http://www.womenwatch.org

Declaration and Programme of Action 5ᵗʰ European Ministerial Conference on Equality Between Women and Men: Democratisation, Conflict Prevention and Peacebuilding: The Perspectives and the Roles of Women, Council of Europe (Skopje, 22-23 January 2003).

Declaration of the Advancement of Women in the ASEAN Region (Bangkok, 5 July 1988).

Implementation of the United Nations Millennium Declaration, Report of the Secretary-General, UN Document A/58/323 (2 September 2003).

Nairobi Forward-looking Strategies for the Advancement of Women, adopted in the World Conference to review and appraise the achievements of the United Nations Decade for Women: Equality, Development and Peace (Nairobi, 14-26 July 1985).

Outcome Document Devoted to Equality of Women and their Contribution to Development and Peace, adopted in the First World Conference on Women (Mexico City, 19 June-2 July 1975).

Outcome Document of the 23ʳᵈ Special Session of the UNGA: 'Women 2000: Gender Equality, Development and Peace for the 21ˢᵗ century, UN Document A/5-23/10/Rev.1 (5-9 June 2000).

Report of the Second World Conference of the United Nations Decade for Women: Equality, Development and Peace, A/CONF.94/35 (Copenhagen, 14-30 July 1980).

UN Security Council Resolution 1325, UN Document S/RES/1325 (2000) (31 October 2000).

Windhoek Declaration: The Namibia Plan of Action on Mainstreaming a Gender Perspective in Multidimensional Peace Support Operations, UN Document S/2000/693 (Windhoek, 31 May 2000).

International Conventions

Convention against Torture (1987).

Convention for the Suppression of the Traffic in Persons and of the Exploitation of the Prostitution of Others (1951).

Convention on Civil and Political Rights (1976).
> Optional Protocol 1 on the Convention on Civil and Political Rights (1976).
> Optional Protocol 2 on the Convention on Civil and Political Rights (1989).

Convention on Economic, Social and Cultural Rights (1976).

Convention on the Consent to Marriage Minimum Age for Marriage and Registration of Marriages (1964).

Convention on the Elimination of All Forms of Discrimination against Women (1979).
> Convention on the Elimination of All Forms of Discrimination against Women Optional Protocol (2000).

Convention on the Elimination of All Forms of Racial Discrimination (1991).

Convention on the Nationality of Married Women (1958).

Convention on the Political Rights of Women (1952).

Convention on the Prevention and Punishment of the Crime of Genocide (1951).

Convention on the Recovery Abroad of Maintenance (1956).

Convention on the Rights of the Child (1989).
> Optional Protocol to the Convention on the Rights of the Child on the Involvement of Children in Armed Conflict (2002).
> Optional Protocol to the Convention on the Rights of the Child on the Sale of Children, Child Prostitution and Child Pornography (2002).

Convention relating to the Status of Refugees (1951).
> Protocol relating to the Status of Refugees (1967).

Geneva Conventions (1949).
> Protocol I to the Geneva Conventions (1977).
> Protocol II to the Geneva Conventions (1977).

Inter-American Convention on the Prevention, Punishment and Eradication of Violence against Women, 'Convention of Belem do Para' (1994).

International Convention on the Protection of the Rights of All Migrant Workers and Members of Their Families (2003).

Protocol to the African Charter on Human and People's Rights on the Rights of Women in Africa (2003).

Rome Statute of the International Criminal Court (1998)
> Rules of Procedure and Evidence (2002).

Internet sources

APC Women's Networking Support Program – aims to increase women's access to training and facilitate information flow between North, South, East and West on gender issues. It offers opportunities to women and women's organisations in all regions of the world, but has a particular focus on redressing inequalities in access to technology related to social and ethnic marginalisation and the North-South technological gap, at http://www.apcwomen.org/

DIANA – a comprehensive database of electronic materials relevant to human rights research. It provides a significant collection of full text articles and bibliography on women's rights, at http://www.law-lib.utoronto.ca/Diana

Gender and Peacekeeping Training Course by Canada's Department of Foreign Affairs and International Trade (DFAIT) and UK's Department for International Development (DFID) – the website includes a comprehensive list of scholarly work on gender, conflict and related issues organised in training modules for teachers and students, at http://www.genderandpeacekeeping.org/menu-e.asp

Peacewomen – the website provides important data and information on women, peace and security. It monitors and works towards rapid and full implementation of United Nations Security Council Resolution 1325 on women, peace and security, at http://www.peacewomen.org/wpsindex.html

The People's Movement for Human Rights Education (PDHRE) – a site devoted to human rights education. It provides substantive informative documents on basic human rights including women's rights. Each write-up offers a list of relevant international documents and citations, at http://www.pdhre.org/

UNIFEM : Women, War, Peace – UNIFEM's portal collecting essential information on the theme of women, war, peace. It provides country profiles, access to numerous news articles and links to NGOs, at http://www.womenwarpeace.org/h_index.htm

WomenWatch – portal on all information and resources regarding its work on gender equality and women's empowerment. It covers up to date information on various women's programmes in the UN, statistics and indicators, publications, training modules and many others, at http://www.un.org/womenwatch/

Key Legal and Political Documents

The following section provides a collection of international legal treaties and political declarations relevant to eliminating violence against women and improving women's status in society. These provide an overview of internationally agreed norms and standards of women's human rights to be guaranteed and protected at times of peace and armed conflict.

- Convention on the Elimination of All Forms of Discrimination against Women

- Optional Protocol to the Convention on the Elimination of Discrimination against Women

- Extracts from the provisions of the 1949 Geneva Conventions and their 1977 Additional Protocols

- Declaration on the Elimination of Violence against Women

- Declaration on the Protection of Women and Children in Emergency and Armed Conflict

- United Nations Security Council Resolution 1325, Women, Peace and Security (25 October 2000)

Convention on the Elimination of All Forms of Discrimination against Women

Adopted and opened for signature, ratification and accession by General Assembly resolution 34/180 of 18 December 1979

entry into force 3 September 1981,
in accordance with article 27(1)

The States Parties to the present Convention,

Noting that the Charter of the United Nations reaffirms faith in fundamental human rights, in the dignity and worth of the human person and in the equal rights of men and women,

Noting that the Universal Declaration of Human Rights affirms the principle of the inadmissibility of discrimination and proclaims that all human beings are born free and equal in dignity and rights and that everyone is entitled to all the rights and freedoms set forth therein, without distinction of any kind, including distinction based on sex,

Noting that the States Parties to the International Covenants on Human Rights have the obligation to ensure the equal rights of men and women to enjoy all economic, social, cultural, civil and political rights,

Considering the international conventions concluded under the auspices of the United Nations and the specialised agencies promoting equality of rights of men and women,

Noting also the resolutions, declarations and recommendations adopted by the United Nations and the specialised agencies promoting equality of rights of men and women,

Concerned, however, that despite these various instruments extensive discrimination against women continues to exist,

Recalling that discrimination against women violates the principles of equality of rights and respect for human dignity, is an obstacle to the participation of women, on equal terms with men, in the political, social, economic and cultural life of their countries, hampers the growth of the prosperity of society and the family and makes more difficult the full development of the potentialities of women in the service of their countries and of humanity,

Concerned that in situations of poverty women have the least access to food, health, education, training and opportunities for employment and other needs,

Convinced that the establishment of the new international economic order based on equity and justice will contribute significantly towards the promotion of equality between men and women,

Emphasising that the eradication of apartheid, all forms of racism, racial discrimination, colonialism, neo-colonialism, aggression, foreign occupation and domination and interference in the internal affairs of States is essential to the full enjoyment of the rights of men and women,

Affirming that the strengthening of international peace and security, the relaxation of international tension, mutual co-operation among all States irrespective of their social and economic systems, general and complete disarmament, in particular nuclear disarmament under strict and effective international control, the affirmation of the principles of justice, equality and mutual benefit in relations among countries and the realisation of the right of peoples under alien and colonial domination and foreign occupation to self-determination and independence, as well as respect for national sovereignty and territorial integrity, will promote social progress and development and as a consequence will contribute to the attainment of full equality between men and women,

Convinced that the full and complete development of a country, the welfare of the world and the cause of peace require the maximum participation of women on equal terms with men in all fields,

Bearing in mind the great contribution of women to the welfare of the family and to the development of society, so far not fully recognised, the social significance of maternity and the role of both parents in the family and in the upbringing of children, and aware that the role of women in procreation should not be a basis for discrimination but that the upbringing of children requires a sharing of responsibility between men and women and society as a whole,

Aware that a change in the traditional role of men as well as the role of women in society and in the family is needed to achieve full equality between men and women,

Determined to implement the principles set forth in the Declaration on the Elimination of Discrimination against Women and, for that purpose, to adopt the measures required for the elimination of such discrimination in all its forms and manifestations,

Have agreed on the following:

PART I

Article 1

For the purposes of the present Convention, the term 'discrimination against women' shall mean any distinction, exclusion or restriction made on the basis of sex which has the effect or purpose of impairing or nullifying the recognition, enjoyment or exercise by women, irrespective of their marital status, on a basis of equality of men and women, of human rights and fundamental freedoms in the political, economic, social, cultural, civil or any other field.

Article 2

States Parties condemn discrimination against women in all its forms, agree to pursue by all appropriate means and without delay a policy of eliminating discrimination against women and, to this end, undertake:

(a) To embody the principle of the equality of men and women in their national constitutions or other appropriate legislation if not yet incorporated therein and to ensure, through

law and other appropriate means, the practical realisation of this principle;

(b) To adopt appropriate legislative and other measures, including sanctions where appropriate, prohibiting all discrimination against women;

(c) To establish legal protection of the rights of women on an equal basis with men and to ensure through competent national tribunals and other public institutions the effective protection of women against any act of discrimination;

(d) To refrain from engaging in any act or practice of discrimination against women and to ensure that public authorities and institutions shall act in conformity with this obligation;

(e) To take all appropriate measures to eliminate discrimination against women by any person, organisation or enterprise;

(f) To take all appropriate measures, including legislation, to modify or abolish existing laws, regulations, customs and practices which constitute discrimination against women;

(g) To repeal all national penal provisions which constitute discrimination against women.

Article 3

States Parties shall take in all fields, in particular in the political, social, economic and cultural fields, all appropriate measures, including legislation, to en sure the full development and advancement of women , for the purpose of guaranteeing them the exercise and enjoyment of human rights and fundamental freedoms on a basis of equality with men.

Article 4

1. Adoption by States Parties of temporary special measures aimed at accelerating de facto equality between men and women shall not be considered discrimination as defined in the present Convention, but shall in no way entail as a consequence the maintenance of unequal or separate standards; these measures shall be discontinued when the objectives of equality of opportunity and treatment have been achieved.

2. Adoption by States Parties of special measures, including those measures contained in the present Convention, aimed at protecting maternity shall not be considered discriminatory.

Article 5

States Parties shall take all appropriate measures:

(a) To modify the social and cultural patterns of conduct of men and women, with a view to achieving the elimination of prejudices and customary and all other practices which are based on the idea of the inferiority or the superiority of either of the sexes or on stereotyped roles for men and women;

(b) To ensure that family education includes a proper understanding of maternity as a social function and the recognition of the common responsibility of men and women in the upbringing and development of their children, it being understood that the interest of the children is the primordial consideration in all cases.

Article 6

States Parties shall take all appropriate measures, including legislation, to suppress all forms of traffic in women and exploitation of prostitution of women.

PART II

Article 7

States Parties shall take all appropriate measures to eliminate discrimination against women in the political and public life of the country and, in particular, shall ensure to women, on equal terms with men, the right:

(a) To vote in all elections and public referenda and to be eligible for election to all publicly elected bodies;

(b) To participate in the formulation of government policy and the implementation thereof and to hold public office and perform all public functions at all levels of government;

(c) To participate in non-governmental organisations and associations concerned with the public and political life of the country.

Article 8

States Parties shall take all appropriate measures to ensure to women, on equal terms with men and without any discrimination, the opportunity to represent their Governments at the international level and to participate in the work of international organisations.

Article 9

1. States Parties shall grant women equal rights with men to acquire, change or retain their nationality. They shall ensure in particular that neither marriage to an alien nor change of nationality by the husband during marriage shall automatically change the nationality of the wife, render her stateless or force upon her the nationality of the husband.

2. States Parties shall grant women equal rights with men with respect to the nationality of their children.

PART III

Article 10

States Parties shall take all appropriate measures to eliminate discrimination against women in order to ensure to them equal rights with men in the field of education and in particular to ensure, on a basis of equality of men and women:

(a) The same conditions for career and vocational guidance, for access to studies and for the achievement of diplomas in educational establishments of all categories in rural as well as in urban areas; this equality shall be ensured in preschool, general, technical, professional and higher technical education, as well as in all types of vocational training;

(b) Access to the same curricula, the same examinations, teaching staff with qualifications of the same standard and school premises and equipment of the same quality;

(c) The elimination of any stereotyped concept of the roles of men and women at all levels and in all forms of education by encouraging coeducation and other types of education which will help to achieve this aim and, in particular, by the revision of textbooks and school programmes and the adaptation of teaching methods;

(d) The same opportunities to benefit from scholarships and other study grants;

(e) The same opportunities for access to programmes of continuing education, including adult and functional literacy programmes, particulary those aimed at reducing, at the earliest possible time, any gap in education existing between men and women;

(f) The reduction of female student drop-out rates and the organisation of programmes for girls and women who have left school prematurely;

(g) The same Opportunities to participate actively in sports and physical education;

(h) Access to specific educational information to help to ensure the health and well-being of families, including information and advice on family planning.

Article 11

1. States Parties shall take all appropriate measures to eliminate discrimination against women in the field of employment in order to ensure, on a basis of equality of men and women, the same rights, in particular:

(a) The right to work as an inalienable right of all human beings;

(b) The right to the same employment opportunities, including the application of the same criteria for selection in matters of employment;

(c) The right to free choice of profession and employment, the right to promotion, job security and all benefits and conditions of service and the right to receive vocational training and retraining, including apprenticeships, advanced vocational training and recurrent training;

(d) The right to equal remuneration, including benefits, and to equal treatment in respect of work of equal value, as well as equality of treatment in the evaluation of the quality of work;

(e) The right to social security, particularly in cases of retirement, unemployment, sickness, invalidity and old age and other incapacity to work, as well as the right to paid leave;

(f) The right to protection of health and to safety in working conditions, including the safeguarding of the function of reproduction.

2. In order to prevent discrimination against women on the grounds of marriage or maternity and to ensure their effective right to work, States Parties shall take appropriate measures:

(a) To prohibit, subject to the imposition of sanctions, dismissal on the grounds of pregnancy or of maternity leave and discrimination in dismissals on the basis of marital status;

(b) To introduce maternity leave with pay or with comparable social benefits without loss of former employment, seniority or social allowances;

(c) To encourage the provision of the necessary supporting social services to enable parents to combine family obligations with work responsibilities and participation in public life, in particular through promoting the establishment and development of a network of child-care facilities;

(d) To provide special protection to women during pregnancy in types of work proved to be harmful to them.

3. Protective legislation relating to matters covered in this article shall be reviewed periodically in the light of scientific and technological knowledge and shall be revised, repealed or extended as necessary.

Article 12

1. States Parties shall take all appropriate measures to eliminate discrimination against women in the field of health care in order to ensure, on a basis of equality of men and women, access to health care services, including those related to family planning.

2. Notwithstanding the provisions of paragraph I of this article, States Parties shall ensure to women appropriate services in connection with pregnancy, confinement and the post-natal period, granting free services where necessary, as well as adequate nutrition during pregnancy and lactation.

Article 13

States Parties shall take all appropriate measures to eliminate discrimination against women in other areas of economic and social life in order to ensure, on a basis of equality of men and women, the same rights, in particular:

(a) The right to family benefits;

(b) The right to bank loans, mortgages and other forms of financial credit;

(c) The right to participate in recreational activities, sports and all aspects of cultural life.

Article 14

1. States Parties shall take into account the particular problems faced by rural women and the significant roles which rural women play in the economic survival of their families, including their work in the non-monetised sectors of the economy, and shall take all appropriate measures to ensure the application of the provisions of the present Convention to women in rural areas.

2. States Parties shall take all appropriate measures to eliminate discrimination against women in rural areas in order to ensure, on a basis of equality of men and women, that they participate in and benefit from rural development and, in particular, shall ensure to such women the right:

(a) To participate in the elaboration and implementation of development planning at all levels;

(b) To have access to adequate health care facilities, including information, counselling and services in family planning;

(c) To benefit directly from social security programmes;

(d) To obtain all types of training and education, formal and non-formal, including that relating to functional literacy, as well as, *inter alia*, the benefit of all community and extension services, in order to increase their technical proficiency;

(e) To organise self-help groups and co-operatives in order to obtain equal access to economic opportunities through employment or self employment;

(f) To participate in all community activities;

(g) To have access to agricultural credit and loans, marketing facilities, appropriate technology and equal treat-

ment in land and agrarian reform as well as in land resettlement schemes;

(h) To enjoy adequate living conditions, particularly in relation to housing, sanitation, electricity and water supply, transport and communications.

PART IV

Article 15

1. States Parties shall accord to women equality with men before the law.

2. States Parties shall accord to women, in civil matters, a legal capacity identical to that of men and the same opportunities to exercise that capacity. In particular, they shall give women equal rights to conclude contracts and to administer property and shall treat them equally in all stages of procedure in courts and tribunals.

3. States Parties agree that all contracts and all other private instruments of any kind with a legal effect, which is directed at restricting the legal capacity of women shall be deemed null and void.

4. States Parties shall accord to men and women the same rights with regard to the law relating to the movement of persons and the freedom to choose their residence and domicile.

Article 16

1. States Parties shall take all appropriate measures to eliminate discrimination against women in all matters relating to marriage and family relations and in particular shall ensure, on a basis of equality of men and women:

(a) The same right to enter into marriage;

(b) The same right freely to choose a spouse and to enter into marriage only with their free and full consent;

(c) The same rights and responsibilities during marriage and at its dissolution;

(d) The same rights and responsibilities as parents, irrespective of their marital status, in matters relating to their children; in all cases the interests of the children shall be paramount;

(e) The same rights to decide freely and responsibly on the number and spacing of their children and to have access to the information, education and means to enable them to exercise these rights;

(f) The same rights and responsibilities with regard to guardianship, wardship, trusteeship and adoption of children, or similar institutions where these concepts exist in national legislation; in all cases the interests of the children shall be paramount;

(g) The same personal rights as husband and wife, including the right to choose a family name, a profession and an occupation;

(h) The same rights for both spouses in respect of the ownership, acquisition, management, administration, enjoyment and disposition of property, whether free of charge or for a valuable consideration.

2. The betrothal and the marriage of a child shall have no legal effect, and all necessary action, including legislation, shall

be taken to specify a minimum age for marriage and to make the registration of marriages in an official registry compulsory.

PART V

Article 17

1. For the purpose of considering the progress made in the implementation of the present Convention, there shall be established a Committee on the Elimination of Discrimination against Women (hereinafter referred to as the Committee) consisting, at the time of entry into force of the Convention, of eighteen and, after ratification of or accession to the Convention by the thirty-fifth State Party, of twenty-three experts of high moral standing and competence in the field covered by the Convention. The experts shall be elected by States Parties from among their nationals and shall serve in their personal capacity, consideration being given to equitable geographical distribution and to the representation of the different forms of civilisation as well as the principal legal systems.

2. The members of the Committee shall be elected by secret ballot from a list of persons nominated by States Parties. Each State Party may nominate one person from among its own nationals.

3. The initial election shall be held six months after the date of the entry into force of the present Convention. At least three months before the date of each election the Secretary-General of the United Nations shall address a letter to the States Parties inviting them to submit their nominations within two months. The Secretary-General shall prepare a list in alphabetical order of all persons thus nominated, indicating the States Parties, which have nominated them, and shall submit it to the States Parties.

4. Elections of the members of the Committee shall be held at a meeting of States Parties convened by the Secretary-General at United Nations Headquarters. At that meeting, for which two thirds of the States Parties shall constitute a quorum, the persons elected to the Committee shall be those nominees who obtain the largest number of votes and an absolute majority of the votes of the representatives of States Parties present and voting.

5. The members of the Committee shall be elected for a term of four years. However, the terms of nine of the members elected at the first election shall expire at the end of two years; immediately after the first election the names of these nine members shall be chosen by lot by the Chairman of the Committee.

6. The election of the five additional members of the Committee shall be held in accordance with the provisions of paragraphs 2, 3 and 4 of this article, following the thirty-fifth ratification or accession. The terms of two of the additional members elected on this occasion shall expire at the end of two years, the names of these two members having been chosen by lot by the Chairman of the Committee.

7. For the filling of casual vacancies, the State Party whose expert has ceased to function as a member of the Committee shall appoint another expert from among its nationals, subject to the approval of the Committee.

8. The members of the Committee shall, with the approval of the General Assembly, receive emoluments from United Nations resources on such terms and conditions as the Assembly may decide, having regard to the importance of the Committee's responsibilities.

9. The Secretary-General of the United Nations shall provide the necessary staff and facilities for the effective performance of the functions of the Committee under the present Convention.

Article 18

1. States Parties undertake to submit to the Secretary-General of the United Nations, for consideration by the Committee, a report on the legislative, judicial, administrative or other measures which they have adopted to give effect to the provisions of the present Convention and on the progress made in this respect:

   (a) Within one year after the entry into force for the State concerned;

   (b) Thereafter at least every four years and further whenever the Committee so requests.

2. Reports may indicate factors and difficulties affecting the degree of fulfilment of obligations under the present Convention.

Article 19

1. The Committee shall adopt its own rules of procedure.

2. The Committee shall elect its officers for a term of two years.

Article 20

1. The Committee shall normally meet for a period of not more than two weeks annually in order to consider the reports submitted in accordance with article 18 of the present Convention.

2. The meetings of the Committee shall normally be held at United Nations Headquarters or at any other convenient place as determined by the Committee.

Article 21

1. The Committee shall, through the Economic and Social Council, report annually to the General Assembly of the United Nations on its activities and may make suggestions and general recommendations based on the examination of reports and information received from the States Parties. Such suggestions and general recommendations shall be included in the report of the Committee together with comments, if any, from States Parties.

2. The Secretary-General of the United Nations shall transmit the reports of the Committee to the Commission on the Status of Women for its information.

Article 22

The specialised agencies shall be entitled to be represented at the consideration of the implementation of such provisions of the present Convention as fall within the scope of their activities. The Committee may invite the specialised agencies to submit reports on the implementation of the Convention in areas falling within the scope of their activities.

PART VI

Article 23

Nothing in the present Convention shall affect any provisions that are more conducive to the achievement of equality between men and women, which may be contained:

(a) In the legislation of a State Party; or

(b) In any other international convention, treaty or agreement in force for that State.

Article 24

States Parties undertake to adopt all necessary measures at the national level aimed at achieving the full realisation of the rights recognised in the present Convention.

Article 25

1. The present Convention shall be open for signature by all States.

2. The Secretary-General of the United Nations is designated as the depositary of the present Convention.

3. The present Convention is subject to ratification. Instruments of ratification shall be deposited with the Secretary-General of the United Nations.

4. The present Convention shall be open to accession by all States. Accession shall be effected by the deposit of an instrument of accession with the Secretary-General of the United Nations.

Article 26

1. A request for the revision of the present Convention may be made at any time by any State Party by means of a notification in writing addressed to the Secretary-General of the United Nations.

2. The General Assembly of the United Nations shall decide upon the steps, if any, to be taken in respect of such a request.

Article 27

1. The present Convention shall enter into force on the thirtieth day after the date of deposit with the Secretary-General of the United Nations of the twentieth instrument of ratification or accession.

2. For each State ratifying the present Convention or acceding to it after the deposit of the twentieth instrument of ratification or accession, the Convention shall enter into force on the thirtieth day after the date of the deposit of its own instrument of ratification or accession.

Article 28

1. The Secretary-General of the United Nations shall receive and circulate to all States the text of reservations made by States at the time of ratification or accession.

2. A reservation incompatible with the object and purpose of the present Convention shall not be permitted.

3. Reservations may be withdrawn at any time by notification to this effect addressed to the Secretary-General of the United Nations, who shall then inform all States thereof. Such notification shall take effect on the date on which it is received.

Article 29

1. Any dispute between two or more States Parties concerning the interpretation or application of the present Convention which is not settled by negotiation shall, at the request of one of them, be submitted to arbitration. If within six months from the date of the request for arbitration the parties are unable to agree on the organisation of the arbitration, any one of those parties may refer the dispute to the International Court of Justice by request in conformity with the Statute of the Court.

2. Each State Party may at the time of signature or ratification of the present Convention or accession thereto declare that it does not consider itself bound by paragraph I of this article. The other States Parties shall not be bound by that paragraph with respect to any State Party, which has made such a reservation.

3. Any State Party, which has made a reservation in accordance with paragraph 2 of this article, may at any time withdraw that reservation by notification to the Secretary-General of the United Nations.

Article 30

The present Convention, the Arabic, Chinese, English, French, Russian and Spanish texts of which are equally authentic, shall be deposited with the Secretary-General of the United Nations.

Optional Protocol to the Convention on the Elimination of Discrimination against Women

Adopted by General Assembly resolution A/54/4 on 6 October 1999 and opened for signature on 10 December 1999, Human Rights Day

entry into force 22 December 2000

The States Parties to the present Protocol,

Noting that the Charter of the United Nations reaffirms faith in fundamental human rights, in the dignity and worth of the human person and in the equal rights of men and women,

Also noting that the Universal Declaration of Human Rights Resolution 217 A (III). proclaims that all human beings are born free and equal in dignity and rights and that everyone is entitled to all the rights and freedoms set forth therein, without distinction of any kind, including distinction based on sex,

Recalling that the International Covenants on Human Rights Resolution 2200 A (XXI), annex. and other international human rights instruments prohibit discrimination on the basis of sex,

Also recalling the Convention on the Elimination of All Forms of Discrimination against Women ('the Convention'), in which the States Parties thereto condemn discrimination against women in all its forms and agree to pursue by all appropriate means and without delay a policy of eliminating discrimination against women,

Reaffirming their determination to ensure the full and equal enjoyment by women of all human rights and fundamental freedoms and to take effective action to prevent violations of these rights and freedoms,

Have agreed as follows:

Article 1

A State Party to the present Protocol ('State Party') recognises the competence of the Committee on the Elimination of Discrimination against Women ('the Committee') to receive and consider communications submitted in accordance with article 2.

Article 2

Communications may be submitted by or on behalf of individuals or groups of individuals, under the jurisdiction of a State Party, claiming to be victims of a violation of any of the rights set forth in the Convention by that State Party. Where a communication is submitted on behalf of individuals or groups of individuals, this shall be with their consent unless the author can justify acting on their behalf without such consent.

Article 3

Communications shall be in writing and shall not be anonymous. No communication shall be received by the Committee if it concerns a State Party to the Convention that is not a party to the present Protocol.

Article 4

1. The Committee shall not consider a communication unless it has ascertained that all available domestic remedies have been exhausted unless the application of such remedies is unreasonably prolonged or unlikely to bring effective relief.

2. The Committee shall declare a communication inadmissible where:

   (a) The same matter has already been examined by the Committee or has been or is being examined under another procedure of international investigation or settlement;

   (b) It is incompatible with the provisions of the Convention;

   (c) It is manifestly ill-founded or not sufficiently substantiated;

   (d) It is an abuse of the right to submit a communication;

   (e) The facts that are the subject of the communication occurred prior to the entry into force of the present Protocol for the State Party concerned unless those facts continued after that date.

Article 5

1. At any time after the receipt of a communication and before a determination on the merits has been reached, the Committee may transmit to the State Party concerned for its urgent consideration a request that the State Party take such interim measures as may be necessary to avoid possible irreparable damage to the victim or victims of the alleged violation.

2. Where the Committee exercises its discretion under paragraph 1 of the present article, this does not imply a determination on admissibility or on the merits of the communication.

Article 6

1. Unless the Committee considers a communication inadmissible without reference to the State Party concerned,

and provided that the individual or individuals consent to the disclosure of their identity to that State Party, the Committee shall bring any communication submitted to it under the present Protocol confidentially to the attention of the State Party concerned.

2. Within six months, the receiving State Party shall submit to the Committee written explanations or statements clarifying the matter and the remedy, if any, that may have been provided by that State Party.

Article 7

1. The Committee shall consider communications received under the present Protocol in the light of all information made available to it by or on behalf of individuals or groups of individuals and by the State Party concerned, provided that this information is transmitted to the parties concerned.

2. The Committee shall hold closed meetings when examining communications under the present Protocol.

3. After examining a communication, the Committee shall transmit its views on the communication, together with its recommendations, if any, to the parties concerned.

4. The State Party shall give due consideration to the views of the Committee, together with its recommendations, if any, and shall submit to the Committee, within six months, a written response, including information on any action taken in the light of the views and recommendations of the Committee.

5. The Committee may invite the State Party to submit further information about any measures the State Party has taken in response to its views or recommendations, if any, including as deemed appropriate by the Committee, in the State Party's subsequent reports under article 18 of the Convention.

Article 8

1. If the Committee receives reliable information indicating grave or systematic violations by a State Party of rights set forth in the Convention, the Committee shall invite that State Party to co-operate in the examination of the information and to this end to submit observations with regard to the information concerned.

2. Taking into account any observations that may have been submitted by the State Party concerned as well as any other reliable information available to it, the Committee may designate one or more of its members to conduct an inquiry and to report urgently to the Committee. Where warranted and with the consent of the State Party, the inquiry may include a visit to its territory.

3. After examining the findings of such an inquiry, the Committee shall transmit these findings to the State Party concerned together with any comments and recommendations.

4. The State Party concerned shall, within six months of receiving the findings, comments and recommendations transmitted by the Committee, submit its observations to the Committee.

5. Such an inquiry shall be conducted confidentially and the co-operation of the State Party shall be sought at all stages of the proceedings.

Article 9

1. The Committee may invite the State Party concerned to include in its report under article 18 of the Convention details of any measures taken in response to an inquiry conducted under article 8 of the present Protocol.

2. The Committee may, if necessary, after the end of the period of six months referred to in article 8.4, invite the State Party concerned to inform it of the measures taken in response to such an inquiry.

Article 10

1. Each State Party may, at the time of signature or ratification of the present Protocol or accession thereto, declare that it does not recognise the competence of the Committee provided for in articles 8 and 9.

2. Any State Party having made a declaration in accordance with paragraph 1 of the present article may, at any time, withdraw this declaration by notification to the Secretary-General.

Article 11

A State Party shall take all appropriate steps to ensure that individuals under its jurisdiction are not subjected to ill-treatment or intimidation as a consequence of communicating with the Committee pursuant to the present Protocol.

Article 12

The Committee shall include in its annual report under article 21 of the Convention a summary of its activities under the present Protocol.

Article 13

Each State Party undertakes to make widely known and to give publicity to the Convention and the present Protocol and to facilitate access to information about the views and recommendations of the Committee, in particular, on matters involving that State Party.

Article 14

The Committee shall develop its own rules of procedure to be followed when exercising the functions conferred on it by the present Protocol.

Article 15

1. The present Protocol shall be open for signature by any State that has signed, ratified or acceded to the Convention.

2. The present Protocol shall be subject to ratification by any State that has ratified or acceded to the Convention. Instruments of ratification shall be deposited with the Secretary-General of the United Nations.

3. The present Protocol shall be open to accession by any State that has ratified or acceded to the Convention.

4. Accession shall be effected by the deposit of an instrument of accession with the Secretary-General of the United Nations.

Article 16

1. The present Protocol shall enter into force three months after the date of the deposit with the Secretary-General of the United Nations of the tenth instrument of ratification or accession.

2. For each State ratifying the present Protocol or acceding to it after its entry into force, the present Protocol shall enter into force three months after the date of the deposit of its own instrument of ratification or accession.

Article 17

No reservations to the present Protocol shall be permitted.

Article 18

1. Any State Party may propose an amendment to the present Protocol and file it with the Secretary-General of the United Nations. The Secretary-General shall thereupon communicate any proposed amendments to the States Parties with a request that they notify her or him whether they favour a conference of States Parties for the purpose of considering and voting on the proposal. In the event that at least one third of the States Parties favour such a conference, the Secretary-General shall convene the conference under the auspices of the United Nations. Any amendment adopted by a majority of the States Parties present and voting at the conference shall be submitted to the General Assembly of the United Nations for approval.

2. Amendments shall come into force when they have been approved by the General Assembly of the United Nations and accepted by a two-thirds majority of the States Parties to the present Protocol in accordance with their respective constitutional processes.

3. When amendments come into force, they shall be binding on those States Parties that have accepted them, other States Parties still being bound by the provisions of the present Protocol and any earlier amendments that they have accepted.

Article 19

1. Any State Party may denounce the present Protocol at any time by written notification addressed to the Secretary-General of the United Nations. Denunciation shall take effect six months after the date of receipt of the notification by the Secretary-General.

2. Denunciation shall be without prejudice to the continued application of the provisions of the present Protocol to any communication submitted under article 2 or any inquiry initiated under article 8 before the effective date of denunciation.

Article 20

The Secretary-General of the United Nations shall inform all States of:

(a) Signatures, ratifications and accessions under the present Protocol;

(b) The date of entry into force of the present Protocol and of any amendment under article 18;

(c) Any denunciation under article 19.

Article 21

1. The present Protocol, of which the Arabic, Chinese, English, French, Russian and Spanish texts are equally authentic, shall be deposited in the archives of the United Nations.

2. The Secretary-General of the United Nations shall transmit certified copies of the present Protocol to all States referred to in article 25 of the Convention.

Extracts from the Provisions of the 1949 Geneva Conventions and their 1977 Additional Protocols

Article 3 common to the Geneva Conventions

In the case of armed conflict not of an international character occurring in the territory of one of the High Contracting Parties, each Party to the conflict shall be bound to apply, as a minimum, the following provisions:

1. Persons taking no active part in hostilities, including members of armed forces who have laid down their arms and those placed hors de combat by sickness, wounds, detention, or any other cause, shall in all circumstances be treated humanely, without any adverse distinction founded on race, colour, religion or faith, sex, birth or wealth, or any other similar criteria.

   To this end, the following acts are and shall remain prohibited at any time and in any place whatsoever with respect to the above mentioned persons:

   a) violence to life and persons, in particular murder of all kinds, mutilation, cruel treatment and torture;

   b) taking of hostages;

   c) outrages upon personal dignity in particular humiliating and degrading treatment;

   d) the passing of sentences and the carrying out of executions without previous judgements pronounced by a regularly constituted court, affording all the judicial guarantees which are recognised as indispensable by civilised peoples.

2. The wounded and sick shall be collected and cared for.

Article 27 of the Fourth Geneva Convention

Protected persons are entitled, in all circumstances, to respect for their persons, their honour, their family rights, their religious convictions and practice, and their manners and customs. They shall at all times be humanely treated, and shall be protected especially against all acts of violence, of threats thereof and against insults and public curiosity.

Women shall be especially protected against any attack on their honour, in particular against rape, enforced prostitution, or any form of indecent assault.

Without prejudice to the provisions relating to their state of health, age and sex, all protected persons shall be treated with the same consideration by the Party to the conflict in whose power they are, without any adverse distinction based, in particular, on race, religion or political opinion.

However, the parties to the conflict may take such measures of control and security in regard to protected persons as may be necessary as a result of the war.

Article 147 of the Fourth Geneva Convention

Grave breaches [...] shall be those involving any of the following acts, if committed against persons or property protected by the present Convention: wilful killing, torture or inhuman treatment, including biological experiments, wilfully causing great suffering or serious injury to body or health, unlawful deportation or transfer or unlawful confinement of a protected person, compelling a protected person to serve in the forces of a hostile Power, or wilfully depriving a protected person of the rights of fair and regular trial prescribed in the present Convention, taking of hostages and extensive destruction and appropriation of property, not justified by military necessity and carried out unlawfully and wantonly.

Article 75 of the Additional Protocol I to Geneva Conventions

The following acts are and shall remain prohibited at any time and in any place whatsoever, whether committed by civilians or by military agents:

violence to the life, health, or physical or mental well-being of persons, in particular:

a) murder;

b) torture of all kinds, whether physical or mental;

c) corporal punishment;

d) mutilation;

e) outrages upon personal dignity, in particular humiliating and degrading treatment, enforced prostitution and any form of indecent assault;

f) the taking of hostages;

g) collective punishments;

h) threats to commit any of the foregoing acts.

Article 76 of the Additional Protocol I to Geneva Conventions:

Protection of women

1. Women shall be the object of special respect and shall be protected in particular against rape, forced prostitution and any other form of indecent assault.

2. Pregnant women and mothers having dependant infants who are arrested, detained or interned for reasons related to the armed conflict, shall have their cases considered with the utmost priority.

3. To the maximum extent feasible, the Parties to the conflict shall endeavour to avoid the pronouncement of the death penalty on pregnant women or mothers having dependant infants, for an offence related to the armed conflict. The death penalty for such offences shall not be executed on such women.

Article 4 of the Additional Protocol II to Geneva Conventions:

Fundamental guarantees

1. All persons who do not take a direct part or who have ceased to take part in hostilities, whether or not their liberty has been restricted, are entitled to respect for their persons, honour and convictions and religious practices. They shall in all circumstances be treated humanely, without adverse distinction. It is prohibited to order that there shall be no survivors.

2. Without prejudice to the generality of the foregoing, the following acts against the persons referred to in paragraph 1 are and shall remain prohibited at any time and in any place whatsoever:

a) violence to the life, health, or physical or mental well-being of persons, in particular murder as well as cruel treatment such as torture, mutilation or any form of corporal punishment;

b) collective punishments;

c) taking of hostages;

d) act of terrorism;

e) outrages upon personal dignity, in particular humiliating and degrading treatment, rape, enforced prostitution and any form of indecent assault;

f) slave and the slave trade in all their forms;

g) pillage;

h) threats to commit any of the forgoing acts.

Declaration on the Elimination of Violence against Women

General Assembly resolution 48/104 of 20 December 1993

The General Assembly,

Recognising the urgent need for the universal application to women of the rights and principles with regard to equality, security, liberty, integrity and dignity of all human beings,

Noting that those rights and principles are enshrined in international instruments, including the Universal Declaration of Human Rights[1], the International Covenant on Civil and Political Rights,[2] the International Covenant on Economic, Social and Cultural Rights,[3] the Convention on the Elimination of All Forms of Discrimination against Women[4] and the Convention against Torture and Other Cruel, Inhuman or Degrading Treatment or Punishment,[5]

Recognising that effective implementation of the Convention on the Elimination of All Forms of Discrimination against Women would contribute to the elimination of violence against women and that the Declaration on the Elimination of Violence against Women, set forth in the present resolution, will strengthen and complement that process,

Concerned that violence against women is an obstacle to the achievement of equality, development and peace, as recognised in the Nairobi Forward-looking Strategies for the Advancement of Women,[6] in which a set of measures to combat violence against women was recommended, and to the full implementation of the Convention on the Elimination of All Forms of Discrimination against Women,

Affirming that violence against women constitutes a violation of the rights and fundamental freedoms of women and impairs or nullifies their enjoyment of those rights and freedoms, and concerned about the long-standing failure to protect and promote those rights and freedoms in the case of violence against women,

Recognising that violence against women is a manifestation of historically unequal power relations between men and women, which have led to domination over and discrimination against women by men and to the prevention of the full advancement of women, and that violence against women is one of the cru-

cial social mechanisms by which women are forced into a subordinate position compared with men,

Concerned that some groups of women, such as women belonging to minority groups, indigenous women, refugee women, migrant women, women living in rural or remote communities, destitute women, women in institutions or in detention, female children, women with disabilities, elderly women and women in situations of armed conflict, are especially vulnerable to violence,

Recalling the conclusion in paragraph 23 of the annex to Economic and Social Council resolution 1990/15 of 24 May 1990 that the recognition that violence against women in the family and society was pervasive and cut across lines of income, class and culture had to be matched by urgent and effective steps to eliminate its incidence,

Recalling also Economic and Social Council resolution 1991/18 of 30 May 1991, in which the Council recommended the development of a framework for an international instrument that would address explicitly the issue of violence against women,

Welcoming the role that women's movements are playing in drawing increasing attention to the nature, severity and magnitude of the problem of violence against women,

Alarmed that opportunities for women to achieve legal, social, political and economic equality in society are limited, *inter alia*, by continuing and endemic violence,

Convinced that in the light of the above there is a need for a clear and comprehensive definition of violence against women, a clear statement of the rights to be applied to ensure the elimination of violence against women in all its forms, a commitment by States in respect of their responsibilities, and a commitment by the international community at large to the elimination of violence against women,

Solemnly proclaims the following Declaration on the Elimination of Violence against Women and urges that every effort be made so that it becomes generally known and respected:

Article 1

For the purposes of this Declaration, the term 'violence against women' means any act of gender-based violence that results in, or is likely to result in, physical, sexual or psychological harm or suffering to women, including threats of such acts, coercion or arbitrary deprivation of liberty, whether occurring in public or in private life.

Article 2

Violence against women shall be understood to encompass, but not be limited to, the following:

a) Physical, sexual and psychological violence occurring in the family, including battering, sexual abuse of female children in the household, dowry-related violence, marital rape, female genital mutilation and other traditional practices harmful to women, non-spousal violence and violence related to exploitation;

b) Physical, sexual and psychological violence occurring within the general community, including rape, sexual abuse, sexual harassment and intimidation at work, in educational institutions and elsewhere, trafficking in women and forced prostitution;

c) Physical, sexual and psychological violence perpetrated or condoned by the State, wherever it occurs.

Article 3

Women are entitled to the equal enjoyment and protection of all human rights and fundamental freedoms in the political, economic, social, cultural, civil or any other field. These rights include, *inter alia*:

a) The right to life;[7]

b) The right to equality;[8]

c) The right to liberty and security of person;[9]

d) The right to equal protection under the law;[10]

e) The right to be free from all forms of discrimination;[11]

f) The right to the highest standard attainable of physical and mental health;[12]

g) The right to just and favourable conditions of work;[13]

h) The right not to be subjected to torture, or other cruel, inhuman or degrading treatment or punishment.[14]

Article 4

States should condemn violence against women and should not invoke any custom, tradition or religious consideration to avoid their obligations with respect to its elimination. States should pursue by all appropriate means and without delay a policy of eliminating violence against women and, to this end, should:

a) Consider, where they have not yet done so, ratifying or acceding to the Convention on the Elimination of All Forms of Discrimination against Women or withdrawing reservations to that Convention;

b) Refrain from engaging in violence against women;

c) Exercise due diligence to prevent, investigate and, in accordance with national legislation, punish acts of violence against women, whether those acts are perpetrated by the State or by private persons;

d) Develop penal, civil, labour and administrative sanctions in domestic legislation to punish and redress the wrongs caused to women who are subjected to violence; women who are subjected to violence should be provided with access to the mechanisms of justice and, as provided for by national legislation, to just and effective remedies for the harm that they have suffered; States should also inform women of their rights in seeking redress through such mechanisms;

e) Consider the possibility of developing national plans of action to promote the protection of women against any form of violence, or to include provisions for that purpose in plans already existing, taking into account, as appropriate, such co-operation as can be provided by non-governmental organisations, particularly those concerned with the issue of violence against women;

f) Develop, in a comprehensive way, preventive approaches and all those measures of a legal, political, administrative and cultural nature that promote the protection of women against any form of violence, and ensure that the re-victimisation of women does not occur because of laws insensitive to gender considerations, enforcement practices or other interventions;

g) Work to ensure, to the maximum extent feasible in the light of their available resources and, where needed, within the framework of international co-operation, that women subjected to violence and, where appropriate, their children have specialised assistance, such as rehabilitation, assistance in child care and maintenance, treatment, counselling, and health and social services, facilities and programmes, as well as support structures, and should take all other appropriate measures to promote their safety and physical and psychological rehabilitation;

h) Include in government budgets adequate resources for their activities related to the elimination of violence against women;

i) Take measures to ensure that law enforcement officers and public officials responsible for implementing policies to prevent, investigate and punish violence against women receive training to sensitise them to the needs of women;

j) Adopt all appropriate measures, especially in the field of education, to modify the social and cultural patterns of conduct of men and women and to eliminate prejudices, customary practices and all other practices based on the idea of the inferiority or superiority of either of the sexes and on stereotyped roles for men and women;

k) Promote research, collect data and compile statistics, especially concerning domestic violence, relating to the prevalence of different forms of violence against women and encourage research on the causes, nature, seriousness and consequences of violence against women and on the effectiveness of measures implemented to prevent and redress violence against women; those statistics and findings of the research will be made public;

l) Adopt measures directed towards the elimination of violence against women who are especially vulnerable to violence;

m) Include, in submitting reports as required under relevant human rights instruments of the United Nations, information pertaining to violence against women and measures taken to implement the present Declaration;

n) Encourage the development of appropriate guidelines to assist in the implementation of the principles set forth in the present Declaration;

o) Recognise the important role of the women's movement and non-governmental organisations world wide in raising awareness and alleviating the problem of violence against women;

p) Facilitate and enhance the work of the women's movement and non-governmental organisations and co-operate with them at local, national and regional levels;

q) Encourage intergovernmental regional organisations of which they are members to include the elimination of violence against women in their programmes, as appropriate.

Article 5

The organs and specialised agencies of the United Nations system should, within their respective fields of competence, contribute to the recognition and realisation of the rights and the principles set forth in the present Declaration and, to this end, should, *inter alia*:

a) Foster international and regional co-operation with a view to defining regional strategies for combating violence, exchanging experiences and financing programmes relating to the elimination of violence against women;

b) Promote meetings and seminars with the aim of creating and raising awareness among all persons of the issue of the elimination of violence against women;

c) Foster co-ordination and exchange within the United Nations system between human rights treaty bodies to address the issue of violence against women effectively;

d) Include in analyses prepared by organisations and bodies of the United Nations system of social trends and problems, such as the periodic reports on the world social situation, examination of trends in violence against women;

e) Encourage co-ordination between organisations and bodies of the United Nations system to incorporate the issue of violence against women into ongoing programmes, especially with reference to groups of women particularly vulnerable to violence;

f) Promote the formulation of guidelines or manuals relating to violence against women, taking into account the measures referred to in the present Declaration;

g) Consider the issue of the elimination of violence against women, as appropriate, in fulfilling their mandates with respect to the implementation of human rights instruments;

h) Co-operate with non-governmental organisations in addressing the issue of violence against women.

Article 6

Nothing in the present Declaration shall affect any provision that is more conducive to the elimination of violence against women that may be contained in the legislation of a State or in any international convention, treaty or other instrument in force in a State.

Declaration on the Protection of Women and Children in Emergency and Armed Conflict

Proclaimed by General Assembly resolution 3318(XXIX) of 14 December 1974

The General Assembly,

Having considered the recommendation of the Economic and Social Council contained in its resolution 1861 (LVI) of 16 May 1974,

Expressing its deep concern over the sufferings of women and children belonging to the civilian population who in periods of emergency and armed conflict in the struggle for peace, self-determination, national liberation and independence are too often the victims of inhuman acts and consequently suffer serious harm,

Aware of the suffering of women and children in many areas of the world, especially in those areas subject to suppression, aggression, colonialism, racism, alien domination and foreign subjugation,

Deeply concerned by the fact that, despite general and unequivocal condemnation, colonialism, racism and alien and foreign domination continue to subject many peoples under their yoke, cruelly suppressing the national liberation movements and inflicting heavy losses and incalculable sufferings on the populations under their domination, including women and children,

Deploring the fact that grave attacks are still being made on fundamental freedoms and the dignity of the human person and that colonial and racist foreign domination Powers continue to violate international humanitarian law,

Recalling the relevant provisions contained in the instruments of international humanitarian law relative to the protection of women and children in time of peace and war,

Recalling, among other important documents, its resolutions 2444 (XXIII) of 19 December 1968, 2597 (XXIV) of 16 December 1969 and 2674 (XXV) and 2675 (XXV) of 9 December 1970, on respect for human rights and on basic principles for the protection of civilian populations in armed conflicts, as well as Economic and Social Council resolution 1515 (XLVIII) of 28 May 1970 in which the Council requested the General Assembly to consider the possibility of drafting a declaration on the protection of women and children in emergency or wartime,

Conscious of its responsibility for the destiny of the rising generation and for the destiny of mothers, who play an important role in society, in the family and particularly in the upbringing of children,

Bearing in mind the need to provide special protection of women and children belonging to the civilian population,

Solemnly proclaims this Declaration on the Protection of Women and Children in Emergency and Armed Conflict and calls for the strict observance of the Declaration by all Member States:

1. Attacks and bombings on the civilian population, inflicting incalculable suffering, especially on women and children, who are the most vulnerable members of the population, shall be prohibited, and such acts shall be condemned.

2. The use of chemical and bacteriological weapons in the course of military operations constitutes one of the most flagrant violations of the Geneva Protocol of 1925, the Geneva Conventions of 1949 and the principles of international humanitarian law and inflicts heavy losses on civilian populations, including defenceless women and children, and shall be severely condemned.

3. All States shall abide fully by their obligations under the Geneva Protocol of 1925 and the Geneva Conventions of 1949, as well as other instruments of international law relative to respect for human rights in armed conflicts, which offer important guarantees for the protection of women and children.

4. All efforts shall be made by States involved in armed conflicts, military operations in foreign territories or military operations in territories still under colonial domination to spare women and children from the ravages of war. All the necessary steps shall be taken to ensure the prohibition of measures such as persecution, torture, punitive measures, degrading treatment and violence, particularly against that part of the civilian population that consists of women and children.

5. All forms of repression and cruel and inhuman treatment of women and children, including imprisonment, torture, shooting, mass arrests, collective punishment, destruction of dwellings and forcible eviction, committed by belligerents in the course of military operations or in occupied territories shall be considered criminal.

6. Women and children belonging to the civilian population and finding themselves in circumstances of emergency and armed conflict in the struggle for peace, self-determination, national liberation and independence, or who live in occupied territories, shall not be deprived of shelter, food, medical aid or other inalienable rights, in accordance with the provisions of the Universal Declaration of Human Rights, the International Covenant on Civil and Political Rights, the International Covenant on Economic, Social and Cultural Rights, the Declaration of the Rights of the Child or other instruments of international law.

United Nations Security Council Resolution 1325, Women, Peace and Security (25 October 2000)

The Security Council,

Recalling its resolutions 1261 (1999) of 25 August 1999, 1265 (1999) of 17 September 1999, 1296 (2000) of 19 April 2000 and 1314 (2000) of 11 August 2000, as well as relevant statements of its President and recalling also the statement of its President, to the press on the occasion of the United Nations Day for Women's Rights and International Peace of 8 March 2000 (SC/6816),

Recalling also the commitments of the Beijing Declaration and Platform for Action (A/52/231) as well as those contained in the outcome document of the twenty-third Special Session of the United Nations General Assembly entitled 'Women 2000: Gender Equality, Development and Peace for the twenty-first century' (A/S-23/10/Rev.1), in particular those concerning women and armed conflict,

Bearing in mind the purposes and principles of the Charter of the United Nations and the primary responsibility of the Security Council under the Charter for the maintenance of international peace and security,

Expressing concern that civilians, particularly women and children, account for the vast majority of those adversely affected by armed conflict, including as refugees and internally displaced persons, and increasingly are targeted by combatants and armed elements, and recognising the consequent impact this has on durable peace and reconciliation,

Reaffirming the important role of women in the prevention and resolution of conflicts and in peacebuilding, and stressing the importance of their equal participation and full involvement in all efforts for the maintenance and promotion of peace and security, and the need to increase their role in decision-making with regard to conflict prevention and resolution,

Reaffirming also the need to implement fully international humanitarian and human rights law that protects the rights of women and girls during and after conflicts,

Emphasising the need for all parties to ensure that mine clearance and mine awareness programmes take into account the special needs of women and girls,

Recognising the urgent need to mainstream a gender perspective into peacekeeping operations, and in this regard noting the Windhoek Declaration and the Namibia Plan of Action on Mainstreaming a Gender Perspective in Multidimensional Peace Support Operations (S/2000/693),

Recognising also the importance of the recommendation contained in the statement of its President to the press of 8 March 2000 for specialised training for all peacekeeping personnel on the protection, special needs and human rights of women and children in conflict situations,

Recognising that an understanding of the impact of armed conflict on women and girls, effective institutional arrangements to guarantee their protection and full participation in the peace process can significantly contribute to the maintenance and promotion of international peace and security,

Noting the need to consolidate data on the impact of armed conflict on women and girls,

1. Urges Member States to ensure increased representation of women at all decision-making levels in national, regional and international institutions and mechanisms for the prevention, management, and resolution of conflict;

2. Encourages the Secretary-General to implement his strategic plan of action (A/49/587) calling for an increase in the participation of women at decision-making levels in conflict resolution and peace processes;

3. Urges the Secretary-General to appoint more women as special representatives and envoys to pursue good offices on his behalf, and in this regard calls on Member States to provide candidates to the Secretary-General, for inclusion in a regularly updated centralised roster;

4. Further urges the Secretary-General to seek to expand the role and contribution of women in United Nations field-based operations, and especially among military observers, civilian police, human rights and humanitarian personnel;

5. Expresses its willingness to incorporate a gender perspective into peacekeeping operations and urges the Secretary-General to ensure that, where appropriate, field operations include a gender component;

6. Requests the Secretary-General to provide to Member States training guidelines and materials on the protection, rights and the particular needs of women, as well as on the importance of involving women in all peacekeeping and peace-building measures, invites Member States to incorporate these elements as well as HIV/AIDS awareness training into their national training programmes for military and civilian police personnel in preparation for deployment and further requests the Secretary-General to ensure that civilian personnel of peacekeeping operations receive similar training;

7. Urges Member States to increase their voluntary financial, technical and logistical support for gender sensitive training efforts, including those undertaken by relevant funds and programmes, *inter alia*, the United Nations Fund for Women and United Nations Children's Fund, and by the United Nations High Commissioner for Refugees and other relevant bodies;

8. Calls on all actors involved, when negotiating and implementing peace agreements, to adopt a gender perspective, including, *inter alia*:

   a) The special needs of women and girls during repatriation and resettlement and for rehabilitation, reintegration and post-conflict reconstruction;

   b) Measures that support local women's peace initiatives and indigenous processes for conflict resolution, and that involve women in all of the implementation mechanisms of the peace agreements;

   c) Measures that ensure the protection of and respect for human rights of women and girls, particularly as they relate to the constitution, the electoral system, the police and the judiciary;

9. Calls upon all parties to armed conflict to respect fully international law applicable to the rights and protection of women and girls as civilians, in particular the obligations applicable to them under the Geneva Conventions of 1949 and the Additional Protocols thereto of 1977, the Refugee Convention of 1951 and the Protocol thereto of 1967, the Convention on the Elimination of All Forms of Discrimination against Women of 1979 and the Optional Protocol thereto of 1999 and the United Nations Convention on the Rights of the Child of 1989 and the two Optional Protocols thereto of 25 May 2000, and to bear in mind the relevant provisions of the Rome Statute of the International Criminal Court;

10. Calls on all parties to armed conflict to take special measures to protect women and girls from gender-based violence, particularly rape and other forms of sexual abuse, and all other forms of violence in situations of armed conflict;

11. Emphasises the responsibility of all States to put an end to impunity and to prosecute those responsible for genocide, crimes against humanity, war crimes including those relating to sexual violence against women and girls, and in this regard, stresses the need to exclude these crimes, where feasible from amnesty provisions;

12. Calls upon all parties to armed conflict to respect the civilian and humanitarian character of refugee camps and settlements, and to take into account the particular needs of women and girls, including in their design, and recalls its resolution 1208 (1998) of 19 November 1998;

13. Encourages all those involved in the planning for disarmament, demobilisation and reintegration to consider the different needs of female and male ex-combatants and to take into account the needs of their dependants;

14. Reaffirms its readiness, whenever measures are adopted under Article 41 of the Charter of the United Nations, to give consideration to their potential impact on the civilian population, bearing in mind the special needs of women and girls, in order to consider appropriate humanitarian exemptions;

15. Expresses its willingness to ensure that Security Council missions take into account gender considerations and the rights of women, including through consultation with local and international women's groups;

16. Invites the Secretary-General to carry out a study on the impact of armed conflict on women and girls, the role of women in peacebuilding and the gender dimensions of peace processes and conflict resolution, and further invites him to submit a report to the Security Council on the results of this study and to make this available to all Member States of the United Nations;

17. Requests the Secretary-General, where appropriate, to include in his reporting to the Security Council, progress on gender mainstreaming throughout peacekeeping missions and all other aspects relating to women and girls;

18. Decides to remain actively seized of the matter.

Endnotes

1 Resolution 217 A (III).

2 See resolution 2200 A (XXI), annex.

3 See resolution 2200 A (XXI), annex.

4 Resolution 34/180, annex.

5 Resolution 39/46, annex.

6 Report of the World Conference to Review and Appraise the Achievements of the United Nations Decade for Women: Equality, Development and Peace, Nairobi, 15-26 July 1985 (United Nations publication, Sales No. E.85.IV.10), chap. I, sect. A

7 Universal Declaration of Human Rights, article 3; and International Covenant on Civil and Political Rights, article 6.

8 International Covenant on Civil and Political Rights, article 26.

9 Universal Declaration of Human Rights, article 3; and International Covenant on Civil and Political Rights, article 9.

10 International Covenant on Civil and Political Rights, article 26.

11 International Covenant on Civil and Political Rights, article 26.

12 International Covenant on Economic, Social and Cultural Rights, article 12.

13 Universal Declaration of Human Rights, article 23; and International Covenant on Economic, Social and Cultural Rights, articles 6 and 7.

14 Universal Declaration of Human Rights, article 5; International Covenant on Civil and Political Rights, article 7; and Convention against Torture and Other Cruel, Inhuman or Degrading Treatment or Punishment.

Organisations Dealing with Women's Rights

Abuse and Sexual Violence

Centre Olame (Democratic Republic of Congo) is a non-profit organisation in eastern Congo dedicated to the promotion of women. It has been operating a rape crisis centre in Bukavu providing counselling to victims of rape and sexual exploitation.

Cowichan Women against Violence Society (Canada) works from a feminist perspective to provide a supportive environment for women and children who have been affected by abuse. It supports diversity, change, choice and growth through counselling, advocacy, emergency shelter, community development and education. Website: http://www.cwav.org

Rape Crisis (Cape Town, South Africa) is a women's organisation committed to ending violence against women. Its counselling service offers free and confidential support, 24-hour telephone service, face-to-face counselling, court preparation, support groups, self-help workshops and advice and counselling to friends and family. Website: http://www.rapecrisis.org.za

Rape Crisis Federation (United Kingdom) provides assistance to individual women victims of sexual assault, training and information to groups and organisations interested in sexual violence and consultation on central governmental level. Website: http://www.rapecrisis.co.uk/index.htm

SOS Help line for Women and Children - Victims of Violence (Ljubljana, Slovenia) provides concrete aid to women, their offspring and children who are victims of physical, psychological or sexual violence, provides shelter for women and children victims of violence and organise prevention programmes for young people. Tel: + 386 61 9782, 441 993

Women's Aid (Dublin, Ireland) is a non-governmental organisation providing information, support and accommodation to women and children who are being physically, emotionally and sexually abused in their own homes. The organisation is run by women for women and its philosophy is based on self-help, with the aim of giving women the power to take back control over their lives and offer them the support they need to do this. E-mail: hetata@in touch.com; Website: http://www.niwaf.org

Development and Empowerment of Women

ADEW, Association for the Development & Enhancement of Women (Cairo, Egypt) was founded in 1987 as the first feminist NGO in Egypt to deal specifically with the issue of empowering female heads of households. Its activities comprise credit programmes, literacy programmes, health services and legal awareness seminars. Website: http://www.adewegypt.org

Afghan Women's Resource Centre (Pakistan) is a non-governmental, non-political, indigenous organisation working for Afghan women in the Afghan border communities. The organisation provides centres for educational and vocational training aimed at empowering Afghan women through the provision of the skills and knowledge needed to support themselves and their families, and to contribute actively in the rebuilding of Afghanistan. Website: ttp://www.w4wafghan.ca/project_partners/awrc/awrc_overview.html

AIDWA, All India Democratic Women's Association (New Delhi, India) is committed to achieving democracy, equality and women's emancipation. AIDWA membership comprises women of all strata, regardless of caste, class or creed and its main focus of attention is work among the poorer sections of women. Website: http://www.aidwa.org/aidwa

Alliance 'Women of the Don' (Russia Federation) aims to raise women's roles in the social, political, economical and cultural spheres of life, as well as advocating women's interests and performing peacemaking and law protection activity. Website: http://www.owl.ru/eng/women/aiwo/wom-don.htm

APWA, All Pakistan Women's Association (Karachi, Pakistan) is a non-profit and non-political organisation whose fundamental aim is to improve the social and economic welfare of women and children in Pakistan. Website: http://www.un.org.pk/unic/apwa.htm

AWID, Association for Women in Development (Toronto, Canada) is an international membership organisation committed to gender equality and a just and sustainable development process.

AWID facilitates a three-way exchange among scholars, practitioners and policymakers in order to develop effective and transformative approaches for improving the lives of women and girls worldwide. Website: http://www.avid.org

CARE (Brussels, Belgium) provides immediate humanitarian relief arising from disaster and assists poverty alleviation and discrimination. It strives to involve women as project participants, decision makers and beneficiaries. Of particular focus are women's issues such as reproductive health, family planning, income generation and girls' education. It provides schooling for young girls to encourage long-term health, self-sufficiency, strong family and community status, and parenting skills. Website: http://www.care-international.org/careswork.html

Donetsk Association of Women Organisations (Donetsk, Ukraine) co-ordinates activities of non-governmental organisations in solving problems relating to the improvement of forms and methods of social support to various categories of women, their employment and self-fulfilment. Website: http://www.iatp.donetsk.ua

Fund for an Open Society (Serbia) supports programmes and activities aimed at developing democratic culture, civil society, human rights, openness, tolerance, and peace and stability in Serbia. It works towards this end by focusing on education, science, culture and art, health systems, and communications. Its Network Women's Programme works to promote the advancement of women's human rights, gender equality and empowerment as an integral part of the process of democratisation. Website: http://www.soros.org/about/foundations/serbia

GROOTS (New York, USA) operates as a flexible network linking leaders and groups in poor rural and urban areas in the South and North in order to strengthen women's participation in the development of communities. It help urban and rural grassroots women's groups identify and share their successful development approaches and methods globally and to focus international attention on grassroots women's needs and capabilities. Website: http://www.groots.org/about.htm

International Center for Research of Women (Washington D.C., USA) aims to improve the lives of women in poverty, advance women's equality and human rights, and contribute to broader economic and social well-being. It works in research, advocacy and sustainable development to support women as economic providers and innovators, nurturers and care givers, community leaders and agents of change. It strives to ensure women's control of economic resources, guarantee reproductive rights, health and nutrition, and increase women's political power. Website: http://www.icrw.org

International Gender and Trade Network (IGTN) (Washington D.C., USA) is a network of gender advocates working to promote equitable, social, and sustainable trade. The network utilises research, advocacy and economic literacy to address the specific trade and development issues of its seven regions: Africa, Asia, Caribbean, Europe, Latin America, North America, and Pacific. The IGTN was established in December 1999 following a Strategic Planning Seminar on Gender and Trade. Website: http://www.coc.org/focus/women/international.html

International Women's Forum (Washington D.C., USA) is an organisation of pre-eminent women of significant and diverse achievement. Members come together across national and international boundaries to share knowledge and ideas to enrich each other's lives, to provide a network of support, and to exert influence. Through the Leadership Foundation, the International Women's Forum helps prepare future generations of women leaders. Website: http://www.iwforum.org

International Women's Tribune Centre (USA) provides information, communication and education to women organisations and community groups, targeting particularly low-income rural and urban women. Website: http://www.iwtc.org

KARAT Coalition (Warszawa, Poland) is a network of women's NGOs from ten Central and Eastern European countries. Its mission is to promote and ensure *de facto* gender equality by promoting the Beijing Platform for Action in the region, and raising this region's visibility at international fora. Website: http://www.geocities.com/woalde/karat.html

Kosovo Women's Network (Serbia and Montenegro) is a network of local women's groups. This includes groups that have over ten years experience in community development, as well as new groups that have been founded since the arrival of the UN in Kosovo. Members of the network provide a variety of community services to vulnerable women, including courses, training, aid, and psychological support. Additionally, they work on social problems affecting women and girls today, such as violence against women, trafficking for prostitution, and low enrolment of girls in schools and university. Website: http://www.womensnetwork.org/english/index.html

MYWO, Maendeleo Ya Wanawake Organisation (Nairobi, Kenya) is a non-profit grassroots women's organisation with branches all over Kenya. Its programmes include maternal and child health and family planning, HIV/AIDS, women leadership development and training programme, income generation project and traditional practices and gender issues. Website: http://www.maendeleo-ya-wanawake.org

Shevolution (Burwash Etchingham, United Kingdom) supports the development of systems, services and media for women and men to work together as equals in work, life and politics. Website: http://www.shevolution.qbfox.com

UNDAW, United Nations Division for Women (New York, USA) advocates the improvement of the status of women of the world and the achievement of their equality with men. Aiming to ensure the participation of women as equal partners with men in all aspects of human endeavour, the Division promotes women as equal participants and beneficiaries of sustainable development, peace and security, governance and human rights. As part of its mandate, it strives to stimulate the mainstreaming of gender perspectives both within and outside the United Nations system. Website: http://www.un.org/womenwatch/daw

UNIFEM, United Nations Women's Fund (New York, USA) provides financial and technical assistance to innovative programmes and strategies that promote women's human rights, political participation and economic security. Within the UN system, UNIFEM promotes gender equality and links women's issues and concerns to national, regional and global agendas by fostering collaboration and providing technical expertise on gender mainstreaming and women's empowerment strategies. Website: http://www.unifem.org/

WEDO, The Women's Environment and Development Organisation (New York, USA) aims to promote women playing a major role in the growing worldwide movement for global security, economic justice, democracy, human rights and women's empowerment. Website: http://www.wedo.org

WiLDAF, Women in Law and Development in Africa (Harare, Zimbabwe) is a pan-African women's rights network dedicated to promoting and strengthening strategies which link law and development to increase women's participation and influence at the community, national and international levels. WiLDAF brings together organisations and individuals who share this objective and who are operating at local, national and regional levels to make it a reality. Website: http://site.mweb.co.zw/wildaf

Women for Free Iraq (Iraq) is a diverse group of over fifty women from Iraq who came together in February 2003 to speak up about the suffering of their people under Saddam's regime, and rally support for the liberation of Iraq. It continues to advocate on behalf of a free, pluralistic Iraq that is based on equal rights, the rule of law and representative democracy. Its aim is to contribute to the building of a new Iraq where women have the same rights and opportunities as men. Website: http://womenforiraq.org

Women's Counselling Service (Ljubljana, Slovenia) provides assistance to all women in distress, informs them on how to get assistance, support, advice, representation, legal advice and help from volunteers. It raises public profile of women's issues and provides education and training.

YWCA, World Young Women's Christian Association (Geneva, Switzerland) is an autonomous community-based non-governmental organisation. As a non-profit membership association, each YWCA is run by and for women of the community and their families. YWCA work includes leadership training, hostels for young women in need of housing, income-generating projects, health programmes, shelters for victims of violence, vocational skills training, development projects, and promoting women's rights. Website: http://www.worldywca.org

Education

FAWE, Forum for African Women Educationalists (Nairobi, Kenya) provides a programme ensuring that girls have access to school and complete their education. E-mail: fawe@fawe.org, Website: http://womensissues.about.com/cs/africa

Movimento das Mulheres Moçambicanas Pela Paz (Maputo, Mozambique) is a non-profit, informal group aiming to promote women's education for a culture of peace as a way to educate the new forthcoming generations in a pacifist conflict resolution environment. E-mail: julieta@letras.uem.ruz

UNESCO, The United Nations Educational, Scientific and Cultural Organization (Paris, France) aims at building a culture of peace. It works to create the conditions for genuine dialogue based upon respect for shared values and the dignity of each civilisation and culture. One of its goals is to promote and advance the right to education for all. It has developed a wide range of gender sensitive training manuals linking education, development and health. Website: http://portal.unesco.org/education/en/

Female Genital Mutilation

Centre for Reproductive Rights (New York, USA) is a non-profit legal advocacy organisation dedicated to promoting and defending women's reproductive rights worldwide. It aims to secure universal, safe and affordable contraception, guarantee safe, accessible, and legal abortion, defend the rights of pregnant women, including the right to safe and healthy pregnancies, and eliminate

practices that harm women and girls such as female genital mutilation. Website: http://www.crlp.org

RAINBO is an African led international non-governmental organisation established in 1994 to work on issues of women's empowerment, gender, reproductive health, sexual autonomy and freedom from violence as central components of the African development agenda. RAINBO specifically strives to enhance global efforts to eliminate the practice of female circumcision and female genital mutilation (FC/FGM) through facilitating women's self-empowerment and accelerating social change. Website: http://www.rainbo.org

Gender Justice

Equal Rights Advocates (San Francisco, USA) is dedicated to a mission to protect and secure equal rights and economic opportunities for women and girls through litigation and advocacy. It provides callers to its toll-free Advice and Counselling hotline individualised legal advice and assistance on issues such as sexual harassment, family and medical leave, pay inequity and pregnancy discrimination. Website: http://www.equalrights.org

Women's Initiatives for Gender Justice (former Women's Caucus for Gender Justice) (New York, USA) is a network of individuals and groups committed to strengthening advocacy on women's human rights and helping to develop greater capacity among women in the use of the International Criminal Court, the Optional Protocol to CEDAW and other mechanisms that provide women's access to different systems of justice. Website: http://www.iccwomen.org/archive/aboutcaucus.htm

Women's Justice Center (California, USA) deals with issues of domestic violence, sexual abuse and justice related to women. It provides advocacy, free of charge, for victims of rape, domestic violence, and child abuse. It is also involved in advocacy training and community education, and coordinates the Task Force on Women in Policing with the goal of increasing the number of women and minorities in law enforcement agencies. Website: http://www.justicewomen.com/index.html

Women's Legal Centre (Cape Town, South Africa) is a non-profit, independently funded law centre based in South Africa. The WLC has been established to advance women's rights by conducting constitutional litigation and advocacy on gender issues. It seeks to advance the struggle for equality for women, particularly black women, who suffer socio-economic disadvantage, through the promotion and development of human rights for women. It provides litigation services and legal briefs free of charge. Website: http://www.wlce.co.za/index.html

Harmful Traditional Practices

Progressive Women's Association of Pakistan works mainly on domestic violence and situations leading to the vulnerability of women in Pakistan. It has launched numerous reports, workshops, seminars and discussion panels on acts of violence against women. It has also compiled significant data on the issue and advocates criminalisation and effective state intervention.

Women's United Nations Report Network (WUNRN) (USA) is a non-governmental coalition working towards the implementation of the conclusions and recommendations of a United Nations Study on Freedom of Religion and Belief and the Status of Women From the Viewpoint of Religion and Traditions. Website: http://www.wunrn.com/

Health of Women

Australian Reproductive Health Alliance's (Australia) mission is to promote public support for enhanced reproductive and sexual health in Australia and internationally, and promote the advancement of the status of women and girls. It promotes knowledge, education and research relating to the development of family planning and other reproductive health services, paying particular attention to the needs of indigenous people, both within Australia and internationally. Website: http://www.arha.org.au/index.htm

CARAL Pro-Choice Education Fund (California, USA) provides people from all walks of life with the tools they need to participate more fully in the democratic process that affects their reproductive choices, from contraception and sex education to abortion and healthy birth. Through public forums, skills and leadership training, issue analysis, media, and computer communication, it promotes an inclusive understanding of choice that reflects the agenda and concerns of all women including young women, poor women and women of all races. Website: http://www.choice.org

GAWH, The Global Alliance for Women's Health (New York, USA) is committed to advancing women's health in all stages of life at all policy levels through health promotion, education, advocacy and programme implementation. The GAWH works with coalitions of international, national and non-governmental organisations, women's groups, health care professionals, religious organisations, academics and individual citizens from all regions of the world to promote and implement improvements in women's health care service and conduct research at the local, national and international levels. Website: http://www.gawh.org

International Women's Health Coalition (New York, USA) works to generate health and population policies, programmes, and funding that promote and protect the rights and health of girls and women worldwide, particularly in Africa, Asia, Latin America, and countries in post-socialist transition. Website: http://www.iwhc.org

Ipas (USA) works to increase women's ability to exercise their sexual and reproductive rights and to reduce deaths and injuries of women from unsafe abortion. Ipas' global and country programmes include training, research, advocacy, distribution of equipment and supplies for reproductive health care and information dissemination. Website: http://www.ipas.org/english

Marie Stopes International Global Partnership (London, UK) provides sexual and reproductive health information and services to 3.6 million people worldwide in 35 countries across Africa, Asia, Australia, Europe, Latin America and the Middle East. Website: http://www.mariestopes.org.uk/index.shtml

Physicians for Human Rights (PHR) (Washington D.C., USA) promotes health by protecting human rights. By using medical and scientific methods, it investigates and exposes violations of human rights worldwide and works to stop them. It supports institutions that hold perpetrators of human rights abuses, including health professionals, accountable for their actions. It has made numerous studies on women's health, specifically the effects of gender-based violence. Website: http://www.phrusa.org

Safe Motherhood Inter-Agency Group (IAG) is a unique partnership of international and national agencies that co-sponsored the first Safe Motherhood Conference. Its goal is to contribute to improved maternal and newborn survival and well-being by promoting and supporting the implementation of cost-effective interventions in the developing world. The IAG carries out policy support and disseminates best practices and other information among policymakers, programme managers, and other stakeholders worldwide. Website: http://www.safemotherhood.org

WHO, World Health Organization (Geneva, Switzerland) is the United Nations specialised agency for health committed to the achievement of the highest level of physical, mental and social well-being by all. Its Department of Gender, Women and Health is responsible for researching and disseminating information on neglected topics directly pertaining to women's health, such as gender-based violence against women. Website: http://www.who.int/gender/en/

Human Rights

BAOBAB (Nigeria) promotes and develops women's human rights in customary, secular and religious laws. It has undertaken research and produced reports on women's rights and laws in Nigeria, including access to justice for the Oputa Human Rights Violations Investigation Panel, and (with other non-governmental organisations) produced reports on Nigeria's record in fulfilling its obligations under the Convention for the Elimination of All Forms of Discrimination Against Women. It has also developed a series of legal literacy leaflets. Website: http://www.baobabwomen.org

Centre for Women's Global Leadership (USA) develops and facilitates women's leadership for women's human rights and social justice worldwide. It promotes the leadership of women and advances the feminist perspectives in policy-making processes in local, national and international arenas. Website: http://www.cwgl.rutgers.edu/index.html

Equality Now (New York, USA) works for the protection and promotion of human rights of women around the world. Working with national human rights organisations and individual activists, Equality Now documents violence and discrimination against women and adds an international action overlay to support their efforts to advance equality rights and defend individual women who are suffering abuse. Website: http://www.equalitynow.org

Global Fund for Women (USA) is an international organisation, which focuses on women's human rights. It deals with issues such as literacy, domestic violence, economic autonomy and the international trafficking of women. It supports women's groups worldwide. Website: http://www.globalfundforwomen.org

Global Rights (USA) is a human rights advocacy group that partners with local activists to challenge oppressive ideologies and power structures, channel international pressure to secure human rights protections, and amplify new voices within the global discourse. It works to promote racial and gender equality and help people and communities feel empowered to change their societies. Website: http://www.globalrights.org

Human Rights Watch (New York, USA) is an independent, non-governmental organisation dedicated to protecting the human rights of people around the world. The Women's Rights Division of Human Rights Watch fights against the dehumanisation and marginalisation of women, promotes women's equal rights and dignity and strives to stop discrimination and violence against women. Website: http://www.hrw.org

International Alliance of Women (Australia) is active in the field of promoting women's human rights, particularly through a campaign for the promotion of the ratification and implementation of CEDAW. Website: http://www.womenalliance.com/index.html

International Human Rights Law Group works towards strengthening human rights norms and institutions around the world. One of its thematic projects is the promotion of women's rights, especially in the economic and social field, as well as in conflict situations. Website: http://www.hrlawgroup.org

MADRE (New York, USA) is an international women's human rights organisation that works in partnership with women's community-based groups in conflict areas worldwide. Its programmes address issues of sustainable development; community improvement and women's health; violence and war; discrimination and racism; self-determination and collective rights; women's leadership development; and human rights education. Website: http://www.madre.org

Minnesota Advocates for Human Rights (USA) is a volunteer-based, non-governmental organisation dedicated to the promotion and protection of internationally recognised human rights. It has launched the Stop Violence against Women website, a resource for individuals and organisations working to eliminate violence against women in Central and Eastern Europe (CEE) and in the Commonwealth of Independent States (CIS). Website: http://www.mnadvocates.org

OSAGI, Office of the Special Adviser to the Secretary-General on Gender Issues and Advancement of Women (New York, USA) promotes the effective implementation of the Millennium Declaration, the Beijing Declaration and the Platform for Action of the Fourth World Conference on Women and the Outcome Document of the special session of the General Assembly on Beijing+5. Website: http://www.un.org/womenwatch/osagi

RAWA, the Revolutionary Association of the Women of Afghanistan (Kabul, Afghanistan) was established in 1977 as an independent political and social organisation of Afghan women fighting for human rights and social justice in Afghanistan. Website: http://rawa.false.net/index.html

Rights & Democracy (Canada) is a non-partisan organisation with an international mandate. Within the women's rights theme it defends and promotes the integration of women's human rights within the United Nations system and other international and regional organisations and advocates in favour of the implementation of international human rights instruments. It has developed a participatory methodology to document violations of women's rights. It works in co-operation with partners on ending impunity on violence against women, in particular, on violence against women in armed conflict. It also works on the implementation of *Security Council Resolution 1325 on Women, Peace and Security* from a grassroots perspective in countries such as Afghanistan and the Democratic Republic of Congo. Website: http://www.ichrdd.ca/splash.html

Sisters in Islam (Malaysia) is a group of Muslim professional women committed to promoting the rights of women within the framework of Islam, including awareness of the true principles of Islam, principles that enshrine the concept of equality between women and men, and strive towards creating a society that upholds the Islamic principles of equality, justice, freedom and dignity within a democratic state. Website: http://www.sistersinislam.org.my

Women Living Under Muslim Laws (London, UK) was created to break women's isolation and to provide linkages and support to all women whose lives may be affected by Muslim laws, to increase women's knowledge about both their common and diverse situations in various contexts in order to strengthen their struggles and to create the means to support them internationally from within and outside the Muslim world. Website: http://www.wluml.org/english/index.shtml

Landmines

Geneva International Centre for Humanitarian De-mining (GICHD) (Geneva, Switzerland) is an independent and impartial foundation working for the reduction of the humanitarian impact of remnants of war by providing operational assistance, creating and sharing knowledge, and supporting instruments of international law. GICHD supports Humanitarian Mine Action through operational assistance and research, and the implementation of the Anti-Personnel Mine Ban Convention. In 2001, state parties to the Ottawa Convention mandated the GICHD to establish an Implementation Support Unit to deal with the issues related to the convention. Website: http://www.gichd.ch

International Campaign to Ban Landmines (ICBL) (Brussels, Belgium) is a global network of organisations working to eradicate anti-personnel mines. The campaign calls for an international ban on the use, production, stockpiling, and transfer of anti-personnel landmines, and for increased international resources for humanitarian mine clearance and mine victim assistance programmes. The network represents over 1,100 organisations in over 60 countries, which work locally, nationally, regionally, and internationally to ban anti-personnel landmines. Website: http://www.icbl.org

Mines Advisory Group (MAG) (Manchester, UK) is an international NGO for mine action that assists people affected by landmines and unexploded ordnance (UXO - bombs, mortars, grenades). MAG clears and destroys the landmines and left-over weapons that make areas unsafe after war. Website: http://www.mag.org.uk/magtest/topintro.htm

Peacebuilding and Peacemaking

International Alert (UK) is an independent, international non-governmental organisation that works to help build lasting peace in countries and communities affected or threatened by violent conflict. Within its Gender and Peacebuilding Programme, it launched in May 1999 an international campaign entitled 'Women Building Peace: From the Village Council to the Negotiating Table' with the support of over 200 women's organisations. It works to support the full implementation of international resolutions and commitments relating to women, peace and security, raise awareness of women's experiences and perspectives of peace and conflict, and promote women's peacebuilding activities, It also advocates for an increase of resources for women and women's organisations involved in peacebuilding, conflict reconstruction and reconciliation. Website: http://www.womenbuildingpeace.org

Northern Ireland Women's Coalition (Northern Ireland) is a cross-community political party working for inclusion, human rights and equality in Northern Ireland. It works to implement the Belfast Agreement and address the every day concerns of women, men and children in Northern Ireland, and tries to widen participation in politics and make sure the voices of young people, older people, ethnic minorities, women and community and voluntary groups are heard. Website: http://www.niwc.org/aboutus.asp

Project Parity – Partnership for Peace, (London, UK) based in the United Kingdom, is a not for profit organisation campaigning for women to be included on equal terms with men in peace discussions and on setting any conflict prevention, peacebuilding and post-conflict reconstruction agenda and for gender considerations to be mainstreamed throughout conflict prevention, peacebuilding and post- conflict reconstruction processes. Website: www.pppp.cswebsites.org

The Suzanne Mubarak Women's International Peace Movement (Cairo, Egypt) is an international initiative in the Middle East that seeks to enhance the active participation of women in the decision and peacemaking processes. Its main objective is to link up with organisations, agencies and peace activists that are working on the various aspects of conflict prevention, resolution and reconstruction, offering a platform for all to join forces and strengthen the impact of individual initiatives, in order to find alternative solutions to conflict and promote the culture peace throughout the world. Website: http://www.womenforpeaceinternational.org

WILPF, Women's International League for Peace and Freedom (USA/Switzerland) is the oldest women's peace organisation in the world that aims to bring together women of different political beliefs and philosophies who are united in their determination to study, make known and help abolish the causes and the legitimisation of war. Website: http://www.wilpf.int.ch

Women in Black is an international peace network. Its members stand in silent vigil to protest war, rape as a tool of war, ethnic cleansing and human rights abuses all over the world. Website: http://womeninblack.net/index.html

Women Waging Peace (Washington D.C., USA) advocates for the full participation of women in formal and informal peace processes around the world. Its programme 'Inclusive Security: Women Waging Peace' strives to build a network of women peacemakers, emphasising women's vital contributions to conflict prevention, peace negotiations and post-conflict reconstruction efforts, and women's agency in promoting security. Website: http://www.womenwagingpeace.net

World Council of Churches (Geneva, Switzerland) is the broadest and most inclusive among the many organised expressions of the modern ecumenical movement, a movement whose goal is Christian unity. In the framework of its Decade to Overcome Violence (2001-2010) it initiated a project entitled Overcoming Violence against Women. It aims to call on churches for reflection on the themes of peace, justice, reconciliation and repenting in complicity for practices of violence. The programme intends to build a comprehensive and accessible resource collection of material for education and organise seminars to highlight the need to overcome gender violence. Website: http://www.wcc-coe.org/wcc/what/index-e.html

Prostitution

Coalition for the Rights of Sex Workers (Canada) is part of the international struggle for the rights of people in the sex trade and for the decriminalisation of their work. Website: http://www.lacoalitionmontreal.com/eng_coalition.htm

Foundation for Women (Thailand) provides information, support, referral, and emergency financial assistance to women who have been victims of exploitation, violence and trafficking.

It offers small-scale credit schemes for alternative economic projects and conducts research on international migration and trafficking, adolescent sexuality, and domestic violence. Website: http://www.humantrafficking.org/countries/eap/thailand/ngos/national/foundation_for_women.html

Frauenbus Lysistrata (Switzerland) is an association established in Olten since 1996 at the core of one of Switzerland's oldest red light districts. In the form of a makeshift 'bus' the association works for dialogue and prevention of HIV/AIDS, hepatitis and violence, as well as other services for people involved in the sex industry.

Prostitution Awareness and Action Foundation of Edmonton (PAAFE) (Canada) is the governing body of the Prostitution Offender Programme, an Edmonton City Police initiative approved in April 1996 by the Alberta Ministry of Justice, which aims at alleviating harm caused by prostitution and creating long-standing solutions through community partnerships. Website: http://www.paafe.org/index.htm

Prostitution Research and Education (USA) is sponsored by the San Francisco Women's Centre, a non-profit corporation. It develops research and educational programmes to document the experiences of people in prostitution. A purpose of PRE is to reflect the voices of one of the world's most disenfranchised groups: prostituted women and children. Website: http://www.prostitutionresearch.com/c-escaping-prostitution.html

Sex Industry Survivors' Anonymous (USA) is a worldwide group of former or current male and female sex workers who wish to leave the sex industry and who have established a network of communication to share their experiences. Website: http://www.sexindustrysurvivors.com/splash.htm

Sex Workers Outreach Project (USA) focuses on safety, dignity, diversity and the changing needs of sex industry workers, to foster an environment which enables and affirms individual choices and occupational rights. Website: http://www.swop-usa.org/

WEDPRO, Women's Education, Development, Productivity and Research Organisation (Quezon City, Philippines) deals with women's human rights, with special attention to prostitution and trafficking, reproductive and sexual rights, micro enterprise development and social investigation. It formulates and implements development programmes to empower women through participatory, women-centred and gender sensitive processes. WEDPRO also engages in action research, training and community-based education and documents and disseminates its findings. Its computer database and information library on prostitution and trafficking is available to networks, organisations and individual users. Website: http://www.wedpro1989.org/

Refugee Women

Association 'Women to Women' (Sarajevo, Bosnia-Herzegovina) is a non-governmental organisation aiming to reinforce the need for community building and to find common ground. It aims to facilitate a safe return for women and their families and to ensure emotional and psychological support. It assists women to gain self-respect and self-confidence. E-mail: ZENEZENAMA_SA@ZAMIR-SA.ztu.apc.org

Refugee Women's Alliance (Washington, USA), first established by women refugees, this organisation aims to improve the life of refugee and immigrant women and their families. It serves primarily women from Southeast Asia, Eastern Europe and the former Soviet Union, and East Africa. http://www.rewa.org

Women's Commission for Refugee Women and Children (New York, USA) works to ensure that refugee and displaced women, children and adolescents are given protection, encouraged to participate in public decisions and have access to education, health services and livelihood opportunities. Website: http://www.womenscommission.org/index.html

Roma Women

International Roma Women's Network is a project of the Network Women's Program of the Open Society Institute, promotes the human rights of Roma women by empowering Roma women activists in Central and Eastern Europe. It encourages and promotes the development of young Roma women's leadership. It also raises public awareness about the human rights of Roma women who face a range of prejudices coming from their communities and the larger society. Website: http://www.romawomensinitiatives.org/main.htm

Roma Women Association (Romania) is a non-governmental organisation defending the rights of Roma women and supporting their development and expression of ethnic, cultural, linguistic and religious identity. It focuses on improving Roma women's access to job opportunities, ensuring the quality of educational opportunities and providing health care and reproductive health for Roma women. Website: http://www.romawomen.ro/pages/ngo.htm

Sexual Exploitation and Armed Conflicts

Centre for Women War Victims (Zagreb, Croatia) is a non-governmental organisation that empowers women and their position in society through psycho-social support, and practical (information, humanitarian, legal and financial aid) and political support. It helps victims overcome violence against women, ethnic divisions and war traumas. E-mail: cenzena_zg@zamir-zg.ztn.apc.org

Profemme/Twese Hamwe (Rwanda) is a network of associations involved in rural development projects helping widows and orphans after the genocide. It addresses women's role and needs in post-conflict reconstruction and development. Website: http://www.profemmes.org/1341.html

Women for Women (Washington D.C., USA) is an international programme aiming to help female victims of armed conflict and to rebuild their lives, families and communities through emotional and financial support, access to income generation support and micro credit loans, while fostering awareness and understanding of women's rights. Website: http://www.womenforwomen.org

Torture

International Rehabilitation Council for Torture Victims (IRCT)) (Copenhagen, Denmark) is an independent, health professional organisation, which promotes and supports the rehabilitation of torture victims and works for the prevention of torture worldwide. Website: http://www.irct.org/usr/irct/home.nsf/

OMCT, Organisation Mondiale Contre la Torture (Geneva, Switzerland) offers protection to female victims of torture or women threatened by torture or other, cruel, inhuman or degrading treatment, taking into account the specific aspects of violence affecting them. Website: http://www.omct.org

Trafficking of Women

Anti Slavery International (UK) collects information on debt bondage, forced labour, forced marriage, the worst forms of child labour, human trafficking and traditional slavery. It publishes research through international bodies in order to promote laws to protect those exploited by these practices. Website: http://www.antislavery.org

CATW, The Coalition against Trafficking in Women (USA) promotes women's human rights, and works internationally to combat sexual exploitation in all its forms. CATW is composed of regional networks and affiliated individuals and groups. It serves as an umbrella that co-ordinates and takes direction from its regional organisations in its work against sexual exploitation and in support of women's human rights. http://www.catwinternational.org

East Asia-US Women's Network against Militarism is a volunteer-based organisation uniting country groups from Japan, South Korea, Philippines, Puerto Rico, and the USA. It is involved in public education, lobbying, and community and transnational organising to develop the leadership of women and communities directly affected by the actions of military personnel. It supports a movement that challenges all forms of militarism and creates models of women's leadership, community service and development. Website: http://www.cfdh.org/womanoeuvres/wmo_ref_ws_okazawa.html

GAATW, The Global Alliance against Traffic in Women (Bangkok, Thailand) is a movement of members consisting of both organisations and individuals worldwide co-ordinating, organising and facilitating work on issues related to trafficking in persons and women's labour migration in virtually every region of the world. Its strategy is to promote the involvement of grassroots women's associations in all work against trafficking. Website: http://www.thai.net/gaatw

IOM, International Organization for Migration (Geneva, Switzerland) encompasses a variety of activities on managing migration throughout the world. One of its main working areas is counter-trafficking which aims at the prevention of trafficking in persons, particularly women and children. Its activities include carrying out information campaigns, providing counselling services, conducting research on migrant trafficking, providing safe and dignified return and reintegration assistance to victims of trafficking, and helping governments to improve their legal systems and technical capacities against trafficking. Website: http://www.iom.int

La Strada Ukraine (Ukraine) is a non-governmental organisation in Ukraine working to prevent trafficking in women and helping victims. Its activities include a broad range of assistance to trafficked persons, maintenance of a hot line for emergency telephone assistance, and research projects on the problem of violence against women. E-mail: lastrada@ukrpack.net, Website: www.brama.com/lastrada

Violence aganist Women

Amnesty International (London, United Kingdom) is a worldwide movement for internationally recognised human rights. Amnesty International has launched a special campaign on ending violence against women. The campaign focuses on increasing general awareness of the problem, defending women's rights activists, exposing violence against women in war, refugee situations and homes. It also advocates for gender justice. Website: http://www.amnesty.org

Arab Women Solidarity Association (Cairo, Egypt) is a non-governmental organisation dealing with violence against women in public and private life. It aims at women's empowerment. E-mail: hetata@in touch.com

Korea Women's Hot Line (Seoul, Republic of Korea) is a national organisation working for women's human rights. KWHL helps women fight against oppression, eliminate violence against women and to become full members of a gender equal society. KWHL empowers women by providing counselling, as well as legal and medical support to victims of gender violence. Website: http://www.hotline.or.kr/english/kwhl.asp

METRAC (The Metropolitan Toronto Action Committee on Violence against Women and Children, Toronto, Canada) is a community-based organisation that seeks to decrease and finally eliminate all forms of violence against women and children. METRAC is committed to the right of women and children to live their lives free of violence and the threat of violence. Website: http://www.metrac.org

STOP Violence Against Women (Zagreb, Croatia) is a non-governmental organisation aiming to raise public awareness on violence against women. It informs, influences and sensitises relevant institutions and social structures involved in countering the problem. It also promotes changes in the legal system and state policy concerning violence against women. E-mail: cenzena_zg@zamir-zg.ztn.apc.org

Women's Aid Federation of England (London, United Kingdom) is an association working to end domestic violence against women and children. Its mission is to advocate for abused women and children and to ensure their safety by working locally and nationally to offer support and a place of safety. It works to empower women and meet the needs of children affected by domestic violence, promote policies and practices to prevent domestic violence and raise awareness of the extent and impact of the problem in society. Website: http://www.womensaid.org.uk

Women's Advocacy Networks

CAFRA (Barbados) is a regional network of feminists, individual researchers, activists and women's organisations that define feminist politics as a matter of both consciousness and action. Its activities to date include projects and programmes on Women in Caribbean Agriculture; Women and the Law; Women's History and Creative Expression; Women, Development and Sustainable Livelihood; Women's Health and Reproductive Rights; and Gender and Youth. Website: http://www.cafra.org

European Women's Lobby/Lobby Européen des Femmes (European Union) (Brussels, Belgium) is a large network of non-governmental women's organisations in the European Union consisting of national women's organisations in the EU member states and of European organisations. Website: http://www.womenlobby.org

FOKUS (Oslo, Norway) is a resource centre for international women's issues and a co-ordinating organ for women's organisations in Norway. Website: http://www.fokuskvinner.no

ProFem (Prague, Czech Republic) provides consultancy and advice for women projects and organisations. It promotes women rights through publications, networking and lobbying. Website: http://www.profem.cz

Sawnet, South Asian Women's Network is a forum dealing with South Asian women's issues. http://www.umiacs.umd.edu/users/sawweb/sawnet/index.html

Women Action is a coalition network from around the world aiming to build on existing collaborations with UN and NGOs networks related to the Beijing+5 Review Process. By establishing a broad information-sharing basis worldwide, Women Action enables NGOs to actively engage in the Beijing+5 Review Process with the long-term goal of women's empowerment, especially focused on women and media. Website: http://www.womenaction.org

Women and HIV/AIDS

International Community of Women Living with HIV/AIDS (London, UK) is an international network which strives to share with the global community the experiences, views and contributions of millions of women worldwide who are also HIV positive. Its most important achievement has been to reach these isolated women and, through support, education and training, empower them to be involved in areas of service delivery and policy that affect their lives and those of their children and family. Website: http://www.icw.org/tiki-view_articles.php

UNAIDS, Joint United Nations Programme on HIV and AIDS (Geneva, Switzerland) has launched the Global Coalition on Women and AIDS (GCWA) to work at global, regional and national levels to highlight the impact of AIDS on women and girls and mobilise actions to enable them to protect themselves from HIV and receive the care and support they need. Website: http://womenandaids.unaids.org/

UNFPA, United Nations Population Fund (New York, USA) is the world's largest funding source for population and reproductive health programmes, with special focus on the needs of women and girls and their access to information and services on reproductive and sexual health, family planning and prevention of HIV/AIDS. Website: http://www.unfpa.org/index.htm

Women and Security

Geneva Centre for the Democratic Control of Armed Forces (DCAF) is an international foundation based in Geneva, Switzerland, which supports states and non-state governed institutions in their efforts to strengthen democratic and civilian control of armed forces, and promotes security sector reform in accordance with democratic standards. The Working Group on Women and Children in an Insecure World addresses the special needs of these two vulnerable groups of the population and increases the general awareness of the gravity and magnitude of violence they suffer in times of peace and conflict. It also advances women's active role in security. Website: http://www.dcaf.ch

WIIS, Women in International Security (USA) is dedicated to increasing the influence of women in the fields of foreign and defense affairs by raising their numbers and visibility while enhancing the dialogue about international security issues. Website: http://wiss.georgetown.edu/home.htm

Women and War/Armed Conflict

CFD-Women's Office of Peace Work (Zurich, Switzerland) is a non-profit organisation aiming to show the reasons and structures of violence against women, in peace and war and to enforce resistance. E-mail: frieda@swix.ch

Co-ordination of Women's Advocacy (Givrins, Switzerland) deals with the protection and promotion of women's rights in situations of war and conflict in co-operation with the International Criminal Tribunals for former Yugoslavia (ICTY) and Rwanda (ICTR). Email: cwa@iprolink.ch

Hague Appeal for Peace (The Netherlands) is an international network of peace and justice organisations dedicated to sowing the seeds for the abolition of war through the implementation of the Hague Agenda for Peace and Justice for the 21ˢᵗ Century, a set of 50 recommendations developed at the Hague Appeal for Peace Conference in 1999. It is focused on promoting a Global Campaign for Peace Education dedicated to the integration of peace education into curricula and communities worldwide as a means of reducing violence and preventing war. The network advances women's active and equal role in peace processes. Website: http:// www.haguepeace.org

International Committee of the Red Cross (ICRC), (Geneva, Switzerland). The ICRC aims to protect the lives and dignity of victims of armed conflict and internal strife, provide people suffering the consequences of war with assistance, and acts as the guardian and promoter of international humanitarian law (IHL). ICRC seeks to ensure that the needs of women and girls affected by armed conflict are appropriately assessed and addressed; that women are included in determining the activities carried out on their behalf; and that the specific protection afforded by IHL to women is promoted widely. Website: http://www.icrc.org

International Fellowship of Reconciliation: IFOR Women Peacemakers Programme (The Netherlands) organises training on non-violence for grassroots women's groups and regional consultations, which bring women from opposite sides of conflicts together to discuss and deepen their understanding of conflict resolution. It also documents women's peacebuilding activities and helps to build networks among women peacemakers through its newsletter - Cross the Lines. Website: www.ifor.org

Women Migrants' Rights

Joint Council for the Welfare of Immigrants (JCWI) (UK), The JCWI is an independent national voluntary organisation, campaigning for justice and combating racism in immigration and asylum law and policy. It provides free advice and casework, training courses, and a range of publications. Website: http://www.jcwi.org.uk/

Migrants Rights International (Geneva, Switzerland) is a nongovernmental organisation and a network of migrant associations worldwide aiming at the promotion of the human rights of migrants. Its purposes are to promote recognition and respect for the rights of all migrants, advocate for the ratification of the 1990 International Convention on the Protection of the Rights of All Migrant Workers and Members of their Families, facilitate the efforts of migrant associations, and monitor trends and developments in the situation of migrants' rights and welfare. Website: http://www.migrantwatch.org/

National Network for Immigrant and Refugee Rights (NNIRR) (USA), The NNIRR is a national organisation composed of local coalitions and immigrant, refugee, community, religious, civil rights and labour organisations and activists in the United States. It serves as a forum to share information, educate communities, and develop and coordinate plans of action on immigrant and refugee issues. It works to promote a just immigration and refugee policy and to defend and expand the rights of all immigrants and refugees, regardless of immigration status. Website: http://www.nnirr.org/about/about_mission.html

Notes on Contributors

Ms. Lesley Abdela is a British consultant specialist in gender, democracy, civil society, media, and post-conflict reconstruction and in participation of women in democracy building. She has post-conflict field experience in Iraq, Kosovo and Sierra Leone. She has advised NATO and Britain's Ministry of Defence and led teams in 40 emerging democracies in Central and Eastern Europe, Central Asia, the Middle East and Africa. From 1995-2000, she served on the global board of the British Council, which has offices in 109 countries. Lesley was chosen as the United Kingdom *'Woman of Europe'* in 1996 for her work in Central Europe, training women to take part in democratic politics and awarded an Honorary Doctorate by Nottingham Trent University for her work on women's human rights.

Ms. Ancil Adrian-Paul is a specialist in refugee studies. She is currently Programme Manager for the Gender and Peacebuilding Programme at International Alert (IA). Along with other colleagues at IA she was instrumental in conceptualising and overseeing the campaign on Women Building Peace: From the Village Council to the Negotiation Table that was launched by IA and partners in 1999 to lobby for the UN Security Council Resolution 1325. Before joining IA, she was the Head of the National Commission on Racism in Children's Books and a consultant for the Commonwealth Institute. During her time in Southern Africa she worked in Mozambique for Save the Children (USA), CIDA (Canada) and the United Nations Mission to Mozambique (ONU-MOZ).

Dr. Krishna Ahooja-Patel served for 25 years in the UN system, specifically at the International Labour Office, Geneva, where she was the editor of the ILO Journal 'Women at Work' (1977-1986) and at INSTRAW, Dominican Republic as Deputy Director (1986-1990). In 1990, she was appointed Chair on Women's Studies at Saint Mary's University, Canada, where she is currently a Visiting Professor teaching courses on United Nations and Development and Gender and Development. In 2003, the university granted her a honorary doctorate in literature as a peace activist. She is also a honorary director of the Institute on Equity and Development at Gujarat Vidyapith, India. In addition, as an international NGO activist, she helped develop the programme activity of the Women's World Summit Foundation on priorities for women and children. In 2000, she was elected the international President of the Women's International League for Peace and Freedom (WILPF), Geneva. She has published extensively on women and employment, international migration and development issues. She is recently searching for methodologies on the emerging inequalities between women and men worldwide, particularly in the Asian region. She is currently working on a book entitled 'Development Has a Woman's Face'.

Dr. Pamela Bell has studied psychology and specialises in women and trauma. She worked in Bosnia during the war and post-war phase and gained seminal experience for her clinical and research work. In Sarajevo, she served on a multi-disciplinary team of local mental health professionals, international agency representatives and experts on trauma. In collaboration with the Universities of Brussels and Sarajevo she has undertaken research work on conflict, drawing attention to the acute lack of systematic data and well-informed psychosocial interventions in crisis regions. She continues as a consultant on trauma and performing research in conflict regions. In addition, she has a psychotherapy practice in Belgium where she works primarily with traumatised women.

Ms. Lea Biason holds a degree from the Graduate Institute of International Studies in Geneva. She has studied public international law, international economics, political science and contemporary history with a specialisation in human rights law, Asian history and economics of development. She has written a research project with Reuters S.A. Geneva, which received an award, and has worked for Reuters Magazine. She has also conceptualised and edited a CD-ROM guide for the International Organization for Migration, Geneva. She joined DCAF Geneva in 2002 and has written on issues of security and violence against women. She is currently working on her masters thesis on international law and women's human rights.

Mr. Martin Bohnstedt is of Austrian and German origin and has studied human rights law, African Studies and political science in Vienna, Salzburg and at London's School of Oriental and African Studies (SOAS), where he received his LL.M. in

1995. He joined the International Affairs Management Training section of the United Nations Institute for Training and Research (UNITAR) in Geneva in 1998. Since 2002 he has been heading UNITAR's Peacekeeping Training Programme on the Special Needs of Women and Children in Conflict. He also served as a trainer and legal adviser with OSCE field missions to prepare and organise elections in Bosnia and Kosovo in 1997 and 2001, respectively.

Ms. Valentina Cherevatenko is a Chair Co-ordinator of the Union Women of the Don Region. She is the initiator and organiser of the international on-going conference 'Women for Life without War and Violence', focusing on women and conflict, peaceful resolution of disputes, peacebuilding and the peace potential of civil society. She has been the Chair of the Interim Co-ordination Board since 1996. She also directed and authored a research project entitled 'Chechen Women and the Armed Conflict 1994 – 2000'. She is the editor of The Newsletter Union 'Women of the Don Region' and has edited other publications on women and war.

Ms. Laurence Desvignes specialises in management and monitoring of international development projects and implementation of information and education programmes. She has initiated and developed an integrated agricultural programme in Cambodia. She has worked for the International Committee of the Red Cross (ICRC) as a translator in prison facilities and as a Mine Awareness Co-ordinator, first in Cambodia and Bosnia-Herzegovina and later for ICRC programmes worldwide. She implemented mine-related and data gathering projects and monitored over twenty community-based mine awareness activities. Her work in mine action not only included the targeting of women as a specific group to be informed about the dangers of mine and unexploded ordnance, but also to be used as a vector to disseminate information to men and children. She has conducted consultancies with UNICEF, UNDP and GICHD.

Ms. Isha Dyfan is Program Director of Human Rights, Human Security and Women in the Peace Building Process at International Women's Tribune Centre (IWTC), US. As a women's human rights activist, she was one of the leaders of the Sierra Leone Women's Movement for Peace, which played a pivotal role in the re-establishment of democratic rule in Sierra Leone in 1996 and pushed for a peaceful resolution of the ten year conflict in 1999. Since 1997, she has worked for international women's non–governmental organisations in the area of women's human rights and peace. In 2003, she was appointed one of ten experts worldwide in the area of women, peace and security issues by the United Nations to prepare a report to the 48th session of the United Nations Commission on the Status of Women. She has written numerous articles on women's role and contribution in the resolution of conflict and peacebuilding. She serves on numerous boards including ISIS WICCE, Uganda and the Human Rights Commission Highland Park, New Jersey, US.

Ms. Anja Ebnöther is Assistant Director of the Geneva Centre for the Democratic Control of Armed Forces and Head of Special Programmes. She currently leads DCAF's programme on 'Women and children in an insecure world' and is the Swiss representative in the Consortium Steering Committee of the PfP Consortium of Defence Academies and Security Studies Institutes and the Chairperson of the DCAF-led PfP-

Consortium Working Group on Security Sector Reform. In 2004 she was the project leader for the 6th International Security Forum, held in Montreux. Prior to joining DCAF in 2000, she has experience working as a scientific collaborator in one of Switzerland's leading parties, mainly dealing with Security Policy, and has also worked for the 'Study Commission on Strategic Issues' in the Federal Department of Defence, Civil Protection and Sports. While in the Ministry, she was engaged in developing the parameters of Swiss involvement in the Partnership for Peace (PfP) programme, as Deputy Head of the EAPC/PfP desk.

Ms. Mona Eltahawy is the managing editor of Arabic Women's eNews, a non-profit New York-based website. She is currently a columnist for the London-based pan-Arab Asharq al-Awsat newspaper, where she frequently writes about Arab women's rights. Her commentaries in English have appeared in The Washington Post, The New York Times and The International Herald Tribune. She has written extensively about women's issues since the start of her journalism career in 1990. She covered the International Conference on Population and Development in Cairo in 1994 for Reuters News Agency and reported on the Fourth United Nations Women's Conference in Beijing in 1995 for Women's Feature Service. Before moving to the United States in 2000, she was a journalist in the Middle East for ten years. She was a Reuters correspondent in Cairo and Jerusalem and also an Egypt correspondent for The Guardian of London.

Dr. Vanessa Farr focuses on women's experiences of violent conflict, including the demobilisation, disarmament and reintegration (DDR) of women combatants after war, the impact on women of prolific small arms and light weapons (SALW), and women's coalition-building in conflict-torn societies. She is currently engaged in analysing gender mainstreaming in weapons collection programmes and DDR processes, undertakes research on the gendered impact of SALW for the Small Arms Survey, and is co-editing a book on SALW for the United Nations University. She is also a volunteer at IANSA's Women's Network. She is a graduate of the Women's Studies Programme at York University, Toronto.

Ms. Hélène Harroff-Tavel has attended the Walsh School of Foreign Service at Georgetown University, Washington D.C. She has previously studied international development, environmental studies, Buddhism and Thai language at the Khon Kaen University in Thailand. She has been very active in volunteer programmes in the US and abroad and has also worked in social projects as a fundraiser. Since January 2004 she has been working with the Senator Hillary Rodham Clinton Internship in the Press Office.

Ms. Agnès Hubert is currently an adviser to the President of the Women's Rights Committee of the European Parliament. An economist by training, she was a journalist specialising in North-South issues and gender until she joined the European Commission. As an official, she headed the unit dealing with equal opportunities for women in the Directorate General for Employment and Social Affairs from 1992 to 1996. In 1998/99 she spent a year in the US as an EU fellow in the Fletcher School of Law and Diplomacy. Back in Brussels, she joined the European Commission's governance team in charge of drafting a white paper on European governance, before she joined the European Parliament in 2002. She is the author of several articles and studies on gender, European integration, governance and the information society. In 1998, she published a book entitled 'L'Europe et les Femmes' (ed. Apogée).

Ms. Cecilia Jimenez is an international human rights lawyer and trainer, specialising in international human rights law, international criminal law and peacebuilding and gender issues. She has had vast practical experience in national and international human rights NGO work, first as a Philippine activist lawyer and later as an international legal NGO expert working in the context of UN standard-setting, national implementation of international law and advocacy within the UN system. Presently based in Geneva, she works as an independent consultant working on NGO capacity building and research, giving policy advice on UN processes and providing training on human rights issues and on advocacy skills.

Ms. Ramina Johal is Senior Co-ordinator of the Participation and Protection Programme at the Women's Commission for Refugee Women and Children where she has worked for five years. She promoted the protection of war-affected women by undertaking field visits, providing technical support to local women's groups, assessing international humanitarian assistance and post-conflict development programmes and policies, and designed advocacy strategies. Her current work centres on developing partnerships with women's groups in Sierra Leone, Colombia, Afghanistan and Pakistan. Her expertise is also drawn from previous postings with the World Bank, the Australian Embassy in Washington D.C. and the Canadian Employment and Immigration Commission.

Dr. Adam Jones is a researcher in the Division of International Studies at the Centre for Research and Teaching in Economics (CIDE) in Mexico City and holds a Ph.D. in political science from the University of British Columbia. He is Executive Director of Gendercide Watch, a web-based educational initiative that confronts gender-selective killing of males and females worldwide. His writings on gender, human rights, and international politics have appeared in Review of International Studies, Ethnic and Racial Studies, Journal of Human Rights, Journal of Genocide Research, and other publications. He is also the editor of Gendercide and Genocide (Vanderbilt University Press, 2004) and Genocide, War Crimes & the West: History and Complicity (Zed Books, 2004).

Ms. Avila Kilmurray is Director of the Community Foundation for Northern Ireland. Initially employed in Derry in community work, she worked in a Community Education Project in Magee College, was active in establishing the Women's Aid organisation and was involved in a range of anti-poverty initiatives. In 1990, she was appointed the first Women's Officer for the Transport and General Workers' Union in Ireland. She has written extensively on community development, women's issues and civil society. She was active in the Northern Ireland Women's Rights Movement and was a founding member of the Northern Ireland Women's Coalition and a member of the coalition's negotiating team for the Belfast Agreement.

Ms. Shukuko Koyama is the Project Assistant for the 'Weapons for Development: Lessons Learned from Weapons Collection Programmes' project at the United Nations Institute for Disarmament Research (UNIDIR) in Geneva. She has carried out field research in Albania, Cambodia and Mali,

and has written on gender aspects of small arms disarmament. Prior to joining UNIDIR, she worked for the Bonn International Centre for Conversion (BICC) in Germany.

Dr. Ida Kuklina studied law at the Leningrad University and obtained a Ph.D. in Economy (1965) and a Ph.D. in Political Sciences (1991). She joined the Union of the Committees of Soldiers Mothers of Russia (UCSMR) in 1993 and has been a member of the UCSMR Co-ordination Council and the Secretary of the UCSMR Analytical and Information Commission. Since 2002 she represents the UCSMR in the Commission on Human Rights of the President of Russian Federation. She has published books and articles on international conflicts, international security, military reform in Russia and human rights.

Ms. Sonja Licht specialises in sociology and social and cultural anthropology. She has conducted research on Eastern Europe, the emergence of social movements and resurgent nationalism until early 1990s. In 1991-2003 she became the first Executive Director of the Soros Fund Yugoslavia. In 2003, she established a new institution, the Belgrade Fund for Political Excellence.

Ms. Charlotte Lindsey is Deputy Director of Communication at the International Committee of the Red Cross (ICRC). From 2002 to 2003, she was Deputy Head of the Division for Policy and Co-operation. From 1999 to 2003 she headed the ICRC's Women and War Project and carried out missions in the Balkans, Africa, Asia and the Middle East. She authored the ICRC publication Women Facing War and has been responsible for a number of other ICRC publications and audio-visual projects on women and war.

Ms. Megan McKenna is the Media Liaison at the Women's Commission for Refugee Women and Children where she works on press outreach. Before joining the Women's Commission, she was a writer for the US Fund for UNICEF, where she wrote speeches and articles about the situation of women and girls worldwide. She is a former press officer for the European Women's Lobby, a reporter for United Press International in London, associate editor for Inside Washington Publishers and a researcher for CNN International.

Ms. Marlea Muñez is a graduate from the University of the Philippines at Los Baños College of Forestry and a forester by profession. She conducted course work in the Master of Public Administration at the University of the Philippines at Diliman, and completed an intensive Project Management Course conducted by ProjektStyrning AB in Sweden. Since 1988, she has been involved in community forestry systems. She worked for fulfilment of the rights of the poor, indigenous peoples, upland and coastal communities. In 1995, she revived the Gender and Development undertakings of the Department of Environment and National Resources and initiated more concrete actions for women's rights. At present, she is the Executive Director of Women's Education, Development and Productivity, Research and Advocacy Organisation, Incorporated (WEDPRO), a collective women's organisation.

Mrs. Ndioro Ndiaye is the Deputy Director General of the International Organization for Migration since 1999. From 1990 to 1995, she was Minister for Women, Children and Family Affairs in Senegal. She was instrumental in the reform of tertiary education through activities with the Cheikh Anta Diop University of Dakar. In 1990, she took part in preparations for the World Summit for Children, and in 1992 for the World Summit on the Economic Advancement of Rural Women held in Geneva. In 1994, she headed the Senegalese delegation to the International Conference on Population and Development in Cairo. In 1995, as chairperson of the Regional Conference of African Women, she was a driving force in the preparations for the Fourth UN Conference on Women in Beijing. As a founding member of the Scientific Commission for Women and Development, she founded an NGO in the mid-1990s, the 'Network of African Women Leaders for Peace and Development', which she co-ordinated until her appointment to IOM.

Dr. 'Funmi Olonisakin is the Director of the Conflict, Security and Development Group (CSDG) at the International Policy Institute, King's College London. Her current areas of interest include the role of the UN and regional actors in conflict resolution in Africa; the protection and reintegration of children affected by armed conflict and the gender dimensions of conflict and reintegration. She has held research positions at the Centre for Defence Studies, King's College; at the Institute for Strategic Studies, University of Pretoria, South Africa; and was MacArthur Post-Doctoral Fellow at the Department of War Studies King's College. She is the author of 'Reinventing Peacekeeping in Africa' and co-author of 'Peacekeepers, Politicians and Warlords', among other publications.

Dr. Leena Parmar is Associate Professor in the Department of Sociology, University of Rajasthan, India. She is currently working on the peace process in the Kashmir valley. She has conducted research on various social aspects of the Indian Army including war-widows and integration of women. For each of these aspects she has tried to use the sociological perspective along with first hand data. She has also participated in various workshops on gender issues and violence against women.

Ms. Athena Peralta is currently a consultant working with the World Council of Churches on issues of Women and Economy. She specialises in economics of development. She was previously Senior Economic Development Specialist with the National Economic and Development Authority of the Philippines. She has participated in numerous international conferences on women's concerns with regard to global trade, finance and sustainable development.

Ms. Charlotte Ponticelli was appointed Senior Co-ordinator for International Women's Issues at the US Department of State in 2003. Prior to assuming her current position, she served as Deputy Senior Co-ordinator for International Women's Issues. Before coming to the department in September 2002, she was Director of Lectures and Seminars at the Heritage Foundation. Ms. Ponticelli has extensive government experience, serving previously at the White House, the US Agency for International Development and the US Commission on Civil Rights. During the Administration of President George W. Bush, she was Director of Human Rights and Women's Affairs in the State Department's Bureau of International Organisation Affairs, and later moved to the International Republican Institute, where she designed and implemented several projects to assist democratic forces in the Balkans. Ms. Ponticelli is the recipient of numerous Superior Honour Awards from the State Department.

Ms. Nadine Puechguirbal currently works at the Policy Development and Studies Branch of the Office for the Co-ordination of Humanitarian Affairs (OCHA) at the United Nations headquarters in New York. Prior to this position, she worked for the UN Department of Peacekeeping Operations (DPKO) in New York and was seconded in 2003 as a Gender Affairs Officer to the UN Mission in the Democratic Republic of the Congo (MONUC). Her recent research interests are 'Gender Perspectives in Post-Conflict Situations: Comparative Study between Somalia, Rwanda and Eritrea'.

Ms. Indai Sajor is a human rights defender and educator for women's human rights. She was a Rockefeller Humanities Fellow for 2002-2003, adviser to Amnesty International on their Violence against Women Campaign and former regional Director of Asian Women's Human Rights Organisation bringing in Asian women's participation in UN world conferences in Vienna, Cairo, Copenhagen and Beijing. She also documented the testimonies of Filipino and other Asian comfort women for their wartime sufferings. From 1998 to 2001, she served as co-convener of the Women's International War Crimes Tribunal on Japan's Military Sexual Slavery. She has edited the book 'Common Grounds. Violence Against Women in War and Armed Conflict Situations' (1998) and has published numerous articles and books on the topic of women's rights in situations of war and armed conflict.

Ms. Josi Salem-Pickartz is a clinical psychologist. From 1995 to 2002 she co-directed the Al Kutba Institute for Human Development in Amman with focus on women's education, political empowerment and research on women's issues. Since 1992 she was a consultant for UNICEF in Jordan, Iraq, Palestine, Armenia and the Regional Office for Middle East and North Africa on child, youth and family protection issues. She has co-ordinated therapy groups with political refugees and survivors of torture and rape. She was also a Visiting Professor at the Universities of Siegen and Oldenburg in Germany on migration and mental health, stress and trauma rehabilitation and women's education.

Ms. Colette Samoya is the founder and co-ordinator of the BANGWE project since 1998. The project is aimed at building a culture of peace and non-violence in Burundi, Rwanda and the Democratic Republic of Congo by women through the education of young people. She has worked as a consultant in various NGOs, such as the Geneva Third World NGO and the African Renaissance Institute. From 1987-1991, she was the Secretary General of Women's Union of Burundi focusing primarily on issues related to women and development. She played a major role in the ratification of the CEDAW and of the Convention on the Protection for the Rights of the Child by Burundi.

Ms. Aida Santos-Maranan is one of the pioneers of the Philippine women's movement since its re-inception in the early 1980s and has co-founded several women's groups working on the issues of human rights, violence against women, migration, trafficking and prostitution. She also works as a gender and development consultant/researcher and teaches women's studies. She is a member of the international network on Feminist Approaches to Bioethics (FAB), the East Asia-US-Puerto Rico Women's Network against Militarism, and is a board member of the Coalition Against Trafficking in Women (CATW)-Asia Pacific. She has written numerous articles and studies on various socio-political concerns, edited publications, and published three anthologies of award-winning poems.

Ms. Mikiko Sawanishi has worked for the Small Arms and Demobilisation Unit of the Bureau for Crisis Prevention and Recovery of UNDP as Capacity Development Adviser. Within UNDP, she also served for the Timor Leste Country Office and the Regional Bureau for Asia and the Pacific. Prior to joining UNDP, she worked for the Japan Bank for International Co-operation and the United Nations Secretariat. She has worked in the field of capacity development and gender. She conducted research on CEDAW's enforcement mechanism and has been a member of the Japanese Association of International Women's Rights.

Mrs. Ivana Schellongová is human rights lawyer working for the DCAF Working Group on Women and Children in an Insecure World. She served as a diplomat and human rights expert for the Ministry of Foreign Affairs in the Czech Republic both in Prague and at the Permanent Mission of the Czech Republic to the United Nations Office in Geneva in 1994-2004. She is a graduate of the Faculty of Law in Brno, Czech Republic, and currently a masters candidate at the Graduate Institute of International Studies in Geneva.

Ms. Darla Silva is the Deputy Director for the Office of Public Policy and Advocacy at the US Fund for UNICEF in Washington DC. Prior to joining the US Fund, she worked for the Women's Commission for Refugee Women and Children as its Washington representative. She also served as counsel to Senator Richard J. Durbin (D-IL) on the Senate Judiciary Committee and Governmental Affairs Committee, where her issue portfolio included immigration, civil rights and civil justice issues. Ms. Silva is a long time children's advocate and has worked as a children's court attorney in New Mexico representing the state in child abuse and neglect proceedings. She is a cum laude graduate of Boston University, where she received a BA in Political Science in 1989 and a law degree from the University of New Mexico in 1992. She is an active member of the DC Bar.

Ms. Melina Skouroliakou holds a masters degree in international relations from the Graduate Institute of International Studies in Geneva. She has also studied international and European law, economics and political science in Thessaloniki, Greece and in Nice, France. She joined DCAF's Working Group on Women and Children in an Insecure World in 2003. Prior to joining DCAF she worked at the United Nations Information Centre in Athens, where she produced a report on the United Nations Observer Mission in Georgia, and as a researcher on Greek foreign policy and European affairs at the Hellenic Foundation for European and Foreign Policy (ELIAMEP) in Athens, Greece.

Ms. Slavica Stojanovic is currently working for the Women's Programme at the Fund for an Open Society Yugoslavia, where one of the priorities is to develop Roma women's initiatives. She is co-founder of the Autonomous Women's Centre and is currently working on establishing a Reconstruction Women's Fund. Since the beginning of the war in former Yugoslavia she was engaged in women's groups dealing with violence against women and feminist pacifist activities. She has a specialised background in world literature and theory and was a freelance translator of Hannah Arendt and Virginia Woolf.

Dr. Biljana Vankovska is a Full Professor of Political Science at the Faculty of Philosophy (Department for Defence and Peace Studies) at the University of Skopje, Macedonia, and member of the faculty staff of the European Peace University (EPU) in Austria. In 2001-2002 she worked as Senior Fellow at DCAF. For three years (1997-2000) she was a guest Senior Research Fellow at the Copenhagen Peace Research Institute (COPRI) and also worked with the Transnational Foundation for Peace and Future Studies (TFF) in Lund (Sweden) as an international adviser. She has published three books, edited two other and authored numerous book chapters and articles.

Ms. Camila Vega has conducted extensive research on security studies, as well as issues related to Colombian politics, including the dynamics of violence in Colombia, drug control policy, human security and the role of women in conflict. She worked for the Geneva Centre for the Democratic Control of Armed Forces (DCAF) and is currently working for the United Nations Office on Drugs and Crime (UNODC) in Myanmar. She holds a masters degree in political science from the Graduate Institute of International Studies in Geneva, and obtained her bachelor degree from the University of Wales, Aberyswyth in International Politics and Strategic Studies.

Dr. Marie Vlachová headed the Research Department at the Ministry of Defence in the Czech Republic in 1995-2001. In 2001 she was seconded to the Geneva Centre for the Democratic Control of Armed Forces. She is a specialist in civil-military relations, defence reforms in Central Europe, and she also works in the field of gender and security, primarily dealing with integration of women into armed forces. She is the co-ordinator of two DCAF working groups, Women and Children in an Insecure World, and Military and Society. She has edited two books and contributed to several publications on civil-military relations and democratic control of armed forces. She held the position of the chairwoman of ERGOMAS (European Group on Armed Forces and Society) in 2000-2002 and is currently the vice-president of the International Association of Sociology, Research Committee 01 on Armed Forces and Society.

Dr. Charlotte Watts is a Senior Lecturer in Epidemiology and Health Policy at the London School of Hygiene and Tropical Medicine. She is a core research team member for the World Health Organization's seven country study on Women's Health and Domestic Violence against Women, and prior to this, spent three years in Zimbabwe working with a local organisation conducting research on domestic violence against women. Her research interests include the international public health burden of violence against women; the linkages between violence against women and HIV/AIDS; trafficking and health; the development and evaluation of community interventions to address violence against women; and the potential importance of female controlled methods of HIV prevention.

Ambassador Dr. Theodor H. Winkler studied political science and international security studies in Geneva and at Harvard University. He subsequently joined the Swiss Department of Defence as an arms control and international security expert. He was appointed Representative of the Chief of Staff for Politico-Military Affairs in 1985, in 1995 became Head of International Security Policy, and in 1998 Deputy Head of Security and Defence Policy. In October 2000 he was nominated by the Federal Council Director of DCAF and promoted to the rank of Ambassador.

Index

crimes against humanity, 9, 132, 201, 238, 259, 261, 266
Croatia, 115, 136, 161, 163, 165, 216
Cuba, 22, 188
custodial violence, 14, 91-98

D

Democratic Republic of the Congo, 19, 131, 143, 194
Denmark, 139
depression, 58, 120, 161-163
DeSalvo, Albert (the Boston Strangler), 22
development, 15, 17, 37-51
disarmament, demobilisation and reintegration (DDR), 194, 268
displacement, 117, 134, 163, 177-181, 191, 252
domestic killings, 23
domestic slavery, 14
domestic violence, 6, 7, 10, 12, 28, 39, 49, 67, 70, 72, 73, 78, 80,
    82, 84, 85, 92, 121, 133, 149, 182, 233, 237, 238, 240, 261,
    265, 273, 284, 289, 297, 323
Dominican Republic, 65, 68, 86
dowry killings, 31

E

education, 6, 13, 15, 17, 18, 21, 27, 29, 33-35, 37, 39, 50, 52,
    64, 69, 73, 75, 76, 77, 84, 109, 138, 144, 159, 160, 170,
    173-175, 182, 184, 189, 190, 191, 194, 208, 213, 216, 218,
    219, 236-238, 239, 245, 251, 252, 267, 277, 278, 279, 281,
    282
El Salvador, 110, 175, 247
employment, 6, 8, 41, 46, 50, 61, 75, 77, 79, 81, 82, 85, 87, 139,
    164, 170, 199, 236, 237
empowerment, 13, 35, 43-48, 51, 64, 68, 95, 160, 175, 184, 208,
    210, 216, 217, 238, 250, 271, 282
Eritrea, 125, 136, 197, 249, 254
ethnic cleansing, 110, 115, 117, 118
European Union, 81, 85, 128, 208, 213, 223, 248, 265, 270
ex-combatants, 197, 198, 199
explosive remnants of war, 187, 189-191

F

female combatants, 137, 155
female deficit, 15, 17
female genital mutilation, 13, 26, 27, 29, 34, 35, 177, 238, 246, 271
female infanticide, 15-17, 22
        China, 16
female suicide bombers, 136
feminicide, 13
feminisation
        of poverty, 13, 38, 85, 239, 278
        of migration, 43, 81
feminist, 2, 8, 46, 47, 49, 140, 163, 197, 211, 216, 217, 233,
    243-246, 278
Finland, 39, 81
forced
        disappearances, 116
        impregnation, 92, 113
        labour, 26, 41, 43, 79, 80, 81, 83, 134
        marriage, 170
        prostitution, 7, 76, 113, 238
        sex, 55, 58
        sterilisation, 92, 113
        termination of pregnancy, 113

former Yugoslavia, 6, 9, 10, 115, 120, 132, 158, 161, 202, 203,
    216, 233, 238, 240, 259, 261, 271, 277
        ICTY (International Crimininal Tribunal for the
        former Yugoslavia), 120, 122, 124, 133, 259, 260
Forward Looking Strategies (Nairobi), 238, 265
France, 22, 36, 249, 259

G

Gaza Strip, 56
gender, 15, 19, 37, 38, 45-50, 57, 64
        and development, 49
        awareness, 127, 156, 197, 221, 252
        discrimination, 48, 79, 84, 85, 88, 132, 175, 214, 243, 244,
        252
        equality, 48, 50, 68, 139, 214-216, 223, 238, 239, 248, 249
        justice, 127, 240, 282
        mainstreaming, 46, 87, 125, 233, 239, 244, 248, 249, 250,
        252, 268, 281
        Roles Framework, 46
        sensitive budgeting, 48, 49
        sensitive policies, 48
gender-based crimes, 259, 262, 279, 281, 282
gender-based violence, 1, 2, 5-10, 13, 26, 64, 65, 85, 92, 94, 96,
    132-134, 145, 155, 169, 170, 174, 238, 243-246, 250, 252,
    257, 259, 260, 270, 271, 277, 278, 279, 280-282
gendercidal institutions, 15, 16
gendercide, 13, 15, 21
Geneva Conventions, 133, 138, 171, 181, 240, 258, 259, 266
genocide, 9, 15, 16, 21, 51, 115, 124, 136, 145, 201, 202, 238,
    247, 259, 266
Georgia, 249
Germany, 22, 52, 74, 75, 139, 204, 245, 259
Ghana, 19, 35, 36, 246, 268
girl-child, 9, 235, 238
girls, 1, 5-10, 13, 14, 16-20, 22, 23, 25-29, 31, 33-38, 43, 48, 52,
    57, 64, 69, 71, 72, 77, 81, 84-87, 98, 107, 109, 113, 115, 116,
    119, 124-128, 143, 145, 146, 169, 170, 171, 173-175, 178,
    179, 190, 193, 196, 197, 199, 206, 209, 211, 218, 238, 245,
    246, 249, 251, 252, 254, 266, 267, 269, 278, 279, 280-282
Great Lakes region, 121, 211, 247
Greece, 139
Green River Killer (Ridgway, Gary), 22
Guatemala, 136, 209, 249, 278
guerrilla forces, 136
Guidelines on the Protection of Refugee Women, 171, 172, 177
Guinea, 7, 20, 35, 39, 124
Gulf War, 139

H

Hague, 122, 124, 202, 203, 208, 261, 266, 270
Haiti, 127, 249
Hamas, 137
harmful cultural practices, 9
health, 13, 15, 17, 18, 21, 22, 26, 27, 29, 33-35, 37, 43, 44,
    48, 50, 52, 56-59, 61, 62, 65, 68, 74, 75, 76, 77, 87, 88, 96,
    121, 134, 144, 146, 157-167, 175, 178, 188, 198, 199, 210,
    213, 216, 218, 220, 236-239, 252, 254, 279, 281
Hezbollah, 137
Hillside Strangler, the (Richard Ramirez) 22
HIV/AIDS, 87, 88, 143, 144, 145, See AIDS

Philippines, 44, 48, 62, 68, 70, 73, 74, 77, 96, 97, 136, 261

Poland, 22, 139

police, 14, 19, 23, 28, 31, 42, 52, 57, 61-63, 67, 70, 72, 74, 76, 77, 85-87, 91, 92, 94, 97, 98, 119, 124, 125, 126, 128, 169, 171, 172, 195, 245, 249, 251-254, 267, 279, 280, 281

pornography, 67, 71, 118, 246, 270

post-traumatic stress disorder (PTSD), 58, 69, 145, 155, 160, 161, 165, 166, 254

post-war situations, 119, 158, 221

poverty, 1, 8, 13, 14, 17, 37, 38, 39, 40, 43-49, 52, 60, 61, 69, 71, 73, 75, 79, 82, 84, 85, 88, 109, 110, 121, 162, 164, 170, 182, 198, 212, 217, 238, 239, 246, 261

pregnancy, 18, 20, 32, 44, 57, 59, 92, 114, 115, 117, 120, 163, 165, 238

prostitution, 6, 8, 13, 14, 16, 52, 67-77, 80-82, 85-87, 98, 174, 236, 259, 270

Protocol to Prevent, Suppress and Punish Trafficking in Persons, Especially Women and Children, 80, 81, 84, 239

PTSD, *See* post-traumatic stress disorder

R

racism, 52

rape, 6, 7, 9, 13, 19, 20, 23, 38, 44, 57, 64, 69, 71, 74, 75, 87, 92, 94, 97, 98, 110, 113-121, 132, 133, 144, 145, 155, 162, 163, 165, 166, 167, 170, 174, 176, 178, 202, 203, 205, 237, 238, 240, 243, 246, 247, 254, 259, 260, 265, 266, 278

reconciliation, 2, 51, 156, 181, 198, 201-203, 205, 206, 208, 210, 211, 248, 249, 253, 262, 282

refugee women, 170-177

reproductive rights, 9, 33, 35, 239

resilience, 1, 64, 110, 159, 162

rest and recreation facilities (R&R), 70, 73, 74

Ridgway, Gary (Green River Killer), 22

Roma women, 52

Romania, 81, 82, 86, 204

Rome Statute of the International Criminal Court (ICC), 9, 132, 240, 266, 271, 278

Russian Federation, 57

Rwanda, 9, 10, 16, 51, 115, 118, 132, 136, 144, 145, 202, 211, 233, 238, 240, 244, 259, 261, 266, 277, 278

S

SALW (small arms and light weapons), 194, 195

security sector reform, 1

Senegal, 29, 35, 36

serial killings of women, 22, 23

servicewomen, 135, 137, 138, 139, 140

sex industry, 14, 40, 42, 67, 68, 70-77, 82, 85, 87

sex work, 75, 76, 79, 82

sexism, 73

sexual exploitation, 7, 41, 43, 44, 64, 68, 73, 79, 80, 81, 85, 87, 124, 125, 126, 127, 270, 271

sexual harassment, 6, 70, 75, 96, 98, 144, 238, 246, 270

sexual slavery, 85, 87, 98, 113, 133, 134, 178, 238, 261, 262, 266

sexual violence, 6, 19, 20, 44, 55, 56, 60, 61, 62, 69, 71, 74, 107, 109, 113-116, 119-122, 127, 128, 145, 155, 177, 238, 251, 254, 258-262, 270, 279

sexuality, 2, 26, 34, 44, 55, 69, 73, 238

Sharia, 217, 220

    Nigeria, 32

Sierra Leone, 7, 20, 36, 87, 115, 124-126, 128, 136, 144, 170, 172, 195-197, 206, 209, 221, 249, 250, 261, 263, 278

Slovakia, 52

Slovenia, 216

Somalia, 19, 20, 39, 136, 209

South Africa, 19, 56, 87, 143, 145, 194, 195, 197, 201, 202, 206, 210, 244, 261

Spain, 52, 249

Special Rapporteur on Trafficking in Persons (UN), 83, 239

Special Rapporteur on Violence against Women (UN), 61, 96

Sri Lanka, 34, 136, 137, 263, 269

statistics, 6, 16, 17, 20, 23, 32, 39, 40, 44, 57, 67, 115, 145, 178, 188, 213, 279, 280

STD (sexually transmitted diseases), 68, 143

stigmatisation, 67, 72, 74, 76, 77, 118, 145, 158, 163, 199, 200, 206

stove deaths, 13, 31

sub-Saharan Africa, 18, 56, 87, 146

Sudan, 19, 34, 87, 136, 174, 249, 278

suicide, 31, 35, 58, 69, 116, 117, 120, 136, 137, 162, 165

Swaziland, 145

Sweden, 29, 36, 68, 77, 81, 245

Switzerland, 56, 57, 75, 245, 249, 269

Syria, 29

T

Taiwan, 50, 71, 261

Taliban, 178, 179, 206, 218

Tanzania, 35, 48, 49, 60, 136, 171

Thailand, 60, 67, 68, 70, 76, 77, 79, 81, 87

Tigrayan People's Liberation Forces, 136

Timor, 86, 125, 221, 247, 249, 250, 252, 254, 261, 278

Togo, 35, 88

torture, 23, 64, 68, 91-98, 114, 116, 117, 118, 124, 131-34, 161, 163-167, 216, 218, 221, 237, 257, 258, 259

trafficking, 67, 71, 79-84, 128, 239, 240, 270

transitional justice, 196, 202, 203, 205, 267

trauma, 1, 19, 26, 59, 68, 69, 86, 109, 114, 117, 118, 120, 121, 155, 159, 160, 162-167, 170, 175, 181, 191, 205, 211, 260

Turkey, 29, 56, 136, 137

Turkmenistan, 39

Tutsi, 136, 259

U

Uganda, 29, 51, 58, 87, 133, 134

unemployment, 60, 76, 82, 85, 117, 162, 166, 217

unexploded ordnance (UXO), 187-190, 194

USA, 74

UXO, *See* unexploded ordnance

V

violence against women, 1, 2, 5, 7, 8, 9, 10, 13, 14, 19, 25-28, 31, 33, 34, 55, 57, 61, 64, 65, 74, 77, 91-98, 115, 133, 146, 175, 200, 233, 236, 237, 238, 239, 243, 245, 246, 260, 261, 266, 267, 270, 271, 277-280

virgin cure myth, 19